D1292352

HUMAN
DIVERSITY

HUMAN DIVERSITY

The Biology of Gender, Race, and Class

CHARLES MURRAY

TWELVE

NEW YORK   BOSTON

Twelve
Hachette Book Group
1290 Avenue of the Americas, New York, NY 10104
twelvebooks.com
twitter.com/twelvebooks

First Edition: January 2020

Twelve is an imprint of Grand Central Publishing. The Twelve name and logo are trademarks of Hachette Book Group, Inc.

The publisher is not responsible for websites (or their content) that are not owned by the publisher.

The Hachette Speakers Bureau provides a wide range of authors for speaking events. To find out more, go to www.hachettespeakersbureau.com or call (866) 376-6591.

Library of Congress Control Number: 2019952691

ISBNs: 978-1-5387-4401-7 (hardcover), 978-1-5387-4400-0 (ebook)

Printed in the United States of America

LSC-C

10 9 8 7 6 5 4 3 2

To Harlan Crow

I remember once being entreated not to read a certain newspaper lest it might change my opinion upon free-trade. "Lest I might be entrapped by its fallacies and misstatements," was the form of expression. "You are not," my friend said, "a special student of political economy. You might, therefore, easily be deceived by fallacious arguments upon the subject. You might, then, if you read this paper, be led to believe in protection. But you admit that free-trade is the true doctrine; and you do not wish to believe what is not true."

—*Charles Sanders Peirce*
"The Fixation of Belief," 1877

Contents

A Note on Presentation

Human Diversity is grounded in highly technical literatures involving genetics, neuroscience, and statistics. It must satisfy two audiences with completely different priorities: my intended reader and the experts.

I've always thought of my intended reader as someone who enjoys reading the science section of the *New York Times*—curious about scientific matters, but someone who wants the gist of the science, not the minutiae. I need to keep the narrative moving. But I am conveying material that often has daunting technical complexities. Readers also need to be able to compare my claims with the details of the underlying evidence. I use my three favorite devices: Boxed text introduces related issues that are interesting but not essential. Appendixes provide full-scale discussions of important ancillary issues. Endnotes expand on points in the main text. But *Human Diversity* uses these devices, especially the endnotes, even more extensively than I have in the past. Some of the endnotes are full-scale essays, complete with tables. Brackets around a callout number for an endnote indicate that it contains at least a substantial paragraph of additional exposition.

For this complicated book, I have had to add a fourth device. In the past, I have usually been able to avoid technical jargon in the main text. *Human Diversity* doesn't give me that option. Too much material cannot be discussed without using technical terms that will be new to many readers. I therefore insert periodic interludes in the text to explain them.

I have also tried to make the book more accessible by my treatment of charts and tables. Sometimes the information in a figure or table is complicated enough to warrant giving it a title and traditional formatting. But often a simple graph of a trendline or a few summary statistics don't need the folderol. They can be integrated into the text so that you can absorb the simple point that's being made and move on.

HUMAN DIVERSITY

Introduction

If you have picked up *Human Diversity* looking for bombshells, you'll be disappointed. I'm discussing some of the most incendiary topics in academia, but the subtext of the chapters to come is that everyone should calm down. The differences among human groups are interesting, not scary or earthshaking. If that sounds boring, this isn't the book for you.

If, on the other hand, you have reached this page convinced that gender, race, and class are all social constructs and that any claims to the contrary are pseudoscience, you won't get past the first few pages before you can't stand it anymore. This book isn't for you either.

Now that we're alone, let me tell you what *Human Diversity* is about and why I wrote it.

The sciences form a hierarchy. "Physics rests on mathematics, chemistry on physics, biology on chemistry, and, in principle, the social sciences on biology," wrote evolutionary biologist Robert Trivers.[1] If so, this century should be an exhilarating time to be a social scientist. Until now, we social scientists—for I am a member of that tribe—have been second-class citizens of the scientific world, limited to data and methods that cast doubt on our claim to be truly part of the scientific project. Now, new possibilities are opening up.

Biology is not going to put us out of business. The new knowledge that geneticists and neuroscientists are providing, conjoined with the kinds of analyses we do best, will enable us to take giant strides in understanding how societies, polities, and economies really function. We are like physicists at the outset of the nineteenth century, who were poised at a moment in history that would produce Ampères and Faradays.

We ought to be excited, but we aren't. Trivers again: "Yet discipline after discipline—from economics to cultural anthropology—continues to resist growing connections to the underlying science of biology, with devastating effects."[2]

Why the resistance? Because the social sciences have been in the grip of an orthodoxy that is scared stiff of biology.

The Orthodoxy

The core doctrine of the orthodoxy in the social sciences is a particular understanding of human equality. I don't mean *equality* in the sense of America's traditional ideal—all are equal in the eyes of God, have equal inherent dignity, and should be treated equally under the law—but equality in the sense of sameness. Call it the sameness premise: *In a properly run society, people of all human groupings will have similar life outcomes.* Individuals might have differences in abilities, the orthodoxy (usually) acknowledges, but groups do not have inborn differences in the distributions of those abilities, except for undeniable ones such as height, upper body strength, and skin color. Inside the cranium, all groups are the same.

The sameness premise theoretically applies to any method of grouping people, but three of them have dominated the discussion for a long time: gender, race, and socioeconomic class. Rephrased in terms of those groups, the sameness premise holds that whatever their gender, race, or the class they are born into, people in every group should become electrical engineers, nurture toddlers, win chess tournaments, and write sci-fi novels in roughly equal proportions. They should have similar distributions of family income, mental health, and life expectancy. Large group differences in these life outcomes are prima facie evidence of social, cultural, and governmental defects that can be corrected by appropriate public policy.

The intellectual origins of the orthodoxy go back more than three centuries to the early days of the Enlightenment and the concept of humans as blank slates. The explicit rejection of a role for biology in the social sciences occurred from the end of the nineteenth through the beginning of the twentieth centuries, with the leading roles played by Émile Durkheim in sociology, Franz Boas in anthropology, and John Watson in psychology.[3]

The political expression of the orthodoxy had its origins in the mid-1960s with the legal triumphs of the civil rights movement and the rise of feminism. In the beginning, the orthodoxy consisted of specific allegations and solutions: Racism keeps black unemployment high. Sexism stunts women's careers. Affirmative action and antidiscrimination laws are needed. But the orthodoxy soon began to incorporate an intellectual movement that gained momentum in the mid-1960s with the publication of *The Social Construction of Reality* by Peter L. Berger and Thomas Luckmann.

The authors were dealing with an ancient problem: Each of us thinks we know what reality is, but different people have different perceptions of it. "The sociologist is forced by the very logic of his discipline to ask, if nothing else, whether the difference between the two 'realities' may not be understood in relation to various differences between the two societies," wrote Berger and Luckmann.[4] This beginning, written in plain English, perfectly sensible, morphed during the 1970s and 1980s into the orthodox position that just about everything is a social construct, often argued in postmodern prose that is incomprehensible to all but the elect.[5] The sources of human inequalities are artificial, made up, a reflection of the particular reality that a dominant segment of society has decided is the one we must all live by.

As I write, three of the main tenets of the orthodoxy may be summarized as follows:

Gender is a social construct. Physiological sex differences associated with childbearing have been used to create artificial gender roles that are unjustified by inborn characteristics of personality, abilities, or social behavior.

Race is a social construct. The concept of race has arisen from cosmetic differences in appearance that are not accompanied by inborn differences in personality, abilities, or social behavior.

Class is a function of privilege. People have historically been sorted into classes by political, economic, and cultural institutions that privilege heterosexual white males and oppress everyone else, with genes and human nature playing a trivial role if any. People can be re-sorted in a socially just way by changing those institutions.

I have stated these tenets baldly. If you were to go onto a university campus and chat privately with faculty members whose research touches on issues of gender, race, or class, you would find that many of them, perhaps a majority, have a more nuanced view than this. They accept that biology plays a role. Why then don't they mention the evidence for a biological role in their lectures? Their writings?

A common answer is that they fear that whatever they write will be misinterpreted and misused. But it's easy to write technical articles so that the mainstream media never notice them. The real threat is not that the public will misuse a scholar's findings, but that certain fellow academicians will notice those findings and react harshly.

Therein lies the real barrier to incorporating biology into social science. It is possible to survive on a university campus without subscribing to the orthodoxy. But you have to be inconspicuous, because the simplistic version of the orthodoxy commands the campus's high ground. It is dangerous for a college faculty member to say openly in articles, lectures, faculty meetings, or even in casual conversations that biology has a significant role in creating differences between men and women, among races, or among social classes. Doing so often carries a price. That price can be protests by students, denial of tenure-track employment for postdocs, denial of tenure for assistant professors, or reprimands from the university's administrators.

The most common penalties are more subtle. University faculties are small communities, with all the familiar kinds of social stigma for misfits. To be openly critical of the orthodoxy guarantees that a vocal, influential element of your community is going to come after you, socially and professionally. It guarantees that many others will be reluctant to be identified with you. It guarantees that you will get a reputation that varies from being an eccentric at best to a terrible human being at worst. It's easier to go along and get along.

The risks that face individual faculty members translate to much broader damage to academia. We have gone from a shared telos for the university, exemplified by Harvard's motto, "Veritas," to campuses where professors must be on guard against committing thought crimes, students clamor for protection against troubling ideas, codes limiting the free expression of ideas are routine, and ancient ideals of scholarly excellence and human virtue are derided and denounced.[6] On an individual level, social scientists have valid rationales to avoid exploring the intersection of biology and society. Collectively, their decisions have produced a form of de facto and widespread intellectual corruption.

Archaeological Digs

The good news is that some scholars have been exploring the intersection of biology and society despite the risks—so many that the orthodoxy is in the process of being overthrown. The heavy lifting is being done not within the social sciences, but by biologists and, more specifically, by geneticists and neuroscientists. They have been accumulating data that will eventually pose the same problem for defenders of the sameness premise that Aristotelian physicists faced when Galileo dropped objects from heights. Everyone could see that they didn't behave as Aristotle's theory predicted. No one could offer a counterargument. When our understanding of the genome and the brain is sufficiently advanced—and it is approaching that point faster than most people realize—the orthodox will be in the same position. Continuing to defend the sameness premise will make them look silly. It is my belief that we are nearing inflection points and that the triumph of the revolution will happen quickly. The key battles are likely to be won within the 2020s. This book is a progress report.

In the course of writing *Human Diversity*, it became apparent to me that progress is at strikingly different points for gender, race, and class. The analogy of an archaeological dig of a buried city comes to mind.

The dig for gender is well along. Excavations have been extensive, the city's layout has been identified, and thousands of artifacts have been found. There's lots yet to be done, but the outlines of the city and its culture are coming into focus.

The dig for race is in its early stages. Topological analysis has identified a promising site, initial clearing of the site has been completed, and the first probes have established that there's something down there worth investigating. Scientists are just beginning excavation.

The dig for class had been largely completed by the end of the twentieth century, and scholars in this century had until recently been kept busy analyzing the artifacts. They are now returning to the site with newly developed tools.

Analogies aren't precise, but this one explains the organization of the book. I begin with gender differences and devote five substantial chapters to them. A *lot* has been securely learned about gender differences. Race gets shorter chapters describing how the site was located, how it has been cleared, and the evidence that there's something down there worth investigating. The chapters on class summarize findings that for the most part have been known for decades.

Why Me?

I am neither a geneticist nor a neuroscientist. What business do I have writing this book?

The answer is that specialists are seldom good at writing overviews of their specialties for a general audience because they know too much—the forest and trees problem. It's often easier for an outsider to communicate the specialists' main findings to other outsiders. There are personal reasons as well. I think I'm skilled at making the findings of technical literatures accessible to a broader audience, I enjoy doing it, and I have been a fascinated observer of developments in genetics and neuroscience for years. I'm also at a point in my career when I'm immune to many of the penalties that a younger scholar would risk.

That career includes the firestorm that followed the publication of *The Bell Curve* more than a quarter of a century ago, an experience that has been on my mind as I have written *Human Diversity*. How can I avoid a repeat? Perhaps it's impossible. The background level of animosity and paranoia in today's academia is much worse than it was in 1994. But here is the reality: We are in the midst of a uniquely exciting period of discoveries in genetics and neuroscience—that's good news, not bad. My first goal is to describe what is being learned as clearly as possible, without sensationalism. I hope you will finish the book understanding that there are no monsters in the closet, no dread doors that we must fear opening.

My second goal is to stick to the low-hanging fruit. Almost all of the findings I report are ones that have broad acceptance within their disciplines. When a finding is still tentative, I label it as such. I know this won't deter critics from saying it's all pseudoscience, but I hope the experts will be yawning with boredom because they know all this already. Having done my best to accomplish those two things, I will hope for the best.

WHY THERE IS SO LITTLE ABOUT EVOLUTIONARY PSYCHOLOGY IN *HUMAN DIVERSITY*

Hundreds of millions of years of evolution did more than shape human physiology. It shaped the human brain as well. A comparatively new discipline, evolutionary psychology, seeks to understand the links between evolutionary pressures and the way humans have turned out. Accordingly, evolutionary psychology is at the heart of explanations for the differences that distinguish men from women and human populations from each other. Ordinarily, it would be a central part of my narrative. But the orthodoxy has been depressingly successful in demonizing evolutionary psychology as just-so stories. I decided that incorporating its insights would make it too easy for critics to attack the explanation and ignore the empirical reality.

I discuss some evolutionary material in my accounts of the peopling of the Earth and the source of greater male variance. That's it, however, ignoring the rest of the fascinating story. The note gives you some sources for learning more.[7]

The 10 Propositions

The propositions that accompany most of the chapters are intended to exemplify low-hanging fruit. I take on an extremely broad range of topics, but with the limited purpose of clarifying a handful of bedrock issues.

I apologize for the wording of the 10 propositions—they are not as snappy as I would prefer—but there's a reason for their caution and caveats. On certain important points, the clamor of genuine scientific dispute has abated and we don't have to argue about them anymore. But to meet that claim requires me to state the propositions precisely. I am prepared to defend all of them as "things we don't have to argue about anymore"—but exactly as I worded them, not as others may paraphrase them.

Here they are:

1. Sex differences in personality are consistent worldwide and tend to widen in more gender-egalitarian cultures.
2. On average, females worldwide have advantages in verbal ability and social cognition while males have advantages in visuospatial abilities and the extremes of mathematical ability.
3. On average, women worldwide are more attracted to vocations centered on people and men to vocations centered on things.
4. Many sex differences in the brain are coordinate with sex differences in personality, abilities, and social behavior.
5. Human populations are genetically distinctive in ways that correspond to self-identified race and ethnicity.
6. Evolutionary selection pressure since humans left Africa has been extensive and mostly local.
7. Continental population differences in variants associated with personality, abilities, and social behavior are common.

8. The shared environment usually plays a minor role in explaining personality, abilities, and social behavior.

9. Class structure is importantly based on differences in abilities that have a substantial genetic component.

10. Outside interventions are inherently constrained in the effects they can have on personality, abilities, and social behavior.

On all 10, the empirical record is solid. The debate should move on to new findings in the many areas where great uncertainty remains. That doesn't mean I expect the 10 propositions to be immutable. On the contrary, I have had to keep in mind that *Human Diversity* is appearing in the midst of a rushing stream, reporting on a rapidly changing state of knowledge. Aspects of it are sure to be out of date by the time the book appears. My goal is to have been so cautious in my wording of the propositions that any outdated aspects of them will have been elaborated or made more precise, not overturned.

How the Phrase Cognitive Repertoires *Is Used Throughout* the Rest of the Book

The 10 propositions repeatedly refer to "characteristics of personality, abilities, or social behavior." As I will occasionally put it, I am talking about the ways in which human beings differ above the neck (a loose way of putting it, but serviceably accurate).

I use *personality* and *social behavior* in their ordinary meanings. *Abilities* is a catch-all term that includes not only intellectual abilities but interpersonal skills and the clusters of qualities that have been described as emotional intelligence and grit. A good way of thinking about the universe of abilities is through Howard Gardner's famous theory of multiple intelligences.[8]

From now on I will usually abbreviate *personality, abilities, and social behavior* to *cognitive repertoires*. *Cognitive* means that it happens in the cranium or is at least mediated there. *Repertoires* refers to different ways of doing things that need not be ordered from "bad" at one extreme to "good" at the other. Some of them can be so ordered, but few have bad-to-good extremes. If you're an employer, where do you want a job applicant to be on the continuum from "extremely passive" to "extremely aggressive"? It depends on whether you're recruiting Navy SEALs or care providers at nursing homes, and in neither case is the most extreme position the ideal one. The same is true even of something generally considered to be an unalloyed good, such as high IQ. Google may be looking for the highest possible visuospatial skills among its applicants for programmers, but the qualities that often accompany stratospheric visuospatial skills would make many of them dreadful choices as SEALs or care providers.

For most of the human qualities we will be discussing, "bad" and "good" don't capture human differences. How many kinds of lovable are there? How many kinds of funny? How many kinds of annoying? Using the word *repertoires* allows for these kinds of apples and oranges too. So take note: For the rest of the book, *cognitive repertoires = characteristics of personality, abilities, and social behavior.*

As we embark on this survey of scientific discoveries about human diversity, a personal statement is warranted. To say that groups of people differ genetically in ways that bear on cognitive repertoires (as this book does) guarantees accusations that I am misusing science in the service of bigotry and oppression. Let me therefore state explicitly that I reject claims that groups of people, be they sexes or races or classes, can be ranked from superior to inferior. I reject claims that differences among groups have any relevance to human worth or dignity. The chapters to come make that clear.

PART I

—⁓—

"GENDER IS A SOCIAL CONSTRUCT"

From earliest recorded human history, everywhere and in all eras, women have borne the children and have been the primary caregivers. Everywhere and in all eras, men have dominated the positions of political, economic, and cultural power.[1] From those two universal characteristics have flowed a cascade of secondary and tertiary distinctions in the status of men and women, many of which have nothing to do with their actual capabilities. In today's language, gender has indeed been partly a social construct. Many of those distinctions were ruthlessly enforced.

The legal constraints on women in the modern West through the eighteenth century were not much short of de facto slavery. Mary Astell, often regarded as the first feminist (though she had precursors), made the point in response to John Locke's cramped endorsement of women's equality in the *Second Treatise*.[2] She italicized phrases borrowed from Locke's philosophical case for freedom: "If *all men are born free*, how is it that all women are born slaves? As they must be if the being subjected to the *unconstant, uncertain, unknown, arbitrary will* of men, be *the perfect condition of slavery*? . . . And why is slavery so much condemned and strove against in one case, and so highly applauded and held so necessary and so sacred in another?"[3]

If Astell's language seems extreme, consider: An English woman at the time Astell wrote and for more than a century thereafter rarely got any formal education and had no access to university education, was prohibited from entering the professions, and lost control of any property she owned when she married. She was obliged to take the "honor and obey" marriage vow literally, with harsh penalties for falling short and only the slightest legal protections if the husband took her punishment into his own hands. Men were legally prohibited from actually killing their wives, but just about anything less than that was likely to be overlooked. When the first wave of feminism in the United States got its start at the Seneca Falls Convention of 1848, women were rebelling not against mere inequality, but against near-total legal subservience to men.

Under those conditions, first-wave feminists were too busy to say much about questions of inborn differences between men and women. An exception was Kate Austin, who compared the plight of women to those of Chinese women with bound feet: "We know that at birth the feet of the little baby girl were straight and beautiful like her brothers, but a cruel and artificial custom restrained the growth. Likewise it is just as foolish to assert that woman is mentally inferior to man, when it is plain to be seen her brain in a majority of cases receives the same treatment accorded the feet of Chinese girls."[4] As Helena Swanwick put it, "There does not seem much that can be profitably said about [the alleged inferiority of women] . . . until the incubus of brute force is removed."[5] Men joined in some of the strongest early statements on nature versus nurture. John Stuart Mill coauthored "The Subjection of Women" with his feminist wife, Harriet Taylor.[6] George Bernard Shaw wrote, "If we have come to think that the nursery and the kitchen are the natural sphere of a woman, we have done so exactly as English children come to think that a cage is the natural sphere of a parrot—because they have never seen one anywhere else."[7]

After the great legal battles of first-wave feminism had been won during the first two decades of the twentieth century, a new generation of feminists began to devote more attention to questions of nature versus nurture. The result was second-wave feminism, usually dated to the publication of Simone de Beauvoir's *Le Deuxième Sexe*, a massive two-volume work published in 1949. Its argument sprawled across philosophy, history, sociology, economics, and psychology. The founding statement of second-wave feminism opened the second volume: "*On ne naît pas femme: on le devient.*" One is not born, but rather becomes, a woman.[8]

It was an assertion that required an explanation of how and why the change from birth to adulthood takes place. The intuitive explanation of "how" is that little girls are taught to be women—what is known now as socialization theory. It refers to the ways that children are exposed to influences that shape their gender identities. The pressure can come from parental interactions in infancy and toddlerhood, as girl babies are dressed differently from boy babies and female toddlers are given dolls to play with while boys are given trucks. The pressure may take the form of encouragement by parents, teachers, or playmates to engage in sex-typed play and discouragement of behaviors that go against type, as in the case of tomboy girls and effeminate boys. Parents may teach different lessons about right behavior, emphasizing the importance of being helpful and cooperative to daughters and the importance of standing up for themselves and taking the initiative to sons. Children may be encouraged to model themselves on the parent of their own sex. In these and many other ways, sometimes subtle or unconscious, children are constantly getting signals that track with the stereotypes of males and females.

This brief characterization of socialization theory skips over a number of intense scholarly debates between learning theorists and cognitive theorists, but the debaters differ about the mechanisms at work. All agree on the basic tenet that girls are taught from infancy to be girls and boys are taught from infancy to be boys.[9]

Is socialization theory true? It's natural to think so, if only because almost everybody can think of something during their childhood that involved references to what girls are supposed to be and what boys are supposed to be. Those of us who have had children of both sexes know that our interactions with our daughters and our sons have been somewhat different even if we tried hard to be gender-neutral in encouraging their abilities and ambitions.

But it's one thing to have such personal experiences and another to demonstrate empirically that these differences in treatment as children produce the sex differences in personality, abilities, and social behavior that we observe in adult women and men. Little boys and little girls are treated differently, but how differently? "Several theoretical models suggest mechanisms that are consistent with the differential treatment of boys and girls," wrote four Dutch scholars of childhood socialization. "However, to date there is no consensus in the literature about the extent to which parents *do* treat their sons and daughters differently, in which areas of parenting this mostly occurs, and whether fathers and mothers differ in the extent of gender differentiation."[10] [Emphasis in the original.]

The literature about differential socialization now consists of hundreds of titles. The note gives an overview of what has been found.[11] The short answer is that while there are lots of reasons to think that little girls and little boys are treated differently, it's surprisingly hard to prove that the differences are more than superficial.

Apart from its empirical problems, socialization theory standing alone is unsatisfying. Yes, it provides a framework for exploring the *how* of the construction of artificial sex differences, but it is silent on the *why*. Why should it be, everywhere and throughout history, that certain differences between the sexes have been so consistent? Isn't it simpler to assume that we're looking at innate sex differences produced by millions of years of evolution? In 1987, psychologist Alice Eagly published *Sex Differences in Social Behavior: A Social-Role Interpretation*, introducing a comprehensive theory of sex differences that embraces evolution, sociology, psychology, and biology, providing an answer to the *why*.[12] She has continued to develop the theory in the decades since, often in collaboration with psychologist Wendy Wood. Reduced to its essentials, the argument goes like this:

In the beginning was evolution, which led to physical sex differences. Males were larger, faster, and had greater upper body strength than females. Only females were capable of gestation and lactation. Given such differences, certain divisions of labor were natural. In hunter-gatherer societies, men's greater upper body strength led societies to funnel males into social roles involving physical strength—for example, hunting and protection against predators—and to funnel women into social roles involving childcare.

Over the millennia, *social* roles gave rise to *gender* roles as people associated the behaviors of males and females with their dispositions. Women are associated with childcare not just because of biology but because of a reflexive assumption that women, more than men, have innate nurturing qualities. It is not just that men's physical attributes make them more efficient hunters than women; it is also reflexively assumed that males have innate advantages—aggressiveness, perhaps, or initiative—that make them better hunters. This conflation of social role and gender role persists after the original physical justification for some social role has disappeared. These beliefs about stable, inherent properties of men and women have solidified without a biological foundation for them.

Enter socialization. If society has come to depend on women caring for children, little girls need to be socialized into the personality traits and skills that facilitate nurturance. If society has come to depend on men being providers and leaders, little boys need to be socialized into the personality traits that facilitate acquiring resources and status.

Social role theory includes a role for biology. "Men and women selectively recruit hormones and other neurochemical processes for appropriate roles, in the context of their gender identities and others' expectations for role performance," Eagly and Wood write. "Testosterone is especially relevant when, due to personal identities and social expectancies, people experience social interactions as dominance contests. Oxytocin is relevant when, due to personal identities and social expectancies, people define social interactions as involving bonding and affiliation with close others."[13] Biology interacts with psychology in two ways. Men and women alike psychologically internalize their gender roles as "self standards" for regulating their own behavior. They also regulate their behavior according to the expectations that others in the community have of them. "Biology thus works with psychology to facilitate role performance."[14]

The interdisciplinary sweep of social role theory means that it calls upon a wide variety of empirical observations about social roles across history and across cultures, evidence from psychology about internalization of norms, social psychological experiments, the nature of sex differences in personality, demographic trends, and economics, among many others. There is no equivalent to the meta-analyses of socialization studies that permits a short characterization of the state of knowledge about the validity of social role theory. But social role theory does what socialization theory does not: It provides a comprehensive explanation of *why* sex is a social construct.

But is sex exclusively a social construct? That the woman in a heterosexual couple does more housework than the man even when both have full-time jobs is at least largely a gender difference—the product of culture. It may have biological roots (perhaps men have evolved to be more tolerant of a messy living space than women are). But the issue is whether differential effort in doing the housework is sustained today by culture or genes. Think of it this way: How many women who can afford to hire someone to clean the house do so? A lot.

But simple quickly becomes complicated. Is the difference between the time men and women spend tending to young children artificially created by culture or driven by inborn male-female differences? How about the attraction of girl toddlers to dolls and boy toddlers to trucks? Male-female differences in college majors? Male-female differences in attraction to casual sex? Are they sex differences or gender differences?

The sensible answer would seem to be "probably some of both," with arguments about how much of which. At one level, that's actually how the academic debate is conducted. The following chapters have hundreds of references to highly technical articles, adhering to normal standards of scientific rigor, published in refereed journals, arguing questions of nature and nurture, with male and female scholars making contributions on all sides on all topics. The tone is usually civil, and the conclusions are usually nuanced and caveated.

But the women and men who are engaged in this endeavor are a rarefied group of neuroscientists and quantitative social scientists. Few of them seek publicity (many do their work as unobtrusively as possible), and they do not set the mood on college campuses. Since American second-wave feminism took off in the 1960s, the most visible feminist academics have rejected the possibility that there are *any* significant sex differences from the neck up. In my terminology, they have denied that men and women have any inborn differences in cognitive repertoires. A person's gender "is an arbitrary, ever-changing socially constructed set of attributes that are culture-specific and culturally generated, beginning with the appearance of the external genitals at birth," in the words of one of the most widely read feminist scientists in women's studies courses, Ruth Bleier.[15] It's not a position with a lot of nuance. Gender is a social construct. End of story.

The most famous illustration of what happens to those who question the orthodoxy is what befell economist Larry Summers. On January 14, 2005, Summers, then president of Harvard University, spoke to a conference on diversifying the science and engineering workforce.[16] In his informal remarks, responding to the sponsors' encouragement to speculate, he offered reasons for thinking that innate differences in men and women might account for some of the underrepresentation of women in science and engineering. He spoke undogmatically and collegially, talking about possibilities, phrasing his speculations moderately. And all hell broke loose.

An MIT biologist, Nancy Hopkins, told reporters that she "felt I was going to be sick," that "my heart was pounding and my breath was shallow," and that she had to leave the room because otherwise "I would've either blacked out or thrown up."[17] Within a few days, Summers had been excoriated by the chairperson of Harvard's sociology department, Mary C. Waters, and received a harshly critical letter from Harvard's committee on faculty recruiting. One hundred and twenty Harvard professors endorsed the letter. Some alumnae announced that they would suspend donations.[18] Summers retracted his remarks, with, in journalist Stuart Taylor Jr.'s words, "groveling, Soviet-show-trial-style apologies."[19] As if to validate that image, Lizabeth Cohen, a Harvard history professor, told reporters after attending the Summers self-criticism session that "[h]e regrets what he said, and I hope that he will prove that by taking constructive steps. We're going to be in intense discussions with him over the next week."[20]

Since 2005, expanding knowledge about male-female differences has substantiated Summers's speculations. The next five chapters review that evidence. The basics have been available to interested lay readers for years.[21] And yet elite gender studies departments still refuse to acknowledge the biological side of gender differences.[22] The degree to which the standard social science disciplines have also ignored this literature is an intellectual scandal. Evolutionary biologist Robert Trivers, whom you met in the introduction, has not held back:

> Once you remove biology from human social life, what do you have? Words. Not even language, which of course is deeply biological, but words alone that then wield magical powers, capable of biasing your every thought, science itself reduced to one of many arbitrary systems of thought.
>
> And what has been the upshot of this? Thirty-five wasted years and counting. Years wasted in not synthesizing social and physical anthropology. Strong people welcome new ideas and make them their own. Weak people run from new ideas, or so it seems, and then are driven into bizarre mind states, such as believing that words have the power to dominate reality, that social constructs such as gender are much stronger than the 300 million years of genetic evolution that went into producing the two sexes—whose facts in any case they remain resolutely ignorant of.[23]

Despite the orthodoxy's devotion to "words that have the power to dominate reality," the state of knowledge about the observable differences in men and women has advanced enormously in the last 20 years. During those same years, the state of knowledge about sex differences in the brain has been transformed. The next five chapters give you an overview of the most important developments.

1

A Framework for Thinking About Sex Differences

A few decades from now, I expect we will have a widely accepted comprehensive theory of sex differences that is grounded in neuroscience, genetics, and evolutionary psychology. Progress has already been made in that regard, but it is still at the frontiers of scholarship and bears no resemblance to low-hanging fruit. In any case, my purposes don't require that level of sophistication. A simple framework for thinking about phenotypic sex differences is supported by a growing number of scholars. This framework also links up with recent findings about sex differences in the brain.

A WORD ABOUT USAGE

From now on I will usually refer to "sex differences" instead of "gender differences." "Gender" was popularized in the 1960s to designate socially constructed differences.[1] But it turns out that there is no clear division between biological and socially constructed differences and no point in trying to pretend otherwise—which is what the widespread use of "gender" amounts to. In the technical literature, many scholars who write on these topics have resumed the use of "sex" to apply to all kinds of differences between males and females. So do I.

The People-Things Dimension

More than a century ago, Edward Thorndike, one of the founders of educational psychology, asserted that the greatest cognitive difference between men and women is "in the relative strength of the interest in things and their mechanisms (stronger in men) and the interest in persons and their feelings (stronger in women)."[2] In 1944, Hans Asperger, for whom Asperger's syndrome is named, hypothesized that the autistic cognitive profile is an extreme variant of male intelligence, which is another way of saying that normal males are more interested in things than people.[3] On the female side, the quantifiable existence of a female advantage in "sociability," as it had come to be called, was developed over the last half of the twentieth century among experts in personality.

Putting these advances together with some discoveries in biology that I will discuss in chapter 5, Simon Baron-Cohen, director of Cambridge University's Autism Research Centre, developed a theory of male-female differences that he described for a general audience in *The Essential Difference: Male and Female Brains and the Truth About Autism*, published in 2003. He coined the words *systemizer* and *empathizer*. In Baron-Cohen's formulation, men are driven to understand and build systems. The defining features of a system are that it has rules and that it does something. It has inputs at one end and outputs at the other. In between are specific operations that translate the inputs into the outputs. "This definition," Baron-Cohen wrote, "takes in systems beyond machines such as math, physics, chemistry, astronomy, logic, music, military strategy, the climate, sailing, horticulture, and computer programming. It also includes systems like libraries, economics, companies, taxonomies, board games, or sports."[4] Whatever the system may be, men are attracted to understanding what makes it tick.

Understanding what makes human beings tick? Not so much. "The baby is crying because it's hungry" is something men can recognize as well as women (ordinarily, anyway). But entering into and responding to the state of someone else's mind is a different matter. Empathy is required for that. Most men can do it, but on average, women are attracted to it more and do it better. It's not just because women devote more attention to it. Entering into someone else's mind calls on a different set of mental capabilities than the ones required for understanding a system.

Empathizer as Baron-Cohen uses the word is not confined to understanding what's going on inside the other person's head. It also involves "the observer's emotional response to another person's emotional state."[5] Sympathy might be one part of the emotional response, but it can also be anger or concern. These responses may be used for altruistic or self-interested purposes. Good empathizers can make effective ministers to the grieving and effective therapists for the psychologically troubled—but, using the same neurocognitive tools, they can also make effective arbitrators of disputes, interrogators of criminal suspects, managers of people, or election-winning politicians.

Other scholars of sex differences have been finding differences in academic interests, careers, and life choices that break along the lines of systemizing and empathizing but that also lend themselves to the broader and simpler difference that Thorndike identified—in choice after choice, men are attracted to options that have more to do with things while women are attracted to options that have more to do with people. That's the simple theory of the case I bring to the chapters on sex differences: Women and men divide along the People-Things dimension.

Lest there be any misunderstanding: *I am talking about statistical tendencies, not binary divisions.* Many men and women possess trait profiles more typical of the other sex.[6] But these tendencies are strong enough to create distinctively different distributions on important traits of personality, abilities, and social behavior.

First Interlude: Interpreting How Big a Sex Difference Is

I warned you in "A Note on Presentation" that I would occasionally be interrupting my narrative to explain technical terms. This is the first such interlude. Some of you are already familiar with the term I will be explaining, *effect size*, but I urge you to continue reading nonetheless. The interpretation of effect sizes plays a significant role in how one interprets the evidence.

In the following chapters, I compare men and women on dozens of traits. They are based on many kinds of measures—answers to questionnaire items, scores on tests, and ratings of observed behavior, to name just a few. Researchers need a common metric for expressing the differences that these comparisons reveal.

To see what this metric must do, think in terms of a simple measure like height. In one sense, an inch gives a common metric for measuring height. You can express the height of anything with it. In another sense, it doesn't tell us much. For example, how big is a difference of six inches in height? In absolute terms, it's always the same. But how big is a six-inch difference if we are talking about the height of elephants? The height of cats? The answer depends on the average height of the things you are measuring and how much height varies among the things you are measuring. You need a way to express *height* in a way that means the same thing for elephants relative to other elephants and cats relative to other cats.

We need the same kind of metric to talk about sex differences across cognitive repertoires. That metric is based on a statistic called the standard deviation, described in detail in Appendix 1. In many cases, including the ones we will be dealing with, the standard deviation applies to a normal distribution, also known as a bell curve. To get from bell curves to effect sizes, let's stick with the example of height.

The contemporary mean height of American women ages 20 or older is 63.6 inches. The comparable mean for men is 69.0 inches. Most people are clustered within a few inches of those means, but successively smaller numbers of people are three, four, five, and six inches from the mean. A tiny proportion of people are a foot or more from the mean. The nationally representative database of people that produced those numbers had these distributions:

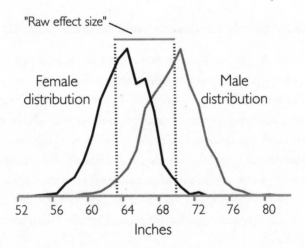

Source: Fryer, Gu, Ogden et al. (2016).

The dotted vertical lines show the means for women and men. The gray horizontal bar shows the difference between the two, which I call the "raw effect size." Dividing it by the pooled standard deviations of the two groups gives us a way to express magnitude that can be compared across different traits.

An effect size is denoted as *d*. To calculate *d* for height, I subtracted the male mean from the female mean, producing a difference of –5.4 inches. The pooled standard deviation is 2.9 inches, so *d* equals –5.4 ÷ 2.9, which works out to an effect size of –1.86. This is an extremely large effect size. Most sex differences are much smaller and the distributions have much more overlap.

Note that the sign of *d* (negative or positive) is arbitrary. If I had subtracted the female mean from the male mean, the effect size wouldn't have changed, but the sign would have been positive. Just so you know, in this book *my default will be to subtract the male mean from the female mean in calculating sex differences. Therefore negative* d *values will always indicate that males are higher than females on the trait in question*, whether "higher" means something good, bad, or neutral.

Two questions are crucial to assessing the importance of sex differences: When is an effect size big enough to be interesting? Should individual effect sizes be treated individually or aggregated?

When Is an Effect Size Big Enough to Be Interesting?

Jacob Cohen, who originated Cohen's *d*, inadvertently set the standard for interpreting effect sizes (he had a different purpose in mind). His list was subsequently expanded by Shlomo Sawilowsky. Under these guidelines, a *d* value of 0.01 = very small, 0.20 = small, 0.50 = medium, 0.80 = large, 1.20 = very large, and 2.00 = huge.[7]

The guidelines were well-intended but have often proved to be pernicious in practice. As Cohen himself took pains to point out, the importance of a given value of Cohen's *d* depends on the specific topic you are examining.[8] In 2019, psychologists David Funder and Daniel Ozer took on what they called the "nonsensical" standard set by Cohen, arguing that the interpretation of effect sizes should be guided by their consequences. In the case of a drug for curing a deadly disease that has a relatively small success rate, the effect of a success is a saved life—a consequence that can be important even if the effect size is small. In the case of a small effect size that has many repetitions, it's the cumulative effect that's important. For example, a study that tracked two million financial transactions found that the correlation between a person's score on a measure of extraversion and the amount spent on holiday shopping is just +.09. "Multiply the effect identified with this correlation by the number of people in a department store the week before Christmas," the authors wrote, "and it becomes obvious why merchandisers should care deeply about the personalities of their customers."[9] They offered a new set of guidelines based on the correlation coefficient (r). In the summary that follows, I have replaced the value of r with the equivalent value of Cohen's d.

The authors argued that an effect size of .10 "is 'very small' for the explanations of single events but potentially consequential in the not-very long run," while an effect size of .20 "is still 'small' at the level of single events but potentially more ultimately consequential."[10] Other scholars have advocated similar guidelines for interpreting small values of d.[11] But their treatment of "small" collides with the position taken by the most influential work arguing for small sex differences in cognitive repertoires—the "gender similarities hypothesis" originated by psychologist Janet Shibley Hyde in the September 1985 issue of *American Psychologist*, the flagship journal of the American Psychological Association. Here is her statement of the hypothesis:

> The gender similarities hypothesis holds that males and females are similar on most, but not all, psychological variables. That is, men and women, as well as boys and girls, are more alike than they are different. In terms of effect sizes, the gender similarities hypothesis states that most psychological sex differences are in the close-to-zero ($d \leq 0.10$) or small ($0.11 < d < 0.35$) range, a few are in the moderate range ($0.36 < d < 0.65$), and very few are large ($d = 0.66{-}1.00$) or very large ($d > 1.00$).[12]

The inclusive definition of "small" to include everything up to a d of .35 dictates her interpretation of the literature. Hyde reviewed 46 meta-analyses of psychological sex differences and concluded that of 124 classifiable effect sizes, 78 percent were small or close to zero by her definition.[13]

For Hyde, Cohen's guidelines "provide a reasonable standard for the interpretation of sex differences effect sizes."[14] She acknowledged that in some cases—cure rates for disease, for example—a small effect size can have important effects. But, she argued, "[I]n terms of costs of errors in scientific decision making, psychological sex differences are quite a different matter from curing cancer. So, interpretation of the magnitude of effects must be heavily conditioned by the costs of making Type I and Type II errors for the particular question under consideration."[15]

Type I error refers to a false positive finding—in this case, wrongly concluding that a sex difference has been found. Type II error refers to a false negative finding—mistakenly concluding that no difference exists. Hyde was worried about the consequences of making a Type I error. She went on to give examples of the ways that inflating sex differences have real-world costs. For example, the idea that women are more nurturing than men backfires when it comes to the workplace: "Women who violate the stereotype of being nurturant and nice can be penalized in hiring and evaluations," Hyde wrote, citing evidence to that effect.[16]

On these issues, everyone who writes about sex differences should put their personal perspectives on the table. Regarding the use of Cohen's guidelines, I think Hyde's reliance on them to defend the gender similarities hypothesis is misplaced. There are too many ways in which effect sizes defined as "small" by Cohen's guidelines can have important aggregate effects when thinking about sex differences. I appeal to the arguments made by the scholars I have cited, including Cohen himself, in defense of my position.

I also disagree with Hyde's position that Type I errors should still be more feared than Type II errors. If we were back in 1960, I would agree with her— many people assumed that men and women were separated by large differences, and research that falsely reinforced that assumption could perpetuate harmful stereotypes, just as Hyde argues. But I'm writing at the end of the second decade of the twenty-first century when so many things, from high school athletic programs to the military's composition of combat units, are guided by the assumption that there are no relevant sex differences. My guess is that the situation in 1960 has been reversed: More harms are now inflicted by incorrectly ignoring sex differences than by incorrectly exaggerating them. At the least, it can be said that there's no clear case that Type I error is still more harmful than Type II error. This is an argument that does not lend itself to data-driven resolution. Differences in perspective are embedded in the literature on sex differences. It is well to be transparent about them.

Should Individual Effect Sizes Be Treated Individually or Aggregated?

My more important difference with Hyde involves her insistence on treating sex differences as independent bits and pieces rather than as profiles. When are traits of personality, ability, and social behavior rightly treated independently? When should they be added up? These questions come up all the time in the social and behavioral sciences, and there are no cookbook recipes to go by.

To illustrate, let's say we're investigating personality differences and discover that people in Group A (the group could be based on any kind of common membership, not just sex) are somewhat more outgoing on average than people in Group B, with "somewhat" meaning that d = +0.35.

We get to know these groups better and determine that Group A is also somewhat warmer on average than Group B, with d = +0.35. Should we represent the two groups as separated by a mean personality difference of +0.35? Add the two effect sizes and say they are separated by a difference of +0.70? Or something in between?

I say that the answer is something close to +0.35. *Outgoing* and *warm* are nearly synonymous. The additional information hasn't given us reason to think that the two groups of people are much more different than we already knew.

Suppose instead that we determine that Group A is also more emotionally stable than Group B, with d = +0.35. Should we continue to represent the two groups as separated by an average of +0.35? An aggregate of +0.70? Or something in between?

This time, I argue that the answer has to be closer to +0.70. We're comparing people who are both warmer and more emotionally stable with people who are more aloof and easily upset. The personalities of the two groups are (on average) definitely more different than we knew before.

We continue to learn more about the two groups. We learn that one group is more prudent, the other more happy-go-lucky; one group is more practical, the other more imaginative; and so on. In some cases, the additional traits on which the groups differ are so closely related that the new knowledge adds only a small amount to the difference; in other cases, the new information adds a lot to the degree of their difference. But whether increments are small or large, my view is that individual differences that are conceptually related should routinely be aggregated.

Psychologist Marco Del Giudice, a leading advocate for aggregating sex differences in personality, uses an analogy with the distance between towns. If I tell you that one town is 35 miles west and 35 miles north of another town and ask you the Euclidean distance between the two, it wouldn't occur to you to take the average of the two and announce that the towns were 35 miles apart. Similarly, it wouldn't occur to you to add the two and say that the towns are 70 miles apart. You realize that we're talking about a right triangle and that the hypotenuse is the distance between the two towns. You remember the Pythagorean theorem and know that the distance is therefore the square root of $35^2 + 35^2$, which works out to about 49.5 miles. If I were then to tell you that the altitude of the two towns differed by 4,000 feet, you would have to recalculate, taking the third dimension of height into account.

I like the analogy in part because the correct answer is so intuitively satisfying: We neither treat the three measures of distance separately nor simply combine the raw measures. Some method of aggregation that falls between averaging and simple addition seems right.

If you still want to average traits or treat them separately, my argument does not compel you to change your mind. I've made it through analogy and an appeal to intuition. But you should come to grips with how radical your solution is. If two indicators are involved, averaging cuts the simple sum of the two effect sizes by half. With three indicators, it cuts the simple sum by two-thirds. Suppose 10 indicators are involved. Averaging the results gives you an estimate of the sex difference that is just one-tenth of the estimate you would get by adding up the effect sizes. Doesn't that seem like too much of a discount? This is a nontechnical way of saying that cognitive repertoires commonly involve multidimensional constructs, and the measure of male-female differences must be multidimensional as well.[17]

In the same way that it is possible to compute the geographical distance separating two towns given two measures of their distance on the cardinal points of the compass, it is possible to compute distance in multidimensional space. The most widely used statistic for expressing multivariate distance is called Mahalanobis D, named after the Indian statistician, Prasanta Mahalanobis, who developed it. The algorithm for calculating D does what I have argued intuition tells us it should, taking correlations into account. Suppose that variables have correlations near zero. D converges on the Euclidean distance. The higher the correlation between variables, the less D is augmented by including them. When a new variable is a linear combination of variables already in the equation, D is not augmented at all.[18] The note also gives you references disputing his position (one of them by Hyde) and Del Giudice's response to them.

In assessing the various arguments for and against, three points need to be kept in mind. First, Mahalanobis D or any other method of aggregation must be used cautiously. In all complex statistical analyses, the validity of the results depends on interpreting the statistic with its limitations in mind.

But that leads to my second point: When I talk about indicators of sex differences being "conceptually related," I am not appealing to esoteric social science abstractions. To go back to my example, traits like warmth and emotional stability are characteristics with which we're all familiar from everyday life. We can effortlessly think of them as continua from coldly aloof to gushingly friendly; from rock-solid calm to emotionally volcanic. We've had experience with people who have different combinations of the two traits. In the same way, given normal standards of technical care in the application of multidimensional measures of distance and a clear narrative description of the logic for combining traits, aggregated measures of multidimensional distance can enhance our understanding of sex differences.

My third point is that in the real world it is taken for granted that small differences add up. Imagine a tennis match. You know that both players are professionals, but that's all you know. You have to bet on one of them. You learn that one player is 10 percent taller than the other. That doesn't give you much to go on; all you need is fractionally better than 1:1 odds to bet on the other guy. But suppose you then learn that the taller player also has 10 percent greater wingspan, 10 percent greater strength, 10 percent more endurance, 10 percent faster foot speed, 10 percent faster serve speed, 10 percent higher percentage of first serves, 10 percent faster reaction time, and 10 percent more emotional control. Now what kind of odds do you require to bet on the other guy?

I should add that my position makes virtually no practical difference to the discussions in the next four chapters. Almost all of the effect sizes I report are plain vanilla Cohen's d. I have given so much space to this topic because I think that treating effect sizes individually or averaging them has underestimated male-female differences. If you are unpersuaded, I will rest my case with the example of sex differences in the human face. Adult female and male faces are distinguished by dozens of tiny morphological differences. But they add up. Consider the following two faces:

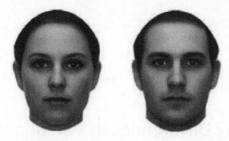

Source: Adapted from Rhodes, Jeffery, Watson et al. (2004).

Describing precisely why those two faces are so obviously a female's on the left and a male's on the right is daunting. The individual differences are almost imperceptible. But one thing is sure: To average out all those tiny individual differences and conclude that "male and female faces are virtually indistinguishable" would be ridiculous. The estimate of overall sex difference in faces must be expressed as some sort of aggregation. I submit that the same holds true for all sex differences comprised of functionally distinctive but conceptually related traits.

2

Sex Differences in Personality

Proposition #1: Sex differences in personality are consistent worldwide and tend to widen in more gender-egalitarian cultures.

Bimbo. Jock. Feminine. Macho. A great lady. A true gentleman. Males and females have been stereotyping each other from time out of mind, positively and negatively. Almost all of the stereotypes are about personality characteristics that are thought to break along the lines of sex. Some do and some don't. At the end of the review of the evidence in this chapter, I defy anyone to conclude that either sex has a superior personality profile. They're just different. Some of the most coherent ways they're different correspond to the People-Things dimension.

Sex Differences in Psychiatric and Neurological Conditions

The most extreme expressions of personality characteristics manifest themselves as personality disorders. All of them are known to have genetic causes; some are also known to have environmental causes. One thing is certain: Their incidence rates differ markedly across the sexes. In a 2017 review article, neuroscientist Margaret McCarthy and her colleagues summarized the sex imbalance of incidence rates in a table that I present in an abbreviated version below.[1]

SEX DIFFERENCES IN PERSONALITY DISORDERS

Condition	Sex with greater prevalence	Approximate proportion of cases
Childhood onset		
Autism spectrum disorder	Male	80–90%
Conduct/oppositional defiance disorder	Male	75%
Attention deficit hyperactivity disorder	Male	66–75%

Condition	Sex with greater prevalence	Approximate proportion of cases
Schizophrenia	Male	60%
Dyslexia and/or reading impairment	Male	66–75%
Stuttering	Male	70%
Tourette syndrome	Male	75–80%
Adult onset		
Major depression	Female	66%
Bipolar II disorder*	Female	Unspecified
Generalized anxiety	Female	66%
Panic disorder	Female	70%
Obsessive-compulsive disorder	Female	60%
Post-traumatic stress syndrome	Female	66%
Anorexia nervosa	Female	75%
Bulimia	Female	75–80%
Alcoholism or substance abuse	Male	Unspecified

Source: Adapted from McCarthy, Nugent, and Lenz (2017): Table 2. The original table includes references.

* Bipolar II is characterized by at least one episode of major depression lasting two or more weeks and at least one hypomanic episode.

At this point, I just want to put the existence of these well-documented and important sex differences on the table.[2] Possible biological causes will be discussed in chapter 5.

Sex Differences in Personality Within the Normal Range

Now I turn to adult personality profiles. We know from everyday experience that personality characteristics tend to cluster. The person who is the life of the party tends to enjoy being around other people elsewhere. The person who is a hypochondriac also tends to fret about other things. In the 1940s, psychometricians led by Raymond Cattell began to explore how personality "facets," the detailed indicators of personality characteristics, clustered into larger constructs—"factors."[3] Over several years, Cattell and his colleagues developed a model that had 16 factors and a self-report personality test called the Sixteen Personality Factor Questionnaire, labeled 16PF. It is now in its fifth edition and continues to be widely used.

By the 1980s, another personality model had gained wide currency. It is known colloquially as the Big Five model, the label I will use.[4] The factor that explains the most variance is neuroticism, which I will relabel *emotional stability* (see the box below). The other four, in descending order of the variance they explain, are extraversion, openness, agreeableness, and conscientiousness. The first widely accepted test was based on work by Paul Costa and Robert McCrae of the National Institutes of Health. I will refer to it as the Five Factor Model (FFM) inventory.[5]

NEUROTICISM OR EMOTIONAL STABILITY?

Every personality characteristic has a continuum that goes from one extreme to the other, and neither extreme is desirable.[6] For example, agreeableness at one extreme indicates an unquestioningly acquiescent person; at the other extreme, it indicates a reflexively antagonistic person. Four of the Big Five factors have labels that describe a moderately positive position on the continuum. One label, neuroticism, is not only negative but, to most ears, extremely negative. In the technical literature, scholars increasingly use a moderately positive label for this factor, *emotional stability*. I do so as well.

Other personality models have been developed, but the 16PF and FFM inventories continue to be the ones with the largest databases and the most cross-national databases.[7] I focus on three surveys of adults: the U.S. standardization sample of Costa and McCrae's FFM inventory in 1992 (n = 1,000), hereafter called the Costa study; a 2018 replication using the open-access version of the FFM inventory by psychologists Petri Kajonius and John Johnson (n = 320,128), hereafter called the Kajonius study; and the analysis by psychologists Marco Del Giudice, Tom Booth, and Paul Irwing of the U.S. standardization sample for the fifth edition of the 16PF inventory (n = 10,261), hereafter called the Del Giudice study.

Personality Sex Differences in the United States

It is appropriate to begin by emphasizing that on many important personality traits, the differences between men and women are quite small. These trivial differences apply to many characteristics that are sometimes ascribed to men (e.g., "assertive or forceful in expression," "self-reliant, solitary, resourceful") and ones that are sometimes ascribed to women (e.g., "open to the inner world of imagination," "lively, animated, spontaneous"). The full list is given in the note.[8]

Among the traits on which men and women differ, some of the largest effect sizes are consistent with the higher prevalence of depression among women. In the FFM inventory, women experienced more free-floating anxiety than men (d = +0.40 and +0.56 for the Costa and Kajonius studies respectively) and were more vulnerable to stress (d = +0.44 and +0.54). In the 16PF inventory, women were more apprehensive, self-doubting, and worried (d = +0.60 in the Del Giudice study).[9]

Some of the substantively significant sex differences correspond to traditional stereotypes about feminine sensibility. In the FFM inventory, women were more appreciative of art and beauty than were men (d = +0.34 and +0.33 for the Costa and Kajonius studies respectively), were more open to inner feelings and emotions (d = +0.28 and +0.64), were more modest in playing down their achievements (d = +0.38 and +0.45), and were more reactive, affected by feelings, and easily upset (d = +0.53). In the 16PF inventory, several stereotypical characteristics were combined into one factor, "sensitive, aesthetic, sentimental," with a whopping d of +2.29.

The characteristics shown in the table below have a special bearing on the People-Things dimension.

PERSONALITY DIFFERENCES RELATING TO THE PEOPLE-THINGS DIMENSION

	Costa	Kajonius	Del Giudice	Inventory
Warm, outgoing, attentive to others			+0.89	16PF
Sensitive, aesthetic, sentimental			+2.29	16PF
Cooperative, accommodating, deferential			+0.54	16PF
Shows warmth toward others	+0.33	+0.07		FFM
Altruistic concern for others	+0.43	+0.51		FFM
Sympathizes with others	+0.31	+0.57		FFM
Enjoys the company of others	+0.21	+0.05		FFM
Straightforwardness, not demanding	+0.43	+0.40		FFM

Source: Costa, Terracciano, and McCrae (2001); Del Giudice, Booth, and Irwing (2012); Kajonius and Mac Giolla (2017); Kajonius and Mac Giolla (2017). Positive scores indicate women score higher.

A person who is warm, sympathetic, accommodating, altruistic, and sociable amounts to the stereotype of a human being, male or female, who is more attuned to people than things. Women are more likely to have that profile than are men.

People who are somewhat to the other side of each trait in the table are reserved, utilitarian, unsentimental, dispassionate, and solitary—which amounts to the stereotype of a human being, male or female, who is more attracted to things, broadly defined, than to people. Men are more likely to have that profile than are women.

With the 16PF inventory, just two factors, sensitivity (d = +2.29) and warmth (d = +0.89), tell most of the story. With the FFM inventory, the individual effect sizes from both studies are modest, with the largest being just +0.57 for "sympathizes with others." But a scan of the table also makes an obvious point: All five of the FFM traits add up. I do not have the raw data for computing the aggregated difference (D) on the traits included in the table, but some other statistics will give you a sense of the overall sex difference in personality that they reflect.

For the 16PF inventory, the Del Giudice study calculated the value of D for all 15 factors. It was 2.71, a huge difference that would leave only 10 percent overlap between two normal distributions.[10] Even when the extremely large difference (+2.29) on just one of the factors, sensitivity, is excluded, the value of D is 1.71, corresponding to 24 percent overlap between two normal distributions.[11] If instead we use the mean of those 15 separate effect sizes (again excluding sensitivity), the overall difference would be estimated at just +0.44—a dramatic illustration of the difference between averaging effect sizes and aggregating them.

With regard to the FFM inventory, we have reason to be confident that aggregating the effect sizes for the five traits most closely related to the People-Things dimension would produce a D much larger than their mean d of +0.32. To give you an idea, a large-sample (n = 8,308) administration of the FFM in 2006 had an average sex difference in d of +0.30.[12] The value of Mahalanobis D for that dataset was 0.98.[13]

THE EVIDENCE FROM INFANCY

Measuring personality sex differences in infancy is tough, and the instruments for doing so are not nearly as precise as instruments for older children. Different studies come up with different estimates of some relationships, and almost all of the studies need replication. The most dramatic example of a finding from infancy, which led to considerable publicity, was a 2002 study presenting evidence that newborn girls no more than two days old after birth showed stronger interest in a human face while the newborn boys showed stronger interest in a mechanical mobile.[14] It is a single, unreplicated study with a sample of 102, not proof to take to the bank, but its finding was in line with many other studies that have found personality sex differences in infants.

On average, infant girls cry longer than boys in response to recordings of another baby crying, believed to be a primitive empathic reaction.[15]

On average, infant girls hold eye contact with an adult human longer than boys do.[16]

On average, infant girls show more expressions of joy than boys at the appearance of the mother.[17]

On average, infant girls are more responsive to maternal vocalizations than infant boys.[18]

On average, infant girls are more distressed by maternal "still face" than infant boys.[19]

On average, infant girls show visual preferences for objects with human attributes while boys show more visual preferences for balls and vehicles.[20]

On average, infant girls are more likely to initiate and respond to joint attention.[21]

In Erin McClure's meta-analysis of 20 studies of facial expression processing in infants, the six studies for which effect sizes were reported or could be calculated had a weighted effect size of +0.92 favoring girls.[22]

Sex Differences in Personality Worldwide

So far, I have presented nothing indicating that these personality differences are hardwired. Maybe that's just the way little girls and little boys are brought up in the United States and other Western cultures. That's where cross-national comparisons come in. The legal and social status of women varies widely around the world. Some Islamic cultures still keep women at a level of legal subservience little better than Western women experienced until the twentieth century. Some sub-Saharan African cultures still take the superiority and dominance of men for granted and organize daily life accordingly. At the other extreme are countries in Western Europe and especially Scandinavia that have erected elaborate structures to require gender parity in all economic and social matters.

Cultures around the world have other deep differences that affect both women and men—for example, the intensely family-oriented cultures of much of Asia compared to the individualism of the Western tradition. And yet despite this extremely wide range of environments in which children are raised, sex differences in personality are remarkably similar around the world.

The same article that reported the results for American adults on the Costa-McCrae inventory also reported them for 25 other countries.[23] In 2005, McCrae and Antonio Terracciano used observer reports from 50 cultures, 22 of which had not been included in previous studies. The next table shows effect sizes for the same five traits from the Costa-McCrae inventory shown in the previous table, adding the results from the international samples.

High-end descriptors	Questionnaire data		Observational data
	U.S.	25-nation sample	50-nation sample
Shows warmth toward others	+0.33	+0.23	+0.29
Appreciates art and beauty	+0.34	+0.35	+0.31
Has altruistic concern for others	+0.43	+0.25	+0.33
Sympathizes with others	+0.31	+0.28	+0.39
Enjoys the company of others	+0.21	+0.14	+0.26

Source: Costa, Terracciano, and McCrae (2001); McCrae and Terracciano (2005). All samples are adults. Positive scores indicate women score higher.

The results show universally higher female means and similar effect sizes on the individual traits. Even taken country by country, the number of anomalies was remarkably small. The Costa study reported effect sizes for extraversion, agreeableness, and openness for 26 populations in 25 countries—78 effect sizes in all. The signs for 77 out of the 78 were positive (women scored higher).[24] The McCrae study of 50 cultures reported country-by-country effect sizes for 49 populations in 46 countries. Of the 147 effect sizes reported, 139 were positive. The largest of the negative effect sizes (i.e., higher for males) was trivially small ($d = -0.05$).[25]

This consistency is all the more remarkable considering that the 50 nations included ones from East Asia, South Asia, the Mideast, Africa, Europe,

South America, and North America, and nations that ranged from the most impoverished and traditional (e.g., Uganda, Burkina Faso) to the wealthiest and most sex-egalitarian (e.g., Sweden, Denmark). The great cultural and economic disparities across these countries make it difficult to see how all of them could produce uniform socialization of girls to be more warm, altruistic, sympathetic, sociable, and artistically sensitive than men.

Sex Differences in Personality and a Society's Gender Egality

I use gender *egality* in preference to gender *equality* to signify not just progress toward diminishing sex differences but also institutional, legal, and social changes intended to put men and women on an equal footing. The question at hand is whether sex differences in personality are smaller in countries that have made the most progress.

The theories of socialization and of social roles that I summarized in chapter 1 necessarily expect that the answer is yes. If sex differences in personality are artificial, diminishing the causes of artificial differences must eventually lead to smaller differences.[26] The only question is how long it will take. This brings us to a counterintuitive finding that seems to cut across a variety of sex differences: *Many sex differences in cognitive repertoires are wider rather than smaller in countries with greater gender egality.* Personality traits offers the first example.

The Evidence for Wider Personality Differences in Advanced Countries

The Costa study. The Costa study discovered this startling result as they examined the scores for individual nations in their pioneering study. The wrong nations had the largest sex differences: "Sex differences are most marked among European and American cultures and most attenuated among African and Asian cultures," they wrote.[27]

To convey this finding more systematically, I employ the UN's annual Gender Inequality Index (GII). It is based on maternal mortality rate, adolescent birth rate, women's share of seats in parliament, percentage of women with at least some secondary education, and women's labor force participation.[28] A high score on the GII indicates high inequality.

The results correspond to widespread impressions that Western Europe has the best record for sex equality. Among the 70 nations with data on personality and a GII score, the five nations with the best (meaning lowest) scores on the GII were Switzerland, Denmark, the Netherlands, Sweden, and Iceland. The five nations with the worst (highest) GII scores were Burkina Faso, Congo, Egypt, Pakistan, and Tanzania.

As noted, both socialization and social role theories of sex differences predict that effect sizes should diminish as gender egality increases. Translated into a prediction about the Costa data, this means that a correlation between the absolute size of the sex difference and the GII should be positive (greater inequality is associated with greater personality differences).[29] In the Costa study, those correlations were not only negative—the "wrong" sign—but substantially so: −.61 for emotional stability, −.57 for extraversion, −.49 for openness to emotion, and −.42 for agreeableness.[30] On average, personality differences were wider in countries with greater gender egality.

The McCrae study. The McCrae study applied the same measures plus one for conscientiousness to a larger sample of nations, using an observational measure of personality traits rather than self-reports. It found the same thing as the Costa study. The correlations between the Gender Inequality Index with the effect sizes for sex differences were once again all in the "wrong" direction and all substantial: −.61 for openness to emotion, −.57 for emotional stability, −.56 for extraversion, −.47 for conscientiousness, and −.43 for agreeableness.[31]

The Schmitt study. In 2008, an international team of behavioral scientists consisting of American David Schmitt, Austrian Martin Voracek, and two Estonians, Anu Realo and Jüri Allik, drew on one of the largest cross-cultural studies of personality ever conducted, part of the International Sexuality Description Project, with three aims in mind.

First, the team wanted to see if the findings of the Costa and McCrae studies generalized to another instrument for measuring personality. The Schmitt study used the Big Five Inventory, consisting of 44 self-report items, rather than the FFM inventory.

Second, the team wanted to increase the range of nations in the database. In all, they obtained personality measures from 55 nations, including 14 that were not part of either the Costa or McCrae studies.

Third, the Schmitt study undertook an elaborate set of tests to determine whether artifacts explained the widening personality differences in advanced countries.

The short version of the answers presented at length in the Schmitt study is that (1) the Big Five Inventory showed essentially the same cross-national patterns that the FFM inventory had produced; (2) the addition of new nations allowed an extension of the conclusions that the Costa and McCrae studies had reached; and (3) the arguments for an artifactual explanation of the widening gap in advanced nations were not borne out by the analyses.[32]

The Giolla study. In 2018, Erik Mac Giolla and Petri J. Kajonius published the results for a database with a more extensive (120-item) version of the FFM for 22 countries with uniformly larger sample sizes per country (at least 1,000) than the samples used by the other studies. Uniquely, this study also calculated Mahalanobis *D*—the method for aggregating individual effect sizes that I described in chapter 1. The index of gender egality used for the study was the Global Gender Gap Index (GGGI) published by the World Economic Forum. The index is scored from 0 to 1, with 1 meaning gender equality (or better conditions for women) on all of the 14 indicators.[33]

In this case, the "right" correlation with the absolute size of the sex difference is negative (a higher score on the GGGI is associated with smaller sex differences). Instead, all of the correlations between personality differences and the GGGI were positive, which means they were all in the "wrong" direction and all were substantial: +.33 for emotional stability, +.33 for openness, +.48 for conscientiousness, +.49 for agreeableness, and +.53 for extraversion. The correlation between the GGGI and the aggregate statistic *D* was 0.69. The size of *D* was much larger than the average value of the effect sizes. Mean *D* was 0.89 compared to a mean for Cohen's *d* of 0.24—further evidence of how much difference aggregating conceptually related indicators makes.[34]

The Falk study. Also in 2018, economists Armin Falk and Johannes Hermle published their analysis of the Global Preferences Survey conducted in 2012. The indicators were not of personality traits per se, but of six preferences that in turn are consistent with personality traits. Four of these preferences were in the social domain: altruism, trust, positive reciprocity (a preference for rewarding positive behaviors), and negative reciprocity (a preference for punishing negative behaviors). Two were nonsocial and had more direct implications for economic behavior: risk-taking and time discounting (preference for a future larger reward than an immediate smaller reward). The sex differences on the four social preferences were all on the side of People-oriented personality traits: On average, women preferred altruism, trust, and positive reciprocity more than men and were more averse to negative reciprocity than men. In the two nonsocial preferences, men preferred risk-taking and waiting for a larger reward more than women. The analysis employed representative samples from 76 countries.

All of the sex differences on these traits became larger as countries became more economically developed and more egalitarian in their social policies. The correlations of preferences with the authors' Gender Equality Index were all in the wrong direction: +.51 for altruism, +.41 for trust, +.13 for positive reciprocity, +.40 for negative reciprocity, +.34 for risk-taking and +.43 for patience.[35] Greater equality was associated with larger sex differences. The authors did not report an aggregated effect size. However, they did create an index incorporating all six preferences. The correlation between the size of the sex difference on the combined index and the Gender Equality Index was +.56. The correlation was even larger (+.67) for a measure of national wealth, per capita GDP. Or as the authors put it, "These findings imply that both economic development and gender equality exhibited an independent and significant association with gender differences in preferences."[36]

—————

Five different studies, based on different measures of personality and national gender egality, analyzing data from dozens of countries, all found the same pattern: overall consistency in male-female differences in personality, but larger differences in the most advanced countries.[37]

Explaining Wider Personality Differences in Advanced Countries

Why haven't the sex differences in personality gotten smaller in countries that have aggressively adopted gender-egalitarian policies? Why instead, and contrary to all expectations, have they tended to widen? Costa and his coauthors hypothesized that in traditional societies with strong sex roles, people see behavioral sex differences as socially mandatory, not the result of personal dispositions, whereas people in advanced societies are more likely to see them as evidence of personal dispositions.[38] Another possibility is that people tend to compare themselves to others of their own sex in traditional cultures, whereas in advanced cultures people compare themselves to the whole population. For example, a woman in a traditional culture may rank herself on kindness relative to other women. She may be of the opinion that women tend to be kinder than men, but that doesn't enter into her self-report. In an advanced culture, perhaps a woman compares her kindness to others of both sexes, and a sex difference emerges.[39]

It should be pointed out that these hypotheses do not argue that the wider sex differences in personality in the more egalitarian countries are illusions. They de facto acknowledge the reality of the large differences in advanced countries; it's just that the differences are masked in countries with strong sex roles. But the Schmitt study argues that in fact the hypotheses cannot be sustained in the face of the patterns in the data. Instead, the authors introduced an important new empirical perspective to explain the phenomenon of widening sex differences: Perhaps we're looking at a general phenomenon that goes far beyond personality traits. For example, the Schmitt study points out, sexual dimorphism in height increases with a country's wealth. So too with sexual dimorphism in blood pressure. So too with competitiveness in sports—as opportunities and incentives increase for women to compete in sports, sex differences in performance increase as well. So too with differences between advantaged and disadvantaged groups in health and education when new opportunities are made available to all. Two years after the Schmitt study made these points, another study led by Richard Lippa found that sexual dimorphism in visuospatial abilities also increased with gender equality.[40]

Another surprise from the Schmitt study was its finding that men do most of the changing, in both the physiological and personality traits. When sexual dimorphism in height increases, for example, it is primarily due to greater height among males. In the case of personality, the Schmitt study found that the wider sex gap in emotional stability in advanced countries is not the result of women becoming less emotionally stable, but of men self-reporting higher levels of emotional stability, and also lower levels of agreeableness and conscientiousness, than men in less advanced countries.

Whatever the explanation turns out to be, the evidence about personality profiles around the world needs to be taken on board by orthodox academics. In 2016, David Schmitt and colleagues returned to the body of evidence that had accumulated since the turn of the twenty-first century, summarizing it this way:

> Psychological sex differences—in Big Five traits, Dark Triad traits, self-esteem, subjective well-being, depression, and values—are demonstrably the largest in cultures with the *lowest* levels of bifurcated gender role socialization or sociopolitical patriarchy. Ultimately, the view that men and women start from a blank slate simply does not jibe with the current findings, and scholars who continue to assert gender invariably starts from a psychological blank slate should find these recurring cross-cultural patterns challenging to their foundational assumptions.[41] [Emphasis in the original.]

I would add that the international story of sex differences in personality is challenging not only to advocates of the sex-is-a-social-construct position. I know of no ideological perspective that would have predicted greater sex differences in personality in Scandinavia than in Africa or Asia.

Recapitulation

The core message of this chapter is that the personality profiles of males and females are different in ways that break along the People-Things dimension worldwide.

Many of the differences conform to stereotypes of masculine and feminine characteristics, which in turn prompts me to remind you once again that we are talking about overlapping distributions. Many males are closer to the female profile than are many females, and vice versa. But neither is it appropriate to minimize those differences. Sometimes the effect size for a single aspect of the personality inventories is huge, as in the effect size of +2.29 for the "sensitive, aesthetic, sentimental" factor in the 16PF standardization sample. Sometimes separate but conceptually related facets point to a large aggregated difference even when such aggregates have not been calculated, as in the case of the facets in the FFM that are related to the People-Things dimension.

The traits that differ along the People-Things dimension are not shocking. The technical studies tell us that women are, on average, warmer, more sympathetic, more altruistic, and more sensitive to others' feelings than men are. I suggest that these technical findings are face-valid. They match up with common human experience.

Why do many of these differences apparently become more pronounced in the most gender-egalitarian nations? I will not try to adjudicate among the explanations that others have advanced, but I will disclose my own, admitting that it is completely ex post facto: The deprivations of freedom that women still suffer in traditional societies sometimes suppress the expression of inborn personality traits. For example, whatever genetic tendencies toward extraversion that women in a strict Muslim culture may have, they are under enormous cultural pressure to modify their expression of those tendencies to meet cultural norms. Perhaps such conditions also warp the expression of male personality. Under this hypothesis, genetically-grounded personality differences widen in the most gender-egalitarian societies for the simplest of reasons: Both sexes become freer to do what comes naturally.

3

Sex Differences in Neurocognitive Functioning

Proposition #2: On average, females have advantages in verbal ability and social cognition while males have advantages in visuospatial abilities and the extremes of mathematical ability.

As groups, men and women have different cognitive profiles. Those differences manifest themselves many different ways, leaving us with a lot of ground to cover in this chapter. I begin with summaries of the state of knowledge about a variety of specific abilities, then turn to cross-national data, and conclude with two syntheses that help tie the pieces together.

Specific Skills and Aptitudes

For some of these summaries, I make use of Diane Halpern's fourth edition of *Sex Differences in Cognitive Abilities* (2012).[1] I do not try to interweave the dozens of references Halpern cites, giving instead a single endnote at the outset with the pages for her book. I add endnotes for material that she did not use or that postdate the fourth edition.

On Average, Females Have Better Sensory Perception Than Males[2]

When it comes to the five senses—taste, touch, smell, sound, vision—the story is mostly one of small female advantages.

- Females tend to be better than males at detecting pure tones.
- Adult females tend to have more sensitive hearing for high frequencies than males.

- Females tend to have better auditory perception of binaural beats and otoacoustic emissions.[3]
- Females tend to detect faint smells better than males.
- Females tend to identify smells more accurately than males.[4]
- Males under 40 tend to detect small movements in their visual field better than females.
- Age-related loss of vision tends to occur about ten years earlier for females than for males.
- Males are many times more likely to be color-blind than females (the ratio varies by ethnic group).
- The balance of evidence indicates that females are more accurate than males in recognizing the basic tastes (sweet, sour, salty, bitter), though some studies find no difference.
- Females tend to be better than males at perceiving fine surface details by touch. This holds true for blind people as well as sighted ones.[5]

Most of these differences have small individual effect sizes consistent with the stereotype that "women are more sensitive than men," For taste, touch, smell, and sound, women are (on average) more sensitive instruments than men are. They are not a lot more sensitive on any single sense, but somewhat more sensitive on all of them. Even when it comes to vision, the male advantage in detecting movement is counterbalanced by a greater male disadvantage in color blindness.[6]

Women are also more sensitive to pain than men. It's not that women aren't as tough as men; rather, the neurological experience of pain is more intense for women.[7] Evidence for greater female sensitivity to pain is found even in infancy.[8] Another aspect of this greater sensitivity is a pronounced sex difference in "disgust," whether in response to exposure to pathogens (e.g., reactions to seeing a rat or to an oozing wound) or with regard to sexual activity that involves risk of disease or decreases reproductive fitness (e.g., incest). Effect sizes for sexual disgust can be large, ranging from +0.60 to +1.54.[9]

On Average, Females Have Better Perceptual and Fine Motor Skills Than Males[10]

Females have an advantage on certain perceptual-motor tasks. On digit-symbol coding, for example, where each symbol corresponds to a number (e.g., "substitute 2 for #"), women code faster than men do. Sometimes these differences involve large effect sizes, with $d = +0.86$ in one major study.

Females have an even larger advantage in a variety of fine motor skills involving hand-eye coordination. Evidence for this advantage goes back to infancy.[11] Diane Halpern observes dryly that while such tests of fine motor skills "are sometimes labeled 'clerical skills tests' ... I note here that fine motor skills are also needed in a variety of other professions such as brain surgery, dentistry, and the repair of small engines."[12] In tests of motor skills, it sometimes happens that men are faster but women are more accurate.

On Average, Males Have Better Throwing Skills Than Females[13]

Men have a substantial advantage in many large motor skills, but few of them have much to do with cognition. The major exception is males' pronounced advantage on tasks that involve throwing objects accurately at stationary or moving targets, because that accuracy is highly dependent on visuospatial processing in the brain. Effect sizes have sometimes exceeded 1.0 and persist when right-handed subjects are throwing with their left hands.[14]

On Average, Females Have Better Memory on Several but Not All Types of Memory[15]

Memory comes in many forms—long-term and short-term, "autobiographical," "episodic," and "semantic," among others. Here are the main themes of the research, mostly drawn from Diane Halpern:

- Females tend to be better than males at remembering faces and names.
- Females tend to be better than males at recognizing facial emotions.
- Females tend to be better at remembering the minutiae of an event (labeled *peripheral detail*), while males tend to be better at remembering the core events (labeled *gist*).[16]
- Females tend to remember speech they have heard better than males, particularly when it relates to emotionally laden events in their past.
- Females tend to retain memories from earlier childhood better than males do.
- Females tend to have better short-term memory than males (e.g., given a list of single-digit numbers, they remember longer lists than males do).

- Females tend to have better verbal working memory (e.g., remembering a list of numbers while answering questions about an unrelated topic).
- Females tend to have better memory for locations of objects (e.g., remembering where the car keys were left).
- Males tend to have better visuospatial memory (e.g., navigating on the basis of a combination of landscape features).[17]

On Average, Females Have Better Verbal Ability Than Males in the Normal Range[18]

There are no official definitions of "normal range" of ability versus "gifted." The most common decision rule for placement in gifted programs is an IQ score of 130 or above, putting someone in the top 2 percent of the population. My purposes in the discussion below don't require a hard-and-fast cutoff. When I discuss scores in the normal range, I report effect sizes and male-female ratios for entire samples. When I discuss scores at the high end, I focus on the top five percentiles. By "extreme high end" I mean the top two percentiles at most.

On tests with nationally representative samples, females can be expected to consistently outperform males on a variety of verbal tasks, with a small advantage in reading and a more substantial advantage in writing. The note describes the details for the Cognitive Abilities Test (CogAT) and the National Assessment of Educational Progress (NAEP), which have produced effect sizes ranging from near zero to +0.20 for verbal reasoning, around +0.20 to +0.30 for reading, and in the +0.40 to +0.60 range in writing.[19]

Reading disabilities. Boys experience dyslexia more commonly than girls. In the past, the size of the discrepancy has been clouded by referral bias, but epidemiological samples have established that the male-female ratio is in the range of 1.5 to 3.3, depending on the criteria for severity of the problem and the minimum IQ used for diagnosis.[20]

EXPRESSING RATIOS

I've just given the first of dozens of ratios that are reported in the book. Unless I specify otherwise, all the ratios I report are produced by dividing the male value by the female value, which means the base for all the numbers is 1, as in, for example, 3.3:1. I omit the base and report the ratio as 3.3, which is easier to read.

Females Probably Retain an Advantage at the Extreme High End of Verbal Ability Before Puberty and Probably Lose It Subsequently

At the beginning of adolescence, girls still have some advantage at the extreme high end of verbal ability, but it does not seem to persist through high school for American students. These are provisional conclusions awaiting further evidence.

Gifted 7th graders. Since 1981, Duke University has sponsored the Duke University Talent Identification Program (Duke TIP), which now operates in a 16-state region of the South and Midwest. Students are invited to participate if they have previously scored in the top five percentiles for their grade level on the composite score of a standardized test or a relevant subtest (usually math or verbal). It attracts more than 100,000 students a year, accumulating more than 2.8 million participants since 1980. Upon entering TIP, participants take either the SAT or the ACT. Because they are taking college entrance tests designed for 17-year-olds, SAT scores obtained in their seventh year of schooling discriminate levels of ability among students in fractions of the top percentile.

The female advantage in the top percentile persisted to the highest levels of verbal ability. For the top 0.01 percent in the SAT (the largest female advantage), there were 1.4 girls for every boy.[21]

Gifted students as of grade 12. I'm still talking about verbal ability as measured by the SAT and ACT, but no longer about 13-year-olds. Rather, I refer to students who take it at the normal time. They are self-selected for academic ability. Stated conservatively, the test-taking populations for both the SAT and ACT are still concentrated in the upper half of the ability distribution.[22]

For the test pools as a whole, the young women who take the SAT have consistently had fractionally lower scores than the young men. The opposite is true of the ACT—the females have fractionally higher scores. The note gives the details.[23]

Sex ratios in the top few percentiles. What goes on in the top few percentiles of verbal skills for adolescents ages 17–18? The only source I have been able to find that casts light on the answer is the SAT data broken down not only by gender but by score intervals (the ACT does not publish such information). The SAT data are internally consistent in showing that the female advantage disappeared in the verbal reasoning test and was trivially small in the writing test at the top levels of ability, but it's a single set of test batteries. The pattern needs to be replicated in other large databases before making much of it.

Sex Differences in Math Ability in the Normal Range Are Inconsistent and Small[24]

Now we turn to mathematics, which has gotten most of the attention in the debate about sex differences in test scores. It's one of the rare cases in which the data are plentiful and the story doesn't vary, at least within the United States:

Females get higher classroom grades than males in math at all K–12 grade levels—but, for that matter, females get higher grades than males in just about everything during the K–12 years. On standardized tests, sex differences in mean scores on mathematics tests usually favor males, but the effect sizes are quite small for representative samples of students. A meta-analysis of the NAEP mathematics test from 1990 to 2011 found effect sizes of –0.07, –0.04, and –0.10 (favoring boys) in grades 4, 8, and 12 respectively.[25] In the most recent test for grades 4 and 8, 2017, the effect sizes were –0.06 and –0.03 respectively. The most recent math test for grade 12 was in 2015, when the effect size was –0.09.[26]

Halpern's review of meta-analyses of differences in math scores includes many other standardized tests showing similarly small effect sizes. To the question, "Is the typical male better at math than the typical female?" the answer is close to settled: "If yes, not enough to be noticeable," with an open possibility that a small gap will close altogether.

Males Have a Persisting Advantage in Math at the Extreme High End

"Sex differences in mathematics become progressively larger as the sample becomes more selective and the type of math skill becomes more advanced," writes Halpern, and herein lies a major issue in the study of cognitive sex differences.[27] The literature has been extensive and aroused contentious reactions, but the dust has settled (as much as any dispute about sex differences is allowed to settle) on a few basic points.[28] We once again have two major sources of data: scores of 12–13-year-olds who are tested in 7th grade using a college entrance exam (SAT or ACT), and for 17–18-year-olds who are tested in their senior year.

Gifted 7th graders. The last 60 years have seen major reductions in the male advantage at the extreme high end for 7th graders. For those in the top two percentiles, a ratio of about 2.0 in 1960 appears to have disappeared. For those in the top percentile, a male ratio of about 7.0 has fallen to around 1.5. At the most stratospheric level, the top 1 percent of the top 1 percent, a male advantage that was measured at about 13 to 1 in the 1970s and the early 1980s has fallen to less than 3 to 1.[29] In short, what was once thought to be an overwhelming male advantage at high levels of math achievement has been greatly reduced during the last six decades. But a second statement is also true: The male advantage for 7th graders at the highest levels of ability shrank mostly during the 1980s and has been relatively stable since the early 1990s.[30]

Gifted 12th graders. For college-bound seniors taking the SAT math, the gap at a broadly defined high end—treating the entire SAT pool as a moderately gifted group—has narrowed since the 1970s. The effect size of the male advantage on the SAT was −0.38 in 1977, its largest since the first published scores in 1972, and stood at −0.25 in 2016, its smallest ever.[31] The shrinkage in the size of the male advantage was relatively steady throughout the period.

A WORD ABOUT THE SAT

The letters *SAT* originally stood for *Scholastic Aptitude Test*, which signaled the test's purpose: to identify high-IQ students regardless of their family circumstances or the quality of their schooling. The College Board has ignored that history since IQ became politically incorrect in the 1960s, but the SAT remained a good measure of IQ for high school graduates into the 1990s.[32] Since the SAT does not release the needed psychometric information, there's no way to be sure, but I surmise that the SAT lost a little of its quality as a measure of IQ in the revision in 1994, more in the revision in 2005, and still more in the revision in 2016. I should add that the SAT is not culturally biased against ethnic minorities or the poor and, at least until the revisions of 2005 and 2016, was far less susceptible to coaching than most parents think.[33]

If we concentrate on students who qualify as gifted by a more demanding definition—those who score 700–800 on the SAT math—a big drop in the male advantage occurred in the 1980s. It continued into the 1990s, but the downward trend flattened after 1995. Since 2010, the ratio of males to females scoring 700–800 in the SAT math has hovered near 1.9.

The male math advantage at the extreme high end for 17- and 18-year-olds remains large. Since 1950, the Mathematical Association of America has sponsored the American Mathematics Competitions (AMC) for high school students. The test used for the competition is far harder than the SAT math test.[34] The following table shows the male-female ratio for students who scored in the top five percentiles for the years 2009 through 2018. *Everyone in this group is in the top percentile of the national population of 17- and 18-year-olds.* Those in the 99th percentile on the AMC are probably around the top 0.01 percent of the national population or even higher.

I show two ways of computing the ratio for each of the top five percentiles. One is the raw ratio: the number of males scoring in that AMC percentile divided by the number of females. The other is the ratio adjusted for the numbers of males and females taking the test.[35]

AMC	Male-female ratio	
Centile	Raw	Adjusted
95th	4.2	2.9
96th	4.4	3.1
97th	4.4	3.1
98th	5.3	3.7
99th	7.8	5.4

For the American Mathematics Competitions, the male-female ratio remains quite high. Which ratio you think is closer to correct depends on your judgment about the population of test-takers. From 2009 to 2018, the population of AMC12 test-takers averaged 59 percent male and 41 percent female. Your opinion about the reason for the sex imbalance in test-takers should push you toward one choice or the other.

One possibility is that students self-select into the AMC testing pool if they think they're good enough at math to do well on the test and otherwise don't bother to take it. To the extent that there is a genuine sex imbalance of talent in the top percentiles of ability, then more males than females will self-select into the pool. If you are attracted by this explanation, you should focus on the raw ratios as the correct ones.

Another possibility is that the larger proportion of male test-takers is an artifact having nothing to do with underlying math talent. Taking the AMC is exceptionally nerdy. Perhaps that's more off-putting to 17-year-old girls than to 17-year-old boys. Perhaps there is a difference (whether biological or socialized doesn't matter) in how much boys and girls enjoy the kind of competition that the AMC represents. If you are attracted by this explanation, you should focus on the adjusted ratios as the correct ones.

I won't try to spin out all the many ways in which the meaning of the ratios is clouded by selection factors. Whichever ratio you think is closer to the truth, they point to an empirical reality: The male-female ratios in the top percentiles of the AMC12 are substantial and they grow larger at the 98th and especially the 99th percentile. In the table, I counted perfect scores of 150 as being in the 99th percentile. When they are broken out separately, it turns out that from 2009 to 2018, 97 males and 7 females got perfect scores: a ratio of 13.9.

On Average, Males Have Substantially Better Visuospatial Skills Than Females[36]

Diane Halpern's review of sex differences in visuospatial skills takes 17 pages. It is so long partly because the concept is complicated (she divides visuospatial skills into five components) and partly because, in her words, "sex differences in spatial tasks are among the largest sex differences."[37] But another good reason for a lengthy discussion is that a male advantage in visuospatial skills has specific implications for real-world sex differences in vocations. In the Paleolithic period, they were useful for throwing spears at edible mammals and finding one's way back home after a long hunting trip. Now they are useful because they seem to be an essential component of extraordinary mathematical and programming skills. Other professions that make extensive use of visuospatial abilities include engineering, architecture, chemistry, aviation, and the building trades.

The first category of spatial aptitude is spatial perception. An example is the Piaget water-level task:

Figure A shows a bottle with some water in it.

In Figure B the bottle has been tilted.
Draw a line to show how the water line would look.

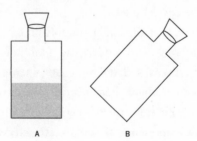

A   B

Source: Halpern (2012): Fig. 3.12.

The test-taker is asked to draw a line to show how the water line would look in the tilted bottle. The correct answer is a horizontal line relative to the earth. Halpern reports that the best estimate, summarizing results over many studies, is that about 40 percent of college women get it wrong.[38] Effect sizes favoring males range from –0.44 to –0.66. In Halpern's words, "It is difficult to understand why this should be such a formidable task for college women."[39] And yet the result has been replicated many times, has been confirmed internationally, and is just about impossible to explain as a product of culture or socialization (if you doubt that, give it a try).[40]

"Mental rotation" refers to the ability to imagine how objects will look when rotated in two- or three-dimensional space. Twenty-five years of research and several meta-analyses have all confirmed a substantial male advantage throughout the age range, with effect sizes ranging from –0.52 to –1.49.

Spatiotemporal ability is another conceptually distinct form of visuospatial skill that calls for judgments about moving objects. For example, the subject of the test might be asked to press a key when a moving object passes a specified point or asked to make an estimate of "time of arrival" of a moving object at a specified destination. Effect sizes have ranged from –0.37 to –0.93.[41] In a large sample, with a carefully executed experimental design, effect sizes ranged from –0.51 to –0.81.[42]

The fourth type of visuospatial skill calls upon participants to generate a visual image from short-term or long-term memory and then use information in that image to perform a task. The tests usually are scored for both speed and accuracy. In one of the best studies, the effect sizes on speed for four different tasks ranged from –0.63 to –0.77, all favoring males, with no sex differences in accuracy.[43]

The last type of visuospatial skill is called spatial visualization, which calls on people to go through a multistep mental process to understand how an object will be changed if something is done to it. For example, the paper-folding test asks: If you fold a piece of paper in half and punch three holes through it, what will the piece of paper look like when it is unfolded? Males usually show an advantage on spatial visualization, but the effect sizes are generally small.

Halpern describes other types of visuospatial skills, all of which show a male advantage.[44] An important outstanding question is how large the aggregate difference in visuospatial skills might be. Many of the effect sizes for sex differences in visuospatial skills are large even when taken individually. But given the parallel with personality facets—conceptually related but distinct traits—a calculation of Mahalanobis D for large samples of males and females who have taken a comprehensive test battery would be instructive. Perhaps many of the different types of skills are so intercorrelated that aggregating them would not add much to the largest individual effect size. It is a question that I hope will be explored.

On Average, Women Have Better Social Cognition Than Men

We take for granted that we can infer what someone else is thinking, but this inference is actually a theory—"theory of mind," often abbreviated as ToM in the literature. It refers to our belief that other people have minds of their own that operate in ways we can understand. It is properly called a theory because the only mind we have direct access to is our own and because we can make predictions based on our theory.[45]

Children acquire ToM as toddlers. As normal people mature, they employ ToM to navigate the social world in increasingly complex ways. But not everybody has a normal human consciousness. The severely autistic have trouble with ToM—one of the features of autism that inspired Baron-Cohen's empathizer-systemizer theory. Even within the normal range, people vary widely in their ability to project themselves into another person's mind and correctly predict how that person will react. These are skills that are encompassed by Howard Gardner's *interpersonal intelligence* and that other scholars refer to as *cognitive empathy, mentalizing, mindreading*, or the label I have chosen to use, *social cognition*. In terms of Simon Baron-Cohen's *empathizing* and *systemizing*, social cognition is to empathizing as visuospatial skills are to systemizing. In both cases, the topic is neurocognitive abilities that contribute to a broad difference between the sexes.

The study of social cognition originated in one of the most durable sex stereotypes, that women are more intuitive than men. Through the early 1970s, researchers were dismissive of evidence that a sex difference existed. As late as 1974, the most comprehensive review of sex differences yet undertaken concluded that "neither sex has greater ability to judge the reactions and intentions of others in any generalized sense."[46] Then in 1978, psychologist Judith Hall produced the first comprehensive study of all the quantitative work that had been done. In "Gender Effects in Decoding Nonverbal Cues," published in *Psychological Bulletin* in 1978, Hall reported mean effect sizes favoring females of +0.32 for visual cues, +0.18 for auditory cues, and a large effect of +1.02 for the seven studies that combined visual and auditory cues.[47] Six years later, Hall extended her meta-analysis to include nine countries around the world. Subsequent work has yielded similar results.[48]

In 2014, psychologists Ashley Thompson and Daniel Voyer undertook a new meta-analysis. Hall's reviews had included studies of accuracy in interpersonal perception of any kind. Thompson and Voyer focused on the ability to detect specific discrete emotions. As in other studies, the results showed a female advantage, but with a smaller effect size that had a lower bound effect size of +0.19 and an upper bound of +0.27.[49]

The Thompson meta-analysis also corroborated Hall's findings that effect sizes are substantially increased when the subjects in the studies have access to a combination of visual and audio information—that is, when they could see both face and body language and also hear tone of voice. The lower bound effect sizes favoring women were +0.17 for visual only, +0.16 for audio only, and +0.38 for a combination of the two.[50]

The publication of Daniel Goleman's bestselling *Emotional Intelligence: Why It Can Matter More than IQ* in 1995 prompted the construction of tests to measure emotional intelligence (EI). The most psychometrically successful and widely used one has been the Mayer-Salovey-Caruso Emotional Intelligence Test (MSCEIT). Version 2 has eight subscales measuring four aspects of EI: perceiving emotion, assimilating emotion in thought, understanding emotion, and reflectively regulating emotion. Of these, the items that most directly measure social cognition as I have been using the term are in the subtests for perceiving emotion. A 2010 meta-analysis found an effect size favoring females of +0.49. On the overall score for performance EI, the female advantage was +0.47.[51]

I will return to other evidence of sex differences in social cognition in chapter 5, reporting the progress that neuroscientists have made in identifying sex differences in brain function that relate to sex differences in social cognition. In the meantime, two points about differences in social cognition need emphasis:

Social cognition consists of a set of abilities, not something that women do better than men just because they are paying more attention to other people than men do.[52] Those abilities often break along the People-Things dimension. For example, it has been found that systemizing skills and empathizing skills are inversely related in men—men who scored high on tests measuring systemizing tended to score low on tests measuring empathizing. Males are rarely good at both systemizing and empathizing. In contrast, these skill sets are largely independent in women. Women can be high in both, low in both, or high in one and low in the other.[53] The same study found evidence that men apply systemizing skills to empathizing tasks. Put another way, even when men do well in social cognition tasks, they are not using the cognitive tools most naturally suited to that purpose.

It has also been established that the relationship of IQ to social cognition is different for men and women. Subtests measuring memory are standard in a full-scale IQ test. They wouldn't be included if they did not correlate with the other subtests seeking to measure g. But the correlation between IQ and certain kinds of memory is different for men and women. In a Swedish study comparing IQ with three episodic memory tasks, women outperformed men in all three—verbal memory, memory for pictures of things, and memory for pictures of faces. The difference was that male performance was substantially correlated with IQ for all three tasks while IQ was substantially less important, especially at the lower levels, for women. Women with IQs of 60–80 had verbal memory as high as men with IQs of 101–120. Women with IQs of 60–80 had substantially *higher* scores on memory for faces than men with IQs of 101–120.[54] Something's going on with memory in females that calls on non-IQ skills that men do not tap (or perhaps possess) to the same degree.

The aggregate sex difference in social cognition has yet to be estimated. Four different clusters of sex differences are relevant to assessing the overall magnitude of the sex difference in social cognition. The first consists of the direct measures that I have reviewed in this section. The second consists of the female advantage in memory for faces, which in turn is presumably related to the ability to discern visual clues about emotional states. The third is the cluster of ways in which the female sensory apparatus is more sensitive than the male's. The fourth cluster has to do with male-female differences in personality that bear on the reasoning aspect of social cognition.[55] In the technical literature, the effect sizes in all four of these categories have been treated separately. The prudent expectation is that if these individual effect sizes, which have usually been in the small to medium range, were aggregated appropriately, they would reveal a much larger overall difference.

Is There a Sex Difference in g*?*

The most famous cognitive measure is the IQ test. The tests are designed to minimize sex differences,[56] but minor sex differences in test scores do exist, and they have usually, though not always, favored males.[57] The Wechsler Adult Intelligence Scale (WAIS), one of the best-known IQ tests, provides a typical example. The U.S. standardization samples for the first version, released in 1955, showed a 1.0-point difference in full-scale IQ favoring males. WAIS-R, released in 1981, showed a 2.2-point difference. WAIS-III, released in 1997, showed a 2.7-point difference. WAIS-IV, released in 2008, showed a 2.3-point difference.[58]

But all of this evidence is based on IQ scores, not on the general mental factor *g*, the thing that IQ tests are imperfectly measuring. The distinction between an IQ score and *g* is crucial. An IQ score is based on a set of subtests. The simple sum or average of scores depends on which tests have more representation in the test battery; therefore, as Arthur Jensen wrote, "the simple sum or mean of various subtest scores is a datum without scientific interest or generality."[59] The question of scientific interest regarding a sex difference in intelligence is whether there is a sex difference on *g*. Jensen's conclusion after assessing *g* in five major test batteries—the WAIS, the Wechsler Intelligence Scale for Children-Revised (WISC-R), the General Aptitude Test Battery (GATB), the Armed Services Vocational Aptitude Battery (ASVAB), and the British Ability Scales (BAS)— was that "the sex difference in psychometric *g* is either totally nonexistent or is of uncertain direction and of inconsequential magnitude."[60]

Jensen made this pronouncement in his magnum opus, *The* g *Factor*, published in 1998. The list of eminent scholars who have shared that view began with Cyril Burt and Lewis Terman in the early part of the twentieth century and continued through the rest of the century and into the twenty-first century with figures such as Raymond Cattell, Nathan Brody, Hans Eysenck, John Loehlin, David Geary, Diane Halpern, Thomas Bouchard, David Lubinski, and Camilla Benbow. I should add that Richard Herrnstein and I took the same position in *The Bell Curve*.

This does not mean that everyone accepts that the question has been settled. A lively and sometimes acrimonious debate has been ongoing in recent years that you may follow by checking the sources in the note.[61] It is still technically unsettled. My own sense—and it's no more than that, from someone who is knowledgeable about IQ but not expert in the abstruse technical issues that are being disputed—is that the possibility of a trivial sex difference in g is still in play but the demonstration of a meaningful one is not.

Do Sex Differences in Abilities Diminish in Countries with Greater Gender Egality?

The question has different answers for academic abilities and measures of visuospatial skills.

Academic Abilities

PISA test results from the early 2000s gave reason to believe that greater gender egality had a meaningful relationship with academic test scores, but data since then have made that case increasingly tough to make.[62] The emerging story is both more complicated and more interesting. It appears that all of the following are likely to be true:

Worldwide, overall sex differences in performance on math and science tests in the normal range are trivially small. The 2015 PISA survey included 67 countries. The overall mean effect size on the math test was −0.05—a tiny difference favoring boys.[63] The overall mean effect size on the science test was +0.01—no difference. The TIMSS survey of 2011 included 45 countries. The overall mean effect size on the math test was +0.04—a tiny difference favoring girls. The overall mean effect size on the science test was +0.05—a tiny difference again favoring girls.

The differences that do appear in some individual countries have a weak and inconsistent relationship with gender egality. Some analyses of the PISA and TIMSS survey in the early 2000s found a negative correlation between the size of the sex difference in mathematics and the indexes of gender equality in the culture.[64] When Gijsbert Stoet and David Geary analyzed all four PISA administrations from 2000 to 2009, they concluded that the patterns in the early 2000s were not sustained:

> If anything, economically developed countries with strong sex-equality and human development scores tended to have a larger sex difference in mathematics than less economically developed countries.... Further, we found considerable variation among lower scoring countries, with some

showing a large sex difference in mathematics achievement favoring boys and others favoring girls. In other words, the sex differences in mathematics were more consistently found among higher-achieving nations, a pattern which coincides with the larger sex difference in mathematics in high-achieving students.[65]

The results of the most recent administrations of the PISA and TIMSS tests are consistent with that finding.

When the standardized scores for the Gender Development Index (GDI), Gender Inequality Index (GII), and Global Gap Index (GGI) are combined, the biggest effect sizes favoring boys in math were Honduras, Austria, and Ghana. In science, they were again Ghana and Honduras, plus Costa Rica. It's hard to make much of that pattern with regard to gender egality in political and social institutions. But it's even harder when you consider the biggest effect sizes favoring girls: Oman, Bahrain, and Jordan for math; Jordan, Albania, and the United Arab Emirates for science—not countries known for their enlightened gender policies. Taking the data from the last two decades as a whole, cross-national academic test scores show no significant relationship to measures of gender egality. Details are in the note.[66]

The most plausible explanation for the substantial effect sizes in math and science that appear in some individual countries is cultural, not biological. Why should some Arab countries that are notorious for legal and cultural discrimination against women produce female high school students who perform better in math than their privileged male classmates while nothing approaching the same gap favoring females is found elsewhere, either in countries with high gender egality or in non-Arab countries with low gender egality? It looks as if something about Arab socialization of children either depresses male incentives to do well in math and science or increases female incentives to do well in math and science.

The most plausible explanation for the consistent female advantage in verbal tests is biological, not cultural. The story for reading achievement in the PISA test echoes the consistent female advantage found in U.S. tests of verbal skills. Girls outscored boys in reading in every single PISA country, with effect sizes that ranged from a low of +0.08 in Peru to a remarkable high of +0.83 in Jordan. Nor was Jordan alone among nations with bad records on gender egality but large effect sizes favoring girl students. Other nations in the bottom half of the gender egality index but with effect sizes of +0.40 or higher were Algeria, the United Arab Emirates, Qatar, and Georgia. The mean effect size across all 67 PISA nations was +0.32. The correlation of the effect size with the egality index was −.11.[67]

It is difficult to reconcile the universal advantage of women in verbal tests with socialization or social role theories, neither of which has ever appealed to the idea that the oppression of women can enhance their cognitive ability. All the social-construct argumentation is based on the proposition that discrimination has suppressed female accomplishment. Nor can the argument be easily shifted by arguing that social roles encourage women to be more social and verbal, which is then reflected in superior verbal skills. The verbal test in PISA is not about sociability. It measures a cognitive ability to assimilate and analyze language that is as cognitively demanding as mathematics is in the nonverbal domain. There is no evidence that underlying verbal ability can be taught, either deliberately or through socialization. The parsimonious explanation for the international female advantage in verbal tests, across cultures that cover the full range from openly oppressive to aggressively gender-equal, is that women have a genetic advantage.

Measures of Visuospatial Skills

Some evidence indicates that sex differences in visuospatial skills are greater in countries with greater gender egality. In 2005, the BBC conducted an Internet survey of sex differences that included tests of mental rotation and line-angle judgment. Total sample sizes were 90,433 and 95,364 respectively, with sample sizes large enough to reliably explore sex differences for 53 countries. An analysis (first author was Richard Lippa) found, "Sex differences in mental rotation and line angle judgment performance were universally present across nations, with men's mean scores always exceeding women's mean scores."[68] The mean national effect size was −0.47 for the mental rotation task and −0.49 for the line-angle judgment task, both favoring men and statistically significant at $p < .001$.[69]

"STATISTICALLY SIGNIFICANT AT $P < .001$"

The phrase *statistically significant* is commonly misunderstood. In assessing the statistical significance of a quantitative relationship, the null hypothesis is that no relationship exists. Suppose we are once again talking about the sex difference in height. The null hypothesis is that the mean heights of men and women are the same. The statistical test asks, "If the null hypothesis is true, how likely is it that I nonetheless got these results by chance?" The statistic p is a proportion. Thus the standard requirement for reaching statistical significance, $p < .05$, means that there must be less than a 5 percent probability that you got your results even though the null hypothesis is true. A result of $p < .001$ means that the probability was less than one in a thousand.

"Statistically significant" doesn't mean much by itself. Given a large enough sample, trivial effect sizes will be statistically significant. Given small enough samples, large effect sizes will fail to reach statistical significance. Sample sizes (n), effect sizes (d), and statistical significance (p) must be considered jointly.

The Lippa study then calculated the correlations between national effect sizes of sex differences and four measures of national development: the UN Gender Development Index, UN Gender Empowerment Index, per capita income, and life expectancy. For all of these measures, "high" equals "good" (more gender egalitarian or economically developed), so, according to social-construct theories, the correlations with the size of the gender difference should be negative (the effect sizes should be smaller for more egalitarian or developed societies). The table below shows the correlation coefficients from the Lippa study after controlling for age and education.

	Correlation after adjusting for age and education	
Index of national development	Mental rotation	Line-angle judgment
UN Gender Development Index	+.42*	+.47*
UN Gender Empowerment Index	+.11	+.31*
Per capita income	+.08	+.42*
Life expectancy	+.33*	+.68*

Source: Adapted from Lippa, Collaer, and Peters (2010): Tables 1 and 2. Asterisk indicates that $p < .05$.

The more advanced the country, the wider the sex differences in both visuospatial tasks. The relationship was stronger on the line-angle judgment task—all four indices were significantly correlated with the effect size, at the $p < .01$ level or better for three of the four. For the mental rotation task, the correlations were significant at the $p < .01$ level for both the UN Gender

Development Index and life expectancy. But the main point of the table is that not a single correlation, large or small, is negative—a finding directly at odds with expectations of the social-construct logic.

Why should these differences in visuospatial skills be wider in more developed countries? Lippa offers potential explanations based on the greater effects of stereotype threat in advanced countries and evolutionary theories that posit greater sensitivity of males to environmental challenges, but these remain only hypotheses.[70] Nobody knows.

Recapitulation (and Integration)

I have bombarded you with a great many numbers about a great many different kinds of male and female differences in neurocognitive functioning. Two integrative analyses, conducted by leading scholars in their respective fields, help to see the broader picture.

Patterns on a Broad Neurocognitive Battery

First, consider the profiles of neurocognitive functioning found in a major recent study of neurocognitive sex differences in children and young adults. It was led by psychologists Ruben and Raquel Gur. They examined the largest and best-documented sample of its kind, the Philadelphia Neurodevelopmental Cohort (PNC). It consists of 9,122 persons ages 8 to 21, divided between 4,405 males and 4,717 females.

The participants were administered the Computerized Neurocognitive Battery (CNB). A neurocognitive battery of tests is not the same as an IQ test battery that is being used to measure different aspects of *g*. Rather, *neurocognitive* refers to bits and pieces of the way a person's brain works, focusing on ones that can be linked to the functioning of specific brain systems. The most common categories covered by the major tests of neurocognitive functioning include executive function (such things as mental flexibility, planning, and strategic decisions), memory, complex cognition (verbal and visuospatial facility), social/emotional cognition, and sensorimotor function. A neurocognitive battery commonly contains at least 10 subtests, and some contain a few dozen.

The battery administered to the Philadelphia Neurodevelopmental Cohort consists of 14 subtests designed to measure executive function, episodic memory, complex cognition, social cognition, and sensorimotor and motor function. Twelve of the subtests have two measures: the accuracy and speed of the participant's performance. The other two measure only the speed of motor and sensorimotor function. In all, the test yielded 26 male-female comparisons. Twelve of them amounted to an absolute effect size of less than 0.1. Women outscored men on six of the seven measures of accuracy with an effect size greater than 0.1, and they outscored men on four of the seven measures of speed with an effect size greater than 0.1.[71] The highlights are similar to findings you have already encountered:

- Females had more accurate memory for items involving words and people.
- On IQ-like items, women did better on the verbal ones; men did better on the spatial ones.
- On the three subtests measuring social cognition, females were both more accurate and faster than males on all of them.
- On the subtest measuring motor speed, males were faster than females.

The authors describe another pattern that did not involve specific subtests, but rather an overall construct called *within-individual variability* (WIV), referring to the evenness or unevenness of performance on the test battery. A participant with high scores on some subtests and low ones on others has high WIV; a participant who is near the same point on the distribution on all the tests has low WIV. In the technical literature, high WIV is associated with cognitive specialization, while people with low WIV are considered to be cognitive generalists.[72] Males in the Philadelphia Neurodevelopmental Cohort had higher WIV than females on both speed and accuracy for almost all ages from 8 to 21, and the difference was most pronounced in the oldest participants.[73]

The magnitude of the effect sizes ranged from small to medium. Given such large sample sizes, all but two of the differences were statistically significant. Ruben and Raquel Gur summarized their findings this way. The full citations for the references they mention are included in the note:

In summary, behavioral measures linked to brain function indicate significant sex differences in performance that emerge early in development with domain variability that relates to brain maturation. Notably, our findings are in line with a robust literature documenting sex difference in laterality and behavior (e.g., Linn and Petersen 1985; Thomas and French 1985; Voyer et al., 1995; Halpern et al., 2007; Williams et al., 2008; Hines 2010; Moreno-Briseño et al., 2010). *These findings support the notion that males and females have complementary neurocognitive abilities, with females being more generalists and outperforming males in memory and social cognition tasks and males being more specialists and performing better than females on spatial and motor tasks.*[74] [Emphasis added.]

We will get to the "sex differences in laterality" reference in chapter 5. For now, the Gurs' summary is a concise way of expressing the pattern of differences that the individual sections of this chapter have described.

Male and Female Differences in Cognitive Toolboxes

Even when men and women get the same answers to their cognitive tasks, they often get there by different routes. For example, people with high verbal skills often get the right answer to mathematics problems, but by using verbal forms of logic rather than mathematical symbols or spatial reasoning. Another well-documented example is how people navigate from point A to point B. Women tend to identify and remember landmarks—a strategy that taps into the female advantage in memory. Men tend to construct a mental map of the route—a strategy that taps into the male advantage in visuospatial skills.[75] Both methods work equally well for a wide variety of navigation tasks.[76] People are just using different sets of tools to get the job done.

In the early 2000s, Wendy Johnson and Thomas Bouchard, senior psychologists at the famed Minnesota Institute for the Study of Twins Raised Apart (MISTRA), decided to extend the metaphor of cognitive tools.[77] Using an analogy, they hypothesized that everyone has an "intellectual toolbox," but no two are exactly alike. They are stocked with varying tools that people use with different frequencies, different degrees of skill, and in different ways, and there are systematic toolbox differences between men and women. On average, men and women can accomplish most intellectual tasks equally well with their different choices and uses of tools. Hence the similarity in overall *g*. "But some tasks can be accomplished much better with certain tools than with others," Johnson and Bouchard write, "and individual performance on these tasks depends not only on skill in tool use, but also to some degree on individual toolbox composition.... The analogy is incomplete, of course, but it makes clear the question we address in this paper, namely, what are the differences in specific tool use (mental abilities) of men and women when overall skill in tool choice and use (*g*) is removed?"[78]

Johnson and Bouchard used the MISTRA sample, consisting of adult twins raised apart along with many of their spouses, partners, adoptive and biological family members, and friends. The sample was not representative, but its members came from a wide range of backgrounds, and the researchers had extraordinarily thorough information about them. All of them had gone through at least one weeklong assessment of medical and physical traits plus psychological tests of cognitive abilities, personality, interests, and attitudes.

Johnson and Bouchard used sophisticated quantitative methods. Describing them would take us far afield (it was a combination of factor analysis and regression analysis), but the result is simple enough to understand.

Imagine a man and woman with equal general intelligence (*g*). The woman uses her elevated verbal skills to help her solve math problems while the man uses his elevated visuospatial skills to help solve him math problems. They take two math tests. One consists entirely of problems expressed in mathematical notation. The other consists of math problems expressed in words. They both get most of the items right on both tests—*g* goes a long way toward enabling people to solve math problems no matter what their special skills might be. But the woman gets a slightly higher score than the man on the word-problem test while the man gets a slightly higher score on the one using mathematical notation. The net result is no sex difference. But actually there was a difference in tools that the man and woman used. What Johnson and Bouchard did was to strip away the role played by *g* and let us see the differences in tools. A more precise description is given in the note.[79]

The Johnson study presented the results for all 42 tests, but calculated effect sizes only for those that met a stricter than normal standard of statistical significance ($p < .01$ instead of $p < .05$) because of the large number of tests involved. Results for the residual effects on 21 of the subtests that met that statistical standard are shown in the following table. I omit the *p* values. All but two of the *p* values for the residual effects were at the .001 level.[80] The effect sizes stripped of *g* are ordered from the largest for females (positive) to the largest for males (negative).

COGNITIVE SEX DIFFERENCES IN THE MISTRA SAMPLE

Assessment activity	Overall effect size	Effect size stripped of g
Coding (ID of symbol-number pairings)	+0.56	+0.83
Perceptual speed (evaluation of symbol pairs)	+0.37	+0.68
Spelling (multiple choice)	ns	+0.66
Word fluency (production of anagrams)	ns	+0.64
ID of familial relationships within a family tree	ns	+0.63
Rote memorization of meaningful pairings	+0.33	+0.60
Production of words beginning and ending with specified letters	ns	+0.57
Vocabulary (multiple choice)	ns	+0.50
Rote memorization of meaningless pairings	ns	+0.42
Chronological sequencing of pictures	−0.28	−0.30
Information (recall of factual knowledge)	−0.29	−0.39
Trace of a path through a grid of dots	−0.42	−0.40
Matching of rotated alternatives to probe	ns	−0.45
Reproduction of 2-D designs of 3-D blocks	−0.34	−0.48
Outline of cutting instructions to form the target figure	−0.39	−0.48
Arithmetic (mental calculation of problems presented verbally)	−0.36	−0.53
ID of unfolded version of a folded probe	−0.44	−0.59
ID of matched figures after rotation	−0.55	−0.75
ID of parts missing in pictures of common objects	−0.60	−0.81
ID of rotated versions of 2-D representation of 3-D objects	−0.92	−1.04
ID of mechanical principles and tools	−1.18	−1.43

Source: Adapted from Johnson and Bouchard (2007): Table 4. "ns" signifies $p > .01$. Negative effect sizes indicate a higher male mean.

First, look at the column showing the overall effect size, calculated the same way as all the other effect sizes you have seen. Among the effect sizes that were statistically significant, four were "small" by the Cohen guidelines, eight were "medium," one was "large," and one was "very large." We can safely assume that most of those that did not meet the $p < .01$ standard of statistical significance fell in the "small" range.

Now look at the right-hand column, showing the difference between males and females on these subtests when the role of g has been extracted. As Johnson and Bouchard anticipated, all of these effect sizes are larger than the overall effect size. Furthermore, only one qualifies as "small" while 13 are "medium," five are "large," and two are "very large." (As you might predict, I think that if these conceptually related effect sizes were aggregated, the value of Mahalonobis D would be huge.) Johnson and Bouchard's work tells us how much that apparent similarity in overall g is illusory: End points are similar, but ways of getting to them are different. Hence the title of their article: "Sex Differences in Mental Abilities: g Masks the Dimensions on Which They Lie."

Linking Sex Differences in Neurocognitive Functioning with the People-Things Dimension

People generally enjoy the things they're good at. They also like the experience of being good at what they do—a fundamental truth about the nature of human enjoyment that goes back to Aristotle. The sex differences in neurocognitive functioning point to a tendency for men and women to enjoy different kinds of activities. When I discussed visuospatial skills, I listed some of the vocations that, to attain excellence, require high visuospatial skills—math, programming, engineering, architecture, chemistry, the building trades. They're all Things occupations. Excellence in verbal skills almost by definition requires one to be able to engage with other people. This is self-evidently true in occupations that require steady interaction with other people—teaching, patient-oriented medicine, and helping professions of all kinds. They're all People occupations.

These days, everyone who has been paying attention knows that the Things and People occupations I just listed are notorious for being disproportionately male and female respectively. You can guess what's coming next.

4

Sex Differences in Educational and Vocational Choices

Proposition #3: On average, women worldwide are more attracted to vocations centered on people and men to vocations centered on things.

The third component of cognitive repertoires is social behavior, but there's no point in cataloging all the ways in which men and women differ in social behavior. They go from the obvious and extreme (e.g., men commit the overwhelming majority of violent crimes) to the obvious and everyday (e.g., women perform the overwhelming majority of child-rearing tasks).[1] I devote this chapter to an extended look at the People-Things thesis regarding education and vocation. More than a century after legal restrictions on women's vocations were lifted and half a century since gender discrimination in hiring, promoting, and firing was outlawed, large disparities continue in the university educations that young men and women attain, the jobs they take, and how their careers unfold. What to do about this is a major policy debate. Here, I lay out some reasons for thinking that the persistence of these observable sex differences constitutes strong circumstantial evidence for underlying biological causes.

The Women of SMPY

From January 2012 to February 2013, a team of Vanderbilt psychologists interviewed 322 men and 157 women in their late 40s about their work preferences and life values. The men and women differed on many of their views. Limiting the list to ones with an absolute effect size of 0.35 or higher, here were the things that men valued more or agreed with more than women did.[2] The effect sizes are shown in parentheses:

"The prospect of receiving criticism from others does not inhibit me from expressing my thoughts." (−0.54)

A merit-based pay system (−0.53)

Having a full-time career (−0.51)

Inventing or creating something that will have an impact (−0.45)

A salary that is well above the average person's (−0.43)

"I believe that society should invest in my ideas because they are more important than those of other people in my discipline." (−0.42)

Being able to take risks on my job (−0.41)

Working with things (e.g., computers, tools, machines) as part of my job (−0.41)

"The possibility of discomforting others does not deter me from stating the facts." (−0.40)

Having lots of money (−0.36)

Stereotypical men.

Meanwhile, here were the things that the women in the sample valued more than the men did, again limiting the list to ones where the absolute effect size was 0.35 or higher:[3]

Having a part-time career for a limited time period (+0.83)

Having a part-time career entirely (+0.78)

Working no more than 40 hours in a week (+0.72)[4]

Having strong friendships (+0.49)

Flexibility in my work schedule (+0.41)

Community service (+0.38)

Having time to socialize (+0.37)

Giving back to the community (+0.35)

Stereotypical women.

Why have I presented such predictable results? Because this chapter is about sex differences in educational and vocational choices, and this particular sample lets me put issues of sex differences in abilities aside. Every one of those middle-aged men and women had an IQ of about 140 or higher.[5] They were part of the Study of Mathematically Precocious Youth—SMPY.

The Unique Advantages of the SMPY Samples

The results I just presented came from members of SMPY's Cohort 2, born in 1964–67, who at age 13 had tested in the top 0.5 percent of overall intellectual ability: the top 1 in 200. All of them were also in the top percentile specifically in math skills.[6] All of the respondents were intellectually qualified to have pursued any undergraduate major they preferred and any cognitively demanding career.[7]

The SMPY sample has other advantages. Every girl in the sample knew she was extremely talented in math by the time she entered her teens. Her mathematical talent was part of her self-image from an early age.

SMPY

Johns Hopkins psychologist Julian Stanley began SMPY in 1971. He recruited large numbers of 12-year-olds to take the SAT math test. The SAT is designed for high school juniors and seniors bound for college. By administering it to 12- and 13-year-olds who had not yet taken high school math courses, Stanley was able to identify students with exceptionally high aptitude for math. Over the years, SMPY established four cohorts of mathematically precocious youth who became part of a longitudinal study that continues as I write, jointly directed since 1991 by Camilla Benbow and David Lubinski.[8] I focus on the results from the 35-year and 40-year follow-ups for Cohort 2 with some supplemental findings regarding Cohort 3.

Virtually all of the parents of these girls were extremely supportive of their daughters' talent. SMPY parents responded positively to their child's invitation to seek admission to the program and then were willing to go through the time and effort to get their child to the testing site, which often meant a significant journey. Apart from these indicators, we also have the results of a study of the SMPY parents in that era. The study found that "(a) parents were treating their children differently based not on their child's gender but apparently rather as a function of their child's talent; (b) fathers did not appear to be more involved with the mathematically talented students than with the verbally talented; and (c) the majority of students, especially females, were not strongly sex typed."[9]

Despite their parents' support, it might be argued that the girls who entered SMPY's Cohort 2 were still socialized to traditional pre-feminist norms. The modern feminist movement was in its first decade when they were born in the mid-1960s. It should be assumed that as little girls the SMPY women had gotten a full dose of socialization to female roles in a country that was still traditional on matters regarding gender roles.

If the girls who entered SMPY had typically come from small towns or from middle-class suburban neighborhoods in the Midwest or South, that argument would have merit. But instead they came from highly educated, upper-middle-class families located in the Washington, Baltimore, and Philadelphia areas. By the early 1970s, these families and neighborhoods were probably more explicitly and emphatically feminist than comparable neighborhoods today. It may be hard for readers not old enough to remember for themselves how long—50 years now—the upper-middle-class milieu has been overwhelmingly feminist, so perhaps a few reminders are in order.

First, consider the timeline of legal reforms:

1963: John Kennedy's Presidential Commission on the Status of Women released its strongly pro-feminist report, and the Equal Pay Act of 1963 mandated equal pay for equal work.

1964: Title VII of the Civil Rights Act of 1964 forbade employer discrimination on the basis of sex. *Griswold v. Connecticut* invalidated legal restrictions on access to birth control.

1967: A presidential executive order extended affirmative action in employment and education to include women.

1968: Sexual harassment was added to federal antidiscrimination law as a basis for bringing actions against employers.

1972: Title IX of the Education Amendments mandated nondiscrimination in any school receiving government aid (effectively all of them) and included broad enforcement powers.

The girls of Cohort 2 were born into a world in which legal equality had been established, but in some respects that was the least of it. Even by the time they were in elementary school, the list of legal victories had been accompanied by a cultural sea change that began in the 1960s and was at its height during the 1970s and early 1980s. In the upper-middle-class schools and neighborhoods where most of the SMPY girls grew up, courses in elementary school were filled with inspirational stories about women scientists, political leaders, artists, and authors. High schools were putting boys and girls in the same gym classes, and high school counselors were urging female students to go into male-dominated careers. On campuses, young women were hearing faculty and their fellow students urging them to forgo marriage and childbearing in favor of a career. Gloria Steinem's famous slogan "A woman needs a man like a fish needs a bicycle" comes from the early 1970s, epitomizing a celebration of women that found cultural expression in films, popular music, and television.[10] When the girls of Cohort 2 reached college age in 1982–85, they all knew that the most famous universities in the nation were eager to add them to their student bodies and even more eager for them to populate their majors in science, technology, engineering, and math, familiarly known as STEM.

That's the female sample we are able to follow through almost 50 years of their lives: extraordinarily talented women who knew they were talented from an early age, were urged to enter STEM fields, and were often urged not to let children and family dictate their lives. Yet they reached their late 40s with a profile of stereotypical sex differences in career and life priorities. What had they been doing in the meantime?

Even Among the Gifted, People Tend to Like Doing What They Do Best

Educationally, males and females in Cohort 2 were in a dead heat, with nearly the same high proportions getting bachelor's, master's, and doctoral degrees.[11] Yet the traditional gender gap in STEM majors persisted. The SMPY women were about twice as likely to take STEM majors as the general population of female undergraduates,[12] but this was true of the men also, and so the male-female ratio in STEM degrees among the SMPY sample (1.6) was fractionally *higher* than the ratio in the general undergraduate population (1.5).[13] Meanwhile, twice as many of these gifted young women were getting degrees in the social sciences, business, and the humanities as were the gifted young men.[14]

Why the persistence of the tilt of men toward STEM and women toward the social sciences and the humanities? The special nature of the SMPY sample enables a test of this proposition: It doesn't make any difference how extremely talented you are in one field; you tend to gravitate toward the field in which you are the most talented.[15] Even though everyone in Cohort 2 was gifted in math skills, those whose verbal skills were even higher than their math skills tended to end up in the social sciences, humanities, business, and law, while those whose math skills were greater than their verbal skills tended to end up in STEM fields. This pattern was true for both males and females.[16]

Much of the theoretical literature assumes that this tendency is driven by students' and their parents' knowledge of grades and test scores—that the numbers tell them they are better at math than verbal or vice versa.[17] But there is good reason to think that the impulse runs deeper than conscious knowledge. This finding emerged first from Project Talent, a 1960 study based on a nationally representative sample (total sample size was about 400,000) of American high school students whose participants were given tests of visuospatial skill to accompany their scores on verbal and mathematics tests. Visuospatial skill is not ordinarily something that schools test or that students think about. And yet it turned out that such skills played an important independent role in shaping the students' academic and vocational choices, strongly reinforcing a tendency for students to go into STEM majors if those skills were high and depressing the likelihood of going into STEM majors if they were low.[18]

Was the same true of students who were gifted in both math and verbal skills? Members of SMPY Cohort 2 completed two visuospatial subtests of the Differential Aptitude Tests.[19] The results mirrored those from Project Talent. The students' visuospatial skills interacted with their verbal and math scores, with high skills pushing them toward STEM and low scores pushing them toward the humanities or social science majors.[20]

What I've just reported applied to Cohort 2, who were in the top 0.5 percent in intellectual ability. Surely (or so it would intuitively seem), this phenomenon has to fade at some level of ability when it doesn't make any difference which skill set is higher—even your "weaker" skill is fabulously high. But apparently not, or so SMPY's Cohort 3 seems to tell us.

SMPY's Cohort 3 is the largest database of profoundly gifted persons ever assembled for systematic longitudinal research: 253 males and 67 females who as 12-year-olds were in the top 0.01 percent of intellectual ability, with an estimated mean IQ of 186.[21] The top 1 in 10,000. The phenomenon they had identified in Cohort 2—even highly gifted people gravitate to the fields where they have the greatest comparative advantage—also applied to Cohort 3. Among those whose SAT math scores were at least a standard deviation above their SAT verbal scores (the "high-math" group), 69 percent had an undergraduate major in math or an inorganic science, compared to 29 percent of those whose SAT verbal scores were at least a standard deviation above their SAT math scores (the "high-verbal" group). Forty-two percent of the high-verbal group had undergraduate degrees in the humanities or arts, compared to 23 percent of the high-math group.[22] The sample size of women is too small to draw strong conclusions from Cohort 3 as a single study, but its consistency with the results for the larger sample in Cohort 2 and the nationally representative Project Talent data make it worth noting: The male-to-female disparity in attraction to STEM even among the profoundly gifted suggests that we may be looking at nothing more complicated than people's attraction to doing what they do best no matter how extraordinarily gifted they are in the things they don't do best.

Even Among the Exceptionally Gifted Who Are Attracted to STEM, Males and Females Gravitate to Different Types of STEM

Hidden within the overall figures is another intriguing story: Even gifted women who are attracted to STEM gravitate toward the life sciences (People-oriented), not math and the physical sciences (Things-oriented). It was not a subtle tendency. Proportionally, males outnumbered females by almost two to one on the Things-oriented sciences, and females outnumbered males by almost two to one on the People-oriented sciences.[23] The implication: Women who are so gifted that they can deal with any intellectually demanding field are not scared off by science per se. They instead tend to prefer those fields that deal with living things rather than nonliving things.

The results from the smaller sample of profoundly gifted woman in Cohort 3 indicate a similar sex difference in interests, except that the female tilt toward STEM disciplines that deal with living things was even stronger among the women of the top 0.01 percent in math than it was for those who were "merely" in the top 1 percent—and it's definitely not because the women of Cohort 3 weren't smart enough to do physics or pure mathematics if they felt like it.[24]

Even Among the Exceptionally Gifted, Women Have Different Life Priorities and Work Priorities Than Men That Affect Their Career Trajectories and Achievements

The SMPY women were similar to the general population of college-educated women in matters of marriage and children. Among the SMPY women at ages 45–49, 75 percent were married, compared to 72 percent of all college-educated women of the same age. Seventy-four percent of the SMPY women had borne children, compared to 80 percent of their college-educated peers. Fifty-seven percent of the SMPY women had more than one child, compared to 61 percent of their college-educated peers.[25]

In light of this, it is not surprising that the list of sex differences in work preferences and life values that began this chapter included several that directly or indirectly involved children, particularly with regard to women's markedly greater unwillingness than men to work long hours. Long hours at work compete with that responsibility. But motherhood doesn't appear to be the whole story. Remember that the women of Cohort 2 were ages 45–49 when they were surveyed in 2012–13. They weren't being asked about how many hours they were willing to work outside the home when they had preschool children at home, but how much they were prepared to work in their late 40s and the years ahead. In that context, the results of one survey question were especially intriguing. How much would they be willing to work, at most, *if given their ideal job*? Thirty percent of these extraordinarily talented women, few of whom had small children to care for, were unwilling to work more than 40 hours per week even if they were given their ideal job, compared to only 7 percent of the men.[26] Add in the other responses indicating the priorities SMPY women put on community service, having time to socialize, not working outside the home, having a meaningful spiritual life, and being available for family and friends, and we are once again faced with a sex difference in profiles. Individually, most of the effect sizes ranged from small to medium. As in the case of personality differences, these effect sizes are found in indicators that are conceptually related but functionally distinct, and I would argue that aggregating them would give us a more accurate picture of the magnitude of the sex differences involved. But, even lacking the data to calculate Mahalanobis *D*, it is safe to conclude that in middle age the SMPY men and women had importantly different life priorities—which makes the next set of results all the more interesting.

*The SMPY Men and Women Saw Themselves as Having Equally
Satisfying Lives*

As part of their survey, the members of Cohort 2 were given some standard instruments for measuring subjective well-being.[27] As a group, their evaluations of their lives as of their late 40s were extremely positive—in the top decile, according to the norms for those instruments. The differences between women and men were uniformly minuscule.[28] The authors' appraisal of these findings seems exactly right:

> In short, marked sex differences in how participants allocated their time and structured their lives were not accompanied by corresponding sex differences in how they viewed their career accomplishments and close relationships, or in their positive outlook on life. One interpretation of the lack of appreciable differences between the sexes across these indicators is that there are multiple ways to construct a meaningful, productive, and satisfying life.[29]

I have given so much space to the SMPY cohorts for two reasons. The first is to emphasize that sex differences in ability profiles are not the whole explanation for differences in educational and vocational choices. As I discussed in chapter 3, sex differences exist in the male and female profiles of abilities, and they do indeed have implications for performance in certain occupations. But the data from the SMPY cohorts convincingly document that STEM sex differences persist at virtually the same levels when women are easily capable of having successful STEM careers if they want them.

Second, the SMPY results pose a challenge to which defenders of social-construct explanations must respond: Suppose we grant that socialization discourages girls from STEM fields. But socialization to avoid STEM fields is not something in the water that all little girls drink in similar quantities. It is fostered by specific inputs from parents, teachers, peers, and the media, among other agents. Different little girls get different amounts.

As noted earlier, we have good reason to think that the SMPY women disproportionately grew up with gender-neutral toys, had mothers who were in professional careers, had parents both of whom proactively told their daughters to transcend gender stereotypes, were educated in progressive upper-middle-class schools, and had peer groups consisting of other girls raised in similar circumstances.

Vulnerability to socialization into traditional female roles also varies by a girl's personal characteristics. We know for sure that the SMPY girls were all extremely smart and knew they were smart. It seems reasonable to assume that they were also disproportionately confident, with keen critical faculties, and resistant to propaganda.

In short, the nature of the SMPY sample tells us that the SMPY females got a smaller dose of socialization to traditional female roles than average and had higher levels of resistance than average. If socialization is the whole explanation for differences in attraction to STEM vocations, how is it possible that the girls of Cohort 2, in the top half percent of academic ability, show the same ratio to the SMPY men that the general population of college-educated girls shows to the general population of college-educated men? The SMPY results imply sex differences that transcend socialization.

GOING BEHIND THE NUMBERS

For a three-dimensional understanding of the priorities of highly accomplished women, you should read Susan Pinker's *The Sexual Paradox: Men, Women, and the Real Gender Gap* (2008). In addition to a still-relevant account of the science of sex differences, the book contains a number of in-depth profiles of women who were extremely successful professionally but made choices in their careers that were different from those men usually make. Pinker's narrative is in effect the SMPY results brought to life.

Three final thoughts before leaving the SMPY women:

First, it's time for another reminder that all the results I have described amount to statistical tendencies. The SMPY cohorts included women who were as professionally driven as stereotypical men and men who were as involved in family and community as stereotypical women. But it's still true that the sex differences in profiles were unmistakable.

Second, where is it written that STEM majors or careers are objectively more valuable than non-STEM majors or careers? Lubinski and Benbow make an important point that should be obvious but isn't: "Given the ever-increasing importance of quantitative and scientific reasoning skills in modern cultures, when mathematically gifted individuals choose to pursue careers outside engineering and the physical sciences, it should be seen as a contribution to society, not a loss of talent."[30]

Third, where is it written that spending years of seven-day, 80-hour workweeks is more fulfilling or more fun than combining a less intense career with richer family life? These gifted women, applying the mature judgment of their late 40s, took great satisfaction from their time and engagement with their children, spouses, and communities. If you try to argue that these women were duped into accepting traditional female roles, you run into a problem: Chances are that the women who made those judgments are a lot smarter than you are.

Extrapolating from the SMPY Experience: The Breadth-Based Model

Psychologists Stephen Ceci, Wendy Williams, Jeffrey Valla, and their colleagues have pulled these strands together in a theoretical explanation of sex differences in attraction to STEM. It is known as the *breadth-based model*. The argument runs like this: It has been demonstrated that the decision to pursue a STEM career depends on two things: high math ability (hardly anyone without high math ability is attracted to STEM) and lower verbal ability.[31] The public and academic debate over female underrepresentation in STEM has focused on the first of those two, but the evidence indicates that the second may be even more important. People with equally high or higher verbal skills (male or female) have an array of attractive alternatives to STEM—the arts, social sciences, law, and business, for example—and many with high math skills *and* high verbal skills choose those alternatives.

Now recall the asymmetry noted in the SMPY sample: Gifted boys tend to be gifted in those skills that go into superior performance in STEM occupations but not in skills that go into superior performance in non-STEM occupations, while gifted girls tend more often than boys to have a choice—they are capable of superior performance in just about any cognitively demanding field.

Next, consider the empirical observation that, on average, females are drawn more to the occupations facilitated by high verbal skills. The breadth-based model argues that this is no accident, nor does it draw from a narrow calculation that financial success is more likely by going with one's best skills. Rather, from an early age, males and females tend to have different interests. Those interests lead to different experiences and acquisition of knowledge, and those in turn lead to different choices of careers. As Valla and Ceci put it in their 2014 article summarizing the breadth-based model, "the 'nature' of cognitive sex differences lies not in absolute ability, but in breadth of intrinsic interests—and its downstream developmental effects on interests, abilities, and career choices."[32]

Valla and Ceci are referring to the choice between STEM careers and their alternatives. But the sex differences in personality traits discussed in chapter 2 suggest that we need not limit the argument to the small proportion of the population that has high math skills. It's time to leave the special case of the gifted and look at sex differences in interests that apply to men and women in general.

The Revolution in Women's Education and Work Since 1960

Any discussion of the trends in vocation and life choices among the general population of women must begin with the transformed opportunities for women since 1960. Sociologist Catherine Hakim has cast these in terms of five specific changes that produced a qualitatively new reality for women:

- The invention of new forms of contraception, especially the pill, gave women reliable and independent control over their own fertility.
- The equal opportunities revolution gave women better access to all careers and positions.
- White-collar occupations, the ones most attractive to women, expanded.
- Jobs for secondary earners expanded, making it easier for women to combine childcare and work outside the home.
- Freedom of lifestyle choices in liberal modern societies increased.[33]

All of these changes began in a concentrated period of time during the 1960s. Without hyperbole, the results have been revolutionary.

In 1960, a few years before second-wave feminism took off in the United States, only 41 percent of women ages 25–54 were in the labor force. In 2018, that figure stood at 75 percent.

By 2015, women had a presence in high-status jobs that was inconceivable in 1960. From 1960 to 2018, women went from 1 percent of civil engineers to 17 percent; from 5 percent of attorneys to 35 percent; from 8 percent of physicians to 42 percent.

Not a single woman was the CEO of a Fortune 500 company in 1960, nor would there be any until 1972.[34] In 2018, 25 women were Fortune 500 CEOs, among them the chief executives of General Motors, IBM, PepsiCo, Lockheed Martin, Oracle, and General Dynamics.

In 1960, there was one woman in the U.S. Senate. After the 2018 election, there were 25. In the 1960 House of Representatives, there were 19 women. After the 2018 election, there were 102.

Female students from elementary school through college have long had higher mean grade point averages than males in most subjects (including math).[35] But in 1960 women were nonetheless a minority of entering college students (46 percent), and the gap grew during the undergraduate years. Almost two males got a bachelor's degree for every woman who did. In 1982, the number of women getting bachelor's degrees surpassed the number of men. The gap continued to widen subsequently. By 2016, 1,082,669 women got bachelor's degrees compared to 812,669 men—a 33 percent difference.[36]

The change in professional degrees was even more dramatic. The figure below shows the number of PhDs, medical degrees, law degrees, dental degrees, and others ordinarily requiring at least three years of graduate work.

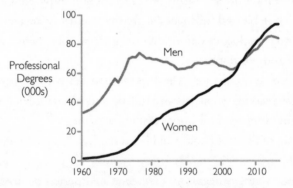

Source: National Center for Education Statistics, *Digest of Education Statistics,* 1995 edition: Table 236, and 2017 edition: Table 318.

In 1960, 20 men got a professional degree for every woman who did. By 1970, the ratio was less than 10 to 1. By 1980, it was less than 3 to 1. In 2005, women caught up with men. Since then, more women have gotten more professional degrees than men in every year. As of 2016, 93,778 women got a professional degree compared to 84,089 men.[37]

Nothing about women's abilities had changed in the interim. Opportunities formerly denied them had opened up, and women were exercising talents and capacities they had possessed all along. That is the overriding headline about gender and occupational changes during second-wave feminism.

It is in this context of progress for women over the course of half a century that I now show you the data on current sex differences in vocational interests and life.

Sex Differences in Vocational Interests and Life Choices in the General Population

The argument here amounts to two mini-propositions: that the vocational preferences of men and women as measured by tests differ in ways that correspond to differences on the People-Things dimension, and that the job choices that people actually make correspond to their preferences.

Men and Women Are Attracted to Different Vocations, and Those Differences Correspond to Differences on the People-Things Dimension

In 1959, psychologist John Holland published an article titled "A Theory of Vocational Choice" that has shaped vocational counseling ever since.[38] At the heart of his theory, which was created without regard to sex differences, was the premise that an adult comes to a vocational choice with "a hierarchy of habitual or preferred methods for dealing with environmental tasks.... The person making a vocational choice in a sense 'searches' for situations which satisfy his hierarchy of adjustive orientations."[39] In its final form, Holland's theory posited six clusters of these orientations:

- *R—Realistic.* Working with tools, instruments, and mechanical or electrical equipment. Activities include building, repairing machinery, and raising crops/animals.
- *I—Investigative.* Investigating and attempting to understand phenomena in the natural sciences through reading, research, and discussion.
- *A—Artistic.* Expressing oneself through activities such as painting, designing, singing, dancing, and writing; artistic appreciation of such activities (e.g., listening to music, reading literature).
- *S—Social.* Helping, enlightening, or serving others through activities such as teaching, counseling, working in service-oriented organizations, and engaging in social/political studies.

- *E—Enterprising.* Persuading, influencing, directing, or motivating others through activities such as sales, supervision, and aspects of business management.
- *C—Conventional.* Developing and/or maintaining accurate and orderly files, records, accounts, etc.; following systematic procedures for performing business activities.[40]

The theory is often referred to as RIASEC, based on its combined initials. I should add that two of the labels were poorly chosen. As the descriptions make clear, "Enterprising" doesn't refer to entrepreneurship or risk-taking. It's about interacting with other people in a leadership or managerial role. "Conventional" doesn't mean timid or boring or stuck with tradition. It refers to a preference for procedure, systematic practices, and orderliness. These more accurate understandings also make it clear why Enterprising is related to the People dimension and Conventional is related to what Baron-Cohen calls systemizing—and, by extension, the Things dimension.

Subsequently, psychometrician Dale Prediger developed a two-dimensional way of assessing the results of inventories testing Holland's orientations. One dimension went from Ideas at one extreme to Data at the other. The second dimension went from Things at one extreme to People at the other. Prediger accompanied his analysis with formulas for computing a People-Things index and an Ideas-Data index.[41]

Schematically, Holland's and Prediger's ideas look like this.

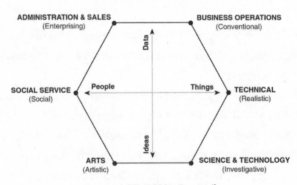

Source: ACT (2009): Fig. 1.1.[42]

Holland's and Prediger's conceptualizations have remained at the center of vocational counseling because they work. Tests of where people stand on the six clusters have proved to be valid descriptors of people's occupational interests and useful in giving people career guidance.[43]

Those tests have also revealed sex differences. In 2009, psychologists at the University of Illinois and Iowa State University conducted a meta-analysis. The first author was psychologist Rong Su. Their question: Taking the literature as a whole, where do men and women come out on the Holland orientations and the Prediger dimensions?

The authors assembled a database from 81 samples that amounted to 243,670 men and 259,518 women. On average, women's vocational interests tilted toward occupations involving work with or understanding of other people; men's vocational interests tilted toward working with things.

The biggest tilts involved the Realistic orientation—a male preference— with an effect size of −0.84, and the Social orientation—a female preference—with an effect size of +0.68. When the data were analyzed along Prediger's two dimensions using his indexes, a striking contrast emerged. On the Data-Ideas dimension, there was virtually no sex difference.[44] On the People-Things dimension, the effect size was +0.93, meaning that women were on the People end and men were on the Things end of the dimension— a large effect size by any standard.

Sex Differences in Vocational Interests Are Replicated in the Jobs That Men and Women Occupy

What about the jobs that people actually hold? Women are overwhelmingly pointed toward People jobs and away from Things jobs, something I will document with regard to all jobs before zeroing in on women's representation in STEM occupations.

All occupations. In 1938, the U.S. federal government started publishing the *Dictionary of Occupational Titles.* Since 1998, it has existed on the Internet as O*NET, a digital database that provides information about the skills, personal characteristics, cognitive requirements, experience requirements, and job outlook for each occupation in the list. As part of that information, O*NET now uses explicit criteria to score each occupation on the six RIASEC orientations on a continuous scale running from 1.0 through 7.0.[45] We can use these data for jobs actually held to replicate the earlier findings from the Su data for test scores of vocational interests. In the following figure the black bars show the results on occupations by employed persons ages 25–54 in the combined Current Population Surveys for 2014–18. The gray bars show the results from the Su meta-analysis of data on vocational interests.

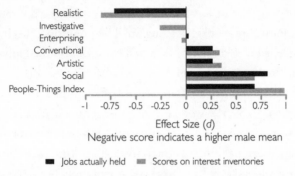

Effect Size (*d*)
Negative score indicates a higher male mean

■ Jobs actually held   ■ Scores on interest inventories

Source: Author's analyses, CPS 2014–18 and Su, Rounds, and Armstrong (2009): Table 3.

It's not often that two completely different databases produce such similar results. The big sex differences on both interests and jobs were for the Realistic and Social orientations—the conceptually clearest Things and People orientations—and on Prediger's overall index combining all the RIASEC data.

STEM occupations. The same thing happens within different kinds of STEM occupations: In 2015, two of the same authors, Rong Su and James Rounds, conducted another meta-analysis focusing on distinctions within scientific and technical occupations. Again, their database of vocational preferences and a database of actual jobs held by the U.S. working-age population produced almost interchangeable results. In both cases, the biggest sex differences favoring men involved the most Things-oriented jobs; the biggest sex differences favoring women involved the most People-oriented jobs.[46] The degree of consistency of the sex differences in vocational interests and occupations is quite remarkable. To draw the discussion together, consider the table below.

SEX DIFFERENCES (*D*) IN VOCATIONAL INTERESTS AND OCCUPATIONS ACROSS DIFFERENT MEASURES AND SAMPLES

RIASEC dimension	Meta-analysis of 503,188 scores on interest inventories	Adult scores of SMPY cohorts 1, 2, 3, and 4	Ratings of occupations held by Americans ages 25–54
Realistic	−0.84	−0.92	−0.77
Investigative	−0.26	−0.28	−0.08
Conventional	+0.33	−0.47	+0.27

RIASEC dimension	Meta-analysis of 503,188 scores on interest inventories	Adult scores of SMPY cohorts 1, 2, 3, and 4	Ratings of occupations held by Americans ages 25–54
Enterprising	−0.04	−0.50	+0.09
Artistic	+0.35	+1.06	+0.22
Social	+0.68	+0.88	+0.84

Source: Su, Rounds, and Armstrong (2009); Author's analysis, combined ACS, 2011–15; Lubinski and Benbow (2006): Table 5. A negative score indicates a higher male mean.

The three columns draw on databases that are quite different in both measures and samples, yet they tell a clear and consistent story.[47] Effect sizes on Realistic favoring men were −0.84, −0.92, and −0.77 for the three sources; effect sizes on Social favoring women were +0.68, +0.88, and +0.84 for the three sources.

Trends in Vocational Interests and Choices Since 1970

Everything I've given you so far is evidence for the existence of a phenomenon—sex differences on the People-Things dimension—but no evidence for its cause. All these effect sizes could simply mean that women and men alike continue to be socialized into certain gender-typical interests as well as gender-typical jobs.

Let's turn to evidence that I believe makes this interpretation difficult to defend. A look back at what has happened to educational and job choices over the last 50 years suggests that vocational doors really did open up for women during the 1970s, that women took advantage of those new opportunities to the extent that they wanted to, and that we fairly quickly reached a new equilibrium.

Women's Undergraduate Majors Since 1970: A Brief Surge in Things-Oriented STEM and Enduring Increases in People-Oriented STEM

Women's undergraduate majors offer a case in point. In 1971, 38 percent of women's bachelor's degrees were in education. That proportion had fallen by half by the early 1980s. Meanwhile, degrees in business grew from 3 percent in 1971 to 20 percent by 1982. Women were no longer limited to K–12 teaching as their major professional option (besides nursing), and they quickly made other professional interests known.

There were also big changes in women's bachelor of science degrees—but of a particular kind. Consider first the most Things-oriented STEM careers—physics, chemistry, earth sciences, computer science, mathematics, and engineering. The percentage of women's degrees obtained in those majors more than doubled from 1971 to 1986—but "more than doubled" meant going from 4 percent to 10 percent.[48] And 1986 was the high point. By 1992, that number had dropped to 6 percent, where it has remained, give or take a percentage point, ever since. It's not that women were unwilling to undertake majors that require courses in math and science. Women's degrees in People-oriented STEM—biology and health majors—doubled in just the eight years from 1971 (9 percent) to 1979 (18 percent), remained at roughly that level through the turn of the century, then surged again, standing at 27 percent of degrees in 2017. Rather, they wanted to use their math and science so that they could study topics that dealt with living things, especially people, rather than topics restricted to inanimate things and abstract concepts.

Occupations of College-Educated Women: Change in the 1970s and Early 1980s, Stability Since the Late 1980s

I turn from trends over time in women's vocational interests and choices of undergraduate majors to trends over time in the jobs they hold as employed adults.[49]

To analyze the trends in the jobs that women hold, I took advantage of the Department of Labor's O*NET database that assigns RIASEC scores to every occupation.[50] I then used Prediger's work to identify jobs that tilt toward the People and Things ends of the spectrum. The specifics are given in the note.[51]

Analyzing women's choices over the years since 1970 is complicated by three contemporaneous trends: Women were rapidly entering the labor force through the mid-1990s, concentrated among married women; the percentage of People jobs as a proportion of all jobs was increasing as the service sector grew and manufacturing declined; and fewer people were getting married. Furthermore, all of these trends played out differently for college-educated women and women with no more than a high school education, so I will present the results separately for those two categories. All numbers refer to employed persons ages 25–54. I begin with the story for college-educated women.

The pair of figures below shows how occupations for college-educated women changed when categorized as People-oriented or Things-oriented.[52] The figure on the left shows percentages of employed women in People jobs versus Things job. The figure on the right shows the sex ratios for the two types of jobs. The dotted lines represent the average for 2014–18, giving you a way to see how long the current situation has lasted.

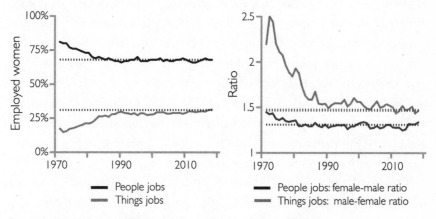

Source: Author's analysis, CPS. Sample limited to women ages 25–54.

Based on either perspective, observers in the late 1980s could be excused for thinking that men and women would converge within a few decades. From 1970 through the mid-1980s, the percentage of women in Things jobs had risen and the male-female ratio had plunged. If those slopes had been sustained, the percentages of men and women in Things jobs would have intersected around 2001. The percentages of men and women in People jobs would have intersected in the mid-1990s.

But convergence was already slowing by the late 1980s and had effectively stalled by 1990. The percentage of women in Things jobs hit 30 percent in 1990 and never subsequently surpassed it. Rounded to one decimal point, the male-female ratio in Things jobs reached 1.4 in 1982 and remained in the narrow range of 1.4–1.6 through 2018.[53]

For college-educated women, the distribution of vocational choices along the People-Things dimension changed substantially from the 1970s into the mid-1980s, but little has changed since then. It looks as if women were indeed artificially constrained from moving into a variety of Things occupations as of 1970, that those constraints were largely removed, and that equilibrium was reached around 30 years ago.

For Women with No More Than a High School Education, Not Much Changed

Overall, the story for high-school-educated women is like the Sherlock Holmes story with the dog that didn't bark. In 1971, 30 percent of women were employed in People jobs. By 2018, that figure had risen to 39 percent. During the same period, the proportion of women employed in Things jobs moved in a narrow range from a high of 53 percent in 1971 to a low of 46 percent in 2004. As of 2018, the figure stood at 51 percent. Most of the rise in People jobs can be associated with the increased role of People jobs in the economy, but not all.[54] The effects of the feminist revolution in the 1970s and early 1980s that were so evident for college-educated women were missing for women with no more than a high school education.

This finding surprised me. From the 1970s onward, well-paying jobs for women without college educations were opening in manufacturing and a wide variety of technical specialties that were formerly closed to them—not only opened up but opened wide. From the 1970s through the mid-1990s, males with no more than a high school education were dropping out of the labor force, working shorter hours, and were more often unemployed, while women with no more than a high school education were joining the labor force and working longer hours.[55] A variety of evidence indicates that during the same period working-class men were becoming more unreliable employees.[56] It appears that the time was right for women to enter these jobs if only for economic reasons, independently of vocational preferences.

Some women took advantage of those new opportunities. For example, among people ages 25–54 employed as mechanics or repairers, only 0.6 percent were women in 1971–75. In 2014–18, 2.1 percent were women—a proportional increase of 350 percent. But seen as a percentage of all employed women with no more than a high school degree, mechanics and repairers constituted 0.1 percent of employed women ages 25–54 in 1971–75 and 0.2 percent of them in 2014–18—such a tiny number that the increase in women mechanics had no effect on the trendline. In other blue-collar jobs, there were remarkably small increases in the percentage of jobs held by women. Among people ages 25–54 with no more than a high school degree employed in manufacturing jobs in 1971–75, an average of 21 percent were women. In 2014–18, that figure was 23 percent.

In sum: The effect of the feminist revolution on the vocations of college-educated women was real but quickly reached a new equilibrium. For women with no more than a high school education, it is as if the feminist revolution never happened.

Cross-National Sex Differences in Vocational Directions

As I discussed in chapter 3, the results of the 2015 administration of the PISA tests were familiar from previous ones, showing a small math effect size (–0.05) favoring boys and a moderate reading effect size (+0.32) favoring girls. In 2018, psychologists Gijsbert Stoet and David Geary published an analysis of the 2015 round of PISA tests that cast a new and informative light on what those results imply for the attraction of males to Things occupations and of females to People occupations.

The authors created a measure of the individual 15-year-old's personal strengths in science, math, and reading scores relative to their overall ability. The details are given in the note,[57] but it comes down to this: Suppose 100 students from a magnet school for the gifted take the PISA tests, and so do 100 students from an ordinary high school. Joan, from the magnet school, has raw science, math, and reading scores of 700, 650, and 600 respectively, for an average of 650 points. Her science score is 50 points above her personal average. Joe, from the ordinary high school, has raw science, math, and reading scores of 400, 350, and 300 respectively, for an average of 350 points. His science score is also 50 points above his personal average. So for both of them, despite the great difference in their raw scores, science is their relative strength. But how can we compare their respective relative strengths? The measure Stoet and Geary devised is a statistically suitable way for doing so— what I will call *relative-strength* scores (the authors called them *intraindividual* scores). We can then add up the 100 relative-strength scores for each school and compare them by sex, making statements about sex differences (if any) between the relative strengths of boys and girls in the two schools.

We can do the same thing comparing nations. The following table summarizes the 2015 PISA results for 62 countries showing mean scores by nation, relative-strength scores, and correlations with the Global Gender Gap Index.[58]

RELATIVE-STRENGTH SCORES FOR PISA-2015 WERE DIFFERENT EVEN WHEN MEAN SCORES WERE ALMOST THE SAME

Subject	Mean scores		Relative-strength scores	
	Effect size (d)	Correlation with GGGI	Effect size (d)	Correlation with GGGI
Mathematics	−0.05	−.18 (ns)	−0.55	−.04 (ns)
Science literacy	+0.01	−.23 (ns)	−0.42	−.42 (.001)
Reading comprehension	+0.32	−.06 (ns)	+0.78	+.30 (.017)

Source: Stoet and Geary (2018): Table S2. The unit of analysis is the country. A negative score indicates a higher male mean. The sample is limited to countries with GGGI (Global Gender Gap Index) scores (*n* = 62).

As I described in chapter 3, there's hardly any sex difference in mathematics and science mean scores—and yet there's a big sex difference favoring males on relative-strength scores. There's a noticeable sex difference favoring females on reading comprehension mean scores—but a bigger one for relative-strength scores. In other words, we could expect a significant male-female disparity toward STEM *even when the mean test scores are the same* just because of the sex difference in relative strengths. Two other quick points:

The global consistency in relative-strength scores is nearly perfect. On the relative-strength score for reading, the effect size favored girls in all of the countries. For math, the relative-strength effect size favored boys in all of the countries. For science, the relative-strength effect size favored boys in 61 out of 62 countries.[59]

The more gender-egalitarian the country, the greater the boys' relative strength in science ($r = -.42$, $p < .001$). To illustrate, the bottom five countries on the Global Gender Gap Index were Jordan, Lebanon, Turkey, Algeria, and Tunisia. The mean relative-strength effect size for sex differences in science literacy was −0.18.[60] The top five countries on the Global Gender Gap Index were Iceland, Finland, Norway, Sweden, and Ireland. The mean relative-strength effect size was −0.55.

The more gender-egalitarian the country, the greater the girls' relative strength in reading ($r = +.30$, $p = .017$). The difference in relative-strength mean effect size for the bottom five countries on the Global Gender Gap Index was +0.69; for the top five countries, it was +0.83.

If you hold to a social-construct theory of sex differences in test scores, it is hard to explain these results. In contrast, it is easy to explain them if you postulate inborn sex differences that influence academic ability. It's a version of the Matthew effect—the rich get richer and the poor get poorer (Matthew 25:29).[61] In the case of education, the Matthew effect takes the form of widening test score differences when good students and poor students are both exposed to improved education. The test scores of the poor students may rise, but those of the good students usually rise more.[62]

A third important finding is not part of the data in the table. Stoet and Geary also calculated the correlation between the percentage of girls with a relative strength in science or math and the Global Gender Gap Index. The result was a correlation of –.41 ($p < .003$).[63] The implication is that the more gender-equal the country, the fewer of the women who are capable of successful STEM careers choose to go into them.

Why? Stoet and Geary point out that perhaps it reflects the greater freedom of talented women in advanced countries. In poorer countries where economic insecurity is high—the ones that tend to be toward the bottom of the Global Gender Gap Index—jobs in STEM fields are among the most secure and well paid. A girl from such a country whose relative strength is verbal skills but who also has high math and science skills has a strong economic incentive to override her preferences and go into a STEM career. In a country near the top of the gender equality ladder such as Norway or Finland, economic security is assured through the welfare state, and good jobs in non-STEM fields are abundant even though they may not pay as well as many STEM jobs. If one postulates an inborn female tendency to be drawn toward People-oriented fields, it is to be expected that as national affluence and economic security increase, more women will choose fields that correspond to their interests rather than STEM fields that offer higher job security and income.[64]

Recapitulation

In the words of Proposition #3, "On average, women worldwide are more attracted to vocations centered on people and men to vocations centered on things." The proposition is true with regard to the general population and to the gifted men and women of SMPY. It is established by scores on tests of vocational interests and by the revealed preferences of the jobs that people take. It applies to those with advanced educations and those with high school educations. It has persisted over a half century of second-wave feminism and has not diminished in the last three decades.

The subtext of this chapter has been that it's not plausible to explain the entire difference in educational and vocational interests as artifacts of gender roles and socialization. If that were the case, the world shouldn't look the way it does. In contrast, a mixed model—it's partly culture, partly innate preferences—works just fine. In this narrative, females really were artificially deterred from STEM educations and occupations through the 1950s and into the 1960s. One of the effects of the feminist revolution was that new opportunities opened up for women and women took advantage of them. The changes in women's choices of college majors dramatically reflect that, along with their movement into professions such as medicine, the law, and business. But something has to explain how quickly those changes settled into a new equilibrium of educational and occupational choices that has lasted for 30 to 40 years now.

Is the patriarchy still to blame? One can try to defend that position, but it has to be done with data. I hope the nationwide, enduring patterns of educational and vocational choices across women of different interests and levels of ability have shown how hard it is to make that case.

5

Sex Differences in the Brain

Proposition #4: Many sex differences in the brain are coordinate with sex differences in personality, abilities, and social behavior.

Twenty years ago, this chapter would have been able to discuss many sex differences in rodent brains but not in human brains.[1] Then, doing that kind of research on humans could be a career-killer. "Be careful, it's the third rail," a senior colleague told neurobiologist Larry Cahill in 2000. "Fortunately, times are changing," Cahill wrote in the introduction to a special double issue of the *Journal of Neuroscience Research* in 2017 devoted to sex differences in the brain:

> The past 15 to 20 years in particular witnessed an explosion of research (despite the prevailing biases against the topic) documenting sex influences at all levels of brain function. So overpowering is the wave of research that the standard ways of dismissing sex influences (e.g., "They are all small and unreliable," "They are all due to circulating hormones," "They are all due to human culture," and "They don't exist on the molecular level") have all been swept away, at least for those cognizant of the research.[2]

This chapter is in no sense a survey of the state of knowledge about sex differences in the brain. There's too much going on, it's far too complex, and too much still consists of tentative findings for anything resembling a comprehensive discussion. My first goal for this chapter is to present some of the most important known sex differences in the brain. My second goal is to give you a sense of the exciting progress that is being made in linking specific differences in the brain to specific behavioral sex differences. Proposition #4 is accordingly modest. Stated informally, the proposition amounts to, "What we see in observable differences between males and females on the People-Things dimension hangs together with things that are being learned about differences in male and female brains. The connections are still approximate, with many unknowns remaining, but they are becoming clearer."

Second Interlude: Things About Genetic Sex Differences and the Brain That You Need to Know to Read the Rest of the Book

Genotype and Phenotype

These words pop up continually from here on out. *Genotype* refers to the genetic makeup of an individual. *Phenotype* refers to the observable characteristics of the organism produced by a combination of the genotype and the environment.

The Basics of Genetic Sex Differences

The human genome is organized into 23 pairs of chromosomes. Twenty-two out of the 23 pairs are called *autosomal*, meaning that they have nothing to do with whether an embryo develops into a male or a female. The remaining pair are the sex chromosomes.

In women, both chromosomes are labeled X. Men have an X chromosome with the same genes as the X chromosome in women. The other chromosome, labeled the Y chromosome, exists only in men. It has about 58 million base pairs and over 200 genes. One specific gene on the Y chromosome, designated *Sry*, initiates sexual differentiation of the gonads, which in turn produces a cascade of specific forms of sexual differentiation.

In females, one of the two X chromosomes is usually inactivated. Currently, it is thought that "usually" means in 80–88 percent of the cells.[3] In the others, both X chromosomes continue to have effects on the phenotype. The inactivation is primarily done by an RNA gene labeled *Xist*. The process has regularly been described as random, though recent work indicates that it is more subtle and interesting than that.[4] This inactivation process means that the cells in a female's body constitute a mosaic. Two adjacent cells can have different activated X chromosomes.

Basics of Brain Structure

The architecture and functioning of the human brain are dauntingly complex. Here are the indispensable basics:

Brain stem, *cerebellum*, and *cerebrum*. All of the dozens of regions in the brain fit into one of these three structures.

The brain stem, at the bottom of the brain and the top of the neck, is the smallest of the three, and structurally continuous with the spinal cord. It is the primal brain and has primal tasks such as respiration and cardiac function. Recent research indicates that the locus coeruleus in the brain stem might have a role in mediating sex differences in the brain.[5]

The human cerebellum, behind and partly above the brain stem, is larger than the brain stem but smaller than the cerebrum. Its functions include emotional processing and other higher cognitive functions, but the cerebellum is most closely associated with motor control. It coordinates and executes signals from other parts of the brain and from the spinal cord.[6]

The cerebrum has by far the largest volume of the three structures. The familiar word *cerebral* comes from *cerebrum*, which indicates its role as the center of intellectual activity. It also has a significant role in emotional processing. The cerebrum and its component regions will be the focus of the discussion in this chapter.

Gray matter, *white matter*, *neuron*, and *axon*. The tissue in the brain consists of a combination of gray matter and white matter. Gray matter is composed primarily of neurons—the billions of cells that process information—though it also includes some axons, blood vessels, and connective tissue.[7] White matter is composed largely of axons—projections of the neurons that transmit information to other neurons. It is called "white" because axons are often sheathed with myelin, a fatty white substance that plays an important role in determining the efficiency and speed of the transmission.

Hemispheres. The cerebrum is divided into hemispheres, left and right, separated by a fissure that runs from the front of the cerebrum to the back. The main connection between the two hemispheres is the *corpus callosum*, a broad, flat bundle of white matter about four inches long, also running from front to back. Most of the regions of the brain are represented in both hemispheres—there is a "left amygdala" and a "right amygdala," for example.

The hemispheres are the origin of phrases you have probably heard, "left brain" and "right brain." The meaning of these labels is often oversimplified—both of the brain's hemispheres are involved to some degree in almost all kinds of processing. The two chief differences relevant to this chapter are that the right hemisphere is dominant for visuospatial activity and the left hemisphere is especially important with regard to language and is thought to have nearly exclusive responsibility for language production.[8]

Each hemisphere is also associated with control of one half of the body but reversed. The left hemisphere interacts primarily with the right side of the body, and the right hemisphere with the left.

Cerebral cortex. The cerebrum contains dozens of specific regions. Of these, the largest in humans is the cerebral cortex. It is only about 2–3 millimeters thick, but it is the outer layer of the cerebrum covering both hemispheres. It is divided into four *lobes*—frontal, parietal, temporal, and occipital. It is involved in all the higher forms of cognition, with some specialization within lobes and within layers of the lobes.

Subcortical regions. Neuroscientists have identified many regions beneath the cerebral cortex—hence the word *subcortical* to describe them. The ones I will be mentioning most often are the amygdala, hippocampus, thalamus, and hypothalamus.

A Word About Brain Scans

Presenting the evidence that male and female brains function in different ways will often call upon the results of brain scans—the method that produces those pictures you have probably seen of different parts of the brain lighting up in bright colors. Neuroscientists use several methods to produce those images. The most powerful are positron emission tomography (PET), magnetic resonance spectroscopy (MRS), magnetoencephalography (MEG), diffusor tensor imaging (DTI), and functional magnetic resonance imaging (fMRI).

None of these techniques directly detect what neurons are doing. Rather, they rely on indirect indicators of activity such as increased blood flow to areas that are active, the diffusion rates of water to measure connectivity across regions of the brain, or the concentrations of chemicals in different parts of the brain. Indirect measures can be statistically reliable—there is no doubt that neuronal activity really does cause increased blood flow, for example—but it's not nearly as simple as a binary "yes, these neurons are active, and no, those other neurons are not."

Furthermore, these dramatic images are not snapshots of an actual, individual brain taken at a moment in time. Rather, millions of bits of data from many scans have been analyzed and combined into a single image. The colors are a method of communicating results, chosen to be visually efficient, with more intense colors indicating higher levels of activity, but they are arbitrary (your brain tissue doesn't actually turn bright orange when you're thinking hard).

The ability to create dramatic images has led to some shoddy work. Many researchers have been guilty of overinterpreting small samples, data mining, failure to use proper controls, or simply not understanding the subtleties of a demanding methodology.[9] But, properly done, brain imaging has produced valuable and replicated findings.[10]

The Argument About Dimorphism in Male and Female Brains

The study of sex differences in the brain proceeds bit by bit, identifying evidence of discrete distinctions. Some of these distinctions remain discrete, with isolated effects (as far as anyone knows now). Sometimes the distinctions add up, forming a pattern that has greater effects than the sum of the parts. But in all cases, it remains true that much brain function and the products of that brain function are shared by males and females.

This truth can be obscured by headlines and titles that are far too catchy—"Men Are from Mars, Women Are from Venus" comes to mind. Recently, some researchers have gone to the opposite extreme. The minimal-differences argument was made most famously in an article titled "Sex Beyond the Genitalia: The Human Brain Mosaic." The first author among 14 was psychologist Daphna Joel. The Joel study argued, "We should shift from thinking of brains as falling into two classes, one typical of males and the other typical of females, to appreciating the variability of the human brain mosaic."[11]

The article contained an empirical assertion: "The lack of internal consistency in human brain and gender characteristics undermines the dimorphic view of human brain and behavior."[12] Specifically, the authors analyzed the 10 regions of the brain that showed the largest sex differences. For each region, the authors classified a subject as being at the "male-end" or "female-end," defining the "male-end" and "female-end" zones as the scores of the 33 percent most extreme males and females, respectively.[13] It was on the basis of these classifications that the authors found that "35 percent of brains showed substantial variability, and only 6 percent of brains were internally consistent."[14] But the definition of "internally consistent" required that all 10 regions show values at the male-end for a man and all 10 at the female-end for a woman. Psychologist David Schmitt summarized his problem with this definition: "That is, for a sex difference in the brain to 'really' exist, men must have relatively masculine brains in *each and every* respect, and women must have relatively feminine brains in *each and every* respect. Otherwise, no sex difference. Really?"[15] Larry Cahill was blunter, going on record in *Scientific American* with his view that the methodology in the Joel article was rigged and "the paper is ideology masquerading as science."[16]

A year later, the same journal published technical rejoinders.[17] The details of the counterarguments were varied, but their broad theme was the one I presented in chapter 1 with regard to personality: Small differences on individual measures routinely constitute large and important differences in the aggregate.

What can be said about where the debate over the "female brain" versus the "male brain" stands? If the question is whether neuroscientists, given data on a wide variety of brain parameters, can accurately identify a specific brain as belonging to a male or a female, the answer is yes. Their accuracy is increasing as more is learned. One response to the Joel study, using the same data as the article had used, classified 69–77 percent of the brains accurately.[18] Another classified 80 percent correctly.[19] A third, using a different dataset, classified 90–95 percent accurately.[20] In 2018, a new method based on multivariate quantification of gray matter correctly classified 93 percent of participants in two separate samples.[21] But it remains true that most of the individual sex differences in the brain (though not all) involve a great deal of overlap.

There's no inconsistency in the two findings. It's a difference of perspective: Are you interested in similarities between male and female brains or differences? The topic of this chapter is differences.

So much for the preliminaries. The next three sections describe some of the most important and securely known biological sex differences in the brain:

the activational effects of the sex hormones, sex differentiation during fetal and neonatal brain development, and the generally greater lateralization of the male brain. I then discuss differences in emotional cognition and their links to specific regions of the brain.

I have consigned discussion of two other securely documented and substantial sex differences to Appendix 3: "Sex Differences in Brain Volumes and Variance." Both types of difference will presumably play into the story of sex differences in cognitive repertoires eventually, but as I write they represent important findings with undetermined or uncertain effects on the phenotype.

The Activational Effects of Sex Hormones

Almost everyone has heard about sex hormones. Both sexes have all of the major sex hormones to some degree, but *androgens* are the ones most identified with males (testosterone being the most famous) and *estrogens* are the ones most identified with females. Their effects on mood and behavior are part of the popular culture. Some of the stereotypes are exaggerated, but not all of them. Journalist Andrew Sullivan once underwent a medically prescribed regimen of testosterone injections. Here is his description of what an injection did to him:

> Within hours, and at most a day, I feel a deep surge of energy. It is less edgy than a double espresso, but just as powerful. My attention span shortens. In the two or three days after my shot, I find it harder to concentrate on writing and feel the need to exercise more. My wit is quicker, my mind faster, but my judgment is more impulsive. It is not unlike the kind of rush I get before talking in front of a large audience, or going on a first date, or getting on an airplane, but it suffuses me in a less abrupt and more consistent way. In a word, I feel braced. For what? It scarcely seems to matter.[22]

Nor were those effects limited to Sullivan's mood. When he began his series of testosterone injections, he weighed 165 pounds.

> I now weigh 185 pounds. My collar size went from a 15 to a 17 1/2 in a few months; my chest went from 40 to 44. My appetite in every sense of that word expanded beyond measure. Going from napping two hours a day, I now rarely sleep in the daytime and have enough energy for daily workouts

and a hefty work schedule. I can squat more than 400 pounds. Depression, once a regular feature of my life, is now a distant memory. I feel better able to recover from life's curveballs, more persistent, more alive. These are the long-term effects. They are almost as striking as the short-term ones.[23]

These effects of hormones are akin to those of alcohol—powerful but varying with their level in the bloodstream, which changes over time. The technical term for these effects is *activational*. Hormones have many such effects on phenotypic differences between males and females, and the hormones are not limited to estrogen and testosterone. For example:

The female advantage in social cognition. A single administration of testosterone in women significantly altered connectivity of the network in the brain (technically known as the IFG-ACC-SMA network) that underlies the integration and selection of sensory information during empathic behavior. This finding suggests a neural mechanism by which testosterone can impair the recognition of emotions.[24]

In a double-blind, placebo-controlled study, testosterone administered to women diminished their accuracy in inferring mental states. Estrogen administered to men increased their emotional reactivity when watching a distressed person.[25]

In a placebo-controlled study, administration of oxytocin to males improved their ability to infer the mental state of others from social cues. The effect was pronounced for difficult items.[26]

The female advantage in prosocial behavior. In a double-blind and placebo-controlled experiment, pharmacologically blocking dopaminergic transmission reduced prosociality in women and selfishness in men. The authors concluded that in females the dopaminergic reward system is more sensitive to shared rewards than to selfish rewards, while the opposite is true for males. Their conclusion is supported both by pharmacological and neuroimaging data.[27]

The higher male level of impulsive behavior. In a placebo-controlled experiment, testosterone administered to males diminished their performance on the Cognitive Reflection Test, which measures capacity to override intuitive judgments with deliberated answers. The independent effect of the testosterone persisted after controls for background variables and 14 other hormones.[28]

The higher female level of risk aversion. Variations in salivary concentrations of testosterone were analyzed in MBA students. Higher levels of testosterone in women were associated with lower levels of risk aversion, with collateral evidence suggesting that testosterone has nonlinear effects on risk aversion. Persons high in testosterone and low in risk aversion were also more likely to choose risky careers in finance.[29]

The higher female level of emotional arousal. Neuroimaging studies have shown that measures of fear and arousal are associated with changes in estradiol levels across the menstrual cycle and correlate with changes in the functional reactivity of the amygdala and hippocampus.[30]

I will leave the discussion of the activational effects of hormones with these examples. The even bigger story about hormones and sex differences is not their temporary activational effects, but their permanent organizational effects on the fetal and neonatal brain.

Sex Differentiation During Fetal and Neonatal Brain Development

The discovery that testosterone permanently changes brain tissue was made 60 years ago but remains remarkably little known among the lay public. What follows is a simplified description. A more complete description (for example, discussing important changes that occur during and after puberty) would include yet other ways in which brains develop differently in males and females.

By the end of week eight, a human embryo's brain and central nervous system already contain their rudimentary structures. By week 26, the primary ridges, folds, and furrows of the human brain have emerged. Most of the 100 billion neurons in the adult human brain have already been created.[31] These basic changes happen for both sexes, driven by processes that are believed to be unrelated (or nearly so) to the embryo's sex.[32]

But long before week 26, sex has entered the picture. Even at the end of the embryonic phase, the embryo's testicles or ovaries have been developing for two weeks. By week 12, the differentiation of the sexual organs is settled, and the differentiation of the brain begins. Specifically, testosterone surges in human males occur twice before birth, during weeks 12–18 and again during weeks 34–41. Another testosterone surge in males, often called *minipuberty*, occurs in the first three months after birth.[33]

The confirmation of this role for hormones dates to 1959 and a seminal article by Charles Phoenix and his colleagues.[34] Before then, biologists knew about the role of the sex hormones in stimulating mating behavior. The Phoenix study presented the first evidence that hormones also had organizational effects that permanently altered the structure of the nervous system. "No other idea in behavioral neuroendocrinology has so transformed how we think about the genesis of masculine and feminine behavior," wrote neuroendocrinologist Kim Wallen. "The notion that hormones at circumscribed times in life predictably and permanently alter the function, and we now know, the structure, of a living being to become phenotypically male, is one of the truly powerful ideas of the twentieth century."[35]

Since 1959, thousands of experiments have been conducted on nonhuman mammals, primarily rodents and primates, in which the experimental animals are exposed to hormone manipulations during critical periods of prenatal and neonatal development.[36] These experiments have established that certain regions of the brain (but not others) have receptors (in different proportions) that accept chemical signals from hormones. These signals can affect a cell's survival, its anatomical connectivity, and its neurochemicals.

It has been found that the default is female—in the absence of a spike in testosterone at the appropriate times during gestation and neonatal life, the brain takes on female characteristics. Feminization is not an entirely passive process, however. Just as some receptors accept chemical signals from testosterone, others accept signals from estrogen. But it is through the spike in testosterone that the brain is both masculinized and defeminized (the testosterone prevents the development of female characteristics).[37] For both males and females, changes that develop during the fetal and neonatal phases also have delayed effects. Some of the circuits that are already formed by three months after birth are quiescent until activated by sex hormones at puberty.[38]

What does *masculinized* mean? Neuroscientist Margaret McCarthy summarized aspects of masculinization in rodents as follows:

Collections of cells that constitute nuclei or subnuclei of the brain differ in overall size due to differences in cell number and/or density, as well as in the number of neurons expressing a particular neurotransmitter. The length and branching patterns of dendrites and the frequency of synapses also vary between males and females—in specific ways in specific regions—as does the number of axons that form projections between nuclei and across the cerebral hemispheres. Even nonneuronal cells are masculinized. Astrocytes in parts of the male brain are more "bushy," with longer and more frequent processes than those in the same regions of the female brain. And microglia, modified macrophages that serve as the brain's innate immune system, are more activated in parts of the male brain and contribute to the changes seen in the neurons.[39]

Indisputably, a variety of physiological and measurable sex differences exist in the brains of rodents. What about in the brains of humans?

WHY RODENT STUDIES, THOUGH IGNORED HERE, ARE REALLY IMPORTANT

The quote from Margaret McCarthy gives you only a glimpse of the many ways in which studies of rodents and primates have documented that the mammalian brain is a highly sexed organ. My approach is akin to going into a fight with one hand voluntarily tied behind my back. One of the largest and most sophisticated bodies of knowledge about biological sex differences in the brain is based on nonhuman mammals, primarily rodents and some species of monkey. I am ignoring it here for the same reason I draw so little from evolutionary psychology. Like the accusation that "Evolutionary psychology is nothing more than just-so stories," the dismissive response that "Knowing something about rats doesn't mean humans work that way" is more effective than it should be. The proper question is not "Why should we think humans are the same as rats?" but rather "Why should we think that one mammalian brain was immune from the evolutionary forces that produced highly sexed brains in other mammals?"

Exploring the Organizational Effects of Prenatal Hormones in Humans

A genetic disorder of the adrenal glands known as congenital adrenal hyperplasia (CAH) has been recognized for more than a century. It can result in the production of too little cortisol or aldosterone, with effects having nothing to do with sexual identity. But it also can result in overproduction of androgens, especially testosterone. Starting in the late 1960s, researchers began to explore the possibility that girls with CAH might be more likely to engage in male sex-typed behavior in their choices of toys and games.[40]

In the 1980s, researchers also began to explore the possibility that the organizational effects of prenatal hormones in animal studies applied to humans as well.[41] In 1995, sociologist and demographer J. Richard Udry and his colleagues put that possibility to the test and found that the model used for animal research did in fact apply to humans: "It is concluded that gendered behavior is not entirely socially constructed, but partly built on a biological foundation."[42] It was a landmark article in the development of an alternative to the social-construction orthodoxy.

Also beginning in the late 1960s, neurologist Norman Geschwind had been studying anatomical asymmetries in the brain. By the early 1980s, Geschwind had integrated diverse empirical evidence to reach a specific hypothesis that would explain links between maleness and the right hemisphere. Along with one of his students, Albert Galaburda, he presented his hypothesis in another landmark article, "Cerebral Lateralization," in 1985:

> It is the intent of this hypothesis to account for the following: (1) Left-handedness is usually found to be more common in men than women. (2) The developmental disorders of language, speech, cognition, and emotion, e.g., stuttering, dyslexia, and autism are strongly male predominant. (3) Women are on the average superior in verbal talents while men tend on the average to be better at spatial functions. (4) Left-handers of both sexes and those with learning disabilities often exhibit superior right-hemisphere functions. (5) Left-handedness and ambidexterity are more frequent in the developmental disorders of childhood. (6) Certain diseases are more common in non-right-handers, e.g., immune disorders.[43]

Simplified, Geschwind's hypothesis was that the prenatal testosterone surge in males led to earlier and faster growth of the male's right hemisphere.[44]

In the late 1990s, Simon Baron-Cohen, whom you met in chapter 1, was inspired by Geschwind's hypothesis to test its validity. To infer levels of prenatal testosterone, Baron-Cohen and his colleagues measured testosterone levels in amniotic fluid.[45] In *The Essential Difference*, Baron-Cohen recalled his reaction to the initial results:

> We found that the toddlers (at twelve and twenty-four months of age) who we had identified as having lower fetal testosterone, now had higher levels

of eye contact and a larger vocabulary; or, putting it the other way around, the higher your levels of prenatal testosterone, the less eye contact you now make and the smaller your vocabulary. This is exactly as Geschwind had predicted.

When we got those results, I had one of those strange feelings, like a shiver down the spine. A few drops more of this little chemical could affect your sociability or your language ability. I found it extraordinary.[46]

In the first two decades of the twenty-first century, these beginnings have been augmented by an array of additional evidence for the role of androgens in masculinizing the human brain.

Evidence from natural variation in prenatal testosterone. Baron-Cohen's Autism Research Centre has generated most of the studies documenting the relationships between prenatal testosterone levels and various measures of male-typical and female-typical behavior. These include visuospatial ability,[47] autism,[48] the empathy quotient,[49] systemizing quotient,[50] social relationships,[51] and interest in children.[52] The pattern of results linking testosterone to the phenotype has been striking but not dispositive. A 2015 review of the literature on early androgen exposure and sex development (first author was Melissa Hines) indicates that the underlying problem may be the use of amniotic fluid: The within-sex variation in testosterone in amniotic fluid may not be sufficient to serve as a reliable measure of natural variation in prenatal exposure to testosterone.[53] It can point research in the right direction, but seldom can conclusively pin down relationships. Measures of neonatal testosterone (which can be tested directly) and studies of people with sexual disorders are producing more robust evidence.

DISSENTING VOICES

The best-known and most detailed critiques of the organizational role of testosterone in particular and biological explanations of phenotypic sex differences in general are Rebecca Jordan-Young's *Brain Storm* (2010), Cordelia Fine's pair of books, *Delusions of Gender* (2010) and *Testosterone Rex* (2017), and Gina Rippon's *The Gendered Brain* (2019).[54] All four books are directed at the general reader and are entertainingly written. They draw attention to some problems that are indeed common such as small samples, inconsistent results, and scarce replications.

The reviews in the mainstream press have been uniformly and sometimes gushingly enthusiastic.[55] *Testosterone Rex* also won the 2017 Royal Society Insight Investment Science Book Prize, awarded by the oldest scientific society in the world.[56] And yet none of these books has had a visible effect on neuroscientists working on sex differences. There were a few critical reviews in the technical literature, and other academics have had scathing things to say in blogs, but that's it.[57] A neuroscientist whom I asked about the lack of reaction to *Testosterone Rex* replied, "One reason you don't find many critiques of Fine's book is that people in the field really don't care. It's so evidently nonsense." In their view, Jordan-Young, Fine, and Rippon are guilty of cherry-picking (they're good at attacking weak studies; they don't come to grips with the strong ones), fail to acknowledge the weaknesses of their favored studies, and set up straw men, demolishing positions that neuroscientists working on sex differences don't take (e.g., treating male and female brains as binary).[58]

If you want to compare the arguments side by side, I recommend a pair of articles easily obtainable online. The first is by Cordelia Fine, Daphna Joel, and Gina Rippon: "Eight Things You Need to Know About Sex, Gender, Brains, and Behavior: A Guide for Academics, Journalists, Parents, Gender Diversity Advocates, Social Justice Warriors, Tweeters, Facebookers, and Everyone Else."[59] The second is a response by Marco Del Giudice, David Puts, David Geary, and David Schmitt: "Sex Differences in Brain and Behavior: Eight Counterpoints."[60]

If you're trying to compare the positions in Jordan-Young, Fine, and Rippon with mainstream science on the crucial issue of masculinization of the male brain, I recommend two evenhanded reviews of the literature on early androgen exposure written by acknowledged experts in the field. One is "Early Androgen Exposure and Human Gender Development" by Melissa Hines, Mihaela Constantinescu, and Debra Spencer.[61] Hines is director of the Gender Development Research Centre at Cambridge University. The other is "Beyond Pink and Blue: The Complexity of Early Androgen Effects on Gender Development" by Sheri A. Berenbaum, professor of psychology and pediatrics at Penn State and member of the Penn State Neuroscience Institute.[62]

Evidence from sexual disorders. Two intersex conditions in which a person's biological sex is ambiguous have served as natural experiments about the effects of testosterone.

The first of these conditions is the one you have already encountered, classic CAH (as distinct from late-onset CAH; see Appendix 2 for details), in which female fetuses are exposed to high levels of testosterone. Except for that exposure, they are genetically normal females with two X chromosomes. CAH causes partial masculinization of the genitalia. Because the effect is visible, CAH is normally diagnosed and treated at birth through surgical feminization of the genitalia and correction of the hormonal abnormality. The overall effects on females with CAH were summarized in a review of the literature as follows:

> Females with CAH differ from unaffected females (their siblings or age-matched comparisons) in a number of domains, including activity interests, personality, cognitive abilities, handedness, and sexuality. Thus, compared to controls, CAH females are more interested in male-typical activities and less interested in female-typical activities in childhood, adolescence, and adulthood, as measured by observation, self-report, and parent-report. The differences are large and, when multiple measures are used, there is very little overlap between females with CAH and control females.[63]

A subsequent study specifically focused on how 125 women with CAH compared to their unaffected siblings on the People-Things dimension. The researchers found that females with CAH had more interest in Things versus People than did unaffected females, and variations among females with CAH reflected variations in their degree of androgen exposure. On Prediger's Things-People dimension, the effect size comparing women with and without CAH was −0.75 (indicating that women with CAH were farther toward the Things end of the continuum).[64]

In terms of their self-defined sexual identity, almost all adult women with CAH self-identify as women. Only about 1–2 percent choose to live as males, but that is far higher than the one per thousands in women without CAH. About 5 percent experience sex dysphoria, also far above the levels for women without CAH.[65]

The other sexual disorder is complete androgen insensitivity syndrome (CAIS). Fetuses with CAIS are genetically male, carrying the XY chromosome pair. Their testes produce prenatal testosterone in normal amounts at the proper times—but their androgen receptors are not functional. The testosterone circulates, but it has no effect. Persons with CAIS are born with externally normal female genitalia, reared as girls, are usually indistinguishable from girls behaviorally, and are usually designated as females in the technical literature despite their Y chromosome.[66] It is also noteworthy that, despite their Y chromosome, CAIS carriers apparently do not have elevated spatial skills.[67]

A 2017 study by Swedish neuroscientists identified specific ways in which fetuses with a Y chromosome but affected by CAIS develop brains that are a mix of characteristically "male" and "female" patterns. Omitting the most abstruse results, women with CAIS displayed a characteristically female pattern of thicker parietal and occipital cortices and thinner left temporal cortex than male controls.[68] On the other hand, the CAIS women displayed a "male" pattern in cortical thickness with regard to a thinner cortex in the precentral and postcentral gyrus. CAIS women were characteristically "female" with regard to the hippocampus volumes and "male" with regard to the caudate volumes. Add in the more abstruse findings, and the authors felt able to conclude that "the results indeed show considerable support" for the hypotheses they took into the study: The CAIS condition—no effect of testosterone on neural tissue—explains the similarities in brain structure between CAIS women and female controls, while the presence of the Y chromosome and its unique genes explains the similarities between CAIS women and male controls.[69]

Exploring the Interplay of Biology and Socialization

Accepting the organizational role of hormones does not require that we reject a role for socialization. Intuition tells us that both are probably involved, and scholars have made progress in exploring the balance.

In 2000, Richard Udry used an elegant experimental design to initiate an investigation of the nature-nurture balance. Udry took advantage of the natural variation in androgen levels among women even in the absence of a genetic disorder such as CAH. He assembled a sample of 163 adult women (ages 27–30 at the time of analysis) who had measures of their testosterone and SHBG[70] values taken in utero (they were drawn from the Child Health and Development Study conducted in the 1960s). Udry's researchers also obtained measures of the women's adult levels of testosterone and SHBG along with a variety of questionnaire information that enabled Udry to assess the participants along four masculinity-femininity continua. The continua involved the importance of home, interests, job status, and personality. The results showed the predicted relationships of both prenatal and adult testosterone and SHBG to adult gendered behavior—but also showed independent relationships of childhood gender socialization to adult gendered behavior. The more interesting finding involved an interaction term: The effects of childhood socialization were confined to women who had low levels of prenatal androgen exposure. In Udry's words, "if a daughter has natural tendencies to be feminine, encouragement will enhance femininity; but if she has below average femininity in childhood, encouraging her to be more feminine will have no effect."[71] A second interesting finding involved scores on a measure of the importance of spending time with one's family. In adolescence, the women in the study had been tightly bunched in the middle of the range regardless of their level of prenatal androgen exposure. When interviewed at ages 27–30, those with above-average prenatal androgen exposure had moved to the "not important" position, while those with below-average prenatal androgen exposure had moved to the "very important" position.

In 2015, Shannon Davis and Barbara Risman drew from the same Child Health and Development Study that Udry used, but with a larger sample. In their article with the main title "Feminists Wrestle with Testosterone," they used an analogous set of instruments, applied them to path analysis, and got complementary results. Their analysis showed effects of both prenatal androgen exposure and childhood socialization, with socialization playing the stronger role in terms of path coefficients.[72] Their finding that the effect of hormones was stronger for masculinity than femininity is consistent with Udry's finding.[73]

Male-Female Differences in Brain Lateralization and Connectivity

So far, I have discussed evidence that the prenatal and neonatal surges of testosterone are causally linked to a variety of phenotypic sex differences, but I haven't directly addressed Geschwind's hypothesis that the male brain is more lateralized than the female brain because of the organizing effects of testosterone.

Lateralization

Lateralization refers to the relative localization of a function in one hemisphere or the other. To apply it to the question we are discussing, Geschwind hypothesized that males primarily use the left hemisphere for verbal tasks and the right hemisphere for spatial tasks, whereas women use both hemispheres for both types of tasks. Another way of expressing it is that males exhibit more *functional asymmetry.*

Even before Geschwind formulated his hypothesis about testosterone and the right hemisphere, scholars had been considering the possibility that sex differences in test scores might point to sex differences in the use of the left and right hemispheres of the cerebrum. As early as 1980, a review of the evidence in *Behavioral and Brain Sciences* cautiously concluded that the literature did not "overwhelmingly confirm" greater functional asymmetry in males, but among those studies that did find a sex difference, "the vast majority are compatible with [that] hypothesis."[74] A meta-analysis in 1996 came to the somewhat more confident conclusion that "it appears that sex differences in verbal and spatial abilities can be explained, at least in part, by the fact that men tend to be more lateralized than women."[75]

Recall that the default in brain development is female. In the case of language processing, this means that the default is to use both hemispheres. The salient issue in analyzing the effects of testosterone on language processing is that something about the development of the male right brain is crowding out the use of the right hemisphere for language processing (which, by default, would also ordinarily be used). The focus of the right hemisphere on spatial processing, driven by the impact of testosterone on the right hemisphere, is a plausible explanation.

Clinical evidence from brain injuries reinforces the probability of sex differences in lateralization. When women suffer brain damage to the left hemisphere, they are less likely than men to develop language difficulties. Women's language test scores after brain damage suffer the same effect whether the damage occurred in the left or right hemisphere, whereas men are more affected by damage to the left hemisphere.[76] Researchers are also able to investigate this difference by anesthetizing just one hemisphere of the brain. Women lose language fluency no matter which hemisphere is anesthetized; men do so only if it is the left hemisphere.[77]

Most of the evidence from brain injuries had been developed before the advent of fMRI. Since then, neuroscientists have made major advances in understanding what's going on inside the brain that produces the circumstantial evidence for greater male lateralization.

Evidence of Sex Differences in Structural Connectivity

Neurons in the brain produce thoughts and behaviors through their inter-connections. But there has to be an architecture to those connections, just as there must be an architecture to any kind of network. That architecture is labeled *structural connectivity*. The map of those connections is called the *connectome*. The word was created to reflect its kinship to the map of the genome. There are many parallels. Maps of both the genome and con-nectome don't answer questions of functionality in themselves, but they do provide a framework within which function can be studied. Both consist of structural elements at different levels of scale—from genetic regulatory net-works to genes to base pairs in the genome; from brain regions to neuronal populations to neurons in the connectome.[78]

Don't expect to see a fully mapped human connectome anytime soon. Whereas the genome has about 3 billion sites, the human brain has about 86 billion neurons. Whereas the sites of the genome lie sequentially along a strip of DNA, neurons can connect with many other neurons. The complexity of a connectome is such that, as I write, neuroscientists are still struggling to complete the connectome of the fruit fly larva, a brain that contains just 15,000 neurons.[79]

Neuroscientists are nonetheless able to construct connectomes using regions as the unit of analysis instead of individual neurons. In the early 2000s, it was established that the connectome follows a "small-world" topol-ogy.[80] The phrase has a precise mathematical description, but the easiest way to understand it is through the popularized concept of "six degrees of separa-tion," referring to the assertion that you can establish a path between yourself and any other person in the world through no more than five intermediary links.[81] The reason you can do it is that your personal cluster of acquain-tances includes at least a few people who have a direct connection with some other distant cluster. That's how the brain is organized: It is characterized by a high degree of local clustering of neurons, forming nodes and hubs, supple-mented with random connections that permit direct pathways between dis-tant nodes.

From the mid-1990s onward, new evidence from fMRI accumulated for greater lateralization among males.[82] A group of neuroscientists at Beijing Normal University hypothesized that connectivity varies by brain size and by sex. They used DTI tractography to analyze MRI images of 72 healthy, right-handed young adults. They found no relationship between path length and either brain size or sex, which the authors interpreted as suggesting that "the global efficiency of structural networks of the brain is not affected by sex or brain size."[83] But their analysis of the efficiency of local clusters told a strikingly different story: The smaller the brain, the higher the efficiency of clusters—but only for women. The correlation between the authors' clustering coefficient and brain size for women was a sizable –.53. For men, the correlation was a trivially small –.09. It's a finding that bears on the similarity of *g* in males and females despite the larger male brain volumes that I discuss in Appendix 3.

In 2014, the state of knowledge saw a major advance through a study titled "Sex Differences in the Structural Connectome of the Human Brain." First author was Madhura Ingalhalikar. She and her colleagues at the University of Pennsylvania and at Children's Hospital of Philadelphia used the same Philadelphia Neurodevelopmental Cohort discussed in chapter 3. Their sample size was large: 428 males and 521 females. The 10 coauthors of the Ingalhalikar study parcellated the cerebrum into 95 regions, then used interregional probabilistic fiber tractography to compute the connection probability between regions, expressed in a 95-network matrix. Analyses were conducted by sex and by each of three age groups corresponding to the developmental stages of childhood (8–13 years), adolescence (13–17 years), and young adulthood (17–22 years).

Here are the main findings:

1. Male brains are structurally optimized for communicating within hemispheres. Female brains are structurally optimized for communicating between hemispheres. "Our analysis overwhelmingly supported this hypothesis at every level."[84]

2. No significant age-by-sex interactions were found in the connection-based analysis—which is to say, there was no evidence that environmental forces operated from age eight onward to augment the contrasting male and female differences in connectivity.

3. A sex difference exists in the degree to which the connectome can be divided into distinct, separate modules (*modularity*), and a sex difference exists in the degree to which a given region is connected to

its neighbors (*transitivity*). Both modularity and transitivity were globally higher in males ($p < .0001$ in both cases). Both results are consistent with a male brain that on average is wired for localized functionality and a female brain that on average is wired for cross-module functionality.

4. A sex difference exists in the degree to which the connections of regional nodes of the connectome are uniformly distributed across all the lobes of the cerebral cortex. The statistic for measuring this quality, the participation coefficient, was significantly higher for women in numerous regions in the frontal, parietal, and temporal lobes, whereas it was never higher for men in the regional nodes of the cerebral cortex. In contrast, the same coefficient was higher for men in the cerebellum.

A study of connectivity by a team of Swiss scientists published later in 2014 confirmed the pattern of connectivity found by the Ingalhalikar study, but argued that it was not the result of a sex difference per se but a function of brain size: "This pattern of connectivity can also be found within genders when comparing small-brained with large-brained women and small-brained with large-brained men."[85] For our purposes, the source of the distinctive connectivity patterns doesn't make any difference. A recent meta-analysis of sex differences in brain volumes reported effect sizes for intracranial volume, total brain volume, and the cerebrum of -3.03, -2.10, and -3.35 respectively (i.e., favoring males).[86] Effect sizes that large mean that the overlap of the male and female distributions is small. It implies a familiar situation—just as many women are taller than the average man, many women have brain connectivity patterns similar to those of a man with average brain volume. Nonetheless, a large sex difference in connectivity pattern remains because the sex difference in brain size is so large—a biological difference that is wholly unaffected by the environment.

The authors of the Ingalhalikar study speculated about the relationship of these structural differences to neurocognitive functioning. For males (or for women with unusually large brains), "Greater within-hemispheric supratentorial connectivity combined with greater cross-hemispheric cerebellar connectivity would confer an efficient system for coordinated action" and was consistent with results from fMRI studies showing "greater focal intrahemispheric activation in males on a spatial task, in which they excelled."[87]

For females (or males with unusually small brains), greater interhemispheric connectivity "would facilitate integration of the analytical and sequential reasoning modes of the left hemisphere with the spatial, intuitive processing of information of the right hemisphere," and was consistent with results from fMRI studies "which have reported greater interhemispheric activation in females on a language task, in which they excelled."[88]

Evidence for Sex Differences in Functional Connectivity

A year after the Ingalhalikar study of structural connectivity, a companion study looked at sex differences in functional connectivity. The first author was Theodore Satterthwaite, who had also been a coauthor of the Ingalhalikar study.[89] Like the Ingalhalikar study, it used the Philadelphia Neurodevelopmental Cohort, restricted to male-female pairs matched on age and in-scanner motion (the results from fMRI studies can easily be contaminated by head motion during the scan). This procedure resulted in a sample consisting of 312 males and 362 females.

Functional connectivity is not based on architecture, but on the activation of neurons. Formally, functional connectivity denotes "temporal correlations between remote neurophysiological events."[90] Think of it this way: *Structural* connectivity maps the anatomical routes whereby neurons connect. *Functional* connectivity doesn't describe what paths the connections took. It simply documents that a set of neurons were active at a given time, without supplying any information about causation.[91]

The Satterthwaite study took the speculations of the Ingalhalikar study and explored them directly. "Our hypothesis was that the extent to which a given subject demonstrated a stereotypically 'male' or 'female' pattern of brain connectivity would be related to the masculinity or femininity of their cognitive profile."[92] To that end, the authors created two continuous indexes. One was a score that represented the degree of masculinity or femininity in a subject's pattern of connectivity. The other did the same thing for the subject's pattern of scores on the Computerized Neurocognitive Battery. The authors also used a model that classified each subject as male or female on the basis of the two patterns, one for functional connectivity, the other based on the pattern on the neurocognitive tests.

In one sense, the results vindicate those who emphasize how much males and females overlap. The classification using cognitive data correctly assigned

63 percent of the subjects to their actual sex; the one using connectivity data was correct for 71 percent. That leaves 37 percent and 29 percent of the subjects for whom the classification was wrong—substantial error rates. On the other hand, the results showed as well that males and females are dimorphic in the normal sense of that term both for test scores and for neural connectivity within the brain.

The authors then demonstrated that the two indexes of masculinity/femininity were correlated. The correlation across the entire sample was +.20—statistically highly significant because of the large sample size. Two things about this result can be, and are, true at the same time. One is that the findings of the Satterthwaite study, like those of the Ingalhalikar study, represent a significant step forward. As the authors correctly note, "Our results show that sex differences in patterns of brain connectivity are related to sex-specific profiles of cognitive performance, for the first time establishing a link between sex differences in cognition and the organization of the brain's functional connectome."[93] The other truth is that the sizes of the male-female differences are substantively modest.

A subsequent study of connectivity in the Philadelphia Neurodevelopmental Cohort (first author was Birkan Tunç) found that males had increased connectivity between the motor and sensory systems, along with increased connectivity in systems that are associated with complex reasoning and control. Males had higher connectivity in the integration of the "default mode network" that is believed to play an important role in the integration of cognitive processes. Females had increased connectivity with subcortical regions including the amygdala, hypothalamus, hippocampus, thalamus, pallidum, and others that have been associated with emotion processing, social cognition, and motivation. Taken as a whole, the results "suggest a better perception-action coordination in males, and better anticipation and subsequent processing of socially and emotionally relevant cues in females."[94]

Sex Differences in the Corpus Callosum

In addition to sex differences in both structural and functional connectivity, explanations of greater interhemispheric connectivity in females naturally led neuroscientists to look at possible sex differences in the corpus callosum. The corpus callosum is a flat ribbonlike bundle of fibers about four inches long that lies at the bottom of the fissure between the two hemispheres. It is the largest white matter structure in the brain, and, as I mentioned earlier, white matter transmits information across neurons. It is the main connection that enables the left and right hemispheres to communicate. All this combines to raise the question of whether the corpus callosum differs between men and women.

In 1982, physical anthropologist Ralph Holloway and one of his students, Christine de Lacoste-Utamsing, published a small-sample study finding that the relative size of the corpus callosum was larger in females than in males and that the splenial portion (toward the back of the cerebral cortex) was more bulbous.[95] For the next two decades, an assortment of technical articles appeared, some supporting and some disputing that dimorphism in the corpus callosum is real.[96] As in so many other aspects of neuroscience, the advent of MRI technology and increasing sophistication in the use of that technology has enabled something resembling a consensus to emerge. In 2013, neuroscientists at the Center for Advanced Brain Imaging of the Nathan S. Kline Institute published the results for a sample of 316 normal subjects ages 18–94, using a sophisticated methodology that responded to the many issues of statistical confounding that had tripped up many earlier studies. The measure was the cross-sectional area of the corpus callosum if you sliced through the middle of it lengthwise. The technical term is the midsagittal plane. After controlling for brain size, it was found that the female corpus callosum is larger than the male corpus callosum. The estimates of the marginal means for females and males were 634 mm^2 and 611 mm^2 respectively, with $p < .03$.[97] They concluded as follows:

> In this paper, it has been shown that on average, for pairs of female and male subjects with equal brain sizes and similar ages, the CCA is larger in the female by a few percent. Given that postmortem studies of callosal fibers in normal subjects have either found no difference in fiber density between sexes or a denser fiber packing in females, it can be inferred that for a given brain size, the female cerebral hemispheres are more extensively interconnected.[98]

Once again, the effect size is modest; once again, it is consistent with other sex differences in the brain indicating greater female symmetry in brain connectivity.

Sex Differences in Gray Matter

In 2012, a study of sex difference in gray matter provided triangulating evidence for the role of fetal testosterone in changing the male right hemisphere. Michael Lombardo was the first author of the resulting article, "Fetal Testosterone Influences Sexually Dimorphic Gray Matter in the Human Brain." Its findings should be treated as provisional until replicated, but it gives a window into the research that is linking brain structure and function to differences in neurocognitive test scores.

The Lombardo analysis was conducted in two phases. First, neuroimaging of 28 normally developing males ages 8–11 whose prenatal testosterone had been measured through amniotic fluid established the relationship between fetal testosterone and the volume of gray matter (adjusted for differences in brain size) in brain regions of interest.[99] Next, neuroimaging of 101 boys and 116 girls, also 8–11 years old, was used to assess sexual dimorphism in the same regions of interest. Boiling down a highly technical presentation, the three regions of interest showed significant sex dimorphism in both gray matter volume and in the correlations of fetal testosterone with adult gray matter volume.[100]

In a region of the brain in the right hemisphere that has been associated with social-cognitive and social-perceptual abilities, including empathy, greater fetal testosterone was predictive of larger gray matter volume, and the mean gray matter volume was larger for boys than for girls. The correlation of +.45 for fetal testosterone and gray matter volume fits in with collateral evidence that higher fetal testosterone correlates negatively with eye contact among infants,[101] attributions of intentionality at four years of age,[102] and empathy at eight years of age.[103]

In a region of the brain that overlaps with key language regions, including Wernicke's area, and extends into Geschwind's territory, greater fetal testosterone was predictive of *smaller* gray matter volume and girls had larger gray matter volume than boys.[104] The sizable negative correlation (–.47) of fetal testosterone with the volume of gray matter is consistent with collateral evidence that higher fetal testosterone is correlated with smaller vocabulary at ages 12 and 24 months and that girls have larger vocabularies than boys at those ages.[105]

In all three regions of interest, the relationships of fetal testosterone to gray matter volume were consistent with other studies involving autism, conduct disorder, and developmental language problems that disproportionately affect males.[106] "In sum," the authors concluded, "this study provides the first evidence that FT [fetal testosterone] has an organizing effect on some sexually dimorphic areas of the human brain. Along with prior work on how FT influences behavior, this work highlights FT as an important developmental mechanism contributing to sex differences in neuroanatomy."[107]

There's more on this topic that I will not try to cover (the note has some more sources for the curious), nor will I try to cover the continuing debate about the details.[108] My limited point is that the debate is being conducted within a consensus among neuroscientists that the male brain is more lateralized than the female brain. The differences are consistent with observed phenotypic sex differences in visuospatial and verbal skills.

Sex Differences in Emotional Cognition and Memory

I promised that I would give you a glimpse of the progress that is being made in directly linking sex differences in the brain to sex differences in the phenotype. I chose progress in understanding sex differences in emotional response because an extensive technical literature has been accumulating and because of the intriguing links between the female phenotypic advantage in certain kinds of memory and the greater female vulnerability to depression.[109] The story that is emerging has not reached the level of settled science, but progress has been remarkable.

Emotions and some types of memory have been identified with a set of regions located deep in the temporal lobes. Five of the most important regions are the amygdala, hippocampus, thalamus, hypothalamus, and cingulate gyrus. For convenience, I will use a familiar label, "limbic system," with the understanding that the term has fallen out of favor among neuroscientists— it amounts to "brain regions that do emotion," with no satisfactory way of delineating what regions do and do not qualify.

The amygdala plays an important role in evaluating the emotional valence of a situation (it is famously involved in fight-or-flight decisions) and in learning through reward and punishment. It also is involved in the consolidation of emotion-laden memory.

The region most closely associated with memory is the hippocampus, located immediately behind the amygdala. Specifically, the hippocampus is key to the consolidation of long-term declarative memory—the inventory of events and facts that we can consciously call to mind. The hippocampus is especially important to episodic memory, based on events that we have observed or participated in.[110]

With the advent of neuroimaging, researchers soon started investigating what parts of the brain were activated when samples of men and women were exposed to emotionally loaded material. The most common stimuli were sets of pictures that evoke negative or positive responses. Negative examples are photographs of a mutilated corpse or of a prison cell. Positive examples are photographs of a child happily blowing out birthday candles or of champagne glasses clinking against a setting sun. More examples are available online.[111]

Male-Female Differences in Response to Sexual Stimuli

Before proceeding to other kinds of emotion, let's get one of the obvious varieties out of the way: sex differences in response to sexual stimuli. The overall conclusion, expressed by one of the leading researchers on sex differences in emotional response, will not come as a shock: "Numerous studies have demonstrated that men are more psychologically and physiologically responsive to visual sexually arousing stimuli and display a greater motivation to seek out and interact with such stimuli."[112] Science marches on.

A biological substrate underlies that observed sex difference. It has been known for some time, through clinical studies of rodents and by studying humans who have suffered seizures near the amygdala, that both the amygdala and hypothalamus are involved in sexual behavior.[113] Neuroimaging studies have now established that the amygdala and hypothalamus in humans also show significant sex differences.

The most obvious difference is that the male amygdala and hypothalamus are significantly larger than the female amygdala and hypothalamus, even after controlling for total brain size.[114] Two collateral findings indicate that size makes a difference. First, the residual size of the amygdala after neurosurgery for epilepsy has been correlated with residual sexual drive.[115] Second, while many regions of the brain do *not* differ in size after controlling for total brain size (see Appendix 3), the ones that do differ tend to have high concentrations of sex hormone receptors.[116] Brain size is most dimorphic in regions where sex hormones have had the greatest organizational effect.

The results of neuroimaging studies are consistent with the proposition that men not only react more strongly to sexual stimuli than women, but also that men and women have different neurocognitive profiles. An initial neuroimaging study in 2002 established a higher level of sexual arousal in neural activation among men, but it left open two interpretations of the results: the arousal hypothesis and the processing mode hypothesis.[117] The arousal hypothesis is that men show greater brain activation because there is a simple sex difference in the magnitude of response to equivalent stimuli. The greater size of the amygdala and hypothalamus might help account for this kind of sex difference.

The processing mode hypothesis, originated by psychologist Stephan Hamann, who tested it, is that men and women use different neural pathways. If so, men and women matched on level of arousal will exhibit different brain activation patterns. That's what Hamann found. Even after equating level of sexual arousal among the male and female participants, both through fMRI data and self-ratings, the amygdala and hypothalamus exhibited substantially more activation among males than among females.[118] The activation among the females was not just less than that of men in the amygdala and hypothalamus, it was slight. As for the rest of the brain, there were no areas at all in which females showed greater activation than males.

Sex Differences in Response to Nonsexual Emotional Stimuli

The larger question is whether men and women also respond differently to emotional stimuli more broadly defined.

Emotional responses and sex differences in memory. It is a familiar conversational event for long-married couples: The wife vividly remembers a family event from many years ago that the husband has completely forgotten. Over the 1980s and 1990s, evidence accumulated that this is not a baseless stereotype. On average, women are better than men at what psychologists call "autobiographical memory."[119] It is not limited to mothers remembering events involving their children; it applies generally. Evidence also accumulated for another sex difference: Women tend to be better at remembering the minutiae of an event (labeled *peripheral detail*), while men tended to be better at identifying the core events (labeled *gist*).[120]

The advent of fMRI has enabled researchers to relate these phenotypic sex differences to sex differences in the functioning of the brain. The basic technique is to expose the subjects to pictures or films while they are undergoing fMRI. A few weeks later, the subjects are tested on their memory for the scenes they saw. With the successfully remembered scenes in hand, the investigators can then go back to the fMRI results and see which brain areas were active.

In 2003, Larry Cahill and Anda van Stegeren drew on the accumulating evidence for two relationships to make a prediction. The two bodies of evidence were, first, that the right hemisphere (which tends to play a relatively larger role in males) is biased toward the more global aspects of a scene, while the left hemisphere (which tends to play a relatively larger role in women) is biased toward finer detail; and, second, that the amygdala's role in memory for emotional material is concentrated in its right hemisphere for men and left hemisphere for women. The prediction was that administration of a drug that impairs amygdala function for memory (propranolol) should have opposite effects on men and women, impairing memory for gist in men and memory for peripheral detail in women. The results confirmed the prediction.[121]

Repeated studies since then have elaborated on the sex differences in functioning of the amygdala. The level of neural activity in the amygdala is consistently predictive of later recall: The higher the level, the greater the probability that the scene will be remembered.[122] But for both sexes, this predictiveness holds for only one hemisphere: the left amygdala in women, the right amygdala in men. An additional finding from one study provides a possible explanation of women's better recall: When asked to rate the level of emotional arousal in the pictures they were shown, the subjects' ratings of emotional arousal correlated with the left amygdala in both men and women. In other words, women use the same region—the left amygdala—both for emotional reactions and for encoding memory. In men, the emotional reactions occur in one hemisphere and the encoding of memory in the other. It could be part of the explanation for the greater vividness and accuracy of women's emotional memories.

The strength and persistence of emotional responses to negative stimuli. By 2012, Jennifer Stevens and Stephan Hamann of Emory University could call upon 80 separate neuroimaging studies with a total of 1,217 participants for a meta-analysis of sex differences in brain activation in response to emotional stimuli.[123]

The meta-analysis indicated that both sexes used all the major elements of the limbic system along with other parts of the brain. But there were also statistically significant differences in several regions, and they formed an intriguing pattern for negative or positive emotions.

Men and women showed significant differences in their response to negative images in a total of 17 regions. The intriguing pattern was that women showed significantly greater activation than males in all of the major regions of the limbic system: the left amygdala, hippocampus, thalamus, hypothalamus, and the medial frontal and anterior cingulate gyri. The only region among the major components of the limbic system with a disproportionately high male activation was the left putamen, a part of the basal ganglia that is not known to have any relationship with emotion (it has many functions, but mostly involving control of motor skills). To put it another way, when it came to negative emotion, females had significantly stronger responses in those parts of the brain that play the most important part in generating emotion; males had significantly stronger responses in regions of the brain that are only peripherally involved in generating emotion.

Now consider what happens when men and women are exposed to positive images. Men showed significantly greater activation than women in the left amygdala, but, with that single exception, neither sex had significantly greater activation in any component, major or minor, of the limbic system traditionally defined. All of the other areas in which there were significant sex differences were elsewhere in the brain. Thus a first and potentially important sex difference: Women have a pronounced neurological tendency to respond to negative stimuli; men have a pronounced neurological tendency to respond to positive stimuli.

The Stevens meta-analysis is useful for establishing the reality of an overall relationship—in this case between regional sex differences in the brain and emotional response—but the best individual studies tell us more about what's going on.

Rumination. In the psychological literature, *rumination* refers to thoughts, typically autobiographical, that a person mentally rehearses over and over, usually not productively. When they are negative thoughts, rumination amounts to brooding. Taken to an extreme, rumination can become depression. In the 1990s, Susan Nolen-Hoeksema led several studies establishing that women were more likely than men to ruminate, particularly in response to negative events.[124] In the early 2000s, two studies using brain imaging established a biological basis for those findings. Instead of showing participants pictures just once, participants saw them several times. The finding in both studies was that males quickly became habituated to a stimulus—the response in the amygdala decreased rapidly after the first few exposures—whereas it persisted among women.[125] In 2013, researchers at the Harvard Medical School (Joseph Andreano was the first author) tested whether this pattern replicated for both positive and negative stimuli. It did not. As in previous studies, men showed higher amygdala activity for novel stimuli than women no matter whether the stimulus was negative, neutral, or positive. For familiar positive stimuli, men again had a higher response than women. But when it came to *negative* stimuli, men quickly habituated while women continued to show substantial amygdala activity even after repeated exposure. The difference was large enough that it reached statistical significance despite the small sample size.[126]

Now recall the table in chapter 2 that showed the prevalence of personality disorders by sex. Men had higher incidence rates on the autism spectrum, conduct disorders, ADHD, and schizophrenia, among others. Women had higher prevalence on another set, including three that involve rumination: major depression, generalized anxiety, and post-traumatic stress disorder. The findings I have just summarized point to a sex difference both in the intensity of initial reaction to negative stimuli and in the persistence of that reaction, which in turn point to a difference in rumination. In discussing the meaning of its findings, the Andreano study put them into the context of the literature on depression and the brain:

- Persons at increased risk for both depression and anxiety disorders exhibit amygdala activity in response to both novel and familiar faces, while controls respond only to novel faces.[127]

- Persons at increased risk for those disorders continue to show increased amygdala response to faces even after extended habituation.[128]
- Persons high in trait anxiety fail to habituate to previously threat-associated stimuli, as these stimuli continue to evoke amygdala activity after extinction training.[129]
- Persons with post-traumatic stress disorder show decreased habituation in amygdala signal to repeated fearful faces.[130]
- Individuals with more persistent amygdala response to negativity in the Andreano sample also self-reported more anxiety and depressive symptoms than those with faster habituation.[131]
- Spontaneous intrusive memories and mood-congruent recall have been related to increased amygdala activity.[132]
- Increased engagement of the amygdala during the encoding of emotions predicts subsequent memory.[133]

Putting together the pieces, Andreano and his coauthors concluded that "a resistance to habituation to negative material in women may represent a potential vulnerability contributing to women's higher rate of affective disorder."[134]

I have given you a typical example of how progress is being made in linking phenotypic sex differences—in this case, a conspicuous sex difference in depression and related disorders—and their biological underpinnings. It comprises an intricate map of related phenomena that have been observed and implications that have been substantiated.

At the end of it, we still are looking at an incomplete picture. But this example is also typical in the velocity of discovery that it represents. At the turn of the twenty-first century, it was known that the incidence of depression was higher among women, that women ruminate more than men, and that there was probably some relationship between those facts. Two decades later, important components of the biological processes of depression are understood and progress continues to be rapid. When the full etiology of depression is known, it may well be that environmental influences explain some of the sex differences in prevalence of depression. But even now, convincing evidence indicates that biology is also part of the story.

Recapitulation

The takeaways from this chapter's complicated discussion can be summarized quickly:

- Circulating sex hormones produce easily observable differences in the phenotype. Those hormones have specific, documented effects that match up with some of the differences in personality and neurocognitive functioning discussed in chapters 2 and 3.
- The underreported news about sex hormones is the permanent effect that prenatal and infant surges of testosterone have on masculinizing the male brain. Those effects also match up with the earlier discussions of personality and neurocognitive functioning.
- The greater lateralization of the male brain has been documented by a variety of evidence about sex differences in structural connectivity and functional connectivity. These findings bear on phenotypic sex differences in visuospatial and verbal skills.
- Differences in the functioning of the amygdala, hypothalamus, and other regions of the limbic system appear to have links with phenotypic sex differences in memory and vulnerability to depression.

These topics barely scratch the surface. For example, I described sex differences in memory as they are related to the amygdala. Researchers are now integrating the findings on the phenotypic sex differences in memory, spatial abilities, and perceptual processing (the temporal order in which a scene and its individual features are recognized) into an explanation that invokes sex differences in the amygdala, hippocampus, and lateralization, all mediated by the locus coeruleus in the brain stem and the adrenal glands (more precisely, the catecholamine system).[135] For those of you who want to get a broader sense of how much has been done and is under way in research on sex differences in the brain and are prepared to cope with some densely technical material, I recommend a 2019 review article, "Sex Differences in the Developing Brain."[136]

Probably the takeaway with the most long-term importance is that it's still early days. The progress in understanding sex differences in the brain over the last two decades has been spectacular, but you can expect it to be eclipsed by what will be learned in the next twenty years.

A Personal Interpretation of the Material in Part I

I reserve an entire chapter at the end of the book for my own interpretation of larger issues, but I also end Parts I, II, and III with personal statements of my reading of the material.

Males and females are different. A lot different. The distinctions that show up in the phenotypic evidence on personality, abilities, educational choices, vocational choices, and career paths are interconnected both conceptually and empirically. The links between these phenotypic differences and the sex differences in the brain are still only partly understood, but what we have learned so far also hangs together. I expect that the more we learn, the more closely phenotypic differences will match up with genetic differences. I will also assert without trying to demonstrate it that this coherent picture fits seamlessly within the context of evolutionary pressures over millions of years that shaped *Homo sapiens*.

But this is also a good time to remind you that "a lot different" does not come close to *comprehensively* different. On the contrary, those who would try to make the case that one sex is superior to another should recall some of the personality traits described in chapter 2 on which males and females do *not* appear to differ. Some of those involve personality traits that many men like to associate with being male, such as forcefulness in expression, self-reliance, and venturesomeness; others involve traits that many women like to associate with being female, such as openness to the inner world of the imagination, spontaneity, and openness to new experiences. In those instances and many other important traits such as commitment to fulfilling moral obligations and thinking things through before acting, males and females are indistinguishable.

As the discussion of abilities in chapter 3 should have made clear, males and females do indeed differ in their profiles of abilities—but in such complicated ways that claiming superiority for one sex or the other is ridiculous. Or I'll put it another way: Claiming superiority can be done only by attaching subjective weights to different strengths. Revealing what those weights are exposes how subjective the claims are.

As for the differences in educational and vocational choices discussed in chapter 4, decisions about what makes for a satisfying vocational life are intimately bound up with personal preferences and priorities. Inborn sex differences in personality and abilities contribute to different distributions of vocational preferences and priorities. Sex differences in this domain will be with us forever. They are not to be deplored but celebrated.

PART II

—⦿—

"RACE IS A SOCIAL CONSTRUCT"

Peoples of the world have probably had words that mean "people different from us" as long as they have had language. A common practice in isolated tribes has been to call one's own tribe humans and everyone else nonhumans. By the end of the sixteenth century, the word *race* had entered the English language, originally used loosely to refer to people of common descent, identified with their common culture and geographic place. Increasing contact with the peoples of Africa and Asia led to distinctions based on differences in appearance. In popular usage, whites in Europe began to group races based on skin color—white, black, yellow, brown, and red.

In the eighteenth century, science got involved. Naturalists Carl Linnaeus and Johann Blumenbach proposed formal groupings of populations into races based on distinctive morphological features. By the middle of the nineteenth century, scholars had decided that the different races were not only cosmetically and morphologically distinctive but also had different personality and intellectual characteristics. The differences amounted to a racial hierarchy, they argued, with whites on top and blacks at the bottom.

These scientific writings occurred in the context of the Europeans' colonization of the New World. In South and North America alike, the intruders displaced and in many cases eradicated the indigenous peoples who already occupied the land. They enslaved and imported African blacks and incorporated slavery into their social systems.

The consequences were devastating. In the opening to Part I, I described the legal status of English women through the eighteenth century as not much short of de facto slavery. The effects of actual slavery experienced by Africans in the New World went far beyond legal constraints, and they were far worse on every dimension of life. The freedom granted by emancipation in America was only marginally better in practice and the situation improved only slowly through the first half of the twentieth century. Meanwhile, all of the indigenous cultures of the New World had been devastated beyond recognition by the end of the nineteenth century. For the United States, founded on ideals of liberty and equality, that record was a fatal flaw that in my view ensured the eventual unraveling of the American project.[1]

Among scholars, the opening of the twentieth century saw a scientific backlash not only against the idea of a racial hierarchy but against the idea of race itself. Its most prominent spokesman was Franz Boas, a pioneering anthropologist and a fierce opponent of what he labeled "scientific racism."[2] A British anthropologist who studied under Boas, Ashley Montagu, took his mentor's position to new levels of passion ("Race is the witchcraft, the demonology of our time") and set the rhetorical tone for today's academic orthodoxy. The book from which that quote is taken, *Man's Most Dangerous Myth: The Fallacy of Race*, was originally published in 1942 and remained in print throughout the rest of the century.[3]

In the 1970s and 1980s, the backlash against the concept of race got new ammunition with two propositions: The genetic differences among human populations are insignificant, and humans left Africa too recently for important differences to have evolved. These arguments were most famously expressed by geneticist Richard Lewontin and paleontologist Stephen Jay Gould, both of Harvard.

In 1972, Lewontin published an article titled "The Apportionment of Human Diversity." In it, he analyzed genetic diversity among the different races with the tools available at the time and found that less than 15 percent of all genetic diversity is accounted for by differences among groups. He concluded with a passage that has since become canonical:

It is clear that our perception of relatively large differences between human races and subgroups, as compared to the variation within these groups, is indeed a biased perception and that, based on randomly chosen genetic differences, human races and populations are remarkably similar to each other, with the largest part by far of human variation being accounted for by the differences between individuals.

Human racial classification is of no social value and is positively destructive of social and human relations. Since such racial classification is now seen to be of virtually no genetic or taxonomic significance either, no justification can be offered for its continuance.[4]

The canonical version of the orthodoxy's second proposition appeared twelve years later, written by Gould for his regular column in *Natural History* magazine. "Equality [of the races] is not given a priori," he wrote.

It is neither an ethical principle (though equal treatment may be) nor a statement about norms of social action. It just worked out that way. A hundred different and plausible scenarios for human history would have yielded other results (and moral dilemmas of enormous magnitude). They didn't happen.

Gould argued for this conclusion along several lines, some of which echoed Lewontin. But he also offered a new proposition that quickly became popular: "[T]he division of humans into modern 'racial' groups is a product of our recent history. It does not predate the origin of our own species, *Homo sapiens*, and probably occurred during the last few tens (or at most hundreds) of thousands of years." For Gould, the implication was obvious:

As long as most scientists accepted the ancient division of races, they expected important genetic differences. But the recent origin of races... squares well with the minor genetic differences now measured. Human groups do vary strikingly in a few highly visible characters (skin color, hair form)—and this may fool us into thinking that overall differences must be great. But we now know that our usual metaphor of superficiality—skin deep—is literally accurate.

And so, he concluded in his 1984 article, "Say it five times before breakfast tomorrow; more important, understand it as the center of a network of implication: 'Human equality is a contingent fact of history.'"[5] Gould stuck to that position for the rest of his life. In an interview in 2000, he made the blanket statement that "natural selection has almost become irrelevant in human evolution. There's been no biological change in humans in 40,000 or 50,000 years. Everything we call culture and civilization we've built with the same body and brain."[6]

The implication was obvious: The concept of race has been made up—or, put more academically, socially constructed. Sociologists Michael Omi and Howard Winant supplied a theoretical framework for the social construction of race in 1986 with the publication of *Racial Formation in the United States: From the 1960s to the 1980s*. Racial formation, they wrote, refers "to the process by which social, economic, and political forces determine the content and importance of racial categories."[7] Race, they went on to argue, is an artificial way of assigning people to groups, consolidating the power of the majority that sets the rules for racial assignment and enabling that majority to control racial minorities.

The orthodox sometimes come surprisingly close (given the obvious cosmetic differences across races) to asserting that biological race is a figment of our imaginations. I'm not talking about people at the fringes of academia. An official statement of the American Sociological Association in 2003 told its members to beware "the danger of contributing to the popular conception of race as biological."[8] Nor am I talking about attitudes that have softened in the face of all that has been learned since the sequencing of the genome. Here is part of the official statement of the American Association of Physical Anthropology on race that was adopted on March 27, 2019:

> The Western concept of race must be understood as a classification system that emerged from, and in support of, European colonialism, oppression, and discrimination. It thus does not have its roots in biological reality, but in policies of discrimination. Because of that, over the last five centuries, race has become a social reality that structures societies.[9]

For Jared Diamond, author of the bestselling *Guns, Germs, and Steel*, "[t]he reality of human races is another commonsense 'truth' destined to follow the flat Earth into oblivion."[10]

It is in this context that Part II sets out to convince you that the orthodoxy about race is scientifically obsolete.

6

A Framework for Thinking About
Race Differences

Of necessity, Part II is organized radically differently from Part I. In Part I, I could assume that most readers came to the discussion accepting that the sexes have major genetic differences with regard to sexual function and reproduction, and thus are open to the idea that those known genetic differences could spill over into effects on personality, abilities, and social behavior. My task was first to describe some phenotypic differences of interest, then show how genetic and neuroscientific findings are linking up with phenotypic differences.

MY MODAL READER

Readers of *Human Diversity* presumably span the range in their opinions on these issues, but I'm writing for what I conceive to be the statistically modal type: reasonably open-minded but also accepting the intellectual received wisdom. My sense of that received wisdom regarding sex differences is that a strict view of "gender is a social construct" is seen as too extreme—it is accepted that gender is largely a social construct, but not entirely so. My experience with race has been different. The intellectual received wisdom seems to be that significant racial differences in cognitive repertoires are known to be scientifically impossible.

In the case of race, there is no equivalent to the Y chromosome and no equivalent reason to assume that significant racial genetic differences are plausible. That being the case, it would be pointless for me to begin with evidence about phenotypic differences in cognitive repertoires across races in the same way that I presented them for the sexes. The logical reaction from many readers would be, "So what? They're not genetic."[1]

My goal in Part II is to get past the first hurdle in thinking about race differences: to lay out the evidence that it is evolutionarily reasonable to expect that phenotypic differences among races in cognitive repertoires could be at least partly genetic and that expanding knowledge about genetic variants supports that expectation. I also want to convey that this is not some new, fringe position, but the result of accumulating knowledge about genes and race that goes back almost 30 years. That's why this presentation takes a historical approach. Recall the analogy with archaeological digs that I offered in the introduction. When it comes to race differences, science has identified a promising site, mapped it, and has a plan for next steps, but the actual excavation of the site is in its early stages. You are going to come away from the discussion in Part II with (I hope) an appreciation of where things stand and curiosity about what comes next—curiosity, not dread. The most likely scenario is that we will find many interesting but usually small distinctions.

My confidence that such distinctions will be found is based on three developments over the last 30 years, concentrated in the years since the genome was sequenced:

- It was discovered that human populations are genetically distinctive in ways that correspond to self-identified race and ethnicity.
- Advances in the ability to date evolutionary changes have revealed that evolutionary selection pressure since humans left Africa has been extensive and mostly local to the different continents.
- Raw race differences in genetic material related to cognitive repertoires are common, not exceptional.

Each of these developments has its own chapter.

What the Orthodoxy Gets Right

As we set out, let me specify what the orthodoxy gets right. Franz Boas and Ashley Montagu were right to say that many nineteenth-century conceptions of race were caricatures divorced from biological reality. Richard Lewontin was right that race differences account for only a small fraction of the biological variation existing among humans. Stephen Jay Gould was right to reject the once widely held belief that humans evolved independently in Europe, Asia, and Africa for hundreds of thousands of years. The orthodoxy is not wrong altogether but goes too far when it concludes that race is biologically meaningless. We have before us an exercise in modifying our understanding of race, not resurrecting nineteenth-century conceptions.

The orthodoxy is also right in wanting to discard the word *race*. It's not just the politically correct who believe that. For example, I have found nothing in the genetics technical literature during the last few decades that uses *race* except within quotation marks. The reasons are legitimate, not political, and they are both historical and scientific.

Historically, it is incontestably true that the word *race* has been freighted with cultural baggage that has nothing to do with biological differences. The word carries with it the legacy of nineteenth-century scientific racism combined with Europe's colonialism and America's history of slavery and its aftermath.

Scientifically, it is an error to think of races as primordial. Part of the story I will tell describes the repeated cycles of mixing, isolation, and remixing that have gone on among the populations that left Africa. Such cycles have also gone on within the populations that remained in Africa, not to mention remixing by populations that revisited Africa. As you will see, the number of groups into which people can be sorted genetically is fluid and depends on how much genetic information is brought to bear on the sorting.

The combination of historical and scientific reasons makes a compelling case that the word *race* has outlived its usefulness when discussing genetics. That's why I adopt contemporary practice in the technical literature, which uses *ancestral population* or simply *population* instead of *race* or *ethnicity*, throughout the rest of Part II.

Third Interlude: Genetic Terms You Need to Know to Read the Rest of the Book

I cannot discuss any of the propositions of Part II without using technical terms regarding genetics. Hence it's time for another interlude, a refresher course in this area of biology.

Genome. A genome consists of two strands of DNA (deoxyribonucleic acid), intertwined in the famous double helix and found in the nucleus of almost every cell of every organism. In humans, each strand of DNA consists of a string of more than three billion occurrences of one of four chemicals: adenine, thymine, guanine, and cytosine, usually referred to by their first letters, A, T, G, or C. Each occurrence in each strand is lightly linked by hydrogen bonds to a corresponding occurrence in the other strand. They are called *base pairs.* Stretched out, the three billion base pairs in the nucleus of just a single cell would be about six feet long. But the strands are curled up into a space about six microns across—six millionths of a meter.

Site is a synonym I will use for base pair. In the technical literature, *locus* is often used for this purpose, but with the advent of genome-wide association studies, *locus* also is often used to designate a larger stretch of the genome.[2] I always use *site* to refer to a single base pair and *locus* when both sites and regions are involved.

WHAT DOES "SEQUENCING OF THE HUMAN GENOME" MEAN?

DNA, like some other complex molecules, has a specific physical sequence of bits. DNA has a sequence of nucleotides arranged in base pairs. To sequence a segment of DNA is to determine the base pair residing at each address (which also requires that you have an exact address for the beginning and end of the segment relative to the rest of the genome). It is like a map of New York's Broadway showing every building and its unique address, but not what any of the buildings are used for. Sometimes you will read about "mapping" or "decoding" the genome. They are probably referring to the same thing as "sequencing."

In the early 1970s, British biochemist Frederick Sanger, who had already won a Nobel Prize for sequencing insulin, joined another British biochemist, Alan Coulson, to invent a method for sequencing up to 80 nucleotides at a time, far more than anyone had been able to do previously. In 1977, they published an improved, faster version that was the foundation for subsequent generations of sequencing technology.[3]

During the 1980s and 1990s, limited segments of the human genome were sequenced, but it was left to the Human Genome Project, begun in 1990, to undertake the huge collaborative effort needed to sequence and stitch together the identities of the three billion base pairs making up the human genome.

Drafts of the complete genome were released starting in June 2000. On April 14, 2003, the National Human Genome Research Institute announced that the Human Genome Project had been successfully completed and published the full sequence.[4] In the rest of this book, I will sometimes refer to 2003 as the date for the sequencing of the genome, with the understanding that work on the human genome had already begun using the earlier drafts.

Chromosome. All the base pairs are contained in chromosomes. A chromosome is a long chunk of DNA, with the helix usually packed in a tight structure. Humans have 46 chromosomes arranged in 23 pairs, one of which is the pair of sex chromosomes that figured so prominently in the discussion of sex differences. Under a powerful microscope, chromosomes can be visually differentiated from one another, and they are also functionally differentiated. The adjective *autosomal* refers to the 44 nonsex chromosomes, their genes, and SNPs.

SNP. Now we come to a term that you will encounter many times: SNP, pronounced "snip," the term for sites that consist of different pairs of letters in different people, and thereby are the major source of variation among human beings. A SNP is one of several kinds of genetic *variants*. The letters stand for *single nucleotide polymorphism*. To qualify as a SNP, a given combination at a given site must occur in at least 1 percent of the genomes of whatever species is being studied.

SNV. This term, which is unpronounceable, stands for *single nucleotide variant.* It includes sites that show variation without any implication for frequency (all SNPs are also SNVs, while a site with a minor allele frequency of less than .01 is a SNV but is not a SNP). I will sometimes use *SNP* loosely to refer to all nucleotide variants when I think that switching back and forth between SNP and SNV would be unnecessarily confusing.

Allele. The letters involved in a SNP are called alleles, emphasis on the second syllable. A large majority of SNPs have only two alleles. Such SNPs are *biallelic.* It is customary to call the allele with the lower frequency the *minor allele,* and to use the frequency of the minor allele as the default when talking about a given site.

Microsatellite. SNPs are not the only bits of genetic material that can show variation among individuals. Sometimes, tandem base pairs are repeated (e.g., CACACACA), but with varying numbers of repeats in different individuals. Unlike SNPs, which usually have only two variations, the number of tandem repeats, sometimes abbreviated *VNTR* (variable number of tandem repeats), goes from two to dozens. A VNTR is called a *microsatellite* if it involves no more than five tandem base pairs. A larger VNTR is called a *minisatellite*.

Genotype. The genotype is an organism's genetic material with regard to a given trait. Writ large, it refers to all of the loci that have a causal effect on the trait. Writ small, it refers to the combination of alleles present on the pair of chromosomes at a given site.[5] In a biallelic site, there can be three such combinations, which are generically denoted as *AA*, *Aa*, or *aa* (respectively indicating two copies of one of the DNA letters, one of each, and two of the other DNA letter).

Genetic marker. A genetic marker is usually a SNP or a microsatellite. Genetic markers are useful because they take different forms—different alleles in the case of SNPs, different numbers of repeats for microsatellites—but they typically do *not* have a known function. On the contrary, analysts often take pains to select genetic markers that are thought to be nonfunctional. The utility of a genetic marker is that it is neutral with regard to natural selection, enabling the researcher to analyze patterns independently of natural selection's confounding effects.

Noncoding. Sites can do a number of things, but a majority of the three billion sites don't seem to have any effect on anything. They used to be called "junk DNA," but that term is falling out of use as subtle functions are discovered, especially involving gene expression. *Coding* is used to describe a site that is part of a region encoding a protein. *Noncoding* refers to all other sites. Some noncoding sites are located in regions with important regulatory functions, but many of them still have no known function.

Gene. That leaves the word you have known since elementary school, *gene.* Its meaning has gotten more complicated as geneticists have learned how DNA works. If you are in your fifties or older, you probably still think of *gene* in the Mendelian sense: the genetic unit that determined a trait, with dominant and recessive versions—the gene for eye color, for example. In modern genetics, the term refers to a contiguous region spanning many sites whose expression or transcription leads to the production of something useful—usually a protein. The number of protein-coding genes is around 20,000.

A mistake to be avoided: People who grew up with Mendelian genetics often still talk about "having a gene for" some trait—a gene for intelligence, for example. It is now known that extremely few traits are determined by a single gene (even using the word in its modern sense). Variation on a relatively simple trait can be determined by hundreds or thousands of SNPs located in many genes. To use the technical term, almost all heritable traits are *polygenic*.

Genetic drift. You are probably already aware that the mother and father each contribute about 50 percent of their genes to their child. Which parent contributes which genes is mostly a matter of figurative coin flips.[6] Suppose (I'm simplifying for the illustration) that for a given SNP with two alleles, *A* and *a*, 80 percent of each sex carry the *AA* combination and 10 percent carry the *aa* combination. Given random mating, 64 percent (.8 × .8) of the couples who produce the children both carry the *AA* combination, and they are guaranteed to pass on the *AA* combination to their offspring. Another 4 percent (.2 × .2) will both carry *aa* and are guaranteed to pass on the *aa* combination. The other 32 percent of the couples carry at least one copy of the *a* allele between them. Whether one or both of the offspring's chromosomes carry the *a* allele is a matter of 50/50 coin flips. For example, suppose that the father is *Aa* and the mother is *AA*. The mother will certainly contribute an *A* allele. The odds that the father will contribute an *A* allele are just 50 percent. It makes no difference that 80 percent of the population carries the *A* allele; in the process of meiosis, when one chromosome from each parent is contributed to the offspring, it's a coin flip.

Repeated coin flips can produce odd results, so it is unlikely that the next generation has exactly 80 percent of *AA* combinations. It could be somewhat higher or somewhat lower. The percentage drifts, for purely statistical reasons. The smaller the population, the greater the expected drift. If you flip a fair coin a million times, the percentage of heads is going to be almost exactly 50 percent. Flip it ten times, and it will often be far from 50 percent. Now suppose that for several generations in a row, the coin flips happen to increase the incidence of allele *A*. Given small populations and enough generations, sometimes the percentage will hit 100—allele *A* will "go to fixation" or become "fixed." It hasn't been a process of natural selection, but of coin flips. Nonetheless, whatever effect allele A has is now universal in this particular population. And, by necessity, whatever effect allele a may have had is also gone from the population.

———

Enough background. It's time to recount how human ancestral populations can be defined not by the color of their skin or any other visible characteristic, but by the profiles of their DNA.

7

Genetic Distinctiveness Among Ancestral Populations

Proposition #5: Human populations are genetically distinctive in ways that correspond to self-identified race and ethnicity.

A good place to start is by understanding a simple truth that was predicted theoretically many decades ago and has since been validated by empirical evidence: Any human population becomes genetically distinctive by the mere fact of separation from others who share the same ancestry.

Suppose a few centuries from now humans invent the warp drive and a coalition of countries—East Asian countries, let's say—launches a ship with 100 humans to colonize another planet. For mysterious reasons, the coalition does not screen the colonists for qualities like intelligence, sociability, physical attractiveness, levelheadedness, or fertility. Instead, it employs a sophisticated algorithm that randomly picks 100 East Asians.[1]

Even as the door of the spaceship closes on the 100, they will already be genetically distinctive from the East Asians who remain on Earth *even though the random selection procedure was perfect.* The reason is that the 100 colonists will carry with them only a portion of the genetic diversity among all East Asians. In the database for Phase 3 of the 1000 Genomes Project, the East Asian sample has about 19,257,000 sites with two alleles.[2] Almost two-thirds of them have a minor allele frequency among East Asians of less than .01.[3] It can be expected that most of those rare variants will not be carried by even one of the 100 colonists. They're gone forever in that subgroup of East Asians (unless, by a fantastic coincidence, they reappear through mutations).

THE PIONEERING ANCESTRAL POPULATION DATABASES

You will be seeing references to these databases in the rest of Part II:

The *HGDP-CEPH database*. Predating the sequencing of the genome, this database consists of lymphoblastoid cell lines from 1,050 individuals in 52 world populations. It was assembled by the Human Genome Diversity Project at Stanford University under the direction of Luigi Luca Cavalli-Sforza.

The *Perlegen database*: In 2005, researchers at Perlegen Sciences genotyped almost 1.6 million SNPs in 71 Americans of European, African, and Asian ancestry.

The *HapMap Project:* The first large database of ancestral populations, Phase 1 of the HapMap Project, released in 2005, genotyped a million SNPs in 269 individuals drawn from four populations—Yoruba in Nigeria, Japanese in Tokyo, Han in Beijing, and Utah residents of northern and western European ancestry.

1000 Genomes Project: This has been the most widely used database for analyzing ancestral populations since the release of Phase 1 in 2012. It is described in detail on pages 163–64.

Among the one-third of the sites that meet the technical definition of SNP (the minor allele frequency is at least .01), almost all will be present in at least one colonist, but their existence will be precarious because they are carried by only a few. Thus the genetic distinctiveness of the colonists will increase with each generation because, in each generation, thousands of SNPs will cease to vary because so few members of the crew carried the unusual variant and the coin flips went against those SNPs.

In addition to losing diversity through SNPs that have ceased to vary (and therefore may no longer be called SNPs), genetic drift will produce different patterns among the SNPs that remain. Suppose we split up our crew into two groups of 50. At the time of the split, let's say that a given SNP has a frequency of 50 percent in both groups. Twenty generations later, suppose it has drifted downward to a percentage of 45 percent in one of the groups and upward to 55 percent in the other. It has been a completely random event without adaptive implications in both cases, but the two groups have nonetheless become genetically distinctive with regard to that particular SNP.

I have described the process in terms of a spaceship crew centuries in the future, but the relevant population genetics theory has been established for decades. In 1943, Sewall Wright explored the mathematics of genetic transmission in a population distributed uniformly over a large area.[4] It had long been accepted that populations separated by geographical barriers such as mountains or oceans would be genetically distinctive (the "island model"). Wright's equations demonstrated that even within an area in which a population is evenly spread without geographic barriers, the parents of any given individual are drawn from a small surrounding region (the "isolation by distance model"). In 1948, Gustave Malécot demonstrated mathematically that population differences in gene frequencies may be expected to increase as a function of geographic distance.[5] In 1964, population geneticists Motoo Kimura and George Weiss integrated these findings into what they labeled the "stepping stone model of population structure."[6] This model postulated that a population expands outward from a single geographic center and that occasionally a band splits off from the larger group. The result is a series of stepwise increases in genetic drift and decreases in genetic diversity within each band. The process came to be called a "serial founder effect."

The model also predicted that the cumulative magnitude of genetic distinctiveness would tend to be associated with geographic distance from the original center, because these migrations would tend to be driven by the subpopulation's need to find unoccupied territory. It may seem odd that such a need existed, given how few humans were around during the Pleistocene, but hunter-gatherers take up a lot of space—usually about 5,000 acres per person, although, depending on local conditions, a band of just 25 could require more than 1,000 square miles.[7] By moving away from occupied territory, humans would also usually be moving farther geographically from the original center.

How the Earth Was Peopled

This body of theoretical work became especially relevant as paleontologists and then geneticists found compelling evidence for what is known as the Out-of-Africa explanation of human expansion. It started out simple. It is now exceedingly complex and becoming more so.

Around 6 million years ago, the first hominins diverged from chimpanzees, becoming fully bipedal sometime more than 4 million years ago.[8] *Homo habilis*, who was bipedal and apparently used stone tools, appeared about

2.5 million years ago. About 2 million years ago came our likely direct ancestor, *Homo erectus*. Hominins first expanded out of Africa around 1.8 to 2.1 million years ago and eventually spread throughout Eurasia.[9]

LABELS FOR OUR ANCESTORS

Hominins: Refers to all branches of the human family, modern and extinct. Another word, *hominid*, formerly had this meaning, but in contemporary usage, *hominid* refers to all modern and extinct great apes, including us. Mnemonic for keeping them straight: *Human* and *hominin* both end with an *n*.

Homo erectus: Simplifying, the hominin that immediately preceded *Homo sapiens*.[10]

Homo sapiens: Us. All humans on planet Earth.

Anatomically modern humans: This term, abbreviated *AMH* in the technical literature, refers to archaic *Homo sapiens* who had globular brain cases and other physiological traits of *Homo sapiens* but did not leave behind substantial evidence of cultural accouterments (art, burials, ornament, musical instruments).[11]

Until the late 1980s, three theories competed to explain where and how *Homo erectus* became *Homo sapiens*.[12] The oldest of these was Franz Weidenreich's multiregional hypothesis, dating back to the 1940s, arguing that evolution from *Homo erectus* to anatomically modern humans happened contemporaneously throughout Africa and Eurasia but with continual gene flow across regions during the process.[13] In the early 1960s, Carleton Coon countered with the "candelabra hypothesis," arguing that anatomically modern humans had evolved along separate lines in Africa, Europe, and Asia.[14] The third theory was the Out-of-Africa hypothesis. It emerged in the 1980s as paleontologists realized that the oldest fossil remains of anatomically modern humans were always being found in eastern Africa, not in Europe or Asia.

Genetics entered the debate in 1987 when geneticist Rebecca Cann used mitochondrial DNA, which is inherited solely from the mother, to argue that all of today's humans are descended from a single female who lived sometime between 99,000 and 148,000 years ago.[15] A year later, paleontologists Christopher Stringer and Peter Andrews combined the genetic evidence with the growing paleontological record to make the case that anatomically modern humans had evolved exclusively within Africa and only thereafter expanded to the rest of the world.[16]

By the end of the 1980s, the circumstantial evidence for the Out-of-Africa model had won over a majority of the scientists working on the problem, but definitive evidence required more detailed access to the genome. In 1991, population geneticist Luigi Luca Cavalli-Sforza of Stanford University initiated the Human Genome Diversity Project (HGDP). Geneticists around the world had been collecting blood samples and other data from different populations. Cavalli-Sforza's idea was to assemble and augment these disparate sources of information, combining them into an integrated database. Eventually, the project brought together cultured lymphoblastoid cell lines from 1,050 individuals in 52 world populations. Preliminary results were included in Cavalli-Sforza's magnum opus, 1,088 pages long, *The History and Geography of Human Genes*, published in 1994.[17] The HGDP data broadly substantiated the theory that the human dispersal had indeed consisted of radiating expansions from a single center somewhere in Africa.

The finishing touch came in 2005 when scholars from Stanford, the University of Illinois, and the University of Michigan applied the newly acquired data from the sequenced human genome to rigorous genetic tests of two key questions: Was Africa the origin of the human dispersal? Was the peopling of the globe characterized by the "serial founder effect" (the loss of genetic diversity that occurs when a subpopulation breaks off from the main population)? The analyses were excruciatingly thorough. To take just one example, the authors performed regressions of genetic distance on geographic distance using each of 4,210 potential centers for human dispersal. By the end of their work, they could conclude confidently that "no origin outside Africa had the explanatory power of an origin anywhere in Africa" and that the geographic patterns were "consistent with a model of a serial founder effect starting at a single origin."[18]

Since 2005, advances in genetics and new paleontological evidence have transformed the state of knowledge about the dispersal out of Africa and have also identified a number of new questions.[19] Some uncertainty has emerged about exactly where anatomically modern humans arose. The consensus answer has long been East Africa, but now it is thought that other regions in the continent may have played a role. Recent fossil evidence for anatomically modern humans comes from Morocco and dates to 315,000 years ago, more than 100,000 years earlier than the previous oldest fossils.[20] A team of physical anthropologists, archaeologists, and geneticists have argued that morphologically and technologically varied populations of *Homo sapiens* lived throughout Africa, supporting a view of a "a highly structured African prehistory that should be considered in human evolutionary inferences, prompting new interpretations, questions, and interdisciplinary research directions."[21] But the core tenet of the Out-of-Africa theory—that hominins became *Homo sapiens* exclusively in Africa—remains uncontested.

The immediate consequence of the exodus was the spaceship effect. Within Africa, interbreeding continued even across substantial geographic distance. The genetic diversity that had already accumulated within Africa was largely conserved. The few hundred people who left Africa carried with them only a fraction of the total genetic diversity that existed there. In that sense, subsequent generations were guaranteed to be distinct from those who remained in Africa, if only because their descendants could not possibly carry the full range of traits that still occurred among the peoples who remained.

Theories about the exodus from Africa have their own uncertainties. More than one dispersal occurred, but by what routes? When? The archaeological record combined with recent paleogenomic evidence strongly suggests that an early wave or waves traveled from northern Egypt across the Sinai Peninsula and were probably present in the Levant around 200,000 years ago—much earlier than had previously been thought.[22]

Tens of thousands of years later, a southern exodus occurred, probably through the Bab-el-Mandeb Strait at the mouth of the Red Sea.[23] The date of the exodus was formerly put at about 60,000 years ago, but emerging evidence points to an earlier date, perhaps as early as 120,000–130,000 years ago.[24]

Until 2016, the evidence for multiple dispersals led naturally to the assumption that at least some members of more than one wave survived. A plausible scenario was that an initial southern wave peopled Southeast Asia and "Sahul," the name that has been given to the Pleistocene landmass that included today's Australia, New Guinea, and Tasmania. It is now usually called Oceania by students of human populations. It was thought that a later northern wave spread through the Levant and peopled Europe, Central Asia, East Asia, and eventually the Americas via the Siberian bridge.[25]

In 2016, a new whole-genome study based on 300 genomes from 142 diverse populations provided evidence for a one-wave scenario, indicating that just one band of anatomically modern emigrants from Africa has descendants among today's humans.[26] The individuals in the study represented a larger and more globally representative set of populations than ever before, with genomes sequenced at a more precise level than ever before. But, as usual, there were complications. The genomes of Papuans in the study gave signs that about 2 percent of their genomes might have come from an earlier population. That's not much, but it suggests something more complicated than a single band of emigrants.

One thing is sure: *Homo sapiens* was not spreading into an unpopulated continent. Whenever they reached Eurasia, it is now accepted that at least two archaic hominins, the Neanderthals and Denisovans, were already in residence and that the anatomically modern newcomers interbred with both groups.[27] The admixture with the Neanderthals was until recently dated to 50,000–65,000 years ago.[28] Other evidence now suggests that introgression with Neanderthals began earlier, with one study finding that it could date as far back as 270,000 years, which opens up still another set of possibilities.[29] It affected the genomes of both modern Europeans and East Asians.[30] Admixture with Denisovans is found in proportions as high as 5 percent in Papuans and the Melanesians and Australian Aboriginals, and in far lower proportions in South, Southeast, and East Asians.[31]

The complications don't stop there. There are the Hobbits to deal with— fossils from the three-foot hominins found on the Indonesian island of Flores.[32] There are the apparent migrations from Europe back into North Africa.[33] There's the unexpected discovery that America was not peopled by a single migration across the Bering Strait but more likely by four separate prehistoric migrations, one of which is a mysterious population Y that has descendants in both the Amazon and in Australasia.[34] In David Reich's words, "the evidence for many lineages and admixtures should have the effect of shaking our confidence in what to many people is now an unquestioned assumption that Africa has been the epicenter of all major events in human evolution."[35]

Reich's 2018 book, *Who We Are and How We Got Here*, also recounts one of the most useful discoveries in modifying the traditional view of race. It is not the case that Europe was settled by emigrants from Africa who then adapted over tens of thousands of years to become the peoples we now identify as European whites. Europe was repeopled several times, as groups from various points in Central Asia and the Middle East displaced the existing populations. What we think of as European whites are indeed an amalgam. So are today's East Asians, South Asians, sub-Saharan Africans, and Amerindians. Ancestral populations did not evolve quietly in isolation. Genetic ancestry is endlessly fluid and dynamic.

The study of the peopling of the Earth has both powerful new analytic methods and a mother lode of ancient DNA data that has barely been tapped. I won't try to give a sense of the mainstream on many open questions, because everything is in such flux. Some accessible overviews are given in the note.[36] I should add that I have had to revise this account several times during the time it took to write *Human Diversity* because of new discoveries. There's no reason to doubt that additional discoveries are on the way over the next several years. Stay tuned.

The Correspondence Between Genetic Differentiation and Self-Identified Race and Ethnicity

The maps in *The History and Geography of Human Genes* revealed for the first time that genetic differentiation of populations showed a continental pattern. This should not have been surprising—if humans began in Africa, population genetics theory predicted that the differentiation would increase along with geographic distance from Africa. But it was nonetheless jarring to see how closely the clusters corresponded with traditional definitions of races at the continental level. The five continents in question were Africa, Europe, East Asia, the Americas, and Oceania.

The First Cluster Analyses of Genetic Distinctiveness Across Populations

During the 1990s and 2000s, Stanford's Human Genome Diversity Project produced a series of cluster analyses that successively expanded on the patterns reported in *The History and Geography of Human Genes*. The first was published the same year, 1994. Cavalli-Sforza collaborated with other scholars—Anne Bowcock was the first author—to analyze a particular type of microsatellite at 30 places on the genome, using a sample covering 14 populations. They used cluster analysis to explore the ways in which the 14 populations fell into groups.

FOUR THINGS TO REMEMBER ABOUT CLUSTER ANALYSIS

Many kinds of statistical cluster analysis are routinely used by disciplines in both the hard and the soft sciences. They all have the same generic purpose: to see whether the members of a sample can appropriately be parsed into groups. The choice of how many groups is specified by the analyst. The usual procedure is to instruct the statistical software to produce K clusters, beginning with $K = 2$ and repeating it for incremental values of K as long as the clusters being produced continue to be informative.

Geneticists use a variety of statistical techniques to assess clustering. They fall into two broad categories: distance-based methods and model-based methods.[37] The ones I will be discussing are all distance-based, bringing no preconceptions to the analysis. The statistical theory and the computational algorithms for cluster analysis are complex, and trying to describe them here would be overkill.[38] Just remember four things about all of the methods that pass methodological muster:

1. A distance-based cluster analysis does not artificially force clusters on the basis of some a priori categorization. The software is trying to find the best statistical fit for the raw data; that's all.

2. The software will dutifully identify whatever number of "clusters" it is told to produce, but the output of the software also usually makes it easy for the investigators to see that the results aren't really clusters in any substantive sense.

3. Cluster analysis is exploratory. It is standard procedure for the investigators to run the cluster analysis several times, specifying incremental numbers of clusters and asking what differences among the subjects correspond to the statistical clusters.

4. When dealing with human populations, the clusters do not define "racial purity." That an individual falls into a single cluster with no admixture indicates statistical coherence given the value of K that happens to be in use for that run. Depending on the number of polymorphic sites in the analysis and the value of K, an individual can fall into a single cluster with no

admixture with one value of *K* and yet show a membership in more than one cluster with another value of *K*. The only consistent aspect of cluster analyses of human populations is that the clusters do fall along geographical lines—which is not a product of the software but is consistent with the population genetics theory that antedated the tools for conducting cluster analyses.

The cluster analysis used by Cavalli-Sforza and Bowcock confirmed (as have all subsequent analyses) that the great bulk of variation in humans is within populations, not between them, just as Lewontin said. But even with the limited measures of genetic variation available in the early 1990s, their clusters corresponded to the geographic origin of the subjects at the continental level.[39] In 1998, a similar analysis conducted by geneticists at Yale produced similar results.[40]

The methods used for this pioneering work were primitive by later standards. In 2000, Stanford geneticists led by Jonathan Pritchard developed a more sophisticated method that they implemented through a software program called Structure.[41] Among other things, the new method allowed for mixed ancestry—individuals could be assigned to more than one cluster, with the percentages in the various clusters summing to 100.

In 2002, a team of scholars with the Human Genome Diversity Project (first author was Noah Rosenberg) applied the Structure software to a sample of 1,056 individuals from 52 populations, using 377 autosomal microsatellites.[42] The individuals were deliberately chosen from so many populations to ensure that the software's clustering algorithms would not be constrained by artificially narrow groups (e.g., a European sample drawn exclusively from Dutch individuals). Their results replicated and expanded upon the 1994 and 1998 findings. The cleanest set of clusters was produced when *K* was set to 5. The five clusters once again clustered according to continents: Africa, Europe, East Asia, the Americas, and Oceania.

The First Cluster Analysis Using Hundreds of Thousands of SNPs

The sequencing of the genome changed everything. In 2008, a team of eleven scholars affiliated with the Human Genome Diversity Project (first author was Jun Z. Li) used the same sample as the Rosenberg study, reduced to 51 populations and 938 persons for technical reasons. The big difference was that the Li study was analyzing 642,690 variants instead of 377.[43] Here's what they found as K went from two to seven:

At $K = 2$, two sets of the 51 populations in the Li study's database had virtually no overlap: populations in sub-Saharan Africa versus populations in East Asia plus a few in the Americas. All the other populations were mixtures of the two clusters.

At $K = 3$, the people who showed virtually no admixture across clusters consisted of individuals from sub-Saharan Africa, today's Europe and Mideast, and the East Asian–Americas group. Those from Central and South Asia had varying mixtures of the European/Mideast and East Asian/Amerind clusters.

At $K = 4$, the Amerindians split off to form a separate cluster.

At $K = 5$, the Oceania populations split off.

At $K = 6$, the Central and South Asians split off.

At $K = 7$, the configuration that the authors assessed as the most informative, those in the Mideast split off from the Europeans.

The figure below graphically shows the results for the analysis at $K = 7$.

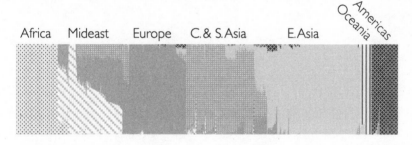

Africa   Mideast   Europe   C. & S. Asia   E. Asia   Oceania   Americas

Source: Li, Absher, Tang et al. (2008). Adapted from Fig. I.

It is a fascinating graphic. It combines 938 vertical lines, one for each person in the sample. Each line is partitioned into segments with lengths that correspond to that person's "ancestry coefficients." When only one pattern is represented, the individual belongs entirely to that cluster—as in large portions of the lines for Africa, Europe, East Asia, and the Americas. In contrast, look at the Mideast segment of the figure. Interpreted colloquially (remember that the labels for the clusters were added only after each individual's ancestry had been estimated), most of the lines have a mix of Mideastern, European, and Central or South Asian ancestry.[44]

What struck me most about the Li analysis is what happened when the number of clusters went from five to seven. As in the 2002 study, the first five clusters corresponded to the five continental ancestral populations. But the two new subsidiary clusters that emerged when $K = 7$ corresponded to commonsense observation. When $K = 5$, the Li study produced a cluster that corresponded to the classic definition of *Caucasian*—an odd agglomeration of peoples from Europe, North Africa, the Mideast, South Asia, and parts of Central Asia. There had been a reason why physical anthropologists had once combined these disparate populations—all of them have morphological features in common—but it had never made sense to people who weren't physical anthropologists.[45] With $K = 7$, one of the new clusters split off the peoples of the Mideast and North Africa and the other split off the peoples of Central and South Asia—precisely the groups that had always been visibly distinctive from Europeans and from each other in the Caucasian agglomeration.

The figure below shows another perspective on the separation of members of the 51 subpopulations. The note gives details of the analysis.[46] Highly simplified, you're looking at the genetic distance of each of the 938 people in the study from the other 937.

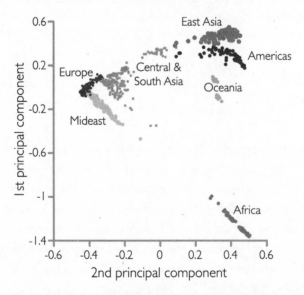

Source: Li, Absher, Tang et al. (2008): Fig. S3B. The authors computed a 938-by-938 Identity-by-State (IBS) matrix using the software package PLINK, which was then factor analyzed for all samples and for seven regions separately.

The graph is necessarily a two-dimensional representation of a multidimensional dataset, but it does provide a useful sense of the varying genetic distances separating the seven clusters. Africa is distinct from all the rest. The traditional Caucasian clusters are grouped but nonetheless distinct. A mixture of Central/South Asian and East Asian populations are between the Caucasian clusters and the two clusters of East Asians and Amerinds. The Oceania subjects are separate, two small blobs representing the Melanesians and Papuans. The signature feature of the graph is not the overlap, which is confined to just two of the seven groups, but the clarity of most of the separations among the rest.

Since the Li Study

In 2010, a consortium of evolutionary geneticists extended the Li study, assembling data from 296 individuals in 13 populations that had not been covered by previous studies. The first author was Jinchuan Xing. The methods differed from those used in the Li study, and the addition of 13 new populations enabled a new level of detail. For example, adding the new populations led to an estimated global differentiation of 11.3 percent, compared to 15.9 percent with the HapMap Project's more restricted samples (and the 15 percent cited by Lewontin).[47] The Xing study also demonstrated, consistent with population genetics theory, that the more granular the analysis, the less discontinuity is seen between adjacent populations.

In both the Li and Xing studies, the first component in the principal component analysis differentiated Africans from all other populations, and the second component differentiated Eurasian populations. In terms of the genetic distances among regions and subpopulations, the Xing study amounts to a confirmation of the Li study. In a replication of the principal components plot shown above for the Li study, Africa was most distant from all the others; Europe, West Asia, and Central Asia were adjacent but distinct; and the Americas, East Asia, and Polynesia were adjacent but distinct. To indicate how little the main conclusions differed, I have included the "Conclusion" section of the Xing study in its entirety in the note.[48]

Since 2010, studies of genetic differentiation among populations have focused on fine structure. The use of large samples of SNPs enables investigators to more or less replicate not just the major populations traditionally defined as races, but subpopulations within the major populations. In their review of the state of the art as of 2016, John Novembre and Benjamin Peter showed what happens when several European subpopulations are plotted with different numbers of sites.[49] When only 100 or even 1,000 sites are used, the subpopulations are indistinguishable. At 10,000 sites, some separation is visible. At 100,000 sites, Italians, Spanish, Germans, and Romanians are all reasonably distinct, with the British, Dutch, Swedish, and Irish fuzzily separated.

The methods for analyzing population structure have multiplied and become more sophisticated. A review published in 2015 listed 25 different software packages for analyzing population structure and demographic history.[50] The methods for ensuring that the genetic markers are drawn from noncoding SNPs have improved.[51] The technical literature has grown accordingly, analyzing population structures at exceedingly fine levels.[52] Geneticist Razib Khan pulled together a sampling of the most important varieties of population structure as of 2016, with illustrative graphics for each.[53]

By now, the ability to classify people not just according to continental ancestral population but also to specific subpopulations has become so routine that you may have already availed yourselves of it in the form of a commercial product that gave you an analysis of your ancestral heritage in return for a cheek swab and a modest payment. Originally, these companies used clusters of genetic markers known as "Ancestry Informative Markers," or AIMs. With the technology now available, most of them no longer bother with AIMs, instead just using hundreds of thousands of markers.

The results can be extremely precise. One of the earliest uses of AIMs, applied to a sample of 3,636 people who self-identified as white, black, East Asian, or Latino, classified 99.7 percent of them—all but five—into the same population as the subjects identified themselves.[54] But such profiles can also be misleading. If you are from Pakistan, for example, and your profile indicates that you are 4 percent Melanesian, don't expect to find anything if you ransack your family tree for a great-great-grandfather from Samoa. The explanation is probably that the reference populations didn't include enough South Asian variation. The algorithm looked for the nearest population, which was Melanesian.

How Have Advocates of "Race Is a Social Construct" Responded to the Cluster Analyses?

Advocates of "race is a social construct" have raised a host of methodological and philosophical issues with the cluster analyses. None of the critical articles has published a cluster analysis that does *not* show the kind of results I've shown.[55]

Many of the critical responses emphasize that genetic differentiation across populations is small compared to the variation within populations, that admixtures do exist in some populations, and that the finer the level of population structure, the smaller the distance between adjacent populations becomes.[56] All of these points are true, but no one conducting the cluster analyses has ever disputed them.

A more direct conflict involves the exploratory nature of cluster analyses, especially the different results that are produced by different values of K and by different numbers of iterations used to produce the results.[57] But none of the critiques I have seen deal with an observation first made in the Rosenberg study: "Each increase in K split one of the clusters obtained with the previous value."[58] That is, different values of K do not produce a radically different pattern of results. Instead, they augment the results, giving a greater degree of definition to a previously identified pattern.

Much of the rest of the criticism of the cluster analyses comes down to semantics. The Rosenberg study in 2002 prompted David Serre and Svante Pääbo of the Max Planck Institute for Evolutionary Anthropology to explore the possibility that the appearance of clusters was illusory, an artifact of the sampling procedure. If a larger number of markers and populations had been used, they argued, it would be seen that variation in human populations occurred gradually—in clines, to use the technical term. They presented evidence that simple geographic distance better explained genetic distance than discrete geographic regions.[59] The authors of the Rosenberg study responded by reanalyzing their clusters after raising the number of genetic markers from 377 to 993. They concluded that "examination of the relationship between genetic and geographic distance supports a view in which the clusters arise not as an artifact of the sampling scheme, but from small discontinuous jumps in genetic distance for most population pairs on opposite sides of geographic barriers, in comparison with genetic distance for pairs on the same side."[60] That conclusion was reinforced by the subsequent Li and Xing studies, with their larger numbers of genomes and hundreds of thousands of SNPs available for the analysis. The principal component analyses from those studies give visual evidence for the discontinuous genetic distances separating continent-wide populations. But the discontinuous jumps were most evident when significant geographic barriers separated populations. The smaller the geographic scale, the more often variation in allele frequencies occurred in clines.[61] Subsequently, the defenders of race as a social construct have expended considerable effort pushing back against *any* existence of genuine, as opposed to statistical, clusters of populations.[62]

Seen in ideological terms, I can understand why the orthodoxy wants genetic differences to be clinal. Geographic discontinuities in genetic variation look a lot more like races, classically construed, than clinal variation does. But substantively, what difference does it make? The genetic distance between Europeans and East Asians shown in the principal components plots looks "big." Now suppose that we zero in on the genetic profiles of Bretons living in the far northwest of France and Hakka Chinese living in the far southeast of China. Suppose that the genetic differentiation between those two populations occurs entirely in clines—that if you sampled each and every population on the route between northwest France and southeast China, the gradations would perfectly correlate with geographic distance and there would be no discontinuities associated with the steppes of Russia or Central Asian deserts. Even in that case, the magnitude of the genetic distinctiveness of the French and Chinese would be unaffected. If the difference is great, it would still be just as great, even though the pairwise differences among the dozens of populations in between were quite small.

More broadly, my view of the orthodox reaction to the cluster analyses is that it constitutes a complicated set of "Yes, buts…" A core truth uncongenial to the orthodoxy goes untouched. A geneticist can say to the orthodox, "Give me a large random sample of SNPs in the human genome, and I will use a computer algorithm, blind to any other information about the subjects, that matches those subjects closely not just to their continental ancestral populations, but, if the random sample is large enough, to subpopulations within continents that correspond to ethnicities." If race and ethnicity were nothing but social constructs, that would be impossible. It's actually a sure bet.

Recapitulation

As I close this discussion, it is time for another reminder that the genetic distinctiveness of populations is minor compared to their commonalities and that all of the clusters and genetic distances are based on SNPs that for the most part are not known to affect any phenotype. The material here does not support the existence of the classically defined races, nor does it deny the many ways in which race is a social construct. Rather, it communicates a truth that geneticists expected theoretically more than half a century ago and that has been confirmed by repeated empirical tests: Genetic differentiation among populations is an inherent part of the process of peopling the Earth. It is what happens when populations successively split off from parent populations and are subsequently (mostly) separated geographically.

The inescapable next question is whether we're looking at a phenomenon that has been confined to SNPs that have no effect on the phenotype, or whether the same thing has been happening to SNPs that do have such an effect. We will explore that topic by looking at what has been learned about evolution since humans left Africa.

8

Evolution Since Humans Left Africa

Proposition #6: Evolutionary selection pressure since humans left Africa has been extensive and mostly local.

A pillar of the orthodox position is that humans left Africa so recently that they haven't had time to differentiate themselves genetically in ways that would affect cognitive repertoires. That position is now known to be wrong, as indicated by Proposition #6. Presenting the evidence for Proposition #6 involves a number of technical issues regarding evolution, and so it's time for another interlude.

Fourth Interlude: Evolutionary Terms You Must Know to Read the Rest of the Book

Evolution refers to the process whereby the first primitive forms of life became the biosphere we know today, a process independently understood in its modern form by Charles Darwin and Alfred Russel Wallace in the 1830s and 1840s and famously described in 1859 by Darwin in *On the Origin of Species*.

Mutation. The evolution of completely new traits—hearing or eyesight, for example—requires mutations. Mutations have several causes. The chemicals that make up the base pairs can decay or be damaged. The process for correcting those errors (a capability for DNA repair is built into every cell) is pretty good, but it sometimes makes mistakes. Similarly, errors can occur during DNA replication. Mutations can be caused by different forms of radiation or exposure to certain chemicals. These and other causes can affect the chemical in one letter of a base pair or the number of repetitions in microsatellites. They can result in small insertions or deletions of bases (*indels*), and structural variations in regions of DNA.[1]

An extensive literature debates the incidence of mutations and whether the rate has increased or decreased over time. The rate is usually expressed in incomprehensibly small numbers (e.g., 1.29×10^{-8} per position per generation). But the same study that produced that estimate thankfully gives an intuitively useful way of thinking about it: It implies that a newborn with 30-year-old parents will carry 75 new SNV mutations and 6 new short indel mutations.[2]

The process of mutation is a matter of chance. The great majority of mutations have no effect or a negative effect—random changes are unlikely to add something positive to highly evolved traits.[3] "Negative effect" in evolutionary terms refers to a reduction in *reproductive fitness* (often just *fitness*), the technical term for describing reproductive success, measured in the simplest case by the number of offspring one produces.[4] Even when a mutation has a positive effect on fitness, it initially happens to a single individual. For that mutation to spread from one individual throughout the population requires a great deal of luck. Exactly how much luck was calculated almost a century ago by British geneticist J. B. S. Haldane: If a given allele has a selective advantage of *s*, the chance that it will sweep through a large population and become fixed is 2*s*.[5] For example, if the selective advantage conferred by an allele is 5 percent (a large advantage for a single allele), it has only a 10 percent chance of eventually becoming fixed. Even a highly favorable mutation has a precarious place in the genome until it has successfully propagated to many people.

Allele frequency. The evolution of population differences in traits that already exist is driven by changes in allele frequency. Suppose that some trait is determined by 100 SNPs and that the average allele frequency for the alleles that promote that trait is .20 among Bretons and .60 among the Hakka. The trait in question will probably be more pronounced or more common among the Hakka than among Bretons, but the trait is not exclusively Hakka. On the contrary, the luck of the draw means that some Bretons will have a more pronounced expression of that trait than some Hakka.

CALCULATING AND EXPRESSING AN ALLELE FREQUENCY

Allele frequency is a proportion ranging from 0 to 1. It can also be expressed as a percentage—an allele frequency of .15 is equivalent to 15 percent of genomes—but I will express it as a proportion instead because most people instinctively interpret a percentage as referring to the percentage of the population. That's incorrect. An allele frequency is the proportion of gene copies within a population, which means the denominator is based on chromosomes, not people.

Since each individual carries two copies of each gene, the total number of gene copies in a population of 100 people is 200. Suppose that the two alleles in a particular site are A and a and we want to calculate the allele frequency of the A-allele. An individual could carry the genotypes AA, Aa, or aa. Suppose that 20 people have the AA combination. They contribute 40 copies of the A-allele. Another 20 people have the Aa combination, contributing 20 copies of the A-allele. The remaining 60 people have the aa combination. So while 40 percent of the population carries at least one A-allele, the allele frequency is (40 + 20)/200, or 30 percent, which I will express as .30.

The five main candidates driving evolution through either mutations or changes in allele frequencies are *natural selection, sexual selection, migration, introgression*, and *genetic drift*. You have already encountered genetic drift in chapter 6. Here are quick summaries of the other four:

Natural selection. The most famous of the mechanisms for translating infusions of new genetic variations into effects on traits is the principle of natural selection, the momentous insight achieved independently by Charles Darwin and Alfred Russel Wallace. Here is the way Darwin put it in *On the Origin of Species*: "If variations useful to any organic being do occur, assuredly individuals thus characterized will have the best chance of being preserved in the struggle for life; and from the strong principle of inheritance they will tend to produce offspring similarly characterized. This principle of preservation, I have called, for the sake of brevity, Natural Selection."[6]

Both Darwin and Wallace were inspired by the same empirical observation: All species are so fertile that their populations should increase exponentially, and yet the sizes of populations are relatively stable. The necessary implication is that significant numbers of any generation fail to reproduce.

Another empirical observation was that no two members of a species are exactly alike. Furthermore, it was obvious to Darwin and Wallace that many of the variations within a species are heritable. Hence Darwin's and Wallace's key inference: Some variations facilitate the transmission of traits to the next generation; some variations impede that transmission. Variations increase or diminish *reproductive fitness*. Evolution selects for reproductive fitness.

Sexual selection. Sexual selection is a form of natural selection, but it doesn't necessarily have anything to do with an organism's abilities to survive threats to life. On the contrary, some signals that attract the opposite sex can reduce reproductive fitness. For example, bright coloring in male birds makes them more attractive to females but also makes them more visible to predators.

Sexual selection is all about finding someone to mate with and having offspring that survive to the age of reproduction. Reproductive fitness is irrelevant. A frivolous example, but one that makes the point: Whether someone is left-handed or right-handed is genetically determined, with left-handers being in a small minority—about 10 percent of the population.[7] There is no reason to think that left-handedness in and of itself augments reproductive fitness. But if for some reason women were to develop a strong sexual preference for left-handed men, it would not take long on an evolutionary time scale for the proportion of left-handed men to increase drastically.

What's your best chance of passing on your genes? It depends on your role in mating versus parenting, which in turn depends on your sex, which in turn depends (you may be surprised to learn) on the size of your gametes. *Gamete* refers to a germ cell that is able to unite with another to sexually reproduce. By biological definition, the male sex is the one that produces the smaller gametes (in human males, spermatozoa), and the female sex is the one that produces the larger gametes (in human females, eggs).[8]

Why is it that so many living things are characterized by two sexes that produce gametes of very different size? Because as an empirical matter, that's the arrangement that gives the best odds that progeny will survive. The process can be modeled mathematically. Assuming a positive correlation between the size of the fertilized cell and its survival, a stable equilibrium is often a bifurcation of the population into two types characterized by extremely different gamete sizes. The intuitive explanation of this result is that any fertilized cell resulting from a large gamete begins the struggle for life with the advantage of a stockpile of nourishment; the production of many small gametes is advantageous because the number of fertilizations is maximized. Two intermediate-sized gametes don't work as well because neither is fully committed either to nourishing the fertilized cell or maximizing the number of fertilizations, and this mediocrity tends not to prosper.

Now comes the evolutionary kicker that is at the source of so much contemporary argument about sex roles and child-rearing: Among almost all living things that reproduce sexually, the sex with the smaller gametes (males) provides less care after fertilization than the sex with the larger gametes (females).

It makes evolutionary sense. In most mammalian species, the most efficient way for a male to ensure that his genes survive is to impregnate as many females as possible.[9] The most efficient way for a female to ensure that her genes survive is to make the most of her limited opportunities to produce offspring, which means being choosy about the quality of the male's fitness and devoting a lot of effort to keeping the offspring alive. In his book *Male, Female,* evolutionary psychologist David Geary makes the point with an extreme case: A male elephant can impregnate several females in a single day. A female elephant must carry a single offspring for 22 months before it is even born, let alone weaned. Female elephants don't get many chances to pass on their genes. The female elephants who succeed tend to be the ones who are most adept at mating with healthy males and who are devoted to the welfare of their babies.[10] *Homo sapiens* is an outlier among mammals, with the male providing more paternal care than is customarily observed—but it's still not a lot compared to the burden carried from fertilization onward by the female.

Migration. Different human populations have lived in contact with each other as long as there have been humans, and occasionally their members have had sex with each other and produced children. Over a long period of time, these offspring alter the gene pool.

Such intermingling through migration has been going on for tens of thousands of years. And yet contemporary human groups, including different ethnicities within the same continental ancestral population, still have distinctive genetic signatures in cluster analyses and are still visually distinguishable to a greater or lesser degree. Why haven't humans long since become a uniform shade of beige with a common set of physiological features?

It's not mysterious. Even though the interbreeding of populations has gone on for so long, usually it has not happened on a large scale over many generations, which means it is easily possible for populations to mingle some aspects of their gene pools and yet remain visually distinct. Suppose that back in the thirteenth century a Chinese woman had borne a child with a visitor from Italy, Marco Polo. That child was half Italian and half Chinese and probably looked like a mix. But the second generation of that initial union was only a quarter Italian, the third generation one-eighth, the fourth generation one-sixteenth—and by that time none of Marco Polo's descendants had the slightest visible trace of their Italian ancestry.

This has been a common experience throughout history: Interbreeding produces a visible blend in the first generation of progeny, but the heritage of one of the parents wins out over the long run. It remains surprisingly true even today: America has one of the most ethnically diverse populations in the world, with the most opportunities for children of mixed parentage to mate with other children of mixed parentage, and yet, for example, among American women who have a European American and a Chinese American parent, 82 percent marry a European American husband, putting their children (now only a quarter ethnically Chinese) on the road toward eventual indistinguishability from fully European Americans.[11]

Even though encounters among human populations have not led to the degree of visible blending one might intuitively expect, those encounters can nonetheless introduce changes that persist in the gene pool forever after. Suppose, for example, that Marco Polo had passed on an allele that conferred protection against a deadly pathogen afflicting the Chinese. In this hypothetical case, it would still be true that several generations later his descendants in China would look exactly like any other Chinese and would carry few distinctively Italian alleles—but one of them could be that highly valuable antipathogen allele, already in the process of spreading among the Chinese population without leaving a visible trace.[12]

Introgression. The fastest way to introduce completely new genes into a species, orders of magnitude faster than mutation, is interbreeding with another species—*introgression*.[13] It's not common. A breeding wall usually prevents different species from producing offspring. If they succeed, those offspring are often infertile (e.g., mules, produced by the interbreeding of horses and donkeys). But some species are interfertile, meaning that introgression produces fertile offspring. Introgression is likely to produce significant evolutionary results because of the sheer quantity of new genetic variants introduced into both genomes.

The 1000 Genomes Project. In addition to the foregoing evolutionary terms, you need to know something about the 1000 Genomes Project that will be referenced in the rest of this chapter and will figure prominently in chapter 9.

The 1000 Genomes Project had its inception in September 2007, when an international group of geneticists convened at Cambridge University to plan a collection of sequenced genomes from individuals around the world. The goal was to find genetic variants with allele frequencies of at least .01 in a broad range of populations. The Phase 1 database for the 1000 Genomes Project assembled information on more than 39 million SNPs and other genetic variants for 1,094 persons grouped into 14 ancestral subpopulations. Five of them came from Western and Northern Europe, three from East Asia, three from sub-Saharan Africa, and three from the Americas. In the subsequent discussion and the next chapter, I limit my use of the Phase 1 data to the subpopulations representing the Big Three continental ancestral populations that are at the center of discussions about race differences: sub-Saharan Africa (hereafter "Africans"), Western and Northern Europe ("Europeans"), and East Asia ("Asians"). The subpopulations for Africa are the Luhya in Western Kenya, Yoruba in Nigeria, and African Americans in the American Southwest. The subpopulations for Europe are British samples drawn from England and Scotland, Finns in Finland, Tuscans from Italy, and Americans of Northern and Western European ancestry from Utah. The subpopulations for East Asia are Han in South China, Han students in Beijing, and Japanese in Tokyo. Details on the populations are given in the note.[14]

Rethinking the Nature of Recent Human Evolution

How much evolution took place after humans left Africa? Before the genome was sequenced, geneticists had few tools for exploring that question. Some things looked as if they must have evolved after the dispersal—most obviously light skin among Europeans and Chinese and lactase persistence in Europeans. But otherwise the story of recent evolution was inaccessible.

Then came the sequencing of the genome, "a turning point in the study of positive selection in humans," as evolutionary geneticist Pardis Sabeti put it.[15] It changed just about everything about the study of human evolution since humans left Africa: the type of natural selection at the center of geneticists' attention, the strategies they used to identify the specific genes and SNPs involved, and the methods for implementing those strategies.

Early on, a team of anthropologists and geneticists (first author was John Hawks) took advantage of the newly sequenced genome to test the provocative hypothesis that adaptive human evolution has recently accelerated. The transition to agriculture in some populations about 10,000 years ago led to drastic changes in diet, population density, technology, economics, and culture in general. Evolutionary biologists are still trying to understand the many intense evolutionary pressures that were generated. Among the most urgent was the need to adapt to the lethal epidemic diseases—smallpox, malaria, yellow fever, typhus, and cholera—that followed the introduction of agriculture. The Hawks study concluded that "the rapid cultural evolution during the Late Pleistocene created vastly more opportunities for further genetic change, not fewer, as new avenues emerged for communication, social interactions, and creativity."[16] It was a radical departure from the conventional wisdom, but just the beginning of a wholesale rethinking of recent evolution.

From Darwin's Insights to the Modern Synthesis

The word *genetics* wasn't even coined until 1905, soon after Gregor Mendel's pioneering work was rediscovered after having been ignored for almost half a century. The first half of the twentieth century saw a series of landmark discoveries about the biology of genetic transmission, led by Thomas Hunt Morgan in the early decades and culminating in the discovery of the double-helix structure of DNA by James Watson and Francis Crick in 1953.[17]

From the beginning, scientists were aware of the potential importance of genetics for explaining how evolution worked at the molecular level. One of the earliest theoretical findings was genetics' equivalent to Newton's first law of motion: identification of the circumstances under which the frequencies of alleles at a given site would remain stable.[18] Discovered independently by Godfrey Hardy and Wilhelm Weinberg, who both published in 1908, it became known as the Hardy-Weinberg equilibrium. It provided the baseline against which to identify and measure disturbances to the equilibrium—the process of evolution.

But there was a problem in reconciling Darwinian evolution and Mendelian genetics. The Darwinian model posited excruciatingly slow and imperceptibly small modifications in continuous phenotypic traits. In Mendelian genetics, the phenotype changed abruptly depending on a few discrete alleles—for example, the alleles determining the color or shape of the seeds among Mendel's pea plants.

The tension was resolved by three giants born within three years of each other: Ronald Aylmer Fisher (1890–1962), J. B. S. Haldane (1892–1964), and Sewall Wright (1889–1988). From 1915 through the mid-1930s, they laid the mathematical foundation for what has become known as the modern evolutionary synthesis, or, within the field, simply "the modern synthesis."

The first among equals was probably Fisher, an authentic genius (in the process of making his seminal contributions to genetics, he also made seminal contributions to modern statistics). His 1918 article "The Correlation Between Relatives on the Supposition of Mendelian Inheritance" is foundational, demonstrating that gradual variation in a trait could be the result of Mendelian inheritance.[19] In so doing, he incorporated the polygenic nature of traits and the importance of allele frequency (though he did not use those terms). I have already mentioned J. B. S. Haldane's coefficient s for expressing the probability that a mutation will go to fixation and Sewall Wright's work in the theory of genetic differentiation among populations. But these are just examples of a cascade of contributions that Fisher, Haldane, and Wright had made by the mid-1930s. They built the theories of population and quantitative genetics that still guide these disciplines today.

A Shift in Focus from Hypothesis-Driven Candidate Gene Studies to Hypothesis-Generating Genome-Wide Studies

Candidate gene studies. From the 1930s through the rest of the century, the number of things that geneticists could do with this magnificent body of theory was limited. Perforce, geneticists had to adopt strategies that worked despite only fragmentary knowledge of what was going on within the genome. One was the "candidate gene" approach.[20]

It began with Anthony Allison's observation back in the early 1950s that sickle cell anemia was geographically limited within Africa to areas where malaria was endemic. Why should people who survived in an environment afflicted by malaria be peculiarly vulnerable to a blood disease unknown elsewhere? Allison hypothesized that a mutation with a huge s value because it protected against malaria had swept through the population even though it had the lesser deleterious effect of susceptibility to sickle cell anemia. A mutation that did both of those things was probably in that part of the genome involving blood. Allison picked the Hemoglobin-B gene as his candidate gene and subsequently identified a specific mutation that had been the target of natural selection.[21]

A more sophisticated way of identifying candidate genes, called *linkage analysis*, enabled progress during the 1980s in understanding genetically based diseases such as Huntington's disease, Alzheimer's disease, and some forms of cancer.[22] But by the mid-1990s, researchers working on diseases such as schizophrenia, bipolar disorder, and diabetes were stymied. Linkage analysis was useful for diseases that were caused by alleles with large effects, but it produced inconclusive and often contradictory results for complex diseases that were caused by many alleles with small effects.

Evolutionary geneticists also used the candidate gene approach for exploring the known adaptations that had occurred after the dispersal from Africa, such as lightened skin. But such obvious examples of recent evolution were rare. As geneticist Joshua Akey explained it, candidate gene studies have two major limitations.[23] One is that they require a priori hypotheses about which genes have been subject to selection, but few traits lend themselves to a priori hypotheses. This is true of many physiological traits, but especially of cognitive ones. The relevant alleles surely involve brain function and might have something to do with hormones, but that's not nearly specific enough to identify a candidate gene. Ingenious attempts to do so failed. Perhaps the most frustrating example was the search for the genetic basis of cognitive ability using the candidate gene approach. Years of intensive effort in the late 1990s and early 2000s failed to identify even a single replicable genetic locus affecting it.[24]

The second limitation of candidate gene studies was how to determine whether natural selection was really involved even if a candidate gene seemed to be panning out. Perhaps the alleles were under selection pressure. But perhaps genetic drift was at work, or some other mechanism that had nothing to do with natural selection. The available theoretical models weren't good enough to yield precise predictions, and the statistical tests were often inadequate for robust conclusions.

Genome-wide association study (GWAS), pronounced "g-wasp" without the "p." GWAS is an acronym now as ubiquitous in the technical literature as SNP. The technique itself is usually abbreviated as GWA. The idea behind it was first expressed in 1996 in an article in *Science* by Stanford geneticist Neil Risch and Yale epidemiologist Kathleen Merikangas. "Has the genetic study of complex disorders reached its limits?" they asked. Their answer put geneticists on course to a new and productive technique:

We argue below that the method that has been used successfully (linkage analysis) to find major genes has limited power to detect genes of modest effect, but that a different approach (association studies) that utilizes candidate genes has far greater power, even if one needs to test every gene in the genome. Thus, the future of the genetics of complex diseases is likely to require large-scale testing by association analysis.[25]

Implementing "association analysis" is complicated, but the idea is simple, involving concepts you learn in the first month of an introductory statistics course or can learn from Appendix 1, but applied on a gigantic scale.[26]

Maybe a simplified illustration will give you a sense of how the process works. I'll use my running example of height. Suppose you are given a SNP that has alleles A and T. You also have a large sample of people who have been genotyped and their height measured in inches. You find that men with TT are on average 70.0 inches tall, men with TA are on average 70.1 inches tall, and men with AA are 70.2 inches. You apply the appropriate statistical test and determine that the relationship is statistically highly significant. It looks as if allele A is associated with greater height.

That's essentially what a GWA does for several million SNPs. There are complications, of course. If you're running a million tests for statistical significance, you would get about 50,000 SNPs that show up as having a "statistically significant" association with schizophrenia at the familiar $p < .05$ level even if none of them had any substantive association whatsoever. Therefore you must require a far stiffer criterion for statistical significance. Risch and Merikangas anticipated that problem, calculating that to achieve a significance level that gives a probability greater than .95 of no false positives among the nominated SNPs from a million SNPs, the level of statistical significance required for any one SNP should be $<5 \times 10^{-8}$, or less than .00000005.[27] This has become the most commonly used standard, though more sophisticated rationales for it have subsequently been developed.[28]

SNPs that are candidates for causality. If you're interested in establishing the causality of specific SNPs with a specific trait, you have the raw material for beginning the process. But even if your SNPs all meet the standard criterion for statistical significance in a GWA ($p < 5.0 \times 10^{-8}$), what you have at this point is no more than the raw material. You need to go through a number of steps to prune and otherwise clean up—"curate"—your set of SNPs. I will discuss those processes subsequently.

What might you eventually be able to do with this information? It depends on the trait. If you are a medical researcher studying the SNPs associated with a specific disease, your set of SNPs will eventually be part of a mosaic that helps understand the genetic origins of that disease and thereby perhaps enables new curative and prophylactic strategies.

If you're a population geneticist, you can use your set of SNPs to ask questions about whether natural selection for the trait in question has been occurring, and if so, in what populations and when. To do that, you will need a second database that contains samples from the ancestral populations you want to study.

A host of procedural and statistical issues attend the production of a valid GWA, but the main data requirement is a large sample. The statistical methods used in the social sciences are routinely applied to samples in the hundreds, and a sample of 10,000 is considered large. In GWA, a sample of 100,000 is no more than okay.

A Shift in Focus from Mutation and Hard Sweeps to Standing Variation and Soft Sweeps

GWA provided a way to get around one of Akey's limitations on the candidate gene approach, but it did not help with the other: how to tell whether changes over time were the product of natural selection. Progress on that front required another change in focus.

Until the genome was sequenced, most of the work of molecular biologists focused on evolution through mutation—it was the "ruling paradigm," in the words of evolutionary biologists Joachim Hermisson and Pleuni Pennings.[29] The ruling theoretical model was "the neutral theory of molecular evolution," introduced in the late 1960s and given full expression by population geneticist Motoo Kimura in 1983.[30] The neutral theory acknowledges that phenotypic evolution is driven by Darwinian natural selection. But the theory posits that the vast majority of differences at the molecular level are neutral, meaning that they do not influence the fitness of the organism. Insofar as selection does occur, it is "purifying" selection, which acts to eliminate harmful mutations. The genetic variation at the molecular level that we observe within and between species is explained, with rare exceptions, by genetic drift.

Given a focus on evolution through mutations of large effect and a theoretical explanation that assigns almost all molecular variation to genetic drift, scientists may have found it natural to believe that humans hadn't had enough time to evolve much since the dispersal from Africa. The number of generations since humans left Africa is probably around 2,000 and almost certainly no more than 5,000. A favorable mutation with an unusually large s value can go to fixation in a few hundred generations, but under commonly observed values of s, a mutation is likely to take thousands of generations to reach fixation.[31] From this perspective, the time since humans left Africa has indeed been "the blink of an eye" in evolutionary terms, just as Gould proclaimed.

This conclusion has been indirectly reinforced by analyses indicating that, as one such study put it, "strong, sustained selection that drives alleles from low frequency to near fixation has been relatively rare during the past ~70 KY [thousands of years] of human evolution."[32]

Long before the genome was sequenced, however, going all the way back to Fisher's early work, quantitative geneticists were aware that mutation wasn't the only way in which evolution worked. Completely new variants weren't needed, just changes in the variation that already existed—"standing variation."

Over the millions of years that led to anatomically modern humans, a great deal of genetic variation has arisen that confers no particular advantage or disadvantage. Perhaps SNPs have phenotypic effects, but these effects are too small to have an appreciable impact on reproductive fitness. Perhaps a mutation spread to some percentage of the population because it was once advantageous but then lost its advantage as the organism adapted to the environment in other ways. Perhaps it had been simply a matter of genetic drift.

Think of standing variation as kindling. For a long time, it has no effect on anything. The allele frequencies drift aimlessly from generation to generation. Then something changes in the environment—the equivalent of a match. Depending on what the change is, an allele that had been more or less neutral can become advantageous and start to spread. To use a completely made-up example, let's say that the SNPs that produce variation in the trait called "thriftiness" existed as standing variation in hunter-gatherer populations. There was no reason for purifying selection to eliminate the variation completely, but neither was there any evolutionary reason for the thriftiness alleles to increase. In an environment where possessions are rudimentary and foodstuffs rot within a few days, thriftiness has no appreciable effect on fitness. When a hunter-gatherer group switched to agriculture, the situation changed radically. Those who were thrifty had many advantages in accumulating surpluses for surviving hard times and for bartering in good times. Aside from direct fitness advantages, the thrifty man or woman who became prosperous obtained advantages in sexual selection. Under these conditions the frequencies of the thrift-promoting alleles would start to exhibit a tendency to increase rather than to fluctuate haphazardly.

The example generalizes to many kinds of standing variation. The frequencies of the newly favored allele may not go to fixation after an environmental change—the spread of any single favorable allele for a polygenic trait slows as the organism's phenotype becomes satisfactorily adapted to the changed environment—but its frequency within the population increases. These alterations in standing variation are known as *soft sweeps*, in contrast to a *hard sweep*, in which an adaptive mutation spreads and eventually goes to fixation.

The role of standing variation in evolution depends in part on the genetic complexity of the trait. It is least applicable to a trait such as resistance to a deadly disease caused by a specific pathogen. The simpler the genetics of the trait, the more likely that a single mutation can have a major effect, with such a large value of s that the mutation has a good chance of going to fixation. In contrast, adaptation through standing variation is most applicable to traits that are affected by hundreds or thousands of alleles contributing tiny effect sizes. A change in the environment may have only modest effects on the allele frequency at any one locus, but it has those modest effects on hundreds of the relevant sites and thereby produces a cumulatively large effect.

Such changes in standing variation can reliably produce dramatic effects in the phenotype through breeding. Humans have known this for millennia, even though they didn't know anything about alleles. Darwin begins *On the Origin of Species* with a chapter titled "Variation Under Domestication," knowing that his readers among England's rural gentry who were proud of their livestock would understand what he's talking about (P. G. Wodehouse fans will think of Lord Emsworth).

It's not just the physiology of animals that can be changed rapidly through breeding. So can fundamental personality traits. A modern experimental example is the Siberian silver fox. In 1959, Soviet biologist Dmitry Belyaev decided to reproduce the evolution of wolves into domesticated dogs.[33] Instead of using actual wolves, he obtained Siberian silver foxes from Soviet fur farms and began to breed them for tameness. The foxes were not trained in any way, nor were they selected for anything except specific indicators of tameness as puppies. In the fourth generation, Belyaev produced the first fox puppies that would wag their tails when a human approached. In the sixth generation, he had puppies who were eager to establish human contact, whimpering to attract attention, licking their handlers—in short, acting like dogs. By the tenth generation, 18 percent of puppies exhibited these characteristics from birth. By the twentieth generation, that proportion had grown to 35 percent.

Even though the rapid effects of breeding were well known, it had generally been assumed until the 1950s that natural selection in the wild must move more slowly. Then British geneticist Bernard Kettlewell realized that within his own lifetime the wings of many types of moths had changed from light to dark in industrial areas of England. He began experiments in which he released light- and dark-winged peppered moths in unpolluted and polluted forests (the bark on trees in polluted forests having been darkened by industrial smoke and soot). He found that the daily mortality rate of the light-winged moths was twice that of the dark-winged variety in the polluted forests and subsequently elaborated on that finding to prove that natural selection was the cause.[34] (Let us pause for a moment: Try to imagine the patience and doggedness it takes to determine daily mortality rates of moths over several acres of land.) Since Kettlewell's work, rapid response to environmental change has been demonstrated in many species—for example, Italian wall lizards, cane toads, house sparrows, and, most famously, in the beaks of finches living on the Galápagos Islands.[35]

All this had been known before the genome was sequenced. But that knowledge didn't have many practical research implications because the technology for analyzing selection pressure on standing variation wasn't up to the job. Using candidate genes was the only game in town.

Population genomics. The sequencing of the genome opened a possibility that had been closed until then: determining what regions of the genome are under selection (i.e., responding to evolutionary pressures) and how long that selection has been going on.[36] The field is still maturing, with refinements on existing methods and new techniques being published every few months, but it has already made dramatic progress in determining the age of evolutionary adaptations and identifying which regions of the genome are currently under selection.

How is it possible to know that a part of the genome has been under selection when you are working with samples of genomes drawn from people who are alive now? Even more perplexing, how could it be possible to know how long the region has been under selection?

I could answer by telling you that such selective sweeps create a valley of genetic diversity around the site under selection, that they leave a deficit of extreme allele frequencies (low or high) at linked sites and an increase in linkage disequilibrium in flanking regions—but that doesn't tell you much unless you're a geneticist.[37] Here is a highly simplified way of thinking about one of the major sources of information about the location of regions under selection:

Keep three things in mind: (1) Base pairs at nearby SNPs in the genome tend to be correlated. (2) When nature recombines the parents' genes, choosing some from the mother and some from the father, it does not conduct its coin flips site by site; instead, the coin flips shift one parent's genes to the offspring in blocks. (3) The placing of the cuts defining the blocks varies from generation to generation, although there are "hot spots" where cuts are more likely to happen than elsewhere. As time goes on, the size of an original block is whittled down.

The record of evolution left by this process has been likened to palimpsests, the parchment medieval manuscripts that were reused but left traces of the older writing. In genetics, the parchment is the chromosome and the DNA sequence the text.[38] A less elegant way to think of it is to imagine that the block of SNPs is a playing card—the nine of clubs, let's say. Every generation, a thirty-second of an inch is sliced off—sometimes from the top, sometimes from the bottom, sometimes from a side.[39] You will still be able to tell it is the nine of clubs through many, many slices. Eventually, you won't. Geneticists are in the position of observing the card already diminished but being able to estimate how many slices were required to reach its whittled-down configuration. If the frequency of the mutant allele at the center of this block is higher than expected from the block's age as inferred from its whittled-down width, we have evidence that natural selection is responsible for the elevated frequency. The process cannot detect the origin of adaptations older than about 30,000 years—which by definition means that it identifies adaptations that occurred long after the dispersal from Africa.

I have given you a colloquial description of only one of the many methods that are used to detect selection pressure. As early as 2006, a review of progress described five "signatures" in the DNA sequence that indicate selection.[40] Those methods have subsequently been refined and augmented.[41] They are now reaching the point where they can identify individual SNPs under selection as well as regions under selection.[42]

Paleogenomics. This progress in the analysis of contemporary genomes has been augmented by progress in the study of the DNA of archaic humans. Unlikely as it seems, DNA can survive in the bones of hominins who died tens of thousands of years ago. Recovering it is a daunting task. Scientists must piece together partial genomes and infer missing sections. Ancient genetic material has to be discriminated from modern contamination. But the development of next-generation sequencing technologies enabled solutions to those problems.[43] In 2009, a team headed by Svante Pääbo at the Department of Genetics at the Max Planck Institute for Evolutionary Anthropology in Leipzig succeeded in completing the first draft of an entire Neanderthal genome.[44] Since then, the genomes of many other Neanderthals and of early anatomically modern humans have been completed, and progress has been made in reconstructing the genomes of other hominins.[45] The availability of archaic genomes lets geneticists do more than infer whether alleles in contemporary genomes have been under recent selection. They can directly compare their inferences with the evidence on those same alleles from DNA tens of thousands of years old.

Fifteen years after the genome was sequenced, the shift in focus from candidate genes to genome-wide analyses and from mutation to changes in standing variation has resulted in a large body of work documenting that recent evolutionary selection pressure has been extensive. And it has been mostly local.

Recent Selection Pressure Has Been Extensive

One of the unexpected findings since the sequencing of the genome has been how much evolution has taken place in the recent past, continuing up to the present. Most of it has occurred through changes in standing variation. Some of it has occurred through introgression.

Evolution Through Selection Within Homo Sapiens

Evolutionary geneticists wasted no time in using the new tools that became available after the sequencing of the genome. In a 2009 article, just six years after the final draft was published, Joshua Akey could assemble the results of 21 studies that had already used genome-wide scans for natural selection.[46] Focusing on the seven studies that used the largest samples at that time, the HapMap and Perlegen databases, he constructed an integrated map of positive selection.[47]

The aggregate numbers from just those seven were startlingly large. A total of 5,110 distinct regions of the genome were identified by at least one study, encompassing 14 percent of the genome and 23 percent of all genes. A total of 722 regions containing 2,465 genes were identified in two or more studies. His conclusion:

> Genomic maps of selection suggest widespread genetic hitchhiking… throughout the genome. Although the veracity of this statement is subject to the limitations described above, it is fair to say that the number of strong selective events thought to exist in the human genome today is considerably more than that imagined less than a decade ago. Again, restricting our attention to the 722 loci identified in two or more genome-wide scans, ~245 Mb (~8%) of the genome has been influenced by positive selection, and an even larger fraction may have been subject to more modest selective pressure.[48]

Since then, the number of loci believed to be under selection has continued to grow. In 2012, a team predominantly from Stanford used a different method, employing a measure called ROH ("runs of homozygosity"), applying it to the combined data from the HGDP-CEPH and HapMap databases.[49] They identified 69 regions that they labeled "ROH hotspots." The top 10 included genes involving cell function, connective tissue development, the brain, vision, the central nervous system, and skin pigmentation. Five of the top 10 regions had not previously been identified as sources of recent selection pressure.

In 2013, Sharon Grossman of the Broad Institute of Harvard and MIT and her colleagues published the results for a method called CMS (Composite of Multiple Signals) designed to pinpoint specific variants within the genetic regions under selection.[50] Initial applications of this method yielded an additional 86 regions showing a high probability of selection pressure, along with hundreds of specific genes that appear to have been under recent selection pressure. These include genes involving hearing, immunity, infectious disease, metabolism, olfactory receptors, pigmentation, hair and sweat, sensory perception, vision, and brain development.

In 2016, another international team made progress in identifying human adaptation within the last 2,000 years. Using a new method, the Singleton Density Score, applied to a sample of the ancestors of modern Britons, they found strong signals in favor of selection for lactase persistence, blond hair, and blue eyes. Their conclusion: "Our results suggest that selection on complex traits has been an important force in shaping both genotypic and phenotypic variation within historical times."[51]

Also in 2016, Daniel Schrider and Andrew Kern published a sophisticated new machine-learning technique called Soft/Hard Inference through Classification. They applied it to six populations that have low levels of historical admixture: three of sub-Saharan Africans (two from West Africa, one from Kenya), one of non-Latino whites in Utah, one of Japanese in Japan, and one of Amerindians in Peru. Their method identified 1,927 "distinct selective sweeps," of which 1,408 were ones not previously identified.[52] The work by Schrider and Kern also substantiated the importance of changes in standing variation. Of the total 1,927 sweeps they identified, 92.2 percent were soft, which accounts for the title of their article, "Soft Sweeps Are the Dominant Mode of Adaptation in the Human Genome." Geneticists Rajiv McCoy and Joshua Akey summarized the implications this way:

> This finding has potentially wide-ranging implications for the dynamics of neutral and slightly deleterious variation.... More generally, a widespread influence of selective sweeps challenges the long-standing neutral theory of molecular evolution, which states that most variation within and between species does not impact fitness and is largely governed by random genetic drift.... If a large proportion of genetic variation is in fact influenced by linked positive selection, null models may need to be updated to better reflect this complexity.[53]

I have restricted myself to a handful of the global and largest studies. The total body of work is far greater. In 2009, Joshua Akey had 21 studies to work with. A 2016 review article titled "Fifteen Years of Genomewide Scans for Selection" included an additional 52 studies.[54]

In response to such findings, a controversy has arisen. Are we really looking at natural selection or at genetic drift due to purifying and background selection?[55] A team of researchers at the Max Planck Institute for Evolutionary Anthropology set out to answer that question through an analysis of contemporary allele frequencies in the 1000 Genomes Project combined with evidence from a high-quality genome of a 45,000-year-old anatomically modern human from Ust'-Ishim in Siberia. Their answer, published in 2016, was that many of the most strongly differentiated alleles between Africans and Eurasians had not risen in frequency after the dispersal from Africa. "Nevertheless, our results provide clear evidence that local adaptation contributed to these allele frequency changes in European populations, as strongly differentiated alleles in Europeans are enriched in likely functional variants."[56]

"Evidence" is the correct word, not "proof." Techniques for discriminating natural selection from other sources of change in standing variation are still being refined. The state of knowledge is still nowhere close to a firm number for specifying how much total evolutionary change there has been, how much of that total has been an adaptive response to natural selection, how much has been a nonadaptive response to selection on correlated traits, and how much has occurred by genetic drift.[57] What can be said more confidently is that the regions under selective pressure since the dispersal from Africa are in fact extensive; that the methods for identifying these regions have steadily improved since the earliest studies at the beginning of the century; and that each new compilation shows a new and substantial amount of the genome has been influenced—both directly and indirectly—by selection.

Evolution Through Introgression

Descendants of those who left Africa experienced significant introgression of genes from other hominins. Two hominins are definitely involved: Neanderthals and Denisovans. Others might eventually be identified.[58]

Scientists have known since the 1860s that a race of advanced hominins other than *Homo sapiens* once lived in Europe. More recently, they have established that Neanderthals lived in Asia as well. They descended from *Homo erectus* along a separate line from *Homo sapiens*. The timing of the split has been estimated as early as 800,000 and as late as 400,000 years ago. It is now established that anatomically modern humans bred with both Neanderthals and another, recently discovered archaic hominin, the Denisovans, whose discovery in a cave near southern Siberia's Altai Mountains was announced in 2010. Introgression between Denisovans and *Homo sapiens* left traces in modern East Asians and in peoples from New Guinea and elsewhere in the Pacific. It is argued that Denisovan gene variants may also account for Tibetans' ability to function at high altitudes.[59]

Interbreeding between Neanderthals and *Homo sapiens* occurred in several places and times in Europe and at least to some extent in East Asia, leaving traces of Neanderthal DNA in modern Europeans and East Asians amounting to about 1 to 2 percent of the genome. It appears that Neanderthal alleles may have helped humans adapt to non-African environments; Neanderthals are argued to have been not only cold-adapted but hyperarctic-adapted.[60] Another study concluded that "the major influence of Neandertal introgressed alleles is through their effects on gene regulation."[61] The safest conclusion at the moment is that most of the story is yet to be told. The balance of probability says that most of the variants picked up from the Neanderthals were neutral or negative, but the Neanderthals had probably been adapting to conditions and pathogens not found in Africa for hundreds of thousands of years and are bound to have carried many variants that would have been advantageous to the newcomers. Chances are good that humans picked up some of them.

The new findings about recent evolution from natural selection and introgression have triggered a spirited debate that is of greater interest to population geneticists than to us. The neutral theory of molecular evolution has been an intellectual centerpiece of population genetics since the early 1980s. It continues to have vigorous defenders. Responding to an attack, an international team of seven population geneticists (first author was Jeffrey Jensen) concludes that "it is now abundantly clear that the foundational ideas presented five decades ago by Kimura and Ohta are indeed correct."[62] On the other side are geneticists who think that the debate is over. "We argue that the neutral theory was supported by unreliable theoretical and empirical evidence from the beginning, and that in light of modern, genome-scale data, we can firmly reject its universality," wrote geneticists Andrew Kern and

Matthew Hahn in 2018. "The ubiquity of adaptive variation both within and between species means that a more comprehensive theory of molecular evolution must be sought."[63] If history is a guide, the best bet is that some sort of theoretical synthesis will arise from this dialectic. Whatever form it takes, it will have to accommodate the evidence for far more recent evolution than was anticipated before the genome was sequenced.

Recent Selection Pressure Has Been Mostly Local

From the dawn of the genomics era, studies of recent selection have also found that "local adaptation" was widespread, with "local" meaning that the genes under selection varied by continent. An early analysis of local adaptation using the HapHap database was published in 2006 by a team of geneticists (first author was Benjamin Voight). They examined regions of the genome under selection pressure for three populations: Yoruba (a Nigerian tribe), Europeans from a mix of Northern and Western European countries, and East Asians (a mix of Chinese and Japanese). Of the 579 regions, 76 percent were unique to one of the three populations, 22 percent were shared by two of the three, and only 2 percent were shared by all three populations.[64] In the authors' judgment, the degree to which selection occurred independently is probably underestimated by these percentages.[65] In any case, these events represent quite recent selection—"average ages of ~6,600 years and ~10,800 years in the non-African and African populations respectively," in the authors' judgment.[66]

The same pattern has been found repeatedly. In Joshua Akey's literature review of 21 early studies of recent selection published in 2009, he found that "~80% of the 722 loci observed in multiple scans show evidence of local adaptation."[67] In that same year, an international team funded by the Max Planck Society and the German government published results using the HGDP-CEPH database you encountered in chapter 7. This study employed its own distinctive method of identifying regions under selection pressure but got familiar results. Grouping the 51 populations into their continental ancestral location (European, East Asian, Central/South Asian, Middle Eastern, Oceanian, and Amerindian), 68 percent of the regions under selection were under selection for a single population. Another 20 percent were under selection in just two of the six. Only 1 percent were under selection in all six populations.[68]

The six ethnic African ethnicities had little overlap with any of the non-African ethnicities.[69] Of the 632 regions identified as under positive selection, at least one of the African populations was represented in 146 of them. Of those 146 regions, 82 percent were represented by a single African ethnicity. Just one was shared by two African populations. Only 18 percent were shared by an African population and one or more non-African populations.[70]

Principal Component Analysis Revisited

Recall from chapter 7 the patterns shown when noncoding genetic markers were analyzed using principal component analysis. There's no reason why the same analysis could not be applied to functional variants. In 2013, an international team of geneticists (first author was Xuanyao Liu) did so, using yet another method of identifying signatures of positive selection, applied to the 14 populations of Phase 3 of the 1000 Genomes Project, that identified 405 regions under selection. The figure below shows the results.

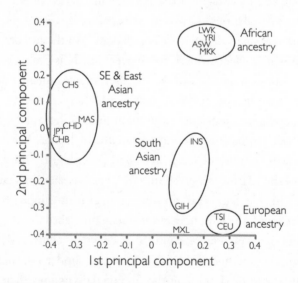

Source: Adapted from Liu, Ong, Pillai et al. (2013): Fig. 5C.

The meaning of the abbreviations: LWK: Luhya in Kenya. YRI: Yoruba in Nigeria. ASW: African Americans in the Southwest. MKK: Maasai in Kenya. JPT: Japanese in Tokyo. CHB: Chinese in Beijing. CHS: Chinese in Singapore. CHD: Chinese in Denver. MAS: Malays in Singapore. INS: Indians in Singapore. GIH: Gujarati Indians in Houston. MXL: Mexicans in Los Angeles. CEU: Europeans in Utah. TSI: Tuscans in Italy. The Mexican population is an unknown mix of European and Amerindian ancestry.

The specifics are different from the profiles in the principal component analysis shown in chapter 7—to be expected, since the nature of the datum entered in each cell of the matrix for the figure above is completely different from those entered in the earlier figure. Some of the subpopulations are different as well.[71] But the clusters formed by the 14 populations are distinct and familiar. When geneticists use noncoding genetic variation from multiple populations, those populations are genetically distinctive in ways that broadly correspond to self-identified race and ethnicity. When geneticists use genetic variation that is not only functional but has been under selection pressure since the dispersal from Africa, the same correspondence usually appears.

Recapitulation

Much has changed since the 1980s when it was still possible for Stephen Jay Gould to believe that evolution since humans left Africa couldn't be more than skin deep. The main events were the sequencing of the genome and then the advent of genome-wide scans. Those analyses in turn shifted the center of attention from evolution through mutation to evolution through changes in allele frequencies. The same analyses uncovered unexpectedly large portions of the genome that have been under recent selection. Like the results of the cluster analyses of noncoding SNPs discussed in chapter 7, the new analyses showed that the regions of the genome under selection varied by geography and population ancestry. Or to summarize it in the words of Proposition #6, evolutionary selection pressure since humans left Africa has been extensive and mostly local.

9

The Landscape of
Ancestral Population
Differences

*Proposition #7: Continental population differences
in variants associated with personality,
abilities, and social behavior
are common.*

This chapter is about raw ancestral population differences in SNPs that are statistically related to cognitive repertoires—"raw" meaning that a great deal of work remains to be done before the significance of such differences is understood.

Until a few years ago, this topic was still *terra incognita*. Only a handful of statistical relationships between specific SNPs and cognitive traits had been identified. But the growth in that number has been phenomenal, paralleling the growth in the number of SNPs associated with diseases and physiological traits. To illustrate what's been happening, consider the GWAS Catalog. It was begun in 2008 by the National Human Genome Research Institute, part of the U.S. National Institutes of Health.[1] The first year with a published GWAS was 2005, when two studies reported a grand total of two SNPs.[2] In 2018 alone, the GWAS Catalog added 17,182 previously unidentified SNPs. Here's what the history looks like:

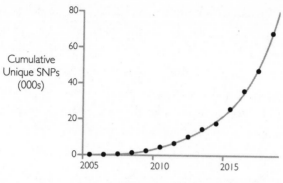

Source: Author's analysis, GWAS Catalog.

As of the end of May 2019, the catalog included 3,469 studies reporting 136,286 variants. The total number of unique variants was 89,544. And that's just a fraction of the total number of variants that have been associated with phenotypic traits at lesser levels of statistical significance. That total is over a million, residing in databases maintained by university and private sector research centers scattered around the world.

Hardly any analyses of this burgeoning knowledge base have compared results for different continental ancestral populations (which for readability I will subsequently abbreviate to "continental populations"). Researchers have been wary of such comparisons because the results can't be trusted. Paradoxically, the reason they can't be trusted has indirectly become the reason that continental population differences will soon be studied intensively.

Why Continental Population Differences Will Be Studied

For the last quarter century, medical researchers have been grappling with evidence that what's true about a disease for one ancestral population isn't necessarily true for another. It's called *population stratification.*

The problem was first suspected in the mid-1990s. Medical researchers looking for candidate genes routinely compared the genetics of a group with the disease being studied with a comparison sample of people without the disease. In choosing those samples, ancestry was initially not a consideration. But as researchers got access to more genetic information, they began to worry that their results were being contaminated because the ancestral populations in the samples had different genetic profiles.[3] A back-and-forth debate ensued in the technical literature. By 2004, the weight of the evidence had become clear. As one of the early DNA-based studies concluded, "Even small amounts of population admixture can undermine an association study and lead to false positive results. These adverse effects increase markedly with sample size. For the size of study required for many complex diseases, relatively modest levels of structure within a population can have serious consequences."[4]

POLYGENIC SCORES

Polygenic scores will be discussed in detail in chapter 14. For now, think of them as analogous to test scores, but based on combined allele frequencies instead of combined answers to test questions. A polygenic score for schizophrenia (for example) measures the genetic risk of schizophrenia.

A decade later, the first studies using polygenic scores verified an explanation for population stratification that generalizes far beyond the study of diseases: Polygenic scores for one continental population don't work as well for other continental populations no matter what the trait may be. In technical terms, the predictive validity of a polygenic score deteriorates as the genetic distance between the test population and the comparison population increases, consistent with population genetics theory.[5] For example, a polygenic score based on a test population of English and Italians usually generalizes accurately for French and Germans, not so accurately for Chinese and Indians, and least accurately for the genetically most distant populations from sub-Saharan Africa.[6]

Population differences in predictive validity could reflect natural selection, genetic drift, or gene × environment interactions. Population geneticists have had strong scientific motivation to learn more about those differences but have been frustrated because the artifacts produced by population stratification are so common.[7] Statistical analysis can correct for some of population stratification's effects, but the only full solution is to have large samples from all the ancestral populations that are being compared. The problem is that genomic data have typically been collected from people who lived in the nations where geneticists worked, dominated by Europe and the United

States, which in turn meant that large genomic databases were overwhelmingly people of European ancestry.

The collection of large samples from non-European populations was on the back burner through the first half of the 2010s. It's understandable—samples in the hundreds of thousands are logistically demanding, and the foundations and government agencies with deep enough pockets to fund such samples have not (until recently) put them on their agendas. There also has been a lack of urgency: Geneticists have been kept busy with an ample supply of GWA research projects that can be done with European samples.

Then murmurings about underrepresentation of non-Europeans in genomic databases began appearing. They reached a broad audience in 2018 when British geneticist David Curtis charged that by using European samples, "UK medical science stands at risk of being institutionally racist."[8] In 2019, an article by a team of American geneticists in *Cell*, "The Missing Diversity in Human Genetic Studies," widely picked up by the media, detailed the many ways in which the bias toward European samples "effectively translates into poorer disease prediction and treatment for individuals of under-represented ancestries."[9]

It now appears likely that large samples from underrepresented populations—notably Africans and South Asians—will be available soon (China and Japan have been building such databases on their own). When they come online, ancestral population differences related to disease are going to be studied minutely.

Those same databases will potentially allow researchers to study genetic differences in personality traits, abilities, and social behavior across continental populations. That potential is likely to generate cross-cutting pressures. For highly charged topics such as IQ, many people will continue to urge that studying population differences does more harm than good. But what happens if findings from European samples about cognitive-related traits such as depression, autism, or schizophrenia lead to more effective treatments for Europeans but not for other populations? It will be ethically imperative to study the genetics of mental disorders in other populations as well, which means studying the ways in which they differ from Europeans. The idea that geneticists could ignore ancestral population differences indefinitely was always implausible. It is now out of the question.

Differences in Allele Frequencies Within and Across Continental Population

When SNPs cause differences in phenotypic traits, evidence for that role surfaces first in differences in target allele frequencies. The *target allele* is usually defined as one that is associated with an increase in the magnitude or intensity of a trait. If the topic is diabetes, the target alleles are the ones associated with an increase in the risk or severity of diabetes. If the topic is IQ, the target alleles are those associated with increases in IQ scores. Other labels used in the literature include *risk allele*, *effect allele*, and *increasing allele*. As in chapter 8, I express target allele frequencies exclusively as proportions ranging from 0 to 1 rather than as percentages of chromosomes.

My purpose in this discussion is limited to the wording of Proposition #7 as it applies to common SNPs: Continental population differences in target allele frequencies associated with personality, abilities, and social behavior are common. *I am not presenting proof that those differences cause phenotypic differences*, but showing you how different the situation actually facing geneticists is from the impression you may have when you hear that "race is a social construct." Virtually all traits, whether physiological, related to disease, or related to cognitive repertoires, exhibit many large differences in target allele frequencies across continental populations.

Comparing Subpopulations from the Same Continent

I'll use a specific example, schizophrenia, as an entry point to the topic. First, consider the landscape for subpopulations within the same continental population. The following graphs show what happens when the target allele frequencies for two populations are plotted against each other for three within-continent pairs: Kenyans and African Americans, British and Italians, and Chinese and Japanese.

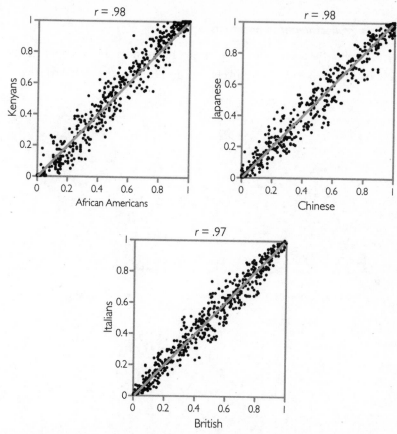

Source: Author's analysis, GWAS Catalog, and Phase I of the 1000 Genomes Project. A total of 962 SNPs in the GWAS Catalog are associated with schizophrenia. For this and the subsequent graphs, I chose 500 to plot (962 in a small graph would produce too many overlays, obscuring the pattern).[10]

The diagonal line identifies SNPs for which the target allele differ-ence is zero. As you can see, the actual differences are closely bunched to either side of the diagonal on all three graphs. Scatter plots like these imply extremely high correlations between the two sets of target allele frequencies, and indeed they are high: +.98 for the African and Asian pairs; +.97 for the European pair. These results are typical. Taking all of the unique SNPs for all traits that are part of both the GWAS Catalog and 1000 Genomes—a sample of 43,543 SNPs—the average correlations were +.98 for the three African pairs, +.98 for the six European pairs, and +.99 for the three Asian pairs.[11]

Comparing Continental Populations

Now look what happens when we repeat the exercise, but comparing Africans with Asians, Asians with Europeans, and Europeans with Africans.

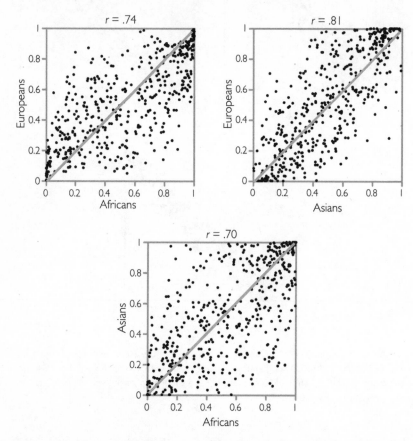

Source: Author's analysis, GWAS Catalog and Phase 1 of the 1000 Genomes Project.

The landscape is completely different. The cross-continent correlations are all high by the standards of social science, but even correlations of +.70, +.81, and +.74 (which are the ones represented in the figure) are associated with large differences between target allele frequencies. Why did I choose schizophrenia for the example? Because the three correlations for schizophrenia are nearly the same as the correlations for all SNPs related to cognitive repertoires in the GWAS Catalog: +.71 for Africans and Asians, +.76 for

Africans and Europeans, and +.81 for Asians and Europeans. The schizophrenia example is typical, not extreme.

And that's the nut of what I am trying to convey with Proposition #7. We don't know what these differences mean yet (with a few exceptions to be taken up later), but the image fostered by "race is a social construct" does not apply. The raw material for investigating genetic sources of population differences in phenotypic traits consists of differences in target allele frequencies. For subpopulations within continents, the raw material is meager. For continental populations, the raw material is abundant.

An Operational Definition of "Large"

To demonstrate that abundance, I need a summary statistic for conveying how many SNPs fall far from the diagonal in the scatter plots. I settled on an operational definition of "large" that defines "large" relative to differences within continental subpopulations: *A difference in target allele frequencies is called "large" if it is bigger than 99 percent of the target allele frequency differences found within continental subpopulations.* To calculate that number, I used all 43,543 unique SNPs in the GWAS Catalog that are also found in Phase 1 of the 1000 Genomes Project. Combining all of the 12 pairs of within-continent subpopulations produced a sample of 522,516 pairs of target allele frequencies. Twenty percent of the absolute differences in target allele frequencies were less than .01, 63 percent were less than .05, and 88 percent were less than .10.[12] Ninety-nine percent were less than .19—to be more precise, less than .186. Thus my operational definition says that the smallest between-continent difference that is "large" is anything greater than .186. For convenience, I will round up and use .20 as the criterion. It's easier to remember.

In other words, if Asians have a target allele frequency of .45 for a certain SNP and Europeans have a target allele frequency of .65 or higher on the same SNP, that difference qualifies as "large." If Europeans have a target allele frequency of .25 or less, that difference also qualifies as "large." What's important is the absolute difference between two populations.

How many SNPs show that large a difference? The following table shows the results for 112 phenotypic traits grouped into three types of noncognitive traits and three types of cognitive traits. The noncognitive traits are major diseases such as breast cancer and Parkinson's disease, physiological biomarkers such as height and weight, and blood parameters such as red cell count and metabolite levels. The cognitive traits are cognitive disorders such as depression, cognitive ability (both IQ and neurocognitive functioning), and personality features such as risk-taking tolerance and life satisfaction. The note gives details.[13]

TARGET ALLELE DIFFERENCES QUALIFYING AS "LARGE" (.20+)

	No. of Unique SNPs	Total	African-Asian	European-African	Asian-European
Physiological Traits	13,431	33%	37%	33%	30%
Diseases	3,718	33%	38%	33%	30%
Biomarkers	5,298	35%	39%	35%	31%
Blood parameters	4,415	31%	35%	31%	28%
Cognitive Traits	9,628	36%	39%	37%	32%
Cognitive disorders	2,594	35%	38%	37%	31%
Mental abilities	5,715	36%	39%	36%	32%
Personality features	1,319	38%	42%	38%	35%

Source: Author's analysis, GWAS Catalog and Phase 1 of the 1000 Genomes Project.

When comparing the three continental populations, about a third of all target allele differences are at least .20.[14] Note that .20 is the smallest difference that qualifies. The mean difference among those that qualify is .33 for both the physiological and cognitive traits.

The results for this subset of traits generalizes to all 2,147 traits in the GWAS Catalog as of May 2019 that also had SNPs represented in Phase 1 of the 1000 Genome Project. For the combined noncognitive traits, 32 percent of target allele differences across continental populations qualified as large. For the combined cognitive traits, 34 percent qualified as large.

One other feature of the results generalizes: The three continental pairs are consistently ordered. Africans and Asians have the highest proportion of large differences, Asians and Europeans have the smallest proportion, and Africans and Europeans are in between. This is consistent with the theoretically expected relationship between geographic and genetic differences between populations discussed in chapter 7.

The Traits Related to Cognitive Repertoires

The table on pages 192–93 presents information on 22 traits related to personality, abilities, and social behavior that have at least 100 SNPs associated with them. Unlike the previous table, this one combines SNPs that are given different labels in the GWAS Catalog but are associated with the same trait. For example, the trait labeled "well-being" in the table combines SNPs from studies in the GWAS Catalog that were for traits labeled "eudaimonic well-being" and "subjective well-being." The note gives additional information about the traits.[15]

The table provides more information than most readers need. Its purpose is to enable skeptical readers to look at the results from a variety of perspectives. Suppose, for example you think that an absolute difference of .20 is not sufficiently big. The table also shows you the percentage of allele differences that met a threshold of .25, which exceeds 99.9 percent of the within-continent differences. It also shows you the between-continent correlations and the mean allele difference for those traits that met the .20 threshold. Proposition #7 claims that "Continental population differences in variants associated with personality, abilities, and social behavior are common." In effect, the table says that the data confirm that proposition no matter how you look at them.

The Inevitability of Interesting Questions to Ask

Even though we don't know what analyses of these data will show, the existence of so many differences in target allele frequencies will raise interesting questions for a simple reason: We already know that the target alleles for two populations seldom balance out. Look again at the Asian-European scatter plot for schizophrenia.

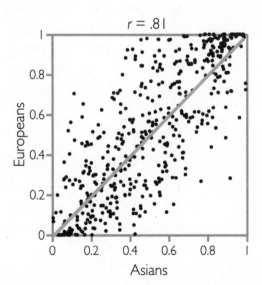

Source: Author's analysis, GWAS Catalog and Phase I of the 1000 Genomes Project.

DIFFERENCES IN TARGET ALLELE FREQUENCIES FOR TRAITS RELATED TO COGNITIVE REPERTOIRES

| | | Correlations of Target Allele Frequencies | | | | | |
| | | Within Continents | | | Across Continents | | |
Trait	Unique SNPs	Africa	Asia	Europe	Africa-Asia	Europe-Africa	Asia-Europe
Cognitive Performance							
Cognitive ability	1,926	0.98	0.98	0.96	0.66	0.72	0.78
Highest math course	1,345	0.98	0.98	0.96	0.68	0.73	0.76
Educational attainment	2,368	0.98	0.98	0.97	0.71	0.78	0.78
Self-reported math ability	1,012	0.98	0.98	0.97	0.70	0.75	0.78
Neurocognitive function	134	0.98	0.99	0.98	0.78	0.78	0.84
Personality/Temperament							
Depression	850	0.98	0.98	0.96	0.73	0.73	0.79
Neuroticism	932	0.98	0.99	0.96	0.66	0.70	0.77
Worry	226	0.98	0.98	0.93	0.49	0.63	0.74
Risk tolerance	420	0.98	0.98	0.96	0.63	0.73	0.74
Adventurousness	162	0.98	0.98	0.97	0.65	0.76	0.78
Positive affect	191	0.97	0.98	0.95	0.69	0.69	0.74
Life satisfaction	176	0.97	0.98	0.95	0.66	0.69	0.72
Well-being	408	0.98	0.98	0.96	0.68	0.71	0.73
Cognitive Disorder							
Schizophrenia	962	0.98	0.98	0.97	0.70	0.74	0.81
Bipolar disorder	134	0.98	0.97	0.97	0.73	0.80	0.77
Autistic traits	215	0.98	0.98	0.97	0.80	0.82	0.87
ADHD	126	0.99	0.99	0.98	0.84	0.87	0.87
Social Behavior							
Conduct disorder	147	0.98	0.98	0.97	0.75	0.80	0.80
Alcohol consumption	284	0.98	0.99	0.96	0.66	0.71	0.71
Alcohol dependence	124	0.97	0.98	0.98	0.73	0.78	0.79
Brain-related							
Brain volumes	160	0.98	0.99	0.98	0.77	0.79	0.86
Cerebrospinal fluid	121	0.98	0.99	0.98	0.76	0.79	0.86

*Within-continent mean differences in target allele frequencies are not shown because they were all from .03 to .06 for all subpopulations and all traits.

**Mean within-continent differences that met the .20 threshold are not shown because there were so few of them.

SNPs Meeting the Two Thresholds						Mean Difference in Target Allele Frequencies					
Africa-Asia		Europe-Africa		Asia-Europe		All SNPs*			SNPs Meeting the .20 Threshold**		
>=.20	>=.25	>=.20	>=.25	>=.20	>=.25	Africa-Asia	Europe-Africa	Asia-Europe	Africa-Asia	Europe-Africa	Asia-Europe
42%	33%	39%	27%	33%	22%	0.18	0.16	0.20	0.37	0.31	0.30
39%	31%	36%	26%	32%	21%	0.20	0.17	0.17	0.36	0.34	0.31
37%	29%	34%	22%	31%	21%	0.16	0.16	0.18	0.36	0.31	0.31
37%	29%	35%	25%	32%	21%	0.19	0.17	0.16	0.37	0.32	0.31
28%	20%	26%	17%	22%	13%	0.15	0.15	0.13	0.34	0.35	0.31
37%	27%	37%	26%	33%	22%	0.17	0.16	0.18	0.34	0.31	0.30
39%	31%	40%	27%	35%	25%	0.18	0.17	0.20	0.38	0.32	0.32
40%	33%	44%	30%	34%	22%	0.20	0.16	0.22	0.43	0.32	0.30
44%	34%	39%	30%	33%	23%	0.18	0.17	0.21	0.38	0.33	0.32
42%	33%	36%	27%	30%	21%	0.18	0.16	0.21	0.38	0.32	0.32
35%	28%	35%	23%	32%	21%	0.17	0.16	0.18	0.36	0.31	0.31
45%	36%	38%	24%	39%	26%	0.17	0.17	0.20	0.34	0.30	0.31
38%	29%	36%	26%	36%	25%	0.17	0.17	0.19	0.37	0.33	0.32
39%	29%	35%	27%	29%	21%	0.17	0.15	0.19	0.36	0.34	0.32
33%	25%	28%	17%	31%	22%	0.15	0.15	0.17	0.34	0.30	0.30
24%	20%	23%	17%	18%	12%	0.14	0.11	0.15	0.35	0.32	0.31
28%	18%	23%	14%	26%	12%	0.13	0.13	0.14	0.30	0.29	0.29
31%	22%	30%	20%	27%	15%	0.15	0.13	0.16	0.35	0.31	0.30
42%	33%	42%	31%	37%	25%	0.19	0.18	0.20	0.37	0.33	0.32
44%	30%	39%	28%	29%	23%	0.17	0.15	0.19	0.33	0.31	0.34
38%	30%	31%	26%	24%	17%	0.16	0.14	0.17	0.34	0.34	0.30
27%	21%	29%	21%	20%	16%	0.14	0.12	0.15	0.36	0.32	0.30

If the investigator's ambition is to identify a role for natural selection in creating population differences, there's no telling whether anything interesting lies in that plot. Getting from raw differences in target allele frequencies to evidence of natural selection is a long and torturous process, and even then the results should be treated provisionally.[16] For that matter, proof of the role of natural selection for many genetic differences will remain unobtainable without methodological breakthroughs. Recall from chapter 8 that one of the most commonly used tools doesn't work for adaptations that occurred more than 30,000 years ago.

But while proving natural selection is difficult, the differences in target allele frequencies across populations can be analyzed without knowing what caused the differences. Such analyses can't be done now with any confidence because of the problems of population stratification, but they will become feasible within a few years when large databases from the major ancestral populations are available.

For purposes of illustration, let's jump ahead to that time and suppose that the schizophrenia scatter plot for Asians and Europeans is free of contamination by population stratification and that target allele frequencies and the weights associated with them can be taken at face value (very big suppositions). The 500 SNPs shown in the scatter plot do not reveal an obvious imbalance between the target allele frequencies above and below the diagonal, but it turns out a modest one does exist. In the full sample of 962 SNPs associated with schizophrenia in the GWAS Catalog, Asians have the higher target allele frequency for 513 SNPs compared to 449 for Europeans. This opens the possibility—only a possibility—that Asians are genetically more susceptible to schizophrenia than Europeans. Whether it is true depends on the magnitude of the differences in target allele frequencies, the effect sizes associated with the SNPs, and a variety of other considerations. Even if population stratification is no longer a problem, the raw difference is useful only for deciding whether it is worthwhile to curate the sample of SNPs to cleanse it of contaminating factors and to analyze polygenic scores for Europeans and Asians. Perhaps the imbalance of 513 to 449 in the raw data will turn out to be meaningful; perhaps it won't.

The imbalance of 513 to 449 for schizophrenia amounts to a 53:47 split per hundred SNPs. The table of 22 traits related to cognitive repertoires presented above has a total of 66 cross-continent pairs. The imbalance is at least

53:47 for 48 of those 66 pairs. It is 55:45 or greater for 33 of them. It is 60:40 or greater for 8 of them. No matter what (reasonable) criterion for a large-enough imbalance you might adopt, many imbalances qualify as large enough to warrant investigation. In time, they will in fact be investigated. It is implausible to expect that *none* of the imbalances will yield evidence of significant genetic differences related to phenotypic differences across continental populations.

The results will often be complex. The same SNPs that affect the trait under investigation will typically be correlated with many other traits as well, which may sometimes mean that SNPs beneficial for a desirable trait also increase vulnerability to undesirable ones, as in the case of the trade-off between protection against malaria versus the risk of sickle cell anemia. Some analyses may reveal that different populations get to similar end points via different processes, as in the case of sex differences in cognitive toolboxes discussed in chapter 3. But simple or complex, the results are in my view bound to be interesting.

Whether my forecast is reasonable depends on the outcome of a larger debate about establishing genetic causation. One side of that debate holds that my optimism is dead wrong. The results cannot possibly be interesting, because causation cannot possibly be established even after the problems of population stratification have been solved. That debate is given a full discussion in chapter 14. It seems fair to say at least this: It is fundamentally wrong to think of the study of genetic population differences as an exercise in ranking populations from top to bottom. The questions to be explored are far more interesting, complex, and potentially more rewarding than filling out an ethnic scorecard.

WHAT ABOUT UNCOMMON AND RARE VARIANTS?

Most single nucleotide variants (SNVs) are found in fewer than 1 percent of chromosomes and therefore do not qualify as common SNPs. The proportion of SNVs with allele frequencies of less than .01 is currently estimated at 74 percent, but that's going to increase as more rare variants are discovered.[17] The closest to a complete inventory as I write is a 2016 sample based on 10,545 genomes that used deep sequencing techniques and identified 150 million variants in the human genome. This is by no means the total. The study reported that each individual added to the sample contributed 8,579 variants not previously identified, leading the authors to estimate that a sample of 100,000 genomes would identify 500 million variants.[18] How much additional variance rare variants explain is still uncertain—a few articles have reported that they explain much of the missing heritability in GWAS analysis, but most analyses show minor effects.[19]

In addition to constituting the bulk of all variants, rare variants are also overwhelmingly confined to a single continental population, on the order of 90 percent or more.[20] However, the importance of rare variants to population differences is uncertain. By one line of argument, they should be minor. By definition, a rare SNV has not spread widely through a population. It is either a new mutation or one that has been only weakly selected if at all. Mutations are random events. They don't happen because there's a need for them (e.g., a mutation giving protection against a disease does not occur because the person was living where the disease was endemic). Thus there is no reason to believe that new mutations occurring in two separated populations will be systematically different with regard to their effects on a given trait. But the literature contains a variety of other perspectives on the role of rare variants.[21] The short story is that comparatively little is known about the role of rare variants, both generally and with regard to population differences. The action for now is with standing variation in common SNPs.

Known Genetic Continental Population Differences

Our expectations for the future should take into account that many genetic population differences are already established.

Hiding in Plain Sight

We have known for years that biologically complex differences in continental populations have evolved since humans left Africa. It is an unlikely assertion on its face—how can "race is a social construct" continue to be the received elite wisdom if such differences are already known? But it's true. Two examples of significant genetic differences across populations have been sitting in plain sight for decades: lactase persistence and susceptibility to sickle cell anemia. Details on both of these adaptations are given in the note.[22] Both of these are major adaptations involving many biological systems. For that matter, lightening of skin pigmentation, passed off as trivial because it is only "skin deep," is genetically more complicated than "skin deep" implies.[23]

Why, given these examples of complex adaptation that obviously occurred after the Africa exodus, should it ever have been assumed that they were the only ones?

Continental Differences Discovered Through Genome-Wide Analysis

Even though the documentation of continental differences has had a low priority among most genetics researchers, several have been found.

Susceptibility to inflammatory and immune-related diseases. In 2014, Jessica Brinkworth and Luis Barreiro examined the GWA results for three chronic inflammatory diseases (celiac disease, Crohn's disease, and ulcerative colitis) and five autoimmune diseases (type 1 diabetes, multiple sclerosis, rheumatoid arthritis, psoriasis, and systemic lupus erythematosus). They found evidence "that at least some of the present-day autoimmune risk loci have been adaptive and conferred some sort of functional benefit to Europeans in the past."[24] The authors hypothesized that a large sample of Africans would yield evidence that "the genetic determinants of susceptibility to chronic inflammatory and autoimmune diseases in individuals of African descent are distinct from those found among Europeans."[25] A 2016 study conducted by a large international team (first author was Yohann Nédélec) found evidence that differences in immune function arose from natural selection rather than genetic drift: "More specifically," the authors wrote, "our results suggest that a significant fraction of population differences in transcriptional responses to infection are a direct consequence of local adaptation driven by regulatory variants."[26]

A study of psoriasis using samples of Europeans (called Caucasians in the study) and Chinese identified European-specific loci that had a cumulative effect that "could explain up to 82.83 percent of the prevalence difference of psoriasis between the Caucasian and the Chinese populations."[27] Overall, the authors concluded, "This study not only provides novel biological insights into the involvement of immune and keratinocyte development mechanism, but also demonstrates a complex and heterogeneous genetic architecture of psoriasis susceptibility across ethnic populations."[28]

Respiratory adaptation to high altitudes. Adaptation to high altitudes has occurred among peoples living on the Qinghai Plateau in Tibet, the Andean Altiplano in Peru, and the Semien Plateau in Ethiopia involving changes in pulmonary function, arterial oxygen saturation, hemoglobin concentration, and maternal physiology during pregnancy. The evolutionary routes taken by each population have involved different genes and produced different responses.[29] Resting ventilation among the Andeans is normal for humans in general; among Tibetans, it is 50 percent higher. Arterial oxygen saturation is elevated for Andeans and Ethiopians; not for Tibetans. Hemoglobin concentration is elevated among Andeans, shows a minimal increase among Ethiopians, and is actually lowered in Tibetans.[30] An exotic complication in the case of the Tibetans is that some of the mutations that helped adapt them to high altitude now appear to have come from introgression with the mysterious Denisovans.[31]

Genetic disorders among Ashkenazi Jews. As early as the 1880s, it was noted that Tay-Sachs disease occurred almost exclusively among Ashkenazi Jews. Over the years, several other genetic disorders have been found to be far more prevalent among Ashkenazi Jews than in any other population. The causes of the difference in prevalence are still unresolved. One possibility is a population bottleneck around a thousand years ago, as argued in a 2018 study that analyzed 5,685 Ashkenazi Jewish exomes. The alleles in question included ones for Tay-Sachs.[32]

Another possibility is that natural selection has been at work. In 2009, before access to GWA, Gregory Cochran and Henry Harpending argued that case, observing that the Jewish genetic disorders are oddly grouped:

> Imagine a fat biochemistry textbook, where each page describes a different function or condition in human biochemistry. Most of the Ashkenazi diseases would be described on just two of those pages. The two most important genetic disease clusters among the Ashkenazim are the sphingoloid storage disorders (Tay-Sachs disease; Goucher's disease; Niemann-Pick disease; and mucolipidosis, type IV) and the disorders of DNA repair (BRCA1 and BRCA2; Fanconi anemia, type C; and Bloom syndrome).[33]

If a population bottleneck were the sole explanation, they calculated that the odds of finding four disorders that affect sphingolipid metabolism would have been about 1 in 100,000.[34] The authors concluded instead that we are looking at recently evolved differences across populations. While the explanation remains unclear, this much is undisputed: The disorders are genetic, and so are population differences separating Ashkenazi Jews from everyone else.

Prostate cancer. In 2018, a team of geneticists (first author was Joseph Lachance) studied the genetic sources of the differential rates of prostate cancer in Europeans and Africans. They used SNPs from the GWAS Catalog, Phase 3 of 1000 Genomes, and the large database of African genomes assembled by Sarah Tishkoff of the University of Pennsylvania. They found that a small proportion of SNPs with large target allele frequency differences and large effect sizes make a disproportionate contribution to population differences in the risk of prostate cancer. "Both neutral and selective evolutionary mechanisms appear to have contributed to disparities in the genetic risk of CaP. These mechanisms include founder effects due to the out-of-Africa migration and genetic hitchhiking of disease susceptibility alleles with locally adaptive alleles."[35]

Evidence of natural selection in height, schizophrenia, and body mass index. A team of geneticists (first author was Jing Guo) examined height, body mass index, waist-hip ratio adjusted for BMI, HDL cholesterol, LDL cholesterol, coronary artery disease, type 2 diabetes, Alzheimer's disease, schizophrenia, and educational attainment for evidence of natural selection. The Guo study tapped a variety of databases instead of limiting itself to the GWAS Catalog. The authors found evidence that SNPs associated with height, schizophrenia, and waist-to-hip ratio have undergone natural selection.[36] They did not find such evidence for the other seven traits in the study.

Blood pressure. A study by a team of Japanese geneticists (first author was Fumihiko Takeuchi) used Europeans and East Asian samples to study continental population differences in blood pressure. They found evidence for two remarkable phenomena: "(1) the colocalization of distinct ancestry-specific variants that are not rare and can exert mutually inverted genetic effects between the ethnic groups and (2) the potential involvement of natural selection in the occurrence of ancestry-specific association signals."[37] They argued that "we have discovered a new model in which genetic effects for transethnic SNPs that form a shared haplotype at a locus are driven by causal variants that are ancestry-specific but are not rare, which can be called a common ancestry-specific variant association model."[38]

And more. Greenlandic Inuits are genetically adapted to a marine diet rich in omega-3 polyunsaturated fatty acids, increasing fitness in a cold and dark environment.[39] The population of San Antonio de los Cobres in Argentina has adapted to high levels of arsenic in the groundwater through positive selection on SNPs involved in the arsenic methylation pathway.[40]

It's early days yet, but the results of the limited genome-wide analyses of differences in continental populations to date point in the same direction: Many continental population differences are out there.

Recapitulation

The story of the raw material for studying continental population differences applies to SNPs related to physiological parameters, diseases, and cognitive repertoires. Substantial between-continent differences in target allele frequencies are common. Around a third of all differences meet a plausible definition of "large." The limited amount of sophisticated genetic analysis of between-continent differences done to date suggests that these extensive differences observed in the raw material will frequently yield productive results about genuine continental population differences.

A Personal Interpretation of the Material in Part II

Part II has described a parallel universe. In the universe inhabited by the elite media and orthodox academia, it has been settled for decades that race is a social construct. In that universe, the lessons taught by Richard Lewontin and Stephen Jay Gould back in the 1970s and early 1980s still apply.

In the universe inhabited by geneticists who study human populations, the 1990s saw glimpses of a new perspective, and the new century opened up fascinating stories that had previously been closed.

The new understandings about the peopling of the Earth have been the most dramatic. New roles in the evolution of *Homo sapiens* were discovered for Neanderthals and previously unknown hominins. Access to ancient DNA enabled the reconstruction of successive human migrations across Eurasia that have revolutionized our knowledge of prehistory.

The understanding of recent evolution that prevailed as recently as the 1990s has also been overturned. Human evolution does not always proceed at a glacial pace dictated by random mutations. Sometimes changes in standing variation can occur quickly in response to environmental selection pressures.

Those environmental pressures have typically been confined to populations in specific geographic areas.

Most recently, the task of assembling the genetic story for specific phenotypic traits has begun. It is still in its early stages, but progress is accelerating nonlinearly. Hence the nervousness that has prevented open discussion of what's going on in the geneticists' parallel universe: the fear that we will discover scary population differences in what I have called cognitive repertoires.

That fear accounts for the taboo that has been attached to discussions of genetics and race. It's no wonder. White Americans' justified guilt about their history of discrimination against blacks, native Americans, and immigrants from Latin America and East Asia gives them reason to worry that white supremacists will use genetics to rationalize that history.

Let me suggest an alternative way of thinking about ethnic differences. Many of the people in elite circles who honor the taboo are also cosmopolitan. They have had professional colleagues of many ethnicities and have traveled extensively, observing the endless variety of ways in which people in different cultures think and behave. They have no trouble believing from personal experience that Chinese think and behave somewhat differently from Saudi Arabians. So do Saudi Arabians and Senegalese, Senegalese and Norwegians, Norwegians and Italians, northern Italians and southern Italians. Viewed from that perspective, ethnic differences in cognitive repertoires are neither to be doubted nor feared. They exist, and everyone who has seen anything of the world knows it. The mix of nature and nurture? That's not the issue. The differences themselves are facts. People around the world are similar in the basics and different in the details. We connect through the basics. We live with and often enjoy the differences.

The material in Part II does not foreshadow discovery of genetically-grounded population differences in the basics. Rather, I hope I have persuaded you that genetically-grounded differences in the details are to be expected. Some of these genetic differences may consist of alternative routes for getting to similar ends, just as has been found with many cognitive sex differences. Many others will be differences that are neither better nor worse, but just differences. Probably some will lend themselves to value judgments, but even those will cut both ways. No population is free of defects nor possessed of all the virtues.

We can expect most of the genetic differences to range from small to moderate and to explain just a portion of the phenotypic differences we already live with. Every population will be represented from one extreme to the other on every trait. There will be no moral or legal justification for treating individuals differently because of the population to which they belong.

I doubt that these assurances will do much good. The prospect of genetic differences across ancestral populations is still too sensitive for calm discussion. But perhaps this will provide perspective:

We already know of a genetically-grounded population difference on a highly sensitive trait that is far, far larger than any ancestral population difference we are going to find. The populations in question are males and females. The highly sensitive trait is the commission of physical violence against other humans. The undoubted genetic source of the difference is the Y chromosome. How big is the difference? Judge it by this: About 90 percent of all homicides are committed by males.[41]

If we can live with a population difference that huge on such an important behavioral trait, we can easily live with the smaller differences in continental populations that are likely to be found. The differences that will be documented during the coming years should be greeted with "That's interesting." I fear that the orthodoxy's insistence that population differences in cognitive repertoires *cannot* exist ensures that they initially won't be greeted that way.[42] But they should be.

PART III

—⁂—

"CLASS IS A FUNCTION OF PRIVILEGE"

The system is rigged in favor of heterosexual white males. The privilege accorded them accounts for who gets ahead in America and who is kept on the bottom. That's one sound-bite version of a core element of the orthodoxy. It began in academia in the 1960s, spilled over into American politics after the turn of the century, and by the 2016 election had become a common position among people who self-identify as progressives. Its more nuanced version is that the system is not completely rigged, but the dice are loaded in favor of whites, males, and heterosexuals—they don't win all the time, but they win far more often than they deserve.

Another sound-bite version of "class is a function of privilege" is that class is a function of wealth: *The system is rigged in favor of the rich, who pass their money to the next generation, who in turn become the next generation of the upper class.* The more nuanced version is that social mobility has diminished in recent decades, symptomatic of an entrenched upper class.

Meanwhile, those who self-identify as conservatives commonly believe that class is a function of character, determination, and hard work. It draws from the traditional American credo: In America, people can become anything they want to be if they try hard enough. The more nuanced version is that people differ in their talents, but for most occupations and roles in life, innate talent is not nearly as important as character, determination, and hard work.

Part III is about a third narrative, not as dark as the orthodoxy's nor as idealistic as the traditional one. Class is a function of the genetic lottery plus character, determination, hard work, and idiosyncratic circumstances. The sociological, economic, and psychometric evidence for it has been available since at least the 1980s and on some topics for longer. That's why a quarter of a century ago, Richard Herrnstein and I were able to write a book of 800-plus pages with the subtitle "Intelligence and Class Structure in American Life."[1]

The book's main title was *The Bell Curve*. In many ways, it documents the ways in which a segment of American society is a indeed morphing into a castelike upper class. But inherited wealth is a tangential contributor. The bare bones of its argument are that the last half of the twentieth century saw two developments of epochal importance: First, technology, the economy, and the legal system became ever more complex, making the value of the intellectual ability to deal with that complexity soar. Second, the latter half of the twentieth century saw America's system of higher education become accessible to everyone with enough cognitive talent. The most prestigious schools, formerly training grounds for children of the socioeconomic elite, began to be populated by the students in the top few percentiles of IQ no matter what their family background might be—an emerging cognitive elite. By 2012, what had been predictions about the emerging cognitive elite as we were writing in the early 1990s had become established social facts that I described in another book, *Coming Apart*.

The purpose of Part III is to bring the third narrative up to date, explicitly addressing not just the role of IQ but of other abilities, the role of genes in determining those other abilities, the distinctions among different kinds of environmental influences, and the interactions between genes and environment.

But What About White Male Privilege and Intersectionality?

In 1989, legal scholar Kimberlé Crenshaw provided a new vocabulary for conceptualizing why class is a function of privilege, not talent. "In race discrimination [legal] cases, discrimination tends to be viewed in terms of sex- or class-privileged Blacks; in sex discrimination cases, the focus is on race- and class-privileged women," she wrote. "This focus on the most privileged group members marginalizes those who are multiply-burdened and obscures claims that cannot be understood as resulting from discrete sources of discrimination."[2] Separating issues of racial discrimination, gender discrimination, and socioeconomic class was theoretically and empirically wrong.

It was not long before Crenshaw's ideas and her introduction of the word *intersectionality* had been expanded into a full-blown theoretical approach that posits an interaction effect across different kinds of oppression. The original focus on women and blacks expanded to apply to all people who suffered from their identities as women, blacks, poor people, gays, the elderly, the disabled, and others. Two leading scholars of intersectionality theory, Margaret Andersen and Patricia Collins, put it this way when introducing the ninth edition of their anthology, widely used as a college textbook:

> Fundamentally, race, class, and gender are *intersecting* categories of experience that affect all aspects of human life; they *simultaneously* structure the experiences of all people in this society. At any moment, race, class, or gender may feel more salient or meaningful in a given person's life, but they are overlapping and cumulative in their effects.[3] [Emphasis in the original.]

Together, the dimensions of intersectionality combine to form what Andersen and Collins labeled a "matrix of domination."

The rhetoric is compelling and fuels endless ideological arguments. But the empirical situation is less fraught. I suggest there is room for agreement on two broad statements: Racism and sexism still play a role in determining who rises to the top, but that role is not decisive. We can have a range of opinions about whether the roles of racism and sexism merit the adjectives "large" or "small," and advocate different public policies depending on our different perspectives, without affecting the relevance of the roles of genes, environment, and their interactions that constitute the topic of Part III.

A COMPROMISE

My proposition is that racism and sexism are no longer decisively important in determining who rises to the top. To support that proposition, I am about to demonstrate that ethnic differences in two major components of class—educational attainment and income—nearly disappear (or in some cases favor ethnic minorities) for people at similar IQ levels. Let's suppose that you think the exercise is meaningless because you reject this use of IQ scores to make racial comparisons. You can nonetheless read Part III profitably if you are willing to consider the evidence that class structure *within* ethnic groups is shaped by the dynamics I describe—that, to take the most important example, white class structure is shaped by these dynamics.

I will also mention, however, that defending your belief that ethnic differences in IQ are meaningless is tough. The ways of defending it that first come to mind don't work, for reasons described in the note.[4]

I use two indicators, educational attainment and earned income, to make that case. The data come from the 2018 Current Population Survey (CPS) and two cohorts of the National Longitudinal Survey of Youth (NLSY). The details for each of the following empirical claims are given in the notes.

Educational attainment by sex. Even without adjusting for anything, there's no female disadvantage to worry about when it comes to educational attainment. Women now have higher mean years of education and a higher percentage of college degrees than men and have enjoyed that advantage for many years. These advantages persist over all IQ levels.[5]

Educational attainment by ethnicity. In terms of the raw numbers, Asians have higher educational attainment than any other ethnic group. Blacks and Latinos have substantially lower educational attainment than whites, but these discrepancies are more than eliminated after adjusting for IQ.[6] Blacks have more mean years of education and higher proportions of college degrees than whites at comparable IQ levels. After taking IQ into account, Latino and white levels of educational attainment are similar. Asians retain their advantage over whites after adjusting for IQ.[7]

Earned income by sex. A substantial female disadvantage in earned income exists, but it is almost entirely explained by marriage or children in the household. Using Current Population Survey data for 2018, earnings for women who were not married, had no children living at home, and worked full-time were 93 percent of the earnings of comparable men.[8] Married women with children in the house have considerably lower earned income even after adjusting for IQ, but the main source of the income discrepancy is not that married women in the labor force earn less than unmarried women, but that married men earn more than unmarried men.[9]

Earned income by ethnicity. Using raw 2018 data from the CPS, Asians have higher mean earned income than whites, while Blacks and Latinos have substantially lower mean earned income than whites.[10] Once again, adjusting for IQ changes that picture dramatically. The note reports multivariate results for two large, nationally representative longitudinal surveys. In the earlier survey, adjusting for IQ wipes out the ethnic income differential among whites, blacks, and Latinos (Asians were not included in this survey). In the latter survey, whites and Latinos have effectively the same earned income while the fitted mean for blacks is 84 percent of the fitted mean for whites. The fitted mean for Asians is 57 percent higher than the fitted mean for whites.[11]

Let me be clear: I am not using these numbers to say that women, blacks, and Latinos do not still face problems because of sexism and racism. These numbers say nothing about individuals being passed over for promotions because of their sex or ethnicity, about glass ceilings, or about discriminatory or harassing interactions in the workplace. But there can be many people who legitimately think they haven't gotten fair treatment without justifying the rhetoric that the orthodoxy uses about white male privilege. If we're comparing men and women with similar IQs or members of different ethnicities with similar IQs, there's only one American group that appears to be privileged for mysterious reasons. Martian sociologists investigating us with an unprejudiced eye would have no trouble identifying it: Americans of Asian ancestry.

There are a host of "Yes, but..." responses that different readers will have. The leading one is probably that IQ is in itself a function of privilege produced by affluence and good schools. And that brings us back to the topic of Part III.

Part III is about the role of genes in shaping this new class structure. Describing that role involves three steps, each of which gets a chapter of its own:

- Establishing the heritability of cognitive repertoires and the relative unimportance of family background.
- Demonstrating that those cognitive repertoires are important causes of success.
- Examining the potential ways to mitigate the role of genes in determining success.

But first you need to be familiar with the framework for disentangling the roles of nature and nurture, to which I now turn.

10

A Framework for Thinking About Heritability and Class

We know a great deal about genes and class, far more than we know about genes and gender or genes and race, and the basics have been known for decades—that's what I meant in the introduction when I said that the archaeological site for exploring class had been effectively closed until the genome was sequenced.

It may sound odd to put it that way, because the orthodoxy still barely acknowledges that genes play any role in human behavior, let alone shape socioeconomic classes. On almost any campus in the country, you can find sociologists who still assure their students that it's all hereditarian pseudoscience.[1] Class is driven by white privilege and the oppression of the patriarchy. But among psychologists who are familiar with the data, such views are exasperating without being an impediment to their work. There are still a few holdouts, but psychologists' debates about heritability generally start from common understandings.[2]

———

Francis Galton was the first person to try to study heritability scientifically. His book *Hereditary Genius* (1869) presented evidence from British history that people with excellence in the same field—judges, parliamentarians, poets, scientists, even wrestlers and oarsmen—tended to be related by blood.[3] Twentieth-century scientists took up where he left off. The intuitive thought here is that if genes are important, people who are more closely related will resemble each other more—siblings will resemble each other more than half siblings, for example.[4] And so it has turned out in practice.

Let's return to our running example, height. If you divide a perfectly random assortment of people into two groups and correlate their heights, the correlation coefficient will be around zero. If the assortment of people consists instead of pairs of half siblings, the correlation will be around +.25. For full siblings it will be about +.50. For identical twins it will approach +1.00.[5] The rising correlation reflects the rising percentage of genes that the pairs share. It forms the basis for a powerful research methodology for calculating the heritability of a trait versus the contribution of the environment: Compare the results for identical twins and fraternal twins—more formally, monozygotic (MZ) twins, formed from a single egg that splits, and dizygotic (DZ) twins, created by two fertilized eggs. But to explain why the method is so powerful, first I need to unpack the meaning of *heritability*.

Heritability

Definition

People from time immemorial have noticed the resemblances of parents and children. Languages around the world have adages reflecting them—in English, for example, "the apple doesn't fall far from the tree" and "a chip off the old block."

The scientific definition of *heritability* is unrecognizably different. Expressed in words, heritability is a ratio calculated as the variance attributable to genes divided by total variance in the phenotype. Mathematically, the kind of heritability that I will be discussing, narrow heritability, is denoted as h^2.

A MINI-INTERLUDE

I don't need to get into as many technicalities about heritability as were required for the discussions of sex and population differences, but you need to be aware of the distinction between *broad heritability* and *narrow heritability*. Broad heritability, denoted as H^2, refers to the combination of both additive and nonadditive sources of variation. Narrow heritability, denoted as h^2, is limited to additive variation.

To illustrate what "additive" means, consider a genetic site in a flower in which one allele codes for red and the other codes for white. The flower is red if the two alleles in the SNP both code for red, white if they both code for white, and pink if one codes for red and the other codes for white. The color of the flower is the result of adding the effects of the pair of alleles in the person's genotype.

If an interaction between the two alleles is involved, the effects of the alleles don't add up in the same simple way. For example, suppose that one site codes for red or white and another site codes for whether color pigment will be produced. To get a pink or red flower not only depends on the site coding for color but also requires that the site coding for pigment production is a "yes." That's one type of nonadditive heritability, called *epistasis*. The other main type of interaction is *dominance*, involving alleles at the same site. Hemophilia is an example. It occurs only if both alleles code for hemophilia. The allele coding for hemophilia is recessive while the "normal" allele is dominant.

Additive variation is the most prevalent form, as I will document. Standard practice has been to fit a model based on additive variation and test to see how well it fits. If the fit is poor, the possibility of nonadditive variance needs to be explored.

Heritability is subject to misunderstandings. A common one is to confuse *heritability*, which refers specifically to the role of genes, with *inherited*, which can refer to things that are passed down through generations whether by genes, parenting, family traditions, or wills.

Another common misunderstanding is to think that the heritability of a trait refers to individuals. Mathematically, heritability refers to a whole population. Suppose that genes explain 70 percent of a population's variance in height. You can use this information to conclude that "genes probably have a lot to do with how tall Joe is," but it does *not* mean that "genes explain 70 percent of how tall Joe is."

Heritability is not a fixed number for a given trait. It can vary by age, for example. We will encounter an example of this when we get to the heritability of IQ: Counterintuitively, it increases as people get older.

Heritability also varies by population. For example, suppose you want to know the heritability of performance on the SAT and you compare two sets of students. One sample is from an ordinary New York City public high school and the other is from Stuyvesant, a famous high school for the intellectually gifted. For practical purposes, Stuyvesant scores will be concentrated in a narrow range—probably 1500 to 1600. The scores for the sample from an ordinary high school will vary from 400 to 1600. The denominator for the heritability ratio calculated from students at Stuyvesant will be smaller than the denominator from the sample from the ordinary high school. Other things equal, the heritability of SAT scores in the Stuyvesant sample will be higher than the heritability for the sample from the ordinary high school.[6]

Heritability can also vary over populations, or over the same population over time, for an important reason that is too seldom recognized: *As society does a better job of enabling all of its citizens to realize their talents, the heritability of those talents will rise.* It is a statistical necessity: The phenotype is the result of genes and environment. In a perfect world where everyone had completely full opportunity to realize their talents, heritability of those talents would converge on 100 percent because the environment relevant to those talents would no longer vary. If it doesn't vary, it can't explain anything.

Heritability rises even in an imperfect world. Consider educational attainment as measured by years of education. For the first half of the twentieth century, Norway was a country in which the amount of schooling you got depended strongly on where you lived (many remote places did not have secondary schools) and your family's social class. In 1960, the average years of education for Norwegian adults was 5.9. After World War II, access to elementary and secondary school became nearly universal. By 2000, the average Norwegian adult had 11.9 years of education. Norwegian allele frequencies for the SNPs that are associated with years of education cannot have changed appreciably from 1960 to 2000. The absolute genetic contribution was effectively constant. But the heritability of educational attainment for Norwegian male twins born before 1940 was 40 percent. For their counterparts born after 1940, it was approximately 70 percent.[7]

A Simple Model

Now for the nuts and bolts of calculating the heritability ratio for narrow heritability, h^2. Let's return to the example of height. For the denominator, the calculation is trivially simple: Measure the height of the people in your sample and do the arithmetic shown in Appendix 1 to calculate variance. The problem comes when you try to estimate the numerator.

By definition, all the variance in a given trait in a population must come from some combination of genes and environment. The simplest model used to operationalize that combination (I will get to the complications later) assumes that total population variance (V_p) consists of the additive effects of three components:

$$V_p = A + C + E$$

In the technical literature, it is commonly referred to as the ACE model. The letter *A* refers to *additive* genetic variance. The letter *C* originally referred to *common environment*, now customarily called *shared environment*. Plausible candidates for the shared environment are such things as parental income, occupation, education, age, parenting practices, family structure, the quality of the neighborhood, and the quality of the schools.[8] The letter E originally stood for *error* but now refers to a combination of two things: measurement error and environmental influences that twins do not share (and that make them different from one another), known as *nonshared environment*.

Both aspects of the nonshared environment need some explanation. *Measurement error* bedevils all the sciences but is especially troublesome in the social sciences. The error can consist not only of inaccurate measurement (e.g., family income is misreported), but also of the gap that separates the construct (what the researcher wants to measure) and the indicator (what the researcher is actually measuring). For example, the number of books in the home is an indicator used to measure the construct "environment for stimulating intellectual development." But such an environment is far more complicated than can be represented by a count of books. Even if the count of books is technically accurate, the indicator will have a lot of error as a representation of the construct. Because of this, the common practice of referring to E as the nonshared environment without mentioning measuring error is seriously misleading.

But some portion of the E component of the ACE model is likely to reflect environmental influences that siblings do not share. In 1987, Robert Plomin, one of the leading students of the nonshared environment, suggested five unshared sources of such phenotypic differences.[9] One is a catch-all nonsystematic category (e.g., accidents, illnesses, trauma). Four others are systematic: family composition (e.g., birth order, sex differences), sibling interaction (e.g., differential sibling jealousy), parental treatment (e.g., differential maternal affection), and extrafamilial networks (e.g., local peer groups, teachers, social media).[10] Actually demonstrating an important role for these potential components of the nonshared environment has proved to be frustrating, as I will discuss in chapter 13. For now, it is enough to recognize that the reality of the nonshared environment is not surprising. If you have siblings, think of all the ways in which you and they had different experiences growing up that were unrelated to your parents' socioeconomic status or to their common parenting practices. You are probably thinking about differences generated by the nonshared environment.

The Analytic Power of Comparing MZ and DZ Twins

This brings us to the unique advantages of studying MZ twins and DZ twins:

- MZ twins share virtually 100 percent of their genes.[11]
- DZ twins share approximately 50 percent of their genes.[12]

Skipping the algebra that lies between, the first two of those advantages mean that you can solve for A, C, and E in the ACE model. Geneticist Douglas Falconer developed the equations for doing so. They look like this:

$$A = 2(R_{MZ} - R_{DZ})$$
$$C = 2R_{DZ} - R_{MZ}$$
$$E = 1 - (A + C)$$

Put in words, narrow heritability equals twice the difference between the correlations of the samples of MZ and DZ twins. The shared environmental contribution equals twice the correlation among DZ twins minus the correlation among the MZ twins. The nonshared environment equals 1 (the total variance) minus the sum of heritability and the shared environment. The note gives an explanation of how this bottom line is reached.[13] In the case of the height example, suppose that the correlation for height of our sample of DZ twins is +.55 and the correlation for our sample of MZ twins is +.95.

$$A = 2 \times (.95 - .55) = .80$$
$$C = 2 \times .55 - .95 = .15$$
$$E = 1 - (.80 + .15) = .05$$

All full siblings share about 50 percent of their genes. The advantage of using DZ twins instead of full siblings who are not twins is that twins are born at the same time. Siblings born several years apart can be born into radically different environments depending on what's happened to the parents' marital relationship, jobs, income, or the location of their home in the meantime. None of those or many other important environmental forces are likely to vary objectively for twins, even though the twins may react to them differently.

TWINS RAISED APART

For many people, "twin studies" brings to mind the famous Minnesota Study of Twins Reared Apart.[14] It got so much publicity because it produced so many dramatic examples of similarities in adults who had never met each other. When the separated twin brothers who inspired the study were reunited in their 30s, it was discovered that as children both had had a dog named Toy. As adults, both had been married twice, first to wives named Linda and then to wives named Betty. They had independently taken family vacations to the same three-block strip of Florida beach, both driving light blue Chevrolets from their homes in the Midwest. Both smoked Salems, both had worked part-time in law enforcement as sheriffs, and both had a habit of scattering love notes to their wives around the house.[15]

Studies of twins raised apart—the Minnesota study was one of several—produced valuable information, but the method's potential was limited. Separation of identical twins at birth happens so seldom that large sample sizes are impossible. The range of environments in which separated twins are raised is narrow—adoption agencies don't knowingly place infants with impoverished or dysfunctional parents.[16] In contrast, it is not difficult to assemble large samples of twins who have been raised together. Their home environments span the range.

The Validity of Twin Studies

The ACE model makes a strong claim: It can disentangle the roles of nature and nurture. You will not be surprised to learn that many challenges to the validity of that model have been mounted.

The logic I have just presented entails five primary assumptions. Three of them, discussed in the note, involve fewer problematic issues.[17] Two of the assumptions are at center stage in the debate over the validity of twin studies:

- Humans mate randomly (no assortative mating).
- DZ and MZ twins experience their common environments equally, known in the literature as the equal environments assumption (EEA).

The Random Mating Assumption

The Falconer equations assume that DZ twins share on average 50 percent of their genes, which in turn depends on their parents having mated randomly for any given trait. When this assumption is violated, the statistical estimate of heritability will be too low.[18]

To see why, suppose that height is 100 percent heritable but that people mate randomly relative to height. In the Falconer equations, the role of shared environment equals twice the correlation among DZ twins minus the correlation among the MZ twins. If true heritability is 100 percent, the MZ twin correlation for height is expected to be +1.0 and the DZ twin correlation is expected to be +.5. Falconer's calculation of the shared environment (C) would be $2 \times .5 - 1.0 = 0$, which is the correct answer.

What happens if the assumption is wrong? Let's say that people tend to marry others who are in the same part of the distribution of height (e.g., shorter-than-average men tend to marry shorter-than-average women). The higher that correlation between the heights of the parents, the more that DZ twins resemble each other over and above the degree that would be predicted by their shared genes, but for a reason that has nothing to do with the environment. Suppose that the assortative mating increased the observed DZ correlation to +.6. In that case, the MZ twin correlation is unchanged at 1.0, but the Falconer formula would determine that the value of the shared environment, C, is $2 \times .6 - .6 = .6$, or 60 percent, which is inflated.

In the real world, assortative mating is routine. At least when it comes to marriage, people tend to marry others who are similar on a wide variety of traits. The empirical reality of that statement has been established for a long time, beginning with Steven Vandenberg's review of the early literature in 1972.[19] Since then, extensive additional research has documented assortative mating for education, intelligence, political affiliation, mental illness, substance abuse, aggressive behavior, and criminal behavior. Often these correlations are substantial, in the region of +.4 to +.5.[20] The expectation must be that assortative mating leads to consistent though modest underestimates of A in the ACE model.

The Equal Environments Assumption

On average, parents of MZ twins treat them more similarly than do parents of DZ twins. As John Loehlin put it, "identical twins are indeed treated more alike—they are dressed alike more often, are more often together at school, play together more, and so forth."[21] But the same scholars who found such differences in treatment of MZ and DZ twins also found, in the words of

Devon LoParo and Irwin Waldman, that "the presence of higher levels of physical and environmental similarity in MZ twins than in DZ twins is a violation of the EEA only if these aspects of the environment are etiologically relevant to the phenotype of interest."[22] LoParo and Waldman found instead that it doesn't seem to make any causal difference that the environments of MZ twins are more similar in some respects than the environments of DZ twins. A few exceptions exist,[23] but such is the finding of the bulk of the literature in twin studies of intelligence, personality, schizophrenia, eating attitudes and behaviors, major depressive disorder, generalized anxiety disorder, phobias, parent-child interactions, hyperactivity, ADHD, PTSD, social attitudes, aggression, alcoholism, and externalizing behaviors.[24] A comprehensive 2014 evaluation of the EEA by Jacob Felson found that controlling for environmental similarity reduced heritability significantly for just one out of 32 outcomes. He concluded, "All things considered, it seems unlikely that the EEA is strictly valid, but it also seems likely that violations of the EEA are relatively modest."[25]

To sum up: Twin studies have come under criticism for overstating the role of genes. The reality is that violations of the random mating assumption are common and lead to modest understatement of the role of genes, whereas violations of the equal environments assumption have even more modest effects in the other direction and are uncommon. Overall, heritability as estimated by twin studies appears to be accurate, with errors tending on net to slightly underestimate heritability rather than overestimate it.[26]

Recapitulation

To understand the causal dynamics that lead to financial and professional success for some people and not for others, and thereby ultimately determine socioeconomic classes, it is essential to understand the comparative roles of environment and genes. Disentangling those roles with ordinary samples of people is extremely difficult and subject to endless disputes. Even before the genome was sequenced, twins offered a uniquely powerful solution. By comparing MZ twins and DZ twins, it is possible to determine the proportional roles of genes and of the environmental conditions shared by children in the same family. Armed with this method, scholars have conducted thousands of twin studies. It's time to look at what they have found.

II

The Ubiquity of Heritability and the Small Role of the Shared Environment

Proposition #8: The shared environment usually plays a minor role in explaining personality, abilities, and social behavior.

This chapter has two purposes. The first is to establish that all cognitive repertoires are heritable to some degree and that the ones most likely to affect success are substantially heritable. You are free to apply your own definition of *substantial* to the many numbers I present. My own interpretation is that substantially heritable doesn't have to mean more than half but it should be at least a third. My second purpose is to ask you to think about environmental factors from a new perspective. The conventional perspective is that the way parents raise a child makes a big difference for all sorts of important qualities. Send children to really good schools, and it will make a big difference in how well they perform intellectually. The right kind of parenting can foster self-discipline and grit, or, for parents with different priorities, foster their children's creativity and free-spiritedness. Proposition #8 says "Not really." The environment in which a child grows up usually makes a difference, but seldom because of the things that parents can control.

The Unexpected Story of the Shared Environment

In the decades since the ACE model was developed, thousands of twin studies have been published. As early as 2000, the pattern of results had been so consistent and so striking that behavior geneticist Eric Turkheimer was led to set out the three laws of behavior genetics:

- *First Law.* All human behavioral traits are heritable.
- *Second Law.* The effect of being raised in the same family is smaller than the effect of genes.
- *Third Law.* A substantial portion of the variation in complex human behavioral traits is not accounted for by the effects of genes or families.[1]

In the two decades since Turkheimer stated them, no one who accepts the validity of twin studies has found reason to dispute them.

Turkheimer's first law is the least interesting of the three. How many people are really surprised to learn that all human traits are heritable to some degree? How can anyone who has been a parent be surprised?[2] The second law is the most provocative. Turkheimer stated it circumspectly, but the typical finding is starker than his wording indicates. It's not just that the role of the shared environment is less than that of genes; that role is usually small, especially with regard to the child's eventual cognitive repertoires as an adult.

This story has been known in broad outline within the behavior genetics community since the 1980s. It was first exposed to a general audience in 1998 when Judith Harris published *The Nurture Assumption*.[3] It got wider attention in 2002 when Steven Pinker recounted it in his bestseller *The Blank Slate*.[4] It has subsequently been referenced in many magazine and book-length discussions of parenting.[5]

At first glance, the claim that parental socialization doesn't make much difference is counterintuitive. The family environment, including socioeconomic status (SES), must surely have a major influence on children's outcomes. That's why psychologists John Loehlin and Robert Nichols of the University of Texas were bemused by the data on 850 twin pairs that they analyzed in the early 1970s. They unveiled their unexpected finding in a book titled *Heredity, Environment, and Personality*, published in 1976.

> Thus, a consistent—though perplexing—pattern is emerging from the data (and it is not purely idiosyncratic to our study). Environment carries substantial weight in determining personality—it appears to account for at least half the variance—but that environment is one for which twin pairs are correlated close to zero....In short, in the personality domain we seem to see environmental effects that operate almost randomly with

respect to the sorts of variables that psychologists (and other people) have traditionally deemed important in personality development.[6]

In 1981, psychologists David Rowe and Robert Plomin named this mysterious source of variation the *nonshared environment*, introduced in chapter 10.[7] A year later, psychologists Sandra Scarr and Susan Grajek put the expanding evidence into language no one could fail to understand:

> Lest the reader slip over these results, let us make explicit the implications of these findings: Upper-middle-class brothers who attend the same school and whose parents take them to the same plays, sporting events, music lessons, and therapists, and use similar child rearing practices on them are little more similar in personality measures than they are to working class or farm boys whose lives are totally different. Now, perhaps this is an exaggeration of the known facts, but not by much.[8]

The findings that Scarr and Grajek described in 1982 have subsequently been confirmed and reconfirmed. The establishment of the truth—for truth it seems to be—that the childhood family environment explains little about the cognitive repertoires of the adult is one of the more important achievements of the social sciences in the last four decades.[9] Do not understand this truth too quickly, however. Three clarifications need to be kept in mind.

First, *I am using the word "explain" in its statistical sense, not an explicitly causal sense.* Proposition #8 says that even though you may think that your parenting style and your family's resources make a big difference in how your children turn out as human beings, using a straightforward model for identifying that effect fails to turn up evidence for it.

Second, *parents can make a negative difference at the extremes.* Really awful parenting, involving severe deprivation and abuse, can damage children permanently.[10] To raise children in really awful neighborhoods, where gangs run the streets and the schools are dangerous and chaotic, increases the chances that your children will be snared in peer groups (part of the nonshared environment) that damage their life chances.[11] Proposition #8 should be understood to refer to parenting and neighborhoods within a broad range but excluding the worst of the worst.

Third, *the limited role of the family environment does not apply to life outcomes that can be directly determined by money.* It applies only to cognitive repertoires. If you are wealthy you can give your children wealth, regardless of their personalities, abilities, or social behaviors. Your socioeconomic class has a causal role in determining your children's material standard of living, but you cannot use your socioeconomic status to make your children more than trivially "better" than they would have been otherwise, whether "better" is defined in terms of personality, abilities, or social behavior.

Can you use your money to make your children professionally more successful than they would otherwise have been? It depends on the profession. The arena in which family wealth can clearly make a huge difference is politics, because wealth can influence nominating committees and finance campaigns, and the powers associated with a political office automatically go to the winner of enough votes, regardless of talent or character. If the parents own the corporation, they can bequeath the power of ownership to the next generation (e.g, the Murdochs, Sulzbergers, and Kochs). Parental wealth and influence can help a child get the appropriate degree and help obtain the first job. It's not so easy for parental influence to get the child promoted. The more competitive the industry and the more cognitively demanding the job, the less influence family wealth has.

The Polderman Meta-Analysis of Twin Studies

The generality of Proposition #8 is most economically established with a single source, a meta-analysis of twin studies published in 2015. The study was conducted by a team of seven Dutch, Australian, and American scholars. It was conceived and led by Danielle Posthuma, head of the Department of Complex Trait Genetics at Vrije Universiteit in Amsterdam. First author was Tinca J. C. Polderman.[12] It was a mammoth undertaking, effectively covering all twin studies from 1958 to 2012. The article reporting the results, "Meta-analysis of the Heritability of Human Traits Based on Fifty Years of Twin Studies," involved 2,748 publications and 14,558,903 twin pairs that explored 17,804 traits.

The authors found that the ACE model, which is limited to additive genetic variance, is usually appropriate. If the difference in the correlations between MZ and DZ twins is solely due to additive genetic variance, then the null hypothesis is that $2r_{DZ} = r_{MZ}$. The authors reported that the "observed pattern of twin correlations is consistent with a simple and parsimonious underlying model of the absence of environmental effects shared by twin pairs and the presence of genetic effects that are entirely due to additive genetic variation."[13]

In instances when the ACE model produced an estimate of the shared environment less than zero ($2r_{DZ} - r_{MZ} < 0$), the model that had to be substituted leads to an *under*estimation of h^2, as explained in the note.[14]

The table below shows the traits that fall into the three categories of cognitive repertoires that I have used throughout the book: characteristics of personality, abilities, and social behavior. I ordered the traits in each category from low to high in the shared environment's estimated role.

TRAITS DIRECTLY RELATED TO COGNITIVE REPERTOIRES

	Shared environment	Nonshared environment	Genes
Personality			
Specific personality disorders	1%	56%	44%
Temperament and personality functions	5%	44%	44%
Emotionally unstable personality	19%	46%	35%
Abilities			
Energy and drive functions	0%	43%	57%
Experience of self and time functions	0%	44%	56%
Psychomotor functions	1%	69%	30%
Attention functions	2%	55%	44%
Memory functions	3%	52%	45%
Calculation functions	13%	32%	56%
Higher-level cognitive functions	18%	27%	55%
Language functions	22%	32%	46%
Mild mental retardation	22%	45%	33%
Social behavior			
Work and employment	0%	63%	37%
Intimate relationships	0%	65%	35%
Attention functions	2%	55%	44%
Family relationships	6%	66%	28%
Informal social relationships	10%	59%	32%
Global psychosocial functions	11%	41%	48%
Societal attitudes	12%	50%	37%
Looking after one's health	13%	43%	44%
Conduct disorders	14%	38%	48%
Disorders due to tobacco use	17%	29%	54%

	Shared environment	Nonshared environment	Genes
Recreation and leisure	18%	27%	55%
Disorders due to alcohol use	19%	38%	44%
Religion and spirituality	21%	43%	36%
Disorders due to cannabinoid use	22%	25%	54%
Educational attainment	25%	26%	50%
Disorders due to multiple drug use	26%	29%	46%
Problems related to upbringing	34%	40%	27%
Basic interpersonal interactions	36%	34%	30%

Source: Polderman, Benyamin, de Leeuw et al. (2015): Supplementary Table 21. Statistics are reported for the "best" model.

In interpreting the numbers, remember that the estimates for heritability are biased downward by about 10 percent for reasons described in the note to the table. Also, only a few of the categories discriminate by age. Thus, for example, the role of the shared environment for "higher-level cognitive functions" is 18 percent—an estimate that is too low if we are thinking about early childhood, too high if we are thinking about adults.

Of the 30 traits in the table, 11 have shared-environment roles of less than 10 percent, 11 have roles of 10–19 percent, 6 have roles of 20–26 percent, and 2 have more than 30 percent. The shared environment had its highest estimated values, 36 percent and 34 percent, for "basic personal interactions" and "problems related to upbringing." (Yes, these data seem to say, you can have some effect on your kids' manners and you can also cause problems.) The 11 traits with a role for the shared environment of less than 10 percent include specific personality disorders, temperament and personality functions, work and employment, intimate relationships, and family relationships.

The next table shows traits that involve serious psychological problems, all of which affect cognitive repertoires in one way or another.

PSYCHOLOGICAL DISORDERS

	Shared environment	Nonshared environment	Genes
Anxiety and depression			
Depressive episode	4%	58%	39%
Recurrent depressive disorder	4%	44%	52%
Other anxiety disorders	9%	49%	42%

	Shared environment	Nonshared environment	Genes
Phobic anxiety disorders	10%	45%	45%
Psychological disorders associated with childhood and adolescence			
Eating disorders	2%	60%	38%
Hyperkinetic disorders	5%	27%	68%
Pre-adult emotional and behavioral disorders	7%	29%	64%
Emotional disorders with onset in childhood	20%	37%	43%
Other psychological disorders			
Stress and adjustment disorders	0%	67%	33%
Nonorganic sleep disorders	0%	55%	45%
Other adult personality and behavior disorders	0%	60%	41%
Obsessive-compulsive disorders	6%	48%	46%
Mood disorders	6%	32%	63%
Pervasive developmental disorders	7%	23%	70%
Bipolar disorder	14%	19%	68%

Source: Polderman, Benyamin, de Leeuw et al. (2015): Supplementary Table 21. Statistics are reported for the "best" model.

Of the 15 traits in the table, only 2 have a role for the shared environment exceeding 10 percent: bipolar disorder (14 percent) and emotional disorders with onset specific to childhood (20 percent). The role of the shared environment for 12 of the 15 is less than 10 percent.

Can parents drive children to distraction? No doubt about it; just as children routinely drive parents to distraction. But when it comes to severe mental disorders, the parents' genes are important while their parenting, by and large, is not.

Before leaving the estimates of heritability, I need to add more detail about two of the most important cognitive repertoires, the general mental factor g and personality characteristics.

The General Mental Factor g

The heritability of IQ scores (the best measures of g) was contested from the 1960s through the 1990s, but the data-driven arguments had subsided even by the time Herrnstein and I published *The Bell Curve* in 1994. At that time, we used a wide range for characterizing heritability, saying that it was somewhere between 40 percent and 80 percent. Since then, the state of knowledge has advanced. Here are two findings for which there was some evidence before the publication of *The Bell Curve* and that have been solidly established since then:

- The shared environment plays a large role in determining IQ during the first few years of life, diminishing thereafter.
- By the time people reach adolescence, almost all studies have found that the shared environment has a negligible relationship to IQ.

Both findings are best documented in a review of the literature by Elliot Tucker-Drob and his colleagues at the University of Texas. The graph below summarizes their results.

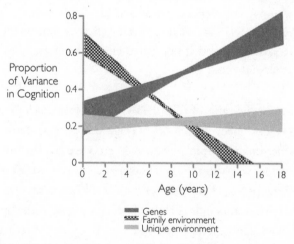

Source: Adapted from Tucker-Drob, Briley, and Harden (2013): Fig. 1. Shaded areas bound ± 1 standard error.

The graph combines the results of publications reporting on 11 different longitudinal twin and adoptions studies. In infancy and the first few years of life, the shared environment explains a large proportion of the variance in scores—around two-thirds. By seven years of age, that figure has dropped to about one-third. By 14, it is zero.

There is more to be said about the relative roles of heritability and the shared environment early in life, but I defer that discussion to chapter 13. For now, I confine myself to the story for IQ in adulthood. After about age 14, there is no evidence from twin and adoption studies that their shared environment as children had anything to do with their IQ scores.

Personality Characteristics

No matter whether researchers use the Big Five or one of the other personality models, the answer to the question "How much effect does the shared environment have on the way that human personalities develop?" is the same: Effectively none.

In 1987, six years after Plomin and David Rowe had named the nonshared environment, Plomin wrote the authoritative review of the state of knowledge at the time. This was his summary with regard to personality:

> In a review of 10 recent twin studies of personality, the average twin correlations were .47 for identical twins and .23 for fraternal twins. This pattern of twin correlations suggests that heredity accounts for 50% of the phenotypic variance and that nonshared environment and error of measurement explain the rest.[15]

In other words, the value of C in the ACE model was zero. "It might seem odd," Plomin continued, "to report average correlations across a domain as diverse as personality." But, he added, there were hardly any exceptions. Whether the topic was a Big Five characteristic such as extraversion or neuroticism or more specific characteristics such as tolerance, sense of well-being, or alienation, twin studies of heritability kept coming up with correlations for MZ twins that were more than twice the correlations for DZ twins, leaving no role for the shared environment.[16] He further noted that studies of non-twin siblings and adoption studies were consistent with those of the twin studies.[17]

In 2014, Turkheimer, with coauthors Erik Pettersson and Erin Horn, published a long article in the *Annual Review of Psychology* that reviewed the history of the study of personality. It's worth quoting in full his summary of the role of the shared environment:

> The Second Law of Behavior Genetics, which states that the shared environmental component of human individual differences is small, is usually true for most traits, but the situation is somewhat starker for personality. It is remarkable, in surveying the genetically informed personality literature

in a very wide context, how completely absent the shared environment is. In fact, it is often the case that identical twins are more than twice as similar as fraternal twins, a violation of the classical twin model that, if uncorrected, produces negative estimates for shared environmental variance.[18]

Before leaving the topic of personality, a reminder is important. The shared environment includes the influences that fall under the headings of both SES and parenting. With regard to parenting, the salient finding is not that parents have no influence on their children, but that whatever influence they have is probably part of the nonshared environment. Plomin put it nicely: "From Freud onwards, theories of socialization had assumed that children's environments are doled out on a family-by-family basis. In contrast, the point of nonshared environment is that environments are doled out on a child-by-child basis."[19]

Recapitulation

The literature on shared environment, nonshared environment, and heritability tells us that a family's SES (income, parental education and occupation) is unimportant in explaining the cognitive abilities and personality traits that parents try hardest to promote. It is a counterintuitive finding. It is an unwelcome finding for parents. But it is based on a technically strong, thoroughly replicated body of evidence.

We cannot jump from this evidence to the conclusion that SES is unimportant for explaining outcomes *across* families. Half a century ago, in a landmark book titled *Inequality*, Christopher Jencks used an example of fallacious reasoning about genes and environment that became iconic: Suppose that red-haired children are arbitrarily denied access to schooling. Their performance on academic tests suffers. Hair color is genetic. A correlation will be found between genetics and test scores, but the relationship is not causal. The causal effect of red hair is the denial of schooling, which in turn is the true cause of worse test scores.[20] For assessing the relationship of SES and heritable traits, we need to turn to other bodies of evidence, the subject of the next chapter.

12

Abilities, Personality, and Success

Proposition #9: Class structure is importantly based on differences in abilities that have a substantial genetic component.

It is time to confront the question directly: To what extent is professional and economic success in life a function of characteristics that have a substantial genetic component? Proposition #9 extrapolates from a famous syllogism that Richard Herrnstein published in 1973:

1. If differences in mental abilities are inherited, and
2. If success requires those abilities, and
3. If earnings and prestige depend upon success,
4. Then social standing (which reflects earnings and prestige) will be based to some extent on inherited differences among people.[1]

The goal of this chapter is to present the case that Herrnstein's syllogism is borne out by the evidence and warrants a somewhat stronger statement when it comes to the role of genes in shaping class structure. If individual success is based even modestly on heritable traits, the aggregate effect on a society's class structure will be important, as I cautiously characterize it in Proposition #9. "Profound" is probably more accurate.

This goal should not obscure a larger truth. I'll say it briefly but italicize it: *The bulk of the variance in success in life is unexplained by either nature or nurture.* Researchers are lucky if they explain half of the variance in educational attainment with measures of abilities and socioeconomic background. They're lucky if they can explain even a quarter of the variance in earned income with such measures. The takeaway for thinking about our futures as individuals is that we do not live in a deterministic world ruled by either genes or social background, let alone by race or gender. But Proposition #9 is about social classes, not individuals. The takeaway for thinking about the future of modern Western societies is that the role of genes is important for shaping class structure.

Heritable Traits and Success: The Primacy of *g*

The most important single heritable trait that explains socioeconomic success is the general mental ability known as *g*, which in turn is best measured by a good IQ test.[2] It is not only the most important, but typically far more important than any other single heritable trait. On the other side of the picture, I will be showing you some evidence that all other heritable traits have combined effects that are quite substantial—in some circumstances and for some measures of success as important in combination as IQ.

Preliminaries

Many of the things that may concern you about IQ tests are not true. For a recent accessible and accurate summary of the state of knowledge about IQ, I recommend Stuart Ritchie's *Intelligence: All That Matters*, a sprightly book that's only 160 pages long.[3] But here are some of the main points that you need to know, along with additional documentation.

IQ tests are not biased against minorities.[4] Education does raise IQ, but within a narrow range (you can't become a genius by staying in school long enough).[5] IQ scores are usually stable, though not perfectly so, after around age six, when the first reliable measures become available, until decline in old age.[6] IQ meets higher standards of reliability and validity in measuring the construct it is intended to measure than any psychological measure of personality or temperament.[7]

All of these statements have abundant, replicated evidence behind them and are not subjects of controversy among specialists. This still leaves a list of "But what about…" questions that people raise about IQ. This is not the place to deal with all of them, but two misapprehensions are so widespread that I must at least briefly deal with them here.

"IQ tests just measure how well you perform on IQ tests." The proper description of what *g* means for daily life goes far beyond performing well on tests. Sociologist Linda Gottfredson's description is the best I've found:

> Intelligence is a very general mental capability that, among other things, involves the ability to reason, plan, solve problems, think abstractly, comprehend complex ideas, learn quickly and learn from experience. It is not merely book learning, a narrow academic skill, or test-taking smarts. Rather, it reflects a broader and deeper capability for comprehending our surroundings—"catching on," "making sense" of things, or "figuring out" what to do.[8]

To put it another way, life is an IQ test.[9] Compared to people with low IQs, people who have high IQs are more likely to see that the tempting short-term payoff will be costly in the long term. They are more likely to eat healthy foods, refrain from smoking, and exercise regularly.[10] They have fewer accidents.[11] More broadly, think of everyday life as a multitude of decisions. For some of those decisions, there's no objectively right or wrong choice; everything depends on personal priorities. That's why some people take up wingsuit gliding despite the mortality statistics—for them, the reward is worth the risk. But many everyday decisions have an option that has an objectively higher probability of producing an outcome that the individual does *not* want. For those thousands of decisions over the course of a year, *g* is useful in reducing the number of mistakes.[12] The general mental factor *g* helps people navigate the caprices and complications of everyday life.[13]

---

g HAS NOTHING TO DO WITH MERIT

I deliberately avoid the word *meritocracy* to describe a society in which able people rise to the top, because the most important single ingredient, g, is a matter of luck. I'm willing to believe that people have some control over their industriousness, perseverance, resilience, and other personal qualities that have brought them success, even though those qualities are partly heritable. g is different. People can make a little or a lot of what they were given; maybe they can even tweak their IQs by a couple of points; but no one gets an IQ score of 130 by trying hard. Merit had nothing to do with it.

"The most successful people I know aren't the ones with the highest IQs." Two separate issues are commonly confused.

First, the image of the intellectual genius who is a social klutz is over-blown. It happens—some people who have extremely high IQs have poor social skills and can be successful only in certain occupations (some genius programmers come to mind). Some people with high IQs seem to have oddly little common sense. They are exceptions, however. The qualities besides IQ that contribute to success tend to be correlated with IQ, and those correlations apply across the full range of IQ.

Second, there's a good reason why people say, "The most successful people I know aren't the ones with the highest IQs." They're probably right. The reason they're right is what statisticians call *restriction of range* or *truncation of range*. Few people these days live their lives in close daily contact with people who have a wide range of IQs. Instead, people mostly hang out with others who are in their own IQ ballpark and are thereby victimized by the illusion created by restriction of range.

More than 30 years ago, sociologist Steven Goldberg told me an analogy for explaining it that I have been borrowing ever since: IQ has the same role for explaining success in many professions as weight has in explaining the success of offensive linemen in the NFL. The best offensive linemen in the NFL are not necessarily the heaviest. The correlation between weight and productivity for all the offensive linemen on the rosters of NFL teams is probably near zero. But you can't get the job unless you weigh at least 300 pounds.[14] Similarly, CEOs of Fortune 500 companies, senior partners in Park Avenue firms, and tenured professors at Harvard may not be the ones with the highest IQs among the potential occupants for such jobs. They distinguished themselves from the others just as smart or smarter through other personal assets. But restriction of range means that you are seeing what role those other personal assets play when everyone figuratively weighs 300 pounds to begin with.

The First Order Effects of g in Producing Success

Having a high level of *g* is a general resource for getting an advanced education and being productive on the job—two of the most elemental building blocks of success.

Educational attainment. Over the last century, the gateway to economic success has increasingly been defined by education, and the ability to take advantage of education is g's most obvious asset. In 2007, sociologist Tarmo Strenze published a meta-analysis of 65 samples with information on IQ and educational attainment. IQ's correlation with eventual educational attainment for persons who had been tested at ages 16–18, before the end of compulsory education, was +.58.[15]

The relationship between IQ and academic success is about as strong for graduate school as for college. A 2010 meta-analysis of the literature on such tests found a correlation between the SAT and first-year college GPA of +.51 and a correlation with cumulative GPAs for the entire college career of +.53. The correlations between scores on various graduate school admissions tests and subsequent graduate school GPAs ranged between +.35 and +.46. The correlation between the Law School Admission Test and scores on bar exams was +.46. The mean correlation of the Medical College Admission Test and scores on medical licensing exams was +.64.[16]

Job productivity. One of the most common assertions about IQ is that it doesn't predict performance in the real world of work. The truth is the opposite. It's not just that IQ predicts job performance for people with cognitively demanding jobs; IQ predicts job performance to some degree for people across the entire range of jobs. People who are responsible for new hires at a workplace should know that an IQ score is a better predictor of job performance than a résumé, evaluation through a job interview, assessment centers, or work samples. The note has details.[17] How important are the effects of IQ? Taking all jobs together, the predictive validity of IQ scores for overall job performance is about +.50 (it's higher than that for high-complexity jobs). You can square that figure and point out that IQ explains only 25 percent of the variance in job performance. If you're an employer, however, and are told that a standard deviation increase in IQ is associated with half a standard deviation increase in overall job performance, a predictive validity of +.50 is a big deal.[18]

Since we live in an age when the social sciences are suffering from a replication crisis, I emphasize again that the generalizations I have made about the relationships of g to educational attainment and job productivity are drawn from hundreds of studies.

Psychometric g *Versus Other Personal Traits*

The popular suspicion of IQ's relationship to success has been tenacious, but for an understandable reason. Anyone who has reached adulthood is aware of all the things besides intelligence that matter in achieving success. The most obvious is simple hard work. In any job setting with more than a few employees, we observe that some people work long hours and others do as little as possible. But other traits also matter. Some people are resilient while others give up when things go badly. Some people have a knack for leading people and others do not. Some people are a pleasure to work with and others are abrasive and off-putting. Industriousness, resilience, charisma, cooperativeness, and many other traits are objectively valuable for productivity in most kinds of jobs and rightly affect supervisors' decisions about who gets ahead.

Since we know these other qualities are so important in everyday life, it seems that good measures of them should explain at least as much about success as an IQ score. People have in fact invested a great deal of effort in coming up with such measures. The ones that have gotten the most public attention are Howard Gardner's "multiple intelligences" and two constellations of qualities that have been labeled "emotional intelligence" and "grit." All three talk about qualities other than *g* that are important to success. I recommend Howard Gardner's *Frames of Mind: The Theory of Multiple Intelligences* (1983), Daniel Goleman's *Emotional Intelligence: Why It Can Matter More Than IQ* (1995), and Angela Duckworth's more recent *Grit: The Power of Passion and Perseverance* (2016) for nontechnical accounts of qualities that aren't directly measured by IQ tests and that are unequivocally important.

The technical validation of these three approaches is another matter. There's a big difference between persuasively arguing that something is important to success and providing a measure of that "something" that is reliable, valid, and not already captured by other measures. Tests of emotional intelligence or grit need to explain variance that measures of IQ and personality traits don't explain. That task has proved to be daunting. Multiple intelligences, emotional intelligence, grit, and other ideas about the causes of success were introduced into a world that already had measures of *g* and personality traits that have passed repeated tests of reliability and construct validity. The new kids on the block have had a hard time demonstrating that they could explain additional variance.[19]

Progress has been made in understanding the role of traits other than IQ, however.[20] A technical literature documents the importance of self-control for success in life independently of IQ.[21] A related concept, locus of control (how much people believe they are in control of what happens to them), has an independent role in explaining both financial success and financial hardship.[22] When it comes to academic performance, simple self-confidence in one's own ability was found to explain variance in academic achievement in mathematics and English (but not in science) even after controlling for IQ.[23] Others have documented an independent role for the importance of intellectual interest and curiosity.[24]

But the most extensive technical literature involves the Big Five personality factors—emotional stability, extraversion, conscientiousness, openness, and agreeableness—so much that a 2014 meta-analysis of the relationship of personality to academic performance by psychologist Arthur Poropat had two dozen samples to work with. Conscientiousness consistently played the most important role, with openness in second place. Poropat reported effect sizes for them of +1.14 and +0.96 respectively, far larger than those for agreeableness (+0.19), emotional stability (+0.36), or extraversion (+0.23).[25] In addition to its value for academic performance, conscientiousness has also been found to predict job performance, salary, promotion,[26] and occupational prestige.[27] These findings make sense. The facets for measuring conscientiousness—competence, orderliness, dutifulness, industriousness, self-discipline, and deliberateness—come close to describing the ideal candidate for many kinds of jobs that require solid day-by-day performance rather than flights of creativity.[28] Other studies have found that emotional stability, openness, and agreeableness have independent associations with similar outcomes that contribute to success. But while such effects have been found, they are quite small compared to the role of *g*.

The effect sizes in the Poropat meta-analysis do not control for IQ—an important omission. I have found three major studies that have analyzed the role of personality in the presence of a good measure of childhood IQ.[29] One (first author was Rodica Damian) is based on 81,075 persons from Project Talent, a subsample of a nationally representative American sample tested in high school in 1961 who were followed up at ages 28–30. Another (first author was Roger Staff) is based on a subset of 443 persons drawn from the Aberdeen Birth Cohort of 1936 who were followed up at age 64. The third study, by Helen Cheng and Adrian Furnham, is based on 4,808 persons from the British National Child Development Study of 1958 who were followed up at age 50. The following table shows what happened when IQ, parental

SES, and the Big Five personality traits were entered together in analyses of adult educational attainment and occupational prestige.

COMPARATIVE ROLES OF IQ AND PERSONALITY TRAITS IN MEASURES OF ADULT OUTCOMES

	Project Talent		Aberdeen Birth Cohort		British NCDP	
	Educational attainment	Occupational prestige	Adult reading	Adult SES	Educational attainment	Occupational prestige
Childhood IQ	**+0.41**	**+0.39**	**+0.65**	**+0.52**	**+0.35**	**+0.14**
Extraversion	+0.08	+0.09	−0.05	+0.07	−0.02	+0.07
Agreeableness	+0.07	+0.08	+0.02	+0.05	0.00	0.00
Conscientiousness	+0.09	+0.09	+0.01	+0.07	0.00	+0.05
Emotional stability	+0.05	+0.05	+0.04	+0.14	+0.03	+0.01
Openness	+0.09	+0.09	+0.15	+0.18	+0.16	+0.05

Sources: Damian, Su, Shanahan et al. (2014): Tables 3, 6; Staff, Hogan, and Whalley (2017): Table 2; Cheng and Furnham (2012): Fig. 2.

You can't compare the size of the effects across the rows in the table. The metrics are all related to standard deviations, but they are too different to make the numbers comparable.[30] Rather, you should scan down the columns. None of the Big Five personality factors has nearly the independent role that childhood IQ has. In fact, even these modest effects are exaggerated, because the results for any one factor control only for childhood IQ, not for the other four personality factors (that is, the multivariate model was run five times, once for each model, not once with all five factors entered as independent variables). The message of the information in the table is not that other personal traits besides *g* are irrelevant after all. But each individual trait plays a subordinate role.

Two ambitious attempts to measure the combined roles of a wide variety of "heritable traits besides IQ" indicates that those other traits do play the significant role in combination that intuition says they should.

The first was produced by an 11-person team of psychologists, mostly from England, using 6,653 sets of twins in the UK Twins Early Development Study (TEDS). The first author was Eva Krapohl.

The dependent variable was the participants' scores on the national examination administered at the end of compulsory education in the UK at age 16. It is known as the GCSE (General Certificates of Secondary Education). The independent variables involving heritable traits were IQ and eight other domains represented by composite scores: personality (including the Big Five and grit), self-efficacy, well-being (e.g., happiness, hopefulness), parent-reported behavioral problems, and child-reported behavioral problems, plus noncognitive scales for health, school environment, and home environment.

In one sense, the Krapohl study is another example of the dominance of IQ. Unlike the studies reported in the table above, the authors did conduct an analysis that entered all nine of the domains in a single model. IQ alone explained 34 percent of the phenotypic variance while the other eight combined explained 28 percent.[31]

What were the independent roles of the other eight? The published tables do not answer that question directly. Twenty-eight percent divided by eight indicates that most of the other roles must have been trivially small. Collateral evidence makes it clear that the measure of self-efficacy was substantially more important than any of the others, followed by the composite measure of personality.[32] As an estimate, IQ had an independent role of about three and a half times that of self-efficacy and more than six times the independent role of personality, the school environment, or parent-reported behavior problems.[33] IQ was much more important than self-efficacy in explaining phenotypic variance, several times more important than personality, the school environment, or parent-reported behavior problems. The independent roles of the home environment, well-being, health, and child-reported behavior problems were virtually zero.

The second study was conducted by a team of psychologists at the University of Texas using a sample of 811 school-age twins from the Texas Twin Project. First author was Elliot Tucker-Drob. The analysis combined several measures of cognitive ability, the Big Five personality factors, and seven character traits that have featured prominently in recent years: grit, intellectual curiosity, intellectual self-concept, mastery orientation, educational value, intelligence mindset, and test motivation.

The seven character traits all loaded on a general character factor that seems to be closely related to intellectual curiosity. The correlation of the general character factor to a combined measure of knowledge and academic achievement (Ach) was +.47. With regard to the Big Five personality factors, openness was as strongly correlated with Ach (r = +.48) but, surprisingly to me, conscientiousness was not (r = +.16).[34] The general character factor contributed a lot to the measure of Ach, but not as much as the measure of fluid intelligence. The same was true of openness.[35]

Which Comes First? Test Scores or SES?

How does the combined influence of heritable ability and personality traits stack up against the influence of the socioeconomic circumstances into which a child is born?

Before turning to the results, I need to point out that any measure of parental SES is not only a measure of the child's environment; it is also partially a measure of the parents' talents (or lack of them) that produced the SES, which in turn are heritable—in the case of IQ and personality, substantially heritable. It is amazing how seldom the authors of technical articles that purport to assess the relative roles of IQ and parental SES in producing adult outcomes mention this large and inescapable confound. Having mentioned it here, I ignore it in the discussion of the following studies, because none of them provides a way to estimate the degree of confounding between IQ and parental SES. I return to the issue with some studies that do provide such estimates in chapter 12.

Performance in College

In the United States, the poster child for the indictment of tests is the relationship between parental SES and performance on college admissions tests such as the SAT: The higher the parental education and income, the higher the scores of the children. How much of this relationship is causal? How much of it is a reflection of the uncomfortable possibility that smart parents attain high SES and also produce smart children?

The exhaustive analysis of this question, presented alongside a comprehensive review of prior studies, was published in 2009 in the *Psychological Bulletin* by a team of psychologists at the University of Minnesota (first author was Paul Sackett). The authors presented results for a meta-analysis of College Board data, a meta-analysis of other studies using a composite measure of parental SES, and a reanalysis of major longitudinal datasets. A table summarizing the results is given in the note.[36] Boiling it down:

- *After controlling for the admissions test score*, the correlation of parental SES and college grades dropped from +.22 to −.01 in the SAT meta-analysis, from .09 to .00 in the meta-analysis of studies with composite SES measures, and from a mean of .06 to .01 among the longitudinal studies.
- *After controlling for the measure of SES*, the correlation between admission test score and grades was reduced only fractionally: from +.53 to +.50 in the SAT meta-analysis, from +.37 to +.36 in the meta-analysis of studies with composite SES measures, and from a mean of +.313 to +.308 among the longitudinal studies.

For practical purposes, parental SES explained nothing about the student's college grades after adjusting for test scores.

Educational Attainment, Income, and Occupation

Quantitative explorations of the comparative roles of IQ and parental SES in producing economic success began with a pair of books in the 1970s for which sociologist Christopher Jencks was the principal investigator and first author: *Inequality*, published in 1972, and *Who Gets Ahead*, published in 1979.[37] The results of subsequent studies have not been consistent in their estimates of the magnitudes of the independent effects of IQ and parental SES, but they have all found such effects.

The following table shows six databases with good pedigrees. Three of them—the Aberdeen Birth Cohort, the National Child Development Study, and Project Talent—were part of the preceding table on IQ and personality factors. The other three are a sample drawn from the Scottish Mental Survey of 1932 (first author was Ian Deary) who were followed up at ages 38–41, and the 1979 and 1997 cohorts of the Longitudinal Survey of Youth project mentioned in the introduction to Part III.[38] They show results over a broad period, from the 1970s up to the present. The members of the earliest cohort reached age 40 in 1972; the oldest members of the most recent cohort are just turning 40 in 2020.

COMPARATIVE ROLES OF IQ AND CHILDHOOD
SES IN ADULT OUTCOMES

	Birth year	Age at follow-up	Childhood IQ	Childhood SES
Scottish Mental Survey of 1932	1932	38–41		
Educational attainment			+0.20	+0.33
Adult social class			+0.53	+0.40
Aberdeen Birth Cohort of 1936	1936	64		
Adult reading test			+0.65	+0.10
Adult SES			+0.52	+0.34
Nat'l Child Development Study (UK)	1958	50		
Educational attainment			+0.40	+0.30
Occupational prestige			+0.28	+0.16
Project Talent (USA)	1933–36	28		
Educational attainment			+0.41	+0.25
Adult income			+0.08	+0.09
Occupational prestige			+0.39	+0.18
NLSY, 1979 Cohort (USA)	1957–64	42–49		
Educational attainment			+0.52	+0.16
Adult income			+0.30	+0.08
NLSY, 1997 Cohort (USA)	1980–84	31–35		
Educational attainment			+0.46	+0.22
Adult income			+0.21	+0.13

Sources: Deary, Taylor, Hart et al. (2005): Fig. 3; Staff, Hogan, and Whalley (2017): Table 3; Cheng and Furnham (2012): Fig. 2; Damian, Su, Shanahan et al. (2014): Tables 3, 5, and 6; and author's analysis, NLSY79 and NLSY97.[39]

All of the metrics represent some form of standardized regression coefficient, but once again there are too many differences across the studies to compare them. Rather, focus on the relative sizes of the coefficients for childhood IQ and childhood SES. The generalizations to be drawn are that all but two of the coefficients for childhood IQ are larger than the coefficients for childhood SES and that in all but one case IQ has a greater effect on educational attainment than it does on adult income or occupation.[40]

Not much should be made of specific magnitudes with a sample of six, but, to get a sense of the table, the median ratio of the effects of childhood

IQ to those of childhood SES was 1.75. And of course, the putative effects of childhood SES were inescapably partly genetic, as I noted earlier.

Recapitulation

Cognitive ability and personality strengths, both substantially heritable, are important to achieving success in life—educationally, in earnings, and in professional achievement. To that extent, class structure is, in the words of Proposition #9, importantly based on differences in abilities that have a substantial genetic component. The relationship between these abilities and success does not amount to genetic determinism for individuals. It is, however, strong enough to decisively shape the social structure of modern Western societies. Of the many abilities involved, the general mental factor g is usually dominant. Proposition #9 is something that we haven't had to argue about for decades, despite all the furor that has accompanied the idea that success is affected by genes. It's demonstrably true.

But it is understandable why that truth still raises hackles for so many people. It smacks of self-satisfaction with the way things are and indifference toward those who were unlucky in the genetic lottery. It is also understandable that scholars and policymakers alike have put a great deal of effort into attempts to use education and other measures to help the unlucky. How well have they succeeded? What are the constraints on helping? Those extremely sensitive issues are up next.

13

Constraints and Potentials

Proposition #10: Outside interventions are inherently constrained in the effects they can have on personality, abilities, and social behavior.

Outside interventions can change people profoundly. An inspiring teacher can fire the imagination of a bored adolescent and change the trajectory of that student's life. Friends who intervene in an alcoholic's life can change its trajectory. It happens all the time. But Proposition #10 is not about individual successes. Rather, Proposition #10 is about whether people can be changed by design in large numbers. That's a more ambitious objective, and it is made more ambitious yet by the material you have read in the preceding three chapters. Those findings lend themselves to another syllogism:

1. If the shared environment explains little of the variance in cognitive repertoires, and
2. If the only environmental factors that can be affected by outside interventions are part of the shared environment,
3. Then outside interventions are inherently constrained in the effects they can have on cognitive repertoires.

In other words, it is not within our power to do much to change personalities or abilities or social behaviors by design on a large scale. This chapter explores some ways in which the conclusion of the syllogism might be challenged:

- "The first premise is wrong for some important outcomes."
- "The first premise is wrong for the early stages of life."

- "The first premise is wrong when it comes to changing self-concept."
- "The second premise is wrong because some aspects of the nonshared environment can be affected by outside interventions."
- "But you're ignoring epigenetics!"

"The First Premise Is Wrong for Some Important Outcomes"

In the Polderman meta-analysis discussed in chapter 11, there were exceptions to the generalization that the role of the shared environment is trivially small. The shared environment explained 36 percent of the variance for basic personal interactions, 24 percent for problems related to upbringing, 26 percent for disorders due to multiple drug use, and 25 percent for educational attainment. If an outside intervention could remediate a high proportion of the shared environmental influences that cause problems in these areas, they would be meaningful accomplishments.

The Comparatively Minor Role of Outside Interventions

The question is whether that's a reasonable expectation. The things that fall into the shared and nonshared environment include all the effects of the family, school, and neighborhood exerted during a young person's waking hours. The usual kinds of outside intervention—counseling, tutoring, mentoring, after-school activities, job training—amount to a few hours per week. Even if the quality of those interventions is excellent (a difficult thing to achieve in itself), we're talking about a tiny fraction of a youth's waking hours. A teenager with a drug counselor might really like and listen to his counselor. But he walks out of his meeting with the counselor into the same shared home, school, and neighborhood environments that explain 26 percent of the variance in drug use. If the shared environment explained 90 percent of the variance, then maybe a few hours a week of an outside intervention might make some measurable difference. If the shared environment explains just 26 percent of the variance, the outside intervention has to be big—boarding school, for example, moving the family out of the neighborhood, or adoption into a new family. Ordinary levels of outside intervention are too small relative to the competing influences.

A similar logic applies to outside interventions that attempt to modify the behavior of parents. Consider the outcome with the largest role for the shared environment (36 percent), basic personal interactions. That number says that parents can legitimately think they've had a major role in raising sociable children. But if a 10-year-old is exhibiting problems with basic personal interactions, a program that tries to change the parents' parenting practices has arrived far too late. Even if the program is successful, the child is not going to turn on a dime just because his parents are behaving somewhat more positively and effectually than they did for the preceding 10 years. If outcomes that are primarily influenced by parenting are the problem, then solutions will have to begin as close to birth as possible.

I will get to the empirical track record of outside interventions later. Now, I'm drawing your attention to underlying realities that are too seldom made explicit. Outside interventions of normal magnitude and intensity make sense for an extremely limited set of problems that are analogous to health problems that can be cured by antibiotics or surgery.

Problems that fit those criteria are rare, but they exist. Here's an example: School systems in large urban areas are notorious for tolerating chaotic classrooms in a handful of schools in the most impoverished part of town. There's no excuse for it. Children who are eager to learn are prevented from doing so, with lifelong consequences, and yet an outside intervention can completely cure that problem in a day: Install strict rules of in-class conduct, and promptly and without exception eject disruptive students from the classroom. Teachers will be able to teach and the remaining students will be able to learn.

The difficulty, of course, is what to do with the students who have been ejected. Solving their problems is a matter of changing their personalities, abilities, or social behavior, or a combination of all three, and that's what the first premise of the syllogism says we don't know how to do.

The underlying point of my example is why the solution works: We know how to help people who already want to do something and are artificially prevented from doing it. My solution doesn't have to change the students who are already trying to learn. It just needs to provide them with an environment in which they are enabled to do what they already want to do. We are not constrained from helping with outside interventions. We're just constrained in whom we can help with what kinds of problems.

If instead we try to change people who aren't ready and able to change, given the opportunity, we're back to a situation in which powerful competing forces, acting through both genes and the nonshared environment, overwhelm the magnitude of the intervention that seeks to produce change. Expecting to see a major impact from outside interventions is usually unrealistic.

How Genes Shape Environment

Interventions intended to change the environment assume that if the environment changes as planned, then, other things being equal, outcomes will be positively affected. Suppose that parents use inconsistent discipline, for example, which is known to be associated with negative outcomes for children. It is assumed that if the parents can be taught to use a reasonable disciplinary style consistently, those negative outcomes will be reduced. But that's not the only way environmental effects work. They can also be mediated by the correlation (r) between the genotype (G) and the environment E, known in the trade as *rGE*. There are three types of rGE: passive, evocative, and active.

Passive rGE can be illustrated with the case of aggressive behavior in a child who was raised by a violent and abusive father. The child is likely to have gotten a double dose of bad luck: the environmental effects of the parental abuse, and a father with a genetic propensity for abusiveness, roughly half of which has also been passed down to the child.[1] *Evocative* rGE (sometimes called *reactive* rGE) occurs when the child's genetically influenced characteristics evoke a response from the environment (which includes other people). Consider the case of parents who use physical punishment on an aggressive child. It could be a case of evocative rGE, whereby parents are reacting to the child's violence by using physical punishment, which then only makes matters worse. *Active* rGE occurs when children shape their environments—for example, by choosing peer groups—for genetically influenced reasons. An adolescent boy who has a genetic propensity for aggression is likely to be attracted to violent teenage gangs and become a member. The environmental influences of the gang then reinforce, or even amplify, the boy's genetic propensity.

Now let's make the example more complicated. In chapter 12, I referenced the Krapohl study of a large sample of British twins. The objective was to identify the causes of the differences among scores that the participants achieved on the General Certificates of Secondary Education. You may recall that IQ explained more of the variance in GCSE scores than any of the other individual measures, but the other variables collectively explained about as much as IQ.[2] This would suggest that even if we don't know how to raise IQ, outside interventions can do a lot to boost students on the other contributions to school achievement. But the authors found that the proportion of the covariance of these other factors with academic achievement was extremely high. "To the extent that children's traits predict educational achievement, they do so largely for genetic reasons, for example, for personality (92%), behavior problems (81% for parent-rated, 89% for child-rated), intelligence (75%), self-efficacy (64%), and well-being (53%)."[3] The authors went on to observe:

> [T]hese results turn some fundamental assumptions about education upside down. For example, one of the reasons that the contribution of intelligence is sometimes considered controversial when discussing educational outcomes is that intelligence is viewed as genetic, whereas achievement is thought to be due to environmentally driven influences.... However, our results suggest the opposite: Genetic influence is greater for achievement than for intelligence, and other behavioral traits are related to educational achievement largely for genetic reasons.[4]

How does this affect the prospects for outside interventions? Correlations between the genotype and the environment lend themselves to two quite different interpretations.

One interpretation focuses on the ways in which genetic causes are mediated by parental behavior. Yes, bad parenting practices are partly driven by parental genes, but if it's the parenting practices that are proximally causal, an outside intervention could still have an effect if it could change the parenting practices.

The other interpretation focuses on the ways in which what we once thought was an environmental cause turns out to be a partly genetic one. When an outside intervention sets out to change bad parenting practices, the already difficult task of changing a person's behavior is fighting a genetic headwind. The behaviors that the intervention is trying to change aren't occurring just because of ignorance about good parenting, but also because of genetic predispositions.

We have a natural experiment that lets us see how these competing forces work out in practice—adoption at birth. Adoption studies routinely show that the correlation between biological children's IQ and the family's socioeconomic status is around twice the correlation between adoptive children's IQ and the adoptive family's socioeconomic status.[5] Can the benefits of competent parenting practices benefit the adopted child? Yes. But adoption is as good as it gets. In effect, adoption at birth to competent parents gives us a glimpse of what would happen if an outside intervention could magically be successful at changing a wide variety of parenting behaviors from bad to good. An outside intervention that makes modest improvements in a small proportion of parenting problems will have a far smaller effect.

"The First Premise Is Wrong for the Early Stages of Life"

Everything we know about human development says that humans are most malleable in the first years of life. The brain is still developing. Habits are not yet set in the child. Some parenting practices can be changed for the better and still have time to work their effects on the child. I fully share the view that if interventions are ever going to work, they're going to work in infancy and early childhood. But it's one thing to believe that; it's another to confront the empirical findings about the difficulties and constraints that have attended a half century of attempts to intervene early in life.

Heritability and Socioeconomic Status

Recall the figure in chapter 12 showing the role of the shared environment in IQ from childhood to adulthood. It hit zero in adolescence, but the shared environment explained more than half of the variance for the preschool years. That finding implies that the second premise of my syllogism doesn't necessarily apply to infants and young children.

The proposition that heritability of IQ is lower for disadvantaged children than for children from ordinary backgrounds was first advanced by psychologist Sandra Scarr in 1971, who found provisional evidence for it.[6] Subsequent studies in 1980 and 1999 provided stronger evidence, but the role of the shared environment remained small even for disadvantaged children.[7]

In 2003, Eric Turkheimer published dramatic evidence that the opportunities for intervening are not only higher at young ages, but that they are

ones that met the criteria for replications) conducted by psychologists Elliot Tucker-Drob and Timothy Bates in 2015 established one intriguing finding beyond doubt: The G×E effects in U.S. samples systematically differ from the effects in non-U.S. samples.[15] The authors conducted extensive tests for the robustness of this finding, all of which it passed. Their main conclusion is worth quoting in full:

> This meta-analysis of published and unpublished data provided clear answers to our three questions. First, studies from the United States supported a moderately sized Gene × SES interaction on intelligence and academic achievement. Second, in studies conducted outside the United States (in Western Europe and Australia), the best estimate for Gene × SES magnitude was very slightly negative and not significantly different from zero. Third, the difference in the estimated magnitude of the Gene × SES effect between the U.S. and the non-U.S. studies was itself significant.[16]

Why should the difference between the United States and the rest of the world be so marked? Tucker-Drob and Bates ran through the options: cross-national differences in the teaching of literacy and numeracy, educational quality, access to education and medical care, social mobility, and income support, each of which has been argued by sources they cite. But no one has done more than speculate about any of them. The note describes some differences in the samples that might also be relevant.[17]

The Empirical Record for Early Childhood Interventions

Few topics in social policy have received more intense empirical scrutiny than the effects of early childhood interventions. Unfortunately, few aspects of social policy have also been as intensely politicized. In 2013, a leading specialist in pre-K programs, economist Greg Duncan, and social policy scholar Katherine Magnuson published a comprehensive review of the evidence up to that time. The authors found these conclusions to be justified by the weight of the evidence:

Effect size at program exit. A meta-analysis of 84 evaluations of preschool programs for disadvantaged students found that "the simple average effects size for early childhood education on cognitive and achievement scores was .35 standard deviations at the end of the treatment periods, an amount equal to nearly half of race differences in the kindergarten achievement gap."[18] In other words, the average effect size was worth noticing on the exit test. But...

Trend in effect sizes over time. The same meta-analysis found that the exit effect sizes have been decreasing over time: "Programs beginning before 1980 produced significantly larger effect sizes (.33 standard deviations) than those that began later (.16 standard deviations)."[19] The authors attributed this to improved conditions for children in the control group from the 1970s to the end of the century.

Fadeout. When participants in preschool programs are tracked after the end of the intervention, programs that achieved an impact at exit consistently show fadeout averaging about .03 standard deviations per year. "With end-of-treatment effect sizes averaging around .30 standard deviations, this implies that positive effects persist for roughly 10 years."[20]

Head Start. From its beginning in 1965, Head Start generated many evaluations, often done by a single school system and poorly designed. As part of the Head Start reauthorization bill in 1998, Congress mandated a large and rigorously designed evaluation that would provide dispositive evidence. The final report of the evaluation was issued in 2010.[21]

After one academic year in the program, effect sizes in six language and literacy areas ranged from .09 to .31, but there was negligible impact on math skills or on children's attention, antisocial, or mental health problems. The limited effects at exit disappeared within two years. "By the end of first grade, both achievement levels and behavioral ratings of treatment group children were essentially similar to achievement levels of control-group children."[22]

Delayed effects. Duncan and Magnuson cite evidence from the Perry Preschool Project, the Abecedarian Project, and Head Start that some effects of the programs emerge only in adolescence or later. For example, a study of siblings found that children who attended Head Start were eight percentage points more likely to graduate from high school. "Taken together, these studies suggest that despite the decline in program impacts on achievement test scores as children progress through elementary school, there may be measurable and important effects of Head Start on children's life chances."[23]

Duncan and Magnuson accurately stated the results of the various programs and were fair-minded in their interpretations of some of the inconsistencies and puzzles in the data. They did not, however, emphasize the reasons why even the modest successes warrant skepticism. In his review of the same programs, Grover Whitehurst, former head of the Department of Education's Institute of Education Sciences, emphasized what Duncan and Magnuson did not:

Not one of the [pre-K] studies that has suggested long-term positive impacts of center-based early childhood programs has been based on a well-implemented and appropriately analyzed randomized trial, and nearly all have serious limitations in external validity. In contrast, the only two studies in the list with both high internal and external validity (Head Start Impact and Tennessee) find null or negative impacts, and all of the studies that point to very small, null, or negative effects have high external validity.[24]

In 2017, the Brookings Institution and the Duke Center for Child and Family Policy put together a task force of 10 of the leading scholars in the field to provide a consensus statement on the findings of the research to date. The specific consensus statements included two that led with the words "Convincing evidence." They can serve as a summary for my account as well:

Convincing evidence shows that children attending a diverse array of state and school district pre-K programs are more ready for school at the end of their pre-K year than children who do not attend pre-K. Improvements in academic areas such as literacy and numeracy are most common; the smaller number of studies of social-emotional and self-regulatory development generally show more modest improvements in those areas.

Convincing evidence on the longer-term impacts of scaled-up pre-K programs on academic outcomes and school progress is sparse, precluding broad conclusions. The evidence that does exist often shows that pre-K-induced improvements in learning are detectable during elementary school, but studies also reveal null or negative longer-term impacts for some programs.[25]

Whether the glass is half full or half empty is a matter of perspective. My own view is that if a four-year-old who is experiencing pain or deprivation at home spends some hours of the day in a warm and nurturing environment, that is a good in itself that does not need to be justified by continued impact 20 years later. Pre-K can also be a positive socializing experience for children who aren't experiencing pain and deprivation at home—that's why pre-K programs are so popular with upper-middle-class parents for their own children. On both counts, I do not oppose spending money on pre-K programs that provide warm and nurturing environments for children in need. However, ascertaining the proportion of programs that actually do provide warm and nurturing environments for children in need is a neglected research topic.

The cautionary aspect of the two "consensus statements" is that they are consistent with Proposition #10. Recall that the mean effect size for programs since 1980 was just 0.16 in the Duncan and Magnuson meta-analysis. That's the effect on exit tests—which then fades out. Teachers in those pre-K programs are using the same methods they've used for the last 50 years, and nothing gives reason to expect some dramatic new pedagogy is in our future. If the potential for helping children in early childhood is to be realized, new tools will have to be found.

"The First Premise Is Wrong When It Comes to Self-Concept"

Over the last half century, psychologists and educators have spent immense effort experimenting with ways in which achievement in life can be enhanced by changing the way people think about their own abilities and potential—*self-concept*. The three major manifestations of this effort have involved self-esteem, stereotype threat, and growth mindset.

The Self-Esteem Movement

The self-esteem movement came first, with its origins often attributed to Nathaniel Branden's *The Psychology of Self-Esteem*, published in 1969.[26] Branden himself, who had first come to public attention as Ayn Rand's principal disciple, treated self-esteem as an internalized sense of self-responsibility and self-sufficiency. But the self-esteem movement took on a life of its own. It soon discarded those core conditions of proper self-esteem and instead focused instead on *having* a favorable opinion of oneself, independently of objective justification for that favorable opinion. Children were to be praised because praise fosters self-esteem. Criticism should be avoided because criticism undermines self-esteem. Classroom competitions should be avoided because they damage the self-esteem of the losers.

From the 1970s through the 1990s, low self-esteem took on the aura of a meta-explanation for many of society's major problems.[27] And since low self-esteem was the problem, high self-esteem was the solution. Psychological health, high educational performance, earnings as an adult—whatever the desired outcome, higher self-esteem would help produce it.

The empirical underpinnings of the self-esteem movement came crashing down in the early 2000s. A team of scholars led by Roy Baumeister, formerly an advocate for self-esteem interventions, reviewed 15,000 studies that had been written on the relationship of self-esteem to the development of children and concluded that improving self-esteem does not raise grades or career achievement, or have any other positive effect.[28] You can still find remnants of the enthusiasm for self-esteem in the public schools (for example, in the persistence of the "everyone gets a trophy" mindset), but the scholarly standing of simple self-esteem as a way to improve childhood outcomes has declined precipitously.

Stereotype Threat

The label *stereotype threat* and the concept itself were introduced in a seminal article by Claude Steele and Joshua Aronson in 1995.[29] The authors administered the same test to two sets of African American students. The test was described as a problem-solving exercise (a neutral description) to one sample and as an IQ test (activating a negative stereotype of the intelligence of African Americans) to the other. The authors concluded that the threatening condition raised concerns about being judged by the stereotype and thereby degraded the performance of the experimental sample. The study got widespread publicity and the concept caught on. Soon stereotype threat was extended to negative stereotypes about women. Its popularity as a concept rose as rapidly as that of self-esteem had climbed a quarter of a century earlier. By 2003, only eight years after the initial article, stereotype threat was covered in two-thirds of introductory psychology textbooks.[30]

From the beginning, the effects of stereotype threat have been widely misunderstood. The original paper by Steele and Aronson was interpreted in the media as showing that once it had been removed, the ethnic difference in test scores disappeared.[31] What Steele and Aronson actually showed is that the ethnic gap can be increased when stereotype threat is activated. That's not the same as evidence that the gap shrinks when it is removed.

The most commonly studied form of stereotype threat involves women and math, using the hypothesis that activating the negative stereotype "women aren't good at math" depresses women's math scores. Five meta-analyses of such studies were published from 2008 through 2016. Despite a host of methodological issues that have been treated differently by the different authors, the estimated effect sizes have clustered within a fairly narrow range, as indicated below.

Author	Effect size (d)
Nguyen and Ryan (2008)	−0.21
Stoet and Geary (2012)	−0.17
Picho et al. (2013)	−0.24
Flore and Wicherts (2015)	−0.22
Doyle and Voyer (2016)	−0.29

Given how closely the effect sizes are grouped, it is bemusing to read the authors' perspectives on whether the glass is half full or half empty. The authors of three of the studies treat their effect sizes more or less at face value and think they have practical implications (Nguyen and Ryan, Picho et al., Doyle and Voyer). In contrast, Stoet and Geary and Flore and Wicherts are both worried about the degree to which there is evidence of publication bias (only studies that find stereotype threat reach publication), a lack of control groups in many studies, and other methodological weaknesses.[32]

The studies of race-based stereotype threat do not have an equivalent body of meta-analytic results, in large part because of the difficulty of assembling large sample sizes. The Nguyen and Ryan meta-analysis reported an effect size for ethnic minorities of −0.32.[33] Psychologists Gregory Walton and Steven Spencer combined three field studies using African American participants to test race-based stereotype threat. Based on the mean level of prior performance, they reported an effect size of −0.27.[34]

In interpreting these results, the overhanging problem is "researcher degrees of freedom"—a phrase that refers to the many decisions researchers have to make in the course of collecting and analyzing data combined with the tendency to make those decisions in ways that favor the hypothesis they are testing.[35] The problem is most acute for topics that have high political and emotional salience. Stereotype threat is a classic example. Researcher degrees of freedom affect both the decisions during the research and the decision whether to publish negative results. There are several indications that such decisions have been a problem with stereotype threat research:

- Replications often fail to confirm the earlier results.[36]
- The evidence for stereotype threat has dissipated over time.[37]
- Publication bias (failure to report negative results) appears to have been a reality.[38]

In 2019, scholars at the University of Minnesota dealt with these and other issues in the most comprehensive meta-analysis of stereotype threat to date, focusing on the high-stakes test settings in which stereotype threat should theoretically cause the most problems. For the studies relevant to high-stakes settings, the effect size of stereotype threat was −.14 (lowering test scores), a small effect that was further reduced to −.09 after correcting for publication bias. The authors summarized their findings as follows:

Based on the results of the focal analysis, operational and motivational subsets, and publication bias analyses, we conclude that the burden of proof shifts back to those that claim that stereotype threat exerts a substantial effect on standardized test takers. Our best estimate of stereotype threat effects within groups in settings with conditions most similar to operational testing is small and inflated by publication bias.[39]

Given this assessment from the largest and most rigorous meta-analysis of a quarter century of attempts to demonstrate stereotype threat, it seems unlikely that a significant role for stereotype threat exists.

The Growth Mindset Movement

For many people, including me, the self-esteem movement as it developed in practice was inherently problematic: Parents and teachers were encouraged to praise children independently of their actual accomplishments. Shouldn't parents and teachers be encouraging earned self-esteem? In 1998, psychologists Carol Dweck and Claudia Mueller put another spin on that concern: When we praise children for an accomplishment, should we praise their intelligence or their effort? They conducted six experiments using items from Standard Progressive Matrices (a widely used test of nonverbal ability that involves no reading) as the task assigned to 5th graders. Subsequently, some of the students were praised for their intelligence, others were praised for the effort that they put into the test, and others received praise that didn't attribute the achievement to anything (e.g., "That's a really high score"). The results showed large and consistent effects. Children who had been praised for being intelligent subsequently displayed less task persistence and less task enjoyment. They became more concerned about getting a good score than about learning new things. They became protective of their image as "smart" and reluctant to jeopardize it.[40] The article, bluntly titled "Praise for Intelligence Can Undermine Children's Motivation and Performance," was especially jarring for a society in which many upper-middle-class parents incessantly tell their children how smart they are.

Concluding the findings was this one: "Children praised for intelligence described it as a fixed trait more than children praised for hard work, who believed it to be subject to improvement."[41] That finding was the seed of the growth mindset movement, which has had at least as much effect on public education in the United States as the self-esteem movement did. It has given birth to nonprofit organizations such as PERTS (Project for Education Research that Scales) and a for-profit company, MindsetWorks, which sells curricula for teaching growth mindset.[42] Advocates of growth mindset have received millions of dollars in research grants from the Department of Education, the Institute of Educational Sciences, and the Bill & Melinda Gates Foundation, among others.[43] "Growth mindset theory has had a profound impact on the ground," wrote educational scholar Carl Hendrick. "It is difficult to think of a school today that is not in thrall to the idea that beliefs about one's ability affect subsequent performance, and that it's crucial to teach students that failure is merely a stepping stone to success."[44]

The essence of the theory is the distinction between *fixed mindsets* and *growth mindsets*. Fixed mindsets see attributes such as intelligence as being fixed and are accompanied by the student's readiness to give up in the face of failure. Growth mindsets see attributes such as intelligence as malleable and are accompanied by a readiness to see failure as an opportunity to try again, try harder, and get better.[45]

Isn't this tantamount to saying that g can be significantly increased— something that runs counter to a large body of literature? Advocates of the growth mindset think of it another way. Students' beliefs can get in the way of realizing their cognitive potential. An unwarranted belief in one's own incompetence is an example. Removing that belief may not increase cognitive potential, but it can increase achievement. Similarly, growth mindset theory does not seek basic changes in personality, but a reorientation of the way the student construes effort or setbacks in school.[46]

In 2018, a team of five psychologists published a meta-analysis (first author was Victoria Sisk) of the effects of growth mindsets regarding two questions: Is there a relationship between a growth mindset and academic achievement? Is there evidence that growth mindset interventions produce improvements in academic achievement?

The relationship of growth mindset to academic achievement. This meta-analysis analyzed the results of 273 studies with a combined sample of 365,915. The mean correlation between growth mindset and academic achievement was .10. Corrected for measurement unreliability, the estimated correlation was .12. The Sisk study analyzed the results relative to a variety of moderators. Academic risk status and family SES did not affect the relationship. There were statistically significant different effects for children, adolescents, and adults, but the effect remained weak for all subgroups.

The effects of growth mindset interventions on academic achievement. The second meta-analysis analyzed 43 studies with a combined sample of 57,155. Thirty-seven of the 43 effect sizes were not significantly different from zero. One was significantly different from zero but in the wrong direction. Only five of the effect sizes were significant and positive. Overall, the effect size was negligible ($d = +0.08$).

The problem in interpreting the meta-analyses is that so few of the sources provided large-sample direct tests of growth mindset theory or interventions (many were conflated with stereotype threat). Among those that did provide direct tests, many were unpublished master's theses and doctoral dissertations of uncertain quality. The advocates of growth mindset theory can point to direct tests of the theory in the published literature that do show effect sizes, occasionally substantial, mixed in with small or zero effect sizes.[47] Most recently, a nationwide longitudinal, double-blind, randomized trial with a sample of more than 12,000 found that a short online growth mindset intervention in public high schools increased the grades of lower-achieving students over the academic year and increased enrollment in advanced math courses in the subsequent year. The overall effect size for students at risk for low achievement was 0.11 overall and 0.17 for those in schools with positive peer norms. The findings were robust.[48] The 0.17 effect size is small by Cohen's guidelines and potentially consequential by Funder and Ozer's guidelines.[49] It is about the same as the mean for pre-K interventions, few of which were subjected to comparably rigorous evaluations.

The validation of growth mindset theory is a work in progress. The key task is to disentangle the effects of growth mindset interventions from preexisting personality characteristics, chiefly openness and conscientiousness, and cognitive ability.[50] The advent of polygenic scores (see chapter 14) offers rich possibilities for such efforts.

"Some Aspects of the Nonshared Environment Can Be Affected by Outside Interventions"

The nonshared environment explains much of the variance in many traits—sometimes more than genes do. Is it really the case that outside interventions cannot affect the nonshared environment?

Answering that question requires knowing how the nonshared environment functions. In their landmark 1987 article "Why Are Children in the Same Family So Different from One Another?," Plomin and Daniels acknowledged the obvious: "One gloomy prospect is that the salient environment might be unsystematic, idiosyncratic, or serendipitous events such as accidents, illnesses, and other traumas.... Such capricious events, however, are likely to prove a dead end for research."[51] But researchers did have something to work with in the form of the systematic components of the nonshared environment that I listed in chapter 10: family composition (birth order, gender differences), sibling interactions (differential responses to the same events), differential parental treatment of their children, and extrafamilial networks such as peer groups.

The phrase "gloomy prospect" hit a nerve. Many scholars, including Plomin, spent the 1990s trying to put the study of the nonshared environment on an empirical footing. Much was learned. Parents really do treat their children differently and siblings really do respond differently to the same events (divorce, for example); and siblings really do have different peer groups that seem to have great influence on their lives.

By 2000, Turkheimer and Mary Waldron could conduct a meta-analysis from a literature search that identified 289 studies, of which 43 qualified for the meta-analysis. Their findings were bleak. When it came to explaining variance for outcomes such as adjustment, personality, and cognition, the largest proportion of explained variance was .053 for differential peer/teacher interactions. "Family constellation" (birth order, age, age spacing, gender) explained .011, differential parental behavior explained .023, and differential sibling interactions explained .024.[52] These are all extremely small numbers. "We emphasize that these findings should not lead the reader to conclude that the nonshared environment is not as important as had been thought," the authors wrote. "Rather, we believe that the appropriate conclusion is that the causal mechanisms underlying nonshared environmental variability in outcome remain unknown."[53]

Plomin was having an equally frustrating experience with a 10-year longitudinal project he had launched with colleagues in the 1990s, Nonshared Environment in Adolescent Development (NEAD). For example, there was the matter of differential parental treatment of children. The researchers knew that parental negativity had been found to make a difference in the likelihood that children would become depressed. But the NEAD research found that parents' negativity was largely a response to, not a cause of, the children's depression and antisocial behavior.[54] What was initially interpreted as an example of parental behavior affecting child outcomes was more appropriately described as a child-based genetic cause of parental behavior—an example of active rGE.

Taking its results overall, NEAD was successful in identifying nonshared environmental influences. Only a few of these seemed to make a difference psychologically, however. Causation also tended to go in the "wrong" direction: The genetics of the child was often what made the twins' environment "nonshared"—for example, as in the case of a child with a genetic personality disorder that prompted the parents to treat the affected twin differently from the unaffected twin.

Subsequently, other research documented another unwelcome aspect of the nonshared environment: One of the securely known features of MZ twins is that their differences in psychological traits cannot be genetic (because they share the same genes); they cannot be caused by differences in the shared environment (by definition); and therefore such psychological differences *must* be due to the nonshared environment. But it has been found that those differences are not stable over time. Cognitive differences last no more than a few years and personality differences change even more quickly. No identical twin differences are stable over many years.[55] The necessary implication: The nonshared environmental factors are not stable, but more like random noise. Writing in 2018, Plomin reflected on what had been learned since he described the nonshared environment in 1987:

> Rather than accepting this gloomy prospect at the outset, it made more sense scientifically to look for possible systematic sources of non-shared environmental effects. However, after thirty years of searching unsuccessfully for systematic non-shared environmental influences, it's time to accept the gloomy prospect. Non-shared environmental influences are unsystematic, idiosyncratic, serendipitous events without lasting effects.[56]

Is it possible that aspects of the nonshared environment can be affected by outside interventions? The prospects are, to borrow a word, gloomy.

"But You're Ignoring Epigenetics!"

Raise the topic of genes' role in affecting human behavior, and chances are good that someone is going to tell you that you're hopelessly behind the times. Epigenetics has proved that alterations in the environment can change our genes, and therefore traditional beliefs about inborn characteristics are outdated and irrelevant.

It's no surprise that this view is so widespread. Respectable media have been reporting it for years. *Time* magazine explained "Why Your DNA Isn't Your Destiny" back in 2010, with the subtitle "The new field of epigenetics is showing how your environment and your choices can influence your genetic code—and that of your kids."[57] In 2013, *Discover* magazine told us that "the genome has long been known as the blueprint of life, but the epigenome is life's Etch A Sketch: Shake it hard enough, and you can wipe clean the family curse."[58] The *New York Review of Books* weighed in with "Epigenetics: The Evolution Revolution" in its issue of June 7, 2018. Authors Israel Rosenfield and Edward Ziff reported, "Epigenetics has also made clear that the stress caused by war, prejudice, poverty, and other forms of childhood adversity may have consequences both for the persons affected and for their future—unborn—children, not only for social and economic reasons but also for biological ones."[59]

It's not just the big events like war that can change our brains. Jogging can do it too. Here's Tara Swart, holder of a PhD in neuropharmacology from King's College London, writing in *Forbes*:

> The new and evolving science [of epigenetics] tells us that our gene expression is malleable, influenced by external stressors and lifestyle choices, from running outside to who you have your coffee break with. Rather than having a set genetic blueprint, epigenetics demonstrates that although our genes themselves are fixed, our genetic expression, much of which is heritable, is also interconnected with a wide range of environmental factors.[60]

With rare exceptions, the mainstream media's reporting on the science behind epigenetics bears little resemblance to what's actually been discovered.

The Basics

Your personal double helix of DNA resides in the nucleus of a cell. The rest of the cell contains the proteins that enable it to perform its particular function, whether it be a cell in a biceps or the brain. For a cell to do that, somehow the small number of relevant genes in the DNA producing those proteins for that cell type must be identified and their information transcribed. Then the transcription must be transferred to the ribosome, the place in the cell where proteins are synthesized.

The steps in the process of getting the information to the ribosome are all part of *gene regulation*, also called *regulation of gene expression*—turning genes off or on and turning them up or down. Some of them involve a class of chemical modifications to DNA or to components of the "packaging" of DNA (chromatin) that has led to what is now called epigenetics.

The word *epigenesis* was first used in 1651 by William Harvey to describe the developmental process that allows the homogeneous fertilized egg to become a complex organism. In 1942, embryologist Conrad Waddington coined *epigenetics*, which he defined as the "whole complex of developmental processes," portraying an "epigenetic landscape" of branching pathways that a cell might take.[61]

In 1958, just a few years after the discovery of the structure of DNA, microbiologist David Nanney recast Waddington's definition. Nanney described two types of cellular control systems. One consisted of "genetics systems" that are involved in transcription. The other consisted of "epigenetic systems" that were auxiliary mechanisms for determining whether expression occurred, and if so, its intensity.[62] Nanney's article also drew attention to what would become a major aspect of epigenetics: "persistent homeostasis," referring to cellular memory that survives cell division.[63]

What caused "persistent homeostasis"? Collapsing decades of research into a few sentences and simplifying, the answer turned out to be *epigenetic marks* of two kinds: those caused by DNA methylation and those caused by histone modifications. I will concentrate on DNA methylation, which has been more commonly studied, and ignore histone genetic marks in this short description.

THE DNA DOESN'T CHANGE

No one claims that the DNA code is modified by environmental events. All the scientific claims involving epigenetics, correct and incorrect, are about changes in gene expression, not changes in DNA.

For DNA methylation, the genetic mark can be thought of as a speck of a chemical in the methyl group[64] deposited onto a gene. The most common effect of methylation is to turn off the gene—to suppress its expression by making it less accessible to the transcription machinery—but in some circumstances it can turn on genes or modulate their intensity.[65]

The task of methylating the genome begins early in life. At conception, a fertilized egg contains not only DNA inherited from the parents but also the parents' methylation patterns. About a week after conception, almost all of those patterns are erased and almost all of the genome is methylated de novo. This new genome-wide methylation pattern paves the way for cell specialization by repressing DNA sequences that aren't supposed to be expressed in a given cell. During pregnancy, methylation and demethylation continue at specific stages of the embryo's development in a programmed sequence until the tissue is fully developed, whereupon it has generated a template that is extremely stable lifelong.

Extremely stable, but not completely so. Abnormal methylation events do occur during the lifespan and have been implicated in various diseases, including some cancers. This brings us to the heart of the excitement over epigenetics: the evidence that changes in methylation can be induced by environmental events.

In the breathless accounts of the epigenetics revolution, a commonplace truth often gets lost: Environmental events routinely change gene expression. If you break a bone in your ankle, expressions of genes in that bone are going to change so that the bone may heal. If you run a mile, a variety of changes in gene expression will have taken place in your respiratory system. That the environment interacts with genes to change the phenotype temporarily is not news. It happens all the time.

The distinctiveness of epigenetic change lies in the cellular memory of methylation that survives cell duplication. Suppose that a negative environmental event early in childhood not only caused temporary changes in gene expression (as in a broken ankle), but changed the methylation patterns, thereby causing permanent genetic changes that damage the phenotype. Suppose that a subsequent positive environmental event could demethylate and thereby reactivate the genes that had been turned off by the negative event. Suppose—and this was the most exciting possibility of all—that cellular memory not only survived during the lifetime of the person who had experienced these environmentally induced genetic changes, but could be passed on to offspring.

That's where the hype over epigenetics originated and why it has been so attractive to the media. Epigenetics seems to promise release from genetic determinism. It seems to offer new explanations for phenotypic differences and new possibilities for remediation. At the extremes, it seems to offer hope for greater equality of capabilities and outcomes across groups.

As these potential extensions of findings about gene expression sank in during the 2000s, the use of the term *epigenetics* expanded to include all forms of transmission of the phenotype by mechanisms that did not involve changes in the DNA sequence—in other words, to expand beyond Nanney's emphasis on cellular memory and instead treat the larger realm of transmission of the phenotype through RNA and transcription factors as part of epigenetics.[66] For John Greally, director of the Center for Epigenomics at the Albert Einstein College of Medicine, this is too broad a definition, conflating changes in transcription regulatory effects with cellular memory. This has created pervasive problems of interpretation—among other reasons because a change in DNA methylation can be an effect instead of a cause.[67] But for better or worse, the broad interpretation of epigenetics has taken hold and a correspondingly broad research agenda based on it has been pursued for two decades. What has been found?

The Claims of the Advocates

The first significant claims for epigenetic change were tailor-made to feed into both the optimism and the media excitement: They dealt with the effects of maternal love in infancy. The article "Epigenetic Programming by Maternal Behavior," published in 2004 (first author was Ian Weaver), reported that rat pups who received high levels of arched-back nursing plus pup licking and grooming had differences in DNA methylation of a specific glucocorticoid receptor in the hippocampus compared to pups who received low levels of such nurturing.[68] That particular receptor has been the focus of attention because it regulates genes known to affect early development, especially including the response to stress.

Media accounts immediately drew the obvious implication of the Weaver study's finding: If these effects occurred in rat pups, perhaps human children who are deprived of such maternal care are permanently less able to cope with stress and more vulnerable to psychological disorders for genetic reasons. The authors further concluded that the effects on methylation were reversed with cross-fostering. "Thus we show that an epigenomic state of a gene can be established through behavioral programming, and it is potentially reversible."[69] The media also fastened on this implication: Something can be done to undo the genetic damage experienced by children who were deprived in infancy.

Since 2004, a flood of articles in technical journals has pursued the possibilities that the Weaver study suggested. The ones that have received the most media attention focus on "natural experiments" in the form of the Dutch famine of 1944–45, the Chinese famine of 1959–61, and the children of Holocaust survivors. Most of these studies are correlational. For example, studies have documented significant increases in the incidence of schizophrenia among children born in both the Dutch and Chinese families.[70]

In the case of the Dutch famine, a team of Dutch scholars compared methylation 60 years later of people who had been in utero during the worst of the famine with siblings who were born before or after the famine. Their conclusion:

> In summary, using a systematic genome-wide approach, we show that DNAm [DNA methylation] at specific CpGs [cytosine-phosphate-guanine dinucleotides] mediates a considerable proportion of the associations between prenatal famine exposure and later-life adiposity and serum TG levels. Our data are consistent with the hypothesis that the associations between exposure to an adverse environment during early development and health outcomes in adulthood are mediated by epigenetic factors. The specific causal mechanism awaits elucidation.[71]

In other words, what happened to the children in utero probably affected DNA methylation in ways similar to those of laboratory studies, but the data didn't permit the authors to determine whether it was the stress on the mother or the stress on the fetus (or both) that caused those effects on methylation, nor could they tell whether the changes were due to changes in DNA sequence variants or other factors.

In 2016, an article on Holocaust survivors and their children got widespread media attention in the *Guardian*, *New York Times*, and *Scientific American*. Based on 32 Holocaust survivors and 22 of their adult offspring, the authors (first author was Rachel Yehuda) reported, "This is the first demonstration of an association of preconception parental trauma with epigenetic alterations that is evident in both exposed parent and offspring, providing potential insight into how severe psychophysiological trauma can have intergenerational effects."[72] The key adjective for the parental trauma was *preconception*. Unlike the study of methylation in the children of the Dutch famine, the Holocaust survivor study claimed to have evidence of transgenerational epigenetic inheritance.

As I write, two systematic reviews of the epigenetics literature have been published. The first, published in 2016, was written by psychiatrist Gustavo Turecki and neurobiologist Michael Meaney. Their review of the literature identified 430 articles, of which 40 met the authors' criteria for inclusion.[73] The other systematic review, published in 2018, was prepared by a team supervised by developmental psychologist Wendy Kliewer. The authors limited their review to studies of infants, using 20 out of 510 unique articles that their literature search had identified.

Neither review found support for epigenetic effects resembling the portrayal of epigenetics in the media. Neither discussed transgenerational epigenetic change. You may check out this characterization of the results for yourself. All of the major findings are presented in the note.[74]

The Responses of the Critics

A familiar story in the history of science is that a paradigm-breaking discovery—the heliocentric solar system, quantum mechanics—is made by Young Turks, resisted by the older generation of scientists, and finally wins acceptance as the geezers die off ("Science advances one funeral at a time").[75] But that's not how the epigenetics debate is being conducted within the profession. Epigeneticists who are still young themselves and doing cutting-edge work see their discipline as the victim of a hijacking. In their view, too many epigenetics enthusiasts are reaching conclusions and publishing them without understanding the science that already exists. For John Greally, the Yehuda study of Holocaust survivors "is pretty typical of all epigenetics studies today for being uninterpretable."[76] Geneticist Graham Coop had a Twitter response to the *New York Review of Books* article that began, "Utter nonsense." And they have allies in the older generation—the week that the *New York Review of Books* article came out, evolutionary biologist Jerry Coyne's blog began with "Another lousy article on epigenetics."

For those who want to pursue the debate, I can point you to an exchange that gives you an overview of the issues and references many of the key sources. The protagonists are neuroscientist Kevin Mitchell and Jill Escher, a well-known advocate for autistic children.

Mitchell's case against the popularized version of epigenetics began with two long scholarly appraisals of the data posted on his blog, *Wiring the Brain*, in January 2013.[77] In May 2018 he returned to the subject in the wake of the Yehuda study of Holocaust victims. He was blunt. "You could be charitable and say the evidence is weak, circumstantial, observational, and correlative, and that it warrants circumspection and careful interpretation (and further research, of course!). I would go further and say that nothing in any of those papers rises to the level of what should properly be called a finding. There's no there there."[78]

A month later, Jill Escher responded on her blog, *Germline Exposures*, with a list of 49 references documenting her allegation that Mitchell cherry-picked studies to make his case and ignored abundant evidence of epigenetic inheritance in mammals. She was as blunt as Mitchell:

> Sloppy overstatement and dogmatism from the Ivory Tower, such as Mitchell's blog post, can breed complacency precisely at a time when we should be deeply alarmed about the intergenerational effects of past and current exposures. It should be clear to all of us by now that molecular insults to the germline can influence disease, behavior or physiology of offspring, perhaps in ways that are staggeringly important for public health. While healthy skepticism is always welcome, research does not progress by allowing outspoken academicians to distort the state of the science, unchallenged.[79]

Four days later, Mitchell responded to Escher with another detailed methodological critique of the epigenetics literature.[80]

If you're wondering how an outsider is to form an opinion, I sympathize. Of the many complex topics in this book, I found epigenetics to be the most impenetrable for an amateur. I come away from the literature thinking of the controversy in terms of two broad issues.

The first is whether events in early childhood change methylation patterns and whether such patterns are reversible. I find Mitchell's skepticism convincing, but this aspect of the research is being conducted using methods that lend themselves to rigorous examination. The more ambitious claims of the enthusiasts are currently unwarranted, but if the enthusiasts are right they will eventually be able to make their case via the scientific method.

The second issue is whether environmentally induced changes in methylation are passed on to the next generation. The scientifically interpretable evidence for this is mostly from work with *C. elegans* (a worm about one millimeter long) and *D. melanogaster* (the fruit fly), which seems a long way from proving that it happens in humans. But some evidence of intergenerational transmission has also come from laboratory versions of the house mouse, a mammal, which strikes closer to home.[81]

The most widely publicized of these was the finding in the early 2000s that feeding pregnant mice extra vitamins during pregnancy altered the coat color and disease susceptibility of newborn mice and that the effects lasted for two generations.[82] At the end of 2018, a team of 10 geneticists, mostly at Cambridge University, published their finding that the methylation marks on the transposable elements thought to be involved were not transmitted to the next generation.[83] In an interview with *The Scientist*, Dirk Schübeler, a molecular geneticist who was not involved in the study, called the analysis "an enormous technical tour de force." Before it had been conducted, he continued, the case of the changed coat color had been treated as the tip of an iceberg. "This study shows there is no iceberg."[84]

The case for intergenerational transmission isn't fully resolved, but the proponents face an uphill battle. The simplest reason it's an uphill battle was explained by the leader of the Cambridge study, Anne Ferguson-Smith. "There's two rounds of epigenetic programming that basically prevent any epigenetic marks from being transmitted from one generation to the next," she told *The Scientist*. "People don't seem to appreciate this."[85]

Bernhard Horsthemke, director of the Institut für Humangenetik at the University of Duisburg-Essen, has expressed the problems at greater length by putting together a "roadmap to proving transgenerational epigenetic inheritance." I've consigned it to a note because it is long and technical—but that's my point.[86] The accounts of the transgenerational epigenetic effects of famines and the Holocaust that have gotten so much press ignore all of these methodological problems.

This much seems uncontroversial: The study of methylation patterns and their manipulability is at an extremely early stage. Even if one takes all of the conclusions in the reviews of the literature at face value, their applications are far down the road. My point with regard to Proposition #10 is limited. Epigenetics properly understood is a vibrant field with findings that have important medical implications. But as far as I can tell, no serious epigeneticist is prepared to defend the notion that we are on the verge of learning how to turn genes on and off and thereby alter behavioral traits in disadvantaged children (or anyone else).

Recapitulation

One of the signature issues dividing conservative and liberal policy analysts for the last 50 years has been the record of outside interventions on behalf of the poor and disadvantaged. From my perch as one of those on the conservative side of the debate, my appraisal is that the liberals have done well in arguing the benefits of income transfers (their downsides notwithstanding) and the conservatives have done well in documenting the overall failure of job training programs, preschool programs, and elementary and secondary educational reforms (their short-term results notwithstanding).

I will reserve my more speculative conclusions for the final chapter. For now, I want to emphasize a few points that can form broadly shared common benchmarks in assessing the ways in which Proposition #10 might be wrong.

We've already tried many, many strategies using the normal tools. For 50 years, social and educational reformers have been coming up with new ideas for interventions. A great many of them have received federal, state, or foundation funding, sometimes lavish funding. As we survey the prospects for better results in the future, it's not as if there is a backlog of untested bright ideas awaiting their chance.

The modest role of the shared environment seems solidly established. As discussed in chapter 10, the validity of twin studies has survived searching examination of its underlying assumptions. Insofar as violations of those assumptions exist, they probably tend to slightly understate the role of genes. The role of "genetic nurture" is greater than we formerly knew, but that too is rooted in biology. The harder people have looked for purely environmental causes, the more they have turned out to have genetic underpinnings.

The gloomy prospect for systematically affecting the nonshared environment seems vindicated. Nothing in the pipeline shows promise of overturning the negative results to date.

Epigenetics as portrayed in the media has no relevance to Proposition #10 for the foreseeable future. The widespread popular belief that environmental pressures routinely and permanently alter gene expression in humans, that those alterations are reversible, and that their effects are passed down through generations is wrong.

Proposition #10 will eventually be wrong. On the bright side, we can look at recent developments and see reasons that Proposition #10 cannot be true forever. The obvious example is the positive and even life-changing effects that pharmaceuticals developed during the last few decades have had on some forms of depression and other mental disorders. Who knows what role future drugs might play in enhancing learning and positively affecting personality traits and social behavior? Their effects might be dramatic. At some point, the promise of CRISPR for gene editing will be realized, and all bets about the ability to change people by design in substantial numbers will be outdated. If we're looking at the long term, Proposition #10 will certainly be wrong eventually. Not now.

A Personal Interpretation of the Material in Part III

We live in a world where certain kinds of abilities tend to be rewarded with affluence and professional prestige. Those abilities have a substantial genetic component. That genetic component is a matter of luck: We don't choose our parents.

The genetic component tends to make social class "stickier," because successful parents pass along not only money but their talents to their offspring. The inheritance of status is far from an ironclad certainty for any individual— on average, the child of parents with very high IQs and outstanding interpersonal skills will have lower IQ and lesser interpersonal skills than their parents.[87] But if we step back and ask where the people with exceptional intelligence and interpersonal skills in the next generation are going to come from, the answer is that they will disproportionately come from high-SES parents.

Putting these facts together—and I submit that the evidence is conclusive enough to warrant treating them as facts—the implication is that advanced societies have replaced one form of unfairness with another. The old form of unfairness was that talented people were prevented from realizing their potential because of artificial barriers rooted in powerlessness and lack of opportunity. The new form of unfairness is that talent is largely a matter of luck, and the few who are so unusually talented that they rise to the top are the beneficiaries of luck in the genetic lottery.

All of these statements apply to frequency distributions and their effects on society as a whole. As individuals, most of our lives are not genetically determined except at the extremes of success. We can't all become rich and famous if we try hard enough, but just about all of us can live satisfying lives, and we have many degrees of freedom in reaching that goal.

PART IV

—◦◦◦—

LOOKING AHEAD

The future of the liberal arts lies, therefore, in addressing the fundamental questions of human existence head on, without embarrassment or fear, taking them from the top down in easily understood language, and progressively rearranging them into domains of inquiry that unite the best of science and the humanities at each level of organization in turn. That of course is a very difficult task. But so are cardiac surgery and building space vehicles difficult tasks. Competent people get on with them, because they need to be done.[1]

—Edward O. Wilson

That's Edward O. Wilson writing in *Consilience: The Unity of Knowledge*, the book that inspired this one. Twenty-two years after I first read it, the social sciences are on the cusp of the future that Wilson foresaw. What next?

I should probably duck the question. Another Wilson, the eminent political scientist James Q. Wilson, had a favorite story about his mentor, the equally eminent Edward C. Banfield. "Stop trying to predict the future, Wilson," Banfield would say to him. "You're having a hard enough time predicting the past." Banfield's excellent advice weighs heavily on me, but I'll give it a try.

Chapter 14 focuses on the problem of establishing causation with genomic material and describes a great debate about the role of genomics in social science that is already well under way. Its resolution will determine whether the social science revolution is upon us or will be deferred indefinitely.

In chapter 15, I offer reflections and speculations about the material I have covered in *Human Diversity*, unabashedly going beyond the data.

14

The Shape of the Revolution

I began *Human Diversity* by asserting that advances in genetics and neuroscience will enable social scientists to take giant strides in understanding how the world works—that we social scientists are like physicists at the outset of the nineteenth century, poised at a moment in history that will produce our own Ampères and Faradays. Can anything more specific be said about how the coming revolution will unfold? The one certainty is that it will be full of surprises. But I can describe a centrally important debate that is already under way and try to tease out some of its implications.

THE DIFFERENCE BETWEEN THE GENOMIC AND NEUROSCIENTIFIC REVOLUTIONS

I focus on the genomics revolution in this chapter because it will have broader direct effects on social science than will developments in neuroscience. To do quantitative neuroscience research, you need to be a neuroscientist and have access to extremely expensive equipment such as MRI machines. The results of the research will inform a variety of social science questions, but the work won't be done by social scientists. In contrast, the products of the genomics revolution, especially polygenic scores, will be usable by social scientists with no training in genomics by the end of the 2020s in the same way that IQ scores are used by social scientists with no training in creating IQ tests.

A Place to Stand

Two hallmarks of genuine science are proof of causation and the ability to predict. Until the 1960s, the social sciences barely participated. Econometrics and psychometrics were already established disciplines, but for the most part social scientists wrote narratives with simple descriptive statistics. Some of those narratives had deservedly become classics—for example, W. E. B. DuBois's *The Philadelphia Negro*, Robert and Helen Lynd's *Middletown*, and Gunnar Myrdal's *An American Dilemma*—but social scientists were powerless to analyze causation or make predictions in quantitative ways except with small samples in psychology laboratories working with rats and pigeons. The multivariate statistical techniques for dealing with larger and messier problems of human society had been invented, but the computational burdens were too great.

In the early 1960s, computers began to arrive on university campuses. They were slow, clumsy things—your smartphone has orders of magnitude more computing power and storage than the most advanced university computers then.[1] Getting access to them was laden with bureaucracy. But they could perform statistical analyses that were too laborious to be done by hand. For the first time, social scientists could explore questions that required adjusting for multiple variables and make cautious quantitative claims about causation. The changes that followed were dramatic and rapid. In 1960, technical journals in sociology and political science were collections of essays. By 1980, they were collections of articles crammed with equations, tables, and graphs. In the subsequent 40 years, the methods have become ever more sophisticated and the statistical packages ever more powerful. The databases on which we work our analyses are better designed, far larger and more numerous, and often downloadable with the click of a mouse.

And yet in one sense we have been stuck where we were in 1960. Archimedes famously promised to move the Earth if he had a long enough lever and a place to stand. When it comes to analyses of human behavior, the social sciences have had a lever for decades, but no secure, solid place to stand.

The debate about nature versus nurture is not just one of many issues in social science. It is fundamental for everything involving human behavior. At the theoretical level, consider economic behavior. To what extent does the assumption that humans are rational actors explain how the market actually works? Answering that question goes to core issues of how human beings function cognitively, which in turn depends on the relative roles of environmental conditions and biologically grounded deviations from rational calculations. On the practical level, almost every social policy analysis, whether it measures the impact of interventions to deter juvenile crime or tries to predict how a piece of legislation will affect the behavior of bankers, ultimately makes sense or not based on scientific findings about human nature. It is a statement of fact: Most of social science ultimately rests on biology.

But we have had no causally antecedent baseline for analyzing human behavior. Twin studies are a case in point—a powerful method to determine when genes must be involved, but unable to push our understanding beyond heritability estimates. Everything more detailed that we try to say about the role of nature is open to question. Triangulating data can make alternative explanations more or less plausible, but ultimately social scientists have had no place to stand in tackling a central question of their profession: What is innate?

Progress in genetics and neuroscience holds out the prospect—a hope for some, a fear for others—that we can peer into the black box. An intense debate is under way about whether that prospect is real or chimerical.

Interpreting Causation in an Omnigenic, Pleiotropic World

Genetic causation is far more complicated than earlier generations expected. It once seemed straightforward: After the genome had been sequenced, geneticists would slowly assemble a jigsaw puzzle. It would be a complicated one, but eventually they would know which variants caused what outcomes.

As recently as 1999, geneticist Neil Risch, one of the originators of genome-wide analysis, led a team of 31 geneticists trying to find loci affecting autism. They made news by reporting that "the overall distribution of allele sharing was most consistent with a model of ≥ 15 susceptibility loci."[2] They characterized 15 as a large number. Eighteen years later, three of the team's Stanford colleagues (first author was Evan Boyle) published an article titled "An Expanded View of Complex Traits: From Polygenic to Omnigenic." In it, they used the Risch study to illustrate how much had changed. A prediction of more than 15 loci for autism "was strikingly high at the time, but seems quaintly low now," they wrote.[3] The intervening years had brought two revolutionary surprises.

The first surprise was that most traits were associated with many, many loci. Effect sizes for common variants were small, and the combined effects of those loci explained only a fraction of predicted genetic variance. As genome-wide analyses became more sophisticated, it was discovered that some loci did have sizable effects, but those loci were usually rare variants—and it began to look as if there might be thousands of them. Almost everything was highly polygenic.

And that's just counting the SNPs that directly code for proteins. "A second surprise," the authors wrote, "was that, in contrast to Mendelian diseases—which are largely caused by protein-coding changes—complex traits are mainly driven by noncoding variants that presumably affect gene regulation."[4] Interpreting a statistical association of a certain allele in a certain SNP with the expression of a trait was going to be arduous.

The numbers of loci involved in a given trait could be staggering. Human height is again a good example. The Boyle study estimated that 62 percent of all common SNPs are statistically associated with a nonzero effect on height—millions of SNPs, in other words. Not all of them are causal, but that's not much comfort. "Under simplifying assumptions," the authors wrote, "the best-fit curve suggests that ~3.8% of 1000 Genomes SNPs have causal effects on height."[5] About 100,000.[6] The Boyle study concluded that complex traits routinely follow a similar pattern, even if not quite so extreme. This finding led them to propose what they called the "omnigenic" model of complex traits, incorporating the evidence that tens of thousands of loci can causally affect a single trait.

Another complexity is that a single SNP can affect many traits. This phenomenon is called *pleiotropy*. Take, for example, a 2018 study that identified 148 loci affecting general cognitive function. The authors tested the genetic correlations between general cognitive function and 52 health-related traits. Thirty-six of them had statistically significant correlations, including traits with no obvious relationship to cognitive function, such as positive correlations with grip strength and negative correlations with angina, lung cancer, osteoarthritis, and heart attack.[7]

Pleiotropy is ubiquitous. In 2016, Joseph Pickrell and his colleagues assembled statistics for genome-wide studies of 42 traits or diseases ranging from anthropometric traits such as height and nose size to neurological diseases (e.g., Alzheimer's, Parkinson's) to susceptibility to infection (e.g., childhood ear infections, tonsillitis). The number of associations ranged from a low of 5 for age at voice drop in men to over 500 for height.[8] Such statistical associations could be coincidental or they could be causal.

If they are causal, causality could work in one of two ways, sometimes called "vertical" and "horizontal" pleiotropy. An example of vertical pleiotropy is a variant that increases LDL cholesterol (bad cholesterol) and also shows an association with the incidence of heart attack—the first causal relationship is direct, the second is downstream from the first.[9] Horizontal pleiotropy occurs when a variant has direct causal effects on traits that are apparently not causally related to each other—for example, when a variant seems to have an effect on both LDL cholesterol levels and schizophrenia. A 2018 analysis limited to horizontal pleiotropy concluded that "horizontal pleiotropy is pervasive and widely distributed across the genome" and that "there are thousands of loci that exhibit extreme levels of horizontal pleiotropy."[10]

Combining these and other discoveries, the task of translating the raw material I described in chapter 9 into statements about causation is daunting. Geneticist Graham Coop devised a vivid thought experiment that enumerates the difficulties.

Coop asks us to imagine that a genome-wide analysis using the UK Biobank has revealed the British to have more alleles that are associated with tea consumption than the French have. He imagines a protagonist named Bob who concludes that the difference between the French and the British in their preference for tea is in part genetic. Bob is judicious. "Bob would assure us that these alleles are polymorphic in both countries, and that both environment and culture play a role. He would further reassure us that there'll be an overlapping distribution of tea drinking preferences in both countries, so he's not saying that all British people drink more tea for genetic reasons. He'll tell us he's simply interested in showing that the average difference in tea consumption is partly genetic."[11]

Coop then turns to the difficulties that Bob has in drawing even that modest causal inference. He begins with a core point: Genome-wide analyses "do not point to specific alleles FOR tea preferences, only to alleles that happen to be associated with tea preference in the current set of environments experienced by people in the UK Biobank." Coop does not argue that nothing causally informative can come from GWAS. Some of the tea-drinking SNPs may be enriched near olfactory receptors. Some may be associated with caffeine sensitivity. These are interesting from a causal point of view. But daunting problems stand between these isolated findings and the conclusion that the differential preference for tea among British and French is partly genetic in origin.

First, there are G×E (gene × environment) interactions to contend with. Maybe people who care about their weight are drawn to tea instead of soft drinks because tea has fewer calories. It is found that alleles correlated with body mass index are also correlated with tea preference. But that won't necessarily permit causal inferences at a national level. Perhaps, for example, what counts is not absolute BMI but one's relative BMI within a country, and the distributions of BMI in the UK and France are different.

A second problem is technical. Sometimes the SNP that shows up in a genome-wide analysis is the one that actually does the work. However, it is often a "tag" SNP that is physically near the functional SNP in the genome but doesn't actually do the work.

In comparing populations, this isn't a big problem if the correlations between the functional SNP and the tag SNP are the same in two populations. But recall from chapter 9 the problems of population stratification. Coop describes how they might affect the tea-drinking analysis. Pretend that British and French ancestral populations have been geographically separated for a long time. The correlation between functional and tag SNPs in one population is likely to have become different from the comparable correlation in the other population if only because of genetic drift and recombination. Let's say that the allele frequencies of the functional SNP in the British and the French are the same as they've always been, but the correlation between the tag SNP and the functional SNP in the British is .90 while the comparable correlation among the French has drifted down to .70. If, unbeknownst to us, our comparison of the two countries is based on the tag SNP, we will wrongly fail to give a bump to French tea-drinking preferences as often as we would if we were working with the functional SNP. Put technically, the predictive validity of the analysis will be lower for the French than it is for the British.

A variant on this problem is assortative mating. Suppose that people who are heavy tea drinkers tend to mate with tall people. Over a few generations, height-increasing alleles will be statistically associated with tea drinking even if there is no causal link. This decreases the predictive validity of that population's genetic score for tea drinking relative to a population that does not falsely include height-increasing alleles in its genetic score.

Coop also discusses another topic that I raised in chapter 9: A great deal of human variation is concentrated in rare variants that the ordinary GWA won't pick up, and these rare variants are commonly private to a single ancestral population. Strong conclusions about between-population comparisons will have to wait until we have far more information about the effects of rare variants in different populations than we have now. Coop concludes:

> Undoubtedly the coming decades of human genomics will see breakthroughs in the identification of functional loci, the size of GWAS performed world-wide, and in the statistical methodologies used to understand trait variation. There is also no doubt that we will come to understand much more about human variation. However, our ability to perform GWAS to identify loci underlying variation in traits among individuals vastly outstrips our ability to understand the causal mechanisms underlying these differences. In many cases, genetic contributions may not be separable from environmental and cultural differences.[12]

The tea-drinking example illustrates just how thoroughly the old jigsaw-puzzle metaphor has been blown up. The process of mapping causal chains from genetic variation to phenotypic trait is immensely more complicated than that.

The Great Debate

Immensely more complicated, yes. But is it impossibly complicated? Seen from another perspective, the progress to date has been stunning. Polygenic scores didn't even exist less than a decade ago. As I write, they already explain significant proportions of the variance in many traits, and progress is rapid. Consider educational attainment, a rough proxy measure for IQ, as an example. In just the five years from 2014 through 2018, the percentage of the variance that could be explained from genetic material alone went from zero to 15 percent.[13] For some, the appropriate reaction is "Wow!" For others, 15 percent is not much, and the appropriate reaction is "So what?"

Two leading behavior geneticists whom you have already met have staked out opposite positions: Robert Plomin and Eric Turkheimer. I will sometimes subsequently refer to "the Plomin school" and "the Turkheimer school." Other scholars have published on these issues, but I think it's fair to say that Plomin and Turkheimer have published earlier and more prolifically on the positions they represent than anyone else.

They are in many ways a matched pair. Plomin and Turkheimer both obtained their PhDs in psychology at the University of Texas at Austin and studied under many of the same luminaries who were teaching there in the 1970s and 1980s. Both have published seminal articles using twin studies. Both have won prestigious awards. But when it comes to nature, nurture, and complex phenotypic traits, they might as well be on separate planets.

Robert Plomin and Polygenic Scores

"What would you think if you heard about a new fortune-telling device that is touted to predict psychological traits like depression, schizophrenia and school achievement?"[14] That's the opening sentence of *Blueprint: How DNA Makes Us Who We Are*, which Plomin published in 2018. He is referring to the advent of the polygenic score.

Polygenic scores are the most exciting and also the most controversial use of GWA data. They work like many other indexes—quarterback performance ratings, fielding averages in baseball, economic indexes predicting GDP growth, and IQ scores—that represent the aggregated score on several indicators. Specifically, a polygenic score is the sum of the number of copies of the alleles that promote or intensify a given trait in an individual. In *Blueprint*, Robert Plomin offered a table of 10 hypothetical SNPs associated with a given trait to illustrate how the calculation works:

THE RAW MATERIAL FOR CALCULATING A POLYGENIC SCORE

	Target allele	Allele 1	Allele 2	Genotypic score	Correlation with trait	Weighted genotypic score
SNP 1	T	A	T	1	0.005	0.005
SNP 2	C	G	G	0	0.004	0.000
SNP 3	A	A	A	2	0.003	0.006
SNP 4	G	C	G	1	0.003	0.003
SNP 5	G	C	C	0	0.003	0.000
SNP 6	T	A	T	1	0.002	0.002
SNP 7	C	C	G	1	0.002	0.002
SNP 8	A	A	A	2	0.002	0.004
SNP 9	A	T	T	0	0.001	0.000
SNP 10	C	C	G	1	0.001	0.001
Polygenic score				**9**		**0.023**

Source: Adapted from Plomin (2018): Table 12.1.

Suppose you are a person whose genome has been sequenced and the target alleles for the ten SNPs in the table are associated with an increase in height. You want to know your polygenic score for height. For SNP 1, you have one copy of the target allele, so you enter 1 in the column labeled "Genotypic score." For SNP 2, neither copy of your two alleles is the target allele, so you enter 0. For SNP 3, both copies are the target allele, so you enter 2. And so on. All told, you have 9 height-increasing alleles out of a possible 20. That's the simple version of a polygenic score. The more sophisticated version is to multiply your score in the "Genotypic score" column by a weight. Plomin uses the correlation of the SNP with the trait (regression weights are also commonly used). Thus your "Weighted genotypic score" for SNP 1 is .005, greater than the weighted score for SNP 8, even though you have only one copy of the target allele in SNP 1 versus two copies for SNP 8. Add up all the weighted scores, and the weighted polygenic score is 0.023.

As you can see, neither the unweighted nor the weighted polygenic scores has a natural interpretation. The polygenic score can be interpreted only relative to a population. Fortunately, polygenic scores are normally distributed. Eventually—this achievement is probably some years down the road—we can hope for polygenic scores with means and standard deviations that can be interpreted in the same way that they are interpreted for IQ scores (which also have no natural interpretation in their raw form).

Polygenic scores are not limited to SNPs that meet the stringent requirement for genome-wide statistical significance. Plomin points out that the goal is the best composite score. "The new approach to polygenic scores is to keep adding SNPs as long as they add to the predictive power of the polygenic score in independent samples.... Some false positives will be included in the polygenic score but that is acceptable as long as the signal increases relative to the noise, in the sense that the polygenic score predicts more variance."[15]

Plomin sees polygenic scores as a game changer for three reasons:

- Predictions from polygenic scores to psychological traits are causal in just one direction (the trait cannot be a cause of the score).
- Polygenic scores can predict from birth.
- Polygenic scores can predict differences between family members, something that twin studies cannot do.

Unweighted polygenic scores have a few other advantages as well. Unlike psychometric measures, which yield somewhat different results when a person is tested more than once, polygenic scores from carefully analyzed DNA samples have 100 percent test-retest reliability. They cannot be influenced by self-esteem, stereotype threat, growth mindset, coaching, or whether the subject got a good night's sleep before giving the DNA sample.

Plomin expects polygenic scores to transform both clinical psychology and psychology research.[16] With regard to clinical psychology, he foresees five such changes:

Polygenic scores will be able to identify the genetic risk that an individual faces for a given disorder before the problem has developed. Psychologists will no longer be confined to observing symptoms and diagnosing problems after they manifest themselves.

Clinical psychology will move away from diagnoses and toward dimensions. One of the revelations of recent research is that polygenic scores are normally distributed, thereby demonstrating that genetic risk for psychological problems is continuous. There is no gene that moves a person from normal to psychologically disordered. In fact, the words "risk" and "disorder" no longer have the same meanings they once did. "There are no disorders to diagnose and there are no disorders to cure. Polygenic scores will be used to index problems quantitatively rather than deciding whether someone 'has' a disorder."[17]

Polygenic scores will enable clinical psychology to create more precise treatments. They will be especially useful for choosing the right drugs and dosages based on genetic evidence—and, as importantly, avoiding the expense and side effects of trying wrong drugs and dosages.

Clinical psychology's focus will shift from treatment toward prevention. Clinical psychologists have no effective broad-based, large-scale prevention strategies. But when we know from polygenic scores that an individual is at risk, we can design, test, and eventually identify effective prevention strategies for individuals.

Polygenic scores will promote "positive genomics." A normal distribution has two tails, and that is as true of psychological states as of any other normally distributed phenomenon. Clinical psychology focuses on the left-hand, negative tail. Knowing where a person stands on the continuum for certain traits can make it easier to identify ways to focus "on strengths instead of problems, abilities rather than disabilities, and resiliencies instead of vulnerabilities."[18]

Polygenic scores will also encourage more attention to the right-hand tail of the distribution, which for many traits can have its own problems—perhaps, for example, the opposite of being at high risk for bipolar disorder is not sunny emotional stability, but instead a flat affect that leaves a person unable to experience the highs and lows of life. What is the sweet spot—the operationalization of Aristotle's golden mean—for a psychological trait? We're going to learn far more about such things as polygenic scores become available.

Psychology research will be similarly transformed, Plomin argues, as polygenic scores make it possible for researchers to ask questions about nature and nurture with far greater precision and sophistication than in the past. Furthermore, the number of researchers who can participate in the research will increase manyfold. Until now, only researchers who had access to databases of twins and adoptees could ask questions about the roles of nature and nurture. Now, researchers can use any database that includes genomic information to do such analyses, and the number of such databases is growing rapidly.

The study of "generalist" genes will be opened up. Researchers have already identified what appears to be a general genetic factor of psychopathology, finding polygenic score correlations of +0.50 or more for schizophrenia, major depressive disorder, and bipolar disorder. The general factor of intelligence, g, is being informed by GWA studies. More broadly, researchers will be able to develop polygenic scores that investigate the genetic links among multiple traits, eventually building a picture of their overall genomic architecture.

All the questions about the relative roles of nature and nurture that twin studies have addressed can be revisited with greater precision. "Polygenic scores can be used to nail down genetic influence on the variance of environmental measures and on their covariance with psychological measures. They can also control for genetic influence in order to study purer environmental effects."[19] And that's just the beginning of the G×E interactions that polygenic scores allow researchers to explore.

Eric Turkheimer's Phenotypic Null Hypothesis

"Science is about causes, period."[20] That's the first sentence in an Eric Turkheimer article about Plomin's work on the shared and nonshared environment.[21] It captures the fundamental difference between the approaches of the two men. Plomin focuses on predictive validity while Turkheimer focuses on ultimate causes.

In 2014, Turkheimer pulled together strands he had been writing about for years into a formal statement of what amounts to a fourth law of behavior genetics to add to the first three I introduced in chapter 11. He calls it the "Phenotypic Null Hypothesis for the Genetics of Personality." It goes like this: "All traits are heritable, and the multivariate structure of the biometric components of behavior does not differ from the phenotypic structure."[22] He subsequently puts the central idea more simply: A phenotypic trait can be heritable without having a genetic mechanism.

To introduce what he means, Turkheimer draws a contrast between Huntington's disease and divorce. If we observe a person exhibiting the symptoms of Huntington's disease, we don't go looking for sociological explanations. Researchers have established an explanation at the genetic level that is theoretically sound and has been verified by test. Causation is known.

Suppose instead we observe a person who is getting a divorce. Marital status is highly heritable—72 percent in one large-sample twin study.[23] The heritability of divorce specifically has been estimated at around 50 percent.[24] Because divorce is heritable, we can be sure that a GWAS will identify a large number of SNPs that are significantly associated with divorce. But what have we really learned?

Suppose, for example, that some of the SNPs are related to the personality trait "irritability." Isn't that a plausible causal link to divorce? It could be, for some fraction of divorces. But we can't be sure of even that. Pervasive pleiotropy probably means that the SNPs related to irritability are also related to a number of other traits that are just as plausibly a cause of divorce—or, conversely, might be related to traits that would more plausibly be related to resistance to divorce. Omnigenetics and pleiotropy both work to create a causal map so sprawling and indeterminate that it is reasonable to conclude that GWAS has taught us nothing new about the causes of divorce and that finding more SNPs in more studies won't teach us anything important. "The heritability of marriage is a by-product of the universal, nonspecific, genetic pull on everything, not an indication that divorce is a biological process awaiting genetic analysis," Turkheimer writes. "Marriage and divorce are heritable, but they do not have a specific genetic etiology."[25]

Turkheimer is not alone in making this point. Geneticists Marcus Feldman and Sohini Ramachandran, who share his position, put it this way:

We must start from recognition that all complex human traits result from a combination of causes. If these causes interact, it is impossible to assign quantitative values to the fraction of a trait due to each, just as we cannot say how much of the area of a rectangle is due, separately, to each of its two dimensions. Thus, in the analyses of complex human phenotypes, such as those described above, we cannot actually find "the relative importance of genes and environment in the determination of phenotype."[26]

It is important to emphasize that Feldman, Turkheimer, and like-minded colleagues are not merely repeating Graham Coop's cautions about how many complications remain unresolved. They aren't just saying that it's early days yet and that we shouldn't get ahead of the data. They are saying that when it comes to complex traits, the GWA enterprise is futile. Turkheimer again: "Causal explanations of complex differences among humans are therefore not going to be found in individual genes or environments any more than explanations of plate tectonics can be found in the chemical composition of individual rocks."[27]

Predictions

On some purely technical issues, the Plomin and Turkheimer schools are not in conflict. Plomin does not argue that polygenic scores are causal as Turkheimer defines it. On the contrary, he acknowledges the disconnect: "The correlation between a polygenic score and a psychological trait does not tell us about the brain, behavioral or environmental pathways by which the polygenic score affects the trait."[28] For his part, Turkheimer does not dispute the existence of the correlations between polygenic scores and phenotypic traits that Plomin describes.

Yet these two schools nonetheless represent radically different understandings of where genomics and neuroscience are going to take us. The great debate for which they are exemplars is going to continue, informed by new developments in analytic methods and results from the huge new genomic databases that are coming online. I have speculative opinions about how the debate will go that I will reserve for the final chapter. Here, I confine myself to some consequences that I think are close to inevitable.

I should begin by stating my own assessment of the great debate, because it undoubtedly affects my predictions: In my field, applied social science, predictive validity trumps causal pathways. The Turkheimer position about our ignorance of causal pathways is certainly correct now and may be correct for decades to come. But applied social science has never been about causal pathways (until now, it's never been an option) and perhaps never will be. It's about explaining enough variance to make useful probabilistic statements.

Regarding the current limitations on predictive validity and the limited ways in which the genomic analyses add anything to what we already know from twins studies, I again think the Turkheimer position is correct about where we stand now. If you want to know a six-year-old's cognitive ability, an IQ score is still much more accurate than a polygenic score. If you want to know the heritability of a trait, polygenic scores still don't tell us much that we don't already know from twin studies. But we're talking about a field that sees methodological advances virtually every month. I think the application of genomic data to social science questions is roughly where aviation was in 1908. Eric Turkheimer thinks the Wright Flyer design has unfixable performance limits (and it does). Robert Plomin foresees the DC-3 (and it's coming).

Polygenic Scores Will Be Useful No Matter What and Will Therefore Be Used

By the end of the 2020s, it will be widely accepted that quantitative studies of social behavior that don't use polygenic scores usually aren't worth reading. More formally, it will be widely accepted that the predictive validity of polygenic scores gives us useful information about causes even though we still don't understand the causal pathways. It's not an unusual situation in science, including the hard sciences. Look at the discovery of laws in physics through the nineteenth century that were validated solely by their predictive validity.

I will use a specific example to illustrate the situation facing applied social science. Suppose it's 2030 and researchers are exploring causes of juvenile crime. In addition to the standard predictors as of 2020 (e.g., parental

SES, education, IQ), researchers have access to polygenic scores for various aspects of criminality. They analyze how the phenotypic measures interact with the polygenic measures as predictors of criminal behavior. In light of the Turkheimer school's objections, can the researchers be sure that the results for the polygenic scores are legitimately interpreted as causal? No. But in an Occam's-razor sense, the results of the analyses will make alternative hypotheses more or less plausible and, as importantly, generate ideas for the next round of analyses that will incrementally clarify what's going on. In 2030, when large databases with genomic information are easily available, I predict it will be akin to professional malpractice to conduct an analysis of social behavior that does *not* include genomic information. In any case, few quantitative social scientists are going to write such analyses because they won't get past peer review. The question, "Why didn't you take genetics into account?" will be universal and will have no good answer.

Broad Swaths of Social Science Will Be Affected

As I write, none of the social sciences have come to terms with genetics. My second prediction is that by 2030 the holdouts will be confined to isolated pockets. The impact of the genomic revolution will have importantly affected all of the traditional social science disciplines.

"Affect" can mean several things. The most important will be the role of genomics in creating novel research strategies that wouldn't have occurred to a social scientist in the pre-genomics era. In the study of genetic effects, twin studies are confining. They require large, hard-to-assemble, expensive samples of twins. The Falconer equations are a blunt tool that enables us to apportion roles to genes, shared environment, and everything else, thereby answering the "how much" question. The new techniques will open up new ways to explore the "how" questions. I've focused on polygenic scores, but a variety of analytic tools are being developed—for example, Genome-Wide Complex Trait Analysis (GCTA).[29] Just as the advent of the university computer did in the 1960s and 1970s, the advent of cheap genomic information will generate new classes of studies that cannot be anticipated. Comparing the eventual power and flexibility of genomic analyses with the ACE model is akin to comparing the power and flexibility of multiple regression analysis with the analysis of a 2×2 contingency table.

With regard to the existing classes of studies, cheap genomic information will also broadly affect studies that analyze a personality trait, ability, or social behavior as it varies by sex, ethnicity, or class. The degree to which such studies are woven into research agendas varies by discipline.

Psychology. The genomics revolution will affect just about everything in psychology that involves the analysis of quantitative data. Psychology is about understanding human personality, emotions, cognitive abilities, and behavior. All of those topics include genetic sources. Plomin's description of the possibilities that I summarized earlier conveys the breadth of the potential effects on both clinical practice and research.

Anthropology. Two of anthropology's subfields, archaeology and physical anthropology, deal in topics that can obviously be informed by ancient DNA, and there's no reason to think scholars in those fields won't take advantage of it. The other two subfields, cultural anthropology and linguistic anthropology, should be as dramatically affected by genomic information as psychology will be, but they are now a battleground between scholars who see their discipline as a science and those who see it as a hybrid of investigation and social justice advocacy.[30] I assume that genomic information will be incorporated to some degree into these latter two subfields, but it is not clear to what extent.

Sociology. Some corners of sociology involve empirical topics that won't be affected, but they are the exception. To give you an idea, consider the 49 articles that were published in America's most prestigious sociological journal, the *American Sociological Review*, in 2018 and the first issue of 2019. Of the 39 articles that presented either survey data or quantitative experimental results, 33 were on topics for which polygenic scores would be directly relevant. In almost half (18 of the 39), the major topic of the article directly involved sex, ethnicity, or class.[31]

Economics and political science. The role of psychological factors in economics goes back to Adam Smith's *Theory of Moral Sentiments.* The work of Daniel Kahneman, Amos Tversky, and Paul Slovic on decision making under conditions of uncertainty and, more recently, the work of Cass Sunstein and Richard Thaler on "nudge" theory, are both rich fields of study that will be informed by genomic data.[32] They are only part of the growing field of behavioral economics. Similarly, questions about how humans act as political agents are at the core of political science. Genomic information is just as relevant to voting decisions as it is to economic decisions. The finding from twin studies that political and ideological views are substantially heritable opens up another set of possibilities.

Social policy. Perhaps the most visible impact of the genomics revolution will be found in public policy analysis. This prediction obviously includes almost any issue involving education, whether pre-K, K–12, or higher education, but it also includes welfare policy, criminality and criminal justice, foster care and adoption, marriage and family, poverty and unemployment—you name it. If it's about social policy, it's almost certainly about topics that genomic data will inform.

We already have one specific example as I write. An international team led by Kathryn Paige Harden and Benjamin Domingue used polygenic scores as a "molecular tracer" to explore how the flow of students through the math pipeline in secondary schools varied in socioeconomically advantaged and disadvantaged schools. Among other things, the analysis revealed that advantaged schools did a better job than disadvantaged schools of getting students with high polygenic scores into advanced math classes and of buffering students with low polygenic scores from dropping out of math. It also revealed that many students with exceptional polygenic scores were unlikely to take the most advanced math classes.[33] If these findings were to be replicated and elaborated, they would have direct implications for better education policy. It's just the beginning.

Some Basics About the Role of the Environment Will Be Better Understood Soon

It will be a long time before the details are fully understood, but the introduction of genomic data will answer some of the most basic questions about the respective roles of genes and environment quickly, for two reasons.

First, genomic data can answer questions about genetic nurture (discussed in chapter 13) that twin studies cannot. In twin studies, the shared environment is the same for both twins, which raises difficult technical problems when there is no variation around the family mean (for example, as in the case of divorce, which is by definition completely shared by both MZ and DZ twins).[34] Analyses using polygenic scores or GCTA are not constrained to twins and thereby escape that problem.

The broader advantage of genomic analyses in this regard is that the complexities of genetic nurture can be unraveled. "Although twin studies have reported for decades that most environments are nearly as heritable as behaviors, this work has been limited to twin-specific environments," write Maciej Trzaskowski and Robert Plomin. "GCTA opens up the possibility of investigating genetic influence on family-, neighborhood-, or even country-wide environmental measures that cannot be studied using the twin design because they are shared in common by members of a twin pair."[35] The same is true of analyses using polygenic scores.

Second, genomic analyses using polygenic scores give us a usable baseline measure of genetic potential. As matters stand, every measure of genetic potential that we use, whether from cognitive tests or personality inventories, is contaminated by potential environmental effects, and the contamination is rightly feared to be worst for people who have come from the most disadvantaged environments. Correlations between polygenic scores and phenotypes cannot be explained by backward causation, and that alone is enough to give us important leverage, despite all the complications.[36]

Eric Turkheimer has used an analogy that illustrates what I mean, comparing polygenic scores to a pile of raw building materials. Let's say that you have many such piles, each of which will be used to construct a building. If you carefully examine the components of different piles, you can determine similarities among them—the buildings' starting places. "That similarity in starting place winds up being correlated with how similar the eventual buildings are," Turkheimer writes. "So pile-similarity is correlated with similarity in how the buildings are used, or what color they are or how big they are, or whatever. These correlations aren't enormous, but they are striking, often in the range of .4–.6. What's more, it turns out that occasionally, there are *identical* piles of materials, and although these identical piles don't produce identical buildings, the buildings they produce are damn similar, often in the range of .7–.9. This is the heritability of building type."[37]

Turkheimer's point is that an individual's genetic potential can lead to a widely dispersed range of phenotypes, which is unquestionably true. My point is that the piles are there at the beginning, constrain the range of possibilities, and are causal in just one direction. By the same token, a polygenic score for IQ or any other trait is causally antecedent, and that makes an enormous difference in the research questions we can answer confidently.

To see how dramatically this will change matters, recall from chapter 12 the vexed question of a G×E interaction between childhood SES and the heritability of IQ. The reason that vexed question is so important is that low heritability for disadvantaged children at young ages could mean an opening for interventions to have major effects. One reason the results have been so equivocal is that measures of IQ before the age of six are so unreliable. A reasonably good polygenic score for IQ fixes that.

Suppose that polygenic scores of children from disadvantaged backgrounds show that their IQ scores as adolescents average 10 points lower than their polygenic scores would have led us to expect. Confident new knowledge of that kind will energize the search for effective interventions in ways that we can scarcely imagine. Conversely, suppose it is found that the relationship of polygenic scores to phenotypic IQ scores in adolescence is about the same regardless of the childhood environment. I realize that many people dread such an outcome. In fact, that too will provide an incentive: to redirect our attention to fostering human flourishing for people with a wide range of ineradicable inequalities in gifts—a topic I take up in the concluding chapter. The most likely scenario is that the results will be less dramatic in either direction but will nonetheless teach us much about untapped potential.

The example generalizes to a wide variety of topics in which the underlying question is the extent to which socioeconomic or cultural disadvantage has affected the realization of a person's potential. I will not spin out all the collateral analyses that could be done or describe how the analytic complications could be dealt with. I do not expect that such analyses will be free of controversy. Rather, I am asserting that many such analyses are technically feasible, will be conducted within the relatively near future, and will offer powerful tests of questions that have been argued for decades.

Eventually Environmental Influences Will Be Demystified

As matters stand, the environment is routinely treated by many social scientists as almost mystically complicated.[38] I will have more speculative comments to make about that assumption in the next chapter, but this much is not speculative: Being freed from the restriction to samples of twins will enable this position to be explored as well, though the process will take much longer than answering the basic questions.

Is socioeconomic environment in a specific culture the issue? We don't need to go out and assemble new longitudinal databases. We already have many large longitudinal databases with detailed data on family structure, parenting practices, SES, education, labor market experience, and just about every other interesting variable you can name. The samples for many of these databases could easily be genotyped. Take, for example, the 1979 and 1997 cohorts of the National Longitudinal Survey of Youth, two of the most widely used American databases. Almost all of the members of those samples are still alive and most of their whereabouts are known. Ask them for cheek swabs in return for the kind of genomic information for which 23andMe charges a few hundred dollars. We may be genotyping people at age 60, but in doing so we get virtually the same baseline information that we would have gotten had we genotyped them at birth.[39] If we want to explore intergenerational effects, we can genotype the parents and the offspring of the members of these samples.

Are we interested in G×E interactions for ancestral populations? Every major ancestral population lives in every conceivable kind of environment. They live in countries in different parts of the world. Within most of those countries, they have varying socioeconomic status, varying numbers of generations of acculturation, and, for that matter, varying degrees of admixture with other ancestral populations. They live in countries that they rule and countries in which they are minorities. As minorities, they live in countries where discrimination against their ethnic group is severe and countries where it is negligible. Do ethnicity and environment interact in complex ways? The natural variation in the environments where ancestral populations live is so great that the raw material for answering that question is plentiful.

If the environment really is as pervasive and subtle a force as so many believe, the comparisons of polygenic scores and phenotypic scores will reveal their complex interactions and be a rich source of information for future research. But it's also possible that for some traits in some populations in some situations, the role of the environment is not particularly complicated or important. That too would be an important finding.

Recapitulation

The great debate will not end soon. The contending parties can continue to make their respective cases on the core issues no matter what the other side says. If proving causation at the molecular level is the goal, the Turkheimer school's pessimism seems well founded. If predictive validity is the goal, the Plomin school has good evidence that usable polygenic scores for many traits are either already available or coming soon.

I will add, however, my own view that one important issue has already been decided: There's no longer any question whether the use of polygenic scores will be widespread. This is already obvious in medical research. In 2010, two technical articles in the U.S. National Library of Medicine contained the phrase "polygenic score" or "polygenic risk score" in the title or abstract. By 2015, that number was up to 47. In 2018, it was 171. Publications during the first half of 2019 were on pace to increase by another third.[40] We can expect the same swift upsurge of publications in the social sciences.

Beyond any of the specifics I have discussed, I share Plomin's belief that we are in the midst of an unfolding and historic revolution in the social sciences. As he put it in *Blueprint*, "The most exciting aspect of polygenic scores is the potential they offer for completely new and unexpected directions for research."[41] He gives examples from his own research involving schools and social mobility, but his enthusiasm is properly open-ended. When a scientific discipline gets a major new tool such as the microscope, electrolysis, or spectroscopy, the eventual uses sprawl far beyond their original ones. Polygenic scores will be a similarly multipurpose tool for expanding the questions that social scientists can ask. Ultimately, the incorporation of genetic information into the social sciences will be transformative.

15

Reflections and Speculations

The study of human diversity fascinates me, and I hope it has captured your interest as well. Ongoing discoveries in genetics and neuroscience are going to change our world in profound ways over the coming decades. I am optimistic that almost all of them will be for the better.

The findings I have presented boil down to just three cautious conclusions:

- Human beings can be biologically classified into groups by sex and by ancestral population. Like most biological classifications, these groups have fuzzy edges. This complicates things analytically, but no more than that.
- Many phenotypic differences in personality, abilities, and social behavior that we observe between the sexes, among ancestral populations, and among social classes have a biological component.
- Growing knowledge about human diversity will inevitably shape the future of the social sciences.

I hope this long and winding account has also made it clear that we need not fear talking about human differences. Nothing we are going to learn will diminish our common humanity. Nothing we learn will justify rank-ordering human groups from superior to inferior—the bundles of qualities that make us human are far too complicated for that. Nothing we learn will lend itself to genetic determinism. We live our lives with an abundance of unpredictability, both genetic and environmental.

Above all, nothing we learn will threaten human equality properly understood. I like the way Steven Pinker put it: "Equality is not the empirical claim that all groups of humans are interchangeable; it is the moral principle that individuals should not be judged or constrained by the average properties of their group."[1]

My conclusions are so cautious that they shouldn't be controversial. If the preceding chapters haven't persuaded you of that, a summing up in this chapter is not going to do the job.

I use this final chapter for another purpose. Writing *Human Diversity* has touched on topics that I have been researching and thinking about for decades. The experience has prompted many reactions on my part that don't belong in the previous chapters because they are based on the totality of my experience. I want to express them, but I do so with trepidation. Remember that you are reading my personal and sometimes idiosyncratic interpretations. *They neither augment nor diminish the empirical case for the ten propositions.* The evidence that those propositions are true needs to be confronted. Having done that, go ahead and form your own opinion of their implications without regard to anything that follows. I am about to go beyond the data.

The Role of Genes in Explaining Human Differences Has Been Misconceived

It's About More Than Traits. It's About Human Nature.

I hope that the twenty-first century will see both social scientists and policy-makers come to peace with the reality of human nature. It's about time.

The Eclipse of Human Nature

From antiquity through the Renaissance, most thinkers took it for granted that human beings come into the world with preexisting characteristics. In the West, little was written about how people could be changed except through Christian salvation. Then toward the end of the seventeenth century came John Locke, intellectual father of the Enlightenment, who popularized the theory of the mind as blank slate—tabula rasa.[2] Locke himself was advocating empiricism and opposing the use of supposedly innate ideas that justified the divine right of kings, hereditary aristocracies, and authoritarian religious institutions.[3] But the blank slate metaphor was powerful. It soon spread to the assumption that human beings are malleable, molded by events and capable of being molded by design.

In the eighteenth century, this position was most flamboyantly proclaimed by the Enlightenment's rock star, Jean-Jacques Rousseau, who was romantically optimistic about education's potential to do the molding by design. Even unromantic Adam Smith believed in a partially blank slate: "The difference between the most dissimilar characters, between a philosopher and a common street porter, for example, seems to arise not so much from nature, as from habit, custom, and education."[4]

But Smith also had a fully realized conception of an inborn human nature (see *The Theory of Moral Sentiments*), and thereby represents a competing stream of eighteenth-century thought in which he was joined by others in the Scottish Enlightenment and by the American founders. Whereas the French First Republic reified the belief that humans could be molded into any shape that rational planners might devise, the American Constitution reified the belief that human nature must shape the structure of government, not the other way around. Why did the founders insist upon the checks and balances? "It may be a reflection on human nature," Madison famously wrote, "that such devices should be necessary to control the abuses of government. But what is government itself, but the greatest of all reflections on human nature?"[5]

During the nineteenth century, unsentimental realism about human nature lost ground to a strange mix of idealism and rationalism that pursued extravagant goals. Karl Marx outdid all the rest with his grand theoretical application of the scientific method (as Marx saw it) to human malleability, blending history, sociology, economics, and politics into a utopian vision of what could be accomplished given the right economic and institutional structures.

The Communists who came to power in Russia didn't think it was just theory; they thought it would work miracles. "Communist life will not be formed blindly, like coral islands, but will be built consciously, will be tested by thought, will be directed and corrected," Leon Trotsky wrote in 1924. "Man, who will learn how to move rivers and mountains, how to build peoples' palaces on the peaks of Mont Blanc and at the bottom of the Atlantic, will not only be able to add to his own life richness, brilliancy and intensity, but also a dynamic quality of the highest degree."[6]

Elsewhere, the pioneers of the new discipline of sociology had less extreme ambitions, but they drew from the same optimism about the power of the scientific method applied to human behavior. "Our main objective," Émile Durkheim wrote of sociology, "is to extend the scope of scientific rationalism to cover human behavior." Causes and effects could be spelled out, he continued, and they in turn "can then be transformed into rules of action for the future."[7] The constraints of inborn human nature? "These individual natures are merely the indeterminate material that the social factor molds and transforms."[8]

At the beginning of the twentieth century, the application of the scientific method to human malleability was extended to another new discipline, psychology. Behaviorism, founded by John B. Watson, took the blank slate to its ultimate expression.[9]

> Give me a dozen healthy infants, well-formed, and my own specified world to bring them up in and I'll guarantee to take any one at random and train him to become any type of specialist I might select—doctor, lawyer, artist, merchant-chief, and yes, even beggar-man and thief, regardless of his talents, penchants, tendencies, abilities, vocations, and race of his ancestors.[10]

By the 1940s, behaviorism had become a major field within academic psychology departments, with B. F. Skinner acquiring considerable fame for, among other things, his Skinner box for studying operant conditioning.[11] Skinner was also convinced that you often didn't need to study humans to understand humans—pigeons and rats would do. Or as one of his former students, Richard Herrnstein, answered, deadpan, when I asked him why behaviorists used pigeons for research: "Given the right reinforcement schedule, pigeons are indistinguishable from Harvard sophomores."[12]

Eventually, the malleability assumption spilled over into policy. The social democratic left in Europe and liberal thinkers in the United States did not aspire to create a "new man" as the Communists had, but they were confident that many of society's problems of poverty, crime, and educational failure were waiting to be solved by rational thinking scientifically applied to malleable human beings. The phrase "social engineering" came into vogue—not used sarcastically as it usually is today, but as a label for policies that would move society closer to utopia. The designers of those programs did not spend time brooding over inborn, intractable characteristics of human beings that might foil their plans.

The mid-1960s through the mid-1970s saw the apogee of American academic optimism for using public policy to change behaviors on a grand scale. But as the evaluations came in, it became apparent that the multibillion-dollar initiatives of the Great Society in education, employment, and criminal justice had not worked out as planned.[13] Aspirations were scaled back. The emphasis changed from an upbeat attitude that "smart social policy can fix that!" to the darker mentality of intersectionality. By the 1990s, the problems of poverty, crime, and educational failure were increasingly ascribed to an intractable, pervasive structure of oppression.

Meanwhile, the psychologists you met in Part III were using twin studies to explore the heritability of human traits. But even those who were comfortable with a major role for heritability of discrete traits were not necessarily comfortable with a role for human nature.

Human nature refers to a coherent conception of the ways that human beings have been shaped by evolution. My idea here goes all the way back to chapter 1 and my reasons for wanting to aggregate effect sizes rather than treat them separately. What makes the differences between male and female personalities interesting and important is not an effect size of +0.24 on one facet in a personality inventory and −0.38 on another, but the way that differences on a dozen facets fit together as a profile. So it is with human nature: The important thing is not the heritabilities of specific traits but the way that the heritability of a variety of linked traits forms an interpretable mosaic.

Even psychologists who are leading scholars of heritability shy away from putting the pieces together or acknowledging that the pieces *can* be put together—such is the shadow that has become associated with human nature. In Steven Pinker's words, "To acknowledge human nature, many think, is to endorse racism, sexism, war, greed, genocide, nihilism, reactionary politics, and neglect of children and the disadvantaged. Any claim that the mind has an innate organization strikes people not as a hypothesis that might be incorrect but as a thought it is immoral to think."[14] That description, written near the turn of the new century, still applies two decades later. Changing it requires a rediscovery of human nature.

The Rediscovery of Human Nature

The rediscovery of human nature has been the province of evolutionary psychology. One of my predictions about the genomics revolution, too speculative to be included in chapter 14, is that evolutionary psychology will finally take its rightful role as a major tool for understanding differences in cognitive repertoires across the sexes, ancestral populations, and social classes. One of the ways it will do so is by tying the elements of cognitive repertoires into a coherent description of human nature.

What we know as evolutionary psychology was anticipated in Darwin's own work, but it was not until 1964 and 1972 that seminal articles by William Hamilton and Robert Trivers respectively provided a rich set of hypotheses for exploring how human nature has been shaped through evolutionary processes.[15] Biologist E. O. Wilson expanded upon their work in *Sociobiology* (1975), and Richard Dawkins popularized some of the key themes in *The Selfish Gene* a year later.[16] Over the course of the 1980s, psychologist Leda Cosmides and anthropologist John Tooby wrote a series of articles on evolutionary psychology that culminated in 1992 with "The Psychological Foundations of Culture," which proposed to replace what they called the Standard Social Science Model (the intellectual version of the orthodoxy) with an Integrated Causal Model that would bring biology into the picture.[17]

Even as evolutionary psychology matured as a discipline and developed ways of dealing with the dangers of just-so storytelling, it was no secret that the underlying objections to evolutionary psychology were political—the virulently hostile reaction to E. O. Wilson's *Sociobiology* left no doubt about it. A familiar figure from Part II, Richard Lewontin, was joined by neurobiologist Steven Rose and psychologist Leon Kamin as authors of a denunciation of evolutionary psychology titled *Not in Our Genes: Biology, Ideology, and Human Nature* (1984).[18] That hostility continues to this day. It is an integral part of the orthodoxy.[19]

Evolutionary psychologists have been fighting back for decades and can claim to have won on points many times over, but it has done little good.[20] One of them, Steve Stewart-Williams, has not repressed his frustration. "Critics who rail against status quo bolstering, genetic determinism, and just-so story-telling are like the crazy person in the bus shelter, fighting with a sparring partner who isn't really there. They've invented their own evolutionary psychology and are arguing loudly with that," he wrote.[21] "Fighting the evolutionary psychologists' corner is like weeding a garden, or cutting the head off a hydra. It's like a Nietzschean eternal recurrence, or pushing

Sisyphus's rock up the hill again and again, forever. And it's also a pain in the butt."[22]

I may sound naïve in predicting that the genomics revolution is going to finally get the rock to the top of the hill. The orthodoxy has not had a problem brushing off hard evidence in the past. Why should the genomics revolution pose a greater problem?

The reason goes back to the antiscientific bulwark that the orthodox are huddling behind. Evolutionary psychology is about the reality of inborn human nature: the role that biology has played in shaping human beings above the neck. The orthodox are saying that it's all socialization. They have felt able to continue to maintain this position because there has not been an ironclad, you-can't-get-around-this-one refutation of it. Polygenic scores will eventually provide that.

Once again, look ahead to 2030. By that time, scientists will be able to make predictions about personality characteristics, abilities, and social behavior of groups on the basis of polygenic scores. If the orthodoxy is right, such statistical predictions should be impossible. If everything is socialization, then DNA samples shouldn't be able to tell you anything about differences in personality characteristics, abilities, or social behavior among adults.

"But they can just soften their position," it may be argued. The orthodoxy can shift to an "it's almost but not entirely a matter of socialization" and carry on as before. Perhaps that's right, but I doubt it. We didn't need to sequence the genome to recognize that human beings have evolved underlying characteristics that are deeply biological. In that sense, the orthodoxy on campuses has been hanging on inexplicably, like a religious cult whose leader's predictions have been contradicted by events time and again. That amounts to a fragile situation. I don't think the orthodoxy can tolerate acknowledging openly that, for example, men and women are biologically different above the neck even a little bit.

This explains my probably starry-eyed expectation: The ability to predict a wide variety of human differences solely from baseline genetic measures will puncture the center of the orthodoxy's beleaguered defense. Evolutionary psychologists will be liberated to make strides in describing human nature, not just individual heritable traits, in an environment where the legitimacy and importance of their contributions is accepted.

Reconciling Human Nature with Ideology

The insistence that only the environment shapes cognitive repertoires has been yet another case, like "gender is a social construct" and "race is a social construct," of taking partial truths and running them into the ground. In the centuries when Locke and Smith wrote, most people with the potential to be philosophers probably really were living out their lives as street porters—and farmers and housewives. People in all eras and places really are shaped to some degree by their environment. But the limits of shaping are governed by hundreds of millions of years of evolution.

An apt example of the clash between utopian plans and human nature comes from Israeli kibbutzes founded in the 1930s and 1940s. Infants and children were cared for by full-time caretakers and lived in a centralized children's quarter, spending only a few hours per day with their parents. The intention was to replace the nuclear family with the extended family of the community. The rationale for doing so was grounded in ideals about human flourishing. The members of the early kibbutzes were themselves idealistic and committed to their utopian goals. The kibbutzes were small enough (a few hundred people) to permit intimate communities to form. The members shared powerful bonds of a common ethnic and cultural heritage. If ever a socialist utopian community could succeed, the kibbutzes had the best chance. For a while, it seemed to work.[23] Over the years, however, the nuclear family ineluctably reasserted itself.[24] It was inevitable. Societies must be made to fit human nature, because human nature cannot be reshaped to fit theoretical utopias.

This brings us to the intersection of scientific findings and political ideology. I have a problem finding the right words here, because the meanings of "conservative" and "liberal" have shifted so radically in recent years. I'm using them as they were popularly understood in the United States from the New Deal until 2016. With those meanings in mind, this much is undeniable: The belief in constraints and limits on government's ability to change people is inherently conservative. The belief in open-ended potential for changing people through the right policies is inherently liberal.

That doesn't mean that liberals are forced into denying human nature; it just means that they need to take it into account. In the case of sex differences, this can often be done by adjusting policy to recognize differences in distributions between men and women. Custody of children after divorce is a case in point. Until the last quarter of the nineteenth century, men were automatically awarded custody of children. By the latter part of the nineteenth century, and largely as a result of first-wave feminism, the "tender years doctrine" automatically gave the mother custody of young children unless there was clear evidence that the mother was unfit. In the 1970s, one effect of second-wave feminism in many states was to remove the mother's legal advantage in custody disputes, substituting "the best interests of the child" as the basis for custody decisions and encouraging joint custody.

What is likely to be in "the best interests of the child" when the child is of "tender years"? By any measure of which sex is better at nurturing young children, there is a big effect size favoring females and an overwhelming evolutionary case that the female advantage is grounded in biology. If that is accepted as scientific reality, what is a principled liberal position toward child custody? One option is to follow Pinker's principle that people should not be judged by the average properties of their group. That's clearly the right call when we're talking about fairness in treating job applicants or criminal defendants. But what about when a helpless third party's "best interests" are involved? In a world where judges in custody disputes often are faced with no clear evidentiary basis for favoring one parent over another and a helpless third party's welfare is at stake, a principled liberal position can acknowledge an important innate difference between men and women.

Similarly, Title IX of the Education Amendments of 1972 had a good rationale (if you aren't a libertarian) for requiring schools to provide equitable opportunity for female students to participate in sports.[25] Some girls love competitive sports, and they weren't being offered enough opportunities to play them. It's also true that by any measure of interest in team sports there's a big effect size favoring males and there is again an overwhelming evolutionary case that the greater male interest is grounded in biology.[26] Title IX should be administered with that difference in mind (it often hasn't been).

Women in combat? It's not an issue of female courage. But from early childhood into adulthood, males are far more attracted than females to physical contests, including ones involving violence, and are more physically aggressive and risk-taking than women. Once again there is an overwhelming case that the sex difference is grounded in biology.[27] Are women as enthusiastic as men about attacking and killing total strangers if the proper institutional framework is provided (i.e., the military in battle)? Are women as obsessively driven to win at all costs in contest situations as men? Some women are, but what proportion? Can male soldiers be trained out of their instinct to protect women? Probably some can—but what proportion? Men and women have different distributions on these traits, with biology playing a major role. The conclusion need not be that women shouldn't be used in combat roles, but that the relevant sex differences need to be taken into account. Women in combat as part of a missile-firing team on a warship sidesteps the potential problems I just mentioned; women in combat as part of a frontline infantry platoon triggers all of them.

Being realistic about human nature goes far beyond sex differences. An acceptance of the constraints imposed by human nature should guide the administration of the civil and criminal justice systems, the regulation of business, the powers granted to bureaucrats—the operations of just about every social, cultural, economic, and political institution. It can be done by conservatives and liberals alike without either side having to abandon core principles. The challenge for conservatives is to accommodate their historic advocacy of freedom and limited government with the role of the genetic lottery in determining success. The challenge for liberals is to acknowledge the constraints of human nature in ways they have historically resisted.

The Role of the Environment in Explaining Human Differences Has Been Misconceived

It's Not the Shared Environment Versus the Nonshared Environment.
It's the Manipulable Environment Versus Happenstance and Milieu.

I cannot prove that the role of the environment in explaining human differences has been misconceived, but I can describe why I think so.

Murray's Conjecture

Analogies have been a popular way to describe the relative roles of genes and the environment for 50 years. Richard Lewontin started it in 1970 with one that Richard Herrnstein and I adapted for *The Bell Curve*: All of the kernels in a strain of hybrid seed corn are genetically identical. But if two handfuls of that seed corn are planted in Iowa and the Mojave Desert, there will be a huge difference in yield.[28] Christopher Jencks continued the tradition in 1979 with his analogy of red-haired children who are denied education (hair color is highly heritable and will be correlated with a difference in academic achievement, but it has nothing to do with genes).[29] Eric Turkheimer used piles of building materials to describe the limits of the genetic contribution in predicting phenotypic traits. Graham Coop produced the most elaborate analogy, the one about differences in French and English tea drinking that I recounted in chapter 14.

What these analogies have in common is that none of them would pose a problem to a real analysis. That's understandable; analogies need to employ simplistic situations to make their point. But social scientists trying to figure out differences in corn yield, educational achievement, the appearance of finished buildings, and tea drinking are not going to spend a nanosecond puzzling over the environmental forces at work. They are blindingly obvious. I think this is true far more often than most social scientists concede, hence Murray's Conjecture: *When a difference really is environmental in origin, it's easy to prove it; when it's hard to prove an environmental cause, it's because the role of the environment is minor.*[30]

Why were there so proportionally few female physicians through the first half of the twentieth century? Guess what: It was the environment. Proving that it was the environment is trivially easy. Why has there been so little change in the vocational choices of women for the last thirty years? It is now difficult to make an empirical case that residual sexism is the culprit. The reason it's so difficult, the conjecture says, is because the environment no longer has much effect.

The conjecture applies to personality traits and abilities, but I must specify that it often does *not* apply to much of social behavior. As I will explain subsequently, I think milieu everywhere and always has pervasive effects on social behavior.

As an elaboration of Murray's Conjecture, I propose a distinction among three types of environmental forces: legal compulsion, hard custom, and soft custom.

Legal compulsion. In the hierarchy of ways in which some human beings can force others to do their bidding, physical coercion is at the top. In a civilized society, that means legal compulsion. Why was European Jewish achievement in the arts and sciences so rare from the Middle Ages until the nineteenth century? Because Jews were prohibited by law from entering universities or engaging in scientific professions. Within two generations of their legal emancipation, Jews were disproportionately represented among the leading figures in both the arts and sciences.[31]

Hard custom refers to means other than laws that entail coercion. An example of physical coercion (and the threat of it) was the extralegal enforcement of segregation in the South to supplement the Jim Crow laws until the Civil Rights Act of 1964 and continuing to some degree thereafter. A nonviolent example of covert prohibition is the de facto ceiling that many medical schools put on the number of women they would admit until the law mandated equal access. Hard custom can persist for a long time even though it is not underwritten by laws. Under some circumstances, legal prohibition of discrimination can shorten its persistence.

Soft custom has no element of covert prohibition or the threat of physical coercion. It consists instead of social incentives to refrain from engaging in a behavior—stigma or social isolation. No one will beat you up, you won't lose your job, nor will any other tangible punishment be administered from on high. But you must bear social punishment—the disapproval of your parents, teachers, or other people who matter to you. Some of your friends become ex-friends. Your coworkers may shun you. For example, if you were one of the first women hired as police patrol officers in the 1960s, you had to put up with a lot, even if you were treated correctly professionally (which often didn't happen). Maybe none of your male coworkers would eat lunch with you and you would be subjected to endless derogatory comments about women's abilities.

My speculative proposition here is that once legal prohibitions and hard custom are no longer an issue, soft custom has a short half-life. The arrival of even a second policewoman on the force is a big relief to the pioneer. Then there are three, five, and 10 women. Many male police officers who were initially hostile see that the women are pretty good cops after all and begin to accept them as equals. I am not saying that soft custom goes away entirely, but that its power to intimidate diminishes nonlinearly, just as the half-life of radioactivity diminishes nonlinearly. Further, I would argue that the half-life is often a matter of years, sometimes a decade or so, but seldom many decades.

Translated into the way I see the role of the environment as it is usually construed, I think that much of the remaining discrimination against women, ethnic minorities, and LGBT people in the United States consists of soft custom and is well into or past its first half-life, albeit to varying degrees in different geographic and socioeconomic settings. That's why proving a large independent role for the environment in differential outcomes is often becoming difficult.

Happenstance, Milieu, and the Manipulable Environment

None of the above means that the environment is unimportant in determining how people's lives turn out. But in conceptualizing the environment, we shouldn't divide it into the shared environment and the nonshared environment. Rather, we should divide it into happenstance, milieu, and the manipulable environment.

Happenstance. Happenstance is equivalent to the nonshared environment seen from a different perspective.

Surely everyone who has reached middle age occasionally stops to muse on how differently life would have turned out except for random events. Certainly it is true of people who are lucky enough to be in happy marriages. Meeting that right person is almost always the result of a series of capricious events, and it's scary to think how your life would have been different if any one of the pieces hadn't fallen into place. With regard to one's children, happenstance amounts to one-in-millions chances that they turned out to be who they uniquely are. And of course, so was the union of egg and sperm that created you. The role of randomness is huge.

But do you feel the same way about the kind of person you have become? Your abilities? Your personality strengths and weaknesses? Speaking for myself, I know that my circles of friends, the places I've lived, the books I have written, and all sorts of other ways in which my personality traits and abilities have been expressed in behavior have been hugely affected by happenstance. So has my happiness. I can easily imagine having reached old age sad and lonely because of happenstance. But I sense that my personality traits and abilities are close to what they would have been no matter what, short of some extreme psychological or physical trauma.

I would argue that happenstance explains why people discover as they get older that they are becoming more like their parents—a common personal experience that is reflected in the technical literature demonstrating that heritability of many traits rises with age. My logic goes like this: In adolescence and young adulthood, people act inconsistently with their genetic predispositions for many reasons. Sometimes they are consciously rebelling against their parents. The broader generic reason is that adolescents and young adults are immature and prone to spectacularly poor judgment. That's why most of us recall things we did in adolescence and into our 20s and say to ourselves, "What could I have been thinking?"

THE REAL MEANING OF CLASS PRIVILEGE

I am generally skeptical of claims about the power of privilege. Growing up in an upper-middle-class or wealthy home has a variety of potential downsides. An exception involves the stupid things that adolescents sometimes do. Upper-middle-class families are often able to rescue their children from adolescent mistakes that can have lifelong disastrous consequences for poor children.

During those same years, we get bounced around by happenstance. Some random influences push us to do foolish things; other random influences push us toward maturity. For most people, this multitude of random events balances out, and we emerge into adulthood less likely to do things that run against genetic predisposition. Whether that's good, bad, or indifferent depends on what genetic predispositions we're talking about. But the nonshared environment has had its heyday. It may have played havoc with our lives for a time, but those effects were temporary (recall evidence to that effect from chapter 13).

Milieu refers to the world into which we are born in its cultural, social, and economic totality—the water in which we swim. Milieu often exerts itself most powerfully on a national scale, but it has many variations. The Amish have managed to preserve a comprehensive milieu in the face of a competitive national milieu. The typical college or university has a milieu that transcends socioeconomic status. So does a black neighborhood in Harlem or a Korean neighborhood in Los Angeles. In America's current polarized state, many of the politically committed of both extremes live in separate milieus. In my view, the current biggest American division is the milieu of small towns and small cities versus the milieu of the megalopolises and their suburbs.

Milieu is pervasively causal. It doesn't just influence the ways we behave. It entirely rules out many possibilities and makes others almost inevitable. A thought experiment may make the point. Imagine that Michelangelo, Mozart, and Shakespeare are all cloned in the twenty-first century as babies with exactly the same DNA as the originals. Let us suppose that as adults they respectively become an artist, a composer, and a writer. It is easily imaginable that they will rise to the top of their professions in our time—their talents would be prodigious in any century. But it is inconceivable that their masterpieces will be anything like the *Pietà*, the *Jupiter* Symphony, or *King Lear*. Expressions of genius are decisively shaped by the milieu into which geniuses are born.

Thinking of the distinction between milieu and environment in this way makes it easy for me to understand why the shared environment explains so little. Go back to our clone of Mozart. Let's say that you and your spouse are the cloned boy's adoptive parents. You know about his talent, and you think classical music would be the highest expression of his talent. What are you going to do that will channel that genius into composing some new string quartets in the classical style? You can try all sorts of things to manipulate the family environment, but you can't affect the milieu. Every moment that the cloned Mozart is not directly under your control, he will be swimming in the milieu—in comparison to which parents are nearly powerless. He may compose some mind-bendingly wonderful popular music or even wonderful atonal music. Not the *Jupiter*.

The milieu exerts a similar influence over everyone's life decisions. The occupations that are in vogue. The age at which people marry and the number of children they have. Sexual mores. Conceptions of virtue. Religiosity. The milieu changes continually, usually in the way that an ocean liner changes course—visibly, but seldom abruptly.[32] Government can affect milieu, but, sadly, the best examples of "successfully" doing so are the regimes of Hitler, Stalin, and Mao. In democratic regimes, changes in the milieu are commonly driven by broad changes in the culture that then prompt expression in public policy. The civil rights movement followed by the Civil Rights Act of 1964 is a recent example in American history—it is inconceivable that the Civil

Rights Act would have been passed in any earlier administration no matter how hard a president or party fought for it. The milieu wasn't yet right.

The manipulable environment refers to discrete aspects of our world that are at least theoretically possible to manipulate. It includes parenting practices, parental SES, the school, and most other aspects of what twin studies call the shared environment. Even if you share my belief that the milieu is a far more powerful influence, doesn't the fact that these influences are manipulable mean that we ought to try to manipulate them for the benefit of those who need help? That brings us to a question that policy analysts have been pondering for many years:

Why Is It So Hard for Outside Interventions to Work?

Of the 10 propositions that I defend in *Human Diversity*, the one that might attract the most vehement criticism is the final one, #10: "Outside interventions are inherently constrained in the effects they can have on personality, abilities, and social behavior." I almost refrained from spelling it out. What's the point, since the amount of money now being spent on such programs is rounding error in the federal budget? I included Proposition #10 nonetheless because among the truths that need to be understood is how incredibly difficult it is to get people to change permanently if they don't already want to—and sometimes even if they do.

One way or another, I have spent more than half a century around programs that were trying to get people to change the way they behave, whether as a "change agent" (how quaint that label sounds now) in the Peace Corps in the 1960s, an evaluator of social programs in the field in the 1970s, or a policy analyst reading the technical literature on social programs from the 1980s onward. These have been experiences that would make a cynic of a far saintlier person than I, and I suppose they account for my instinctive reaction to reports of success: "Oh yeah?" I have indeed grown cynical listening to glowing descriptions of programs that turned out to bear no resemblance to what was happening on the ground. I grew cynical because of technical articles in which the upbeat "Conclusions" section about a program's accomplishments didn't match up with the numbers in the "Results" section.

But those were not the experiences that most affected me. I alluded to my most dispiriting ones in the acknowledgments for *Losing Ground*, written soon after I had stopped evaluating social programs. My first debt, I wrote, was to the people who had run the social programs I had observed:

> Whether they have been counseling inner-city students in Atlanta, trying to keep Chicago delinquents out of jail, or teaching prenatal care to Thai villagers, they have shared an uncommon energy and dedication.... [But] the people who were doing the helping did not succeed nearly as often as they deserved. Why, when their help was so obviously needed and competently provided, was it so often futile?[33]

I am under the impression that I now know some answers to that question that I did not know in 1984.

The Fragility of Induced Effects

Effects of outside intervention are fragile. In a scientific sense, this is most apparent in the hundreds of attempts since the 1960s to positively affect the capabilities and behavior of disadvantaged populations, such as the pre-K programs I discussed in chapter 13. This is not the place to hash out the contentious literature on other types of interventions, but I think that four generalizations drawn from that literature are easily defended.

The first one is positive: Programs for people who self-select into the program can work. Alcoholics Anonymous is the most famous example, but there are others. KIPP and Success Academy are charter schools that have had success in educating students who include many minority children from low-income households.[34] The parents self-select on behalf of their children and the children themselves also have to buy into KIPP's and Success Academy's rigorous expectations. This is not to say that programs with self-selected clients are universally successful. But we do know how to help people who consciously want to help themselves and are prepared to try hard.

The other three generalizations apply to programs that try to help people without self-selection, and they are pessimistic:

- Substantively significant short-term effects have been observed, but even these have been comparatively rare.
- Fadeout of those immediate effects over a period of a few years has been nearly universal.

■ Over the last six decades, not a single major improvement in the education or socialization of the disadvantaged has been scaled up to the state or national level.

What makes this dismal experience puzzling is that everyone who has spent time with these efforts has seen anecdotal cases of not just "substantively significant" but what looked like dramatic change. I remember observing classes in an inner-city school in Atlanta where an experimental method of teaching math was being used. The same kids who had been somnolent or sullen in other classes were on the edge of their seats, completely engaged in an extremely fast-paced, intensive instruction in honest-to-god math. This was in the late 1970s. The method was never scaled up, and I can understand why. It required teachers to expend an enormous amount of nervous energy over the entire class period. I can't imagine being able to summon that kind of energy for more than two periods a day at most. I can't imagine that more than a small fraction of teachers have the skillset required to do it successfully even for two periods a day. Is it possible to take a class of ordinary students in a school in a socioeconomically deprived neighborhood and make them excited about math? Yes, I've seen it done. Do I have the remotest practical idea for how to do it on a large scale? No.

There are success stories of all kinds out there, but they seldom last. The school dropout whose mentor convinced her to return to school is enthusiastic for a few months and then drops out again. The drug user relapses. The student who got special tutoring in reading and whose grades went up in the first semester flunks the second semester. If failure to follow up the initial success were the explanation, then the solution would be simple: Provide follow-up support. But this leads to a second theme regarding the fragility of environmentally induced change:

The Relapse Syndrome

It is striking and even mysterious how hard it is to sustain a good effect. I'm not talking about disadvantaged children, but about you and me.

Does the word "diet" come to mind? Losing weight is something that large numbers of Americans have successfully accomplished—temporarily. But the number of people who are able to maintain their new, lower weight is minuscule compared to the number who gain all the weight back within a few months.

What makes this especially odd is that the experience of the diet is often positive. After a few days, you find that you aren't suffering from terrible hunger after all, and you have more energy. As you lose weight, you like the way you look in the mirror and like the compliments you get from friends. You are getting exactly the positive reinforcement that you hoped to get. And yet a few months later you are off the diet and have gained back all the weight. Why? Different people have different answers, but it comes down to this: You theoretically *should* be able to manipulate the environment to produce a change in your phenotype, but it's as if there were an ineluctable gravitational force pulling you back to a genetic baseline, whether that genetic baseline is grounded in your metabolism, your self-discipline, or some other complicated set of personal tendencies over which you don't seem to have enough control.

The same may be said of other self-initiated attempts at improvement, whether it's a resolution to stick to an exercise regime or to keep your desk tidy. It's not that we fail, nor that we find we don't like being fit or having a tidy desk. We succeed for a while and enjoy the results. But it all fades away.

I will use another personal example, because it involves an achievement that has eluded educators despite their most strenuous attempts: dramatically raising cognitive function—not an effect size of +0.35 or +0.50, but of two or three standard deviations.

One summer while I was in graduate school, I enrolled in the Evelyn Wood speed-reading course. When I entered the course, a pretest revealed that I read at about 500 words per minute—okay but nothing special. At the end of the course (as I recall, it was about six weeks) I was reading at around 2,500 words per minute. It is hard to convey what a phenomenal experience it is to be turning the pages of a book every few seconds with full comprehension. Furthermore, the change was not as straightforward as losing weight. The program had drastically raised my ability on a complex cognitive task. As a graduate student with a crushing reading load, it seemed too good to be true.

And it was. There was a catch, and my Evelyn Wood teacher was stern about it: You've got to read everything using the Evelyn Wood technique. You can't decide to pick up a detective novel and read it slowly just for fun. If you do, you'll lose your speed. I can't complain that I wasn't warned. And of course, I didn't follow through, and within a few months I was back at baseline. The experience often comes to mind when people ask me if there's any way to raise IQ and I have to answer that there's no way to raise it dramatically. Then some corner of my mind goes back to that brief, shining moment when one of my own cognitive abilities shot upward like a rocket, and I add, "not permanently."

Nutritionists have a phrase for what happens with diets. Each person has a "set point" (or "settling point"): a weight range that the body will defend if weight falls below or above that range. I'm not going to get into the science of diets, but the concept applies to a wide variety of traits that technically can be changed by environmental stimuli, but seldom are permanently changed by those stimuli. A heritability of, say, 50 percent means that half of the expression of that trait is environmental, but it does not necessarily mean that any nontrivial proportion of that environment can be manipulated to achieve a preferable expression of that trait over the long term. It's another reason I think the environmental role assigned to traits by twin studies overestimates the plasticity of human beings. We are not made of soft plastic that can be molded and then hardens into place. We are balls of Silly Putty. We can be molded into interesting shapes—temporarily. Leave us alone for a while and we're flat again.

Toward the Best of All Possible Worlds

Custom dictates that policy analysts finish books by presenting politically realistic policy recommendations. But despite being a policy analyst by profession, I have never done so. I can't think of any that I believe would make a difference. Instead, I have advocated changes that I think would work if they were implemented but that I know are politically impossible—replacing all welfare and income transfer programs with a universal basic income, legal defense funds to support systematic civil disobedience to the federal government, and universal education vouchers, among others.

Valued Places and the Four Wellsprings for Human Flourishing

However, I do have beliefs about policy implications more sweepingly defined. Readers who don't know what they are have an ample choice of sources. I've touched on them in all but a few of the books I've written from *Losing Ground* on, most comprehensively in *In Pursuit* (1988). I'm not going to write another full-scale description here. But since the broad policy implications I have in mind bear intimately on what motivated me to write *Human Diversity*, a few paragraphs are appropriate.

DOCUMENTATION

I am about to level a series of sweeping criticisms of public policy and the new upper class without documentation. For those who are curious, here are the past discussions I am drawing on.

On the proper dependent variable for assessing public policy: *In Pursuit*, chapters 1, 2, and 8.

On valued places and the four wellsprings for human flourishing: *In Pursuit*, chapter 12; *The Bell Curve*, chapter 22; *In Our Hands*, chapters 8, 9, 10, and 11; *Coming Apart*, chapter 15.

On the forces creating the new upper class: *The Bell Curve*, chapters 1, 2, 3, and 4; *Coming Apart*, chapters 1 and 2.

On the segregation of the new upper class: *The Bell Curve*, chapter 21, and *Coming Apart*, chapters 3 and 4.

On elites changing the rules in ways that they approve but which make life difficult for ordinary Americans: *Losing Ground*, chapters 1, 2, 3, 12, 13, 14; *In Pursuit*, chapters 5 and 12; *The Bell Curve*, chapters 21 and 22; *Real Education*, chapters 3 and 5; *Coming Apart*, chapters 14, 15, and 17; *By the People*, chapters 2, 3, and 4.

My argument begins with two apparently unrelated propositions. First, the ultimate goal of public policy is not to do things like raise incomes or increase college graduation rates but to enable people to flourish and to achieve deep satisfactions in life—to pursue happiness in the Aristotelian sense of that word. Second, recent decades have seen the development of the new upper class that I described in *Coming Apart*—not just influential and affluent, but smart, highly educated, with its own distinctive culture, significantly cut off from mainstream American society. It is the same group, no longer emergent but having come to power, that Richard Herrnstein and I called the "cognitive elite" in *The Bell Curve*. The new upper class includes (though is not limited to) the people who have the leading roles in shaping the nation's economy, culture, and politics.

As individuals, most members of the new upper class are fine people, personally and professionally. As a group, however, I think they have much to answer for. They have created a world that is ideal for them, filled with the kind of complexity that they are able to navigate and through which they can extract both money and power. At the same time, they have abdicated their role as stewards of the culture. The new upper class has been attentive to issues of economic inequality and inequality of opportunity but has refused to take seriously other questions that invoke human flourishing—the ways in which *all* human beings, not just those with IQs of 130-plus, can reach old age satisfied with who they have been and what they have done. For me, what matters most is not material equality, but access to the wellsprings of human flourishing, which in turn requires that society be structured so that people across a wide range of personal qualities and abilities are able to find valued places.

My definition of *valued place* is the same now as when Richard Herrnstein and I coined the term in *The Bell Curve*: "You occupy a valued place if other people would miss you if you were gone."[35] The central valued places are located in four domains that I have argued are the wellsprings of human flourishing: family, community, vocation, and faith. The valued places those wellsprings offer for adults are spouse, parent, relative, friend, neighbor, congregant, and colleague. It is my view that social policies since the mid-twentieth century, continuing to the present, have inadvertently stripped ordinary people of valued places while leaving intact the ones enjoyed by the new upper class.

I accept a role for economics. Hunger and homelessness are not conducive to human flourishing. The government can provide resources that enable people to be not homeless and not hungry. My own favored solution is a universal basic income that replaces the existing system of transfers. I have written at length about why I think that such a system would eliminate involuntary poverty and revitalize civil society.[36] But this is not the place to make the case for a specific solution. Rather, I want to stress that satisfactions and dignity both arise from occupying valued places, and valued places have to be formed gradually by the people who occupy them. What the new upper class can do is honor the wellsprings. That means, for example, celebrating marriage not just as one of many options, but as the institution that gives the most people the best chance of creating a deep and fulfilling intimate relationship with another adult. It means celebrating Tocquevillian community, whether it is found in a small town or a neighborhood in a megalopolis. It means celebrating productive work of all kinds. It means celebrating the fulfillment that people of faith derive from their faith.

"Celebrating" does not mean passing laws. It means that the people who sit at the apex of the nation's politics, economics, and culture need to be advocates for marriage, community, productive work, and, at the least, to treat religion with respect. Large numbers of them fail that test and have failed it for decades. The members of the new upper class avail themselves of the wellsprings. They marry, raise children, live in communities they find satisfying, work hard, and some of them are religious. But they don't even acknowledge that they are tapping into the traditional sources of human flourishing, let alone celebrate ordinary Americans who do. Instead, their attitude toward ordinary Americans is too often covertly condescending if they are people of color and openly disparaging if they are white. What are the policy implications of *Human Diversity*? They don't constitute a policy agenda. They involve the human heart, not legislation or regulations. The first step is to reconstruct a moral vocabulary for discussing human differences.

Reconstructing a Moral Vocabulary for Discussing Human Differences

A century ago, Walter Lippmann, then one of the nation's most influential public intellectuals, wrote of IQ tests, "I hate the impudence of a claim that in fifty minutes you can judge and classify a human being's predestined fitness in life. I hate the pretentiousness of that claim. I hate the abuse of scientific method which it involves. I hate the sense of superiority which it creates, and the sense of inferiority that it imposes."[37] Among many people, polygenic scores prompt the same anger and revulsion. They foresee dystopian futures in which polygenic scores are used to judge and classify a human being's predestined fitness in life according not just to IQ but other cognitive traits as well. Personality traits. Potential for mental illness. Potential for criminality.

The dystopian dangers are real, but so are wonderful opportunities to use our new knowledge to do good. We won't avoid the dangers and take advantage of the opportunities until we are able to talk easily and realistically about human differences. And yet so few try to do it. The conversation today within the new upper class seems always to be about the ways in which individual differences are created by environmental conditions that we must fix. It is seldom about how to deal with differences that can't be fixed.

Why? I think at the root is the new upper class's conflation of intellectual ability and the professions it enables with human worth. Few admit it, of course. But the evolving zeitgeist of the new upper class has led to a misbegotten hierarchy whereby being a surgeon is *better* in some sense of human worth than being an insurance salesman, being an executive in a high-tech firm is *better* than being a housewife, and a neighborhood of people with advanced degrees is *better* than a neighborhood of high school graduates. To put it so baldly makes it obvious how senseless it is. There shouldn't be any relationship between these things and human worth. And yet, among too many in the new upper class, there is.

The conflation of intellectual ability with human worth helps to explain the new upper class's insistence that inequalities of intellectual ability must be the product of environmental disadvantage. Many people with high IQs really do feel sorry for people with low IQs. If the environment is to blame, then those unfortunates can be helped, and that makes people who want to help them feel good. If genes are to blame, it makes people who want to help them feel bad. People prefer feeling good to feeling bad, so they engage in confirmation bias when it comes to the evidence about the causes of human differences.

I expect the genomics and neuroscientific revolutions to give us undeniable evidence that differences in personality, abilities, and social behavior exist across individuals and groups alike and that those differences cannot be much reduced by the kinds of public policy changes that are available to us. For America, the old way of dealing with that reality was the moral vocabulary of Christianity. We are all deeply flawed—sinners—and we are all the beneficiaries of God's unearned love and grace. We are all equal in God's eyes. That theological foundation, combined with America's devotion to individual freedom, underwrote a signature feature of American exceptionalism: our egalitarianism. One of our proudest boasts was that in the

United States, people aren't better than anyone else just because they have more money or a higher position. We didn't live by that ideal perfectly, but we did much better than many people realize. In living memory, it was considered un-American to be a snob, to look down on other Americans, and to think you were better than anyone else.

The moral vocabulary we must reconstruct for twenty-first century America cannot be Christian nor even ecumenically religious. Society in general and the new upper class in particular are too secular for that. The only choice left to us is a secular understanding of the truth behind the old formulation, "We are all equal in God's eyes." That secular understanding begins with the recognition that personality humility is not optional but compulsory. If you possess unusual beauty, charm, intellect, or talent of any sort, pride is inappropriate. Go ahead and take satisfaction in the use you have made of your gifts (with a mental caveat that some of the resources you called on are partly heritable too), but live with the consciousness of how incredibly lucky you were to have been born that way and try to be worthy of it.

Humility is the first step in coming to grips with a secular version of "we are all equal in God's eyes," but the fullness and depth of that truth cannot be apprehended abstractly. It needs to be understood through experience. That starts with realizing that most people are good, competent, and likeable, including those who don't have much in common with you—even, amazingly, people who don't share your politics. The more kinds of people you know and the better you know them, the easier it is to recognize that "equality of human worth" isn't just rhetoric. You will also find it is easy to talk about the reality of human differences if you know in your gut how unimportant those differences are in deciding whether the person next to you is someone you respect. My prescription for the new upper class: Get out more.

When we are able once again to talk easily about human differences, a difficult and elusive next step remains. The wellsprings of human flourishing have been going dry for many Americans, and the damage done by the new upper class—however inadvertently—has been importantly to blame. Replenishing and revitalizing those wellsprings should be our first priority. But developing policies that replenish and revitalize them must begin with a drastic shift in the thinking of most of the people who run the nation's economy, culture, and politics. It is time for America's elites to try *living* with inequality of talents, understanding that each human being has strengths and weaknesses, qualities we admire and qualities we do not admire, and that our good opinion seldom turns on a person's talents, but rather on a person's character. We need a new species of public policy that accepts differences and works with people as they are, not as we want to shape them. I hope this book contributes to that process.

Acknowledgments

I began work on *Human Diversity* with curiosity but only an informed amateur's knowledge about either genetics or neuroscience. As I always have done when taking on an unfamiliar discipline, my first step was to find recent technical articles on topics of interest and use the literature reviews to start tunneling into the subject matter.

The difference between this time and all the previous times was the breathtaking complexity of the articles I was reading. The nomenclature alone was daunting, but that was nothing compared to the substance. The processes required to go from a SNP to a synthesized protein and then from proteins to effects on the phenotype were not only stranger than I knew, but stranger than I could have imagined. Neuroscience was no easier, with nomenclature as unfamiliar and brain structure and function as complicated.

As I promised in the introduction, I stuck to the low-hanging fruit, but it was obvious that I would need experts to save me from blunders. I adopted two strategies. First, I emailed drafts of my work to the lead authors of the technical articles that I discussed at length, asking them to tell me what I'd gotten wrong. Second, I asked geneticists, neuroscientists, and behavior geneticists who were most well versed in these topics to read long sections of text and vet them for errors of fact or interpretation.

I am a controversial figure. The last thing a geneticist or neuroscientist working on a college campus needs is to be thanked publicly by me. I therefore added a promise to all my requests for review: "Your response will not be used in any way except to improve the accuracy of the text. You will not be listed in the acknowledgments nor will I disclose in any forum that you saw the draft." That's why I'm not going to give you a single name of the many who responded to my requests (many did not) and to whom I am so indebted. I hope they understand how grateful I am. I have a special soft spot for those who responded to drafts that contained criticism of their work. In return, I did my best to revise the text until they saw the presentation as fair, even though residual disagreements remained.

I can safely thank a few people by name. E. O. Wilson, the pioneer of sociobiology, planted the seeds of *Human Diversity* by writing *Consilience: The Unity of Knowledge*, which I read when it first appeared in 1998. I was immediately convinced that Wilson was right, and my excitement about the integration of the social sciences with biology has stuck with me ever since. Arthur Brooks, AEI's president, and Karlyn Bowman and Ryan Streeter, successively the directors of social and political studies at AEI as I worked on *Human Diversity*, were wholly supportive. Sean Desmond, editor of two of my earlier books, returned to lend his wise editorial counsel and to make the text much more readable. Roland Ottewell, my official copy editor, and Miles Hoffman, my unofficial one and friend of 35 years, meticulously scrutinized a late draft of the complete text. My agent, Amanda Urban, operated as she has since she took me on in 1984: the good shepherd making sure her author is treated right, morphing into a lioness as needed. None of this help means that no errors remain. An anxious aspect of publishing a complicated book is knowing that mistakes must still be hiding in there.

My wife and editor, Catherine, who has featured in so many acknowledgments, initially tried to talk me out of writing *Human Diversity*. When I began work in the fall of 2016, the nastiness associated with the reaction to *The Bell Curve* was a distant memory. Did I really want to go through that again? I didn't think it would be a big deal one way or the other, but I was concerned that she was concerned. Then came the radicalization of the campuses, when we learned that the bad old days were back no matter what. "Confound it!" said Catherine, or two syllables to that effect, on the day I returned from the riot at Middlebury. "If they're going to do this kind of thing anyway, go ahead and write it." *Human Diversity* appears with her blessing, which was absolutely essential. She is the coauthor of my life.

Charles Murray
Burkittsville, Maryland
July 29, 2019

Appendix I
Statistics for People Who Are Sure
They Can't Learn Statistics

The following is aimed at the liberal arts graduate who has not taken a math course since high school and knows nothing whatsoever about statistics but wants to understand the statistical concepts used in the text.

Distributions and Standard Deviations

Why Do We Need "Standard Deviation"?

Every day, formally or informally, people make comparisons—among people, among apples and oranges, among dairy cows or egg-laying hens, among the screws being coughed out by a screw machine. The standard deviation is a measure of how spread out the things being compared are. "This egg is a lot bigger than average," a chicken farmer might say. The standard deviation gives him a way of saying precisely what he means by "a lot."

What Is a Frequency Distribution?

To get a clear idea of what a frequency distribution is, imagine yourself back in your high school gym, with all the boys in the senior class assembled

---

Adapted from *The Bell Curve: Intelligence and Class Structure in American Life* by Richard J. Herrnstein and Charles Murray. Copyright © 1994 by Richard J. Herrnstein and Charles Murray. Reprinted with permission of The Free Press, a Division of Simon & Schuster Trade Publishing Group. I have made a few minor changes to the original text, eliminating some material specific to issues in *The Bell Curve* and rewording a few sentences to fit the context of *Human Diversity*.

before you (including both sexes would complicate matters, and the point of this discussion is to keep things simple). Line up these boys from left to right in order of height.

Now you have a long line going from shortest to tallest. As you look along the line you will see that only a few boys are conspicuously short and tall. Most are in the middle, and a lot of them seem identical in height. Is there any way to get a better idea of how this pattern looks?

Tape a series of cards to the floor in a straight line from left to right, with "60 inches and shorter" written on the one at the far left, "80 inches and taller" on the card at the far right, and cards in one-inch increments in between. Tell everyone to stand behind the card that corresponds to his height.

Someone loops a rope over the rafters and pulls you up in the air so you can look straight down on the tops of the heads of your classmates standing in their single files behind the height labels. The figure below shows what you see.

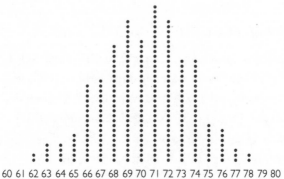

60 61 62 63 64 65 66 67 68 69 70 71 72 73 74 75 76 77 78 79 80

This is a frequency distribution. What good is it? Looking at your high school classmates standing around in a mob, you can tell little about their height. Looking at those same classmates arranged into a frequency distribution, you can tell a lot, quickly and memorably.

How Is the Distribution Related to the Standard Deviation?

We still lack a convenient way of expressing where people are in that distribution. What does it mean to say that two different students are, say, six inches different in height? How "big" is a six-inch difference? That brings us back to the standard deviation.

When it comes to high school students, you have a good idea of how big a six-inch difference is. But what does a six-inch difference mean if you are talking about the height of elephants? About the height of cats? It depends. And the things it depends on are the average height and how much height varies among the things you are measuring. *A standard deviation gives you a way of taking both the average and that variability into account, so that "six inches" can be expressed in a way that means the same thing for high school students relative to other high school students, elephants relative to other elephants, and cats relative to other cats.*

How Do You Compute a Standard Deviation?

Suppose that your high school class consisted of just two people, who were 66 inches and 70 inches tall. Obviously, the average is 68 inches. Just as obviously, one person is 2 inches shorter than average, one person is 2 inches taller than average. The standard deviation is a kind of average of the differences from the mean—2 inches, in this example. Suppose you add two more people to the class, one who is 64 inches and the other who is 72 inches. The mean hasn't changed (the two new people balance each other off exactly). But the newcomers are each 4 inches different from the average height of 68 inches. So the standard deviation, which measures the spread, has gotten bigger as well. Now two people are 4 inches different from the average and two people are 2 inches different from the average. That adds up to a total of 12 inches, divided among four persons. The simple average of these differences from the mean is 3 inches, which is almost (but not quite) what the standard deviation is. To be precise, the standard deviation is calculated by squaring the deviations from the mean, then summing them, then finding their average, then taking the square root of the result. In this example, two people are 4 inches from the mean and two are 2 inches from the mean. The sum of the squared deviations is 40 (i.e., 16 + 16 + 4 + 4). Their average is 10 (40 ÷ 4). The square root of 10 is 3.16, which is the standard deviation for this example. The technical reasons for using the standard deviation instead of the simple average of the deviations from the mean are not necessary to go into, except that in normal distributions, the standard deviation has wonderfully convenient properties. *If you are looking for a short, easy way to think of a standard deviation, "the average difference from the mean" is close enough.*

As an example of how a standard deviation can be used to compare apples and oranges, suppose we are looking at members of the Olympic women's gymnastics team and professional basketball players. You notice a woman who is 5 feet 6 inches and a man who is 7 feet. You know from watching gymnastics on television that 5 feet 6 inches is tall for a woman gymnast and 7 feet is tall even for a basketball player. But you want to do better than a general impression. Just how unusual is the woman, compared to the average gymnast on the U.S. women's team, and how unusual is the man, compared to the average professional basketball player?

We gather data on height among the women gymnasts and determine that the mean is 5 feet 1 inch with a standard deviation (SD) of 2 inches (made-up numbers for this example). For professional basketball players, we find that the mean is 6 feet 6 inches and the SD is 4 inches. Thus the woman who is 5 feet 6 inches is 2.5 standard deviations taller than the average; the seven-foot man is only 1.5 standard deviations taller than the average. These numbers—2.5 for the woman and 1.5 for the man—are also the basis for *effect sizes* introduced in chapter 1. Now we have an explicit numerical way to compare how different the two people are from their respective averages, and we have a basis for concluding that the woman who is 5 feet 6 inches is a lot taller relative to other female Olympic gymnasts than a 7-foot man is relative to other professional basketball players.

How Much More Different? Enter the Normal Distribution

Everyone has heard the phrase *normal distribution* or *bell-shaped curve,* or, as in the title of a controversial book, *bell curve.* They all refer to a common way that natural phenomena arrange themselves approximately (the true normal distribution is a mathematical abstraction that is never perfectly observed in nature). If you look again at the distribution of high school boys that opened the discussion, you will see the makings of a bell curve. If we added several thousand more boys to it, the kinks and irregularities would smooth out, and it would actually get close to a normal distribution. A perfect one looks like the one in the figure below.

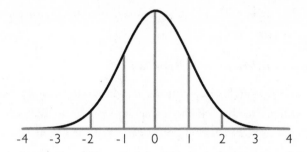

It makes sense that most things will be arranged in bell-shaped curves. Extremes tend to be rarer than the average. If that sounds like a tautology, it is only because bell curves are so common. Consider height again. Seven feet is "extreme" for humans. But if human height were distributed so that equal proportions of people were five feet, six feet, and seven feet tall, the extreme would not be rarer than the average. It just so happens that the world hardly ever works that way.

Bell curves (or close approximations to them) are not only common in nature, they have a close mathematical affinity to the meaning of the standard deviation. In any true normal distribution, no matter whether the elements are the heights of basketball players, the diameters of screw heads, or the milk production of cows, 68.3 percent of all the cases fall in the interval between one standard deviation above the mean and one standard deviation below it.

In its mathematical form, the normal distribution extends to infinity in both directions, never quite reaching the horizontal axis. But for all practical purposes, when we are talking about populations of people, a normal distribution is about six standard deviations wide. The numbers below the axis in the figure above designate the number of standard deviations above and below the mean. As you can see, the line has virtually touched the surface at ±3 standard deviations.

A person who is one standard deviation above the mean in IQ is at the 84th percentile. Two standard deviations above the mean puts him at the 98th percentile. Three standard deviations above the mean puts him at the 99.9th percentile. A person who is one standard deviation below the mean is at the 16th percentile. Two standard deviations below the mean puts him at the 2nd percentile. Three standard deviations below the mean puts him at the 0.1th percentile.

Why Not Just Use Percentiles to Begin With?

Why go to all the trouble of computing standard scores? Most people understand percentiles already. Tell them that someone is at the 84th percentile, and they know right away what you mean. Tell them that he's at the 99th percentile, and they know what that means. Aren't we just introducing an unnecessary complication by talking about "standard scores"?

Thinking in terms of percentiles is convenient and has its legitimate uses. I often speak in terms of percentiles in the text. But they can also be highly misleading, because they are artificially compressed at the tails of the distributions. It is a longer way from, say, the 98th percentile to the 99th than from the 50th to the 51st. In a true normal distribution, the distance from the 99th percentile to the 100th (or, similarly, from zero to the 1st) is infinite.

Consider two people who are at the 50th and 55th percentiles in height. Using a large representative sample from the National Longitudinal Study of Youth (NLSY) as our estimate of the national American distribution of height, their actual height difference is only half an inch. Consider another two people who are at the 94th and 99th percentiles on height—the identical gap in terms of percentiles. Their height difference is 3.1 inches, six times the height difference of those at the 50th and 55th percentiles. The farther out on the tail of the distribution you move, the more misleading percentiles become.

Standard scores reflect these real differences much more accurately than do percentiles. The people at the 50th and 55th percentiles, only half an inch apart in real height, have standard scores of 0.0 and 0.13. Compare that difference of 0.13 standard deviation units to the standard scores of those at the 94th and 99th percentiles: 1.55 and 2.33 respectively. In standard scores, their difference—which is 0.78 standard deviation units, equivalent to an effect size of 0.78—is six times as large, reflecting the sixfold difference in inches.

Correlation and Regression

So much for describing a distribution of measurements. We now need to consider dealing with the relationships between two or more distributions—which is, after all, what scientists usually want to do. How, for example, is the pressure of a gas related to its volume? The answer is the Boyle's law you learned in high school science. In social science, the relationships between variables are less clear-cut and harder to unearth. We may, for example, be interested in wealth as a variable, but how shall wealth be measured? Is it yearly income, yearly income averaged over a period of years, the value of one's savings or possessions? And wealth, compared to many of the other things social scientists study, is easy, reducible as it is to dollars and cents.

Beyond the problem of measurement, social scientists must cope with sheer complexity. It is rare that any human or social relationship can be fully captured in terms of a single pair of variables, such as that between the pressure and volume of a gas. In social science, multiple relationships are the rule, not the exception.

For both of these reasons, the relations between social science variables are typically less than perfect. They are often weak and uncertain. But they are nevertheless real, and with the right methods, they can be rigorously examined.

Correlation and regression are the primary ways to quantify weak, uncertain relationships. For that reason, the advances in correlational and regression analysis since the late nineteenth century have provided the impetus to social science. To understand what this kind of analysis is, we need to introduce the idea of a scatter plot.

A Scatter Plot

We left your male high school classmates lined up by height, with you looking down from the rafters. Now imagine another row of cards, laid out along the floor at a right angle to the ones for height. This set of cards has weights in pounds on them. Start with 90 pounds for the class shrimp and continue to add cards in 10-pound increments until you reach 250 pounds to make room for the class giant. Now ask your classmates to find the point on the floor that corresponds to both their height and weight (perhaps they'll insist on a grid of intersecting lines extending from the two rows of cards). When the traffic on the gym floor ceases, you will see something like the following figure.

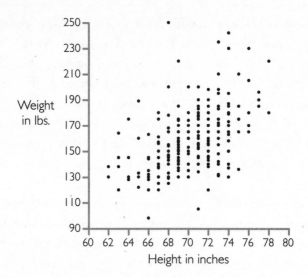

Some sort of relationship between height and weight is immediately obvious. The heaviest boys tend to be the tallest, the lightest ones the shortest, and most of them are intermediate in both height and weight. Equally obvious are the deviations from the trend that link height and weight. The stocky boys appear as points above the mass, the skinny ones as points below it. What we need now is some way to quantify both the trend and the exceptions.

Correlations and *regressions* accomplish this in different ways. But before we go on to discuss these terms, be assured that they are simple. Look at the scatter plot. You can see just by looking at the dots that as height increases, so does weight, in an irregular way. Take a pencil (literally or imaginarily) and draw a straight, sloping line through the dots in a way that seems to you to best reflect this upward-sloping trend. Now continue to read and see how well you have intuitively produced the basis for a correlation coefficient and a regression coefficient.

The Correlation Coefficient

Modern statistics provide more than one method for measuring correlation, but we confine ourselves to the one that is most important in both use and generality: the Pearson product-moment correlation coefficient (named after Karl Pearson, the English mathematician and biometrician). To get at this coefficient, let us first replot the graph of the class, replacing inches and pounds with standard scores. The variables are now expressed in general terms. Remember: *Any* set of measurements can be transformed similarly.

The next step on our way to the correlation coefficient is to apply a formula that finds the best possible straight line passing through the cloud of points—the mathematically "best" version of the line you just drew by intuition.

What makes it the "best"? Any line is going to be wrong for most of the points. Take, for example, the boys who are 64 inches tall and look at their weights. Any sloping straight line is going to cross somewhere in the middle of those weights and will probably not cross any of the dots exactly. For boys 64 inches tall, you want the line to cross at the point where the total amount of the error is as small as possible. Taken over all the boys at all the heights, you want a straight line that makes the sum of all the errors for all the heights as small as possible. This "best fit" is shown in the new version of the scatter plot shown below, where both height and weight are expressed in standard scores and the mathematical best-fitting line has been superimposed.

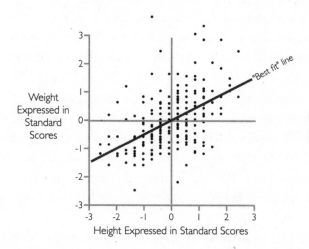

This scatter plot has (partly by serendipity) many lessons to teach about how statistics relate to the real world. Here are a few of the main ones:

1. *Notice the many exceptions.* There is a statistically substantial relationship between height and weight, but, visually, the exceptions seem to dominate. So too with virtually all statistical relationships in the social sciences, most of which are much weaker than this one.

2. *Linear relationships don't always seem to fit very well.* The best-fit line looks as if it is too shallow—notice the tall boys and see how consistently the line underpredicts how much they weigh. Given the information in the diagram, this might be an optical illusion—many of the dots in the dense part of the range are on top of each other, as it were, and thus it is impossible to grasp visually how the errors are adding up—but it could also be that the relationship between height and weight is not linear.

3. *Small samples have individual anomalies.* Before we jump to the conclusion that the straight line is not a good representation of the relationship, we must remember that the sample consists of only 250 boys. An anomaly of this particular small sample is that one of the boys in the sample of 250 weighed 250 pounds. Eighteen-year-old boys are rarely that heavy, judging from the entire NLSY sample, only one or two per 10,000. And yet one of those rarities happened to be picked up in a sample of 250. That's the way samples work.

4. *But small samples are also surprisingly accurate, despite their individual anomalies.* The relationship between height and weight shown by the sample of 250 18-year-old males is identical to the third decimal place with the relationship among all 6,068 males in the NLSY sample (the correlation coefficient is .501 in both cases). This is closer than we have any right to expect, but other random samples of only 250 generally produce correlations that are within a few points of the one produced by the larger sample. (There are mathematics for figuring out what "generally" and "within a few points" mean, but we needn't worry about them here.)

Bearing these basics in mind, let us go back to the sloping line in the figure above. Out of mathematical necessity, we know several things about it. First of all, it must pass through the intersection of the zeros (which, in standard scores, correspond to the averages) for both height and weight. Secondly, the line would have had exactly the same slope had height been the vertical axis and weight the horizontal one.

Finally, and most significant, the slope of the best-fitting line cannot be steeper than 1.0. The steepest possible best-fitting line, in other words, is one along which one unit of change in height is exactly matched by one unit of change in weight, clearly not the case in these data. Real data in the social sciences never yield a slope that steep. Note that while the line in the graph above goes uphill to the right, it would go downhill for pairs of variables that are negatively correlated.

We focus on the slope of the best-fitting line because it *is* the correlation coefficient—in this case, equal to .50, which is quite large by the standards of variables used by social scientists. The closer it gets to ±1.0, the stronger is the linear relationship between the standardized variables (the variables expressed as standard scores). When the two variables are mutually independent, the best-fitting line is horizontal; hence its slope is 0. Anything other than 0 signifies a relationship, albeit possibly a very weak one.

Whatever the correlation coefficient of a pair of variables is, squaring it yields another notable number. Squaring .50, for example, gives .25. The significance of the squared correlation is that it tells us how much the variation in weight would decrease if we could make everyone the same height, or vice versa. If all the boys in the class were the same height, the variation in their weights would decline by 25 percent. Perhaps you have heard the phrase "explains the variance," as in, for example, "Education explains 20 percent of the variance in income." That figure comes from the squared correlation.

In general, the squared correlation is a measure of the mutual redundancy in a pair of variables. If they are highly correlated, they are highly redundant in the sense that knowing the value of one of them places a narrow range of possibilities for the value of the other. If they are uncorrelated or only slightly correlated, knowing the value of one tells us nothing or little about the value of the other.

Regression Coefficients

Correlation assesses the strength of a relationship between variables. But we may want to know more about a relationship than merely its strength. We may want to know what it is. We may want to know how much of an increase in weight, for example, we should anticipate if we compare 66-inch boys with 73-inch boys. Such questions arise naturally if we are trying to explain a particular variable (e.g., annual income) in terms of the effects of another variable (e.g., educational level). "How much income is another year of schooling worth?" is just the sort of question that social scientists are always trying to answer.

The standard method for answering it is regression analysis, which has an intimate mathematical association with correlational analysis. If we had left the scatter plot with its original axes—inches and pounds—instead of standardizing them, the slope of the best-fitting line would have been a regression coefficient, rather than a correlation coefficient. For example, the regression coefficient for weight regressed on height tells us that for each additional inch in height, we can expect an increase of 3.9 pounds. Or we could regress height on weight and discover that each additional pound of weight is associated with an increase of .065 inches in height.

Multivariate Statistics

Multiple regression analysis is the main way that social science deals with the multiple relationships that are the rule in social science. To get a fix on multiple regression, let us return to the high school gym for the last time. Your classmates are still scattered about the floor. Now imagine a pole, erected at the intersection of 60 inches and 80 pounds, marked in inches from 18 inches to 50 inches. For some inscrutable reason, you would like to know the impact of both height and weight on a boy's waist size. Since imagination can defy gravity, you ask each boy to levitate until the soles of his shoes are at the elevation that reads on the pole at the waist size of his trousers. In general, the taller and heavier boys must rise the most, the shorter and slighter ones the least, and most boys, middling in height and weight, will have middling waist sizes as well. Multiple regression is a mathematical procedure for finding that plane, slicing through the space in the gym, that minimizes the aggregated distances (in this instance, along the waist size axis) between the bottoms of the boys' shoes and the plane.

The best-fitting plane will tilt upward toward heavy weights and tall heights. But it may tilt more along the pounds axis than along the inches axis or vice versa. It may tilt equally for each. The slope of the tilt along each of these axes is again a regression coefficient. With two variables predicting a third, as in this example, there are two coefficients. One of them tells us how much of an increase in trouser waist size is associated with a given increase in weight, holding height constant; the other, how much of an increase in trouser waist size is associated with a given increase in height, holding weight constant.

With two variables predicting a third, we reach the limit of visual imagination. But the principle of multiple regression can be extended to any number of variables. Income, for example, may be related not just to education, but also to age, family background, IQ, personality, business conditions, region of the country, and so on. The mathematical procedures will yield coefficients for each of them, indicating again how much of a change in income can be anticipated for a given change in any particular variable, with all the others held constant.

Appendix 2
Sexual Dimorphism in Humans

Homo sapiens is a normally dimorphic species consisting overwhelmingly of heterosexual males and females with a small proportion of exceptions. I realize that I am writing in the LGBT era when some argue that 63 distinct genders have been identified. But while that opening statement constitutes fighting words in some circles, it is not scientifically controversial. If you are already convinced that human beings are a normally dimorphic species, you may want to skip this appendix.

———

Here's a definition of *dimorphism* as given in *The Encyclopedia of Evolutionary Biology*: "Any trait that differs on average between sexes is considered sexually dimorphic, even if the trait distributions overlap considerably between sexes."[1] You will sometimes read claims that a trait is not sexually dimorphic unless it is completely different in the two sexes. That definition has no scientific standing.

For all organisms that reproduce sexually, the biological definition of sex is based on the comparative size of their *gametes*—the germ cells that can unite to produce offspring. Males are defined as the sex with the smaller gamete and females are defined as the sex with the larger gamete.[2] The gametes in humans are sperm and the ovum. The sperm is the smallest cell in the human body and the ovum is one of the largest. In that sense, there's no question about whether humans come in just two sexes nor about who is which sex.

Physiologically and psychologically, there is more room for variation, but the basics may also be stated simply: Physiologically, human sexuality comes in two forms, male and female, with an extremely small proportion of exceptions. Psychologically, human sexuality forms a continuum from "completely heterosexual" to "completely homosexual," but proportionately few people self-identify as anything other than heterosexual.

As I set out to review the data, I will state explicitly what should go without saying: Human dignity and human rights are universal, unconnected to sexual identity. I am presenting data on frequency distributions that have no relevance to value judgments. The reason I need to present the data on those frequency distributions here is because of the descriptions of sex differences in the main text. I write in the face of a yawning gap between popular perceptions about gender identity and scientific reality. For example, Gallup polls since 2000 have consistently found that Americans think that about 23 percent of the population is gay or lesbian.[3] As you will see, the actual figure is closer to a fifth of that. Hence the need to provide proof that all but a few percent of humans are heterosexual males or heterosexual females.

Here are brief answers to four questions: What proportion of people have biologically ambiguous sexual identity—to use the contemporary term, are intersexuals? What proportion of people self-identify as homosexual or bisexual? What proportion of people acknowledge any same-sex attraction or behavior? What proportion of people self-identify (regardless of their biological sex) as transsexual?

Biological Sexual Identity

Before genetics got into the picture, the definition of biological sex was based on physiological differences in the genitalia, leaving one option for identifying intersex persons: people whose genitalia had some of the characteristics of both males and females, known as hermaphrodites. Once the sex distinction in chromosomes was discovered early in the twentieth century—females have the XX pair and males have the XY pair—cleaner definitions of three types of intersexuals were possible: true hermaphrodites (persons born with both testicular and ovarian tissue), people with the XX chromosome pair but significant components of male sexual anatomy, and people with the XY chromosome pair but with significant components of female sexual anatomy.[4]

The three conditions that are consensually accepted as evidence that a person is intersex are as follows:

True hermaphrodites. Individuals born with both testicular and ovarian tissue.[5] Some of the people with the other two conditions appear to have the characteristics of both male and female genitalia, but they don't meet the technical definition.

Classic congenital adrenal hyperplasia (CAH) among females, discussed in chapter 5. Classic CAH is the result of prenatal exposure to abnormally high levels of male hormones (androgens). In female infants, CAH usually presents as ambiguous genitalia. In children and adults, it is associated with masculinization of features, facial hair, menstrual problems, and male-typical personality characteristics. In males, sexual ambiguity is rarely involved nor are there usually any symptoms at birth.[6] Classic CAH in males is accompanied by abnormally rapid growth in childhood, early signs of puberty, and shorter than expected height as an adult.

Androgen insensitivity syndrome (AIS), also discussed in chapter 5. AIS affects only genetically male (XY) fetuses. The condition impairs masculinization of male genitalia. In its mild form, the external genitalia at birth are those of a normal male; in its extreme form, "complete" AIS (CAIS), the external genitalia are those of a normal female.

The table below summarizes incidence of the three conditions. The note gives the source and additional information about the numbers.[7]

	Percent
True hermaphrodites	0.0012
Classic congenital adrenal hyperplasia (CAH)	0.0077
Androgen insensitivity syndrome (partial or complete)	0.0084
Total	0.0173

Limited to the three conditions that are consensually accepted as evidence of an intersex individual (including all levels of AIS), the proportion of intersex persons is 0.0173 percent—less than two-hundredths of a percentage point, or about one in 5,800 persons. That number is slightly inflated because the estimate for CAH includes males as well as females.

In 2000, this core definition was broadened by a team of scholars (first author was Melanie Blackless).[8] Their criteria for a "typical" male or female were, in the authors' own words, "exacting":

> We define the typical male as someone with an XY chromosomal composition, and testes located within the scrotal sac. The testes produce sperm which, via the vas deferens, may be transported to the urethra and ejaculated outside the body. Penis length at birth ranges from 2.5 to 4.5 cm; an idealized penis has a completely enclosed urethra which opens at the tip of the glans. During fetal development, the testes produce the Mullerian inhibiting factor, testosterone, and dihydrotestosterone, while juvenile testicular activity ensures a masculinizing puberty. The typical female has two X chromosomes, functional ovaries which ensure a feminizing puberty, oviducts connecting to a uterus, cervix and vaginal canal, inner and outer vaginal lips, and a clitoris, which at birth ranges in size from 0.20 to 0.85 cm.[9]

The authors subsequently referred to this as "the Platonic ideal of sexual dimorphism." The additional conditions that fall short of the Platonic ideal of sexual dimorphism under that definition fall into three categories (plus a small one of "other"): some chromosomal arrangement other than XX for women and XY for males, vaginal agenesis, and late-onset CAH. The difficulty with counting these conditions as evidence of an intersex individual is that they rarely involve sexual ambiguity. Affected males almost always think of themselves as male; affected females almost always think of themselves as female.

Males with non-XY chromosomes. This includes males with Klinefelter syndrome (an XXY chromosomal makeup) and XXY, XO, XYY, and XXYY variants. These conditions sometimes cause infertility and other physiological and cognitive problems in males, but none of them are associated with confusion in sexual identity. They are biologically males in every clinical sense of the term.

Females with non-XX chromosomes. This includes females with either Turner syndrome or an XXX genotype (Triple X). Women with Turner syndrome are partly or completely missing one of their X chromosomes. The condition brings with it a variety of problems, including infertility, short stature, and short life expectancy. The literature has found that women with

Turner syndrome have a tendency to be hyperfeminine.[10] Women with the XXX configuration sometimes have developmental cognitive difficulties, but once again function normally as women without an association with sexual ambiguity.[11]

Vaginal agenesis. In its simplest form, vaginal agenesis consists of fibrous tissue that displaces a portion of normal vaginal tissue. Correcting it surgically is a straightforward procedure that has been likened to correcting a cleft palate.[12] Vaginal agenesis does have one serious and common characteristic however: The uterus is absent or underdeveloped. But this makes a female no less female than infertility makes a male less male. Women with vaginal agenesis have the XX genotype and normal hormonal exposure for females both in utero and after birth.[13]

Late-onset CAH. That leaves us with late-onset CAH, which in the Blackless study is assigned an incidence rate of 1.5 percent. "Late-onset CAH" refers to a mild form of CAH that appears in childhood or near puberty.

For females and male infants alike, the genitalia appear normal at birth and correspond to the normal chromosomal makeup: All the XY individuals have penises and testicles and all the XX individuals have vaginas and ovaries. For females, menstrual irregularities account for over half of the presenting signs for diagnosis among adolescents.[14] Other symptoms can include rapid growth in childhood but shorter than expected eventual height, early signs of puberty, and acne, but the average woman with late-onset CAH does not present until about age 24.[15] For adult women, presenting symptoms may include enlargement of the clitoris, excess facial or body hair, and, for about 10–15 percent of cases, fertility problems.[16]

Since late-onset CAH is an autosomal recessive disease; it presumably occurs equally in men and women, but far fewer men than women are identified in the technical literature. The reason, as the authors of a 2017 systematic review of the literature noted, is that "the great majority of male patients are asymptomatic and most are identified during genetic screening carried out for purposes of genetic counseling."[17] In adolescent males, the symptoms are most likely to be early appearance of pubic hair, rapid growth during childhood but shorter-than-average eventual height, and early male pattern baldness.[18]

This is not to claim that late-onset CAH never has symptoms that introduce sexual ambiguity in the sense that classic CAH does. Rather, the evidence is clear that such cases are extremely rare among females diagnosed with late-onset CAH and close to zero among males diagnosed with late-onset CAH.

Here are the estimated incidence rates for the Blackless study's additions to the core intersex conditions. See the note for sources and details.[19]

	Percent
Turner syndrome	0.0369
Klinefelter syndrome	0.0922
Other non-XY chromosomes for males, non-XX for females	0.0639
Vaginal agenesis	0.0169
Late-onset CAH in both men and women	1.5000
Unspecified, cause unknown	0.0009
Total	1.7108

Perhaps the most important point about all the above departures from a "Platonic ideal of sexual dimorphism" is that none of the sources I have listed discuss sexual ambiguity as among the presenting symptoms. Is it appropriate to define these people as "intersexuals"?

I leave it as a question. The answer doesn't matter in any practical sense for establishing that humans consist of two sexes with a small number of exceptions. Depending on what you think of the additional departures from the Platonic ideal—and especially what you think of late-onset CAH—either 98.3 percent or 99.8 percent of the population are unambiguously male or female in the biological sense. Either figure makes my point.

I should add, however, that the answer does matter from the clinician's point of view. The total proportion of people considered intersexual in the Blackless study is 1.728 percent, which is almost exactly 100 times the total proportion of people—0.0173 percent—considered intersexual based on the three core categories of intersexuality. One clinician (also a psychologist and physician), Leonard Sax, observed that the total for the three core categories "suggests that there are currently [2002] about 50,000 true intersexuals living in the United States. These individuals are of course entitled to the same expert care and consideration that all patients deserve.

Nothing is gained, however, by pretending that there are 5,000,000 such individuals."[20]

Self-Identified Sexual Orientation

I begin with the ways in which people describe their sexual orientation independently of measures of sexual behavior or attraction.

In 2011, Gary Gates of the Williams Institute published a synthesis of the major studies up to that time that had asked adults to identify their orientation as heterosexual, gay, lesbian, or bisexual. The Gates study combined the results from five American surveys conducted from 2004 through 2009 to reach overall estimates. For males, the results were estimates of 2.2 percent gay and 1.4 percent bisexual. For females, the numbers were 1.1 percent lesbian and 2.2 percent bisexual. Overall, Gates put self-identified lesbian, gay, and bisexual (LGB) individuals at 3.5 percent of the population.[21]

READING INTO THE STATE OF KNOWLEDGE ABOUT SEXUAL IDENTITY

Standing apart from the rhetoric about gender fluidity and the existence of multiple genders is a body of empirical work that still includes many controversies, but ones that are being argued out in the technical literature the old-fashioned way, with actual data. For an overview of where things stand on the major issues, including reviews of the literature on definitions, measurement issues, prevalence, sex differences in expression of sexual orientation, sex differences in category-specific sexual arousal, sexual fluidity, developmental and psychological correlates of sexual orientation, bisexuality, and the environmental and genetic causes of sexual orientation, I recommend a 56-page article, "Sexual Orientation, Controversy, and Science," published in 2016 by a team of the field's leading scholars of varying perspectives (Michael Bailey, Paul Vasey, Lisa Diamond, Marc Breedlove, Eric Vilain, and Marc Epprecht).[22]

One of those sources was the General Social Survey, which had asked the question for the first time in 2008 and has continued to ask it through 2016. We also have subsequent data from an annual poll question about sexual identity that Gallup introduced in 2012 and estimates from the National

Health Interview Survey (NHIS). The latest published percentages as I write are as follows:[23]

	Year	Sample	Total LGB
Gallup Daily Tracking Poll	2017	340,604	4.5%
General Social Survey	2016	1,743	5.9%
Nat'l Health Interview Survey	2015	103,789	2.4%

Both the Gallup data and the General Social Survey show steady though small increases over time. An unweighted average of the three is 4.3 percent; an average weighted by sample size is 4.0 percent.

These estimates of the LGB population may strike you as absurdly low (recall that in polls, Americans estimate that about 23 percent of the population is gay or lesbian). But they are actually higher than the estimates that have been found in the other Western countries that have reported on self-identified sexual orientation for nationally representative samples.[24] Here are the results of the most recent major studies conducted outside America that I have been able to find:

	Gay/lesbian	Bisexual	Total
Norwegian Living Conditions Survey (2010)	0.7%	0.5%	1.2%
UK Integrated Household Survey (2016)	1.2%	0.8%	2.0%
Canadian Community Health Survey (2014)	1.7%	1.3%	3.0%
Australian Study of Health and Relationships (2014)	1.6%	1.7%	3.3%
New Zealand Attitudes and Values Study (2013–14)	2.6%	1.8%	4.4%

There may well be some degree of undercount. But there has been a revolution in openness about homosexuality in all of these countries that is now several decades old. Homosexuality has even acquired cachet among some circles in all of these countries. The answers to all of these surveys were anonymous. It is hard to come up with a scenario whereby all of the reported results are radical undercounts of authentic proportions of self-identified gays, lesbians, and bisexuals.

Prevalence of Same-Sex Attraction or Behavior

Self-identified sexual orientation is an undercount in another sense, however. How does one characterize a person who had a few homosexual experiences as a teenager and not thereafter? A person who was once sexually attracted to another of the same sex but didn't act on it? A person who has been sexually attracted to others of the same sex several times but never acted on it? A person who has had sexual relations with both sexes, but has a decided preference for one of them? For that matter, how does one classify people who have never felt same-sex attraction but have occasional curiosity about what it's like? That must include just about everyone.

In the same 2011 study I have been referencing, Gates included a synthesis of major studies that had tried to assess the proportion of people who have ever experienced any homosexual attraction.[25] Gates reported an American incidence of 11.0 percent, much higher than an Australian incidence of 6.5 percent and a Norwegian incidence of 1.8 percent. But only a minority of those who have experienced any homosexual attraction are equally attracted to both sexes—in the American study that produced the 11.0 percent figure, only 3.3 percent of all respondents said they were equally attracted to both sexes.[26]

Gates also reported the proportion of people who have ever engaged (even if just once) in same-sex sexual behavior. The answer for Americans was about 8 percent (two studies came up with incidence rates of 8.8 percent and 7.5 percent respectively) and 6.9 percent for Australians.[27]

One common way of trying to capture the continuum from "completely heterosexual" to "completely homosexual" is to ask respondents to put themselves on a five-point scale with the options of "heterosexual," "mostly heterosexual," "bisexual," "mostly gay/lesbian," or "gay/lesbian," or else on the similar six-point Kinsey scale. In 2013, Ritch Savin-Williams and Zhana Vrangalova compiled a systematic literature review on people who answered "mostly heterosexual."

The "mostly heterosexuals" make up a variety of people. As the authors point out, some may actually be bisexuals or homosexuals who refrain from identifying as a sexual minority; some could be completely heterosexual "but claim a nonheterosexual label, attraction, or behavior for reasons other than their sexual orientation, such as liberal social views, political correctness, or a desire for the gaze of the same sex." Some may have answered out of confusion or failure to understand the question.[28] There is no way to estimate the size of these groups from the data at hand.

Those who genuinely fit the authors' definition of "mostly heterosexual" can include those who have never acted on their same-sex attractions. Here are the two examples of "mostly heterosexual" respondents that the authors described in the article:

> For example, an 18-year old New England girl identified as mostly heterosexual because "I sort of like that it doesn't just have a *completely* or just a *bisexual*, but it has in between...there isn't always that black and white picture." A boy in the same study explained, "I'm basically attracted to girls, but I've felt like kind of attracted to guys before, but not to like some great extent....I've never felt I was attracted enough to a guy to like go out with them or something like that or like having a relationship with a guy."[29]

The authors presented data on 60 studies published from 1994 to 2012 with samples from the United States, Canada, the United Kingdom, Norway, Australia, and New Zealand and including a wide range of age groups. The authors of the Bailey survey article used a subset of these studies that comprised 71,190 adult males and 117,717 adult females. Here are the results by sex:[30]

	Women	Men
Completely heterosexual	86.8%	93.2%
Mostly heterosexual	10.1%	3.9%
Bisexual	1.4%	0.6%
Mostly homosexual	0.5%	0.7%
Completely homosexual	0.6%	1.4%

The results reinforce the point made earlier: The estimates of homosexuality for the United States from the Gallup polls and the General Social Survey are much higher than those from other studies. For current purposes, the main point of the results is the small proportion of people who self-identify as "mostly heterosexual" and the extremely small proportion who self-identify as bisexual.[31] Are bisexuals undercounted by these studies? Ritch Savin-Williams and Kenneth Cohen argue that the answer is yes, giving a "best estimate" (the authors' phrase) of male bisexual prevalence of about 10–20 percent.[32]

It's partly a technical issue: The two "mostly" categories actually identify bisexuals. If the table above had done that, the male bisexual figure would have been 5.2 percent instead of 0.6 percent. The figure would be augmented by the small percentages of men who do not answer "bisexual" but identify as pansexual, transgender, fluid, questioning, or kink-oriented. In most cases these individuals are deleted from the calculations of prevalence rates. Savin-Williams also argues that some men who don't answer the question are actually bisexual, and points to nonresponse rates in national studies that sometimes reach 10 percent.

The problem ranked first on Savin-Williams's list is definitional. He argues that a major contributor to the undercount is the failure of many assessments to include "nonsexual domains such as romantic attractions, infatuations, and relationships."[33] But should romantic but nonsexual attraction be classified as evidence of bisexuality? For example, consider a man who had a one-time crush on another man as a teenager but never was sexually aroused by him and has had enthusiastic sex exclusively with women all his subsequent life. In trying to characterize the sexual orientation of the population, it doesn't seem realistic to categorize him as bisexual. On the other hand, one may argue that a man who has had many such crushes on men throughout his life but never acted upon them is psychologically bisexual.

No matter how detailed the data collection becomes, people with different perspectives will make different judgments about such cases. A common assumption in the technical literature is that to move someone off the "completely heterosexual" end of the continuum, "attraction" needs to include actual sexual arousal by someone of the same sex. If there's no arousal, it doesn't count. I share that position. A same-sex attraction without any desire for sex is too easily confused with the genuine but nonerotic love that heterosexual women can have for other women and heterosexual men can have for other men.

The Transgender Phenomenon

Transgendered identity has become a major issue in academia and the media. In the popular understanding, transgender people see themselves as trapped in the body of the other sex. It's more complicated than that.[34]

Childhood-onset gender dysphoria. This comes closest to the popular under-standing, and it occurs in both girls and boys. It is characterized by behavior typical of the opposite sex from an early age. In the published literature, findings are that the majority (60–90 percent) of children with this kind of gender dys-phoria have become comfortable with their sex of birth by adulthood, and thus have avoided the need for a sex change.[35] Adults whose childhood-onset gender dysphoria persists typically do report that they have felt more like the other sex from their earliest memories. Childhood-onset gender dysphoria is highly cor-related with adult sexual attraction to one's birth sex, especially in males.

Autogynephilic gender dysphoria. This form occurs only in males. Auto-gynephilia taken alone refers to sexual arousal at the idea of having a female body or behaving like a female. It is usually a gradual process that begins in adolescence or later. Many men with autogynephilia live their lives as hetero-sexual men with wives and children while often engaging in practices such as cross-dressing in private. Males with autogynephilic gender dysphoria (as distinct from autogynephilia alone) are more likely to live as homosexuals and often possess a strong desire to obtain sex reassignment surgery, after which they often identify as lesbian.[36]

Rapid-onset gender dysphoria (ROGD). This is a newly documented phe-nomenon that might not even have existed a decade ago. It is characterized by adolescents, mostly female, who showed no signs of gender dysphoria as children and apparently abruptly decide they are transgender as teenagers.

As I write, only one systematic study of the ROGD phenomenon is avail-able, based on 256 surveys from parents who had reported that their teenage and young adult children had exhibited rapid onsets of gender dysphoria.[37] The author, Lisa Littman, a gynecologist specializing in gender dysphoria, reported that none of the parents' children in the study (83 percent were girls) would have been likely to have met diagnostic criteria for gender dysphoria in childhood. They did have a variety of psychiatric problems, however. Many (48 percent) had experienced a traumatic event prior to their declaration of gender dysphoria, and 63 percent had one or more diagnoses of a psychiatric or neurodevelopmental disability.

The results implicated an important role for social influences. Sixty-seven percent of the adolescents had one or more friends who declared they were transgender at about the same time. Increased time on social media was com-mon, and 69 percent of the parents believed (for reasons they explained) that their children were using language that they had found online. "Within friendship groups," Littman writes, "the average number of individuals who became transgender-identified was 3.5 per group. In 36.8% of the friend groups described, the majority of individuals in the group became transgender-identified....Parents described intense group dynamics where friend groups praised and supported people who were transgender-identified and ridiculed and maligned non-transgender people. Where popularity status and activities were known, 60.7% of the [children] experienced an increased popularity within their friend group when they announced a transgender-identification and 60.0% of the friend groups were known to mock people who were not transgender or LGBTIA (lesbian, gay, bisexual, transgender, intersex, or asexual)."[38]

Littman's is the only systematic study, but two leading scholars of LGBTIA issues, Michael Bailey and Ray Blanchard, have expressed some preliminary thoughts based on interviews with mothers of ROGD children and clinicians who work with ROGD children and parents, case studies, and the limited quantitative data. They surmise that "ROGD is a socially contagious phenomenon in which a young person—typically a natal female—comes to believe that she has a condition that she does not have. ROGD is not about discovering gender dysphoria that was there all along; rather, it is about falsely coming to believe that one's problems have been due to gender dysphoria previously hidden (from the self and others)."[39]

One thing seems clear: The rise in ROGD is concentrated among adolescent females. Historically and internationally, males have had higher rates of gender dysphoria than females. For childhood-onset gender dysphoria, this continues to be true in data from Canada, the Netherlands, and the UK.[40] But these same sources also found that the ratio reversed itself among adolescents during the period 2006–10.[41] In the UK, which operates the largest child and adolescent gender services in the world, the Gender Identity Development Service (GIDS), the sex ratio has become rapidly more disproportionate. In 2010, 52 percent of adolescent referrals were female; by 2016, that figure had risen to 72 percent.[42] The UK data also show a steep rise in referrals of adolescents, from 92 in 2010 to 1,497 in 2016, but it is difficult to disentangle how this growth is divided among increases in incidence, awareness of the existence of the service, and GIDS's area of coverage.

Taken together, how many people qualify as transgender? The fifth

(2013) edition of the *Diagnostic and Statistical Manual of Mental Disorders* of the American Psychiatric Association put the incidence rate at 0.5–1.4 percent for males and 0.2–0.3 percent for women. A 2015 meta-analysis of prevalence studies reached much smaller estimates of 0.0068 percent for women and 0.0026 percent for men.[43] Kenneth Zucker pulled together the available epidemiological data in a 2017 article and reached an overall estimate of 0.5–1.3 percent.[44] Whichever of these numbers is closest to the truth, only a small proportion of such people have undergone the major sex reassignment surgery that is popularly associated with transgender identity.[45]

———

I have left many aspects of sexual identity unaddressed not because they are intrinsically unimportant but because of my limited objective: The first five chapters of *Human Diversity* discuss sex differences, making it important to establish that those chapters are not ignoring large proportions of people who do not fit the ordinary definition of male or female. The evidence is incomplete in many respects, but not the basics. *Homo sapiens* is a typically dimorphic species with regard to sexuality. It consists of two sexes with an extremely small proportion of biological anomalies. Self-identified homosexuality or bisexualism in the United States is somewhere around 5 percent and usually less than that elsewhere. There is room for disagreement about the precise percentages, but not about the truth that humans are a normally dimorphic species.

Appendix 3

Sex Differences in Brain Volumes and Variance

This appendix deals with two important ways in which males and females differ biologically: larger male brain volumes and generally greater male variance in a wide variety of physiological and cognitive traits.

Brain Volumes

The biological reality of larger male brain volumes has been established, but no consensus has been reached on what they mean.

Human Males Have Much Larger Mean Brain Volume Than Human Females

In the 1990s, the first studies of sex differences in brain volume using MRI scans began to be published.[1] By 2014, the literature had grown so large that an international team of neuroscientists drawn primarily from Cambridge University (first author was Amber Ruigrok) could publish "A Meta-analysis of Sex Differences in Human Brain Structure" that combined 77 different studies involving 14,597 individuals.

The table below shows the results for the basic volume measures.

METACANALYSIS OF SEX DIFFERENCES IN THE MAJOR VOLUMES

Volume	Studies	Sample size	Mean difference (ml)	Percentage difference	Effect size (d)
Intracranial volume	77	14,957	135.3	12.0	−3.03
Total brain volume	31	2,532	131.0	10.8	−2.10
Cerebrum	22	1,851	51.1	9.8	−3.35
Gray matter	60	7,934	56.5	9.4	−2.13

Volume	Studies	Sample size	Mean difference (ml)	Percentage difference	Effect size (d)
White matter	57	7,515	44.4	12.9	−2.06
Cerebrospinal fluid	35	4,484	18.7	11.5	−1.21
Cerebellum	19	1,842	7.8	8.6	−1.68

Source: Ruigrok, Salimi-Khorshidi, Lai et al. (2014): Table 3.

The effect sizes for two of the measured volumes qualify as "very large" by Cohen's guidelines, while the other five of them are "huge."

Sex Differences in Brain Volume Extend to the Subcortical Regions

Good information on volumes of the regions of the brain in vivo had to wait for MRI technology. The last half of the 1990s saw more than a dozen early studies showing that a variety of subcortical volumes were larger in males, but small sample sizes left uncertainty about the consistency and magnitude of the differences.[2] That problem continued into the 2000s. In the Ruigrok meta-analysis of 2014, the median sample size of the 25 studies that examined sex differences in specific regions was just 86 and only 10 of them had samples of more than 100.[3]

In 2018, many of the uncertainties of earlier work were put to rest by a team of British scholars (first author was Stuart Ritchie) who analyzed subcortical regional means and variances based on a sample of 5,216 persons from the UK Biobank data.[4] The average male total brain volume was 1,234 cm^3 compared to 1,116 cm^3 for females, which amounts to a difference of 118 cm^3, representing an effect size of −1.41, smaller than the −2.10 effect size in the Ruigrok meta-analysis.

The Ritchie study reported volume estimates for the 68 subcortical regions in the Desikan-Killiany neuroanatomical atlas.[5] Males had larger volumes in all 68. The smallest effect size was −0.24 and the largest was −1.03, with a mean of −0.67. All were highly statistically significant. The table below shows the Ritchie results for some of the most important subcortical regions. Highly statistically significant effect sizes are shown in boldface.

EFFECT SIZES (D) FOR RAW AND ADJUSTED DIFFERENCES IN BRAIN VOLUMES

		Adjusted for...	
	Raw	Height	Total volume
Total brain	−1.41	−0.42	
Gray matter	−1.28	−0.31	*
White matter	−1.49	−0.47	*

| | Raw | Adjusted for... | |
		Height	Total volume
Left hippocampus	−0.55	−0.17	−0.02
Right hippocampus	−0.54	−0.18	−0.01
Left accumbens	−0.39	−0.06	+0.08
Right accumbens	−0.31	−0.05	+0.10
Left amygdala	−0.59	**−0.21**	**−0.18**
Right amygdala	−0.51	**−0.18**	**−0.18**
Left caudate	−0.66	−0.20	−0.01
Right caudate	−0.65	−0.19	0.00
Left pallidum	−0.77	**−0.24**	**−0.16**
Right pallidum	−0.78	**−0.24**	**−0.12**
Left putamen	−1.01	**−0.30**	**−0.22**
Right putamen	−1.08	**−0.35**	**−0.25**
Left thalamus	−0.98	−0.26	+0.01
Right thalamus	−1.03	−0.27	−0.02

Source: Adapted from Ritchie, Cox, Shen et al. (2018): Tables 1 and S1. Figures in bold indicate that $p < 10^{-4}$.

*Adjustments for gray and white matter for total brain volume were not performed because of collinearity.

The effect sizes in the "Raw" column represent the expected magnitudes of difference in brain volumes in a randomly chosen man and a randomly chosen woman. The effect sizes in the "Height" column represent the expected differences in brain volumes of a man and woman of the same height. The effect sizes in the "Adjusted for total volume" column represent the expected differences in regional brain volumes for a man and a woman with the same total brain volume.

The raw effect sizes for the subcortical volumes ranged from −0.31 to −1.08, with a median of −0.660. Adjusted for height, the effect sizes ranged from −0.05 to −0.35, with a median of −0.24. The "Adjusted for total volume" column shows men retaining larger volumes in all but two regions, but with effect sizes that are no larger than −0.25 and a median of −0.12.

Which of these three ways of looking at differences in brain volume should we use? This question only raises more questions. It makes sense that we should adjust for body size for some traits. A plausible reason that elephants have brains twice the weight of human brains is that it takes a lot more neurons to control large muscular structures and nervous systems than to control small ones. But the logic of adjusting for body size is not obvious when it comes to the intellect and emotions. It's all happening in the brain. Why should it take more neurons to solve a quadratic equation in a person who is 5 foot 8 than in a person who is 5 foot 4?

According to neuroscientists whom I have asked, there is oddly little in the technical literature that systematically explores when it is appropriate to adjust for differences in body size. But there is a clear reason to adjust for total brain size for certain purposes: It is the appropriate method for finding interesting sex differences in the relative sizes of different regions. The question that must still be at the back of the investigator's mind is the extent to which adjusting for total brain size produces another kind of artifact, removing variance that does in fact contribute to sex differences in overt traits. That brings us to the fraught question of brain size and how smart people are.

Brain Size and g

The progress of hominids from chimpanzees to anatomically modern humans has been marked by increases in skull volume.[6] Paleontologists, physical anthropologists, evolutionary biologists, and neuroscientists have broadly agreed that greater skull volume means greater brain volume, and greater brain volume across species is associated with greater cognitive capacity.[7]

It is also established that brain volume in humans is correlated with IQ scores, and hence with *g*. That knowledge has been hard-won in the face of controversy. The early correlations were based on indirect measures of brain size—for example, measuring head circumference—that left much room for doubt.[8] Then MRI technology made it possible to determine in vivo volume of the brain with precision—and not just total brain volume, but the volumes of the dozens of subcortical regions.

The size of the correlation of overall brain volume with IQ has varied from sample to sample. Two meta-analyses of all such studies concluded respectively that the correlation is +.33 and +.24.[9] Subsequently, a reanalysis of the literature argued that the scientifically most rigorous studies show an average correlation of +.39.[10] Furthermore, this relationship holds within sexes. On average, men with larger brains have higher IQ than men with smaller brains, and women with larger brains have higher IQ than women with smaller brains.[11]

Is the relationship causal? After all, bigger brains mean more neurons. But what counts for cognitive functioning in mammals is the number of neurons in the cerebral cortex and the subcortical regions.[12] On this score, humans stand apart from all other mammals. The human cerebral cortex contains about 16 billion neurons. The next largest, found in gorillas and orangutans, is just 9 billion.[13]

Several studies have found evidence for this causal link in humans. Cerebellar brain volume has been found to explain variance in g in older adults, even after controlling for frontal lobe volume (which tends to atrophy with age).[14] In 2018, neuroscientists reinforced the evidence for a causal link through a study with a large sample ($n = 2,904$) of brain development in youths and young adults (first author was Kirk Reardon).[15] The cortical surface area expands threefold between infancy and adulthood. A priori, one might expect that human brains of different sizes scale uniformly—a brain with larger total volume also has a linearly larger hippocampus, amygdala, and so forth. But that's not what the Reardon study found. "Rather," as David Van Essen summarized it, "larger brains show greater expansion in regions associated with higher cognition and less expansion in regions associated with sensory, motor, and limbic (emotion- and affect-related) functions."[16] The Reardon study also found that overall cortical surface area correlated significantly with IQ after factoring out age and sex.[17] Thus there is good reason to expect a causal relationship not only between brain volume and IQ, but between brain volume in specific regions and IQ. Other things being equal, more neurons are a good thing for cognitive functioning.[18]

But other things are not equal.

Sexual Dimorphism in Brain Volumes Does Not Necessarily Mean Dimorphism in Cognitive Function

Chapter 5 describes sex differences in connectivity that make female brains more efficient. There's much more work being done in this area. Sex differences in receptor density could be at work independently of regional brain size or overall brain size. Furthermore, volume isn't the only relevant measure of size. Two other measures that were considered in the Ritchie study were the convoluted cortical surface areas and cortical thickness. Those two features have been found to be independent of each other, both globally and regionally.[19] The male-female differences in surface area for all 68 subcortical regions were even larger than those found for overall volume, with effect sizes ranging from −0.43 to −1.20 and a mean of −0.83.[20] This was not true of cortical thickness, however. Consistent with an earlier study of sex differences in cortical thickness,[21] females had significantly thicker cortex across most of the brain (47 of the 68 areas). Males had significantly thicker cortex in just 1 of the 68. The differences in the remaining 20 areas did not reach statistical significance. The effect sizes in the 47 ranged from +0.07 to +0.45, with a mean of +0.22 (a positive *d* indicates greater cortical thickness among females). These differences remained significant after adjusting for total brain size.

Other brain parameters can and do vary by sex; among them, cerebral blood flow, glucose metabolism in the limbic system, dopamine transporter availability, the percentage of gray matter tissue in some parts of the brain, and the percentage of white matter tissue in other parts. The links between these parameters and behavior were summarized by Ruben and Raquel Gur in a review article. "For example," the Gurs write, "differences in gray and white matter volumes have been related to performance on verbal and spatial tasks, sex differences in hippocampal volume and in dopamine availability have been linked to memory performance, and sex differences in limbic activity and orbitofrontal volume have been associated with differences in emotion regulation."[22] What all this shows, the Gurs conclude, is a set of differences that cannot be ranked from good to bad, but that tend to be complementary.

Neuroendocrinologist Geert de Vries has argued that sex differences in brain structure may work to *prevent* phenotypic differences. "Intuition tells us that sex differences in brain structure beget sex differences in brain function," he wrote in 2005. "There is nothing wrong with that. If, for example, a brain area has three times more cells that produce a specific neurotransmitter in one sex vs. the other, and if these cells send, accordingly, three times denser projections to target neurons in another area, stimulation of these cells will probably cause sex-specific responses in the target neurons."[23] But researchers have drawn their hypothesis too narrowly, de Vries argues. Sex differences in brain structure "may indeed generate differences in overt functions and behavior, but they may just as well do the exact opposite, that is, they may prevent sex differences in overt functions and behavior by compensating for sex differences in physiology"—hence the subtitle to his article, "Compensation, Compensation, Compensation."[24] In 2015, de Vries and Nancy Forger elaborated on such compensatory mechanisms. Every organ in the body is sexually differentiated to some degree, the authors argue, and they present a variety of examples whereby sexual differentiation in organs and tissues throughout the body eventually affect neural function or morphology.[25]

These are just some of the many reasons for caution. The reality of sex differences in brain volumes is firmly established. Collateral evidence indicates that these myriad differences must have implications at many levels of brain function. But our understanding of the specifics, and what those differences mean for phenotypic traits, is still rudimentary.

Generally Greater Male Variance

If you followed the furor about James Damore's internal memo at Google that got him fired in 2017, or if you're old enough to have followed the furor over Larry Summers's comments about male-female differences in attraction to STEM back in 2005, you've encountered the phrase "greater male variance hypothesis." The reason the hypothesis has gotten so much attention is its implication for explaining male dominance at the highest levels of achievement in the arts and sciences throughout recorded history.[26] If general cognitive ability g is normally distributed, then even if males and females have the same mean g, greater variation in males will mean that men are overrepresented at the tails of the normal distribution.

A lot of "ifs" lie between the existence of greater male variance and the explanation for male dominance at the highest levels of achievement. That's why I am not prepared to defend a statement that begins, "Greater male variance in measures of abilities explains…" That's a leap too far. But this less ambitious statement is no longer controversial: Greater male variance in a wide variety of traits is a fundamental biological characteristic of humans and of dimorphic species more generally. It doesn't happen with every trait for which data are available, but with a substantial majority of them. The greater male variance hypothesis isn't a hypothesis anymore.[27] It is now known to be generally true.

The Evolutionary Context for Greater Male Variance

I will break my own rule for this book and introduce a little evolutionary biology into the conversation, because the reasons for greater male variance go so extremely deep into the evolutionary dynamics that have been operating for hundreds of millions of years among all species that reproduce sexually.

The simple observation that the males of many species show more visible variation goes back to the 1700s and was remarked upon by Darwin in *The Descent of Man.*[28] It has an elemental evolutionary driver: the necessity of having progeny if one's genes are to be passed on. In 1948, A. J. Bateman, a botanist, presented the first hard evidence for what became known as Bateman's principle: In most species, variability in reproductive success is greater in males than in females. He used that staple of genetic research, the fruit fly, for his evidence.[29] Through a series of experiments, Bateman established three important sex differences in reproductive success:

- Males' reproductive success varied much more widely than females'— only 4 percent of females failed to produce offspring, compared to 21 percent of males.
- Being able to attract the opposite sex was far more important for males than for females. Female reproductive failure wasn't because of a failure to attract males. The 4 percent of females who failed to reproduce were vigorously courted; they just weren't interested. Conversely, the 21 percent of males who failed to reproduce gave every appearance of trying hard to copulate. They just couldn't get accepted.
- Engaging in lots of sex is extremely helpful for male reproductive success, but not for female reproductive success. For males, the number of offspring increased almost linearly with the number of copulations. For females, reproductive success increased only marginally after the first copulation.[30]

In 1972, Robert Trivers drew on Bateman's research and collateral findings to make a seminal contribution: "What governs the operation of sexual selection is the relative parental investment of the sexes in their offspring," with *parental investment* defined as "any investment by the parent in an individual

offspring that increases the offspring's chances of surviving (and hence reproductive success) at the cost of the parent's ability to invest in other offspring."[31]
The optimal strategy for a sex that made little parental investment, Trivers
argued, is to mate with as many partners as possible. The optimal strategy for
a sex that made high parental investment is to be choosy about the choice of
mate. Evolutionary psychologist David Geary put it this way:

> The sex that provides more than his or her share of parental investment is
> an important reproductive resource for members of the opposite sex. The
> result is competition among members of the lower-investing sex (typically
> males) over the parental investment of members of the higher-investing sex
> (typically females). Competition for parental investment creates demand
> for the higher-investing sex that in turn allows them to be choosey when it
> comes to mates.[32]

In more than 95 percent of mammalian species, males make extremely
small parental investments and females make huge ones.[33] This imbalance
can produce greater male variability via different routes that have been the
subject of an extensive literature.[34]

Reviewing that literature here would take us far afield. Think of it this
way: To pass on your genes, you must mate. If you are a male and females are
choosy, you need to have traits that attract females in the first place and other
traits that enable you to fight off, figuratively or literally, other members of
your own sex. If you are a female and the males of your species will copulate
with anything that moves, you do not face any of those sources of evolutionary pressure.[35] On the contrary, deviations from the normal range may exact
fitness costs.

If we are talking about modern human males and females, the dynamic
I just described may now be weak. Contemporary human males typically
make far higher parental investment than most mammals. Humans have
been an example of what Steve Stewart-Williams and Andrew Thomas call
the "mutual mate choice" model, in contrast to the "males-compete/females-
choose" model.[36] But the role that evolution is argued to have played in
generating greater male variability is not something that started with *Homo
sapiens*. It has been going on since sexual dimorphism began. In all cases of
greater choosiness in one sex, wider variability of traits improves your odds

of passing on your genes if you are a member of the less choosy sex. In the overwhelming majority of cases, the less choosy sex has been male. When the process involves unimaginable trillions of reproductive events over millions of years, the fractional fitness advantages of greater variability add up.

A ROLE FOR THE SEX CHROMOSOMES IN PRODUCING GREATER MALE VARIABILITY

The fact that females have two X chromosomes while the male has only one suggests a straightforward explanation for traits that are influenced by genes in the X chromosome. The explanation is based on elementary arithmetic: Women can average, males can't. Here's the more precise statement by evolutionary biologists Klaus Reinhold and Leif Engqvist: "Binomial sampling of the large X chromosomes leads to the intuitive prediction that males should show larger variation. In females, the traits that are influenced by X-chromosomal genes will be under the average influence of the two parental copies, whereas in males, the effect of the single X-chromosome will not be averaged. As a result, male mammals are expected to show larger variability than females in all traits that are, at least to some extent, influenced by X-chromosomal alleles," given certain conditions described in the note.[37] The overall effect of the sex chromosomes on greater male variability is limited to traits affected by the X chromosome, which means that greater male variability in most traits must be driven by other forces.

So much for the evolutionary explanation of greater male variability. You're free to ignore it. The topic here is not an explanation of greater male variability, but the empirical evidence for it. Nowhere is that biological truth more unequivocal than in greater male variance in the brain.

Males Have Greater Variance Than Females at Both the Whole Brain and the Regional Levels

The table below shows the variance ratios for the same three versions—raw, adjusted for height, and adjusted for total brain volume—that I reported for effect sizes in regional volumes. *Variance ratio* (VR) is computed as the variance of one population. In the case of the following table and all other references to VRs in this discussion, male variance is divided by female variance. Therefore a VR greater than 1.0 signifies greater male variance.

VARIANCE RATIOS FOR RAW AND ADJUSTED
DIFFERENCES IN BRAIN VOLUMES

	Raw	Adjusted for...	
		Height	*Total volume*
Total brain	1.22		
Gray matter	1.23	*	*
White matter	1.22	*	*
Left hippocampus	1.16	1.15	1.16
Right hippocampus	1.30	1.28	1.35
Left accumbens	1.23	1.23	1.22
Right accumbens	1.20	1.20	1.20
Left amygdala	1.35	1.35	1.37
Right amygdala	1.27	1.28	1.27
Left caudate	1.18	1.18	1.16
Right caudate	1.19	1.19	1.20
Left pallidum	1.14	1.10	1.09
Right pallidum	1.19	1.16	1.15
Left putamen	1.20	1.22	1.20
Right putamen	1.23	1.23	1.23
Left thalamus	1.22	1.18	1.33
Right thalamus	1.20	1.18	1.30

Source: All ratios are implicitly compared to 1.0. For example, the entry of 1.22 for Total brain volume represents a male-to-female ratio of 1.22. Adapted from Ritchie, Cox, Shen et al. (2018): Tables 1 and S1. For all variance ratios, $p < .001$ (all but the variance ratio for the left hippocampus adjusted for height had $p < 10^{-4}$). All variables are adjusted for age and ethnicity. Ratios greater than 1.0 indicate greater male variance.

*Adjustments for gray and white matter for total brain volume were not performed because of collinearity.

The remarkable aspect of the table is how little the VRs are affected by controlling for height or total brain volume, unlike the story for regional brain volumes presented earlier. The mean of the 28 differences was a trivial 0.0014. The largest of all 28 of the differences between the adjusted ratios and the raw ratio was just 0.04.

The table shows the results for only 14 subcortical regions. The full analysis in the Ritchie study included 68 regions, with measures not just of volume but for surface area and cortical thickness. Males had greater variance in all 68 regions, and those differences were significant for 64 out of the 68. The surface area variance ratio was significant in 66 of the 68 regions. The exception was the measure of cortical thickness, where women had a thicker

cortex than men across almost the entire brain. The variance ratios for cortical thickness were nonsignificant with a single exception.[38]

Greater Male Variance in Other Biological Traits

Greater male variance is found in a wide variety of physiological traits. I won't
try to list them all, but these examples will give you a sense of the prevalence
of greater male variance.

The U.S. National Health and Nutrition Examination Survey (NHANES)
for 2015–16 included 10 basic physiological measures. The variance results for
adults ages 20–39 (936 males, 1,017 females) are shown below:[39]

	Effect size (d)	Variance ratio
Weight	−0.62	1.15
Height	−1.91	1.25
Body mass index (BMI)	−0.02	0.77
Upper leg length	−1.49	1.19
Upper arm length	−1.45	1.09
Waist circumference	−0.24	0.99
Saggital abdominal diameter	−0.36	1.01
Pulse	+0.35	1.08
Systolic blood pressure	−0.68	1.23
Diastolic blood pressure	−0.32	1.33

Of the 10 parameters in the NHANES data, seven show greater male
variability, two show effectively equal male and female variability, and only
one, BMI, shows clearly greater female variability.[40] The mean variance ratio
was 1.10.[41]

In 1988, the U.S. Army conducted an anthropometric survey of its uniformed personnel, taking 132 measurements of length, breadth, and circumference of various portions of the body plus a measure of overall weight using
a sample of 1,774 men and 2,208 women balanced to reflect the racial/eth-
nic and age groups in the active-service Army.[42] The measures ranged from
the basic (height, weight) to the arcane (bitragion coronal arc, bispinous
breadth). Of the 132, 3 percent had variance ratios of 1.0, 14 percent had
variance ratios less than 1.0 (women had greater variance), and 83 percent
had ratios greater than 1.0 (men had greater variance). The average VR for
the 132 anthropometric measures was 1.12.

A team of British scholars analyzed grip strength across the lifespan, combining 12 British studies with 49,964 subjects. From the ages of 5 to 9, girls had slightly higher grip strength than boys (d = +.10) and slightly greater variability (VR = 0.88). Thereafter, males had higher grip strength and greater variability. By the age of 20 and for each 5-year age group through the oldest group (90–94), both the effect sizes and the VRs were at least 1.8.[43]

MRI was used by Canadian and U.S. scholars to measure skeletal muscle mass in 200 women and 268 men ages 18–88 and of varied adiposity.[44] The results are shown below.

	d	VR
Total skeletal muscle (SM)	–2.60	1.95
SM relative to BMI	–1.47	0.86
Lower body SM	–2.10	1.54
Upper body SM	–2.55	2.09

The effect sizes not adjusted for BMI are so large that there was virtually no overlap between the males and females. The variance ratios were large as well. When adjusted for BMI, the effect size remained large, but women were more variable than men.[45]

This is just a sampling. The generalization seems secure: In childhood, the sex differences in variability are scattered and small. Male variability increases after puberty. As adults, greater male variability extends from the regions of the brain throughout the body—not on every parameter, but on a large majority of them.

Greater Male Variance in Sexually Selected Attributes

In 1989, psychologist David Buss conducted a study of sex differences in human mate preferences across 37 cultures worldwide. Using parental investment and sexual selection theory, he predicted the results for five target attributes: In choosing mates, males would value youth, physical attractiveness, and chastity more than females do; females would value good providers (operationally defined as "good financial prospects" and ambition/industriousness) more than men do. All of the five predictions were empirically supported, though to different degrees.[46]

Fourteen years later, psychologists John Archer and Mani Mehdikhani returned to Buss's data with an additional hypothesis, based on Trivers's theory of parental investment but also on the prevalence of men who make high parental investment. Some men behave as if they are pursuing the primordial male reproductive strategy of impregnating as many females as possible; others behave as if they are pursuing a strategy of attracting women through the promise of being good fathers. "If there are alternative reproductive strategies among men but not among women, we would predict greater variability among males than among females in psychological characteristics associated with sexual selection," the authors hypothesized, and used Buss's database to test the hypothesis. They also used meta-analyses of sex differences in physical aggression, another trait predicted to be sexually selected.[47]

The weighted means for effect size and variance ratio are shown below:[48]

	Effect size (d)	VR
Physical aggression	−0.70	2.04
Good looks	−0.59	0.95
Chastity	−0.30	1.82
Ambition and industriousness	0.50	1.91
Good financial prospects	0.76	1.41
Age difference	2.00	2.09

"Good looks" was the exception, with a VR slightly under 1.0. Males showed substantially more variability than females on the other five, with ratios ranging from 1.41 to 2.09, consistent with their hypothesis.[49]

Greater Male Variance in Personality

The database used for the McCrae cross-national study in personality described in chapter 2, based on observations rather than self-reports, has also been analyzed for variability. In the United States, males had greater variability than females on all five factors of the Five Factor Model, with VRs 1.05 for neuroticism, 1.21 for extraversion, 1.14 for openness, 1.08 for agreeableness, and 1.20 for conscientiousness. The mean for all five was 1.13.[50]

This pattern applied to Anglophone and European countries generally. Excluding the United States, the mean VR for 24 other Anglophone and European countries was 1.08. Those 24 countries did not show a higher male variance on neuroticism (mean VR = 0.97). The mean VRs for the other factors were 1.08 for extraversion, 1.13 for openness, 1.11 for agreeableness, and 1.13 for conscientiousness.[51]

The results also differed markedly by personality factor. Males had greater variability in conscientiousness (84 percent of the countries), openness (75 percent), and agreeableness (69 percent), but a majority of countries had greater female variability in neuroticism (59 percent) and extraversion (53 percent). Overall, greater male variability in personality is not nearly as consistent as for the other topics I cover.

Greater Male Variance in Mental Tests

In the early 1990s, testing experts Larry Hedges and Amy Nowell set out to conduct a comprehensive study of sex differences in mental test scores, variability, and high-scoring individuals in the United States for all of the large and nationally representative datasets over the period from 1960 to 1992.[52] Their article, published in *Science* in 1995, was the definitive statement of where things stood when they wrote. They presented variability ratios for 37 different mental test measures. Male variance was higher in 35 of the 37.[53] The exceptions were a test of word memory and one of coding speed—and, the authors noted, "In both cases, measures of the same constructs in other surveys showed greater male variability."[54] Overall, Hedges and Nowell concluded, "These data demonstrate that in U.S. populations, the test scores of males are indeed more variable than those of females, at least for the abilities measured during the 32-year period covered by the six national surveys. Moreover, there is little indication that variance ratios are changing over time."[55]

The National Assessment of Educational Progress (NAEP) now provides an even longer trendline—44 years for reading and 37 years for math. From the first test in 1971 to the most recent one in 2015, 12th-grade boys have had higher variance than girls on all 13 tests for which I have data, with ratios ranging from 1.07 to 1.20, with a mean of 1.12. The trendline is absolutely flat. And yet in all of those tests, girls outscored boys at the mean.[56] On the nine math tests for which I have data, all showed greater male variance, with ratios also ranging from 1.07 to 1.20 and a mean of 1.13. The SAT shows even more consistent but quite small variance ratios. From 1996 to 2016, the variance ratio on the math test was never smaller than 1.03 and never larger than 1.09. For the reading test, variance was almost but not quite equal, ranging from 1.02 to 1.05. There has been no trend in either test.

VARIABILITY IN MENTAL TESTS DURING CHILDHOOD

I concentrate on test scores in adolescents and older because so many sex differences, physiological and mental, change during adolescence and persist thereafter. But greater male variability on mental tests emerges early as well. Psychologists Rosalind Arden and Robert Plomin explored variance in g in large British samples at ages 2, 3, 4, 7, 9, and 10. They found significantly greater variance among boys at every age except 2.[57]

Internationally, greater male variability in test scores was formerly thought to be inconsistent. A 1994 review by psychologist Alan Feingold found a median VR of 0.95 in tests of vocabulary (six countries), 1.01 for reading comprehension (three countries), 1.09 for math (20 countries), and 1.14 for spatial ability (nine countries).[58] The variance ratios were often 1.0 or less, indicating greater female variance. But Feingold had to work with a heterogeneous set of tests from a comparatively small number of nations. Since the PISA tests began in 2000, the picture has come into clearer focus.

Thirty-nine countries plus Macao and Hong Kong participated in the 2003 PISA administration.[59] The mean scores for reading and math showed the pattern you saw in chapter 3: a small male advantage in math (mean $d = -0.11$), a greater female advantage in verbal ($d = +0.36$). But when it came to variance ratios, 38 of the 41 countries showed higher male variance in the math test, with a mean VR of 1.16. The difference in girls' and boys' ratios was statistically significant ($p < .05$) for 37 of the 41 countries. For reading, despite the universal female advantage in mean scores, 40 of the 41 showed higher male variance (Indonesia had a VR of exactly 1.0), with a mean VR of 1.19. The difference in girls' and boys' ratios was statistically significant ($p < .05$) for 35 of the 41 countries.[60]

The most recent PISA results have not changed much since 2003, except that more countries are participating. For the 2015 math and science tests, males had higher variability in 65 out of 67 countries; for the reading, in 63 out of 67. The table below shows the average variance ratios grouped by geographic region.[61]

	Mean variance ratio		
	Reading	Math	Science
Anglosphere	1.15	1.14	1.18
East Asia	1.12	1.18	1.18
Eastern Europe	1.12	1.12	1.14
Latin Am./Caribbean	1.09	1.12	1.13

	Mean variance ratio		
	Reading	Math	Science
Mideast/No. Africa	1.17	1.16	1.14
Scandinavia	1.19	1.14	1.18
SE Asia	1.12	1.10	1.07
Western Europe	1.12	1.14	1.15

The table shows remarkably consistent greater male variability in regions that are culturally, socioeconomically, and educationally diverse. Furthermore, this uniformity of greater male variability existed across three tests that showed quite different effect sizes by sex. Averaged across countries, boys slightly outscored girls on the math test (d = −0.05) while girls fractionally outscored boys on the science test (d = +0.01). Girls substantially outscored boys on the reading test (d = +0.32). And yet the mean VRs for those countries were −1.14, −1.14, and −1.15 for reading, math, and science respectively.

How Big Does a Variance Ratio Have to Be
Before It Becomes Important?

In his 1994 review of greater male variance in mental tests, Alan Feingold pronounced that a VR between 0.9 and 1.1 was "negligible,"[62] and thereby established a guideline that others who discuss variance ratios have often followed. I consider this to be an important error. VRs between 0.9 and 1.1 can be socially and culturally important for any trait for which performance at the extremes has consequences.

Consider the implications for a normally distributed trait if the VR is just 1.09. Assume that male and female means are equal, so that the only source of a disparity is the greater male variance. With a VR of 1.09, we can expect males to outnumber females by 31 percent in the 99th percentile, 38 percent in the top half of the top percentile, and 57 percent in the top tenth of the top percentile. Those are noteworthy disproportions in the abstract, but even more noteworthy when we consider the consequences. The social consequences of this seemingly small disparity can be great.

In a population of 250 million adults—roughly the number of Americans ages 20 and older—the top 0.1 percent amounts to 250,000 people. Think about the 250,000 people with the nation's highest visuospatial and math skills. They constitute some substantial proportion of the top programmers and hardware designers in Silicon Valley, the staffs of quantitative hedge funds, and the nation's most eminent mathematicians, physicists, chemists, biologists, and engineers. Apply the same logic to other fields requiring different abilities—the 250,000 most gifted attorneys, the 250,000 most gifted managers, the 250,000 most gifted in the performing arts. America is far from having tapped the talents of all 250,000 of the most gifted in any field, but it is probable that a large proportion of the most important accomplishments in all fields are done by those who are in the top 0.1 percent, three standard deviations above the mean. Add in the accomplishments and positions of the much larger numbers of people in the entire 99th percentile—2.5 million people—and even the 31 percent disparity at that level, given a VR of only 1.09, will have a large aggregated impact.

Once I leave behind a minimal case—equal means and VR of only 1.09—the disproportions produced by normal distributions increase rapidly. For equal means and a VR favoring males of 1.15, there will be 54 percent more males in the 99th percentile and more than twice as many males in the 99.9th percentile. Start to combine a VR with an effect size favoring males, and the sex imbalance increases even more. Given a VR of 1.15 and an effect size of just $d = -0.10$ favoring males—"very small" by Cohen's definition—and you can expect twice as many males as females in the 99th percentile and almost three times as many in the 99.9th percentile.

Do Statistical Expectations for the
Tails Correspond to Actual Distributions?

The key issue here is the assumption that the distribution of the trait is perfectly normal all the way out through three standard deviations. The only way to be sure what the male-to-female ratios are at the extremes is to have such a large and representative sample that you can see the actual numbers, not the theoretically predicted ones. But this means extremely large samples. For example, if you are interested in knowing the male-to-female ratio of people with IQs of 145 and higher, you are talking about the ratio for the 99.865th percentile. With a mean of 100 and a standard deviation of 15, even a sample of 10,000 people can be expected to produce only about 13 people with IQs that high, far short of the number you need to have any confidence in the male-female ratio. Many national assessments such as the NAEP in America and the Cognitive Abilities Test in Great Britain have samples with hundreds of thousands or even millions of scores, but to my knowledge they have not published breakdowns by gender within the top five percentiles. We do have two solid pieces of evidence bearing on the question, however.

The Early Childhood Longitudinal Study. The first comes from a test of the common assertion that more people are in the gifted range of intelligence than the statistics of the normal distribution would predict. The study of 10 large, nationally representative samples (first author was Russell Warne) indicated that the numbers of people in the top percentiles are generally about what they should be—somewhat more for some tests, somewhat less for others, but overall close to expectations.[63]

For the question I'm asking—does greater male variance really predict disproportionate numbers of males at the extremes?—the Warne study was valuable because one of the studies it used, the Early Childhood Longitudinal Study, had a nationally representative sample that was large enough (18,000) to assess disparities up to the top half of the 99th percentile and information broken down by sex. They were given standardized cognitive tests at six points during their observation from kindergarten through 8th grade.

The effect sizes were typical: small female advantages on the reading tests, small male advantages on the math and science tests, and trivial effect sizes on the general knowledge test. The largest effect size was −0.24 on the science test; none of the rest reached an absolute value of 0.17. But VRs for all of the tests were greater than 1.0, ranging from 1.01 on the science test to 1.32 on one of the math tests. First, here are the actual results—the ratios of boys to girls in various high-end categories ranging from the top five percentiles to the top half of the top percentile.

Test	Top 5%	Top 2%	Top 1%	Top 0.5%
C1 General Knowledge	1.44	1.66	1.69	2.83
C2 General Knowledge	1.39	1.78	2.27	5.25
C3 General Knowledge	1.62	2.42	3.63	3.10
C4 Reading	0.93	0.97	0.95	1.07
C4 Math	1.84	2.22	2.91	2.72
C5 Reading	0.95	1.10	1.16	
C5 Math	2.09	2.79	4.35	3.90
C5 Science	2.10	2.68	2.64	4.38
C6 Science	2.28	2.55	1.77	
Average, all tests	1.63	2.02	2.37	3.32

Source: Data from Warne, Godwin, and Smith (2013), provided by Russell Warne, personal communication.

The numbering of the tests reflects the increasing ages at which they were administered. To interpret the table, look at the top row, left-hand column—"1.44" indicates that there were 44 percent more boys than girls in the top five percentiles for the initial test of general knowledge. The two blank cells for the right-hand column indicate that no more than a few students scored in that range.

The table shows two broad trends: Throughout elementary and middle school, more boys than girls were represented in the top percentiles in general knowledge and math, with roughly equal proportions for the reading test; and the ratios favoring boys tended to increase as the criteria got more restrictive. Taking the mean for all the tests, the ratios increased from 1.57 for the top five percentiles to 3.15 for the top half percentile.

Next, how did the predictions for those categories based on the assumption of a normal distribution work out? The graph below shows a scatter plot of the predicted ratios and the actual ratios.

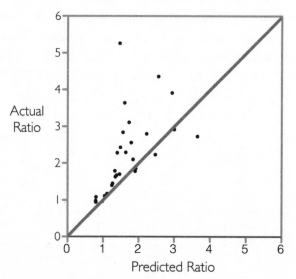

Source: Data provided by Russell Warne, personal communication.

Dots falling above the diagonal represent underprediction of the actual ratio; dots falling below the diagonal represent overprediction of the actual ratio. What it comes down to is that for this test battery administered to a large representative sample of children, the disproportion of males at the right tail of the distribution was usually even larger than the VRs would have predicted.[64]

The Scottish Mental Surveys of 1932 and 1947. The second piece of evidence comes from the Scottish Mental Surveys of 1932 and 1947, which tested 87,498 and 75,211 Scottish 11-year-olds respectively, representing 95 percent and 93 percent of the populations. Psychologists Wendy Johnson, Andrew Carothers, and Ian Deary exhaustively analyzed the actual distributions of both tests. Males outnumbered females at both the low and high ends of the IQ distribution for both cohorts. At IQs of 60 and 140 (the low and high points of the range), the male-female ratios in both cohorts were concentrated in a narrow range, from 2.0 to 2.3.[65] At IQs of 132 (about the 98th percentile), the ratio of boys to girls had dropped to about 1.4 in both cohorts. These results are roughly consistent with recent ratios of boys to girls for the samples of gifted children of the TIP that I reported in chapter 3.

How well did expectations based on a perfectly normal distribution match up with the actual frequency distributions? For the 1932 survey, the prediction for an IQ at exactly 140 was 1.7 males per female, an underprediction of the actual 2.3 males per female. For IQ at exactly 132, the prediction was 1.4 males per female, the same as the actual result of 1.4. For the 1947 survey, the prediction at IQ 140 was also 1.4 males per female, an underprediction of the actual 2.0. At IQ 132, the prediction was of 1.2 males per female compared to an actual 1.4.[66] Overall, taking the Warne and Johnson studies together, the consequences of greater male variance at the tails of actual distributions are at least as great as the assumption of a normal distribution would lead one to expect.

Another lesson of the Scottish surveys is that small variance ratios can make a difference. The VRs for both surveys were quite small, less than 1.1.[67] The frequency distributions for the tests were left-skewed, and in other respects fell short of a perfectly normal distribution. And yet both cohorts produced male-to-female ratios at both tails that represent differences easily big enough to have real-world consequences. As for the greater male variance hypothesis, the authors concluded as follows:

In this article, we reviewed the history of the hypothesis that general intelligence is more biologically variable in males than in females and presented data from two samples consisting of almost entire populations that test this hypothesis. These data, which in many ways are the most complete that have ever been compiled, substantially support the hypothesis.[68]

Generally greater male variance is no longer a hypothesis but a proven phenomenon. *Generally* greater male variance does not mean *universal*. How close to universal depends on the characteristic in question. In brain volumes and surface areas, it applied to 134 of the 136 measures. In the physiological traits I reviewed, it appeared in 83 percent of the measures in the Army's Anthropometric Survey. For cognitive tests, all of the results for the NAEP and the SAT, covering decades in both cases, showed greater male variability in both reading and math. Internationally, the 2003 PISA administration included 41 countries, meaning there were 82 measures of variability for the reading and math tests. Seventy-eight of them showed greater male variability (95 percent). In the 2015 PISA administration with 67 countries and three tests (reading, math, and science), 96 percent showed greater male variability. The weakest evidence for greater male variability I have found is the cross-national data on personality. Of the 255 measures (51 countries, five personality factors), greater male variability was found in just 63 percent of them.

Notes

Many of the books I used for *Human Diversity* were e-book editions, few of which let the reader know the page numbers of the print version. Most of the technical articles, magazine articles, reports, and databases I cite were found on the Internet. In both cases, standards for citations are still evolving. I have followed the *Chicago* style with a few simplifying adaptations. For e-books, I give the chapter from which my material was drawn, and the figure or table number when appropriate. For sources taken from the Internet, I give the website's name and the URL for the home page. I do not give the specific web page because websites change their indexes so frequently, nor do I include the date when I accessed the website.

The full citations of articles in newspapers, magazines, and websites are given in the notes. The references section is reserved for books, journal articles, and other scholarly works.

Introduction

1. Trivers (2011): chapter 13. For a full-scale exposition of the proposition that social science must rest on biology, see Rosenberg (2017). Throughout the book, I use an inclusive definition of *social sciences*, treating psychology as a social science along with anthropology, sociology, economics, and political science.
2. Trivers (2011): chapter 13.
3. For the roots of the orthodoxy, see Tooby and Cosmides (1992) and Pinker (2002): Part I. I give a fuller account of this story in chapter 15.
4. Berger and Luckmann (1966): 2.
5. For a sympathetic account of the subsequent development of social constructionism, see Lock and Strong (2010).
6. This case was memorably made first in Bloom (1987) and brought up to date in Lukianoff and Haidt (2018).
7. Two classics that introduced the field now called evolutionary psychology are E. O. Wilson's *Sociobiology* (1975) and Richard Dawkins's *The Selfish Gene* (1976). For those who are prepared for deep dives, there's David Geary's *The Origin of Mind: Evolution of Brain, Cognition, and General Intelligence* (2004) and the sixth edition of David Buss's classic *Evolutionary Psychology: The New Science of the Mind* (2019). A shorter and breezier account (but still

scientifically serious) is Steve Stewart-Williams's *The Ape That Understood the Universe: How the Mind and Culture Evolve* (2018).

8. Gardner (1983) and Gardner (2008). Gardner has nine intelligences in the most recent version: visual-spatial, verbal-linguistic, logical-mathematical, interpersonal, intrapersonal, musical, bodily-kinesthetic, naturalistic, and existential. The labels for the last two are not intuitively understandable. *Naturalistic* refers to relating to one's natural surroundings and making accurate judgments, as in hunting, farming, and Charles Darwin's genius. *Existential* encompasses what others have called spiritual intelligence. Bodily-kinesthetic intelligence is outside the purview of this book. It has a significant cognitive component, involving a sense of timing, understanding the goal of the physical action, and the mental qualities that go into training the physical abilities. But the core of bodily-kinesthetic ability involves capabilities below the neck. Otherwise, I discuss all of the intelligences (or talents; call them what you will) represented by Gardner's theory insofar as they have entered the technical literature.

Part I: "Gender Is a Social Construct"

1. For the universality of male social and political dominance, see Goldberg (1993b). The original version, titled *The Inevitability of Patriarchy: Why the Biological Difference Between Men and Women Always Produces Male Domination*, inspired a variety of attacks claiming to identify tribes or societies in which men did not rule. Goldberg addressed all of them in the 1993 revision, making an empirical case for the universality of male domination that has not subsequently been challenged with data.

2. Locke's case was limited to arguments that a woman is not the property of the husband, she retains power over her children in the absence of the father, and a woman has as much right as a man to dissolve the marriage compact. Locke (1960).

3. Astell (1700): Preface to the third edition.

4. Kate Austin, "Woman," unpublished MS, 1901. en.wikisource.org.

5. Swanwick (1913): 28.

6. Mill (1869).

7. Shaw (1891): 42. The advent of evolutionary theory in the mid-nineteenth century provided ammunition for those who saw biologically grounded differences. In 1875, Antoinette Blackwell published *The Sexes Throughout Nature*, based on Darwin, concluding that men and women were importantly different emotionally and intellectually, but equal. Blackwell (1875). *The Evolution of Sex*, by Patrick Geddes and Arthur Thomson (1889), concluded that men and women were primordially different: "We have seen that a deep difference in constitution expresses itself in the distinctions between male and female, whether these be physical or mental. The differences may be exaggerated or lessened, but to obliterate them it would be necessary to have all the evolution over again on a new basis. What was decided among the prehistoric Protozoa cannot be annulled by Act of Parliament." Geddes and Thomson (1889): 247.

8. "*On ne naît pas femme: on le devient.*" de Beauvoir (2009): 283. The sentence comes at the opening of the first chapter of volume 2. The 2009 translation by Constance Borde and Sheila Malovany-Chevallier reads, "One is not born, but rather becomes, woman," which I prefer. I have given the customary translation in the text because it is so widely accepted.

9. Martin, Ruble, and Szkrybalo (2002) has a nice account of the different strands of social role theory.

10. Endendijk, Groeneveld, Bakermans-Kranenburg et al. (2016): 1 of 33.

11. The meta-analyses that combine the studies of socialization have found only modest evidence for differential treatment from the second half of the twentieth century onward. The first assessment of the literature was Maccoby and Jacklin (1974). They documented the reality of what are called sex-typed activities (e.g., little girls are given dolls, little boys are encouraged

to play sports), but found that otherwise "the reinforcement contingencies for the two sexes appear to be remarkably similar." (p. 342). A spirited debate ensued, led by Jeanne Block, who argued in a series of articles that Maccoby and Jacklin had underestimated the role of differential socialization (e.g., Block (1978), Block (1983)).

Lytton and Romney (1991), a subsequent meta-analysis of 172 studies of gender socialization, examined socialization regarding eight topics: amount of interaction, achievement encouragement, warmth, nurturance, responsiveness (including praise), encouragement of dependency, restrictiveness/low encouragement of independence, disciplinary strictness, encouragement of sex-typed activities, sex-typed perception, and clarity of communication/ use of reasoning. The meta-analysis found few differences on any of them. "The effect sizes for most socialization areas are nonsignificant and generally very small, fluctuating in direction across studies," the authors wrote in their conclusion. In the North American studies, the one exception was moderately more encouragement of sex-typed activities in boys. In the studies from other Western countries, parents use moderately more physical punishment for boys than for girls. Lytton and Romney (1991): 286 and Tables 4 and 5. The term *effect size* is explained in chapter 1. The effect size for sex-typed activities was −0.43 (boys got more encouragement) and the effect size for physical punishment was −0.37 (boys got more physical punishment).

Seven years later, another meta-analysis, Leaper, Anderson, and Sanders (1998), focused specifically on studies that observed the language that parents use with their children. There were sex differences in the types of speech that parents employed (e.g., supportive speech, directive speech, informative speech). Not surprisingly, mothers tend to talk more to their children than fathers do. But fathers used the same patterns of language with daughters and sons alike. So did mothers, with just two exceptions: Mothers talked somewhat more to daughters than to sons and used somewhat more supportive speech with daughters than with sons. The effect sizes were +0.29 and +0.22 respectively. This was not the stuff of pervasive socialization through language.

Since 1998, one of the major areas in which researchers continue to look for socialization effects has been differences in the ways parents exert parental control over daughters and sons. In the theoretical literature there is a good strategy (*autonomy-supportive*) and a bad one (*controlling*). Autonomy-supportive strategies combine an appropriate amount of control with an appropriate amount of choice, take the child's perspective into account, and explain the reasons when the parent's decision overrules the child's preference. Endendijk, Groeneveld, Bakermans-Kranenburg et al. (2016): 2 of 33. An extensive literature provides evidence that autonomy-supportive strategies are associated with lower levels of oppositional, aggressive, and hyperactive child behaviors. E.g., Kawabata, Alink, Tseng et al. (2011); Karreman, van Tuijl, van Aken et al. (2006); Stormshak, Bierman, McMahon et al. (2000).

The bad strategy is *controlling*. As the label implies, it is a "You will do it because I tell you to do it" approach to child-rearing. The two chief ways in which parents can be controlling are harsh physical control and psychological pressure or manipulation (examples are shaming, inducing feelings of guilt, or withdrawing affection). An extensive literature documents a variety of negative consequences of controlling strategies, especially during adolescence. E.g., Karreman, van Tuijl, van Aken et al. (2006); Rothbaum and Weisz (1994); Kawabata, Alink, Tseng et al. (2011).

In 2016, the Dutch scholars cited earlier published a meta-analysis of the literature on gender-differentiating parenting regarding control strategies. Their conclusion was generically similar to those of the other meta-analyses: The evidence showed little difference in the way parents treat daughters and sons. Parents were slightly more controlling with sons, but the effect was negligible (d = −0.08). The difference was even smaller regarding autonomy-supportive behavior (d = −0.03). The analysis showed an effect over time, with boys receiving more autonomy-supportive parenting in studies from the 1970s and 1980s, while girls received more autonomy-supportive parenting in studies published from 1990 on. But the fitted effect sizes remained small throughout, with an absolute *d* of no more than about 0.10. Endendijk, Groeneveld, Bakermans-Kranenburg et al. (2016): Fig. 2.

The authors' conclusion resembles those of others who have studied gender differentiation in parenting:

> These findings question the importance of gender-differentiated parental control as a means of gender socialization and as a mechanism underlying gender differences in child behavior. However, the large differences between studies and the individual differences within studies suggest that some parents do treat their sons and daughters differently with regard to parental control. Parents' gender stereotypes might explain why some parents do treat their sons and daughters differently and others do not, but this mechanism has yet to be confirmed empirically. (Endendijk, Groeneveld, Bakermans-Kranenburg et al. (2016): 23 of 33).

12. Eagly (1987). This abbreviated description is drawn from Eagly and Wood (2011). For a detailed description of social role theory, see Wood and Eagly (2012).
13. Eagly and Wood (2011): 468.
14. Eagly and Wood (2011): 459.
15. Bleier (1991) quoted in Halpern (2012): 178.
16. Summers's remarks were subsequently transcribed and released by the Office of the President at Harvard. Summers (2005).
17. Stuart Taylor Jr., "Why Feminist Careerists Neutered Larry Summers," *Atlantic*, February 2005.
18. Sam Dillon and Sara Rimer, "No Break in the Storm over Harvard President's Words," *New York Times*, January 19, 2005.
19. Taylor, "Why Feminist Careerists Neutered Larry Summers."
20. Sam Dillon and Sara Rimer, "President of Harvard Tells Women's Panel He's Sorry," *New York Times*, January 21, 2005; Dillon and Rimer, "No Break in the Storm over Harvard President's Words."
21. For those who want to look into sex differences more thoroughly, here's a brief reading list.

    The book that for me best integrates the findings from the technical literature with compelling narratives about real cases is Susan Pinker's *The Sexual Paradox: Men, Women, and the Real Gender Gap*. Much has been learned since she published it in 2008, but none of her technical positions have been discredited and many have been reinforced by subsequent work.

    Simon Baron-Cohen's *The Essential Difference: Male and Female Brains and the Truth About Autism* (2003) is that rarity, a book that is both scientifically seminal and readable.

    A new edition of David Geary's magisterial *Male, Female: The Evolution of Human Sex Differences* is in press as I write. I expect it to be, like the earlier editions in 1998 and 2010, the definitive statement of the existing state of knowledge.

    Diane Halpern's *Sex Differences in Cognitive Ability* (2012) is focused on a narrower topic and is somewhat denser than the others, but she tells you all you need to know about her topic in one source.

    If you want to work your way into a broader discussion of sex differences in smaller chunks, I recommend a series of columns that David Schmitt wrote for *Psychology Today* from 2013 to 2016, easily accessible online at www.psychologytoday.com. Engagingly written, they are also fully documented and accompanied by bibliographies.
22. As of early 2017, the Women's Studies Online Resources webpage listed 673 American institutions of higher education that have women's studies programs, departments, or research centers. I didn't try to review the course offerings for all of them, but I did examine the course catalogs during the 2016–17 school year for the women's studies programs at 13 of the most prestigious universities in the country—the eight Ivy League schools plus MIT, Stanford, Duke, the University of Chicago, and the University of California at Berkeley. I was searching

for courses in women's studies programs that provided systematic discussions of biological evidence for sex differences in cognitive repertoires. I found a single example: Cornell University's course FGSS 3210, "Gender and the Brain," cross-listed as biology course BIONB 3215, which tells prospective enrollees, "Reading the original scientific papers and related critical texts, we will ask whether we can find measurable physical differences in male and female brains, and what these differences might be." I can't guarantee that the online course listings were complete. And while I found no courses dealing with hormones or other genetically-grounded sources of male-female differences, I presume that these topics, along with differences in the brain, are sometimes raised in courses not specifically devoted to them. But compare what I found with what should be the norm. At a reputable university—and these 13 are at the top of the heap—to get a degree in women's studies should include as an obvious requirement a solid foundation in evolutionary biology and in the differential biology of the two sexes, including biology above the neck. None of these 13 prestigious schools did.

23. Trivers (2011): 314–15.

1: A Framework for Thinking About Sex Differences

1. In the 1971 edition of the *Oxford English Dictionary*, the only definition of *gender* as a noun applied to the sexes was as a jocular transfer of the linguistic use of *gender* (masculine and feminine genders) to apply to humans. By the 1989 edition, it had added a new meaning: "In modern (especially feminist) use, a euphemism for the sex of a human being, often intended to emphasize the social and cultural, as opposed to the biological, distinctions between the sexes." The *OED* dated the earliest known example of that meaning to 1963, but the rationale for using *gender* instead of *sex* was first introduced a decade earlier in Money (1952).

2. Thorndike (1911): 32.

3. Quoted in Baron-Cohen (2002): 251.

4. Baron-Cohen (2003): 61.

5. Baron-Cohen (2003): 26.

6. Baron-Cohen and his colleagues devised tests for measuring systemizing and empathizing, with scores labeled SQ and EQ respectively. In the largest sample of people (5,186 total) who were administered both tests, the effect sizes (a term explained later in this chapter) were +0.63 (females had a higher mean) for EQ and −0.47 (males had a higher mean) for SQ. Wright and Skagerberg (2012). Effect sizes in the samples used by Baron-Cohen and his colleagues have been +0.50 and +0.76 for EQ and −0.59 for SQ. Baron-Cohen, Richler, Bisarya et al. (2003): Table 1; Baron-Cohen and Wheelwright (2004): Table II.

7. Sawilowsky (2009).

8. Cohen used the descriptors to guide researchers in characterizing an expected *d* value when there was no prior research available. He repeatedly told his readers not to make too much of them. For example: "The terms 'small,' 'medium,' and 'large' are relative, not only to each other, but to the area of behavioral science or even more particularly to the specific content and research method being employed in any given investigation." Cohen (1988): 25. And "A reader who finds that what is here defined as 'large' is too small (or too large) to meet what his area of behavioral science would consider appropriate standards is urged to make more suitable operational definitions." Cohen (1988): 79.

9. Funder and Ozer (2019).

10. Funder and Ozer (2019).

11. See Rosnow and Rosenthal (2003) for a critique of Cohen's guidelines antedating Hyde (2005). See Gignac and Szodorai (2016) for suggested guidelines corresponding to those proposed by Funder and Ozer (2019).

12. Hyde (2005): 581. I have reproduced the inequality symbols as they appear in the article, which apparently treats "<" as equivalent to "≤."

13. Hyde (2005): 585–86.
14. Hyde (2005): 587.
15. Hyde (2005): 587.
16. Hyde (2005): 590.
17. In his technical discussion of this issue, Del Giudice put it this way: "When measuring a multidimensional construct, the overall difference between two groups is not the average of the effects measured on each dimension, but a combination of those effects in the multidimensional space: Many small differences, each of them on a different dimension, can create an impressive effect when all the dimensions are considered simultaneously. Crucially, such overall differences are likely to matter more than their individual components, both in shaping people's perceptions and in affecting social interaction." Del Giudice (2009): 268.
18. See Del Giudice (2009). He augmented the discussion in Del Giudice, Booth, and Irwing (2012). Janet Hyde responded in the comments to Del Giudice (2009) with "The Distance Between North Dakota and South Dakota." Stewart-Williams and Thomas (2013) critiques the use of Mahalanobis D in its appendix.

2: Sex Differences in Personality

1. Adapted from McCarthy, Nugent, and Lenz (2017): Table 2. I have omitted neurological and neurodegenerative diseases that were included in the table: migraine, stroke, multiple sclerosis, Alzheimer's disease, Parkinson's disease, amyotrophic lateral sclerosis, and myasthenia gravis.
2. As with almost all sex differences, a minority literature disputes the magnitude of differences. In the case of depression, for example, see Martin, Neighbors, and Griffith (2013).
3. In statistics, *factor* has a technical meaning. In its most basic form, the statistical procedure (factor analysis) creates a first component—a factor—that explains as much of the variation among the observations as possible. The algorithms then create a second factor that explains as much of the remaining variation as it can, and so on through successive iterations, each of which produces a new factor, until all of the variation has been assigned to a factor.
4. Lewis Goldberg, who had been instrumental in resuscitating interest in personality studies after a lull in the 1960s and 1970s, coined the phrase "Big Five." See his review of the development of the Big Five model in Goldberg (1993a).
5. Costa and McCrae (1985). The 1985 version had measures of neuroticism, extraversion, and openness. Agreeableness and conscientiousness were added later. The official name of the current version is NEO-PI-3.
6. For a full discussion of this issue, see Pettersson, Mendle, Turkheimer et al. (2014).
7. Other personality models include HEXACO, which adds an honesty-humility factor to the Big Five, and a model focused on three problematic aspects of the personality: narcissism, Machiavellianism, and sadism. It's called variously the Dark Triad or the Dark Tetrad model. For a review of the literature, see Furnham, Richards, and Paulhus (2013).
8. Among the 30 FFM facets (the detailed characteristics that make up the five factors), here are the ones that showed absolute effect sizes of less than 0.20 in both the Costa and Kajonius studies: experiences anger or bitterness, assertive or forceful in expression, open to the inner world of imagination, open to new experiences in life, open to reexamining one's own values, trust in others' sincerity or intentions, values orderliness, believes in fulfilling moral obligations, uses self-discipline in fulfilling tasks, and thinks things through before acting. In the Del Giudice study using the 16PF, these were the factors showing an absolute difference of less than 0.20: Self-reliant, solitary, resourceful, lively, animated, spontaneous, abstracted, imaginative, absentminded, organized, perfectionistic, compulsive private, discreet, nondisclosing, socially bold, venturesome, and thick-skinned.
9. Effect sizes are reported for latent variables corrected for specific variance and measurement error. See the discussion in Del Giudice, Booth, and Irwing (2012).

10. Del Giudice, Booth, and Irwing (2012).
11. Del Giudice, Booth, and Irwing (2012).
12. Noftle and Shaver (2006). Averages of *d* are computed using the absolute value. In this case, the values were corrected for attenuation due to scale unreliability.
13. Del Giudice (2009): Table 1.
14. Connellan, Baron-Cohen, Wheelwright et al. (2000): Table 1.
15. Sagi and Hoffman (1976); Simner (1971); Hoffman (1973). This and subsequent citations in the list are drawn from Alexander and Wilcox (2012).
16. Hittelman and Dickes (1979); Leeb and Rejskind (2004); Lutchmaya, Baron-Cohen, and Raggatt (2001).
17. Cossette, Pomerleau, Malcuit et al. (1996).
18. Gunnar and Donahue (1980).
19. Mayes and Carter (1990).
20. Alexander, Wilcox, and Woods (2009); Benenson, Duggan, and Markovits (2004); Campbell, Shirley, and Heywood (2000). The doll-truck contrast shows up in nonhuman primates as well: Male vervet and rhesus monkeys prefer trucks while female ones prefer dolls. Alexander and Hines (2002); Hassett, Siebert, and Wallen (2008).
21. Mundy, Block, Delgado et al. (2007); Olafsen, Ronning, Kaaresen et al. (2006).
22. McClure (2000). Another 14 studies simply reported that the results were "nonsignificant" without including the information necessary to calculate effect sizes. Half of those studies had samples of 48 or fewer. Large effect sizes can be statistically insignificant with sample sizes that small. McClure calculated a lower bound effect size of +0.26 if all of the nonsignificant results had an effect size of zero—unrealistically low. The true value is somewhere between +0.26 and +0.92, probably well toward the +0.92 end of the range. Even the lower bound of 0.26 was statistically significant.
23. Costa, Terracciano, and McCrae (2001).
24. Costa, Terracciano, and McCrae (2001): Table 3. The only exception was agreeableness in Zimbabwe, which was a trivial –0.02.
25. McCrae and Terracciano (2005): Table 5. The inconsistent effect sizes, all of them only fractionally different from zero, were for Nigeria (N = 0, A = 0, E = –0.04, O = 0, C = 0), India (E = –0.05, O = +0.03), Botswana (E = –0.01), Ethiopia (A = –0.02), Russia (A = –0.02), and Uganda (O = 0).
26. The prediction is necessary, but it has also been explicitly acknowledged. See Eagly, Wood, and Johannessen-Schmidt (2004), quoted in Schmitt, Long, McPhearson et al. (2016).
27. Costa, Terracciano, and McCrae (2001): 327. For the sake of consistency in the interpretation of results, the countries in this and the subsequent discussion are limited to those for which the UN has calculated a score on the Gender Inequality Index. The median effect sizes for emotional stability, agreeableness, openness to emotion, and extraversion for adults across 21 countries were –0.51, +0.45, +0.26, and +0.23 respectively. The Costa study omitted the fifth factor, conscientiousness, because none of its facets showed consistent sex differences. The Costa study also addressed a problem with the facets for measuring extraversion and openness. The facets for measuring extraversion included warmth/affiliation, which is higher in females, and dominance/venturesomeness, which is higher in males. Behaviorally, these traits are completely different, but they more or less cancel each other out in the combined measure of extraversion. A similar problem occurs with openness to experience (women are higher on measures of openness to emotion and males are higher on openness to ideas). The Costa study dealt with this problem by creating measures of extraversion and openness that specifically focused on the warmth/affiliation aspect of extraversion and the emotional aspect of openness. The discussion in Del Giudice, Booth, and Irwing (2012) of these masking tendencies when traits are aggregated into the Big Five includes citations of the relevant sources.

28. Indicators are given in Jahan et al. (2016): Statistical Annex, Tables 4 and 5. The UN also has a Gender Development Index based on women's life expectancy, years of schooling, and women's per capita gross national income. The correlation between the Inequality and Development indexes is –.66 ("high" means "bad" on the Inequality Index, "good" on the Development Index). Both indexes capture measures of health (maternal mortality rate versus life expectancy) and education (percent with at least some secondary education versus years of education). In deciding whether to combine the two indexes, the issue is how much is added by the measure unique to the Development Index, per capita gross national product. I judged that to be minor, outweighed by the potentially distorting effects of double-counting education and health. Data were downloaded from the Human Development Reports website, www.hdr.undp.org.

29. Absolute size, because it doesn't make any difference whether females or males score higher on a personality trait—theoretically, sex differences on all personality traits should be diminishing.

30. Author's analysis using GII scores and Costa, Terracciano, and McCrae (2001): Table 3.

31. For a more concrete sense of how these correlations translate into scores for nations at the extremes, compare the nations in the McCrae sample with the five lowest GII scores (Switzerland, Denmark, Iceland, Germany, Denmark) with the nations with the five highest GII scores (Burkina Faso, India, Uganda, Ethiopia, and Morocco). On all five factors, the mean effect sizes for the most gender-egalitarian countries ranged from two times to more than three times the effect size for the least gender-egalitarian countries: +0.46 compared to +0.22 for agreeableness, +0.18 compared to +0.09 for conscientiousness, +0.27 compared to +0.13 for extraversion, +0.36 compared to +0.12 for openness to emotion, and –0.58 compared to –0.26 for emotional stability. Author's analysis using GII scores and McCrae and Terracciano (2005): Table 5.

32. Schmitt, Realo, Voracek et al. (2008).

33. A description of the index and the annual scores may be found at the World Economic Forum's website, www.weforum.org.

34. The countries with the five largest values of D, indicating the largest sex differences in personality, were the Netherlands (1.17), Norway (1.13), Sweden (1.11), Canada (1.07), and the UK (1.06). The countries with the five smallest values of D, indicating the smallest sex differences in personality, were China (0.47), Malaysia (0.58), Japan (0.59), South Korea (0.59), and India (0.70). Author's analysis of Mac Giolla and Kajonius (2018): Appendix B.

35. Falk and Hermle (2018): 3 of 6. The author's Gender Equality Index is an inversion of the UN's Gender Inequality Index.

36. Falk and Hermle (2018): 3 of 6.

37. A cross-national study conducted two years after the Schmitt study, Lippa (2010), provides additional evidence for these patterns but poses problems in interpretation. Psychologist Richard Lippa used a BBC Internet survey conducted in 2005 that attracted 255,114 people who responded to at least some items in each of six modules. From these data, Lippa compared 53 nations on measures he constructed for extraversion, agreeableness, and emotional stability using indicators from the Cattell inventory. The effect sizes for the three were +0.18, +0.61, and –0.41 respectively. The effect sizes in Lippa's data showed significant widening of the difference in agreeableness (r = –.41 for agreeableness and the Gender Inequality Index), minor widening for emotional stability (r = –.14), and no significant effect for extraversion (r = +.04). Lippa (2010): Table 1. The difficulty with interpreting the Lippa findings arises from the nature of the sample. The Internet survey was conducted exclusively in English. This means that the sample is self-selected for people who speak English and use the BBC and the Internet. Among those for whom English is a second language, there are problems of misunderstanding the questions. Despite the reasons for expecting that Lippa's sample could produce quite different results from the other cross-national studies (and there were indeed some differences), the same pattern of results was found: "In summary, the current results strongly supported Costa et al.'s (2001) and Schmitt et al.'s (2008) findings that sex differences in personality are

highly replicable across cultures. However, they were sometimes inconsistent with Costa et al.'s conclusion that sex differences in personality are necessarily 'modest in magnitude' (p. 328). The mean effect sizes for sex differences in agreeableness and emotional stability, although moderate in magnitude, were still well within the range of effect sizes for many classic person and situation effects in psychology (Eagly, 1995; Lipsey & Wilson, 1993). More dramatically, when analyzed at the aggregated level of men's and women's national means, sex accounted for 93% of the variance in MF-Occ means, 75% of the variance in agreeableness means, 68% of the variance in emotional stability means, and 23% of the variance in extraversion, and in each case, sex accounted for much greater amounts of variance than did either UN gender equality or the interaction of sex and gender equality." Lippa (2010): 634.

38. Costa, Terracciano, and McCrae (2001): 329.
39. Costa, Terracciano, and McCrae (2001). A more elaborate version of this argument is given in Guimond, Branscombe, Brunot et al. (2007).
40. Lippa, Collaer, and Peters (2010).
41. Schmitt, Long, McPhearson et al. (2016): 6.

3: Sex Differences in Neurocognitive Functioning

1. The subsequent list of findings is taken from Halpern (2012): 104–8.
2. Halpern (2012): 104–8.
3. Binaural beats are an auditory phenomenon that occurs when two slightly different frequencies of sound are played into each ear. Otoacoustic emissions are caused by the motion of the cochlea's sensory hair cells.
4. Halpern (2012): 106. In childhood, part of the sex difference may be explained by girls' superior verbal skills, but other studies have found the female advantage in identifying smells in adult samples as well.
5. Halpern (2012): 109.
6. Females are not noticeably better at judging the passage of time, but there is a systematic sex difference in direction of error. Men tend to overestimate a time interval while women tend to underestimate it. Halpern (2012): 107–8.
7. Fillingim, King, Ribeiro-Dasilva et al. (2009); Rosen, Ham, and Mogil (2017).
8. Fuller (2002).
9. Fleischman (2014); Al-Shawaf, Lewis, and Buss (2017).
10. Halpern (2012): 108–10.
11. Nagy, Kompagne, Orvos et al. (2007); Piek (2002).
12. Halpern (2012): 109.
13. Halpern (2012): 110.
14. Watson and Kimura (1991).
15. Halpern (2012): 115–18.
16. Heuer and Reisberg (1990); Cahill, Haier, White et al. (2001).
17. Geary (2010).
18. Halpern (2012): 118–28.
19. *Verbal reasoning.* The Cognitive Abilities Test (CogAT) is a test of three types of reasoning: verbal, quantitative, and nonverbal. Since it was first published in 1984, it has undergone three revisions, in 1992, 2000, and 2011. In the four standardization samples, girls performed better than boys in virtually all grades in all standardizations (out of 28 combinations of grade level and standardization, the difference favored girls in 24). Lakin (2013): Table 3. Effect sizes were uniformly small, averaging +0.07 over all grades and standardizations. Only one of the 28 grade/standardization combinations reached an effect size of +0.20. A British sample of 320,000 students ages 11–12 who took the CogAT in 2001–3 showed a larger female advantage ($d = +0.15$).

Reading. America's National Assessment of Educational Progress (NAEP) is administered periodically to large, nationally representative samples, in grades 4, 8, and 12. In the reading test, girls outperformed boys in every grade and every assessment from 1988 to 2015, with an overall effect size of +0.27. Reilly, Neumann, and Andrews (2018), which was also the source of subsequent reading and writing NAEP statistics. Twelfth-grade girls have had an advantage in the reading test that goes back to the first administration of the test in 1971. Effect sizes from 1971 to 1992 were in the +0.21 to +0.30 range. Hedges and Nowell (1995): Table 3. There was no trend across the years in the size of the difference, but grade level had a marked effect, with *d* rising from +0.19 in grade 4 to +0.30 in grade 8 and +0.32 in grade 12. The +0.19 effect size for grade 4 is consistent with an analysis of 2015 performance on the federally required Reading/Language Arts assessments, which found an effect size for reading of +0.19, combining scores from grades 3 through 6. Peterson (2018): Table 1. These effect sizes translate into substantial differences in the number of boys who failed to reach the minimum standard of literacy by grade 12 (1.5 times as many boys as girls) and the number of girls reaching the advanced literacy standard (1.9 times as many girls as boys).

Writing. The female advantage in writing tests is larger than in reading tests. In NAEP writing tests from 1988 to 2011, the overall effect size was +0.54. As in the case of the reading test, there was no significant trend over the years but there was a significant change in effect size from grade 4 to grade 8, when it rose from +0.42 to +0.62. It stood at +0.55 in grade 12. Reilly, Neumann, and Andrews (2018). Once again, the results from the Reading/Language Arts assessment in 2015 correspond with the NAEP results. The same study that found a female advantage of just +0.19 on the reading test for grade 3 to grade 6 found an effect size of +0.45 on the writing test. Peterson (2018): Table 1. These effect sizes translated into even larger disparities at the low and high ends, with 2.2 times as many boys failing to meet the minimum writing standard and 2.5 times as many girls reaching the advanced standard. For additional evidence of a larger effect size for writing than for reading and literature reviews, see Reynolds, Scheiber, Hajovsky et al. (2015) and Scheiber, Reynolds, Hajovsky et al. (2015).

20. Arnett, Pennington, Peterson et al. (2017).
21. In the most recent follow-up, combining 320,000 TIP students from 2011 to 2015, the male-female ratio for the top percentile was 0.88 for the SAT verbal, 0.79 for the ACT English test, and 1.09 for the ACT reading test. For the top 0.5 percent, the corresponding ratios were 0.96, 0.94, and 0.88. For the top 0.01 percent, the corresponding ratios were 0.73, 0.86, and 0.95. Makel, Wai, Peairs et al. (2016): Table 6. For tests administered until 1994, SAT scores could be interpreted relative to the national population because the Educational Testing Service conducted periodic norm samples explicitly designed for that purpose. But then the SAT was "recentered" in 1995 so that the mean was once again set at 500 (it had fallen to 428 on the verbal test and 482 on the math test). The substance of the test was revised in 2005 and again in 2017. Whether these changes were good or bad is debated (for the record, I think mostly bad), but without question those changes have made trends over time impossible to interpret relative to the general population.

   Data from the standardizations of the CogAT, representing tests of children from grades 4 to 7, show virtual equality in the top five percentiles and the top percentile of the verbal/reading domain from 1992. In the original 1984 standardization, the male-female ratios were 1.15 and 1.25 for the top five percentiles and the top percentile respectively. Girls had a fractional advantage for both categories in the 1992 and 2000 standardizations, while boys had a fractional advantage for both categories in the 2011 standardization. Lakin (2013): Table 4.
22. The statement is based on information from the last national norm study conducted by the Educational Testing Service in the mid-1980s. Braun, Centra, and King (1987) combined with College Board (2016). I used the 2016 scores because the College Board introduced

major changes in the test in 2017, making scores from 2017 onward incomparable with previous administrations. The table showing scores from 1972 to 2016 used a correction for the recentering of the test in 1995. Standard deviations were retrieved from the individual annual reports for college-bound seniors. The two sources together indicate that about 67 percent of the SAT pool had scores above the mean that would have been obtained if all juniors took the SAT. Extrapolating that 1983 number to recent decades involves some guesstimates (25 percent of 17-year-olds took the SAT in 1983 compared to 40 percent in recent years), but that the test-taking population is still concentrated in the upper half of the ability distribution seems incontestable.

23. In terms of effect sizes, the SAT and ACT tell the same story—small—but they have inconsistent signs. For the 45 years from 1972 to 2016, females have always had slightly lower SAT verbal scores than males—a surprising contrast to the universal female advantage for verbal tests of nationally representative samples. The effect size moved in a narrow range from −0.02 to −0.12 during those decades, with a mean of −0.06. College Board (2016): 2. The table showing scores from 1972 to 2016 used a correction for the recentering of the test in 1995. Standard deviations were retrieved from the individual annual reports for college-bound seniors.

On the SAT writing test introduced in 2006 and discontinued as of 2017, females had a small advantage that was never less than +0.10 and never larger than +0.12. There was no trend over time on either test. But for the ACT from 1995 to 2016, females have maintained an advantage in both the reading and the English tests. Effect sizes for the reading test moved in a range from +0.02 to +0.09, with a mean of +0.06. Effect sizes for the English test moved in a range from +0.11 to +0.17, with a mean of +0.14. Tables from the *Digest of Educational Statistics* for 2009 (Table 147) and 2016 (Table 226.50), downloadable from the National Center for Education Statistics website, nces.ed.gov/programs/digest.

One of the imponderables about SAT scores is the growing imbalance in the numbers of males and females taking the test. In 1981, about 22 percent of male 17-year-olds took the SAT compared to 25 percent of female 17-year-olds. (More precisely, that percentage represents the number of test-takers divided by the number of 17-year-olds. Some test-takers are older or younger than 17, but the percentage would change only fractionally if broken down by age at testing.) The gap first hit four percentage points in 1987, five percentage points in 1992, six percentage points in 1996, and seven percentage points in 2000. The difference is large enough that it must be assumed to deflate the female mean because the female test-taking pool dips deeper into the cognitive distribution than does the male pool. The effect is unlikely to be much, but it should be kept in mind. My wordings of the conclusions I draw are intended to tolerate such a bias.

This inconsistency in the results from the SAT and ACT mirrors the earlier data reported in a major review of the nationally representative populations from 1960 to 1995. Larry Hedges and Amy Nowell reported the male-female ratio among top scorers in reading comprehension for two major surveys of high school seniors: the National Longitudinal Study of the High School Class of 1972 and the 1980 High School and Beyond dataset. For scores in the 90th percentile and higher, the ratios were 0.94 and 1.03—meaning females retained a small advantage in one of the two. For those in the 95th percentile and higher, the ratios were 0.81 and 1.06 respectively, thereby showing the same inconsistency. It appears that for 17–18-year-olds from the upper half of the distribution to the 95th percentile, results can go both ways, depending on the test, sometimes favoring females and sometimes favoring males, always by small margins. The minimal conclusion is that the extremely consistent female advantage in the normal range of verbal ability becomes less dependable as the ability level rises.

24. Halpern (2012): 146–50.

25. Reilly, Neumann, and Andrews (2015): Table 1. The effect sizes for the 2015 NAEP in grades 4, 8, and 12 were −0.07, 0.00, and −0.08 respectively. Author's analysis of data downloaded

using the NAEP Explorer tool of a National Center for Education Statistics website, www .nationsreportcard.gov.

26. Author's analysis of data downloaded using the NAEP Explorer tool.

27. Halpern (2012): 146.

28. For literature reviews, see Penner (2003) and Wai, Cacchio, Putallaz et al. (2010).

29. The Study of Mathematically Precocious Youth, which figures prominently in the next chapter, found ratios of about 13 favoring males in this range. Benbow and Stanley (1980), as did Wai, Cacchio, Putallaz et al. (2010) for TIP students in 1981–85.

30. The earliest reliable estimates of differentials at the extremes of mathematical ability come from Project Talent, a study based on a nationally representative sample of American 15-year-olds conducted in 1960. The male-female sex ratio was 1.3 for scores in the top 10 percent, 1.5 in the top 5 percent, 2.1 in the top 3 percent, and 7.0 in the top 1 percent. Hedges and Nowell (1995): 44. The best longitudinal data since then come from Duke's TIP program. Makel, Wai, Peairs et al. (2016): Table 5.

31. 2016 College-Bound Seniors: Total Group Profile Report, College Board: 2, downloadable from a College Board website, reports.collegeboard.org. Halpern does not report ACT results by gender for the math test, and the ACT does not publish those data.

32. For a history of the SAT, see Lemann (1999). For a presentation of the psychometric properties of the test that tacitly confirm its measurement of the general mental factor known as *g*, see Donlon (1984).

33. For the technical debate about test bias, see Mattern and Patterson (2013) and Aguinis, Culpepper, and Pierce (2016). Insofar as there is bias (it is minor), it favors blacks—SAT scores slightly overpredict college grades for blacks. Aguinis, Culpepper, and Pierce (2016) provide evidence that there is differential predictive validity at the level of individual institutions, but even that differential prediction does not systematically favor whites or males. For a nontechnical discussion of the SAT, including issues about what it measures and how much good coaching does, see my article "Abolish the SAT," available at the AEI website, www.aei.org.

34. AMC tests are given in over 3,000 high schools. I focus on AMC12, the test that is taken by 11th and 12th graders. From 2009 to 2018 (the years for which detailed data are available), the AMC12 has been taken by 59,000 to 115,000 students per year. This is a small number compared to the million-plus students who took the SAT during the same period, but the schools that give the test are concentrated among the top high schools in major urban areas, which in turn, for demographic reasons, probably contain most of the extremely talented math students in the country. Furthermore, talented math students who are applying to elite colleges have a strong incentive to take the AMC12—it's a much more difficult test than either the SAT or ACT math tests, and a high score on the AMC can set their applications apart from the many applicants to elite colleges who have an 800 on the SAT.

    The test has a score range of 0 to 150. In their analysis of the AMC competitions, Ellison and Swanson (2010) concluded that a score of 100 on the AMC12 is equivalent to a score of 780–800 on the SAT math. I conducted the analysis of the 2009–18 administrations of AMC12, using data downloaded from the AMC website. Depending on the year, a score of 100 put a student at anywhere from the 94th to the 98th percentile among those who took the AMC. Thus the AMC12 gives us a glimpse into sex differences deep into the top percentile of the total population.

35. The percentiles are based on the distribution for the entire population of test-takers in a given year. The ratio divides the percentage of male test-takers who scored within that percentile that year by the percentage of female test-takers who scored within that percentile that year.

36. Halpern (2012): 128–45.

37. Halpern (2012): 138.

38. Halpern (2012): 130.

39. Halpern (2012): 130.
40. For a literature review, see Vasta and Liben (1996). For international results, see de Lisi, Parameswaran, and McGillicuddy-de Lisi (1989).
41. Law, Pellegrino, and Hunt (1993).
42. Contreras, Rubio, Peña et al. (2007).
43. Huguet and Régner (2007) found that girls performed worse than boys at such a memory task when it was described as testing memory for geometry but better than boys when it was described as testing memory for drawing. The more recent literature on stereotype threat and math and visuospatial skills more commonly has found little or no effect and also found evidence of publication bias; e.g., Pennington, Litchfield, McLatchie et al. (2018); Stoet and Geary (2012); Ganley, Mingle, Ryan et al. (2013). For more on stereotype threat, see chapter 13.
44. Men also have an advantage in visuospatial knowledge and memory. For example, they learn a route from a two-dimensional map in fewer trials and with fewer errors than females. This does not seem to be a function of greater male driving experience. Rather, men and women tend to use different strategies in finding their way from point A to point B, with women likely to use landmarks ("turn right at the bank"), while men are more likely to use points of the compass ("turn north") and distances ("turn after three miles"), and to create mental maps. Boone, Gong, and Hegarty (2018). In this regard, Halpern describes at length the curious story of the National Geography Bee—a competition similar to the National Spelling Bee, except that it asks questions about geographical features. An article by Lynn Liben in 1995 pointed to what she described as "a shocking gender disparity among winners at every level." In 1993, about 14,000 of 18,000 school winners had been boys, as were 55 of the 57 winners in states and territories. That disparity has persisted undiminished in the quarter century since Liben's article. Through 2018, 27 of the 29 winners were male. What makes this especially intriguing is the contrast with the National Spelling Bee. Both competitions require extraordinary memorization. Neither geography nor spelling plays to stereotypical male or female interests. And yet while 27 of 29 National Geography Bee winners have been male, the 95 winners of the Spelling Bee have been split almost equally between girls and boys, with girls holding a 49-to-47 advantage as of 2018. Furthermore, girls have more than held their own since the earliest years—girls won 7 of the first 10 contests.
45. The classic test for ToM is called a "false-belief task." For example, a child is given pictures of another child (Bill), a playground, and a classroom. The child is told that Bill is going to look for his lunch bag. Bill's lunch bag is really on the playground, but Bill thinks his lunch bag is in the classroom. "Where do you think Bill will look for his lunch bag?" Until they're about three, children expect Bill to look for it where the child knows it is—on the playground. Around age four, children are able to predict Bill's behavior on the basis of Bill's false belief, not their own true belief. See Premack and Woodruff (1978).
46. Maccoby and Jacklin (1974): 214.
47. Hall (1978): Table 4.
48. E.g., Rosip and Hall (2004); Schmid, Schmid Mast, Bombari et al. (2011).
49. Thompson and Voyer (2014): 1175. The authors followed a common practice of establishing a lower bound by assigning an effect size of zero to any study reporting that the effect size was statistically insignificant but without reporting its magnitude. This amounted to 147 out of 551 effect sizes in the meta-analysis. When they were excluded, the mean effect size was +0.27.
50. Thompson and Voyer (2014): Table 2. I cannot resist noting a detail of the analyses reported in Table 2. Almost all of the 551 effect sizes in the studies used for the meta-analysis had a mix of male and female subjects, and they showed a lower-bound female advantage of +0.17. Thirty-one studies had only female subjects, and the female advantage was +0.18. Just eight of the studies had exclusively male subjects. The female advantage was +0.61. To put it another

way, women may be only modestly better than men at figuring out the emotions that women are feeling, but they are definitely better than men at figuring out the emotions that men are feeling.

Another interesting finding in the Thompson meta-analysis involved variations in effect size depending on the kind of emotion involved. In the most widely used classification, the six basic emotions are happiness, anger, sadness, fear, surprise, and disgust. Ekman (1999). Past research has established that negative emotions are more difficult to identify than positive ones—and that's where women's advantage over men was concentrated. The lower bound effect sizes were +0.24 for negative emotions, compared to +0.19 for positive emotions. Thompson and Voyer (2014): Table 2.

51. Joseph and Newman (2010): Table 6.
52. There is intriguing experimental evidence on this point. In one set of experiments, participants were given a variety of incentives that would encourage them to "try harder" to understand the emotional states of others. It didn't seem to make any difference, just as "trying harder" doesn't make any difference in being able to mentally rotate objects in three dimensions. Hall, Blanch, Horgan et al. (2009).
53. Valla, Ganzel, Yoder et al. (2010).
54. Herlitz and Yonker (2010): 112.
55. Allen, Rueter, Abram et al. (2017).
56. Full-scale IQ tests such as the Wechsler or Stanford-Binet are designed to minimize sex differences. From the earliest versions of such tests, each item in each subtest has been examined to see whether it is easier for one sex than the other. If so, either a counterbalancing item favoring the other sex has been included in that subtest or the item has been removed altogether. For a discussion of the methods for eliminating gender differences in IQ subtests (which extends to a citation of a book written in 1914), see Matarazzo (1972): 352–58. This practice cannot altogether remove gender differences in the final published test, because the sample used for the item analysis and the sample used for establishing the national norms are different, but the process introduces a heavy thumb on the scale that prevents large gender differences from emerging.
57. The standardization sample for the 1988 revision of the Woodcock-Johnson battery of cognitive tests showed a female advantage of 2.4 points in the 1988 revision (author's analysis, data provided courtesy of the Woodcock-Johnson Foundation). The results apply to test-takers ages 18 through 65. In one of the largest surveys ever conducted, the nearly universal Scottish Mental Survey of 1947, females had a mean that was 1.7 points higher than the male mean. Johnson, Carothers, and Deary (2008): 521. In the large British sample of children ages 11–12 who took CogAT in 2001–3, the total score slightly favored girls, with an effect size of +0.05. Strand, Deary, and Smith (2006): Table 3.
58. Data are taken from the WAIS technical manuals published with each standardization.
59. Jensen (1998): 536.
60. Jensen (1998): 538. Colom, Juan-Espinosa, Abad et al. (2000); Colom, García, Juan-Espinosa et al. (2002); and Deary, Thorpe, Wilson et al. (2003) conducted analyses of the issue and came to the same conclusion.
61. Lynn and Irwing (2004) reopened the debate, arguing that there are no sex differences or a slight female advantage in early adolescence, but a nontrivial male advantage opens by late adolescence. Lynn has continued to compile additional data supporting the existence of a nontrivial sex difference in *g*, most recently in Lynn (2017), a target article that attracted 11 detailed commentaries. Taken together, they will give you a good overview of the state of the debate. Other articles for the affirmative since the question was reopened in 1994 are Lynn (1999); Irwing and Lynn (2005); Jackson and Rushton (2006); and Irwing (2012). Others for the negative are Colom, Juan-Espinosa, Abad et al. (2000); Halpern and LaMay (2000); Blinkhorn (2005); van der Sluis, Posthuma, Dolan et al. (2006); and Iliescu, Ilie, Ispas et al.

(2016). For a recent article with new data and an overview of previous research, see Arribas-Aguila, Abad, and Colom (2019).

62. The most widely publicized study that made the case for a relationship between test scores and gender egality, Else-Quest, Hyde, and Linn (2010), analyzed data from the 2003 round of the Trends in International Mathematics and Science Study (TIMSS) and the 2004 PISA round.

63. Author's analysis, 2015 PISA scores downloaded from the OECD website, www.oecd.org /pisa/. That database includes the standard deviation for each country, enabling effect sizes to be based country-specific in both their means and standard deviations. The means given in the text are calculated as the mean of the individual effect sizes for the 67 countries. If instead the effect size is calculated from the mean male and female test scores and the standard deviations of those means, the female advantage is not +0.32, as given in the text, but +0.62. The effect sizes for math and science are −0.09 and +0.01 respectively, not much different from those reported in the text.

64. Guiso, Monte, Sapienza et al. (2008); Marks (2008); Else-Quest, Hyde, and Linn (2010).

65. Stoet and Geary (2013). See also Stoet and Geary (2015).

66. The sign for the GII was reversed to make it correspond to the sign of the other two (so that "high" = "good" on all three). The correlations among the three separate indexes for 2015 are +.64 for the GDI and GII, +.64 for the GDI and GGI, and +.52 for the GII and GGI. The face validity for the combined indexes is good. The top-fifteen-ranked nations in gender egality are, in order, Iceland, Finland, Norway, Sweden, Slovenia, Switzerland, Ireland, Estonia, Lithuania, Latvia, Denmark, Germany, France, Belarus, and Belgium. The bottom fifteen, starting with the last-ranked, were Yemen, Pakistan, Chad, Mali, Côte d'Ivoire, Syria, Mauritania, Morocco, Liberia, Iran, Benin, Jordan, Burkina Faso, Gambia, and Swaziland.

In some individual countries, the effect sizes of the PISA or TIMSS surveys were nontrivial. Here are the countries with an absolute difference on the math test of $d \geq 0.20$ on either the PISA or the TIMSS surveys:

Male advantage	Female advantage
Honduras (−0.31)	Oman (+0.60)
Austria (−0.29)	Bahrain (+0.44)
Ghana (−0.28)	Jordan (+0.29)
Argentina (−0.24)	Thailand (+0.21)
Costa Rica (−0.24)	
Tunisia (−0.22)	
Chile (−0.22)	
Lebanon (−0.22)	
Italy (−0.21)	
Ireland (−0.21)	

The greatest female advantage was in Oman, ranked 104 out of 134 countries on a combined index of gender egality. Jordan was ranked 123rd, Bahrain 86th, and Thailand 60th. Meanwhile, the countries with a male advantage were evenly split among nations in the top and bottom half of the rankings. This explains the weak correlations between the index of gender egality and the effect size on the math test: just −.17 for the PISA dataset and −.05 for the TIMSS dataset.

Now for the science test, again showing the countries with an absolute difference of $d \geq 0.20$.

Male advantage	Female advantage
Ghana (−0.27)	Jordan (+0.47)
Honduras (−0.26)	Albania (+0.31)
Costa Rica (−0.26)	United Arab Emirates (+0.25)
Tunisia (−0.25)	Qatar (+0.23)
New Zealand (−0.24)	Trinidad (+0.23)
Hungary (−0.22)	Finland (+0.21)
Chile (−0.21)	Algeria (+0.20)
Italy (−0.20)	

Countries far down the list on the egality index—Jordan (123rd), Qatar (102nd), United Arab Emirates (78th)—were associated with a female advantage on science, while two of the countries where males had an advantage were well into the upper half—New Zealand (16th) and Italy (28th). The correlation of the egality index with the effect size in science was −.31 in the PISA dataset and −.22 in the TIMSS dataset.

67. Author's analysis of the 2015 PISA results.

68. Lippa, Collaer, and Peters (2010): 993.

69. Lippa, Collaer, and Peters (2010): 993.

70. The problems in interpreting the Lippa findings for personality traits (see note 37 for chapter 2) were less problematic for interpreting the results for visuospatial skills. It remains true that the test was effectively restricted to English speakers, but the instructions for completing the visuospatial questions were insensitive to level of English ability (unlike questions about personality that used vocabulary with subtle distinctions in meaning).

71. Gur and Gur (2017): Fig. 2.

72. Roalf, Gur, Ruparel et al. (2014).

73. Roalf, Gur, Ruparel et al. (2014).

74. Gur and Gur (2017): 191. The references are Linn and Peterson (1985); Thomas and French (1985); Voyer, Voyer, and Bryden (1995); Halpern, Benbow, Geary et al. (2007); Williams, Mathersul, Palmer et al. (2008); Hines (2010); and Moreno-Briseño, Diaz, Campos-Romo et al. (2010).

75. Boone, Gong, and Hegarty (2018).

76. Men and women perform equally on many navigational tasks, but Nazareth, Huang, Voyer et al. (2019), a meta-analysis of human navigation literature covering 694 effect sizes from 266 studies, found an overall d of −.34 to −.38 (favoring males).

77. Johnson and Bouchard (2007). See also Johnson and Bouchard (2005).

78. Johnson and Bouchard (2007): 24.

79. By using factor analysis and regression analysis in tandem, Johnson and Bouchard were able to calculate residual effect sizes. Johnson/Bouchard's hypothesis about different toolboxes posited two conditions: First, g makes use of a problem-solving toolbox that differs from individual to individual. Second, the overall usefulness of the tools and skill in their use are evenly distributed between men and women. "In the presence of these conditions," the authors wrote, "g should tend to mask sex differences in the specialized tools that contribute to more specialized abilities. Thus, its removal from the scores on a battery of tests through statistical regression should reveal greater sex differences in the residual scores than in the original full scores, and the sex differences in the scores on the residual factor scores should also be larger than commonly observed sex differences in mental ability test scores." They also hypothesized that, given these conditions, it would be possible to understand more clearly the dimensions on which cognitive abilities tend to differ between men and women—that is, differences

either in the tools that tend to be in their boxes or the ways they use them, or both. Johnson and Bouchard (2007): 25.

80. The exceptions were picture arrangement ($p < .009$) and WAIS information ($p < .002$).

4: Sex Differences in Educational and Vocational Choices

1. In the United States, males account for about 80 percent of arrests for violent crime. Federal Bureau of Investigation, Uniform Crime Report for 2017: Table 33. For broader evidence on predominantly male antisocial behavior, see Heidensohn and Silvestri (2012) and Del Giudice (2015).

2. Lubinski, Benbow, and Kell (2014): Figs. 4–5. The numbers for the effect sizes depicted in the bar chart were provided by David Lubinski, personal communication.

3. None of the statements in quotes with which respondents agreed or disagreed reached an effect size of +0.35 for Cohort 2. Lubinski, Benbow, and Kell (2014): Fig. 5.

4. There were also questions about working no more than 50 and 60 hours a week, which women also answered affirmatively more than men (effect sizes were +0.53 and +0.44 respectively).

5. "IQs of about 140 or higher" is an estimate, since the SMPY youngsters weren't given IQ tests. The cutoff for percentile 99.5 for full-scale IQ tests, which are normed to a mean of 100 and a standard deviation of 15, is 139.

6. A student could qualify for SMPY by getting an SAT verbal score of at least 430 regardless of SAT math score, but all of the students chosen for the follow-up had SAT math scores of at least 390, putting them in the top percentile on math among 7th graders. Lubinski, Benbow, Shea et al. (2001): 310.

7. A caveat: SMPY students who were toward the bottom of the top percentile in math (equivalent to an IQ of 135) might have struggled with a mathematics or physics major at a demanding school like MIT or Caltech. But that's a pretty small caveat.

8. Cohort 1 was recruited in 1972–74 (n = 2,188) from those who scored in the top 1 percent on the SAT math. Beginning with the second wave of Cohort 1 and continuing for the rest of the cohorts, students could qualify via either the SAT math or the SAT verbal. Technically, a student with an extremely high verbal score could be selected without being in the top 1 percent on the SAT math. In practice, almost all of those in Cohorts 2 and 3 who qualified via the SAT verbal were in the top 1 percent on math as well. Cohort 2 was recruited in 1976–79 (n = 778) from the top 0.5 percent. Cohort 3 was recruited in 1980–83 (n =501) from the top 0.01 percent. Cohort 4 was recruited in 1992–97 (n =1,130) and consisted of students who were in the top 3 percent of students in academic ability, with a large majority qualifying for the top 0.5 percent. Cohort 5, a form of control group, was recruited in 1992 (n = 714) from graduate students ages 23–25 enrolled in a STEM field at the 15 top-ranked graduate programs in engineering, math, or science. Lubinski and Benbow (2006): Table 1.

Full disclosure: One of my daughters was part of the Talent Search program that generated the SMPY (though not part of any of the follow-up cohorts) in the late 1980s. My description of SMPY parents in the text matches the way her parents were proud of her math talent and urged her to consider STEM fields. She listened attentively. She reached Harvard in the early 1990s while Richard Herrnstein and I were working on *The Bell Curve*. Herrnstein, who had become her friend, urged her to major in applied math. She listened attentively. And decided on Renaissance history and literature. Why? "It's complicated," she says.

9. Raymond and Benbow (1986): 816.

10. The slogan was made famous by Steinem, but she confirmed in a letter to *Time* magazine (September 16, 2000) that the saying was originated in 1970 by Irina Dunn, an Australian educator.

11. Twenty-five percent of the men and 29 percent of the women had stopped at the bachelor's degree. The same proportion (32 percent) of men and women had completed master's degrees. Forty percent of the men and 38 percent of the women had completed PhDs.

12. Almost half (46 percent) of the Cohort 2 of SMPY women got their degrees in STEM fields, nearly twice the proportion among all female undergraduates during 1986–89 (the years when Cohort 2 students graduated from college). Lubinski and Benbow (2006): Table 2; *Digest of Education Statistics*: Online tables supplementing section 322. The categories classified as STEM in the *Digest of Education Statistics* tables were mathematics, engineering, architecture, computer science, physical sciences, biology, and health.

13. Lubinski and Benbow (2006): Table 2. The statistic for the general population is based on college majors for all American undergraduates during 1986–89. *Digest of Education Statistics*: Online tables supplementing section 322, downloadable at nces.ed.gov/programs/digest.

14. Lubinski and Benbow (2006): Table 2.

15. A technical literature exists on this topic. It goes under the label of "expectancy-value theory." Eccles (1983).

16. Lubinski and Benbow (2006).

17. E.g., Eccles, Vida, and Barber (2004).

18. Humphreys, Lubinski, and Yao (1993).

19. A total of 563 out of the 778 members of Cohort 2 completed two subtests of the Differential Aptitude Tests (DAT): Mechanical Reasoning and Space Relations. Shea, Lubinski, and Benbow (2001).

20. Shea, Lubinski, and Benbow (2001): Fig. 3.

21. Lubinski, Webb, Morelock et al. (2001). The male-female ratio in Cohort 3 was 11.2. This is not the result of randomized testing of a nationally representative sample, but of a talent search that may have been unrepresentative for a variety of reasons. But there is also no reason to think that the search was drastically tilted in favor of boys. It represents evidence for a large male-female disproportion at the extreme right-hand tail of the IQ distribution, but 11.2 should be treated as a ballpark figure.

22. Lubinski, Webb, Morelock et al. (2001).

23. More precisely: For math, engineering, computer science, and the physical sciences, the male-to-female ratio for Cohort 2 was 1.88. For biology, health, and medicine, the female-to-male ratio was 1.84. The disparity in the most Things-oriented STEM fields was far greater yet for PhDs and professional degrees. Among the men who got PhDs, 42 percent got them in the most Things-oriented STEM disciplines, compared to 7 percent of the women—a ratio of 6.0. But the disparity reversed for the life sciences. Among SMPY men who got either a PhD or a professional degree, 23 percent got it in either medicine or biology. For women, the comparable statistic was 36 percent. Lubinski and Benbow (2006): Table 2.

24. The male-to-female ratio of young women in Cohort 3 who got undergraduate degrees in the most Things-oriented STEM majors was 1.8, almost identical to the ratio of 1.9 for Cohort 2. Meanwhile, the female-to-male ratio in the life sciences for Cohort 3 was 3.7, double the 1.8 ratio for Cohort 2. Lubinski and Benbow (2006): Table 2.

25. Data for college-educated women ages 45–49: Author's analysis, fertility samples for the CPS, combined 2012 and 2014 surveys. Data for SMPY Cohort 2: David Lubinski, personal communication.

26. Lubinski, Benbow, and Kell (2014): 2224.

27. Diener, Emmons, and Griffin (1985); Diener, Wirtz, Tov et al. (2010).

28. The SMPY women were fractionally lower than the men on satisfaction with their success in their professional career but fractionally higher regarding the current direction of their professional career. The women were also fractionally higher than the men on their psychological flourishing, positive feelings, and overall satisfaction with life. The men and women were equally satisfied with their relationships. Lubinski, Benbow, and Kell (2014): Fig. 7.

29. Lubinski, Benbow, and Kell (2014): 2229.

30. Lubinski and Benbow (2006): 316.

31. Wang, Eccles, and Kenny (2013).
32. Valla and Ceci (2014): 220.
33. The wording is adapted from Hakim (2002): 433–34.
34. Katharine Graham broke that barrier by becoming CEO of the *Washington Post*'s parent company upon the death of her husband.
35. Voyer and Voyer (2014).
36. Author's analysis, CPS. The trendline in bachelor's degrees is remarkable not only for the steep upward climb in women's degrees that had yet to level off as of 2015 but also for a sudden turnaround for men, from a steep increase through 1973 to the beginning of a long secular decline in 1975. The advent of the drop is not an artifact of a drop in the population of men eligible for college (defined as ages 18–23). The number in that age cohort increased slightly through 1983. And although it decreased from 1983 to 1993, it is hard to blame the drop on a shortage of males when the number of women getting BAs continued to increase during the same period. Were women crowding out men? It might have been true for private colleges that have unchanging undergraduate enrollments, but undergraduate enrollment in public universities is more flexible, and new schools continued to open throughout the period in question.
37. The male decline in graduate programs mirrors a similar phenomenon in male undergraduate enrollment, but it was proportionately larger and lasted even longer—30 years—than among undergraduates. In part, this may represent a crowding-out effect. Many graduate programs are relatively inflexible in size, and schools everywhere were eager to increase the number of women both for ideological reasons and in response to the passage in 1972 of Title IX of the Education Amendments, which prohibited discrimination by sex in any school receiving federal funds. But while crowding out may explain part of the change in the male trendline, this remarkable development is a rich subject for study.
38. For an account of the magnitude of Holland's influence, see Nauta (2010).
39. Holland (1959): 35.
40. Wording for the six categories is taken from the technical manual for a widely used RIASEC test, UNIACT: ACT (2009).
41. Prediger (1982). The People-Things and Data-Ideas dimensions have worked as tools for vocational counseling, but there is continuing debate from a statistical standpoint about whether they should be conceived as bipolar dimensions. See Tay, Su, and Rounds (2011).
42. I took this version of the hexagon from the manual describing ACT's version of Holland's Vocational Preference Inventory with the labels that ACT prefers. Holland's own labels are in parentheses. Holland (1977).
43. Holland's Vocational Preference Inventory does not predict actual majors and occupations well—too many competing considerations can override preferences. Su (2018).
44. The effect size was +0.10, with women slightly closer than men to the Data end of the spectrum. This might seem surprising because the word *data* is so closely associated with the kinds of analysis done in STEM fields, but that's the result of semantics. The research chemist may do extensive analysis of data, but typically for the purpose of testing a hypothesis grounded in theory—Ideas. Successful real estate agents are good with people, but their work is grounded in numbers—Data.
45. The O*NET database can be accessed at www.onetcenter.org. In the O*NET system, a job is classified according to the orientation that has the highest rating.
46. The Su study's effect sizes showed the biggest sex differences in vocational interests favoring men to be (in order from high to low) mechanical and electronic repairers, engineering technicians, engineers, physical scientists, computer scientists, and mathematicians. From 2014 to 2018, among employed Americans ages 25–54 with BAs, the biggest ratios favoring males were, in the same descending order, mechanical and electronic repairers, engineers, computer scientists, engineering technicians, applied mathematicians, and physical scientists. The Su

study's only three effect sizes favoring women were, in descending order, medical services (primarily nurses and other assistants to physicians and dentists), social scientists, and medical scientists. For employed Americans, the ratios favoring women were, in descending order, medical services, social scientists, and medical scientists. Overall the correlation of sex differences in vocational interests and employment ratios for 12 STEM job categories was +.79. Su and Rounds (2015): Table 4; author's analysis, Current Population Survey combined for the 2014–18 surveys.

The ratios take into account sex differences in the total number of employed people. Rather than using the raw numbers of employed males and females for calculating the ratio, I use the proportions of employed males and females—e.g., the percentage of employed males who are engineers divided by the percentage of employed females who are engineers.

47. The first column shows a meta-analysis of more than half a million scores on interests. The second column shows the scores of the exceptionally talented members of the four SMPY samples. The third column shows the RIASEC ratings for the jobs actually held by Americans in the combined American Community Surveys of 2011–15, consisting of a cross section of American adults based on a sample of more than five million. The first two columns use the same type of measures for two widely divergent populations. The third column uses a different measure (scores for occupations instead of scores for interests). The only cells that show a notable discrepancy are the Enterprising and Artistic cells for the SMPY sample, in which the sex differences were *larger* than for either of the two results based on the general population. For that matter, note that the effect sizes for all six RIASEC dimensions were largest for the SMPY sample. Men and women who are exceptionally intellectually talented have greater sex differences on this topic than do men and women in the population as a whole.

48. The percentages are based on professional and academic majors. These consist of agriculture, architecture, behavioral sciences, biology, business, communications/journalism, computer science, education, engineering, humanities, health sciences, mathematics, physical sciences, public administration, and social sciences. The numbers are drawn from the relevant table in the *Digest of Education Statistics* published annually by the National Center for Education Statistics.

49. I limit the discussion to descriptive statistics. For a multivariate examination of these issues see Lippa, Preston, and Penner (2014), which examined employment in 60 specific jobs from 1972 to 2010. The study analyzed two issues. One was the extent to which the best jobs go to men, with women excluded or hindered from access to high-status jobs. On this score, the news was good. The link between job status and occupational sex segregation as of 2010 was weak, with women entering high-status occupations in large numbers. Furthermore, the link had been weakening since 1972.

The same study also explored trends in the People-Things orientation that accounted for so much of the sex segregation in occupations. In this regard, they found that little had changed: "Thus, one factor—job status—has led to a reduction in occupational sex segregation over the past 40 years (i.e., increasing numbers of women have entered many formerly male-dominated high-status occupations), whereas another factor—jobs' people-things orientation—has served to maintain occupational sex segregation (women continue to be found more in people-oriented than in things-oriented occupations at all job status levels)." Lippa, Preston, and Penner (2014): 8. Both models also revealed an increase over time in the probability that women were employed in people-oriented jobs, but the statistic in question did not reach statistical significance. (Tables 2 and 3).

50. The data files may be found and downloaded at www.onetonline.org.

51. The following table gives an overview of the types of jobs that fell into each category in the CPS over the period 1971–2015. The percentages refer to the number of people in jobs in that category divided by the total number of people in jobs classified as People or Things respectively.

MAJOR CATEGORIES OF PEOPLE JOBS AND THINGS JOBS

People	Things
Managers of staffs (31%)	Low-skill labor (14%)
Teachers (13%)	Uncategorized skilled jobs (11%)
Salespeople (13%)	Procedural health care (10%)
Health care work with patients (11%)	Food and restaurant jobs (10%)
Restaurant workers (11%)	Construction trades (8%)
Personal services workers (3%)	Some low-level white-collar jobs (8%)
Childcare workers (3%)	Mechanics and repairers (5%)
Lawyers, judges, paralegals (2%)	Skilled administrative support (5%)
Social workers (2%)	Vehicle drivers (5%)
Advisors, counselors (1%)	STEM professionals (5%)
Customer service workers (1%)	Farmers and farm labor (4%)
Designers (1%)	Managers of operations (4%)
Entertainment workers (1%)	Protective services (3%)
Religious workers (1%)	Garment and textile workers (2%)
Human resources workers (1%)	STEM technicians (2%)
Hospitality work with customers (1%)	Manufacturing workers (1%)
All others (4%)	All others (3%)

Source: Author's analysis, CPS 1970–2015. "Procedural health care" refers to occupations such as surgeon, pathologist, radiologist, health technician, or low-skill hospital service staff, in contrast to health care occupations that center on direct delivery through personal interaction between health care worker and patient.

Prediger's equation for calculating the People-Things index score is $2R + I + C - 2S - A - E$. The problem with using the index score is that occupations with strong components of both Things *and* People orientations end up with a middling score that conceals their dual nature. An example is the job of physician—intensely Social in some respects, intensely Realistic and Investigative in others. The Prediger People-Things index score for physicians is 1.51, near the 50th percentile. But that is produced by adding a score of 17.56 for the Things half of the equation and 16.03 for the People half—both of which are well into the upper percentiles of their respective distributions. For analyzing the orientation of jobs toward People and/or Things, I therefore separate the equation into halves: one for calculating a Things score ($2R + I + C$) and the other for calculating a People score ($2S + A + E$). Each occupation has one score for the People dimension and another score for the Things dimension. The potential range of scores for any occupation on either dimension is 4 through 28. The actual range was 4 through 23.3 for People scores and 5.3 through 24.7 for Things scores, with means of 13.0 and 15.4 respectively.

My first requirement for classifying occupations was that any occupation rated 6–7 (the two highest scores) on the Social orientation be classified as a People job and any occupation rated 6–7 on the Realistic orientation be classified as a Things job. The maximum threshold score that ensured this outcome was 15. Occupations with less than a 6 on the Social orientation were classified as a People occupation if they had enough additional points on the Artistic and Enterprising orientations to reach 15; occupations with less than a 6 on the Realistic orientation were classified as Things occupations if they had enough additional points on the Investigative and Conventional orientations to reach 15. Note that an occupation can be classified as *both* a People and Things job, as in the example of physicians.

Presenting CPS occupational data over time requires dealing with the different job classifications that have been used. The Census Bureau has recoded the 1990 and 2010 versions so that each is intended to be consistent across years. But reclassifications inevitably produce discontinuities that cannot be fully reconciled. The O*NET RIASEC ratings are matched most closely with the Census Bureau's 2010 job classification, and I assigned them accordingly, using them to designate occupations as People or Things as described in the text. I replicated all the analyses using the 1990 and 2010 job classifications. The results were effectively the same for college-educated women, but the 2010 version reclassified a variety of low-level People jobs in ways that showed a substantially larger rise in the proportion of high-school-educated women in People jobs from 2003 onward than is shown by the 1990 classification. I chose to present the more conservative results given by the 1990 version, and they are used for all the figures and percentages given in the text. The trendline for occupations starts in 1971 instead of 1970 because both the 1990 and 2010 job classifications involved major changes between 1970 and 1971. For example, the number of jobs in a category such as "Managers not elsewhere categorized" in the 1970 version becomes radically smaller in the occupational categories that began to be used in 1971 because the new version included many new specific managerial categories. Such shifts created an artifactual difference between the 1970 figures and subsequent years. Rather than try to correct for them, it is cleaner to begin the time series in 1971.

Using these classification rules, 35 percent of employed Americans in 2015 were in People jobs, 44 percent were in Things jobs, 8 percent were in jobs that were both People and Things, and 13 percent were in jobs that fell in between. The mean People score (2S + A + E) of employed persons was 17.9. The mean Things score (2R + I + C) of employed persons was 19.0. The correlation of the Things and People scores for employed persons in 2015 was −.75, strongly negative.

The 13 percent of jobs that were in between, classified as neither People nor Things jobs by my RIASEC algorithm, were tilted toward ones that I think most observers would intuitively classify as People jobs. The ones with the largest numbers were secretaries, cashiers, and receptionists. Thirty percent of them were jobs that intuitively seem like Things jobs. The ones with the largest numbers were bookkeepers, accountants, and auditors. Few jobs (2 percent of all jobs, by my estimate) are ones that don't seem to have much tilt in either direction (paralegals, bank tellers, financial managers). By excluding the in-betweens from the analysis, I'm probably short-changing People jobs by a tad.

52. Among employed women ages 25–54 with at least a BA, the percentage in STEM professions increased from less than 1 percent in 1970 to 3.7 percent in 2015, a big proportional change. But the main point of the discussion in the text is to understand women's changes in occupations along the People-Things dimension. Over the time period I'm using, STEM professions amounted to only about 3 percent of all occupations, involving a trivial proportion of the job choices that women (and men) made.

53. Current Population Survey, 1971–2015, author's analysis.

54. Among employed persons ages 25–43, the proportion of People jobs rose from 21 percent to 28 percent of all jobs from 1971 to 2018, while the same figure for Things jobs fell from 44 percent to 37 percent. Author's analysis, Current Population Survey.

55. Murray (2012): ch. 9, 16.

56. Eberstadt (2016).

57. Each student's score in math, reading, and science was standardized to a z-score based on the scores of that nation. (A standardized score, or z-score, has a mean of zero and a standard deviation of 1.) The average of the three z-scores formed a general score, which was subtracted from the individual z-scores. The three differences (zMath−zGeneral, etc.) were themselves standardized within nations. The result could be used to express each student's score in math, reading, and science relative to that student's overall skills and relative to the mean and distribution of his nation's students. The authors use the example of a U.S. student who had z-scores of zScience

= –1.39, zMath = –0.69, and zReading = –1.61. The student's zGeneral score was –1.23. The relative-strength differences produced by the algorithm were –0.71 for science, +2.23 for math, and –1.34 for reading. The authors' explanation of the interpretation: "Note that although this student's scores in all three subjects are below the standardized national mean (i.e., 0), his personal strength in mathematics deviates more than two standard deviations from the national mean of relative mathematics strengths. In other words, the gap between his mathematics score and his overall mean score is much larger (> 2 SDs) than is typical for U.S. students. Using these types of scores, we could calculate the intraindividual sex differences for science, mathematics, and reading for the United States (and similarly for all other nations and regions)." Stoet and Geary (2008): 4.

58. In Stoet and Geary (2018), effect sizes were determined by subtracting female means from male means. I have reversed the signs to be consistent with usage throughout the book (positive *d* indicates a higher female mean), which reverses the signs of the correlations as well.

59. Stoet and Geary (2018): Table S2. Lebanon, with an effect size of +0.09 favoring girls, was the lone exception.

60. This and subsequent effect sizes are calculated from Stoet and Geary (2018): Table S2.

61. Merton (1968) coined the term *Matthew effect*. The relevant verse (25:29) is: "For whoever has will be given more, and they will have an abundance. Whoever does not have, even what they have will be taken from them."

62. Duff, Tomblin, and Catts (2015); Stanovich (1986). It so happens that the Global Gender Gap Index is highly correlated with economic wealth, which is also correlated with the quality of the educational systems. If you postulate that girls have a biologically grounded tendency to have better verbal skills than math and science skills, it may be expected that their relative strength will be accentuated as their educational opportunities increase. The same applies in reverse if boys' inborn math and science skills tend to be better than their verbal skills. The better their educational opportunities, the larger the disparity between what they do best and their overall ability.

63. Stoet and Geary (2018): 5.

64. Stoet and Geary (2018): 10. In the main text I restrict the discussion to relative strengths based on the actual test scores. But the questions about students' opinions of their own abilities in the 2015 PISA also allowed the authors to create a measure of self-efficacy for each field. For example, a boy's positive self-efficacy score in mathematics meant that he was more confident than his performance warranted; a negative score means that he underestimated his math ability. The more gender-equal the country, the greater the sex difference favoring boys in science self-efficacy, interest in science, and joy in science (r = –.60, –.41, and –.43 respectively; p < .001, .003, and .001 respectively).

5: Sex Differences in the Brain

1. To get a sense of how much that was known about sexual differentiation through studies of rodents, birds, and other species has turned out to apply to humans, see de Vries and Södersten (2009).

2. Cahill (2017): 12.

3. Balaton and Brown (2016).

4. Migeon (2017).

5. Herrera, Wang, and Mather (2018).

6. Giedd, Raznahan, Alexander-Bloch et al. (2014).

7. Braitenberg (2001).

8. E.g., Riès, Dronkers, and Knight (2016); de Schotten, Dell'Acqua, Forkel et al. (2011).

9. Sahakian and Gottwald (2017); Satel and Lilienfeld (2015); Poldrack, Mumford, and Nichols (2011).

10. See Jahanshad and Thompson (2017) for a concise review of findings from neuroimaging as of 2017.
11. Joel, Berman, Tavor et al. (2015): 5.
12. Joel, Berman, Tavor et al. (2015): 5.
13. Joel, Berman, Tavor et al. (2015): 3.
14. Joel, Berman, Tavor et al. (2015): 3.
15. David Schmitt, "Statistical Abracadabra: Making Sex Differences Disappear," *Psychology Today*, December 2, 2015.
16. Denworth (2017).
17. Del Giudice, Lippa, Puts et al. (2016); Rosenblatt (2016); Chekroud, Ward, Rosenberg et al. (2016); Glezerman (2016). The authors' reply is Joel, Persico, Hänggi et al. (2016).
18. Del Giudice, Lippa, Puts et al. (2016).
19. Rosenblatt (2016).
20. Chekroud, Ward, Rosenberg et al. (2016).
21. Anderson, Harenski, Harenski et al. (2018).
22. Andrew Sullivan, "The He Hormone," *New York Times Magazine*, April 2, 2000.
23. Sullivan, "The He Hormone."
24. Bos, Hofman, Hermans et al. (2016).
25. Olsson, Kopsida, Kimmo et al. (2016).
26. Domes, Heinrichs, Michel et al. (2007). Oxytocin's effects on behavior have been the subject of many articles, but as a meta-analysis by Bartz, Zaki, Bolger et al. (2011) made clear, the effects vary by context, and especially by sex. My citations are limited (Domes (2007) is an exception) to recent ones that have incorporated these complications into the design and analysis of their experiments.
27. Soutschek, Burke, Beharelle et al. (2017). The authors point out that the results could have been produced by socialization (since response to dopamine can be affected by reward systems) as well as by hardwired biological sex differences.
28. Nave, Nadler, Zava et al. (2017).
29. Sapienza, Zingales, and Maestripieri (2009). Risk aversion is one of the aspects of executive function. Grissom and Reyes (2019) found relatively few and minor sex differences in executive function in terms of the ability to process relevant information in making decisions, but acknowledged that observed gender differences in decision making as measured by the Iowa Gambling Task (the most frequently used decision-making task in such research) "are driven by [women] wishing to avoid frequent loss, not by a gender difference in the ability to detect loss magnitude." The authors added that "observations that women avoid frequent losses in the IGT may be the other side of the coin wherein men are willing to make choices associated with a higher probability of loss, even when loss is highly probable." (p. 2).
30. Goldstein, Jerram, Poldrack et al. (2005).
31. Stiles and Jernigan (2010).
32. The wording refers to the arguments in McCarthy and Arnold (2011) and Arnold (2017) for genetic sex differentiation that occurs during the embryonic phase. It is already known that such genetic differentiation occurs in other species prior to gonadal differentiation. Davies and Wilkinson (2006); Dewing, Shi, Horvath et al. (2003).
33. Savic, Garcia-Falgueras, and Swaab (2010).
34. Phoenix, Goy, Gerall et al. (1959).
35. Wallen (2009): 561.
36. Hines (2010).
37. See Cohen-Bendahan, van de Beek, and Berenbaum (2005) for a discussion of the role of other hormones in the feminization process.
38. Savic, Garcia-Falgueras, and Swaab (2010).
39. McCarthy (2015).

40. For a review of the early literature and an example, see Berenbaum and Hines (1992).

41. E.g., Ehrhardt and Meyer-Bahlburg (1981); Dittmann, Kappes, Kappes et al. (1990).

42. Udry, Morris, and Kovenock (1995): 367. The full text: "A substantial part of the variance in women's gendered behavior in a normal, non-clinical sample is explained by an empirical application of the two-stage behavioral endocrinological theory derived from vertebrate and non-human primate research. This supports other previous research on clinical samples and on normal samples confirming separate parts of the theoretical model for selected ranges of gendered behavior in females. It is concluded that gendered behavior is not entirely socially constructed, but partly built on a biological foundation."

43. Geschwind and Galaburda (1985): 431. Source numbers in the text have been omitted from the quotation.

44. This summary of the linked hypotheses in Geschwind and Galaburda (1985) is taken from Baron-Cohen (2003): 98.

45. Fetal testosterone seeps into amniotic fluid. Amniocentesis, a procedure for women whose pregnancies carry higher than normal risks of birth defects, involves the collection of amniotic fluid. Addenbrooke's Hospital in Cambridge near Baron-Cohen's lab routinely kept the samples of amniotic fluid until the babies were born. Amniocentesis carries a small risk of causing a miscarriage, but using the amniotic fluid for research did not raise ethical issues because the pregnant women had chosen to accept the risk of amniocentesis independently of the research. With the mothers' consent, it was thus possible to assemble a sample of children whose traits as infants and toddlers could be analyzed relative to their prenatal levels of testosterone.

46. Baron-Cohen (2003): 100. The technical accounts of the results are given in Lutchmaya, Baron-Cohen, and Raggatt (2001) and Lutchmaya, Baron-Cohen, and Raggatt (2002).

47. Auyeung, Knickmeyer, Ashwin et al. (2012).

48. Auyeung, Ahluwalia, Thomson et al. (2012); Auyeung, Baron-Cohen, Ashwin et al. (2009).

49. Knickmeyer, Baron-Cohen, Raggatt et al. (2006); Chapman, Baron-Cohen, Auyeung et al. (2006).

50. Auyeung, Baron-Cohen, Chapman et al. (2006).

51. Knickmeyer, Baron-Cohen, Raggatt et al. (2005).

52. Knickmeyer, Baron-Cohen, Raggatt et al. (2005).

53. Hines, Constantinescu, and Spencer (2015).

54. In the U.S. version, *The Gendered Brain* is titled *Gender and Our Brains*.

55. Here are links to reviews in prestigious mainstream outlets. The URLs were current as of May 2019.

Annie Murphy Paul, "Not from Venus, Not from Mars: What We Believe About Gender and Why It's Often Wrong," *New York Times*, February 23, 2017, nytimes .com/2017/02/23/books/review/testosterone-rex-myths-of-sex-science-and-society -cordelia-fine.html.

Antonia Macaro, "Testosterone Rex by Cordelia Fine—Men, Women and Myths," *Financial Times*, February 17, 2017, ft.com/content/946956e6-f2df-11e6-95ee-f14e55513608.

Sarah Ditum, "Testosterone Rex by Cordelia Fine Review—The Question of Men's and Women's Brains," *Guardian*, January 18, 2017, www.theguardian.com/books/2017 /jan/18/testosterone-rex-review-cordelia-fine.

Sheri Berenbaum, "A Spirited Polemic Takes Aim at Biological Sex Differences but Misses Opportunities to Highlight Relevant Science, *Science* blog *Books, Et Al.*, January 18, 2017, blogs.sciencemag.org/books/2017/01/18/723/.

Rachel Cooke, "The Gendered Brain by Gina Rippon Review—Demolition of a Sexist Myth," *Guardian*, March 5, 2019, www.theguardian.com/books/2019/mar/05/the -gendered-brain-gina-rippon-review.

56. The panel of judges consisted of a paleontologist, a psychologist, a television journalist, a novelist, and one neuroscientist. The neuroscientist, Sam Gilbert, has posted a defense of *Testosterone Rex* at his web page, www.samgilbert.net.

57. For reviews in the technical literature of *Brain Storm* and *Delusions of Gender*, see Halpern (2010) and McCarthy and Ball (2011). For *Delusions of Gender*, also see Brown (2017). For *Testosterone Rex*, see Berenbaum (2017). Simon Baron-Cohen reviewed *The Gendered Brain* for the *Sunday Times* of London, March 8, 2019.

For online responses: Robert J. King is a psychologist specializing in biological psychology. He is currently a lecturer at the School of Applied Psychology, University College Cork. His review of *Testosterone Rex* ("Estrogen Promise") was posted on the website of *Psychology Today*, April 11, 2017 (www.psychologytoday.com). Stuart Ritchie is a psychologist specializing in psychometrics and the genetics of cognitive ability. He is currently a lecturer in the Social Genetic & Developmental Psychiatry Centre at King's College London. His review of *Testosterone Rex* was posted on *Quillette*, March 21, 2017 (www .quillette.com). Jerry Coyne is an evolutionary biologist at the University of Chicago. He posted three long essays about Fine's work at his blog, *Why Evolution Is True*, on January 20, 2017, March 9, 2017, and September 21, 2017 (whyevolutionistrue.wordpress.com). Gregory Cochran, coauthor of *The 10,000 Year Explosion*, posted his review of *Testosterone Rex* at his blog, *West Hunter*, on March 20, 2017 (westhunt.wordpress.com). Larry Cahill, a neurobiologist at UC Irvine, reviewed *The Gendered Brain* on *Quillette*, March 29, 2019 (www.quillette.com).

58. The straw man problem is also an issue with a 2018 major technical article published in *American Psychologist*. Titled "The Future of Sex and Gender in Psychology: Five Challenges to the Gender Binary," the first author was Janet Shibley Hyde, originator of the gender similarities hypothesis, and one of her coauthors was Daphna Joel, first author of the controversial article on the brain mosaic discussed in chapter 5. Here is the abstract of the article:

> The view that humans comprise only two types of beings, women and men, a framework that is sometimes referred to as the "gender binary," played a profound role in shaping the history of psychological science. In recent years, serious challenges to the gender binary have arisen from both academic research and social activism. This review describes 5 sets of empirical findings, spanning multiple disciplines, that fundamentally undermine the gender binary. These sources of evidence include neuroscience findings that refute sexual dimorphism of the human brain; behavioral neuroendocrinology findings that challenge the notion of genetically fixed, nonoverlapping, sexually dimorphic hormonal systems; psychological findings that highlight the similarities between men and women; psychological research on transgender and nonbinary individuals' identities and experiences; and developmental research suggesting that the tendency to view gender/sex as a meaningful, binary category is culturally determined and malleable. Costs associated with reliance on the gender binary and recommendations for future research, as well as clinical practice, are outlined. (Hyde, Joel, Bigler et al. (2018): 171).

> There is a distinction to be made between *dimorphic* and *binary*. *Dimorphic* means two forms but allows for substantial overlap. This is an empirically accurate description of humans' biological sexuality, as discussed in Appendix 2. But when it comes to sex differences in the brain, hormonal systems, personality, cognitive functioning, or social behavior, the Hyde study is criticizing a scholarly school that doesn't exist. No one who is cited in *Human Diversity* argues for the "gender binary." Everyone accepts large degrees of overlap.

59. Cordelia Fine, Daphna Joel, and Gina Rippon, "Eight Things You Need to Know About Sex, Gender, Brains, and Behavior: A Guide for Academics, Journalists, Parents, Gender

Diversity Advocates, Social Justice Warriors, Tweeters, Facebookers, and Everyone Else," *S&F Online*, issue 15.2 (2019), sfonline.barnard.edu/neurogenderings/eight-things-you -need-to-know-about-sex-gender-brains-and-behavior-a-guide-for-academics-journalists -parents-gender-diversity-advocates-social-justice-warriors-tweeters-facebookers-and-ever/.

60. Marco Del Giudice, David A. Puts, David C. Geary et al., "Sex Differences in Brain and Behavior: Eight Counterpoints," *Psychology Today*, April 8, 2019, www.psychologytoday.com/us /blog/sexual-personalities/201904/sex-differences-in-brain-and-behavior-eight-counterpoints.

61. Hines, Constantinescu, and Spencer (2015).

62. Berenbaum (2018).

63. Cohen-Bendahan, van de Beek, and Berenbaum (2005): 359.

64. Beltz, Swanson, and Berenbaum (2011): Table 3.

65. Hines, Pasterski, Spencer et al. (2016), summarizing the literature. Dessens, Slijper, Drop et al. (2005) found 5.2 percent incidence of sex dysphoria (not necessarily living as a male) among CAH females raised as females.

66. Hines (2010); Cohen-Bendahan, van de Beek, and Berenbaum (2005).

67. Imperato-McGinley, Pichardo, Gautier et al. (1991).

68. Savic, Frisen, Manzouri et al. (2017).

69. Savic, Frisen, Manzouri et al. (2017): 9.

70. SHBG stands for *sex hormone binding globulin*, a large protein molecule that binds testosterone. Increased levels of SHBG imply less androgenization of the fetal brain.

71. Udry (2000): 451.

72. The authors took three specific hypotheses into the research: one regarding the role of hormones, one regarding the role of childhood socialization, and one regarding a "cultural interactionist frame," which draws from the social-roles theory discussed in the introduction to Part I—in the words of Davis and Risman, that "gender is not the property of individuals, but is instead the product of social interactions which reproduce and legitimate institutional arrangements based on sex categories." Davis and Risman (2015): 112. Their analysis did not support the cultural interactionist hypothesis—which they acknowledged in a straightforward way that one wishes were more common in social science: "As sociologists whose work has been primarily within a gender structure approach, we expected that the cultural interactionist frame would be most strongly supported by the data, that normative pressure to 'do gender' in adult social roles and the current social context would be most influential in shaping gendered selves.... To foreshadow the findings, we found the results much more complicated than the cultural interactionist framework predicted. We were wrong." Davis and Risman (2015): 113. I have reported their findings in accordance with their own conclusion that socialization played a stronger role than prenatal testosterone, but I will note another way of thinking about the situation: One independent variable, exposure to testosterone, was limited to the second trimester in the womb. The other, gender socialization, presumably acted upon them every day after birth for decades.

73. For another study that explored both the contributions of early androgen exposure and parental socialization, see Constantinescu, Moore, Johnson et al. (2018).

74. McGlone (1980): 226.

75. Voyer (1996): 64.

76. Baron-Cohen (2003): 105.

77. Baron-Cohen (2003): 105–6.

78. Sporns (2011).

79. Smith (2017).

80. E.g., Sporns (2006); He, Chen, and Evans (2007). The model was initially proposed in Watts and Strogatz (1998).

81. The idea was made famous by Stanley Milgram. His data didn't actually prove his point in the real world, though the idea behind it makes mathematical sense. Stanley Milgram, "The Small World Problem," *Psychology Today*, May 1967: 60–67.

82. E.g., Kansaku, Yamaura, and Kitazawa (2000); Gur, Alsop, Glahn et al. (2000); Clements, Rimrodt, Abel et al. (2006).
83. Yan, Gong, Wang et al. (2011): 452.
84. Ingalhalikar, Smith, Parker et al. (2014): 825.
85. Hänggi, Fövenyi, Liem et al. (2014): 10.
86. Ruigrok, Salimi-Khorshidi, Lai et al. (2014). See Appendix 3 for details.
87. Ingalhalikar, Smith, Parker et al. (2014): 826.
88. Ingalhalikar, Smith, Parker et al. (2014): 826.
89. Satterthwaite, Wolf, Roalf et al. (2015).
90. Karl Friston, quoted in Yeo, Krienen, Sepulcre et al. (2011): 1127.
91. The method for observing functional connectivity is known as blood-oxygen-level-dependent (BOLD) imaging.
92. Satterthwaite, Wolf, Roalf et al. (2015): 2383.
93. Satterthwaite, Wolf, Roalf et al. (2015): 2390.
94. Tunç, Solmaz, Parker et al. (2016).
95. de LaCoste-Utamsing and Holloway (1982).
96. For an account of the pre-MRI years of the battle, see Holloway (2017).
97. Ardekani, Figarsky, and Sidtis (2013), which also contains a review of the reasons that previous studies found so many discrepant results. A subsequent study, Luders, Toga, and Thompson (2014), with a sample of 24 males and 24 females, argued that individual differences in brain size account for apparent sex differences in callosal anatomy, an argument made previously in the literature. Ralph Holloway, who started the debate with de LaCoste-Utamsing and Holloway (1982) and was invited to summarize the state of knowledge in the 2017 special edition of *Journal of Neuroscience Research*, concluded as follows: "I would like to end this commentary by breaking out in a happy dance, thanks to the most definitive article to date by Ardekani et al. (2012), which showed that, when males and females (N=316) were analyzed, the female CC [corpus callosum] was larger than that in males. A separate analysis (N=74) performed with a younger sample matched for brain size showed the same thing, and significantly so. It should be pointed out that a later article by Luders et al. (2014) with smaller samples and using different methods found no significant sex differences, but it does not mention the results of Ardekani et al. (2012). The recent article by Ingahalikar et al. (2014) on connectome differences between males and females clearly reinforces our findings on the CC. We always did our best to take the high road on these issues, and it is gratifying that many authors today mostly stay with the facts rather than political issues, which should not be playing a role in scientific discourse. May I say: 'we told you so'?" Holloway (2017).
98. Ardekani, Figarsky, and Sidtis (2013): 2518. The text omits embedded citations contained in the original quotation.
99. Lombardo, Ashwin, Auyeung et al. (2012). Specifically, total white matter volume, total gray matter volume, and total cerebrospinal fluid volume were entered as covariates in the statistical analyses.
100. The regions in question were the right temporoparietal junction/posterior superior temporal sulcus (RTPJ/pSTS), planum temporale/parietal operculum (PT/PO), and posterior lateral orbitofrontal cortex (plOFC).
101. Lutchmaya, Baron-Cohen, and Raggatt (2001).
102. Knickmeyer, Baron-Cohen, Raggatt et al. (2006).
103. Chapman, Baron-Cohen, Auyeung et al. (2006).
104. Catani, Jones, and ffytche (2005).
105. Lutchmaya, Baron-Cohen, and Raggatt (2002).
106. Shaywitz, Shaywitz, Pugh et al. (1998); Rojas, Bawn, Benkers et al. (2002); Pelphry, Morris, and McCarthy (2005).
107. Lombardo, Ashwin, Auyeung et al. (2012): 679.

108. See, for example, Rubin, Yao, Keedy et al. (2017) and Koscik, Dan, Moser et al. (2009).
109. For the most complete available catalog of areas of the brain that are differentially activated by men and women in response to emotional perception, see Filkowski, Olsen, Duda et al. (2017), a meta-analysis of 56 studies limited to those that report direct contrasts between men and women participating in the same visual emotion-eliciting task within each study. The meta-analysis focused on which regions were activated, with broad characterizations of the results rather than specific hypotheses about how they related to phenotypic differences. Here is the authors' overall conclusion (omitting references embedded in the text):

> Here we have assembled 56 human functional imaging studies that each reported a reliable sex difference in neural activity elicited by emotional cues in the visual modality. This analysis reveals regions of the brain that are differentially recruited across men and women across a range of emotion-evoking experiments, including frontal, insular, and medial temporal cortex, as well as amygdala, brainstem, and high-order thalamus. This pattern of differences is consistent with a perspective in which men more strongly engage volitional control processes when faced with emotional cues, recruiting frontal cortical regions, perhaps resulting in dampened amygdala reactivity. Medial PFC activity in men could also be a result of enhanced reactivity to reward cues, although valence-specific effects cannot be determined in the current effort. Women, by comparison, show evidence of enhanced subcortical sensitivity to emotional cues, consistent with an evolutionary bias toward harm avoidance. (p. 930).

110. *Declarative memory* ("knowing what") is distinct from *procedural memory* ("knowing how"), the kind of memory that lets us tie our shoelaces or touch-type without consciously thinking about it. Declarative memory is sometimes labeled *explicit memory*, and procedural memory is sometimes labeled *implicit memory*.
111. These examples are taken from Kurdi, Lozano, and Banaji (2016). The photos are in the public domain and available at www.benedekkurdi.com. Another common form of stimulus also uses pictures, but exclusively of faces. Other types of stimulus, used rarely, are films, words, autobiographical recall, script-driven imagery, prosody, and odors. Stevens and Hamann (2012).
112. Hamann (2005): 291.
113. Hamann (2005); Karama, Lecours, Leroux et al. (2002).
114. This is the predominant finding. For a literature review of studies of sex differences in amygdala volume, see Kaczkurkin, Raznahan, and Satterthwaite (2019), which notes that amygdala volumes increase rapidly in females in early puberty before peaking and decreasing, while males show increasing amygdala volumes throughout puberty. Marwha, Halari, and Eliot (2017), a recent meta-analysis that found no significant difference in amygdala size after correcting for total brain volume, disputes this, reporting that "our findings do not support a marked change in the sex difference at puberty, for either raw or corrected AV." Quotation taken from p. 15 of the accepted manuscript.
115. Baird, Wilson, Bladin et al. (2004).
116. Goldstein, Seidman, Horton et al. (2001).
117. Karama, Lecours, Leroux et al. (2002).
118. Hamann, Herman, Nolan et al. (2004). Hamann (2005) notes that the previous study, Karama, Lecours, Leroux et al. (2002), had not found greater male activity in the amygdala, but that the same authors had conducted a follow-up using a method more sensitive to rapid changes in amygdala activity and had obtained results replicating the Hamann study's finding of greater left amygdala activity in men.
119. For a review of the literature, see Seidlitz and Diener (1998).
120. One common instruction given to judges in such experiments is to classify as gist "any fact or element pertaining to the basic story that could not be changed or excluded without

changing the basic story line," while classifying all other facts or elements as peripheral. This wording is drawn from Heuer and Reisberg (1990): 499. The authors continued: "Thus, for example, a description of a slide as showing 'a woman crossing an intersection' would be considered basic. To describe the same scene as 'a person outside' would be too general, while 'a red-haired woman with a handbag on her left arm stepping onto the first third of the cross walk' would be regarded as too specific. The judges agreed on almost all items; in cases of disagreement, items were replaced. Some sample peripheral items were the color of the door in front of which the mother stood in a particular slide; whether the boy was carrying a lunchbox or a soccer ball; and so forth. Some sample central items were whether the mother and son were going to the gas station, to school, or shopping; whether the son watched the repair, or played in the back room; and so forth."

121. Cahill and van Stegeren (2003).
122. The initial identification of this effect was Cahill, Haier, White et al. (2001). For a review of the studies, see Hamann (2005).
123. Stevens and Hamann (2012).
124. Nolen-Hoeksema, Morrow, and Fredrickson (1993); Nolen-Hoeksema, Parker, and Larson (1994).
125. Thomas, Drevets, Whalen et al. (2001); Williams, Barton, and Kemp (2005).
126. Andreano, Dickerson, and Barrett (2013). The sample consisted of 25 females and 16 males.
127. Blackford, Avery, Cowan et al. (2011); Schwartz, Wright, Shin et al. (2003).
128. Blackford, Allen, Cowan et al. (2012).
129. Barrett and Armony (2009); Sehlmeyer, Dannlowski, Schöning et al. (2011).
130. Shin, Wright, Cannistraro et al. (2005).
131. Andreano, Dickerson, and Barrett (2014).
132. Brohawn, Offringa, Pfaff et al. (2010); Ramel, Goldin, Eyler et al. (2007).
133. Cahill, Uncapher, Kilpatrick et al. (2004); LaBar and Cabeza (2006).
134. Andreano, Dickerson, and Barrett (2014): 1393.
135. Herrera, Wang, and Mather (2018).
136. Kaczkurkin, Raznahan, and Satterthwaite (2019).

Part II: "Race Is a Social Construct"

1. In *By the People*, I defined it this way: "By *the American project*, I mean the continuing effort, begun with the founding, to demonstrate that human beings can be left free as individuals, families, and communities to live their lives as they see fit as long as they accord the same freedom to everyone else, with government safeguarding a peaceful setting for those endeavors but otherwise standing aside." Murray (2015): xiii. The book argues that the American project is effectively already dead because of proximal causes other than slavery, but I believe that the ultimate cause was slavery and its aftermath.

2. Boas collected his writings on race in *Race, Language, and Culture* (New York: Macmillan, 1940), available online at monoskop.org. For a detailed description of Boas's opposition to the biological interpretation of race and his allies in sociology, see Degler (1991): chapters 2 and 3.

3. Montagu (1997).

4. Lewontin (1972): 397. In the introduction, I noted that many aspects of the sameness premise have long since been disproved by ordinary social science evidence. Similarly, it has been widely argued since Lewontin published his dictum in 1972 that it was scientifically unjustified. For a full review of the technical literature that followed Lewontin (1972), see Rosenberg (2018). Nontechnically, Lewontin's mistake was to conclude that if 85 percent of genetic variance is within populations, then it follows that the effects of the remaining 15 percent must be trivial. The effects *could* be trivial, but there was no a priori reason to assume so. Sewall Wright's

measure of genetic population differentiation, F_{ST}, proposed in 1943, is one of the most commonly used statistics in population genetics. Ranging in theory from 0 to 1.0, it expresses the ratio of variance among subpopulations to the total variance. But a value of 1 requires that each subpopulation be fixed for a different allele—an extreme seldom seen in practice—and anything less than fixation in each subpopulation produces far lower values of F_{ST}. Wright himself suggested guidelines for interpreting F_{ST}: Values from 0 to .05 indicate "little" genetic differentiation, from .05 to .15 indicate "moderate" differentiation, from .15 to .25 indicate "great" differentiation, and values of .25 and higher indicate "very great" differentiation. Wright (1978). If one applies these guidelines to humans, .15 is on the borderline between "moderate" and "great." The meanings of .15 for F_{ST} and in Lewontin's analysis are somewhat different, but Lewontin's version of .15 is also not obviously trivial. In 1982, three geneticists from the University of Michigan and the University of Pennsylvania raised a more specific statistical issue. "There are a few marker loci which yield almost categorical separation of some human populations, but most loci vary modestly for allele frequencies across populations. The central taxonomic point is that for purposes of classification, which is a direct measure of taxonomic separation (distributional nonoverlap), a large number of small differences is equivalent to a small number of large differences." Smouse, Spielman, and Park (1982): 445–46. The authors proceeded to demonstrate the applicability of their model to seven tribes of South American Indians. In 2003, an eminent British geneticist at Cambridge, A. W. F. Edwards, published "Human Genetic Diversity: Lewontin's Fallacy." He wrote that "this article could, and perhaps should, have been written soon after 1974 [when Lewontin published *The Genetic Basis of Evolutionary Change*]." Edwards then pointed out what statisticians had understood since the 1920s, that it was fallacious to analyze data "on the assumption that it contains no information beyond that revealed on a locus-by-locus analysis.... The 'taxonomic significance' of genetic data in fact often arises from correlations among the different loci, for it is these that may contain the information which enables a stable classification to be uncovered." Edwards (2003): 801, 799.

5. Stephen Jay Gould, "Human Equality Is a Contingent Fact of History," *Natural History*, November 1984: 26–33.
6. Stephen J. Gould, "The Spice of Life: An Interview with Stephen Jay Gould," *Leader to Leader* 15 (Winter 2000): 14–19.
7. Omi and Winant (1986): 65.
8. American Sociological Association (2003).
9. American Association of Physical Anthropologists, "AAPA Statement on Race & Racism," March 27, 2019, physanth.org/about/position-statements/aapa-statement-race-and-racism -2019/.
10. Diamond (1994).

6: A Framework for Thinking About Race Differences

1. I focus exclusively on the genetics in hopes of avoiding the problem faced by Nicholas Wade, who began his book, *A Troublesome Inheritance*, with chapters recounting developments in population genetics and evidence for recent evolutionary adaptation (corresponding to my chapters 7 and 8). Then Wade devoted the second half of his book to a larger set of topics that linked phenotypic differences to possible evolutionary explanations. Wade explicitly warned the reader that arguments in these latter chapters were speculative and "fall far short of proof." But the response to the book conflated the explicitly labeled speculations with the hard science in the first half of the book. See, for example, David Dobbs, "The Fault in Our DNA," *New York Times*, July 10, 2014.
2. Okbay, Beauchamp, Fontana et al. (2016): 60–61.
3. Sanger was awarded the 1980 Nobel Prize for Chemistry, which he shared with American biochemists Walter Gilbert and Paul Berg. Gilbert had invented another method for sequencing

DNA that subsequently was bypassed in favor of Sanger's. Berg's award was for work on the chemistry of nucleic acids, especially those involving recombinant DNA.

4. More precisely, the sequence was said to cover 99 percent of the euchromatic human genome with 99.99 percent accuracy. *Euchromatin* refers to the 95 percent of the active genome that does not stain strongly with basic dyes when the cell is not dividing. The sequencing did not include a tightly packed form of DNA known as heterochromatin.

5. Cells in humans are *diploid*, meaning that the cell carries two copies of each chromosome.

6. There are some rare exceptions to this rule, in which one allele in a SNP is consistently passed on to more than half of the offspring. The technical term for this phenomenon is *meiotic drive* (Sandler and Novitski (1957)), and it also is a source of evolutionary change.

7: Genetic Distinctiveness Among Ancestral Populations

1. I stipulate a particular population so that I can use actual data from Phase 3 of the 1000 Genomes Project. The subsequent numbers in the discussion are based on the allele frequencies for the EAS (East Asian) aggregation, using data downloaded from the 1000 Genomes website, www.internationalgenome.org. The selection criteria for being included in the download were that VT = SNP (i.e., the variant type is a SNP, not another form of variation) and AA = [ACGT] (i.e., the ancestral allele is A, C, G, or T, which culls most SNPs with more than two alleles). The calculation of probabilities uses the Wright-Fisher model for a biallelic SNP.

2. I use a round number because the selection criterion AA = [ACGT] does not cull all SNPs with more than two alleles and because counts of SNPs don't yet stand still. They're still changing as new methods yield more detailed and accurate maps of the genome.

3. I've greatly understated the number of rare variants by using Phase 1 of the 1000 Genomes Project, which was not intended to identify a complete inventory of variants with a minor allele frequency less than .01. More on this in chapter 9.

4. Wright (1943).

5. Malécot (1948).

6. Kimura and Weiss (1964).

7. Wilson (1975).

8. Glazko and Nei (2003); McHenry (2012).

9. Zhu, Dennell, Huang et al. (2018).

10. Other *Homo* species are placed at dates contemporaneous with or following *Homo erectus*. For example, *Homo heidelbergensis* has been thought by some to have been intermediate between *Homo erectus* and both the Neanderthals and *Homo sapiens*. Stewart and Stringer (2012); Papagianni and Morse (2015). But a controversy continues about whether *Homo heidelbergensis* is appropriately treated as a separate hominin. Bermúdez de Castro, Martinón-Torres, Rosell et al. (2016).

11. This wording for the definition of AMH is adapted from Gamble, Gowlett, and Dunbar (2014): Table 1.1. The specification of "globular brain case and other traits" comes from Reich (2018).

12. For a fascinating personal account of the struggle to figure out the origins of *Homo sapiens*, see a long conversation with Christopher Stringer, one of the leading protagonists. John Brockman, "Rethinking 'Out of Africa': Conversation with Christopher Stringer," *Edge*, November 12, 2011. www.edge.org.

13. Weidenreich (1946).

14. Coon (1962).

15. These dates, from Poznik, Henn, Yee et al. (2013), are the most recent estimate as I write.

16. Stringer and Andrews (1988). Schiffels and Durbin (2014) use an innovative method to estimate genetic divergence that leads them to conclude that separation of today's non-Africans from those who remained in Africa began around 150,000 years ago. If that is correct, and

it is also correct that the dispersal that led to today's humans occurred 40,000–80,000 years ago, the implication is that those who left Africa were already distinct from other Africans while still living in Africa. But this analysis has yet to be confirmed as I write.

17. Cavalli-Sforza, Menozzi, and Piazza (1994).

18. Ramachandran, Deshpande, Roseman et al. (2005): 15942.

19. The following account was pieced together from the various sources that are cited subsequently. The most authoritative summary of the state of knowledge as I write is Nielsen, Akey, Jakobsson et al. (2017).

20. Richter, Grün, Joannes-Boyau et al. (2017); Callaway (2017).

21. Scerri, Thomas, Manica et al. (2018): 1.

22. Hershkovitz, Weber, Quam et al. (2018); Posth, Wißing, Kitagawa et al. (2017).

23. Lopez, van Dorp, and Hallenthal (2016).

24. Nielsen, Akey, Jakobsson et al. (2017); Henn, Botigue, Peischl et al. (2016); Schiffels and Durbin (2014); Timmermann and Friedrich (2016); and Seguin-Orlando, Korneliussen, Sikora et al. (2014).

25. For a summary of the various models for the dispersal of humans, see Groucutt, Petraglia, Bailey et al. (2015): Table 1 and accompanying text.

26. The results of the study were presented in three papers: Mallick, Li, Lipson et al. (2016); Malaspinas, Westaway, Muller et al. (2016); and Pagani, Lawson, Jagoda et al. (2016). A commentary, Tucci and Akey (2016), summarizes them. The DNA analyses for the large databases when this study was done had sequenced each region of the genome only a few times, meaning that some errors go undetected and some SNPs are missed.

27. Günther and Jakobsson (2016); Nielsen, Akey, Jakobsson et al. (2017).

28. Nielsen, Akey, Jakobsson et al. (2017).

29. Posth, Wißing, Kitagawa et al. (2017).

30. Other evidence suggests Neanderthal introgression as early as 100,000 years ago, but those encounters apparently did not contribute to modern humans. Lopez, van Dorp, and Hallenthal (2016).

31. Browning, Browning, Zhou et al. (2018).

32. Brown, Sutikna, Morwood et al. (2004) and Argue, Donlon, Groves et al. (2006).

33. Fregel, Méndez, Bokbot et al. (2018).

34. Reich (2018): chapter 7.

35. Reich (2018): chapter 3.

36. Reich (2018) is the book-length account. Bae, Douka, and Petraglia (2017) provides a concise overview with emphasis on the peopling of Asia. For an account of the one-wave evidence, see Tucci and Akey (2016). For an overview of admixture with archaic hominins, see Wolf and Akey (2018).

37. Pritchard, Stephens, and Donnelly (2000).

38. For a discussion of the pitfalls of overinterpreting cluster analyses, see Lawson, van Dorp, and Falush (2018).

39. Bowcock, Ruiz-Linares, Tomfohrde et al. (1994).

40. Calafell, Shuster, Speed et al. (1998).

41. Pritchard, Stephens, and Donnelly (2000). The current version of the program they developed, Structure, is available for download at no cost from the Pritchard Lab's website at Stanford, web.stanford.edu/group/pritchardlab. Structure is a model-based method. The method used by Bowcock, Ruiz-Linares, Tomfohrde et al. (1994) is known as "distance-based," and produces useful graphical representations but poses interpretive problems that Structure avoids.

42. Rosenberg, Pritchard, Weber et al. (2002).

43. Li, Absher, Tang et al. (2008). The Li study used a new software package similar to Structure called Frappe. The authors used the same sample as the 2002 study (reduced to 51 subpopulations and 938 cases for technical reasons). As before, no information about the subpopulations

played into the software's algorithms or "knowledge." The program was allowed to run for 10,000 iterations, with pre-specified cluster numbers, from $K = 2$ to 7. Herráez, Bauchet, Tang et al. (2009) used the same database and found essentially the same results.

44. This interpretation of ancestry coefficients, expressed as percentage of ancestry, follows the usage in Li, Absher, Tang et al. (2008) and in the article that fully explains the Frappe software. The measure is created by a vector of scores. Each score "corresponds to the probability that a randomly sampled allele from individual *i* originates from a specific ancestral population, *k*." Tang, Peng, Wang et al. (2005): 290.

45. Christoph Meiners, the physical anthropologist who named Caucasians in 1785, thought people from the Caucasus to be unusually handsome. The label is arbitrary, but it had to be. Try to think of any descriptive term that would cover everyone indigenous to the variety of regions where Caucasians are found.

46. The plot is based on the value of a statistic, F_{ST}, discussed in note 4 of the introduction to Part II. It measures population differentiation due to genetic structure for each pair of individuals in the sample. It is one of the most widely used statistics in population genetics. The team conducted a principal component factor analysis on the F_{ST} matrix. Such an analysis takes a set of correlated observations—in this case, the 938-by-938 matrix of F_{ST} values—and creates a smaller number of uncorrelated variables, which are called the "principal components" (PCs). Colloquially: The program's algorithms create a first component that explains as much of the variation among the observations as possible. It then creates a second component that explains as much of the remaining variation as it can, subject to the restriction that the second component must be uncorrelated with the first component—and so on through successive PCs until all of the variation has been explained. In the Li study, the first and second PCs explained 52 percent and 28 percent of the F_{ST} respectively, for a total of 80 percent. The first PC primarily described the contrast between sub-Saharan Africans and non-Africans, and the second PC primarily described the differences among the populations in Eurasia.

47. Xing, Watkins, Shlien et al. (2010): 202.

48. The conclusion reads in full:

> In this study, by sampling populations from previously undersampled regions, we sought to assess the effect of more even sampling on human genetic diversity and to investigate the evolutionary history of these populations. We found support for a relationship between the initial founding populations of America and Central/North Asian populations. We demonstrated high genetic diversity in Central Asian and South Asian populations, especially in Nepal. We also found that Iraqi Kurds have a closer relationship to European populations than Asian populations. These results increase our understanding of human population relationships and evolutionary history. In addition, our data provide a resource for understanding patterns of linkage disequilibrium, natural selection and the differential distributions of SNP and CNV alleles among populations, all of which have important implications in genome-wide association studies and the identification of loci with functional, biomedical significance. (Xing, Watkins, Shlien et al. (2010): 209).

49. Novembre and Peter (2016): Fig 2.

50. Schraiber and Akey (2015): Table 1.

51. Schraiber and Akey (2015).

52. An excellent review of the state of knowledge as of 2014 is Elhaik, Tatarinova, Chebotarev et al. (2014), which also describes the Geographic Population Structure algorithm that successfully placed 83 percent of individuals from a worldwide selection into their country of origin.

53. Razib Khan, "How to Look at Population Structure," *Gene Expression*, October 3, 2016, gnxp.com.

54. Tang, Quertermous, Rodriguez et al. (2005).

55. Long, Li, and Healy (2009) conduct an analysis based on nucleotide diversity, defined as the number of differences per site between two copies of a locus, and gene diversity, defined as the probability that two randomly drawn copies of a locus differ in state (are different alleles). Using these variables, the authors concluded that "the clustering methods in popular use produce human population groups that have a simpler structure than even the TLIM.... This structure is clearly a weak description of the true human population structure, because it does not capture the complete nested arrangement of populations." (p. 33). This conclusion is surely true. Genetic diversity across African subpopulations as measured with these variables is greater than the genetic diversity among non-African populations, for the same reason that the genetic diversity of the East Asians left behind in the thought experiment is greater than the genetic diversity on the spaceship crew. Campbell and Tishkoff (2008). But that fact does not engage the clustering phenomenon that separates the populations in the cluster analyses (and would separate the populations in the spaceship thought experiment).

56. Bolnick (2008); Feldman and Lewontin (2008); Feldman (2010). How has Richard Lewontin himself responded to the cluster analyses? In 2006, twelve years after Bowcock, Ruiz-Linares, Tomfohrde et al. (1994) and four years after Rosenberg, Pritchard, Weber et al. (2002), the Social Science Research Council posted a web forum under the title *Is Race "Real"?* One of the contributors was Richard Lewontin. "A clustering of populations that does correspond to classical continental 'races' can be achieved," he wrote, "by using a special class of non-functional DNA, microsatellites. By selecting among microsatellites, it is possible to find a set that will cluster together African populations, European populations, and Asian populations, etc. These selected microsatellite DNA markers are not typical of genes, however, but have been chosen precisely because they are 'maximally informative' about group differences." Richard C. Lewontin, "Confusions About Human Races," *Is Race "Real"?*, June 7, 2006, raceandgenomics.ssrc.org.

Two years later, Lewontin coauthored a paper with Marcus Feldman (Feldman was first author), "Race, Ancestry, and Medicine." Feldman and Lewontin (2008). The paper includes a discussion of Rosenberg, Pritchard, Weber et al. (2002) and Rosenberg, Mahajan, Ramachandran et al. (2005), acknowledging the main results without dissent. But it does not back off from Lewontin's 1972 position. "The repeated and consistent results on the apportionment of genetic diversity reviewed in the previous section show that the genes underlying the phenotypic differences used to assign race categories are atypical of the genome in general and are not a reliable index to the amount of genetic differentiation between groups. Thus, racial assignment loses any general biological interest." Feldman and Lewontin (2008): 96. The article was written before the Li or Xing studies using hundreds of thousands of SNPs as the basis for the cluster analyses.

57. Bolnick (2008).

58. Rosenberg, Pritchard, Weber et al. (2002): 2382.

59. Serre and Pääbo (2004).

60. Rosenberg, Mahajan, Ramachandran et al. (2005): 660.

61. Novembre and DiRienzo (2009).

62. For an extended back-and-forth on this issue see Shiao, Bode, Beyer et al. (2012), which proposed an integration of clines with clusters as "clinal classes," and the subsequent special issue of *Sociological Theory*, 32 (3), 2014, "A Symposium on 'The Genomic Challenge to the Social Construction of Race.'"

8: *Evolution Since Humans Left Africa*

1. Escaramís, Docampo, and Rabionet (2015).

2. Besenbacher, Sulem, Helgason et al. (2016).

3. Kimura (1983).

4. Geneticists distinguish between absolute fitness (in an individual, defined as the number of offspring left behind) and relative fitness (the ratio of the number of one's offspring to the number produced by another).

5. Haldane (1927).

6. Darwin (1859): 127. Available at darwin-online.org.uk.

7. Hardyck and Petrinovich (1977).

8. Kodric-Brown and Brown (1987) summarize the long scholarly effort to understand why sex exists at all, given its evolutionary costs, and why gametes of different size are so universal across diploid organisms. Since then, progress has been made on many outstanding issues. See Parker (2014) and Sharp and Otto (2016).

9. In one of the rare exceptions, the big-belly seahorse, the female deposits fertilized eggs in the male's pouch. And that is accompanied by another rare exception: For that variety of seahorse, it's the female who mates promiscuously and the male who is choosy. Geary (2010): chapter 3.

10. Geary (2010): chapter 3.

11. Author's analysis, 2010–14 aggregated American Community Survey.

12. For more on this, see Cochran and Harpending (2009): 42–44.

13. Anderson and Stebbins (1954), elaborated in Arnold (1997).

14. 1000 Genomes Project Consortium (2012). The following descriptions of the samples are taken from the website of the Coriell Institute for Medical Research, which is a repository for the 1000 Genomes population samples. Retrieved from coriell.org/1/NHGRI/Collections /1000-Genomes-Collections. The sample sizes (the number of genomes used in Phase 1 of the 1000 Genomes database) are taken from Moore, Wallace, Wolfe et al. (2013): Table 1. The final sample sizes in Phase 3 were somewhat larger, and are given in Oleksyk, Brukhin, and O'Brien (2015).

The populations in Phase 1 that I used for the analyses were as follow:

Luhya in Kenya (LWK): From Webuye Division of Bungoma district in western Kenya, who identified themselves as having four Luhya grandparents. Sample: 97.

Yoruba in Nigeria (YRI): From one community in Ibadan, Nigeria, who identified themselves as having four Yoruba grandparents. Sample: 88.

African Ancestry in USA (ASW): From the American Southwest, who self-identified as primarily African American and had four African American grandparents. Sample: 61.

Han Chinese in Beijing, China (CHB): From persons living in the residential community at Beijing Normal University (who came from many different parts of China). Sample: 97.

Han Chinese South (CHS): From Hunan and Fujian provinces, who identified themselves as having at least three out of four Han Chinese grandparents. Sample: 100.

Japanese in Tokyo, Japan (JPT): From the Tokyo metropolitan area. "Because it is considered culturally insensitive in Japan to inquire specifically about a person's ancestral origins, prospective donors were simply told that the general aim was to include samples from people whose grandparents were all from Japan." Sample: 89.

Tuscans in Italy (TSI): From a small town near Florence, who identified themselves as having at least three out of four Tuscan grandparents. Sample: 98.

British from England and Scotland (GBR): From Cornwall and Kent (England), Argyll and Bute (a unitary authority council area in western Scotland), and Orkney, all of whom identified themselves as having all four of their grandparents born in the same rural area. Sample: 89.

Finnish in Finland (FIN): From throughout Finland, who identified themselves as having at least three out of four grandparents born in Finland (98 percent had all four). Sample: 93.

Northern and Western Europeans in Utah, USA: This sample is not described at the Coriell Institute website. They are described on the 1000 Genomes website as being of Northern and Western European extraction. Sample: 85.

The three subpopulations from the Americas are omitted. As stated explicitly in the sample recruitment descriptions at the Coriell Institute website, these samples were not selected for Amerindian ancestry. They are representative of the populations of Puerto Rico and Colombia, and of Americans of Mexican parentage in Los Angeles, which in turn comprise a diverse mix of European and Amerindian subpopulations. I also omitted the Iberian sample from the European subpopulations because of its small sample size (14) in Phase 1.

15. Sabeti, Schaffner, Fry et al. (2006): 1614.
16. Hawks, Wang, and Cochran (2007): 3 of 5. For an elaboration of these issues by two of the coauthors, see Cochran and Harpending (2009): chapter 4.
17. With important contributions from Rosalind Franklin. See Sayre (2000).
18. I owe the analogy with Newton's first law to Avise (2014): chapter 11.
19. Fisher (1918).
20. Akey (2009).
21. Sabeti, Schaffner, Fry et al. (2006).
22. Dick, Agrawal, Keller et al. (2015).
23. Akey (2009).
24. Plomin, McClearn, Smith et al. (1994); Plomin and Spinath (2004).
25. Risch and Merikangas (1996).
26. See Clarke, Anderson, Pettersson et al. (2011) for a step-by-step description of the analytic protocol.
27. Risch and Merikangas (1996).
28. Jannot, Ehret, and Perneger (2015).
29. Hermisson and Pennings (2005): 2335.
30. Kimura (1968); King and Jukes (1969); Kimura (1983).
31. E.g., Hermisson and Pennings (2005): Fig. 2.
32. Coop, Pickrell, Novembre et al. (2009).
33. This account is taken from Trut (1999).
34. Kettlewell (1955); Kettlewell (1956).
35. Weiner (1994). For a full list of examples of rapid evolution in nonhuman animals, see Winegard, Winegard, and Boutwell (2017): Table 1.
36. Hedges (2000).
37. The wording of the sentence is adapted from Schrider and Kern (2017).
38. Delwiche (2004).
39. Cochran and Harpending (2009).
40. Sabeti, Schaffner, Fry et al. (2006).
41. E.g., Schrider and Kern (2017); Field, Boyle, Telis et al. (2016).
42. E.g., the Singleton Density Score for timing and the Composite of Multiple Signals (CMS) for identifying specific areas within regions. Field, Boyle, Telis et al. (2016); Grossman, Andersen, Shlyakhter et al. (2013).
43. Mardis (2008).
44. Ewen Callaway, "First Draft of Neanderthal Genome Is Unveiled," *New Scientist*, February 12, 2009.
45. Olalde and Lalueza-Fox (2015).
46. Akey (2009).
47. "The criteria [for inclusion] were that the study was performed in the HapMap or Perlegen data, lists of all loci deemed as outliers were available as supplemental data, and sufficient information provided information about what genome build was used for the reported map positions." Akey (2009): 714.
48. Akey (2009): 717.
49. *HGDP* refers to the Human Genome Diversity Project and *CEPH* refers to the Centre d'Étude du Polymorphisme Humain.
50. Grossman, Andersen, Shlyakhter et al. (2013).
51. Field, Boyle, Telis et al. (2016).

52. Schrider and Kern (2017).

53. McCoy and Akey (2017): 142.

54. Haasle and Payseur (2016): Table 1.

55. *Purifying selection* refers to the selective removal of deleterious alleles. *Background selection* refers to removal of nondeleterious alleles that are linked to alleles that are removed by purifying selection.

56. Key, Fu, Romagné et al. (2016): 8.

57. The literature on methods of identifying SNPs and regions under recent selection pressure is extensive. Recent articles that also contain excellent literature reviews and bibliographies are Alcala and Rosenberg (2016) and Haasle and Payseur (2016).

58. Fossil evidence of another hominin living outside Africa, *Homo floresiensis*, was discovered on the Indonesian island of Flores in 2003. The evidence that *Homo floresiensis* is a separate species in genus *Homo* has accumulated since then, but doubts remain. Perhaps other, still undiscovered species of hominins existed outside Africa. See Detroit, Mijares, Corny et al. (2019).

59. Callaway (2016).

60. Stewart and Stringer (2012). Neanderthal alleles may have increased the risk for certain diseases. It also seems possible that interbreeding with Neanderthals may have reduced human male fertility. Sankararaman, Mallick, Dannemann et al. (2014).

61. Dannemann, Prüfer, and Kelso (2017): 1 of 11.

62. Jensen, Payseur, Stephan et al. (2018).

63. Kern and Hahn (2018): 1366.

64. Voight, Kudaravalli, Wen et al. (2006).

65. "In principle, sharing of signals between populations might also be due to haplotypes that are inherited from the ancestral populations. However, this is probably a small effect since such unusually long haplotypes would be unlikely to survive the effects of recombination for >1,000 generations, separately in each population. Instead, the data suggest that most of the selective events that we detect are local to a single population, but that a significant fraction of the selective events are experienced by more than one population." Voight, Kudaravalli, Wen et al. (2006): 452.

66. Voight, Kudaravalli, Wen et al. (2006): 451.

67. Akey (2009): 716. See also Ronald and Akey (2005).

68. Herráez, Bauchet, Tang et al. (2009): Table S2.

69. Herráez, Bauchet, Tang et al. (2009): Table S1.

70. Also in 2009, a team comprised primarily of Stanford geneticists analyzed the same database as Herráez, Bauchet, Tang et al. (2009) using still another method of identifying genetic regions subject to selection pressure. They found the same geographic pattern—moderate overlap among European, Middle Eastern, and South Asian populations; little overlap between those three regions and East Asia; and almost no overlap between African and non-African populations. Pickrell, Coop, Novembre et al. (2009).

71. For this figure, the unit of analysis was the population, and the cell entry was the proportion of genetic regions under selection shared by the two populations for that cell. For the visually similar figure in chapter 7, the unit of analysis was the individual and the cell entries were measures of genetic distance—Wright's fixation index, F_{ST}.

9: The Landscape of Ancestral Population Differences

1. Responsibility for the GWAS Catalog was subsequently shared with the European Bioinformatics Institute (EBI). The GWAS Catalog is downloadable free of charge at its website, ebi.ac.uk/gwas. The level of statistical significance required for entry in the GWAS Catalog is p <1.0×10^{-5}, which is more inclusive than the standard for statistical significance in the

published literature ($p < 1.0 \times 10^{-8}$). To be eligible for the database, the study must meet certain technical criteria and have been published in an English-language journal.

2. These numbers and those in the figure include all unique SNPs, excluding other kinds of variants in the GWAS Catalog.

3. Lander and Schork (1994), Thomas and Witte (2002).

4. Marchini, Cardon, Phillips et al. (2004): 516. See also Freedman, Reich, Penney et al. (2004).

5. Scutari, Mackay, and Balding (2016).

6. One of the first systematic evaluations of population stratification using polygenic scores (first author was Alicia Martin) calculated polygenic scores for eight well-studied phenotypes and concluded that polygenic scores based on a single-ancestry population have numerous problems. For example, polygenic scores based on a European sample predict that Africans are shorter than Europeans, which is not true except for a few pygmy populations. Polygenic scores for risk of schizophrenia show a lower score for Africans than for Europeans, whereas the actual incidence rates are similar. Alicia Martin (2017): 645.

Since the Martin study, Reisberg, Iljasenko, Läll et al. (2017) and Luo, Li, Wang et al. (2018) have found other traits that are differentially predicted for different populations. Kerminen, Martin, Koskela et al. (2018) and Berg, Harpak, Sinnott-Armstrong et al. (2018) have demonstrated such differences not just across continental populations but within subpopulations of Finns and British respectively.

Duncan, Shen, Gelaye et al. (2018), a systematic review of population differences in the predictiveness of polygenic scores, identified 29 studies that lent themselves to comparisons of a European population with another. Overall, the Duncan study found that the median effect size of polygenic scores was lower in non-European populations. Median effect sizes were 93 percent of that of a matched European sample for East Asians, 80 percent for South Asians, and 36 percent for Africans. The greater attenuation of predictive performance was "consistent with, on average, greater genetic distance between European and African ancestry populations, than between European and other ancestry populations." (6 of 21). The median effect sizes for the South Asian and African comparisons were consistently smaller than those for the matched European sample. Results for the European/East Asian comparison were intriguingly inconsistent: in six out of the thirteen studies, the median effect size was *larger* for the East Asians than for the matched European population (fig. 2).

7. Duncan, Shen, Gelaye et al. (2018): 9–10 of 21. Regarding bias in polygenic scoring methods, the authors wrote: "Specifically, linkage disequilibrium (LD) structure and variant frequency are captured imperfectly with current methods (including genotyping and imputation), and they vary across populations, and currently available data resources are unequally representative of diverse global populations."

8. Hannah Devlin, "Genetics Research 'Biased Towards Studying White Europeans,'" *Guardian*, October 8, 2018. Examples of earlier murmurings are Bustamante, Burchard, and De la Vega (2011); Lindsey Konkel, "The Racial Discrimination Embedded in Modern Medicine," *Newsweek*, October 20, 2015; and Denise Grady, "Genetic Tests for a Heart Disorder Mistakenly Find Blacks at Risk," *New York Times*, August 17, 2016.

9. Sirugo, Williams, and Tishkoff (2019): 30.

10. I used a random number generator to order the 962 SNPs and chose the first 500 contiguous pairs that produced correlations matching the correlations for the full sample of 962 to the second decimal place.

11. African: Nigerians, Kenyans, and African Americans. East Asian: Japanese and two samples of Chinese. European: British, Finns, Italians, and European Americans.

12. Author's analysis based on the GWAS Catalog as of May 2019.

13. The GWAS Catalog associates each SNP with a trait (the variable name is *diseasetrait*) based on the description of the trait in the journal article in question. The catalog uses the same

label for traits studied in different journal articles if the measure is exactly the same. If there is any meaningful difference, the labels differ as well. For example, three labels for risk-taking are "General risk tolerance," "Risk-taking tendency," and "Self-reported risk-taking behavior." Limiting the analysis of broad types of traits to studies that reported at least 100 unique SNPs under the same label in the GWAS Catalog served as a screen for recent studies (and therefore usually more sophisticated ones) with very large samples and required no judgment calls about whether two similar studies should be aggregated.

Major diseases (combined sample = 3,718). The diseases were atrial fibrillation, breast cancer, chronic lymphocytic leukemia, colorectal cancer, coronary artery disease, Crohn's disease, diisocyanate-induced asthma, diverticular disease, inflammatory bowel disease, lung cancer, multiple sclerosis, Parkinson's disease, prostate cancer, rheumatoid arthritis, systematic lupus erythematosus, type 2 diabetes, and ulcerative colitis.

Physiological biomarkers (combined sample = 5,298 unique SNPs). The traits were total cholesterol, total HDL cholesterol, LDL cholesterol, triglycerides, BMI, waist circumference adjusted for BMI, waist-to-hip ratio adjusted for BMI, diastolic blood pressure, systolic blood pressure, pulse pressure, intraocular pressure, hand grip strength, height, weight, total body bone mineral density, heel bone mineral density, and menarche (age at onset).

Blood parameters (combined sample = 4,415). Blood parameters were blood metabolite levels, eosinophil percentage of white cells, granulocyte percentage of myeloid white cells, hematocrit, hemoglobin concentration, mean corpuscular volume, mean corpuscular hemoglobin, mean platelet volume, monocyte count, monocyte percentage of white cells, myeloid white cell count, platelet count, platelet distribution width, plateletcrit, red blood cell count, and white blood cell count. This list does not exhaust all the blood parameters that are associated with at least 100 unique SNPs in the GWAS Catalog as of May 2019, but they are representative of the entire inventory.

Cognitive disorders (combined sample = 2,594). Cognitive disorders were autism spectrum disorder or schizophrenia, bipolar disorder, depression, depressive symptoms, major depressive disorder, neuroticism, schizophrenia, and "worry."

Mental abilities (combined sample = 5,715). Mental abilities were cognitive performance, educational attainment, general cognitive ability, highest math class taken, intelligence, and self-reported math ability.

Personality features (combined sample = 1,319). Personality features were adventurousness, alcohol consumption (drinks per week), general risk tolerance, risk-taking tolerance, life satisfaction, positive affect, subjective well-being, and well-being spectrum.

14. The choice of the particular traits used for this illustrative table doesn't make much difference. If all of the SNPs in the GWAS Catalog are used, 32 percent of the physiological traits and 34 percent of the cognitive traits have target allele differences that qualify as "large."

15. The following traits consisted of the SNPs under the same label in the GWAS Catalog: Adventurousness, Positive affect, Life satisfaction, and Schizophrenia. The other traits combined SNPs from more than one label in the GWAS Catalog. Those labels are as follow:

Cognitive ability: Cognitive performance, Cognitive performance (MTAG), Extremely high intelligence, General cognitive ability, Intelligence, Intelligence (MTAG).

Highest math course: Highest math class taken, Highest math class taken (MTAG).

Educational attainment: Educational attainment, Educational attainment (MTAG), Educational attainment (college completion), Educational attainment (years of education).

Self-reported math ability: Self-reported math ability, Self-reported math ability (MTAG).

Neurocognitive function: Cognitive function, Episodic memory, Information processing speed, Logical memory (delayed recall), Logical memory (delayed recall) in mild cognitive impairment, Logical memory (delayed recall) in normal cognition, Logical memory (immediate recall) in mild cognitive impairment, Logical memory (immediate recall) in normal cognition, Reading and spelling, Verbal declarative memory, Verbal memory, Verbal memory performance (immediate recall change), Verbal memory performance (immediate recall level), Verbal memory performance (residualized delayed recall change), Verbal memory performance (residualized delayed recall level), Visual memory, Word reading, Working memory.

Depression: Depressed affect, Depression, Depression (quantitative trait), Depressive symptoms, Depressive symptoms (MTAG), Depressive symptoms (SSRI exposure interaction), Depressive symptoms (stressful life events interaction), Major depressive disorder, Major depressive disorder (broad), Major depressive disorder (probable), Current major depressive disorder.

Neuroticism: Neuroticism, Neuroticism (MTAG).

Worry: Feeling worry, Worry, Worry too long after an embarrassing experience.

Risk tolerance: General risk tolerance (MTAG), Risk-taking tendency (4-domain principal component model).

Well-being: Eudaimonic well-being, Hedonic well-being, Subjective well-being, Subjective well-being (MTAG), Well-being spectrum (multivariate analysis).

Autism: Autism, Autism spectrum disorder, Obsessive-compulsive disorder or autistic spectrum disorder, Social autistic-like traits.

ADHD: Attention function, Attention function in attention deficit hyperactive disorder, Attention deficit hyperactivity disorder, Attention deficit hyperactivity disorder (combined symptoms), Attention deficit hyperactivity disorder (hyperactivity-impulsivity symptoms), Attention deficit hyperactivity disorder (inattention symptoms), Attention deficit hyperactivity disorder (time to onset), Attention deficit hyperactivity disorder and conduct disorder, Attention deficit hyperactivity disorder motor coordination, Attention deficit hyperactivity disorder symptom score, Attention deficit hyperactivity disorder (maternal expressed emotions interaction).

Bipolar disorder: Binge-eating behavior and bipolar disorder, Binge-eating behavior in bipolar disorder, Bipolar I disorder, Bipolar disorder, Bipolar disorder (age of onset <21) or attention deficit hyperactivity disorder, Bipolar disorder (early onset), Bipolar disorder (mania), Bipolar disorder and eating disorder, Bipolar disorder and schizophrenia, Bipolar disorder or attention deficit hyperactivity disorder, Bipolar disorder with mood-incongruent psychosis, Eating disorder in bipolar disorder.

Conduct disorder: Aggressiveness in attention deficit hyperactivity disorder, Anger, Behavioral disinhibition (generation interaction), Callous-unemotional behavior, Childhood and early adolescence aggressive behavior, Conduct disorder, Conduct disorder (maternal expressed emotions interaction), Conduct disorder (symptom count), Early childhood aggressive behavior, Middle childhood and early adolescence aggressive behavior, Non-substance related behavioral disinhibition, Oppositional defiant disorder dimensions in attention-deficity hyperactivity disorder.

Alcohol consumption: Alcohol consumption, Alcohol consumption (drinkers vs non-drinkers), Alcohol consumption (drinks per week), Alcohol consumption (heavy vs. light/non-drinkers), Alcohol consumption (transferrin glycosylation), Alcohol consumption in current drinkers, Alcohol consumption over the past year.

Alcohol dependence: Alcohol dependence, Alcohol dependence (age at onset), Alcohol dependence or chronic alcoholic pancreatitis or alcohol-related liver cirrhosis, Alcohol dependence symptom count, Alcohol use disorder (consumption score), Alcohol use disorder (dependence and problematic use scores), Alcohol use disorder (total score), Alcoholism (12-month weekly alcohol consumption score), Alcoholism (alcohol dependence factor score), Alcoholism (alcohol use disorder factor score), Alcoholism (heaviness of drinking).

Brain volumes: Brain connectivity, Brain structure, Brain structure (hippocampal volume), Brain structure (temporal lobe volume), Brain volume in infants (cerebrospinal fluid), Brain volume in infants (gray matter), Brain volume in infants (intracranial brain volume),

Brain volume in infants (white matter), Cortical thickness, Dentate gyrus granule cell layer volume, Dentate gyrus molecular layer volume, Heschl's gyrus morphology, Hippocampal atrophy, Hippocampal fissure volume, Hippocampal sclerosis, Hippocampal subfield CA1 volume, Hippocampal subfield CA1 volume (corrected for total hippocampal volume), Hippocampal subfield CA3 volume, Hippocampal subfield CA4 volume, Hippocampal tail volume, Hippocampal tail volume (corrected for total hippocampal volume), Hippocampal volume, Hippocampal volume in mild cognitive impairment, Hippocampal volume in normal cognition, Intracranial volume, Maximum cranial length, Maximum cranial width, Mesial temporal lobe epilepsy with hippocampal sclerosis, Presubiculum volume (corrected for total hippocampal volume), Subcortical brain region volumes, Subiculum volume (corrected for total hippocampal volume), Superior frontal gyrus gray matter volume, Total hippocampal volume.

Cerebrospinal fluid: Cerebrospinal AB1-42 levels in mild cognitive impairment, Cerebrospinal AB1-42 levels in normal cognition, Cerebrospinal p-tau181p levels, Cerebrospinal t-tau levels, Cerebrospinal fluid AB1-42 levels, Cerebrospinal fluid beta-site APP cleaving enzyme levels, Cerebrospinal fluid biomarker levels, Cerebrospinal fluid levels of Alzheimer's disease–related proteins, Cerebrospinal fluid p-tau181p:AB1-42 ratio, Cerebrospinal fluid p-tau levels, Cerebrospinal fluid p-tau levels in mild cognitive impairment, Cerebrospinal fluid p-tau levels in normal cognition, Cerebrospinal fluid t-tau levels, Cerebrospinal fluid t-tau levels in mild cognitive impairment, Cerebrospinal fluid t-tau levels in normal cognition, Cerebrospinal fluid t-tau:AB1-42 ratio, Cerebrospinal fluid Î±-synuclein levels.

16. Novembre and Barton (2018). For an example of the development of a new method for identifying natural selection, its application to natural selection for height, and the problems introduced by population stratification, see the sequence of Berg and Coop (2014), Berg, Zhang, and Coop (2017), Sohail, Maier, Ganna et al. (2018), and Berg, Harpak, Sinnott-Armstrong et al. (2018).

17. Marth, Yu, Indap et al. (2011).

18. Telenti, Pierce, Biggs et al. (2016): 1, 5 of 6.

19. Examples of reviews of techniques and findings are Auer and Lettre (2015) and Bomba, Walter et al. (2017). Examples of studies finding a significant contribution of rare variants are Gilly, Suveges, Kuchenbaecker et al. (2018), Mancuso, Rohland, Rand et al. (2015), Fournier, Abou Saada, Hou et al. (2019), and Wainschtein, Jain, Yengo et al. (2019).

20. Gravel, Henn, Gutenkunst et al. (2011), Marth, Yu, Indap et al. (2011).

21. A few examples: Moore, Wallace, Wolfe et al. (2013) studied low-frequency (.005 to .030) SNPs and found that high proportions of bins of SNPs from DNA regions that showed indications of natural selection were significantly different across continental populations. There was also a clear ordering: Asia and Europe had the fewest significantly different bins (51 percent), compared to Africa and Europe (81 percent) and Africa and Asia (83 percent). Marth, Yu, Indap et al. (2011) studied rare variants (frequency less than .01) using the 1000 Genomes Exon Pilot database and found that "coding variants below 1 percent allele frequency show increased population-specificity and are enriched for functional variants."

22. *Lactase persistence* (LP). Human infants everywhere have always been able to digest the milk sugar lactose, but for tens of thousands of years after humans left Africa that ability universally faded after weaning. The advent of cattle and goat domestication led to strong selection pressure for the ability to drink milk. A variety of explanations for the increase in fitness have been advanced (Gerbault, Liebert, Itan et al. 2011). The simple food value of milk, which provides protein, micronutrients, calcium, and carbohydrates, was surely a factor, but there are other ways in which LP might have had survival value. When crops failed, the availability of milk would have been of great survival value for adults who were lactose persistent and would have increased the mortality rate of those who tried to drink it but were not lactose

persistent (by inducing dehydration through diarrhea). Because milk contains vitamin D and calcium, LP might have been especially valuable at northern latitudes where sunlight was comparatively scarce. However the benefits combined, lactose persistence spread rapidly after mutations fostering it appeared. In Eurasia, LP began to occur around 9,000 years ago and spread throughout Europe during the last 4,000 years. In Africa, LP also occurred among East African tribes that domesticated cattle around 5,000 years ago, but through a distinctive genetic route (Fan, Hansen, Lo et al. 2016). Field, Boyle, Telis et al. (2016) found strong evidence that selection pressure in Europeans has persisted into the last 2,000 years.

Sickle cell anemia. I mentioned the discovery of the genetic cause of susceptibility to sickle cell anemia in the discussion of candidate genes in chapter 8. It is an example of a gene variant that confers what is called a "heterozygote advantage": Having one copy of an allele is a good thing (protecting against a common form of malaria); having two copies carries the good thing but also carries a bad thing (susceptibility to sickle cell anemia). If the proportion of people who carry just one copy of the target allele is enough larger than the proportion who carry two copies and/or the fitness advantage of carrying the allele is enough larger than the fitness disadvantage of carrying two copies of it, then a harmful allele under some circumstances can nonetheless spread in frequency among a population through natural selection. The net effect is that the allele is fitness enhancing.

23. Darwin thought that light skin was a result of sexual selection. Narasimhan, Rahbari, Scally et al. (2016). But instead the primary cause seems to have been that intense sunlight is damaging to some essential nutrients, especially folate, which is necessary for DNA synthesis and repair. Folate deficiency has a variety of other bad effects—complications during pregnancy and fetal abnormalities including spina bifida, and damage to spermatogenesis. Parra (2007). All of these effects of high UVR exposure have direct effects on reproductive fitness. The humans who left Africa had dark skin because they had evolved to have a high level of melanin, an enzyme that acts as a photoprotective layer, filtering UVR—what commercial sunblocks now do. Jablonsky and Chaplin (2010). Among other things, Parra (2007) had argued that a high level of exposure to ultraviolet radiation (UVR) led directly to all the harmful effects association with sunburn, including (besides pain) edema, disruption of thermoregulation, and increased risk of infection. It also causes skin cancer. But it now appears that none of those had a significant effect on reproductive fitness. Jablonsky and Chaplin (2010). So why did skin eventually lighten among all of the African emigrants who moved north? It's not as obvious as saying "They didn't need dark skin anymore." Nor does skin naturally get lighter across generations in the absence of intense sunlight. The main reason that light skin was advantageous in high latitudes appears to have been that UVR is essential for the synthesis of vitamin D in the skin, and lighter skin allows greater absorption of UVR. Vitamin D deficiency is implicated in rickets in children and softening of the bones in adults, and impedes other recently discovered functions involving immunoregulation and regulation of cell differentiation and proliferation.

Along with skin lightening, populations in Europe also evolved a capacity for tanning. To make things still more complicated, it has been genetically verified that at least three independent evolutionary lines for lightening were taken. The three lines all involved different genetic and physiological mechanisms. Jablonsky and Chaplin (2010). Positive selection for skin color within western Eurasia has continued into the last 5,000 years. Wilde, Timpson, Kirsanow et al. (2013).

24. Brinkworth and Barreiro (2014): 69.
25. Brinkworth and Barreiro (2014): 69.
26. Nédélec, Sanz, Baharian et al. (2016): 666.
27. Yin, Low, Wang et al. (2015): 5 of 11.
28. Yin, Low, Wang et al. (2015): 1 of 11.

29. Bigham (2016).
30. Bigham (2016): 9.
31. Huerta-Sanchez, Jin, Asan et al. (2014).
32. Rivas, Avila, Koskela et al. (2018).
33. Cochran and Harpending (2009): 213–14.
34. Cochran and Harpending (2009): 217. Their hypothesis is that natural selection occurred "because of the unique natural-selection pressures the members of this group faced in their role as financiers in the European Middle Ages." Their proposition is that the fitness-reducing effects of the harmful diseases were more than counterbalanced by their fitness-increasing effects on cognitive ability. It is a provocative hypothesis, but whether it is true is not the point for this discussion.
35. Lachance, Berens, Hansen et al. (2018): 16.
36. Guo, Wu, Zhu et al. (2018): 1 of 9.
37. Takeuchi, Akiyama, Matoba et al. (2018): 6 of 15.
38. Takeuchi, Akiyama, Matoba et al. (2018): 7 of 15.
39. Fumagalli, Moltke, Grarup et al. (2015).
40. Fan, Hansen et al. (2016).
41. Historical and contemporary statistics and sources on commission of homicide by sex are available at ourworldindata.org/homicides.
42. That unyielding insistence is what led geneticist David Reich to write in the pages of the *New York Times*, "It is important, even urgent, that we develop a candid and scientifically up-to-date way of discussing any such differences, instead of sticking our heads in the sand and being caught unprepared when they are found." David Reich, "How Genetics Is Changing Our Understanding of 'Race'," *New York Times*, March 23, 2018.

Part III: "Class Is a Function of Privilege"

1. Herrnstein and Murray (1994).
2. Crenshaw (1989): 140.
3. Andersen and Collins (2019): 4.
4. If you believe that adjusting for IQ is meaningless because racism completely accounts for the observed black/white (B/W) difference in IQ, then let's walk through the logic step by step.

    An initial implication would seem to be that the mean black IQ will be close to the same as the white mean in societies where blacks have been the ruling population for several decades—most sub-Saharan African countries and Haiti. That doesn't work, because the observed means for black IQ in those countries are uniformly lower than the mean of blacks in the United States. Wicherts, Dolan, and van der Maas (2010).

    If your reaction is that these results reflect poor educational systems in Africa and Haiti (in part, they certainly do) and the legacy of colonial racism, then the next step in defending your position that adjusting for IQ is meaningless is to think about why racism would affect IQ. The most obvious answer is through socioeconomic status—racism accounts for disproportionate black poverty and underrepresentation in high-prestige jobs, which in turn deleteriously affects the environments in which black children grow up and thereby their IQs.

    To test that proposition, the B/W difference needs to be examined after adjusting for parental SES. This has been done frequently. The technical literature consistently shows that doing so diminishes the size of the B/W difference by about a third. I could leave it at that (two-thirds of the difference is *not* explained by parental SES), but it is also important to note that in most studies the size of the B/W difference expressed in standard deviations increases as parental SES rises. These statements are documented in *The Bell Curve*. Herrnstein and

Murray (1994): 286–88. Given that I was a coauthor, it may be useful to draw on an independent and authoritative source.

In the wake of the controversy over *The Bell Curve*, the American Psychological Association assembled a Task Force on Intelligence consisting of 11 of the most distinguished psychometricians in the United States, chaired by Ulric Neisser. Their report, titled "Intelligence: Knowns and Unknowns," was published in the February 1996 issue of the APA's flagship journal, *American Psychologist*. It was a consensus statement with no minority dissents. In the interests of concision, I am going to quote from the report when nothing needs to be added that has emerged since it was prepared. I have omitted references embedded in the report's text. The reference for the following quotes is Neisser, Boodoo, Bouchard et al. (1996).

Regarding SES as an explanation of the B/W difference:

> Several considerations suggest that this cannot be the whole explanation. For one thing, the Black/White differential in test scores is not eliminated when groups or individuals are matched for SES. Moreover, the data reviewed in Section 4 suggest that if we exclude extreme conditions, nutrition and other biological factors that may vary with SES account for relatively little of the variance in such scores. Finally, the (relatively weak) relationship between test scores and income is much more complex than a simple SES hypothesis would suggest. The living conditions of children result in part from the accomplishments of their parents: If the skills measured by psychometric tests actually matter for those accomplishments, intelligence is affecting SES rather than the other way around. We do not know the magnitude of these various effects in various populations, but it is clear that no model in which "SES" directly determines "IQ" will do. (Neisser, Boodoo, Bouchard et al. (1996): 94).

Another obvious way to discount the value of adjusting for IQ is that the tests are biased against blacks. This is the Task Force's statement regarding cultural bias because of language:

> The language of testing is a standard form of English with which some Blacks may not be familiar; specific vocabulary items are often unfamiliar to Black children; the tests are often given by White examiners rather than by more familiar Black teachers; African Americans may not be motivated to work hard on tests that so clearly reflect White values; the time demands of some tests may be alien to Black culture. (Similar suggestions have been made in connection with the test performance of Hispanic Americans.) Many of these suggestions are plausible, and such mechanisms may play a role in particular cases. Controlled studies have shown, however, that none of them contributes substantially to the Black/White differential under discussion here. Moreover, efforts to devise reliable and valid tests that would minimize disadvantages of this kind have been unsuccessful. (Neisser, Boodoo, Bouchard et al. (1996): 93–94).

With regard to cultural bias in predictive validity, the Task Force wrote:

> From an educational point of view, the chief function of mental tests is as predictors.... Intelligence tests predict school performance fairly well, at least in American schools as they are now constituted. Similarly, achievement tests are fairly good predictors of performance in college and postgraduate settings. Considered in this light, the relevant question is whether the tests have a "predictive bias" against Blacks. Such a bias would exist if African American performance on the criterion variables (school achievement, college GPA, etc.) were systematically higher than the same subjects' test scores would predict. This is not the case. The actual regression lines (which show the mean criterion performance for individuals who got various scores on the predictor) for Blacks do not lie above those for Whites; there is even a slight tendency in the other direction. Considered as predictors of

future performance, the tests do not seem to be biased against African Americans. (Neisser, Boodoo, Bouchard et al. (1996): 93).

Postdating the Task Force's report, Fagan and Holland (2007) presented experimental evidence that score differences between black and white students were effectively eliminated when they were tested on the basis of newly learned information, and argued that the black/white difference was the result of differences in specific previous knowledge, which in turn reflected test bias. A similar strategy was also used in the Siena Reasoning Test. Goldstein (2008); Scherbaum, Hanges, Yusko et al. (2012). The problem with such tests is that answering these kinds of questions relies in part on short-term memory, a much less g-loaded cognitive skill than those captured by other test batteries. Michael McDaniel analyzed the Siena Reasoning Test data (he did not have access to the data necessary to analyze the Fagan test) and found that the "findings are consistent with the inference that the reported lower mean racial differences in the Siena Reasoning Test are due to its lower g saturation relative to other g tests. If this inference is correct, one could also infer that the apparent lower g saturation of the Siena Reasoning Test would be associated with lower validity and larger prediction errors." McDaniel and Kepes (2014): 339. In a 2018 presentation to the Personnel Testing Council of Metropolitan Washington based on his research conducted for the U.S. Army to evaluate alternative g tests, McDaniel summarized "Ways to build a g test with low mean group differences" as "1. Use easy items in the test. 2. Use items with low g saturation in the test. 3. Reduce the reliability of the test so it measures g less well." McDaniel (2018): 7.

Suppose you posit a broader role for bias, one that cannot be captured by assessments of language and predictive validity. Call it the "background radiation" theory of racism's effect on IQ. This position holds that the United States is so steeped in the conditions that produce the B/W difference that it affects every performance measure, not just IQ scores. If this position is true, it is useless to look for evidence of test bias. We have no criterion measure that is independent of this culture and its history. The bias pervades everything.

If you take that position, I can't argue you out of it with data. None can conceivably exist. But you should understand the implications of that position. The background radiation hypothesis implies that the performance yardsticks in our society are not only biased but so similar in the degree to which they distort the truth—in every type of educational institution from kindergarten through graduate school, at every level of every occupation, for every performance measure—that no differential distortion is picked up by the data. Is this plausible? Everyday experience suggests that the environment confronting blacks in different sectors of American life is not uniformly hostile. Assuming that the background radiation hypothesis is true represents a considerably longer leap of faith than the limited assumption that racism is still a factor in American life.

5. Source: the Census Bureau's 2018 Annual Social and Economic Supplement of the Current Population Survey, hereafter referred to as CPS-2018. The data were downloaded from cps .ipums.org. The numbers for sex differences in educational attainment refer to persons ages 25–54 after applying the CPS sample weights. The means for highest grade completed in 2018 were 14.5 for women and 14.1 for men. Women have had a higher mean every year from 1997 through 2018. The means for the percentages of persons with college degrees in 2018 were 41.0 percent for women and 35.7 percent for men. Women have had a higher percentage than men every year from 2003 through 2018.

The sources for analyses that control for IQ are the 1979 and 1997 cohorts of the National Longitudinal Survey of Youth, hereafter referred to as NLSY79 and NLSY97. The surveys are sponsored by the Bureau of Labor Statistics of the U.S. Department of Labor. Data were downloaded from the NLS Investigator (nlsinfo.org/investigator/pages/search.jsp). They represent two of the handful of large American datasets that have a full-scale measure of cognitive ability and a long follow-up period, combined with detailed data on education, marital status, fertility, income, and labor market experience. The application of sample weights permits nationally representative estimates.

The measure of cognitive ability is the score on the Armed Forces Qualification Test (AFQT). For a detailed description of the NLSY79, see Herrnstein and Murray (1994): Appendix 2. For a detailed discussion of technical issues regarding the AFQT as a measure of IQ, see Herrnstein and Murray (1994): Appendix 3. The short story is that the AFQT is one of the most highly *g*-loaded paper-and-pencil tests. By way of comparison, the median factor *g*-loading for the subtests of the AFQT is .85, compared to a median of .69 for the subtests of the most widely used IQ test for adults, the Wechsler Adult Intelligence Scale (WAIS). The first factor, *g*, accounts for over 70 percent of the variance in the AFQT compared to 53 percent in the WAIS. Herrnstein and Murray (1994): 607. AFQT scores were normalized by year of age at testing and converted to the IQ metric, with a range of 55–145. They are hereafter referred to as IQ scores.

The analyses adjusting for IQ are ordinary least squares regressions for years of education and earned income, and logit analyses for the probability of getting a college degree. All of the analyses were replicated with and without interaction terms. Few of the interaction terms even approached statistical significance, and the fitted values for the analyses including interaction terms were extremely close to the fitted values for those that were restricted to main effects. I therefore report the analyses based on main effects.

To facilitate comparisons of the results for the two NLSY cohorts, I limited the samples to comparable age ranges at the date of the follow-up I report. At the date of the most recent interview for the NLSY97 in 2015, 99 percent of the cohort were ages 30–35, with a small number (69) who were 36. The sample for analysis was limited to ages 30–35. I selected 1994 as the follow-up survey for the NLSY79 cohort and limited the analysis for both cohorts to those who were ages 30–35 on the date of the interview (the NLSY79 cohort was chosen from a wider range of birth years, 1957–64, than the NLSY97 cohort, who were born from 1980 to 1984). Income figures for both cohorts were converted to 2018 dollars.

The table below shows results for years of education and percentage of persons with a college degree for both of the NLSY cohorts. For both indicators, the dependent variable was regressed on IQ and a binary variable denoting sex. The first table shows the fitted values for years of education when IQ is set to 80, 100, and 120, which correspond approximately to the 10th, 50th, and 90th percentiles of IQ in a normal distribution.

	Years of education			
	NLSY79		NLSY97	
IQ	Men	Women	Men	Women
80	11.4	11.7	11.6	12.3
100	13.3	13.6	13.9	14.6
120	15.3	15.5	16.1	16.8

Females had higher values for years of education than males for every IQ category in both NLSY samples. Consistent with the story for sex differences in educational attainment in chapter 4, the female advantage in fitted values for years of education is greater for the NLSY97, whose members were born in 1980–84, than for the NLSY79, whose members were born in 1957–64.

The next table shows the results for achievement of a college degree. Since college degrees are rare among people with measured IQs of less than 100, I show the results for fitted values of IQ set to 100, 110, and 120.

	College degree			
	NLSY79		NLSY97	
IQ	Men	Women	Men	Women
100	15%	19%	24%	35%
110	35%	42%	44%	57%
120	61%	68%	66%	77%

Women had an advantage for all three fitted values in both cohorts. As in the case of years of education, the female advantage increased from the NLSY79 cohort to the NLSY97 cohort.

6. Since 2003, the Census Bureau has used a set of options for self-identified ethnicity that permits combinations of two or three ethnicities. The numbers that follow are based on those who self-identified as white only, black only, or Asian only, and also reported that they were not Latino. The Latino number is based on all those who self-identified with a specific Latino population (e.g., Puerto Rican, Cuban, Chicano, Mexican American), regardless of their self-identified race. Mean years of education for 2018 are shown below:

	CPS 2018	
	Years of education	College degree
White	14.8	44.1%
Black	14.1	28.3%
Latino	12.6	19.4%
Asian	15.4	64.6%
Other	14.2	28.8%

Source: CPS 2018, for persons 25–54.

Before adjusting for IQ, Asians have advantages in both years of education and the percentage with college degrees.

7. The table below shows IQ by ethnicity for the two cohorts of the NLSY and, to demonstrate how typical these results are, ethnic means for the three standardizations of the WAIS over the last 40 years. Asians are not reported for NLSY79 because that survey was limited to whites, blacks, and Latinos. The ethnic designations for NLSY79 use the Sample ID variable (variable no. R0173600). The ethnic designations for NLSY97 combine information from the Key!Race and Key!Race_Ethnicity variables (nos. R538700 and R1482600) and follow the pattern for the CPS: non-Latino whites, blacks, and Asians; and Latinos of any self-identified race.

	Mean IQ by ethnicity			
	White	Black	Latino	Asian
NLSY (1979)	103.1	86.7	90.5	
NLSY (1997)	103.2	89.6	94.0	105.9
WAIS-R (1981)	101.4	86.9		
WAIS-III (1995)	101.4	86.8		
WAIS-IV (2008)	103.2	88.7	91.6	106.1

Sources: Reynolds, Chastain, Kaufman et al. (1987): Table 1; Dickens and Flynn (2006): Supplemental data provided by the authors.

The table below shows the results, expressed in years of education, when the number of years of education is regressed on IQ and ethnicity. The sample was limited to persons whose age at the most recent measure of years of education was 30 or above.

	Years of education						
	NLSY79			NLSY97			
IQ	White	Black	Latino	White	Black	Latino	Asian
80	11.0	12.0	11.2	11.7	12.3	11.8	12.9
100	13.2	14.2	13.4	14.0	14.6	14.2	15.2
120	15.4	16.4	15.6	16.4	17.0	16.5	17.6

For the NLSY79, blacks had an advantage of 1.1 years of education over whites after adjusting for IQ, and Latinos had an advantage of 0.2 years over whites. For the NLSY97, the black advantage was 0.6 years of education and the Latino advantage was 0.1 years.

The next table shows the results of a logit regression of achievement of a college degree (yes or no) on the same independent variables. The table shows the percentages of each group obtaining a college degree. The fitted values of IQ shown in the table are 100, 110, and 120, corresponding approximately to the 50th, 75th, and 90th percentiles.

	College degree						
	NLSY79			NLSY97			
IQ	White	Black	Latino	White	Black	Latino	Asian
100	15%	26%	13%	28%	34%	26%	54%
110	36%	53%	33%	49%	56%	47%	75%
120	65%	78%	61%	71%	76%	69%	88%

Blacks got more college degrees than whites in both of the NLSY cohorts for comparable IQs. So did Asians in the NLSY97. Latinos and whites with comparable IQs have close to the same percentage of college graduates in both NLSY cohorts, with a slight advantage for whites.

8. The indispensable source for understanding the nature of the remaining male-female income disparities is Goldin (2014). I limit this presentation to the basics provided by the CPS and the NLSY. The table below shows median earned income (combined wages or salary, income from business, income from farm) from the 2018 CPS for men and women ages 25–54 with various combinations of marital status, children in the home, and labor force status. The results use the CPS sample weights for persons.

	CPS 2018		
	Median earned income (000s)		Female-male ratio
	Men	Women	
Married with at least one child in the house	$60	$38	63%
Married, child, worked 52 weeks	$63	$43	68%
Married, child, worked 52 40-hr. weeks	$60	$45	75%
Married, no child in the house	$52	$40	77%
Married, no child, worked 52 weeks	$56	$45	80%

	CPS 2018		
	Median earned income (000s)		Female-male ratio
	Men	Women	
Married, no child, worked 52 40-hr. weeks	$55	$45	82%
Single with at least one child in the house	$40	$29	73%
Single, child, worked 52 weeks	$42	$33	79%
Single, child, worked 52 40-hr. weeks	$42	$35	83%
Single, no child in the house	$38	$35	92%
Single, no child, worked 52 weeks	$42	$40	95%
Single, no child, worked 52 40-hr. weeks	$40	$40	100%

Women had a "marriage premium": Married women in every category earned more than single women, and yet the female-male earnings ratio for married people was lower than the ratio for single women. The explanation: The marriage premium for men was even larger than it was for women.

9. The patterns in the CPS data are evident as well after adjusting for IQ. The table below shows the fitted value of annual earned income for people who self-reported being in the labor force throughout the year and who worked at least one hour. The regression analysis was conducted separately for men and women. The independent variables were IQ, a binary variable for marriage (no-yes), and a binary variable for children living in the home (no-yes). I also conducted analyses discriminating between the presence of children under the age of five and of children five years and older, but do not report them because they did not show substantively different results. Income in the NLSY surveys refers to the calendar year (CY) prior to the interview.

TWO INCOME MEASURES AT AGES 30–35 BY IQ, SEX, MARITAL STATUS, AND PRESENCE OF CHILDREN (2018 DOLLARS)

		Unmarried, no children					
		NLSY79, CY 1993			NLSY97, CY 2014		
Income measure	IQ	Men	Women	Ratio	Men	Women	Ratio
Earned income	80	$26,837	$27,324	1.02	$27,685	$24,142	0.87
Earned income	100	$37,365	$37,676	1.01	$36,909	$35,458	0.96
Earned income	120	$52,023	$51,949	1.00	$49,206	$52,077	1.06
Total family income	80	$25,053	$22,519	0.90	$32,395	$29,637	0.91
Total family income	100	$36,845	$34,602	0.94	$47,646	$49,203	1.03
Total family income	120	$54,187	$53,170	0.98	$70,079	$81,684	1.17

		Married with children					
		NLSY79, CY 1993			NLSY97, CY 2014		
Income measure	IQ	Men	Women	Ratio	Men	Women	Ratio
Earned income	80	$37,408	$22,968	0.61	$42,799	$22,706	0.53
Earned income	100	$52,084	$31,669	0.61	$57,058	$33,349	0.58
Earned income	120	$72,517	$43,667	0.60	$76,067	$48,979	0.64
Total family income	80	$49,393	$48,440	0.98	$56,657	$44,090	0.78
Total family income	100	$72,641	$74,434	1.02	$83,332	$73,197	0.88
Total family income	120	$106,832	$114,375	1.07	$122,566	$121,518	0.99

Unmarried women without children. The cohort of women in their early 30s in 1994 earned as much as men at comparable IQ levels. For the cohort of women in their early 30s in 2015, that held true for high-IQ women. Judging from these results, there was a meaningful male advantage only for quite low levels of IQ (e.g., the fitted value for earned income when IQ was set at 80 was 87 percent of income for unmarried males with no children in the home).

Married women with at least one child in the home. Compare the earned income for unmarried and married women. Married women in the labor force earned noticeably less than unmarried women. But the larger factor that drove down the ratio of female to male earnings was that married men earned much more than unmarried men.

Family income. I show family income in addition to earned income to make a point that will come as no surprise. Married women with children are, on average, much more prosperous than unmarried women at comparable IQ levels. For the NLS79 cohort, married women with children had more than double the fitted family income of unmarried women without children (115 percent). That marriage premium had dropped for the NLSY97 cohort but was still a substantial 49 percent.

10. The raw differences in earned income in the 2018 CPS are shown for two groups: those who were in the labor force at the time of the interview (not necessarily employed) and those who reported working for 52 weeks at 40 hours per week during the year.

	CPS 2018 Median earned income (000s)	
	In the labor force	*Employed full-time year-round*
White	$48	$50
Black	$35	$40
Latino	$30	$35
Asian	$54	$65

The ethnic differences are substantial, with fully employed blacks and Latinos earning only 80 percent and 70 percent of the white median respectively. Fully employed Asians made 30 percent more than the white median.

11. The next table shows the fitted values of earned income expressed in 2018 dollars for IQ set at 80, 100, and 120 for the two cohorts of the NLSY. Logged earned income was regressed on IQ and ethnicity. The sample was limited to persons ages 30–35 who reported being in the labor force (though not necessarily employed) throughout the previous calendar year and reported working at least one hour.

	Earned income (2018 dollars)						
	NLSY79, CY 1993			*NLSY97, CY 2014*			
IQ	*White*	*Black*	*Latino*	*White*	*Black*	*Latino*	*Asian*
80	$28,632	$28,519	$26,973	$29,883	$25,144	$30,596	$46,975
100	$40,514	$40,355	$38,166	$40,584	$34,147	$41,553	$63,796
120	$57,327	$57,101	$54,005	$55,117	$46,375	$56,432	$86,641

For NLSY79, blacks and whites with comparable IQs had effectively identical fitted earned incomes, with Latinos only fractionally behind. For NLSY97, blacks had a fitted mean that was 84 percent of the white mean, Latinos and whites were effectively equal, and the fitted Asian mean was 57 percent higher than the white mean.

10: A Framework for Thinking About Heritability and Class

1. See Horowitz, Haynor, and Kickham (2018) for a survey of the ideological positions of 479 sociologists in U.S. colleges and universities.
2. For exceptions, see Moore and Shenk (2017) and Burt and Simons (2014).
3. Galton (1869). I am drawing from the account in Herrnstein (1973): chapter 4, which contains an excellent discussion of the history of scholarship about heritability of IQ as of the early 1970s.
4. Sewall Wright wrote the classic papers on measuring degrees of relatedness in 1921. For an accessible discussion of them, see Hill (1995).
5. For a nice illustration of correlations on phenotypic outcomes for different degrees of relatedness, see Cesarini and Visscher (2017): Fig. 1.
6. I adapted this example from Turkheimer, Pettersson, and Horn (2014): 519. "A heritability coefficient represents the proportion of phenotypic variability that is associated with variability in genotype. As such, it is an effect size, a variance ratio, an R^2 coefficient; and like any variance ratio it is sensitive to characteristics of the population in ways that means are not. In particular, variance ratios depend crucially on the variability of both the predictor and the outcome. For example, the question, 'How much of the variance in college performance is explained by differences in SAT scores?' has no meaningful answer, other than, 'It depends on the variability of SAT scores and other factors at the institutions where the study is conducted.'" Turkheimer, Pettersson, and Horn (2014): 519.
7. Tucker-Drob, Briley, and Harden (2013).
8. Technically, these influences are obvious *potential* components of the shared environment. They do not qualify as part of the shared environment unless they do in fact make persons raised together more similar. At an anecdotal level, consider the school that two siblings attend some years apart. It is "shared" in the sense that both siblings walked into the same building every day. But the siblings necessarily had different peer groups. Suppose also that the siblings shared none of the same teachers. Those elements of the school are not shared. There's no a priori reason to assume that other elements of the school experience made "school" meaningfully shared between the two siblings born even a year or two apart. Now suppose that the solution to the ACE equation for large MZ and DZ twins' samples indicates no role for the shared environment and a substantial role for the nonshared environment. It could well be that the effects of schooling were real, but they were part of the effect attributed to the nonshared environment.
9. Plomin (2011): Table 1. It is adapted from Rowe and Plomin (1981).
10. Of these, different peer groups appear to be especially important, as documented by Harris (1998).
11. The 100 percent figure for MZ twins is accurate when rounded to within half a dozen decimal places. A study of SNPs in 66 adult twins found differences that amount to one SNP per 1.2×10^{-7} nucleotides—an exceedingly small fraction. Li, Montpetit, Rousseau et al. (2013). MZ twins can also fail to share 100 percent of their genes because of rare conditions.
12. DZ twins share only approximately 50 percent because the coin flips that decide the blocks of DNA donated by the mother and father don't always produce exactly equal totals from each.
13. To see the logic, start by thinking about a trait that is 100 percent heritable and perfectly measured. The correlation of that trait among a sample of MZ twins, who share 100 percent of their genes, has to converge on +1.0. What is going to be the correlation among samples of DZ twins who share 50 percent of their genes? It will just as inevitably converge on +.5. That difference in shared genes in MZ and DZ twins gives the mathematical leverage for disentangling genes from the shared environment.

Let's say that we want to understand the heritability of obsessive-compulsive disorder. Among a large sample of MZ twins raised together, we find the correlation of the diagnosis of obsessive-compulsive disorder to be +.53. If one MZ twin has obsessive-compulsive disorder, the other is much more likely than chance to exhibit the disorder as well. Next, we assemble a large sample of same-sex DZ twins raised together and discover that the correlation of their rate of obsessive-compulsive disorder is +.28. (These percentages are taken from Polderman, Benyamin, de Leeuw et al. (2015): Supplementary Table 21.) If obsessive-compulsive disorder were caused entirely by environmental influences, then the correlations for the samples of MZ and DZ twins would be the same. The larger correlation for the MZ twins *must* be caused by their additional shared genes.

This is a classic example of the distinction between specific people and large samples. For the sake of argument, assume that it is possible for parenting to produce obsessive-compulsive disorder. You observe that MZ twins both have obsessive-compulsive disorder. There is no way to tell whether it came about through shared genes or shared parents. But if you have 1,000 randomly chosen pairs of MZ twins and another 1,000 pairs of DZ twins, and you find that twice as many MZ twins as DZ twins have obsessive-compulsive disorder, then that difference (with an ascertainable margin of error) can be explained only by their additional shared genes. There's no other possibility except that your samples weren't really random after all.

The equations for implementing this logic that I give in the text are called the Falconer formulas after their originator, Douglas Falconer. What I've just given you is the most basic treatment of Falconer's formulas. Falconer (1960). The results from the technical literature that I report in chapter 11 are usually based on fitted models that use more complicated statistics. This is necessary because, apart from any other reason, the basic ACE model must be elaborated whenever the correlation among MZ twins is more than twice the correlation among DZ twins—i.e., whenever solving for Falconer's equations leads to a negative value for *C*. But these refinements generally tweak the results of the basic Falconer formulas by only a few percentage points.

14. Bouchard, Lykken, McGue et al. (1990). This is the study that you are likely to have heard about. In fact, the first scientific study of twins goes back to 1937. Newman, Freeman, and Holzinger (1937).

15. Segal (1999): 117–18.

16. The Minnesota study attracted charges that the heritability measures were radically too high (e.g., Taylor (1980), Farber (1981)). Bouchard and his colleagues responded with additional analyses that confirmed their main findings. See Bouchard (1982) and Bouchard (1983).

17. The three other assumptions are: (1) Either nonadditive genetic effects (*D* and *I*) or shared environmental effects (*C*) are zero; (2) there are no gene × environment (G×E) interactions and no gene-environment correlations (rGE); and (3) twins are representative of the non-twin population. For a discussion specifically of number 3, see Barnes and Boutwell (2013). For general discussion of these assumptions with additional references, see Verweij, Mosing, Zietsch et al. (2012) and Appendix A of Barnes, Wright, Boutwell et al. (2014).

18. Genetic assortative mating needs to be discriminated from cultural transmission, which also tends to inflate the estimate of shared environmental effects. For a discussion of the assumptions of the classical twin model and an empirical assessment of assortative mating for intelligence, see Vinkhuyzen, van der Sluis, Maes et al. (2012).

19. A separate issue is the genome-wide genetic similarity of mates (e.g., see Domingue, Fletcher, Conley et al. (2014)). Here I am reporting evidence for phenotypic assortative mating on discrete traits that are known to be substantially heritable.

20. For citations, see the literature review in Barnes, Wright, Boutwell et al. (2014): 7.

21. Loehlin (1978): 72.

22. LoParo and Waldman (2014): 606.
23. E.g., Fosse, Joseph, and Richardson (2015); Hettema, Neale, and Kendler (1995); Kaprio, Koskenvuo, and Rose (1990).
24. For citations on each of these outcomes, see LoParo and Waldman (2014): 606–7. For a comprehensive list of studies of EEA as of 2014, see Barnes, Wright, Boutwell et al. (2014): Appendix D. The authors summarize the table as follows:

> The studies included in Appendix D in the online supporting information tested for violations of the EEA across 1,233 environments and violations were detected in only 112 of them (9 percent). Of the 61 studies available, only 13 concluded that the EEA was invalid (21 percent), but of these only 6 performed any empirical analysis (10 percent), and none of these studies actually estimated the impact of the presence of unequal environments on heritability estimates. However, several studies examined directly the effect of violating the EEA on heritability estimates. Appendix D in the online supporting information includes 11 studies that estimated the impact of unequal environments on heritability estimates, with the average effect being an upward bias of about .012 (or about one percentage point) in the heritability estimate. What this necessarily means is that the widely cited heritability estimate of .50 for antisocial behaviors may be upwardly biased by .012 and the "true" A is actually closer to .488. However, we should note that these estimates do not take into account violations of other assumptions (e.g., assortative mating; the presence of evocative gene-environment correlation) that may downwardly bias heritability estimates. (Barnes, Wright, Boutwell et al. (2014): 11–12).

25. Felson (2014): 195.
26. These bodies of evidence will not prevent yet more assertions that twin studies are worthless. If you wish to get a sense of the scholarly rigor of the two sides of the debate, I recommend a matched pair of 2014 articles in the journal *Criminology*. For the case against twin studies, Callie Burt and Ronald Simons wrote "Pulling Back the Curtain on Heritability Studies" (Burt and Simons (2014)). For the defense, a team of seven scholars wrote "Demonstrating the Validity of Twin Research in Criminology" (Barnes, Wright, Boutwell et al. (2014)). The initial articles were followed by responses from both sides: Burt and Simons (2015) and Wright, Barnes, Boutwell et al. (2015). In my view, it is instructive as a case study. Put bluntly, I find the Burt and Simons articles to be transparently weak. But you don't need to take my word for it. The issues regarding the Burt and Simons use of evidence are not subtle. If you have a basic grasp of statistical evidence, you can decide for yourself.

11: The Ubiquity of Heritability and the Small Role of the Shared Environment

1. Turkheimer (2000): 160.
2. The public's intuitive judgment is remarkably accurate. Willoughby, Love, McGue et al. (2018) found that the public's estimate of the heritability of 21 traits was correlated at +.77 with published heritabilities. With regard to cognitive repertoires (as opposed to physical resemblances), some parents hold out. In the words of psychologist Marvin Zuckerman, "All parents are environmentalists until they have their second child." Quoted in Turkheimer (2019).
3. Harris (1998).
4. Pinker (2002).
5. E.g., Caplan (2011).
6. Loehlin and Nichols (1976): 92.
7. Rowe and Plomin (1981).
8. Scarr and Grajek (1982): 361.
9. For a review of Loehlin's continuing exploration of the heritability of personality traits after the initial 1976 study, see Turkheimer, Pettersson, and Horn (2014).

10. I assert this, confident that it is true at the extreme, but I do not know of good studies proving it. Many badly abused children live seemingly normal adult lives. And for children who are obviously damaged, the problem is distinguishing between the effects of the abuse and a genetic confound when the child is the biological child of the abusers. That said, I continue to believe that my wording, "*can* damage children permanently," is incontestable.

11. Why do I ignore the advantages of choosing the best neighborhood and thereby increasing the chances of positive peer groups? Because defining what constitutes a "good" neighborhood is so intensely a matter of personal opinion and the childhood's particular characteristics. For example, some parents yearn for a home in a prestigious zip code with the children enrolled in an exclusive private school. Other parents think that is a terrible environment for bringing up children and prefer a socioeconomically normal neighborhood and public schools filled with a wide range of children. I know of no data that could adjudicate these different views about the best places to raise children. For that matter, children with different traits will thrive in different environments.

12. Polderman, Benyamin, de Leeuw et al. (2015). The Center for Neurogenomics and Cognitive Research is part of Vrije Universiteit in Amsterdam.

13. Polderman, Benyamin, de Leeuw et al. (2015): 707.

14. The Polderman study's "best" model was the standard ACE model when $2(rMZ - rDZ) > 0$. When $2(rMZ - rDZ) < 0$ (i.e., showing a negative value for the shared environment), the "best" model was an ADE model, with D standing for nonadditive genetic influences. This is a conservative approach to estimating h^2. In the words of the study, "such per-study choices cause bias and can lead to a 10% downward bias in the reported estimates of h^2 in comparison to those based on twin correlations, consistent with the observed discrepancy between our meta-analysis of variance component estimates calculated from twin correlations and the reported variance components." Polderman, Benyamin, de Leeuw et al. (2015): 705.

15. Plomin (2011): 568.

16. Plomin (2011): 568.

17. Plomin (2011): 568.

18. Turkheimer, Pettersson, and Horn (2014).

19. Plomin (2011): 582.

20. Jencks, Smith, Acland et al. (1972): 66–67.

12: Abilities, Personality, and Success

1. Herrnstein (1973): 197–98.

2. The concept of *g* was famously derided by Stephen Jay Gould in his bestselling book *The Mismeasure of Man*. Gould (1981). The book was extremely successful in shaping public opinion about IQ and yet was irrelevant to the state of psychometrics at the time Gould was writing. For technical reviews, see Blinkhorn (1982); Davis (1983); Humphreys (1983); and Carroll (1995). For a recent deep dive into the details of Gould's errors, see Warne (2019). In 1998, Arthur Jensen published his magnum opus, *The g Factor*. Jensen (1998). In the 20 years since then, the biological reality of *g* has been established in new ways by advances in neuroscience. See Haier (2016).

3. Ritchie (2015).

4. See note 4 about test bias in the introduction to Part III.

5. A recent review of the effects of education on IQ is Ritchie and Tucker-Drob (2018).

6. On this issue, the Task Force on IQ that I cited extensively in the notes to Part III wrote:

> Intelligence test scores are fairly stable during development. When Jones and Bayley (1941) tested a sample of children annually throughout childhood and adolescence, for example, scores obtained at age 18 were correlated $r = +.77$ with scores that had been obtained at age 6 and $r = +.89$ with scores from age 12. When scores were averaged across

several successive tests to remove short-term fluctuations, the correlations were even higher. The mean for ages 17 and 18 was correlated r = +.86 with the mean for ages 5, 6, and 7, and r = +.96 with the mean for ages 11, 12, and 13. (Neisser, Boodoo, Bouchard et al. (1996): 81).

7. Jensen (1998): chapter 4.
8. Gottfredson (1997a).
9. I have not found a source with the actual phrase "Life is an IQ test," but I (and many others who write about IQ) picked up the idea from Gordon (1997); Gottfredson (1997b); and Gottfredson (2003).
10. Gottfredson (2003).
11. Batty, Wennerstad, Smith et al. (2008).
12. The full discussion of this role of IQ is Gordon (1997).
13. High IQ also apparently reflects broader physiological well-being. In a 68-year follow-up of the Scottish Mental Survey of 1947, whose members were born in 1936, childhood intelligence was inversely associated with all major causes of death. Calvin, Batty, Der et al. (2017).
14. This is not the same as saying that beyond a certain threshold, higher IQ is unrelated to measures of success, despite a claim to that effect in Malcolm Gladwell's bestselling book *Outliers*. Gladwell (2008). Most evidence indicates that more is better across the IQ range for a wide variety of outcomes. Gottfredson (1997a).
15. Strenze (2007): Table 2. The numbers represent correlations corrected for unreliability and dichotomization weighted by sample size.
16. Kuncel and Hezlett (2010): Fig. 1. Correlations are corrected for restriction of range and criterion unreliability.
17. The relationship of IQ to job performance has been so exhaustively studied that by 2012 when the Oxford University Press included a chapter titled "Cognitive Abilities" in *The Oxford Handbook of Personnel Assessment and Selection*, it consisted of a meta-review of meta-analyses. Here are the "operational validities"—equivalent to correlations—of tests of mental abilities with measures of overall job performance for a variety of different job types.

	Operational validity of the IQ score
Low complexity jobs	.38
Medium complexity jobs	.56
High complexity jobs	.59
Police	.24
Drivers	.45
Salespeople	.46
Clerical jobs	.54
Engineers	.63
Managers	.67
Computer programmers	.73

Source: Ones, Dilchert, and Viswesvaran (2014): Table 3.

The results are limited to meta-analyses incorporating corrections for restriction of range and criterion unreliability using conservative criterion reliability estimates. When more than one meta-analysis reported operational validities for a given category, I report the mean of those results.

The chapter also includes analyses comparing the operational validities of different kinds of information that employers use. In all of those cases, it is not just that the operational validity for the IQ test is higher than for another measure. When IQ and another measure are combined, the other measure adds comparatively little. For example, if an IQ score and the evaluation from a job interview are combined, they jointly have an operational validity of .61, but the increment attributable to the interview (compared to the operational validity of the IQ test alone) is just .07. If an IQ score and biographical data about the job candidate are combined, their joint operational validity is .56—but the increment attributable to the biographical data is just .02. Ones, Dilchert, and Viswesvaran (2014): Table 8. "Cognitive ability tests are generalizably valid predictors of overall job performance across a large number of jobs, organizations, occupations, and even countries," the authors concluded. "No other individual differences predictor produces as high validities as consistently as cognitive ability tests or has proven its validity in such a variety of settings." Ones, Dilchert, and Viswesvaran (2014): 186.

For a dissent to the consensus about the relationship of IQ to job performance, see Richardson and Norgate (2015). The article presents a variety of measurement and aggregation problems associated with meta-analyses in general and assessments of job performance in particular.

18. Kuncel, Ones, and Sackett (2010): 333.
19. *Multiple intelligences* (MI). Gardner himself has never accepted that MI can be judged by psychometric standards, nor has he tried to develop measures of the various intelligences that would permit falsification of his theory, as he has acknowledged. For a technical exchange by critics, Gardner's response, and a rejoinder by the critics, see Visser, Ashton, and Vernon (2006a); Gardner (2006); and Visser, Ashton, and Vernon (2006b). For a literature review of the evidence for MI, see Waterhouse (2006).

In 2016, Gardner offered this retrospective on MI's relationship to classic theories of intelligence: "But, in truth, most psychologists, and particularly most psychometricians, have never warmed to the theory. I think that psychologists are wedded to the creation and administration of short-answer tests, and particularly ones that resemble the IQ test. While such tests can probe linguistic and logical capacities, as well as certain spatial abilities, they are deficient in assessing other abilities, such as interpersonal intelligence (social intelligence), intrapersonal intelligence (akin to emotional intelligence), and other nonacademic intelligences. I have not devoted significant effort to creating such tests." Gardner (2016): 169.

I should emphasize that if you read *Frames of Mind* mentally substituting the word *talent* for *intelligence* and ignoring Gardner's critique of *g*, there's a lot to be learned from him. In that regard, Gardner has an amusing and I think correct observation in a 2018 interview: "I have never been able to reconstruct when I made the fateful decision not to call these abilities, talents, or gifts, but rather to call them 'intelligences.' Because if I had called them anything else, I would not be well known in different corners of the world and journalists like you wouldn't come to interview me. It was picking the word 'intelligence' and pluralizing it." Liz Mineo, "'The Greatest Gift You Can Have Is a Good Education, One That Isn't Strictly Professional,'" *Harvard Gazette*, May 2018.

Emotional intelligence (EI). As mentioned in chapter 3, the most widely used test of EI is the Mayer-Salovey-Caruso Emotional Intelligence Test (MSCEIT). Version 2 has eight subscales measuring four aspects of EI: perceiving emotions, using emotions to facilitate thought, understanding emotions, and managing emotions. For discussions of its psychometric properties, see Mayer, Caruso, and Salovey (1999); Ciarrochi, Chan, and Caputi (2000); Palmer, Gignac, Manocha et al. (2005); and Landy (2005). Matthews, Zeidner, and Roberts (2007) is a book-length critique of EI after the years in which it got the most attention. Van Rooy and Viswesvaran (2004) provide a meta-analysis of the literature. Assessments of the utility of EI independently of IQ and traditional personality factors vary widely, from enthusiastic to dismissive, and characterizing the strengths and weaknesses of the various positions would take us deep into the psychometric weeds. For me, a single source that is both rigorous and judicious is a 2010 integrative meta-analysis by psychologists Dana Joseph and Daniel Newman. They conclude the article with "Practical Advice for Using Emotional Intelligence Measures in Personnel Selection" that seems to do a good job of drawing lessons from a complicated literature of widely varying quality. Quoting directly from their text:

1. *Choose your EI measure carefully.* There are two, distinct definitions of the term "Emotional Intelligence": (a) ability to perform emotional tasks, and (b) a grab-bag of everything that is not cognitive ability. It is critical to distinguish these two, because measures based on the two EI definitions do not have the same content, predictive validity, or subgroup differences.
2. *Exercise extreme caution when using mixed EI measures.* Grab-bag measures of EI (i.e., self-report mixed measures) appear to exhibit some incremental validity over cognitive ability and personality measures on average (based on nine studies), but it is not clear why. As such, use of these measures for personnel decisions may be difficult to defend, without extensive local validation.
3. *Know that ability EI measures may add little to the selection system.* Ability-based measures of EI (performance-based and self-report) exhibit little incremental validity over cognitive ability and personality, on average.
4. *Base the decision to use an EI measure on the job type* (i.e., consider the emotional labor content of the job). When dealing with high emotional labor jobs (jobs that require positive emotional displays), all types of EI measures exhibit meaningful validity and incremental validity over cognitive ability and personality. In contrast, for low emotional labor jobs, EI validities are weaker or can even be negative.
5. *Be aware of subgroup differences on EI.* Although more data are needed, preliminary evidence suggests that performance-based EI measures favor women and Whites, which may produce adverse impact against men and African Americans. (Joseph and Newman (2010): 72).

Grit. Labels can be effective, and "grit" is a great one. It captures a human quality that we recognize in some people and not in others and it has an obvious and persuasive relationship to success in all sorts of human endeavors. But grit as a psychological construct overlaps substantially with one of the Big Five factors, conscientiousness. There are other psychometric issues as well. Marcus Credé has published an excellent review of the literature and presentation of the major issues. He sums up as follows:

> For all its intuitive appeal, the grit literature is currently characterized by a number of serious theoretical and empirical challenges ranging from a lack of construct validity, discriminant validity, and predictive validity. At present there is no empirical support for the idea that grit is the combination of perseverance and passion or for the claim that grit adds to our understanding of success and performance. Indeed, the best available evidence strongly suggests that grit is largely a repackaging of conscientiousness—a widely studied personality trait. If grit is to represent a meaningful contribution to our understanding of success, researchers should focus on three broad areas. First, future work will have to pay particularly close attention to whether the combination of perseverance and passion into a single construct can be theoretically or empirically justified or whether the two facets are best studied individually. Second, future work should consider whether grit or grit facets interact with ability to predict success or whether grit facets represent necessary-but-not-sufficient conditions for success. Third, efforts should be made to improve the measurement of grit and grit facets because any empirical investigation of the role of grit requires that grit be measured better than current scales allow. (Credé (2018): 611).

20. For a systematic discussion of the criteria for establishing that a noncognitive factor in academic achievement is involved in gene-environment transactions, see Tucker-Drob and Harden (2017).
21. Gottfredson and Hirschi (1990); Moffitt, Poulton, and Caspi (2013); Moffitt, Arseneault, Belsky et al. (2011); Duckworth and Carlson (2013).
22. von Stumm, Gale, Batty et al. (2009); Lim, Teo, and Loo (2003); Furnham and Cheng (2017).
23. Chamorro-Premuzic, Harlaar, Greven et al. (2010); Spinath, Spinath, Harlaar et al. (2006); Stankov (2013).
24. von Stumm, Hell, and Chamorro-Premuzic (2011).
25. Poropat (2014): Table 2. In addition to Poropat (2014), Shanahan, Bauldry, Roberts et al. (2014) has an excellent literature review in addition to making its independent contribution. Important subsequent studies include Lechner, Danner, and Rammstedt (2017) and Damian, Su, Shanahan et al. (2014).
26. Borghans, ter Weel, and Weinberg (2008).
27. Cheng and Furnham (2012).
28. These facets and the facets for neuroticism are taken from Costa, Terracciano, and McCrae (2001): Table 2.
29. A fourth study, Borghans, Golsteyn, Heckman et al. (2016), found too late to include in the main text, reports the independent and joint effects of personality and IQ on academic outcomes without a measure of childhood SES.

    In a sample of 298 from a Dutch high school, conscientiousness explained more of the variance for grades than any other personality trait or IQ. For scores on the Differential Aptitude Test, which the authors classified as an achievement test, IQ was the most important predictor, but openness was also highly significant (supplemental tables 7.1 and 7.2).

    A study of a sample of 8,501 from the British Cohort Study had 11 dependent variables representing test scores and grades. Locus of control consistently had a positive effect on test scores while disorganization consistently had a negative effect. The roles of IQ and the combined personality traits were roughly equal on five of the dependent variables, while IQ and the combined personality traits each had a somewhat larger role on three of the remaining dependent variables (supplemental tables 7.3–7.7).

    An analysis of 638 members of the NLSY79 found a dominant role for IQ over measures of locus of control and self-esteem for scores on the Armed Forces Qualification Test (which the authors treated as an achievement test) and grades. On other dependent variables, neither IQ nor the personality inventories explained more than trivial amounts of the variance (supplemental tables 7.8 and 8.1–8.6).

    An analysis of 1,561 members of the National Survey of Midlife Development (US) found that the Big Five personality traits explained more of the variance than IQ on dependent variables measuring adult wages, physical health, mental health, and depression (supplemental tables 8.7–8.11).
30. The Project Talent variables for intelligence, personality traits, and parental SES were standardized prior to the analysis while the measures of educational attainment, log of earned income, and occupational prestige were not. The tables in the article reported unstandardized regression coefficients. I express them in the table on page 235 as quasi effect sizes (the unstandardized regression coefficient divided by the sample standard deviation) to make them more easily interpretable relative to the standardized total effects in a structural equation model for the Aberdeen Birth Cohort, and path coefficients for the British NCDP.

    Both the Project Talent and Aberdeen cohort analyses used structural models that were run five times, once for each of the Big Five factors. The total effects for childhood IQ and parental SES given in the table represent the median of the main effects for IQ and parental

SES for the five coefficients (which with few exceptions were within .01 of each other in all five runs).

31. Krapohl, Rimfeld, Shakeshaft et al. (2014): Table S7.

32. Given the results of the bivariate analyses showing the extent to which the heritability of GCSE scores can be explained by each of the nine predictors without considering any of the other eight, the contributions of well-being, child-reported behavior problems, health, and the home environment after controlling for the other predictors cannot have been more than a percent or so, and those of personality, parent-reported behavior problems, and the school environment cannot have been much more than 5 percent. Self-efficacy was the domain that accounted for perhaps half of the 28 percent explained by eight non-IQ predictors. Based on the implications of Krapohl, Rimfeld, Shakeshaft et al. (2014): Table S6.

33. Krapohl, Rimfeld, Shakeshaft et al. (2014): The distribution of loadings in Table S6 applied to the estimate of the total contribution to phenotypic variance of the eight domains other than IQ of 28 percent in Table S7.

34. Tucker-Drob, Briley, Engelhardt et al. (2016): 800.

35. These statements are drawn from Tucker-Drob, Briley, Engelhardt et al. (2016): Figs. 3 and 5. The figures report decomposed standardized path coefficients that do not lend themselves to intuitive interpretation.

36. The table below is adapted from Sackett, Kuncel, Arneson et al. (2009): Table 4. The figures for the SAT meta-analysis are corrected for national population range restriction.

| | | Correlation | | | Partial correlation | |
| | | | | | Test–grade controlling for SES | SES–grade controlling for test |
Sample	N	SES–test	SES–grade	Test–grade		
Meta-analysis of College Board data		+.42	+.22	+.53	+.50	−.01
Meta-analysis of studies with composite SES	17,235	+.15	+.09	+.37	+.36	+.03
Individual longitudinal studies						
1995. Nat'l Study of Law School Performance	3,375	+.16	+.07	+.38	+.38	+.01
Harvard Study of the Class of 1964–65	486	+.07	+.05	+.30	+.29	+.03
LSAC Nat'l Longitudinal Bar Passage Study	19,264	+.13	+.05	+.35	+.35	+.01
Nat'l Education Longitudinal Study of 1988	6,314	+.40	+.10	+.24	+.23	+.02
Nat'l Longitudinal Study of the Class of 1972	5,735	+.30	+.04	+.31	+.31	−.01
Project Talent	749	+.18	+.05	+.30	+.29	+.01

37. I mark the beginning of this literature with Jencks, Smith, Acland et al. (1972), though an argument could be made for Coleman et al. (1966).

38. Other examples are Jencks (1979); Korenman and Winship (2000); Firkowska-Mankiewicz (2002); and Richards and Sacker (2003).

39. The Project Talent, Aberdeen Birth Cohort, and NCDP databases were part of the table on page 239 about IQ and personality factors.

NLSY79. The analysis for educational attainment (*n* = 8,693) regressed highest grade completed on AFQT scores and the measure of parental SES used in *The Bell Curve,* which combined measures of parental education, family income, and occupational status. Herrnstein and Murray (1994): Appendix 2. The sample was limited to those 35 or older at the time of their most recent information about highest grade completed. The analysis for income (*n* = 5,801) regressed the log of earned income in 2005 on the same independent variables, limited to those with reported earned incomes greater than zero. The logged value was set to 6.0 for incomes of $1 to $999. The data reported in the table are standardized regression coefficients.

NLSY97. The analysis for educational attainment (*n* = 4,078) regressed highest grade completed on AFQT scores and an index of parental SES that combined the resident parents' educational attainment and family income (occupational data for the parents were not collected for the NLSY97). The sample was limited to those who were interviewed in the 2015 follow-up when 97 percent of them were ages 31–35 and the rest were 30 or 36. The analysis for income (*n* = 3,025) regressed the log of earned income in 2005 on the same independent variables, limited to those with reported earned incomes greater than zero. The logged value was set to 6.0 for incomes of $1 to $999. The data reported in the table are standardized regression coefficients.

40. The one instance in which childhood SES had more effect on educational attainment than childhood IQ was for the cohort born in 1932 in Scotland, whereas the relative importance of IQ is greatest in the two most recent cohorts, both from the United States, which suggests two obvious explanations: The influence of SES on schooling diminishes over time as educational opportunities for all have expanded; and SES is less important in the United States than in the UK, where the class system has historically been a much bigger deal. But the Aberdeen data are conspicuously inconsistent with those explanations, so skepticism of this interpretation is appropriate.

The one analysis in which childhood SES had more effect on adult occupations or income than childhood IQ was for the Talent database, which found small effects of either IQ or childhood SES on income, but the effect of childhood SES was slightly larger. Both the small size of the effects and the comparatively small role of IQ are probably explained by the follow-up age for the Talent sample: just 11 years after high school graduation, usually meaning 29–30 years old, years when many who will eventually become high earners (e.g., physicians or attorneys) are either still in school or in entry-level positions and many who are blue-collar workers in the skilled trades are at the peak of their earning power.

13: Constraints and Potentials

1. Moffitt, Caspi, and Rutter (2005).
2. Krapohl, Rimfeld, Shakeshaft et al. (2014): Table S7.
3. Krapohl, Rimfeld, Shakeshaft et al. (2014): 4 of 6.
4. Krapohl, Rimfeld, Shakeshaft et al. (2014): 3 of 6. A 2019 study using the Twins Early Development Study (first author was Saskia Selzam) argued that it had found additional evidence of a major role for passive rGE. The authors used a polygenic risk score (described in chapter 14) derived exclusively from genetic variants evaluated in a large sample of unrelated people. These polygenic risk scores had been shown to predict both cognitive ability and noncognitive traits such as height and BMI. Using a sample of fraternal twins, they asked whether the same polygenic risk scores predicted cognitive and noncognitive traits equally well within families and between families. For the noncognitive traits, the answer was yes. For the cognitive traits, the within-family prediction was significantly lower than the between-family prediction. Then the authors examined the effect on the findings of including SES (assessed on age of mother and parental education) in the analysis. They found that the entire difference in

prediction between families and within families was accounted for by SES and concluded that the explanation was passive rGE. Selzam, Ritchie, Pingault et al. (2019).

The difficulty in interpreting this conclusion is the generic one I discussed in chapter 11: SES is partly a function of parental personality traits and cognitive ability. But SES also has a genuinely environmental component. Some degree of passive rGE is surely at work; it's just hard to know how much. It would be interesting to replicate the analysis for height (one of the traits included in the study) after controlling for the midpoint of parental height to get a sense of how much the predictive validity for a highly heritable trait is reduced.

5. E.g., Horn, Loehlin, and Willerman (1979); Plomin and DeFries (1983).

6. Scarr-Salapatek (1971). Scarr (she later dropped Salapatek) used the following logic: (1) Heritability is a ratio of variance explained by genes divided by total variance; (2) children in disadvantaged families usually have lower mean IQs than children from other families; (3) if those differences are entirely environmental in origin, then something in the environment is depressing the scores of disadvantaged children. If that is the case, then the environment is explaining more of the variance in IQ for disadvantaged children than for other children. If the environment is explaining more, then necessarily genes (the numerator in the heritability ratio) are explaining less, and it necessarily follows that the estimate of heritability for disadvantaged children will be lower than for other children. Scarr found evidence for that hypothesis in a sample of Philadelphia twins.

7. Fischbein (1980) found that among Swedish 12-year-old twins, heritability for the children of employers on a verbal test was much higher (.76) than among children of manual workers (.21). Rowe, Jacobson, and Van den Oord (1999) analyzed scores on a measure of verbal IQ for 523 twin pairs and reached strikingly similar results. Using parental education as the moderating variable, heritability for the highly educated families was .72 compared to Fischbein's .76. Among poorly educated families, heritability was .26 compared to Fischbein's .21. The role of the shared environment, .23 in both studies, remained small even for children from low-SES families.

8. Turkheimer, Haley, Waldron et al. (2003).

9. Specifically, the SES scores were based on the 100-point system from Myrianthopoulos and French (1968).

10. The values for h^2 and c^2 are estimates based on Fig. 3 in Turkheimer, Haley, Waldron et al. (2003).

11. One widely-used social science method is multivariate regression analysis, described in Appendix 1. A multivariate regression equation has a coefficient associated for each independent variable (recall that "independent" causes "dependent") that represents the effect of each independent variable after taking the other independent variables into account. For example, if the dependent variable is years of education and one of the independent variables is family income measured in thousands of dollars, then a coefficient of .003 would mean that an income of $100,000 is associated with an increase in years of education equaling 100 × .003, or .3 years of education. These coefficients are the *main effects*. To test for an *interaction effect* in regression analysis, the two variables in question are multiplied by each other. The coefficient associated with that combined variable is the interaction effect.

A common error when people talk about interaction effects informally is to conflate an interaction effect with an additive effect. Suppose that two independent variables each have a sizable main effect. In a regression analysis, both of those sizable effects are combined. The fact that the interaction term is small or insignificant doesn't diminish the importance of the additive main effects. Thus family income and genetic endowment for IQ could each have important effects on years of education; failure to find an interaction simply means that their added main effects aren't significantly augmented by an interaction between the two.

Two other comments about interaction effects: First, big interaction effects are rare. The main effects usually extract most of the juice from the two independent variables under examination. Second, unless the interaction effect is really big or the sample size is really big, it is unlikely that a significant interaction effect will be found. Most of the analyses that include interaction terms are drastically underpowered—reliably estimating an interaction effect requires a sample about 16 times as large as the sample needed to estimate a main effect. Gelman (2018). If you want to get into the statistical subtleties of interaction effects and your math is up to speed, a basic resource is Cox (1984).

12. The phrase "interpretable as replications" is borrowed from Kirkpatrick, McGue, and Iacono (2015), which selected five studies between 2003 and 2015 that qualified: Harden, Turkheimer, and Loehlin (2007); van der Sluis, Willemsen, de Geus et al. (2008); Grant, Kremen, Jacobson et al. (2010); Hanscombe, Trzaskowski, Haworth et al. (2012); and Bates, Lewis, and Weiss (2013). The results from three other studies shown in Fig. 6.02 are the Kirkpatrick study itself; Bates, Hansell, Martin et al. (2016), which postdated the Kirkpatrick study; Tucker-Drob, Rhemtulla, Harden et al. (2011); Rhemtulla and Tucker-Drob (2012); Spengler, Gottschling, Hahn et al. (2018); and the U.S. sample in Tucker-Drob and Bates (2015). The last two were not selected by Kirkpatrick, McGue, and Iacono (2015). I surmise that they were not selected because they dealt with very young samples (tested at ages two and four respectively), when mental tests are much less reliable than with older children.

A meta-analysis of the literature in 2015, Tucker-Drob and Bates (2015), included other studies that were too different in their measures of cognitive ability and/or SES to qualify as "interpretable as replications." These additional studies and some summary comments are given below:

Asbury, Wachs, and Plomin (2005). This article used a British twins sample, employing a detailed characterization of the shared environment, of which SES was just one component. The others were family chaos, maternal depression, harsh parental discipline, negative parental feelings, maternal medical problems in pregnancy, twin medical risk, instructive parent-child communication, informal parent-child communication, and educational toys. The study had separate cognitive measures for verbal and nonverbal IQ. With regard to SES, the authors (who included Robert Plomin) wrote, "Previous G×E research in the field of cognitive development has focused almost exclusively on SES. In the case of the current research it could be argued that interactions between SES and cognitive abilities do not exist. However, what our data actually suggest is that only very low SES has an effect that, in the case of verbal ability, is to raise group heritability." (p. 657). In other words, the interaction of genes and SES was in the opposite direction of the one observed in Turkheimer, Haley, Waldron et al. (2003) and other studies. The authors speculated that this might reflect British-U.S. differences in culture and child-rearing practices.

Bartels, van Beijsterveldt, and Boomsma (2009). The primary purpose of this study was to assess the effects of breastfeeding. The raw data were reanalyzed by Tucker-Drob, Rhemtulla, Harden et al. (2011), and failed to show a G×E interaction.

Jacobson and Vasilopoulos (2012).

Soden-Hensler (2012) is an unpublished PhD dissertation. Tucker-Drob and Bates (2015) included it in their meta-analysis and described it as one of the studies that failed to find a G × SES effect.

13. van der Sluis, Willemsen, de Geus et al. (2008); Hanscombe, Trzaskowski, Haworth et al. (2012); Grant, Kremen, Jacobson et al. (2010); Bates, Hansell, Martin et al. (2016).

14. Four of the sources for the table contained graphs plotting c^2 against percentiles of SES. In two cases, Rhemtulla and Tucker-Drob (2012) and Tucker-Drob, Rhemtulla, Harden et al. (2011), the metric for the horizontal axis was standard deviations instead of percentiles, and the metric for the vertical axis was variance instead of c^2, which I converted to their percentile and c^2 equivalents. The numbers used for the table for those studies and for Tucker-Drob and Bates (2015) were retrieved from the figures in those articles, which means they are accurate to within a few percentiles. For Harden, Turkheimer, and Loehlin (2007), the

figures are based on parental income (the interaction effect for the parental education representation of SES was not significant). For Rhemtulla and Tucker-Drob (2012), the figures are based on the mathematics score (the interaction effect for the reading score was not significant).

15. Tucker-Drob and Bates (2015).
16. Tucker-Drob and Bates (2015): 9.
17. A major reason to do a meta-analysis is that sampling variability is often the source of inconsistent results across studies. Therefore it is intrinsically dangerous to focus on the studies that found a major effect and discount the others: There's too much chance of finding what you want to find rather than what's true. With that in mind, I will mention some interesting aspects of the three studies that found a large substantive effect.

All of them dealt with very young children. The Rhemtulla and Tucker-Drob studies used the same twins dataset, with the Tucker-Drob study measuring cognitive ability at ages 12 and 24 months while the Rhemtulla study measured it at 4 years of age. The other study that found a large substantive effect, the original Turkheimer study, used measures of children at age seven. The neuroscience literature about the rapid development of children's brains during the first years of life is consistent with the findings of these three studies. Consider the ages in the other studies that showed small interaction effects or no interaction effects. The youngest age group was 11 (one of the cohorts in the Kirkpatrick study), and the rest were adolescents or adults. The broader finding that the heritability of IQ increases with age is also consistent with the failure of studies to find large interaction effects among subjects who are adolescents or older. I should add, however, that there are problems with this inference. The Kirkpatrick study and the meta-analysis by Tucker-Drob and Bates both tested for an age-related trend and found none.

Another issue was suggested by the authors of the Kirkpatrick study, who noted that the samples for all of the attempted replications were overwhelmingly white, while the original Turkheimer study consisted of 54% blacks and 43% whites. "[P]erhaps low SES must be combined with membership in a disadvantaged minority group," they speculated, "whose place in and experience of American society is unique due to the historical legacy of slavery." Kirkpatrick, McGue, and Iacono (2015): 209. It's worth noting in this regard that the sample used by the Rhemtulla and Tucker-Drob studies included 16 percent blacks, a much higher proportion than in any of the other studies.

The Turkheimer sample was also unique in that it included a far higher proportion of severely impoverished families than the other samples. The median years of education for the head of household was less than 11. The median occupation was "service worker." Twenty-five percent were classified as "laborers." Twenty-five percent were below the poverty line. If the most powerful interaction between genes and SES occurs at the very bottom of the distribution, the Turkheimer study had the only sample that could identify it.

I offer these as interesting possibilities. What we need at this point is a study with a large enough and varied enough sample. Simulations conducted in the course of the Tucker-Drob meta-analysis indicated that an adequately powered study would require a minimum of 3,300 twin pairs. Comparing the results from the initial Turkheimer study with subsequent results, the Tucker-Drob and Bates meta-analysis concluded: "It therefore appears that the inconsistency of previous U.S. studies to replicate Gene × SES effects on intelligence may have stemmed from low power associated with overly optimistic expectations regarding the magnitude of the true interaction effect." Tucker-Drob and Bates (2015): 146.

18. Duncan and Magnuson (2013): 114.
19. Duncan and Magnuson (2013): 114.
20. Duncan and Magnuson (2013): 120.
21. U.S. Department of Health and Human Services (2010).
22. Duncan and Magnuson (2013): 117.

23. Duncan and Magnuson (2013): 119.
24. The paragraph continues:

    In general, a finding of meaningful long-term outcomes of an early childhood intervention is more likely when the program is old, or small, or a multi-year intervention, and evaluated with something other than a well-implemented RCT [random controlled trial]. In contrast, as the program being evaluated becomes closer to universal pre-K for four-year-olds and the evaluation design is an RCT, the outcomes beyond the pre-K year diminish to nothing. I conclude that the best available evidence raises serious doubts that a large public investment in the expansion of pre-K for four-year-olds will have the long-term effects that advocates tout. (Whitehurst (2013): 8–9).

25. Phillips, Lipsey, Dodge et al. (2017): 12.
26. Branden (1969).
27. Mecca, Smelser, and Vasconcellos (1989).
28. Baumeister, Campbell, Kreuger et al. (2003). See also Twenge (2006): chapter 2.
29. Steele and Aronson (1995).
30. Sackett, Hardison, and Cullen (2004).
31. Sackett, Hardison, and Cullen (2004).
32. The original article by Steele and Aronson statistically adjusted the results from the experimental test (using items from the Graduate Record Examination) based on the participants' SAT scores when they had entered college. This often happens in studies of stereotype threat. It intuitively seems like a reasonable thing to do. In reality, it introduces a serious statistical confound. Readers who already know some statistics can get the details in Miller and Chapman (2001). Stoet and Geary (2012) explain it this way: "An important assumption of a covariate analysis is that the groups do not differ on the covariate. But that group difference is exactly what stereotype threat theory tries to explain! This is an irreconcilable difference between the theory and the statistical assumptions underlying covariate analysis." (p. 96). The practice of adjusting scores has diminished in recent years as word about the confound has spread, but it creates problems in interpreting much of the literature. For example, the Stoet and Deary meta-analysis of gender-based stereotype threat literature as of 2012 reported two effect sizes. The effect size for the studies that adjusted for prior test scores was a sizable −0.61. The effect size for studies that didn't adjust for prior test scores was just −0.17. Stoet and Geary (2012): 97.
33. Nguyen and Ryan (2008): Table 4.
34. Walton and Spencer (2009): 1137. At low levels of prior performance, $d = -0.31$. At high levels of prior performance, $d = -0.23$. They also reported an effect size of $+0.17$ (the plus sign means that stereotyped students performed better than nonstereotyped students) for tests under "safe conditions that reduce threat." (p. 1137). The study also reported results from a meta-analysis of 39 samples that included several studies of race-based stereotype threat but did not break out separate effect sizes for the race-based studies. The overall effect size, based on mean level of prior performance, was −0.48. They also reported an effect size of $+0.18$ for tests under safe conditions. (p. 1135).
35. The problem of unconscious researcher bias has been recognized for many decades. Simmons, Nelson, and Simonsohn (2011) pulled these arguments together and coined the phrase "researcher degrees of freedom." The authors write, "This exploratory behavior is not the by-product of malicious intent, but rather the result of two factors: (a) ambiguity in how best to make these decisions and (b) the researcher's desire to find a statistically significant result." (p. 1359).
36. Stoet and Geary (2012) concluded that 11 of 20 studies that met their criteria for replications succeeded in replicating the original effect. When the sample was limited to studies that were not confounded by adjusting the results for prior test scores (see note 32), only 3 out of 10 studies replicated the original effect. Finnigan and Corker (2016) report a clear failure to

replicate. Chalabaev, Major, Sarrazin et al. (2012), despite having a much larger sample, and Protzko and Aronson (2016) both failed to replicate a "self-affirmation" intervention effect that had been reported by a variety of earlier studies.

37. Lewis and Michalak (2019).
38. Stoet and Geary (2012); Flore and Wicherts (2015). The senior author of the latter study was Jelte Wicherts, a Dutch psychometrician who is one of the most highly regarded experts on all things technical about the analysis of test scores. Because so much of the controversy involves abstruse psychometric issues, I take his conclusion seriously:

> To conclude, we estimated a small average effect of stereotype threat on the MSSS [math, science, and spatial skills] test-performance of school-aged girls [$d = -0.22$]; however, the studies show large variation in outcomes, and it is likely that the effect is inflated due to publication bias. This finding leads us to conclude that we should be cautious when interpreting the effects of stereotype threat on children and adolescents in the STEM realm. To be more explicit, based on the small average effect size in our meta-analysis, which is most likely inflated due to publication bias, we would not feel confident to proclaim that stereotype threat manipulations will harm mathematical performance of girls in a systematic way or lead women to stay clear from occupations in the STEM domain. (Flore and Wicherts (2015): 41).

39. Shewach, Sackett, and Quint (2019): 16 of 21.
40. Mueller and Dweck (1998). For a nontechnical account of subsequent literature on the dangers of praise, see Po Bronson, "How Not to Talk to Your Kids: The Inverse Power of Praise," *New York*, February 11, 2007, 24–29.
41. Mueller and Dweck (1998): 33.
42. The scholarly work on growth mindset is insulated from these offshoots of the growth mindset movement. Carol Dweck and the other scholars whom I cite have no financial interest in them.
43. Sisk, Burgoyne, Sun et al. (2018).
44. Carl Hendrick, "The Growth Mindset Problem," *Aeon*, March 20, 2019, aeon.co.
45. A nontechnical description of the growth mindset movement and its techniques by Carol Dweck is available online at www.nais.org/magazine. For a book-length description, see Dweck (2006).
46. For a recent full-scale description of growth mindset theory and its empirical record, see Dweck and Yeager (2019).
47. Aronson, Fried, and Good (2002); Blackwell, Trzesniewski, and Dweck (2007); Paunesku, Walton, Romero et al. (2015); Yeager, Lee, and Jamieson (2016); Yeager, Johnson, Spitzer et al. (2014).
48. Yeager, Hanselman, Walton et al. (2019).
49. Cohen (1988), Funder, and Ozer (2019).
50. Tucker-Drob, Briley, Engelhardt et al. (2016).
51. Plomin and Daniels (1987): 8.
52. Turkheimer and Waldron (2000): Table 7.
53. Turkheimer and Waldron (2000): 91.
54. Pike, McGuire, Hetherington et al. (1996).
55. Plomin (2018): 80. See also Burt, Klahr, and Klump (2015); Tucker-Drob, Briley, and Harden (2013).
56. Plomin (2018): 80.
57. John Cloud, "Why Your DNA Isn't Your Destiny," *Time*, January 6, 2010.
58. Dan Hurley, "Grandma's Experiences Leave a Mark on Your Genes," *Discover*, May 2013.
59. Israel Rosenfeld and Edward Ziff, "Epigenetics: The Evolution Revolution," *New York Review of Books*, June 7, 1918.
60. Tara Swart, "Epigenetics: The Brain-Booster You've Never Heard Of," *Forbes*, September 17, 2018.

61. Waddington (1942).
62. Nanney (1958): 712.
63. Nanney (1958): 713–14.
64. A methyl group is a carbon atom bonded to three hydrogen atoms. It is one of the commonest structural components of organic compounds.
65. This description is drawn from Dor and Cedar (2018).
66. Deichmann (2016).
67. Greally (2018): 1–2 of 2.
68. The glucocorticoid receptor is variously called *GR*, *GCR*, and *NR3C1* in the literature.
69. Weaver, Cervoni, Champagne et al. (2004): 847.
70. Susser and Lin (1992), St Clair, Xu, Wang et al. (2005).
71. Tobi, Slieker, Luijk et al. (2018): 5 of 10.
72. Yehuda, Daskalakis, Bierer et al. (2016): 372.
73. "The studies included in this systematic review met the following criteria: 1) use of a case-control or cohort design; 2) use of at least one analysis investigating DNA methylation of the GR gene in response to a change or perturbation in social environment; and 3) inclusion of studies independent from one another." Turecki and Meaney (2016): 88.
74. Turecki and Meaney (2016) has the following summary statements (pp. 91–93):

    ■ Taken together the studies "show a compelling consensus" of increased methylation in conjunction with stress in early life.
    ■ "We found multiple reports of associations between the quality of childhood experience and the methylation status of the [relevant receptors]."
    ■ "Recent evidence supports the hypothesis that epigenetic plasticity is sustained in the brain throughout adulthood, potentially as a mechanism to cope with the evolving demands of the environment; yet, there are clear moments during development when plasticity is heightened, and these may be more strongly associated with the establishment of life-long epigenetic modifications."
    ■ "Recent rodent studies suggest that epigenetic programming of HPA function [the hypo-thalamic pituitary adrenal axis that constitutes humans' stress response system] occurs at multiple levels of the HPA axis in addition to effects on hippocampal GR expression."
    ■ "The initial reports of epigenetic regulation of hippocampal GR expression are now accompanied by reports of environmentally regulated alterations in the methylation status of multiple genes directly implicated in HPA function."

    The Turecki review also reported a variety of relationships between childhood maltreatment and characteristics of cerebrospinal fluid, cortisol levels, and other forms of sensitization of neural and endocrine responses to stress, but without relating these to changes in methylation.
    Sosnowski, Booth, York et al. (2018) has the following summary statements (8–9):

    ■ *11β-HSD2.* "Overall, the evidence suggests an equivocal association between maternal prenatal stress and infant 11β-HSD2 methylation."
    ■ *OXTR.* "Given the equivocal findings, no conclusions can be drawn regarding prenatal stress and infant OXTR methylation."
    ■ *SLC6A4.* "To date, the findings provide no conclusive evidence that maternal prenatal stress is associated with variable infant SLC6A4 methylation."
    ■ *CRH, CRHBP, and FKBP5.* "Overall, the evidence linking prenatal stress and methylation of these genes is limited, but given the significant findings, further examination of each gene is warranted."

    The Sosnowski review also reported the results of four epigenome-wide association studies (EWAS). EWAS is analogous to GWAS, but for the epigenome instead of the genome. One of the four EWAS found 3,405 genes with infant methylation that were statistically associated with maternal prenatal stress, but none of them were in the HPA axis. Two of the four found no effects of maternal depression or psychotropic medication on infant DNA methylation. EWAS studies have the advantage of being hypothesis-free. The fourth study found 42 such associations, but 33 of them revealed *decreased* levels of infant DNA methylation. None of them were located within the HPA axis. Sosnowski, Booth, York et al. (2018): 6. These studies cannot be treated as strong disconfirmation of a role for methylation in the HPA—the sample sizes were too small for that—but they fail to support the findings of the candidate gene studies.

75. This is a common paraphrase of Max Planck's original version: "A new scientific truth does not triumph by convincing its opponents and making them see the light, but rather because its opponents eventually die, and a new generation grows up that is familiar with it." It was made famous by Kuhn (2012): 150.

76. Greally (2015).

77. Kevin Mitchell, "The Trouble with Epigenetics (Part 1)," *Wiring the Brain*, January 7, 2013, wiringthebrain.com; Kevin Mitchell, "The Trouble with Epigenetics (Part 2)," *Wiring the Brain*, January 14, 2013.

78. Kevin Mitchell, "Grandma's Trauma—A Critical Appraisal of the Evidence for Transgenerational Epigenetic Inheritance in Humans," *Wiring the Brain*, May 29, 2018, wiringthebrain.com.

79. Jill Escher, "No Convincing Evidence? A Response to Kevin Mitchell's Reckless Attack on Epigenetic Inheritance," *Germline Exposures*, July 18, 2018, germlineexposures.org.

80. Kevin Mitchell, "Calibrating Scientific Skepticism—A Wider Look at the Field of Transgenerational Epigenetics," *Wiring the Brain*, July 22, 2018, wiringthebrain.com.

81. Perez and Lehner (2019).

82. Perez and Lehner (2019); Waterland and Jirtle (2003).

83. Kazachenka, Bertozzi, Sjoberg-Herrera et al. (2018).

84. Yeager (2019).

85. Yeager (2019).

86. Horsthemke (2018). The author is the director of the Institut für Humangenetik at the University of Duisburg-Essen. Here is his account of "the roadmap to proving transgenerational epigenetic inheritance" on pages 2 and 3 of 3:

1. Rule out genetic, ecological and cultural inheritance. For studies in mice and rats, inbred strains and strictly controlled environments need to be used. When a pregnant female animal is exposed to a specific environmental stimulus, F3 offspring and subsequent generations must be studied in order to exclude a direct effect of the stimulus on the embryos' somatic cells and germ cells. Even more desirable is the use of in vitro fertilization (IVF), embryo transfer and foster mothers. When a male animal is exposed to an environmental stimulus, F2 offspring must be studied in order to exclude transient effects on germ cells. To ensure that any phenotype is exclusively transmitted via gametes, IVF must be used, controlling for possible artifacts relating to IVF. In contrast with laboratory animals, it is impossible to rule out ecological and cultural inheritance in humans, but genetic effects should and can be excluded. If an epimutation apparently follows Mendelian inheritance patterns, be cautious: you are more likely looking at a secondary epimutation and genetic inheritance. Study the haplotype background of the epimutation: if in a given family it is always on the same haplotype, you are again most likely dealing with a secondary epimutation. Do whole genome sequencing… to search for a genetic variant that might have caused the epimutation and be aware that this variant might be distantly located. Good spots to start looking are the two neighboring genes, where a mutation might cause transcriptional read-through in sense or antisense orientation into the locus under investigation. Unfortunately, if you don't find anything, you still cannot be 100% sure that a genetic variant does not exist.

2. Identify the responsible epigenetic factor in the germ cells. Admittedly, this is easier said than done, especially in female germ cells, which are scarce or unavailable. Be aware that germ cell preparations may be contaminated with somatic cells or somatic DNA. Use swim-up (sperm) or micromanipulation techniques to purify germ cells to the highest purity. Exclude the presence of somatic cells and somatic DNA by molecular testing, for example by methylation analysis of imprinted genes, which are fully methylated or fully unmethylated only in germ cells.

3. Demonstrate that the epigenetic factor in the germ cells is responsible for the phenotypic effect in the next generation. If possible, remove the factor from the affected germ cells and demonstrate that the effect is lost. Add the factor to control germ cells and demonstrate that the effect is gained....In light of [the problems of doing such experiments in humans], this might currently be too much to ask for to prove transgenerational epigenetic inheritance in humans, but should, nevertheless, be kept in mind and discussed.

Despite some unfamiliar technical language, enough of Horsthemke's description of the roadmap is comprehensible to a layperson to convey a sense of how difficult proof is going to be. Much of the roadmap also applies to the requirements for proving epigenetic effects within a generation among humans. It seems safe to conclude that the gap between what has actually been accomplished to date and what has been conveyed to the public is enormous. As for a technical pronouncement about the state of knowledge, here is Horsthemke's closing paragraph:

In conclusion, in my opinion, even if the molecular mechanisms exist to transmit epigenetic information across generations in humans, it is very likely that the transgenerational transmission of culture by communication, imitation, teaching and learning surpasses the effects of epigenetic inheritance and our ability to detect this phenomenon. Cultural inheritance has certainly had an adaptive role in the evolution of our species, but the evidence for transgenerational epigenetic inheritance, as laid out above, is not (yet) conclusive. For now, I remain skeptical.

87. I am referring to the phenomenon known as regression to the mean. It is a statistical phenomenon that applies far beyond heritable traits. See Humphreys (1978).

Part IV: Looking Ahead

1. Wilson (1998): 269.

14: The Shape of the Revolution

1. "Orders of magnitude" is often misused. In this case, it is the correct descriptor. The mainframe used by Mission Control for the moon landing in 1969 was IBM's most advanced model. It had one megabyte of storage.
2. Risch, Spiker, Lotspeich et al. (1999): 504.
3. Boyle, Li, and Pritchard (2017): 1177.
4. Boyle, Li, and Pritchard (2017): 1177.
5. Boyle, Li, and Pritchard (2017): 1179.
6. This number refers to the Boyle study but is given in Jordan, Verbanck, and Do (2018).
7. Davies, Lam, Harris et al. (2018).
8. Pickrell, Berisa, Liu et al. (2016): 709–10.
9. The terminology and example are taken from Jordan, Verbanck, and Do (2018), though the concepts originated earlier.
10. Jordan, Verbanck, and Do (2018).
11. Graham Coop, "Polygenic Scores and Tea Drinking," *The Coop Lab*, March 14, 2018, gcbias.org.

12. Coop, "Polygenic Scores and Tea Drinking."
13. Allegrini, Selzam, Rimfeld et al. (2018).
14. Plomin (2018): vii.
15. Plomin (2018): 137.
16. The following discussion is taken from Plomin (2018): 161–77.
17. Plomin (2018): 165.
18. Plomin (2018): 166.
19. Plomin (2018): 170.
20. Turkheimer (2011).
21. Turkheimer's article was one of the commentaries on the 30th-anniversary republication (of Plomin and Daniels (1987)). Plomin (2011).
22. Turkheimer, Pettersson, and Horn (2014): 532.
23. Johnson, McGue, Krueger et al. (2004).
24. McGue and Lykken (1992).
25. Turkheimer, Pettersson, and Horn (2014): 532.
26. Feldman and Ramachandran (2018). The phrase in quotes is taken from Lewontin (1974).
27. Turkheimer (2011): 600.
28. Plomin (2018): 162.
29. Trzaskowski and Plomin (2015). For an example of its application, see Trzaskowski, Harlaar, Arden et al. (2014).
30. For the position of the advocacy school, see Scheper-Hughes (1995) and Angel-Ajani and Civico (2006). For an account by an anthropologist with a traditional perspective, see Glynn Custred, "Turning Anthropology from Science into Political Activism," James G. Martin Center for Academic Renewal, February 17, 2016, www.jamesgmartin.center. In 2010, the executive committee of the American Anthropological Association, the discipline's major professional association, dropped the word "science" from its mission statement. See Nicholas Wade, "Anthropology a Science? Statement Deepens a Rift," *New York Times*, December 9, 2010.
31. The titles of those that I classified as directly involving sex were: "The Mark of a Woman's Record: Gender and Academic Performance in Hiring"; "Precarious Sexuality: How Men and Women Are Differentially Categorized for Similar Sexual Behavior"; "Unemployment, Temporary Work, and Subjective Well-Being: The Gendered Effect of Spousal Labor Market Insecurity"; "Policy Generosity, Employer Heterogeneity, and Women's Employment Opportunities: The Welfare State Paradox Reexamined"; "Is There a Male Marital Wage Premium? New Evidence from the United States"; "The Evolution of Gender Segregation over the Life Course"; and "Women in the One Percent: Gender Dynamics in Top Income Positions." The ones I classified as directly involving ethnicity were: "Sharing the Burden of the Transition to Adulthood: African American Young Adults' Transition Challenges and Their Mothers' Health Risk"; "Firm Turnover and the Return of Racial Establishment Segregation"; "Compounding Inequalities: How Racial Stereotypes and Discrimination Accumulate Across the Stages of Housing Exchange"; and "The Paradox of Persistence: Explaining the Black-White Gap in Bachelor's Degree Completion." The ones I classified as directly involving class were: "Social and Genetic Pathways in Multigenerational Transmission of Educational Attainment"; "Income Inequality and Class Divides in Parental Investments"; "Education, Smoking, and Cohort Change: Forwarding a Multidimensional Theory of the Environmental Moderation of Genetic Effects"; "Relative Education and the Advantage of a College Degree"; "Political Consequences of Survival Strategies Among the Urban Poor"; "Educational Inequality, Educational Expansion, and Intergenerational Income Persistence in the United States"; and "Encultured Biases: The Role of Products in Pathways to Inequality."
32. E,g,, Kahneman, Slovic, and Tversky (1982) and Thaler and Sunstein (2008).
33. Harden, Domingue, Belsky et al. (2019).

34. "On the bottom line, a variable that has no within-family variation cannot covary with the within-family variation in another variable." Turkheimer, D'Onofrio, Maes et al. (2005): 1226.
35. Trzaskowski and Plomin (2015): 9.
36. Population stratification does not change the situation. Population stratification can cause major errors in interpretation of the polygenic scores, but it's irrelevant to backward causation.
37. The subsequent discussion and direct quotes are based on Eric Turkheimer, "The Blueprint Metaphor," GHA Project: Turkheimer's Projects: Genetics and Human Agency, October 30, 2018, geneticshumanagency.org.
38. I reviewed the evidence on G×E interactions at early ages in chapter 13, but I did not give a full account of the degree to which many psychologists believe that G×E interactions are pervasive and, once understood, will fundamentally alter our conception of the heritability of traits. Many expressions of this position are akin to heritability denial—for example, Burt and Simons (2014), discussed in note 26 for chapter 10. A knowledgeable and nuanced expression of this position, combining both theory and empirical examples, is Sauce and Matzel (2018).
39. Methylation changes during the lifespan come into the picture here, but what we know to date does not give reason to think that they will prove to be a major confounding factor. See the discussion of epigenetics in chapter 13.
40. I owe the idea for this search to Steven Hsu, who conducted a similar search for his blog, *Pessimism of the Intellect, Optimism of the Will* (infoproc.blogspot.com), May 25, 2019.
41. Plomin (2018): 172.

15: Reflections and Speculations

1. Pinker (2002): 340.
2. The concept of the mind as initially a blank surface that experience writes upon goes back to the Greeks and has a long pedigree thereafter. But Locke's formulation in *An Essay Concerning Human Understanding* has been the main source for the modern era. Locke actually used the phrase "white paper" ("Let us suppose the mind to be, as we say, white paper, void of all characters, without any ideas"). Book II, chapter 1.
3. Pinker (2002): 5.
4. Smith (1776): vol. I, chapter 2. Smith (1979).
5. Hamilton, Madison, and Jay (1982): No. 51.
6. Leon Trotsky, "Socialism Will Bring Giant Advances for Mankind," *The Militant* 5, no. 34 (1924): 5.
7. Durkheim (1982): 33.
8. Durkheim, *The Rules of Sociological Method*, quoted in Tooby and Cosmides (1992): 24–25.
9. E.g., Watson (1914); Skinner (1938).
10. Watson (1924), quoted in Pinker (2002): 19.
11. Contrary to rumor, the Skinner box was not used to experiment with operant conditioning on Skinner's infant daughter, though Skinner did invent an "air crib" that was intended to reduce the tasks of caring for an infant.
12. On a personal note, my coauthor on *The Bell Curve*, Richard Herrnstein, was a behavioral psychologist who succeeded B. F. Skinner as the Edgar Pierce Professor of Psychology at Harvard. As you will find if you read *The Bell Curve* or *Crime and Human Nature*, coauthored with James Q. Wilson, Herrnstein was a behaviorist who did not go off the deep end.
13. Murray (1984).
14. Pinker (2002): viii.
15. Hamilton (1964); Trivers (1972).
16. Wilson (1975); Dawkins (1976).

17. Tooby and Cosmides (1992). The book in which it appeared, Barkow, Cosmides, and Tooby (1992), is considered a foundational text for evolutionary biology.
18. Stewart-Williams (2018): Appendix A.
19. von Hippel and Buss (2017).
20. For a systematic discussion of the science of evolutionary psychology, see Low (2015). For two technical book-length accounts of the sociobiology controversy presenting the arguments on both sides, see Segerstråle (2000) and Alcock (2001).
21. Stewart-Williams (2018): 291. My characterization of the attacks on evolutionary psychology are a condensation of Steve Stewart-Williams's presentation in Appendix 1.
22. Stewart-Williams (2018): 292.
23. Spiro (1954).
24. Beit-Hallahmi (1981).
25. Technically, it applies only to colleges and universities that accept federal funds. But you can count the ones that don't on the fingers of one hand.
26. For greater male attraction to team sports from childhood onward, see Lever (1978); Sandberg and Meyer-Bahlburg (1994); and Deaner, Geary, Puts et al. (2012). For cross-national data, see Deaner and Smith (2012).
27. For rough-and-tumble play, see DiPietro (1981) and Pellegrini (2007). For sex-typical competition and exposure to testosterone in utero, see Hines and Kaufman (1994). For sex differences in aggression, see Card, Stucky, Sawalani et al. (2008). Byrnes, Miller, and Schafer (1997) is a meta-analysis of the literature on risk-taking as of 1997. Subsequent work includes Zuckerman and Kuhlman (2000) and Morrongiello and Dawber (2004). For the effects of testosterone on an increase in risk-taking in women, see van Honk, Schutter, Hermans et al. (2004).
28. Lewontin (1970).
29. Jencks (1979).
30. My conjecture was inspired by Cheverud's conjecture that genetic correlations and phenotypic correlations are similar. Cheverud (1984); Cheverud (1988). Subsequent research (e.g., Dochtermann (2011); Sodini, Kemper, Wray et al. (2018)) indicates that the conjecture is usually correct.
31. Murray (2003): 275–83. From 1400 to 1800 CE, the only famous Jewish figure living as a Jew was Spinoza (Montaigne had a Jewish mother but was a lifelong Catholic).
32. There are exceptions to the slow pace of change in milieu. For example, even though the sexual revolution in America was brewing throughout the twentieth century, there was a gaping discontinuity in the course of a few years in the mid-1960s.
33. Murray (1984): x.
34. For AA, see Kelly and Yeterian (2011); for KIPP, see Angrist, Dynarski, Kane et al. (2012); for Success Academy, see Unterman (2017).
35. Herrnstein and Murray (1994): 535. The subsequent discussion draws directly from the concluding pages of *The Bell Curve*.
36. Murray (2006).
37. Walter Lippmann, "The Great Confusion," *New Republic*, January 3, 1923: 46.

Appendix 2: Sexual Dimorphism in Humans

1. Fairbairn (2016): 105.
2. Kodric-Brown and Brown (1987). For a nontechnical account, see Paco Garcia-Gonzalez, Damian Dowling, and Magdalena Nystrand, "Male, Female—Ah, What's the Difference?," *The Conversation*, March 26, 2013, theconversation.com.
3. Frank Newport, "Americans Greatly Overestimate Percent Gay, Lesbian in U.S.," *Gallup News*, May 21, 2015, galluppoll.com.
4. I adapted this formulation from Sax (2002).

5. This definition is taken from Blackless, Charuvastra, Derryck et al. (2000).

6. Khalid, Oerton, Dezateux et al. (2012) found incomplete masculinization in 2 out of 33 male cases diagnosed at birth. For 44 female cases, 33 presented with virilization of female genitalia.

7. All the percentages in the table are taken unchanged from Blackless, Charuvastra, Derryck et al. (2000) to avoid needless arguments. These additional points should be noted:

   Classic CAH. Blackless, Charuvastra, Derryck et al. (2000): Table 8 puts the incidence of classic CAH for females and males combined at 0.0077 percent (1 in about 13,000). A 2012 epidemiological study of classic CAH in Great Britain found a smaller incidence of 0.0055 percent for males and females combined (1 in about 18,000). Khalid, Oerton, Dezateux et al. (2012). Forty-three percent of the cases were male.

   Androgen insensitivity syndrome. The Blackless study puts incidence at .0084 percent (about 1 in 12,000) for all forms combined. Subsequent national epidemiological studies in Denmark (Berglund, Johannsen, Stochholm et al. (2016)), and the Netherlands (Boehmer, Brüggenwirth, van Assendelft et al. (2001)) found incidence rates of 0.0064 percent (about 1 in 15,600) and 0.0010 percent (1 in 10,000) respectively.

8. Although the authors searched for incidence studies worldwide, they caution that because the bulk of the studies were from Europe and North America, their generalizations hold only for a "generic Euro-American, Caucasian population." Blackless, Charuvastra, Derryck et al. (2000): 159. The 1.728 percent estimate of the incidence of intersexuality in Blackless was given prominence in Fausto-Sterling (2000) and attracted considerable media attention.

9. Blackless, Charuvastra, Derryck et al. (2000): 152. The original text includes two references that are omitted here.

10. Ranke and Saenger (2001). Hyperfemininity is such a common symptom of XXX women that the identification of a lesbian woman with Turner syndrome warranted a note in a technical journal. Fishbain and Vilasuso (1980).

11. Otter, Schrander-Stumpel, and Curfs (2010).

12. Sax (2002).

13. About 7–8 percent of persons with vaginal agenesis also have AIS, but they would be classified as intersex under the AIS criterion. Foley and Morley (1992).

14. Carmina, Dewailly, Escobar-Morreale et al. (2017).

15. Speiser, Knochenhauer, D'ewailly et al. (2000).

16. Moran, Azziz, Carmina et al. (2000); Witchel and Azziz (2010).

17. Carmina, Dewailly, Escobar-Morreale et al. (2017): 12.

18. Witchel and Azziz (2010).

19. As in the case of hermaphrodites, classic CAH, and AIS, the incidence rates for the other departures from the Platonic ideal of sexual dimorphism are as reported in Blackless, Charuvastra, Derryck et al. (2000): Table 8. Subsequent research gives reason to think the estimate of 1.5 percent is too high. Carmina, Dewailly, Escobar-Morreale et al. (2017), a systematic literature review and analysis published 17 years after the Blackless study, studied late-onset CAH women who presented symptoms of androgen excess. They estimated a worldwide prevalence of 4.2 percent among such women. Azziz, Carmina, Dewailly et al. (2009) estimated that ~10 percent of women are affected by hyperandrogenism. The authors declined to extrapolate an estimate of prevalence of late-onset CAH from those numbers both because of the imprecision of the 10 percent prevalence rate and because of the uncertainty about the numbers of asymptomatic women. At a minimum, it seems unlikely that the prevalence of symptomatic late-onset CAH as a percentage of the female population could reach 1.5 percent.

20. Sax (2002): 177.

21. Gates (2011): Fig. 1.

22. Bailey, Vasey, Diamond et al. (2016).

23. Sources: Frank Newport, "In U.S., Estimate of LGBT Population Rises to 4.5%," *Gallup News*, May 22, 2018; Tables from the National Health Interview Survey 2015 on the survey's website, www.cdc.gov/nchs/nhis; author's analysis, General Social Survey 2016.

24. Studies were limited to those that claimed nationally representative samples of adults, usually ages 18 and above, and obtained self-identified sexual orientation limited to the categories of gay/lesbian, bisexual, and heterosexual. Percentages are based on persons who chose one of those categories. I omitted studies where more than a few percent of the answers were "other" or more than a few percent of the participants refused to answer (because large numbers of such responses might indicate people who were homosexual or bisexual but didn't want to say so). The sources were: Norway: Gates (2011); UK: Sexual Orientation dataset available at the Office for National Statistics website, www.ons.gov.uk; Canada: Canadian Community Health Survey, Cycle 2.1, available at the Statistics Canada webside, www.stat.can.gc.ca; Australia: Richters, Altman, Badcock et al. (2014): Table 1; New Zealand: Greaves, Barlow, Lee et al. (2017).

25. Gates (2011). The Williams Institute is a think tank attached to the UCLA Law School that is devoted to law and public policy regarding sexual orientation and gender identity.

26. Bailey, Vasey, Diamond et al. (2016): 53.

27. Gates (2011): Fig. 4.

28. Savin-Williams and Vrangalova (2013): 60.

29. Savin-Williams and Vrangalova (2013): 59.

30. Bailey, Vasey, Diamond et al. (2016): Fig. 1.

31. Bailey (2009).

32. Savin-Williams and Cohen (2018).

33. Savin-Williams and Cohen (2018): 197.

34. For an overview of scholarly opinion on the varieties of transsexualism, see Blanchard (2008) and Bailey and Blanchard (2017).

35. Bailey, Vasey, Diamond et al. (2016).

36. Bailey, Vasey, Diamond et al. (2016).

37. The publication of Littman (2018) in August 2018 caused an uproar among transgender advocates. See Meredith Wadman, "New Paper Ignites Storm over Whether Teens Experience 'Rapid Onset' of Transgender Identity," *Science*, August 30, 2018, www.sciencemag.org/news. The protests led the online journal in which it was published, *PLoS ONE*, to conduct a post-publication review and require Littman to issue a correction, posted on March 19, 2019, that emphasized the study was based on parents' reports and was intended as a hypothesis-generating study. She was also required to include an expanded discussion about limitations and biases. The revisions did not lead to any substantive changes in the results reported in the original article. The reaction to Littman's cautiously analyzed and mildly worded research could serve as a case study for my observation in the introduction that for an academician to depart openly from the orthodoxy usually carries a price.

38. Littman (2018): 15–16 of 41.

39. J. Michael Bailey and Ray Blanchard, "Gender Dysphoria Is Not One Thing," *4thWaveNow*, December 7, 2017, 4thwavenow.com.

40. de Graaf, Giovanardi, Zitz et al. (2018).

41. Zucker (2017).

42. de Graaf, Giovanardi, Zitz et al. (2018): Fig. 1.

43. Arcelus, Bouman, Van Den Noortgate et al. (2015).

44. Zucker (2017).

45. From the *Encyclopedia of Surgery*, available online at www.surgeryencyclopedia.com: "Reliable statistics are extremely difficult to obtain. Many sexual reassignment procedures are conducted in private facilities that are not subject to reporting requirements. Sexual reassignment surgery is often conducted outside of the United States. The number of gender reassignment

procedures conducted in the United States each year is estimated at between 100 and 500. The number worldwide is estimated to be two to five times larger."

Appendix 3: Sex Differences in Brain Volumes and Variance

1. The earliest was Willerman, Schultz, Rutledge et al. (1991).
2. For a review of the 1990s literature, see Goldstein, Seidman, Horton et al. (2001).
3. Based on the 25 unique studies listed in Ruigrok, Salimi-Khorshidi, Lai et al. (2014): Table 2.
4. Ritchie, Cox, Shen et al. (2018).
5. Desikan, Ségonne, Fischl et al. (2006).
6. Caspari (1979).
7. Holloway (1979); Epstein (1979).
8. Willerman, Schultz, Rutledge et al. (1991).
9. McDaniel (2005), a meta-analysis of in vivo brain volume and full-scale IQ, reported an average correlation of +.33. Pietschnig, Penke, Wicherts et al. (2015) argued for a comparatively low average of +.24.
10. Gignac and Bates (2017) reanalyzed the 2015 set of studies in Pietschnig, Penke, Wicherts et al. (2015), restricting them to ones with samples of healthy adults and correcting for restriction of range. They reached an estimated correlation of +.31. The 2017 meta-analysis also classified studies according to their quality of measurement—"fair," "good," and "excellent." The estimated correlations for these subsets were +.23, +.32, and +.39 respectively.
11. van der Linden, Dunkel, and Madison (2017): Table A1.
12. Perhaps the number of neurons in the cerebellum is also important. See Buckner (2013).
13. Herculano-Houzel (2017). Comparing brain volumes of men and women does not pose the same problem. The Ruigrok meta-analysis found that the male-female ratios for the volumes of the cerebrum and cerebellum were close (9.8 percent and 8.6 percent larger in males respectively). Ruigrok, Salimi-Khorshidi, Lai et al. (2014): Table 3.
14. See Hogan, Staff, Bunting et al. (2011), which also has a good literature review of similar work.
15. Reardon, Seidlitz, Vandekar et al. (2018).
16. Van Essen (2018): 1184.
17. Reardon, Seidlitz, Vandekar et al. (2018): Table S3.
18. There is an active research program questioning whether this is true. Neves, Guercio, Anjos-Travassos et al. (2018) found that "whereas neuronal number is a good predictor of cognitive skills across species, it is not a predictor of cognitive, sensory or motor ability across individuals within a species, which suggests that other factors are more relevant for explaining cognitive differences between individuals of the same species." The species in question was mice, however, so much remains to be learned.
19. Winkler, Kochunov, Blangero et al. (2010).
20. Ritchie, Cox, Shen et al. (2018).
21. Sowell, Peterson, Kan et al. (2007).
22. Gur and Gur (2017): 9.
23. de Vries (2004): 1063.
24. de Vries (2004): 1064.
25. de Vries and Forger (2015).
26. Murray (2003).
27. A good one-source summary of the evidence is Lehre, Lehre, Laake et al. (2009).
28. Darwin (1900).
29. Remarkably, eight Nobel Prizes had been won using research on fruit flies through 2017: Thomas Hunt Morgan, 1933; Hermann Muller, 1946; George W. Beadle and Edward L. Tatum, 1958; Max Delbrück, Alfred D. Hershey, and Salvador E. Luria, 1969; Edward B.

Lewis, Christiane Nüsslein-Volhard, and Eric F. Wieschaus, 1995; Richard Axel and Linda Buck, 2004; Jules Hoffmann, Bruce Beutler, and Ralph Steinman, 2011; Jeffrey Hall, Michael Rosbash, and Michael Young, 2017.

30. Bateman (1948). My summary is drawn from Trivers (1972): 53–54.
31. Trivers (1972): 56, 55. See also Williams (1966).
32. Geary (2017): 357.
33. Clutten-Brock (1989).
34. For the most comprehensive literature review of sexual selection in humans and across species, see Geary (2010): chapters 2–8. Archer and Mehdikhani (2003) has a concise review of the major theoretical approaches. See also Pomiankowski and Møller (1995).
35. Del Giudice, Barrett, Belsky et al. (2018).
36. Stewart-Williams and Thomas (2013).
37. The quotation from Reinhold and Engqvist continues:

> Theoretical considerations reveal a slightly more complicated picture. Under the simplest genetic assumptions—alleles contribute additively to trait expression (heterozygotes are intermediate to homozygotes), and they have equal hemizygous and homozygous effects on trait expression (e.g., due to dosage compensation)—a polymorphic sex chromosome-linked locus will contribute twice as much to trait variance in the heterogametic sex, as it will to variance in the homogametic sex. Quantitative traits are of course polygenic and are likely influenced by genes spread across the sex chromosome and the autosomes. The contribution of the sex chromosome to trait variance should therefore depend on its relative size within the genome (i.e., the proportion of genes that it carries), with trait variance differences between the sexes being less pronounced in species with small sex chromosomes, and more pronounced in species with large sex chromosomes. In addition, differences will be dampened by environmental effects (i.e., will be lower for traits with low heritability). Even so, qualitative predictions of the model remain valid for any trait that is to some extent heritable irrespective of sex chromosome sizes. (Reinhold and Engqvist (2013): 3662–63).

38. Ritchie, Cox, Shen et al. (2018): 8.
39. Author's analysis, National Health and Nutrition Examination Survey, 2015–2016 (www.cdc.gov). The sagittal abdominal diameter represents the mean of four measures. The blood pressure results represent the mean of the first three readings.
40. The greater female variability in BMI must be assessed in light of the much larger effect size for height (–1.91) than for weight (–0.62), which are the two components used to calculate BMI. The equation for computing BMI is w/h^2, where w is weight in kilograms and h is height in meters.
41. Following Katzman and Alliger (1992), all mean VRs reported in this appendix use the mean of log-transformed values of the VRs. To see why using logged values is necessary when calculating means, recall that a ratio is the arbitrary choice of a numerator and denominator. Consider two tests in which the male variance is divided by the female variance. In the first test, the male variance is 100 and the female variance is 80, giving a VR of 1.25. In the second test, the male variance is 80 and the female variance is 100, giving a VR of 0.80. The simple mean of 1.25 and 0.80 is 1.025, falsely indicating that average male variance is slightly higher than female variance. The logged values of 1.25 and 0.80 are +0.223 and –0.223, leading to a mean of zero, which correctly transforms to a VR of 1.00.
42. Author's analysis, Gordon, Churchill, Clauser et al. (1989).
43. Author's analysis, Dodds, Syddall, Cooper et al. (2014): Table 2.
44. Author's analysis, Janssen, Heymsfield, Wang et al. (2000): Table 1.
45. It is not clear how much the adjustment for BMI was affected by sample selection. The authors specify that they built variability in adiposity into the sample. One indication that

this significantly affected the male-female distribution of BMI is that the variance ratio for weight was higher for women than for men (VR = 0.79). This is in striking contrast with the results from the NHANES nationally representative sample (VR = 1.25), the Nordic Reference Interval Project used in the Norwegian study (VR = 1.13), and the Army's anthropometric study (VR = 1.77), which was representative of active-duty uniformed Army personnel.

46. Buss (1989).
47. The authors also used meta-analyses of two traits that are *not* believed to be involved in sexual selection: anger as a personality trait ("touchiness") and self-esteem. Neither showed a significant sex difference in either effect size or variance ratio. Archer and Mehdikhani (2003): Table 4.
48. Archer and Mehdikhani (2003): Table 4. The reported means were expressed in log-transformed variance ratios. I converted them back to the standard metric.
49. The huge effect size of 2.00 for preferred age difference is explained by the way the question was asked, which resulted in men in all cultures universally giving a negative number of years and women giving a positive number of years. The actual means across the 37 cultures were –2.66 years for men and +3.42 years for women. That's appropriately seen as a big sex difference in preferred age, but it's a small one—just 0.76 years—if instead the respondents had been asked to give the preferred age difference between the man and the woman (men and women alike agree that it's better if the man is older, and by a similar age difference).
50. This and the rest of the statistics are based on Borkenau, McCrae, and Terracciano (2013): Table 1.
51. There was a tendency for male variability to be greater in the more gender-egalitarian countries. The mean VR for the 10 most gender-equal countries on the Gender Inequality Index (GII) was 1.10; for the ten most gender-unequal countries, it was 1.03. But the relationship was not strong or consistent.
52. The six studies were Project Talent, with a sample of 73,425 15-year-olds (1960); the National Longitudinal Study of the High School Class of 1972 (1972), with a sample of 16,860 12th-grade students; the National Longitudinal Study of Youth (1980), with a sample of 11,914 noninstitutionalized 15- to 22-year-olds; the High School and Beyond Study (1980) with a sample of 25,069 12th-grade students; the National Educational Longitudinal Study (1992) with a sample of 24,599 8th-grade students as of 1988; and the National Assessments of Educational Progress from 1971 to 1992, with varying but extremely large samples of 17-year-olds enrolled in school. Hedges and Nowell (1995).
53. Hedges and Nowell (1995): Table 2.
54. Hedges and Nowell (1995): 44.
55. Hedges and Nowell (1995): 44.
56. Data for 1971–92 from Hedges and Nowell (1995): Table 3. Data from 2002 to 2015 from the Department of Education Statistics Data Explorer.
57. Arden and Plomin (2006).
58. Feingold (1994).
59. The "other political entities" were Macau and Hong Kong.
60. Machin and Pekkarinen (2008): Supplemental Tables 1 and 2. The authors also analyzed TIMSS and PIRLS scores, reporting that both showed significantly higher male variance in most (though not all) countries. Table S4.
61. Author's analysis, PISA-2015 data. Variance ratios were averaged using logged values, and the result converted back to the ratio metric.
62. Feingold (1994): 83. He had also taken that position in earlier articles.
63. Warne, Godwin, and Smith (2013).
64. The figure shows the predicted and actual values calculated using the observed male and female means. A parallel plot that assumed equal means showed the same pattern with only mild attenuation. For values based on sex-specific means, 83 percent of the actual ratios were

higher than predicted; for values based on the assumption of equal means, the corresponding figure was 73 percent. The minority of cases that were below the diagonal (the actual values were smaller than the predicted values) were even closer to the diagonal in the case of the equal-means calculation than in the sex-specific calculation.

Russell Warne also provided breakdowns by sex for subtests in the Armed Services Vocational Aptitude Battery (ASVAB) administered to the 1979 cohort of the National Longitudinal Survey of Youth. But the sample size was 11,914, meaning that only the 95th percentile and 98th percentile categories could be expected to have interpretably large samples. A further problem was that the VRs and effect sizes for three of the subtests (on auto shop info, mechanical comprehension, and electronics information) were so large that hardly any females got scores in the top percentiles. That said, the results were consistent with those from the Early Childhood Longitudinal Study. For the 95th percentile, the most interpretable category, the median predicted male-female ratio was 2.16 compared to 2.11 for the actual male-female ratio (the median is given rather than the mean because of the extremely large VRs for auto shop info, mechanical comprehension, and electronics information).

65. Johnson, Carothers, and Deary (2008): 526.
66. Author's calculations of the predicted values based on Johnson, Carothers, and Deary (2008): Table 1. Actual values were given in Johnson, Carothers, and Deary (2008): 526.
67. Johnson, Carothers, and Deary (2008): Table 1.
68. Johnson, Carothers, and Deary (2008): 529.

References

ACT. 2009. *Act Interest Inventory Technical Manual.* Iowa City, IA: ACT.

Aguinis, Herman, Steven A. Culpepper, and Charles A. Pierce. 2016. "Differential Prediction Generalization in College Admissions Testing." *Journal of Educational Psychology* 108 (7): 1045–59.

Akey, Joshua M. 2009. "Constructing Genomic Maps of Positive Selection in Humans: Where Do We Go from Here?" *Genome Research* 19 (5): 711–22.

Alcala, Nicolas, and Noah A. Rosenberg. 2016. "Mathematical Constraints on F_{ST}: Biallelic Markers in Arbitrarily Many Populations." *Genetics* 206 (3): 1581–600.

Alcock, John. 2001. *The Triumph of Sociobiology.* Oxford: Oxford University Press.

Alexander, Gerianne M., and Melissa Hines. 2002. "Sex Differences in Response to Children's Toys in Nonhuman Primates." *Evolution of Human Behavior* 23: 467–79.

Alexander, Gerianne M., and Teresa Wilcox. 2012. "Sex Differences in Early Infancy." *Child Development Perspectives* 6 (4): 400–406.

Alexander, Gerianne M., Teresa Wilcox, and Rebecca Woods. 2009. "Sex Differences in Infants' Visual Interest in Toys." *Archives of Sexual Behavior* 38 (23): 427–33.

Allegrini, Andrea, Saskia Selzam, Kaili Rimfeld et al. 2018. "Genomic Prediction of Cognitive Traits in Childhood and Adolescence." *bioRxiv.*

Allen, Timothy A., Amanda R. Rueter, Samantha V. Abram et al. 2017. "Personality and Neural Correlates of Mentalizing Ability." *European Journal of Personality* 31 (6): 599–613.

Al-Shawaf, Laith, David M. G. Lewis, and David M. Buss. 2017. "Sex Differences in Disgust: Why Are Women More Easily Disgusted Than Men?" *Emotion Review* 10 (2): 149–60.

American Sociological Association. 2003. *The Importance of Collecting Data and Doing Social Scientific Research on Race.* Washington, DC: American Sociological Association.

Andersen, Margaret L., and Patricia H. Collins, eds. 2019. *Race, Class, Gender: Intersections and Inequalities.* 10th ed. Boston: Cengage Learning.

Anderson, Edgar, and G. Ledyard Stebbins. 1954. "Hybridization as an Evolutionary Stimulus." *Evolution* 8: 378–88.

Anderson, Nathaniel E., Keith A. Harenski, Carla L. Harenski et al. 2018. "Machine Learning of Brain Gray Matter Differentiates Sex in a Large Forensic Sample." *Human Brain Mapping* 40 (5): 1496–506.

Andreano, Joseph M., Bradford C. Dickerson, and Lisa Feldman Barrett. 2014. "Sex Differences in the Persistence of the Amygdala Response to Negative Material." *Social Cognitive and Affective Neuroscience* 9: 1388–94.

Angel-Ajani, Asale, and Aldo Civico, eds. 2006. *Engaged Observer: Anthropology, Advocacy, and Activism.* New Brunswick, NJ: Rutgers University Press.

Angrist, Joshua D., Susan M. Dynarski, Thomas J. Kane et al. 2012. "Who Benefits from KIPP?" *Journal of Policy Analysis and Management* 31 (4): 837–60.

Arcelus, Jon, Walter Bouman, Wim Van Den Noortgate et al. 2015. "Systematic Review and Meta-analysis of Prevalence Studies in Transsexualism." *European Psychiatry* 30 (6): 807–15.

Archer, John. 2019. "The Reality and Evolutionary Significance of Human Psychological Sex Differences." *Biological Reviews*. Advance online publication.

Archer, John, and Mani Mehdikhani. 2003. "Variability Among Males in Sexually Selected Attributes." *Review of General Psychology* 7 (3): 219–36.

Ardekani, Babak A., Khadija Figarsky, and John J. Sidtis. 2013. "Sexual Dimorphism in the Human Corpus Callosum: An MRI Study Using the Oasis Brain Database." *Cerebral Cortex* 23: 2514–20.

Arden, Rosalind, and Robert Plomin. 2006. "Sex Differences in Variance of Intelligence Across Childhood." *Personality and Individual Differences* 41: 39–48.

Argue, Debbie, Denise Donlon, Colin Groves et al. 2006. "Homo Floresiensis: Microcephalic, Pygmoid, Australopithecus, or Homo?" *Journal of Human Evolution* 51 (4): 360–74.

Arnett, Anne B., Bruce F. Pennington, Robin L. Peterson et al. 2017. "Explaining the Sex Difference in Dyslexia." *Journal of Child Psychology and Psychiatry, and Allied Disciplines* 58 (6): 719–27.

Arnold, Arthur P. 2017. "A General Theory of Sexual Differentiation." *Journal of Neuroscience Research* 95 (1–2): 291–300.

Arnold, M. L. 1997. *Natural Hybridization and Evolution.* New York: Oxford University Press.

Aronson, Joshua, Carrie B. Fried, and Catherine Good. 2002. "Reducing the Effects of Stereotype Threat on African American College Students by Shaping Theories of Intelligence." *Journal of Experimental Social Psychology* 38 (2): 113–25.

Arribas-Aguila, David, Francisco J. Abad, and Roberto Colom. 2019. "Testing the Developmental Theory of Sex Differences in Intelligence Using Latent Modeling: Evidence from the Tea Ability Battery (Bat-7)." *Personality and Individual Differences* 138: 212–18.

Asbury, Kathryn, Theodore D. Wachs, and Robert Plomin. 2005. "Environmental Moderators of Genetic Influence on Verbal and Nonverbal Abilities in Early Childhood." *Intelligence* 33 (6): 643–61.

Astell, Mary. 1700. *Some Reflections upon Marriage.* London: John Nutt.

Auer, P. L., and G. Lettre. (2015). "Rare Variant Association Studies: Considerations, Challenges and Opportunities." *Genome Medicine* 7 (1): 16.

Auyeung, B., Aneesha Ahluwalia, L. Thomson et al. 2012. "Prenatal Versus Postnatal Sex Steroid Hormone Effects on Autistic Traits in Children at 18 to 24 Months of Age." *Molecular Autism* 3 (17): 1–5.

Auyeung, B., S. Baron-Cohen, E. Ashwin et al. 2009. "Fetal Testosterone and Autistic Traits." *British Journal of Psychology* 100 (Pt. 1): 1–22.

Auyeung, B., S. Baron-Cohen, Emma Chapman et al. 2006. "Foetal Testosterone and the Child Systemizing Quotient." *European Journal of Endocrinology* 155: 123–30.

Auyeung, B., R. Knickmeyer, E. Ashwin et al. 2012. "Effects of Fetal Testosterone on Visuospatial Ability." *Archives of Sexual Behavior* 41: 571–81.

Avise, John C. 2014. *Conceptual Breakthroughs in Evolutionary Genetics: A Brief History of Shifting Paradigms.* New York: Elsevier.

Azziz, Ricardo, Enrico Carmina, Didier Dewailly et al. 2009. "The Androgen Excess and PCOS Society Criteria for the Polycystic Ovary Syndrome: The Complete Task Force Report." *Fertility and Sterility* 91 (2): 456–88.

Bae, Christopher J., Katerina Douka, and Michael D. Petraglia. 2017. "On the Origin of Modern Humans: Asian Perspectives." *Science* 358 (6368).

Bailey, J. Michael. 2009. "What Is Sexual Orientation and Do Women Have One?" In *Contemporary Perspectives on Lesbian, Gay, and Bisexual Identities*, edited by D. A. Hope, 43–64. New York: Springer.

Bailey, J. Michael, Paul L. Vasey, Lisa M. Diamond et al. 2016. "Sexual Orientation, Controversy, and Science." *Psychological Science in the Public Interest* 17 (2): 45–101.

Baird, A. D., S. J. Wilson, P. F. Bladin et al. 2004. "The Amygdala and Sexual Drive: Insights from Temporal Lobe Epilepsy Surgery." *Annals of Neurology* 55: 87–96.

Balaton, Bradley P., and Carolyn J. Brown. 2016. "Escape Artists of the X Chromosome." *Trends in Genetics* 32 (6): 348–59.

Barkow, J. H., L. Cosmides, and J. Tooby, eds. 1992. *The Adapted Mind: Evolutionary Psychology and the Generation of Culture*. Oxford: Oxford University Press.

Barnes, J. C., and Brian Boutwell. 2013. "A Demonstration of the Generalizability of Twin-Based Research on Antisocial Behavior." *Behavior Genetics* 43 (2): 120–31.

Barnes, J. C., John Paul Wright, Brian B. Boutwell et al. 2014. "Demonstrating the Validity of Twin Research in Criminology." *Criminology* 52 (4): 588–626.

Baron-Cohen, Simon. 2002. "The Extreme Male Brain Theory of Autism." *Trends in Cognitive Sciences* 6 (6): 248–54.

———. 2003. *The Essential Difference: Male and Female Brains and the Truth About Autism*. New York: Basic Books.

Baron-Cohen, Simon, Jennifer Richler, Dheraj Bisarya et al. 2003. "The Systemizing Quotient: An Investigation of Adults with Asperger Syndrome or High–Functioning Autism, and Normal Sex Differences." *Philosophical Transactions of the Royal Society B: Biological Sciences* 358 (1430): 361–74.

Baron-Cohen, Simon, and Sally Wheelwright. 2004. "The Empathy Quotient: An Investigation of Adults with Asperger Syndrome or High Functioning Autism, and Normal Sex Differences." *Journal of Autism and Developmental Disorders* 34 (2): 163–75.

Barrett, J., and J. L. Armony. 2009. "Influence of Trait Anxiety on Brain Activity During the Acquisition and Extinction of Aversive Conditioning." *Psychological Medicine* 39 (2): 255–65.

Bartels, M., C. E. M. van Beijsterveldt, and D. I. Boomsma. 2009. "Breastfeeding, Maternal Education and Cognitive Function: A Prospective Study in Twins." *Behavior Genetics* 39: 616–22.

Bartz, J. A., J. Zaki, N. Bolger et al. 2011. "Social Effects of Oxytocin in Humans: Context and Person Matter." *Trends in Cognitive Sciences* 15 (7): 301–9.

Bateman, A. J. 1948. "Intra-sexual Selection in Drosophila." *Heredity* 2: 349.

Bates, Timothy C., Narelle K. Hansell, Nicholas G. Martin et al. 2016. "When Does Socioeconomic Status (SES) Moderate the Heritability of IQ? No Evidence for G × SES Interaction for IQ in a Representative Sample of 1176 Australian Adolescent Twin Pairs." *Intelligence* 56: 10–15.

Bates, Timothy C., Gary J. Lewis, and Alexander Weiss. 2013. "Childhood Socioeconomic Status Amplifies Genetic Effects on Adult Intelligence." *Psychological Science* 24 (10): 2111–16.

Batty, G. David, K. M. Wennerstad, George D. Smith et al. 2008. "IQ in Early Adulthood and Mortality by Middle Age: Cohort Study of One Million Swedish Men." *Epidemiology* 20 (1): 100–109.

Baumeister, Roy F., Jennifer D. Campbell, Joachim I. Kreuger et al. 2003. "Does High Self-Esteem Cause Better Performance, Interpersonal Success, Happiness, or Healthier Lifestyles?" *Psychological Science in the Public Interest* 7 (4): 1–44.

Beit-Hallahmi, Benjamin. 1981. "The Kibbutz Family: Revival or Survival." *Journal of Family Issues* 2 (3): 259–74.

Beltz, Adriene, Jane Swanson, and Sheri Berenbaum. 2011. "Gendered Occupational Interests: Prenatal Androgen Effects on Psychological Orientation to Things Versus People." *Hormones and Behavior* 60 (4): 313–17.

Benbow, Camilla P., and Julian C. Stanley. 1980. "Sex Differences in Mathematical Ability: Fact or Artifact?" *Science* 210: 1262–64.

———. 1983. "Sex Differences in Mathematical Reasoning Ability: More Facts." *Science* 222: 1029–31.

Benenson, J. F., V. Duggan, and H. Markovits. 2004. "Sex Differences in Infants' Attraction to Group Versus Individual Stimuli." *Infant Behavior and Development* 27: 173–80.

Berenbaum, Sheri. 2017. "Born This Way?" *Science* 355 (6322): 254.

———. 2018. "Beyond Pink and Blue: The Complexity of Early Androgen Effects on Gender Development." *Child Development Perspectives* 12 (1): 58–64.

Berenbaum, Sheri, and Melissa Hines. 1992. "Early Androgens Are Related to Childhood Sex-Typed Toy Preferences." *Psychological Science* 3 (3): 203–6.

Berg, Jeremy J., and Graham Coop. 2014. "A Population Genetic Signal of Polygenic Adaptation." *PLoS Genetics* 10 (8): e1004412.

Berg, Jeremy J., Arbel Harpak, Nicholas Sinnott-Armstrong et al. 2018. "Reduced Signal for Polygenic Adaptation of Height in UK Biobank." *bioRxiv*.

Berg, Jeremy J., Xinjun Zhang, and Graham Coop. 2017. "Polygenic Adaptation Has Impacted Multiple Anthropometric Traits." *bioRxiv*.

Berger, Peter L., and Thomas Luckmann. 1966. *The Social Construction of Reality: A Treatise in the Sociology of Knowledge*. New York: Doubleday.

Berglund, Agnethe, Trine H. Johannsen, Kirstine Stochholm et al. 2016. "Incidence, Prevalence, Diagnostic Delay, and Clinical Presentation of Female 46,XY Disorders of Sex Development." *Journal of Clinical Endocrinology and Metabolism* 101 (12): 4532–40.

Bermúdez de Castro, José María, María Martinón-Torres, Jordi Rosell et al. 2016. "Continuity Versus Discontinuity of the Human Settlement of Europe Between the Late Early Pleistocene and the Early Middle Pleistocene. The Mandibular Evidence." *Quaternary Science Reviews* 153: 51–62.

Besenbacher, Søren, Patrick Sulem, Agnar Helgason et al. 2016. "Multi-nucleotide *de novo* Mutations in Humans." *PLoS Genetics* (November 15).

Bigham, Abigail W. 2016. "Genetics of Human Origin and Evolution: High-Altitude Adaptations." *Current Opinion in Genetics and Development* 41: 8–13.

Blackford, J. U., A. H. Allen, R. L. Cowan et al. 2012. "Amygdala and Hippocampus Fail to Habituate to Faces in Individuals with an Inhibited Temperament." *Social Cognitive and Affective Neuroscience* 8 (2): 143–50.

Blackford, J. U., S. N. Avery, R. L. Cowan et al. 2011. "Sustained Amygdala Response to Both Novel and Newly Familiar Faces Characterizes Inhibited Temperament." *Social Cognitive and Affective Neuroscience* 6 (5): 621–29.

Blackless, Melanie, Anthony Charuvastra, Amanda Derryck et al. 2000. "How Sexually Dimorphic Are We? Review and Synthesis." *American Journal of Human Biology* 12 (2): 151–66.

Blackwell, Antoinette. 1875. *The Sexes Throughout Nature*. New York: G. P. Putnam's Sons.

Blackwell, Lisa S., Kali H. Trzesniewski, and Carol Sorich Dweck. 2007. "Implicit Theories of Intelligence Predict Achievement Across an Adolescent Transition: A Longitudinal Study and an Intervention." *Child Development* 78 (1): 246–63.

Blanchard, R. 2008. "Deconstructing the Feminine Essence Narrative." *Archives of Sexual Behavior* 37 (3): 434–38.

Bleier, Ruth. 1991. *Gender Ideology and the Brain: Sex Differences Research*. Washington, DC: American Psychiatric Press.

Blinkhorn, Steve. 1982. "What Skullduggery?" *Nature* 296 (April 8): 506.

———. 2005. "Intelligence: A Gender Bender." *Nature* 438 (November 3): 31–32.

Block, Jeanne H. 1978. "Another Look at Sex Differentiation in the Socialization Behaviors of Mothers and Fathers." In *The Psychology of Women: Future Directions in Research*, edited by J. A. Sherman and F. L. Denmark, 29–87. New York: Psychological Dimensions.

———. 1983. "Differential Premises Arising from Differential Socialization of the Sexes: Some Conjectures." *Child Development* 54 (6): 1335–54.

Bloom, Allan. 1987. *The Closing of the American Mind: How Higher Education Has Failed Democracy and Impoverished the Souls of Today's Students.* New York: Simon & Schuster.

Boehmer, Annemie L. M., Hennie Brüggenwirth, Cissy van Assendelft et al. 2001. "Genotype Versus Phenotype in Families with Androgen Insensitivity Syndrome." *Journal of Clinical Endocrinology and Metabolism* 86 (9): 4151–60.

Bolnick, Deborah A. 2008. "Individual Ancestry Inference and the Reification of Race as a Biological Phenomenon." In *Revisiting Race in a Genomic Age*, edited by Barbara A. Koenig, Sandra Soo-Jin Lee, and Sarah S. Richardson, 4–85. New Brunswick, NJ: Rutgers University Press.

Bomba, L., K. Walter, and N. Soranzo (2017). "The Impact of Rare and Low-Frequency Genetic Variants in Common Disease." *Genome Biology* 18 (1): 77.

Boone, Alexander P., Xinyi Gong, and Mary Hegarty. 2018. "Sex Differences in Navigation Strategy and Efficiency." *Memory and Cognition* 46 (6): 909–22.

Borghans, Lex, Bart H. H. Golsteyn, James J. Heckman, et al. 2016. "What Grades and Achievement Tests Measure." *Proceedings of the National Academy of Sciences* 113 (47): 13354.

Borghans, Lex, Bas ter Weel, and Bruce A. Weinberg. 2008. "Interpersonal Styles and Labor Market Outcomes." *Journal of Human Resources* 43 (4): 815–58.

Borkenau, Peter, Robert R. McCrae, and Antonio Terracciano. 2013. "Do Men Vary More Than Women in Personality? A Study in 51 Cultures." *Journal of Research in Personality* 47 (2): 135–44.

Bos, Peter A., Dennis Hofman, Erno J. Hermans et al. 2016. "Testosterone Reduces Functional Connectivity During the 'Reading the Mind in the Eyes' Test." *Psychoneuroendocrinology* 68: 194–201.

Bouchard, Thomas J., Jr. 1982. "Identical Twins Reared Apart: Reanalysis or Pseudo-analysis?" *Contemporary Psychology* 27: 190–91.

———. 1983. "Do Environmental Similarities Explain the Similarity in Intelligence of Identical Twins Reared Apart?" *Intelligence* 7 (2): 175.

Bouchard, Thomas J., Jr., David T. Lykken, Matthew McGue et al. 1990. "Sources of Human Psychological Differences: The Minnesota Study of Twins Reared Apart." *Science* 250 (October 12): 223–28.

Bowcock, A. M., A. Ruiz-Linares, J. Tomfohrde et al. 1994. "High Resolution of Human Evolutionary Trees with Polymorphic Microsatellites." *Nature* 368 (6470): 455–57.

Boyle, Evan A., Yang I. Li, and Jonathan K. Pritchard. 2017. "An Expanded View of Complex Traits: From Polygenic to Omnigenic." *Cell* 169 (7): 1177–86.

Braitenberg, Valentino. 2001. "Brain Size and Number of Neurons: An Exercise in Synthetic Neuroanatomy." *Journal of Computational Neuroscience* 10 (1): 71–77.

Branden, Nathaniel. 1969. *The Psychology of Self-Esteem: A New Concept of Man's Psychological Nature.* Los Angeles: Nash Publishing.

Braun, Henry I., John Centra, and Benjamin F. King. 1987. *Verbal and Mathematical Ability of High School Juniors and Seniors in 1983: A Norm Study of the PSAT/NMSQT and the SAT.* Princeton, NJ: Educational Testing Service.

Brinkworth, J. F., and L. B. Barreiro. 2014. "The Contribution of Natural Selection to Present-Day Susceptibility to Chronic Inflammatory and Autoimmune Disease." *Current Opinion in Immunology* 31 (December): 66–78.

Brohawn, K. H., R. Offringa, D. L. Pfaff et al. 2010. "The Neural Correlates of Emotional Memory in Posttraumatic Stress Disorder." *Biological Psychiatry* 68 (11): 1023–30.

Brown, Gillian R. 2017. "Book Review: The Dangerous Battles over Sex and Gender." *Trends in Ecology and Evolution* 32 (12): 881–82.

Brown, P., T. Sutikna, M. J. Morwood et al. 2004. "A New Small-Bodied Hominin from the Late Pleistocene of Flores, Indonesia." *Nature* 431 (7012): 1055–61.

Browning, Sharon R., Brian L. Browning, Ying Zhou et al. 2018. "Analysis of Human Sequence Data Reveals Two Pulses of Archaic Denisovan Admixture." *Cell* 173 (1): 53–61.

Bryc, Katarzyna, Eric Y. Durand, J. Michael Macpherson et al. 2015. "The Genetic Ancestry of African Americans, Latinos, and European Americans Across the United States." *American Journal of Human Genetics* 96 (1): 37–53.

Buckner, Randy L. 2013. "The Cerebellum and Cognitive Function: 25 Years of Insight from Anatomy and Neuroimaging." *Neuron* 80 (3): 807–15.

Burt, Callie H., and Ronald L. Simons. 2014. "Pulling Back the Curtain on Heritability Studies: Biosocial Criminology in the Postgenomic Era." *Criminology* 52 (2): 223–62.

———. 2015. "Heritability Studies in the Postgenomic Era: The Fatal Flaw Is Conceptual." *Criminology* 53 (1): 103–12.

Burt, S. Alexandra, Ashlea M. Klahr, and Kelly L. Klump. 2015. "Do Non-shared Environmental Influences Persist over Time? An Examination of Days and Minutes." *Behavior Genetics* 45 (1): 24–34.

Buss, David M. 1984. "Evolutionary Biology and Personality Psychology: Toward a Conception of Human Nature and Individual Differences." *American Psychologist* 39 (10): 1135–47.

———. 1989. "Sex Differences in Human Mate Preferences: Evolutionary Hypotheses Tested in 37 Cultures." *Behavioral and Brain Sciences* 12: 1–49.

———. 2019. *Evolutionary Psychology: The New Science of the Mind*. 6th ed. New York: Routledge.

Bustamante, Carlos D., Esteban González Burchard, and Francisco M. De la Vega. 2011. "Genomics for the World." *Nature* 475 (7355): 163–65.

Byrnes, J. P., D. C. Miller, and W. D. Schafer. 1997. "Gender Differences in Risk-Taking: A Meta-analysis." *Psychological Bulletin* 125: 367–83.

Cahill, Larry. 2017. "An Issue Whose Time Has Come." *Journal of Neuroscience Research* 95: 12–13.

Cahill, Larry, Richard J. Haier, Nathan S. White et al. 2001. "Sex-Related Difference in Amygdala Activity During Emotionally Influenced Memory Storage." *Neurobiology of Learning and Memory* 75 (1): 1–9.

Cahill, Larry, Melina Uncapher, Lisa Kilpatrick et al. 2004. "Sex-Related Hemispheric Lateralization of Amygdala Function in Emotionally Influenced Memory: An fMRI Investigation." *Learning and Memory* 11 (3): 261–66.

Cahill, Larry, and Anda van Stegeren. 2003. "Sex-Related Impairment of Memory for Emotional Events with B-Adrenergic Blockade." *Neurobiology of Learning and Memory* 79 (1): 81–88.

Calafell, F., A. Shuster, W. C. Speed et al. 1998. "Short Tandem Repeat Polymorphism Evolution in Humans." *European Journal of Human Genetics* 6 (1): 38–49.

Callaway, Ewen. 2016. "Evidence Mounts for Interbreeding Bonanza in Ancient Human Species." *Nature News* (February 17).

———. 2017. "Oldest Homo Sapiens Fossil Claim Rewrites Our Species' History." *Nature News* (June 7).

Calvin, Catherine M., G. David Batty, Geoff Der et al. 2017. "Childhood Intelligence in Relation to Major Causes of Death in 68 Year Follow-Up: Prospective Population Study." *BMJ* 357 (j2708).

Campbell, A., L. Shirley, and C. Heywood. 2000. "Infants' Visual Preference for Sex-Congruent Babies, Children, Toys and Activities: A Longitudinal Study." *British Journal of Developmental Psychology* 18: 479–98.

Campbell, Michael C., and Sarah A. Tishkoff. 2008. "African Genetic Diversity: Implications for Human Demographic History, Modern Human Origins, and Complex Disease Mapping." *Annual Review of Genomics and Human Genetics* 9: 403–33.

Caplan, Bryan. 2011. *Selfish Reasons to Have More Kids: Why Being a Great Parent Is Less Work and More Fun Than You Think*. New York: Basic Books.

Card, N. A., B. D. Stucky, G. M. Sawalani et al. 2008. "Direct and Indirect Aggression During Childhood and Adolescence: A Meta-analytic Review of Gender Differences, Intercorrelations, and Relations to Maladjustment." *Child Development* 79: 1185–229.

Carmina, Enrico, Didier Dewailly, Héctor F. Escobar-Morreale et al. 2017. "Non-classic Congenital Adrenal Hyperplasia Due to 21-Hydroxylase Deficiency Revisited: An Update with a Special Focus on Adolescent and Adult Women." *Human Reproduction Update* 23 (5): 580–99.

Carroll, John B. 1995. "Reflections on Stephen Jay Gould's *The Mismeasure of Man* (1981): A Retrospective Review." *Intelligence* 21: 121–34.

Caspari, Ernst W. 1979. "Evolutionary Theory and the Evolution of the Human Brain." In *Development and Evolution of Brain Size*, edited by Craig Jensen and Bruce C. Dudek, 9–28. New York: Academic Press.

Catani, Marco, Derek K. Jones, and Dominic H. Ffytche. 2005. "Perisylvan Language Networks of the Human Brain." *Annals of Neurology* 57: 8–16.

Cavalli-Sforza, Luigi Luca, Paolo Menozzi, and Alberto Piazza. 1994. *The History and Geography of Human Genes*. Princeton, NJ: Princeton University Press.

Cesarini, David, and Peter M. Visscher. 2017. "Genetics and Educational Attainment." *npj Science of Learning* 2.

Chalabaev, Aïna, Brenda Major, Philippe Sarrazin et al. 2012. "When Avoiding Failure Improves Performance: Stereotype Threat and the Impact of Performance Goals." *Motivation and Emotion* 36 (2): 130–42.

Chamorro-Premuzic, Tomas, Nicole Harlaar, Corina Greven et al. 2010. "More Than Just IQ: A Longitudinal Examination of Self-Perceived Abilities as Predictors of Academic Performance in a Large Sample of UK Twins." *Intelligence* 38 (4): 385–92.

Chapman, Emma, Simon Baron-Cohen, Bonnie Auyeung et al. 2006. "Fetal Testosterone and Empathy: Evidence from the Empathy Quotient (EQ) and 'Reading the Mind in the Eyes' Test." *Social Neuroscience* 1 (2): 135–48.

Chekroud, Adam M., Emily J. Ward, Monica D. Rosenberg et al. 2016. "Patterns in the Human Brain Mosaic Discriminate Males from Females." *Proceedings of the National Academy of Sciences* 113 (14): E1968.

Cheng, Helen, and Adrian Furnham. 2012. "Childhood Cognitive Ability, Education, and Personality Traits Predict Attainment in Adult Occupational Prestige over 17 Years." *Journal of Vocational Behavior* 81 (2): 218–26.

Cheverud, James M. 1984. "Quantitative Genetics and Developmental Constraints on Evolution by Selection." *Journal of Theoretical Biology* 110 (2): 155–71.

———. 1988. "A Comparison of Genetic and Phenotypic Correlations." *Evolution* 42 (5): 958–68.

Ciarrochi, Joseph V., Amy Y. C. Chan, and Peter Caputi. 2000. "A Critical Evaluation of the Emotional Intelligence Construct." *Personality and Individual Differences* 28 (3): 539–61.

Clarke, Geraldine M., Carl A. Anderson, Fredrik H. Pettersson et al. 2011. "Basic Statistical Analysis in Genetic Case-Control Studies." *Nature Protocols* 6 (2): 121–33.

Clements, A. M., S. L. Rimrodt, J. R. Abel et al. 2006. "Sex Differences in Cerebral Laterality of Language and Visuospatial Processing." *Brain and Language* 98 (2): 150–58.

Clutten-Brock, T. H. 1989. "Mammalian Mating Systems." *Proceedings of the Royal Society of London B* 236: 339–72.

Cochran, Gregory, and Henry Harpending. 2009. *The 10,000 Year Explosion: How Civilization Accelerated Human Evolution*. New York: Basic Books.

Cohen, Jacob. 1988. *Statistical Power Analysis for the Behavioral Sciences*. Hillsdale, NJ: Erlbaum.

Cohen-Bendahan, Celina C. C., Cornelieke van de Beek, and Sheri A. Berenbaum. 2005. "Prenatal Sex Hormone Effects on Child and Adult Sex-Typed Behavior: Methods and Findings." *Neuroscience and Biobehavioral Reviews* 29: 353–84.

Coleman, James S. et al. 1966. *Equality of Educational Opportunity*. Washington, DC: U.S. Office of Education.

College Board. 2016. *College-Bound Seniors: Total Group Profile Report*. New York: College Board.

Colom, Roberto, Luis F. García, Manuel Juan-Espinosa et al. 2002. "Null Sex Differences in General Intelligence: Evidence from the WAIS-III." *Spanish Journal of Psychology* 5 (1): 29–35.

Colom, Roberto, Manuel Juan-Espinosa, Francisco Abad et al. 2000. "Negligible Sex Differences in General Intelligence." *Intelligence* 28 (1): 57–68.

Connellan, Jennifer, S. Baron-Cohen, Sally Wheelwright et al. 2000. "Sex Differences in Human Neonatal Social Perception." *Infant Behavior and Development* 23: 113–18.

Constantinescu, Mihaela, David S. Moore, Scott P. Johnson et al. 2018. "Early Contributions to Infants' Mental Rotation Abilities." *Developmental Science* 21 (4): e12613.

Contreras, María José, Víctor J. Rubio, Daniel Peña et al. 2007. "Sex Differences in Dynamic Spatial Ability: The Unsolved Question of Performance Factors." *Memory and Cognition* 35 (2): 297–303.

Coon, Carleton S. 1962. *The Origins of Races*. New York: Alfred A. Knopf.

Coop, G., J. K. Pickrell, J. Novembre et al. 2009. "The Role of Geography in Human Adaptation." *PLoS Genetics* 5.

Cossette, Louise, Andrée Pomerleau, Gérard Malcuit et al. 1996. "Emotional Expressions of Female and Male Infants in a Social and a Nonsocial Context." *Sex Roles* 35 (11): 693–709.

Costa, Paul T., and Robert R. McCrae. 1985. *The Neo Personality Inventory Manual*. Odessa, FL: PAR.

Costa, Paul T., Jr., A. Terracciano, and Robert R. McCrae. 2001. "Gender Differences in Personality Traits Across Cultures: Robust and Surprising Findings." *Journal of Personality and Social Psychology* 81 (2): 322–31.

Cox, D. R. 1984. "Interaction." *International Statistical Review* 52 (1): 1–24.

Credé, Marcus. 2018. "What Shall We Do About Grit? A Critical Review of What We Know and What We Don't Know." *Educational Researcher* 47 (9): 606–11.

Crenshaw, Kimberlé. 1989. "Demarginalizing the Intersection of Race and Sex: A Black Feminist Critique of Antidiscrimination Doctrine, Feminist Theory and Antiracist Politics." *University of Chicago Legal Forum* 140: 139–67.

Damian, Rodica, Rong Su, Michael Shanahan et al. 2014. "Can Personality Traits and Intelligence Compensate for Background Disadvantage? Predicting Status Attainment in Adulthood." *Journal of Personality and Social Psychology* 109 (3): 473–89.

Dannemann, Michael, Kay Prüfer, and Janet Kelso. 2017. "Functional Implications of Neandertal Introgression in Modern Humans." *Genome Biology* 18 (1): 61.

Darwin, Charles. 1859. *On the Origin of Species by Means of Natural Selection*. London: John Murray.

———. 1900. *The Descent of Man and Selection in Relation to Sex* (A Library of Universal Literature). New York: P. F. Collier and Son. Original edition 1871.

Davies, Gail, Max Lam, Sarah E. Harris et al. 2018. "Study of 300,486 Individuals Identifies 148 Independent Genetic Loci Influencing General Cognitive Function." *Nature Communications* 9 (1): 2098.

Davies, William, and Lawrence S. Wilkinson. 2006. "It Is Not All Hormones: Alternative Explanations for Sexual Differentiation of the Brain." *Brain Research* 1126 (1): 36–45.

Davis, Bernard D. 1983. "Neo-Lysenkoism, IQ, and the Press." *The Public Interest* no. 73: 41–59.

Davis, Shannon N., and Barbara J. Risman. 2015. "Feminists Wrestle with Testosterone: Hormones, Socialization and Cultural Interactionism as Predictors of Women's Gendered Selves." *Social Science Research* 49: 110–25.

Dawkins, Richard. 1976. *The Selfish Gene*. Oxford: Oxford University Press.

Deary, Ian J., Michelle D. Taylor, Carole L. Hart et al. 2005. "Intergenerational Social Mobility and Mid-life Status Attainment: Influences of Childhood Intelligence, Childhood Social Factors, and Education." *Intelligence* 33 (5): 455–72.

Deary, Ian J., Graham Thorpe, Valerie Wilson et al. 2003. "Population Sex Differences in IQ at Age 11: The Scottish Mental Survey 1932." *Intelligence* 31 (6): 533–42.

de Beauvoir, Simone. 2009. *Le Deuxième Sexe*. Translated by Constance Borde and Sheila Malovany-Chevallier. New York: Vintage. Original edition 1949.

Degler, Carl N. 1991. *In Search of Human Nature: The Decline and Revival of Darwinism in American Social Thought.* New York: Oxford University Press.

de Graaf, Nastasja M., Guido Giovanardi, Claudia Zitz et al. 2018. "Sex Ratio in Children and Adolescents Referred to the Gender Identity Development Service in the UK (2009–2016)." *Archives of Sexual Behavior* 47: 1301–4.

Deichmann, Ute. 2016. "Epigenetics: The Origins and Evolution of a Fashionable Topic." *Developmental Biology* 416: 249–54.

de LaCoste-Utamsing, Christine, and Ralph L. Holloway. 1982. "Sexual Dimorphism in the Human Corpus Callosum." *Science* 216: 1431–32.

Del Giudice, Marco. 2009. "On the Real Magnitude of Psychological Sex Differences." *Evolutionary Psychology* 7 (2): 264–79.

———. 2015. "Gender Differences in Personality and Social Behavior." In *International Encyclopedia of the Social and Behavioral Sciences,* edited by J. D. Wright. New York: Elsevier.

Del Giudice, Marco, Emily S. Barrett, Jay Belsky et al. 2018. "Individual Differences in Developmental Plasticity: A Role for Early Androgens?" *Psychoneuroendocrinology* 90: 165–73.

Del Giudice, Marco, Tom Booth, and Paul Irwing. 2012. "The Distance Between Mars and Venus: Measuring Global Sex Differences in Personality." *PLoS ONE* 7 (1): e29265.

Del Giudice, Marco, Richard A. Lippa, David A. Puts et al. 2016. "Joel et al.'s Method Systematically Fails to Detect Large, Consistent Sex Differences." *Proceedings of the National Academy of Sciences* 113 (14): E1965.

de Lisi, Richard, Gowri Parameswaran, and Ann V. McGillicuddy-de Lisi. 1989. "Age and Sex Differences in Representation of Horizontality Among Children in India." *Perceptual and Motor Skills* 68 (3, Pt. 1): 739–46.

Delwiche, Charles F. 2004. "The Genomic Palimpsest: Genomics in Evolution and Ecology." *BioScience* 54 (11): 991–1001.

Denworth, Lydia. 2017. "Is There a 'Female' Brain?" *Scientific American* (September).

de Schotten, Michel Thiebaut, Flavio Dell'Acqua, Stephanie J. Forkel et al. 2011. "A Lateralized Brain Network for Visuospatial Attention." *Nature Neuroscience* 14: 1245.

Desikan, Rahul S., Florent Ségonne, Bruce Fischl et al. 2006. "An Automated Labeling System for Subdividing the Human Cerebral Cortex on MRI Scans into Gyral Based Regions of Interest." *NeuroImage* 31 (3): 968–80.

Dessens, Arianne B., Froukje M. E. Slijper, and Stenvert L. S. Drop. 2005. "Gender Dysphoria and Gender Change in Chromosomal Females with Congenital Adrenal Hyperplasia." *Archives of Sexual Behavior* 34 (4): 389–97.

Détroit, Florent, Armand Salvador Mijares, Julien Corny, et al. 2019. "A New Species of Homo from the Late Pleistocene of the Philippines." *Nature* 568 (7751): 181–86.

de Vries, Geert J. 2004. "Sex Differences in Adult and Developing Brains: Compensation, Compensation, Compensation." *Endocrinology* 145 (3): 1063–68.

de Vries, Geert J., and Nancy G. Forger. 2015. "Sex Differences in the Brain: A Whole Body Perspective." *Biology of Sex Differences* 6 (1): 15.

de Vries, Geert J., and Per Södersten. 2009. "Sex Differences in the Brain: The Relation Between Structure and Function." *Hormones and Behavior* 55 (5): 589–96.

Dewing, P., T. Shi, S. Horvath et al. 2003. "Sexually Dimorphic Gene Expression in Mouse Brain Precedes Gonadal Differentiation." *Brain Research* 118 (1–2): 82–90.

Diamond, Jared. 1994. "Race Without Color." *Discover Magazine* (November).

Dick, Danielle M., Arpana Agrawal, Matthew C. Keller et al. 2015. "Candidate Gene-Environment Interaction Research: Reflections and Recommendations." *Perspectives on Psychological Science* 10 (1): 37–59.

Dickens, William T., and James R. Flynn. 2006. "Black Americans Reduce the Racial IQ Gap: Evidence from Standardization Samples." *Psychological Science* 17 (10): 913–20.

Diener, Edward F., R. A. Emmons, and S. Griffin. 1985. "The Satisfaction with Life Scale." *Journal of Personality Assessment* 49: 71–75.

Diener, E., D. Wirtz, W. Tov et al. 2010. "New Well-Being Measures: Short Scales to Assess Flourishing and Positive and Negative Feelings." *Social Indicators Research* 97: 143–56.

Di Pietro, Janet A. 1981. "Rough and Tumble Play: A Function of Gender." *Developmental Psychology* 17 (1): 50–58.

Dittmann, Ralf W., Michael H. Kappes, Marianne E. Kappes et al. 1990. "Congenital Adrenal Hyperplasia I: Gender-Related Behavior and Attitudes in Female Patients and Sisters." *Psychoneuroendocrinology* 15 (5): 401–20.

Dochtermann, Ned A. 2011. "Testing Cheverud's Conjecture for Behavioral Correlations and Behavioral Syndromes." *Evolution* 65 (6): 1814–20.

Dodds, Richard M., Holly E. Syddall, Rachel Cooper et al. 2014. "Grip Strength Across the Life Course: Normative Data from Twelve British Studies." *PLoS ONE* 9 (12): e113637.

Domes, Gregor, Markus Heinrichs, Andre Michel et al. 2007. "Oxytocin Improves 'Mind-Reading' in Humans." *Biological Psychiatry* 61: 731–33.

Domingue, Benjamin W., Jason Fletcher, Dalton Conley et al. 2014. "Genetic and Educational Assortative Mating Among US Adults." *Proceedings of the National Academy of Sciences* 111 (22): 7996–8000.

Donlon, Thomas F., ed. 1984. *The College Board Technical Handbook for the Scholastic Aptitude Test and Achievement Tests*. New York: College Entrance Examination Board.

Dor, Yuval, and Howard Cedar. 2018. "Principles of DNA Methylation and Their Implications for Biology and Medicine." *Lancet* 392 (10149): 777–86.

Doyle, Randi A., and Daniel Voyer. 2016. "Stereotype Manipulation Effects on Math and Spatial Test Performance: A Meta-Analysis." *Learning and Individual Differences* 47: 103–16.

Duckworth, Angela Lee, and Stephanie M. Carlson. 2013. "Self-Regulation and School Success." In *Self-Regulation and Autonomy: Social and Developmental Dimensions of Human Conduct*, edited by Bryan W. Sokol, Frederick M. E. Grouzet, and Ulrich Müller, 208–30. Cambridge: Cambridge University Press.

Duff, Dawna, J. Bruce Tomblin, and Hugh Catts. 2015. "The Influence of Reading on Vocabulary Growth: A Case for a Matthew Effect." *Journal of Speech, Language, and Hearing Research* 58 (3): 853–64.

Duncan, Greg J., and Katherine Magnuson. 2013. "Investing in Preschool Programs." *Journal of Economic Perspectives* 27 (2): 109–32.

Duncan, Laramie, Hanyang Shen, Bizu Gelaye et al. 2018. "Analysis of Polygenic Score Usage and Performance Across Diverse Human Populations." *bioRxiv*.

Durkheim, Émile. 1982. *The Rules of the Sociological Method*. Translated by W. D. Halls. New York: Free Press. Original edition 1895.

Dweck, Carol S. 2006. *Mindset: The New Psychology of Success*. New York: Random House.

Dweck, Carol S., and David S. Yeager. 2019. "Mindsets: A View from Two Eras." *Perspectives on Psychological Science* 14 (3): 1745691618804166.

Eagly, Alice H. 1987. *Sex Differences in Social Behavior: A Social-Role Interpretation*. Hillsdale, NJ: Erlbaum.

Eagly, Alice H., and Wendy Wood. 2011. "Social Role Theory." In *Handbook of Theories in Social Psychology*, edited by P. van Lange, A. Kruglanski, and E. T. Higgins, 458–76. Thousand Oaks, CA: Sage Publications.

Eagly, Alice H., Wendy Wood, and M. C. Johannessen-Schmidt. 2004. "Social Role Theory of Sex Differences and Similarities: Implications for the Partner Preferences of Women and Men." In *The Psychology of Gender*, edited by Alice H. Eagly, A. E. Beall, and Robert J. Sternberg, 269–95. New York: Guilford Press.

Eberstadt, Nicholas. 2016. *Men Without Work: America's Invisible Crisis*. West Conshohocken, PA: Templeton Press.

Eccles, Jacquelynne S. 1983. "Expectancies, Values, and Academic Behaviors." In *Achievement and Achievement Motives: Psychological and Sociological Approaches*, edited by J. T. Spence, 75–146. San Francisco: W. H. Freeman.

Eccles, Jacquelynne S., Mina N. Vida, and Bonnie Barber. 2004. "The Relation of Early Adolescents' College Plans and Both Academic Ability and Task-Value Beliefs to Subsequent College Enrollment." *Journal of Early Adolescence* 24 (1): 63–77.

Edwards, A. W. F. 2003. "Human Genetic Diversity: Lewontin's Fallacy." *BioEssays* 25: 798–801.

Ehrhardt, A. A., and H. F. Meyer-Bahlburg. 1981. "Effects of Prenatal Sex Hormones on Gender-Related Behavior." *Science* 211 (4488): 1312.

Ekman, Paul. 1999. "Basic Emotions." In *Handbook of Cognition and Emotion*, edited by T. Dalgleish and M. Power, 45–60. New York: John Wiley & Sons.

Elhaik, Eran, Tatiana Tatarinova, Dmitri Chebotarev et al. 2014. "Geographic Population Structure Analysis of Worldwide Human Populations Infers Their Biogeographical Origins." *Nature Communications* 5 (3513).

Ellison, Glenn, and Ashley Swanson. 2010. "The Gender Gap in Secondary School Mathematics at High Achievement Levels: Evidence from the American Mathematics Competitions." *Journal of Economic Perspectives* 24 (2): 109–28.

Else-Quest, N. M., J. S. Hyde, and M. C. Linn. 2010. "Cross-National Patterns of Gender Differences in Mathematics: A Meta-Analysis." *Psychological Bulletin* 136 (1): 103–27.

Endendijk, Joyce J., Marleen G. Groeneveld, Marian J. Bakermans-Kranenburg et al. 2016. "Gender-Differentiated Parenting Revisited: Meta-analysis Reveals Very Few Differences in Parental Control of Boys and Girls." *PLoS ONE* 11 (7): e0159193.

Epstein, Herman T. 1979. "Correlated Brain and Intelligence Development in Humans." In *Development and Evolution of Brain Size*, edited by Craig Jensen and Bruce C. Dudek, 111–31. New York: Academic Press.

Escaramís, Gèorgia, Elisa Docampo, and Raquel Rabionet. 2015. "A Decade of Structural Variants: Description, History and Methods to Detect Structural Variation." *Briefings in Functional Genomics*: 14 (5): 305–14.

Fagan, Joseph F., and Cynthia R. Holland. 2007. "Racial Equality in Intelligence: Predictions from a Theory of Intelligence as Processing." *Intelligence* 35 (4): 319–34.

Fairbairn, D. J. 2016. "Sexual Dimorphism." In *Encyclopedia of Evolutionary Biology*, edited by Richard M. Kliman, 105–13. Oxford: Academic Press.

Falconer, Douglas S. 1960. *Introduction to Quantitative Genetics*. London: Oliver & Boyd.

Falk, Armin, and Johannes Hermle. 2018. "Relationship of Gender Differences in Preferences to Economic Development and Gender Equality." *Science* 362 (6412).

Fan, Shaohua, Matthew E. B. Hansen, Yancy Lo et al. 2016. "Going Global by Adapting Local: A Review of Recent Human Adaptation." *Science* 354 (6308): 54–58.

Farber, S. L. 1981. *Identical Twins Raised Apart: A Reanalysis*. New York: Basic Books.

Fausto-Sterling, Anne. 2000. *Sexing the Body: Gender Politics and the Construction of Sexuality*. New York: Basic Books.

Feingold, Alan. 1994. "Gender Differences in Variability in Intellectual Abilities: A Cross-Cultural Perspective." *Sex Roles* 30 (1): 81–92.

Feldman, Marcus W. 2010. "The Biology of Ancestry: DNA, Genomic Variation, and Race." In *Doing Race: 21 Essays for the 21st Century*, edited by Hazel Rose Markus and Paula M. L. Moya, 136–59. New York: W. W. Norton.

Feldman, Marcus W., and Richard C. Lewontin. 2008. "Race, Ancestry, and Medicine." In *Revisiting Race in a Genomic Age*, edited by Barbara A. Koenig, Sandra Soo-Jin Lee, and Sarah S. Richardson, 89–101. New Brunswick, NJ: Rutgers University Press.

Feldman, Marcus W., and Sohini Ramachandran. 2018. "Missing Compared to What? Revisiting Heritability, Genes and Culture." *Philosophical Transactions of the Royal Society B: Biological Sciences* 373 (1743): 20170064.

Felson, Jacob. 2014. "What Can We Learn from Twin Studies? A Comprehensive Evaluation of the Equal Environments Assumption." *Social Science Research* 43: 184–99.

Fenstermaker, Sarah, and Candace West, eds. 2002. *Doing Gender, Doing Difference*. New York: Routledge.

Field, Yair, Evan A. Boyle, Natalie Telis et al. 2016. "Detection of Human Adaptation During the Past 2000 Years." *Science* 354 (6313): 760–64.

Filkowski, M. M., R. M. Olsen, B. Duda et al. 2017. "Sex Differences in Emotional Perception: Meta-analysis of Divergent Activation." *NeuroImage* 147: 925–33.

Fillingim, R. B., C. D. King, M. C. Ribeiro-Dasilva et al. 2009. "Sex, Gender, and Pain: A Review of Recent Clinical and Experimental Findings." *Journal of Pain* 10 (5): 447–85.

Finnigan, Katherine M., and Katherine S. Corker. 2016. "Do Performance Avoidance Goals Moderate the Effect of Different Types of Stereotype Threat on Women's Math Performance?" *Journal of Research in Personality* 63: 36–43.

Firkowska-Mankiewicz, A. 2002. *Intelligence and Success in Life*. Warsaw: IFiS.

Fischbein, Siv. 1980. "IQ and Social Class." *Intelligence* 4: 51–63.

Fishbain, David A., and Adolfo Vilasuso. 1980. "Exclusive Adult Lesbianism Associated with Turner's Syndrome Mosaicism." *Archives of Sexual Behavior* 9 (4): 349.

Fisher, Ronald Aylmer. 1918. "The Correlation Between Relatives on the Supposition of Mendelian Inheritance." *Transactions of the Royal Society of Edinburgh* 52: 399–433.

Fleischman, Diana Santos. 2014. "Women's Disgust Adaptations." In *Evolutionary Perspectives on Human Sexual Psychology and Behavior*, edited by V. A. Weekes-Shackelford and Todd K. Shackelford, 277–96. New York: Springer Science + Business Media.

Flore, Paulette C., and Jelte M. Wicherts. 2015. "Does Stereotype Threat Influence Performance of Girls in Stereotyped Domains? A Meta-analysis." *Journal of School Psychology* 53 (1): 25–44.

Foley, Sallie, and George W. Morley. 1992. "Care and Counseling of the Patient with Vaginal Agenesis." *The Female Patient* 17 (October): 73–80.

Fosse, Roar, Jay Joseph, and Ken Richardson. 2015. "A Critical Assessment of the Equal-Environment Assumption of the Twin Method for Schizophrenia." *Frontiers in Psychiatry* 6: 62.

Freedman, Matthew L., David Reich, Kathryn L. Penney et al. 2004. "Assessing the Impact of Population Stratification on Genetic Association Studies." *Nature Genetics* 36: 388.

Fregel, Rosa, Fernando L. Méndez, Youssef Bokbot et al. 2018. "Ancient Genomes from North Africa Evidence Prehistoric Migrations to the Maghreb from Both the Levant and Europe." *Proceedings of the National Academy of Sciences* 115 (26): 6774–79.

Fryer, C. D., Q. Gu, C. L. Ogden, et al. 2016. "Anthropometric Reference Data for Children and Adults: United States, 2011–2014." *Vital Statistics* (39).

Fuller, Barbara F. 2002. "Infant Gender Differences Regarding Acute Established Pain." *Clinical Nursing Research* 11 (2): 190–203.

Fumagalli, Matteo, Ida Moltke, Niels Grarup, et al. 2015. "Greenlandic Inuit Show Genetic Signatures of Diet and Climate Adaptation." *Science* 349 (6254): 1343.

Funder, David C., and Daniel J. Ozer. 2019. "Evaluating Effect Size in Psychological Research." *Advances in Methods and Practices in Psychological Science*. Advance online publication.

Furnham, Adrian, and Helen Cheng. 2017. "Socio-demographic Indicators, Intelligence, and Locus of Control as Predictors of Adult Financial Well-Being." *Journal of Intelligence* 5 (2).

Furnham, Adrian, Steven C. Richards, and Delroy L. Paulhus. 2013. "The Dark Triad of Personality: A 10 Year Review." *Social and Personality Psychology Compass* 7: 199–216.

Galton, Francis. 1869. *Hereditary Genius: An Inquiry into Its Laws and Consequences*. 1892 ed. London: Macmillan.

Gamble, Clive, John Gowlett, and Robin Dunbar. 2014. *Thinking Big: How the Evolution of Social Life Shaped the Human Mind*. London: Thames & Hudson.

Ganley, Colleen M., Leigh A. Mingle, Allison M. Ryan et al. 2013. "An Examination of Stereotype Threat Effects on Girls' Mathematics Performance." *Developmental Psychology* 49 (10): 1886–97.

Gardner, Howard. 1983. *Frames of Mind: The Theory of Multiple Intelligences*. 1985 ed. New York: Basic Books.

———. 2006. "On Failing to Grasp the Core of MI Theory: A Response to Visser et al." *Intelligence* 34 (5): 503–5.

———. 2008. *Multiple Intelligences: New Horizons*. New York: Basic Books.

———. 2016. "Multiple Intelligences: Prelude, Theory, and Aftermath." In *Scientists Making a Difference: One Hundred Eminent Behavioral and Brain Scientists Talk About Their Most Important Contributions*, edited by Robert J. Sternberg, Susan T. Fiske, and Donald J. Foss, 167–70. Cambridge: Cambridge University Press.

Gates, Gary J. 2011. *How Many People Are Lesbian, Gay, Bisexual, and Transgender?* Los Angeles: Williams Institute.

Geary, David. 2004. *The Origin of Mind: Evolution of Brain, Cognition, and General Intelligence*. Washington: American Psychological Association.

———. 2010. *Male, Female: The Evolution of Human Sex Differences*. 2nd ed. Washington, DC: American Psychological Association. Original edition 1998.

———. 2017. "Evolutionary Framework for Identifying Sex- and Species-Specific Vulnerabilities in Brain Development and Functions." *Journal of Neuroscience Research* 95 (1–2): 355–61.

Geddes, Patrick, and J. Arthur Thomson. 1889. *The Evolution of Sex*. New York: Humboldt Publishing.

Gelman, Andrew. 2018. "You Need 16 Times the Sample Size to Estimate an Interaction Than to Estimate a Main Effect." *Statistical Modeling, Causal Inference, and Social Science* (March 15).

Geschwind, Norman, and Albert M. Galaburda. 1985. "Cerebral Lateralization, Biological Mechanisms, Associations, and Pathology: I. A Hypothesis and a Program for Research." *Archive of Neurology* 42 (5): 428–59.

Giedd, Jay N., Armin Raznahan, Aaron Alexander-Bloch et al. 2014. "Child Psychiatry Branch of the National Institute of Mental Health Longitudinal Structural Magnetic Resonance Imaging Study of Human Brain Development." *Neuropsychopharmacology* 40: 43.

Gignac, Gilles E., and Timothy C. Bates. 2017. "Brain Volume and Intelligence: The Moderating Role of Intelligence Measurement Quality." *Intelligence* 64: 18–29.

Gignac, Gilles E., and Eva T. Szodorai. 2016. "Effect Size Guidelines for Individual Differences Researchers." *Personality and Individual Differences* 102: 74–78.

Gilly, A., D. Suveges, K. Kuchenbaecker et al. (2018). "Cohort-wide Deep Whole Genome Sequencing and the Allelic Architecture of Complex Traits." *Nature Communications* 9 (1): 4674.

Gladwell, Malcolm. 2008. *Outliers: The Story of Success*. Boston: Little, Brown.

Glazko, G. V., and M. Nei. 2003. "Estimation of Divergence Times for Major Lineages of Primate Species." *Molecular Biology and Evolution* 20 (3): 424–34.

Glezerman, Marek. 2016. "Yes, There Is a Female and a Male Brain: Morphology Versus Functionality." *Proceedings of the National Academy of Sciences* 113 (14): E1971.

Goldberg, Lewis R. 1993a. "The Structure of Phenotypic Personality Traits." *American Psychologist* 48 (1): 26–34.

Goldberg, Steven. 1974. *The Inevitability of Patriarchy: Why the Biological Difference Between Men and Women Always Produces Male Domination*. New York: Morrow.

———. 1993b. *Why Men Rule: A Theory of Male Dominance*. Chicago: Open Court.

Goldin, Claudia. 2014. "A Grand Gender Convergence: Its Last Chapter." *American Economic Review* 104 (4): 1091–119.

Goldstein, H. 2008. "Building Cognitive Ability Tests with Reduced Adverse Impact." Paper presented at Mid-Atlantic Personnel Assessment Consortium, New York.

Goldstein, Jill M., M. Jerram, R. A. Poldrack et al. 2005. "Hormonal Cycle Modulates Arousal Circuitry in Women Using Functional Magnetic Resonance Imaging." *Journal of Neuroscience* 25: 9309–16.

Goldstein, Jill M., Larry J. Seidman, Nicholas J. Horton et al. 2001. "Normal Sexual Dimorphism of the Adult Human Brain Assessed by *in vivo* Magnetic Resonance Imaging." *Cerebral Cortex* 11 (6): 490–97.

Goodman, Alan H., Yolanda T. Moses, and Joseph L. Jones. 2012. *Race: Are We So Different?* Arlington, VA: American Anthropological Association.

Gordon, Claire C., Thomas Churchill, Charles E. Clauser et al. 1989. *1988 Anthropometric Survey of U.S. Army Personnel: Summary Statistics; Interim Report.* Natick, MA: United States Army.

Gordon, Robert A. 1997. "Everyday Life as an Intelligence Test: Effects of Intelligence and Intelligence Context." *Intelligence* 24 (1): 203–320.

Gottfredson, Linda S. 1997a. "Mainstream Science on Intelligence: An Editorial with 52 Signatories, History, and Bibliography." *Intelligence* 24 (1): 13–23.

———. 1997b. "Why *g* Matters: The Complexity of Everyday Life." *Intelligence* 24 (1): 79–132.

———. 2003. "*g*, Jobs, and Life." In *The Scientific Study of General Intelligence: A Tribute to Arthur R. Jensen,* 293–342. Oxford: Pergamon.

Gottfredson, Michael R., and Travis Hirschi. 1990. *A General Theory of Crime.* Stanford, CA: Stanford University Press.

Gould, Stephen J. 1981. *The Mismeasure of Man.* New York: W. W. Norton.

Grant, Michael D., William S. Kremen, Kristen C. Jacobson et al. 2010. "Does Parental Education Have a Moderating Effect on the Genetic and Environmental Influences of General Cognitive Ability in Early Adulthood?" *Behavior Genetics* 40 (4): 438–46.

Gravel, Simon, Brenna M. Henn, Ryan N. Gutenkunst et al. 2011. "Demographic History and Rare Allele Sharing Among Human Populations." *Proceedings of the National Academy of Sciences* 108 (29): 11983.

Greally, John M. 2015. "Over-interpreted Epigenetics Study of the Week." *EpgntxEinstein* (August 23).

———. 2018. "A User's Guide to the Ambiguous Word 'Epigenetics.'" *Nature Reviews Molecular Cell Biology* 19: 207–8.

Greaves, Lara M., Fiona Kate Barlow, Carol H. J. Lee et al. 2017. "The Diversity and Prevalence of Sexual Orientation Self-Labels in a New Zealand National Sample." *Archives of Sexual Behavior* 46 (5): 1325–36.

Grissom, Nicola M., and Teresa M. Reyes. 2019. "Let's Call the Whole Thing Off: Evaluating Gender and Sex Differences in Executive Function." *Neuropsychopharmacology* 44 (1): 86–96.

Grossman, Sharon R., Kristian G. Andersen, Ilya Shlyakhter et al. 2013. "Identifying Recent Adaptations in Large-Scale Genomic Data." *Cell* 152 (4): 703–13.

Groucutt, Huw S., Michael D. Petraglia, Geoff Bailey et al. 2015. "Rethinking the Dispersal of Homo Sapiens out of Africa." *Evolutionary Anthropology: Issues, News, and Reviews* 24 (4): 149–64.

Guimond, S., N. R. Branscombe, S. Brunot et al. 2007. "Culture, Gender, and the Self: Variations and Impact of Social Comparison Processes." *Journal of Personality and Social Psychology* 92: 1118–34.

Guiso, L., F. Monte, P. Sapienza et al. 2008. "Culture, Gender, and Math." *Science* 320: 1164–65.

Gunnar, M. R., and M. Donahue. 1980. "Sex Differences in Social Responsiveness Between Six Months and Twelve Months." *Child Development* 51: 262–65.

Günther, Torsten, and Mattias Jakobsson. 2016. "Genes Mirror Migrations and Cultures in Prehistoric Europe—a Population Genomic Perspective." *Current Opinion in Genetics and Development* 41: 115–23.

Guo, Jing, Yang Wu, Zhihong Zhu et al. 2018. "Global Genetic Differentiation of Complex Traits Shaped by Natural Selection in Humans." *Nature Communications* 9 (1): 1865.

Gur, Ruben C., D. Alsop, David C. Glahn et al. 2000. "An fMRI Study of Sex Differences in Regional Activation to a Verbal and a Spatial Task." *Brain and Language* 74 (2): 157–70.

Gur, Ruben C., and Raquel E. Gur. 2017. "Complementarity of Sex Differences in Brain and Behavior: From Laterality to Multimodal Neuroimaging." *Journal of Neuroscience Research* 95 (1–2): 189–99.

Haasle, Ryan J., and Bret A. Payseur. 2016. "Fifteen Years of Genomewide Scans for Selection: Trends, Lessons and Unaddressed Genetic Sources of Complication." *Molecular Ecology* 25: 5–23.

Haier, Richard J. 2016. *The Neuroscience of Intelligence*. New York: Cambridge University Press.

Hakim, Catherine. 2002. "Lifestyle Preferences as Determinants of Women's Differentiated Labor Market Careers." *Work and Occupations* 29 (4): 428–59.

Haldane, J. B. S. 1927. "A Mathematical Theory of Natural and Artificial Selection, Part V: Selection and Mutation." *Proceedings of the Cambridge Philosophical Society* 23: 838–44.

Hall, Judith A. 1978. "Gender Effects in Decoding Nonverbal Cues." *Psychological Bulletin* 85 (4): 845–57.

Hall, Judith A., Danielle C. Blanch, Terrence G. Horgan et al. 2009. "Motivation and Interpersonal Sensitivity: Does It Matter How Hard You Try?" *Motivation and Emotion* 33 (3): 291.

Halpern, Diane F. 2010. "How Neuromythologies Support Sex Role Stereotypes." *Science* 330 (6009): 1320.

———. 2012. *Sex Differences in Cognitive Ability*. 4th ed. New York: Psychology Press. Original edition 1986.

Halpern, Diane F., Camilla P. Benbow, David C. Geary et al. 2007. "The Science of Sex Differences in Science and Mathematics." *Psychological Science in the Public Interest* 8: 1–51.

Halpern, Diane F., and Mary L. LaMay. 2000. "The Smarter Sex: A Critical Review of Sex Differences in Intelligence." *Educational Psychology Review* 12 (2): 229–46.

Hamann, Stephan. 2005. "Sex Differences in the Responses of the Human Amygdala." *Neuroscientist* 11 (4): 288–93.

Hamann, Stephan, Rebecca A. Herman, Carla L. Nolan et al. 2004. "Men and Women Differ in Amygdala Response to Visual Sexual Stimuli." *Nature Neuroscience* 7: 411–16.

Hamilton, Alexander, James Madison, and John Jay. 1982. *The Federalist Papers*. New York: New American Library. Original edition 1787.

Hamilton, W. D. 1964. "The Genetical Evolution of Social Behaviour." *Journal of Theoretical Biology* 7 (1): 1–52.

Hänggi, Jürgen, Laszlo Fövenyi, Franziskus Liem et al. 2014. "The Hypothesis of Neuronal Interconnectivity as a Function of Brain Size—a General Organization Principle of the Human Connectome." *Frontiers in Human Neuroscience* 8: 915.

Hanscombe, Ken B., Maciej Trzaskowski, Claire M. A. Haworth et al. 2012. "Socioeconomic Status (SES) and Children's Intelligence (IQ): In a UK-Representative Sample SES Moderates the Environmental, Not Genetic, Effect on IQ." *PLoS ONE* 7 (2): e30320.

Hanselman, Paul, Christopher S. Rozek, Jeffrey Grigg et al. 2017. "New Evidence on Self-Affirmation Effects and Theorized Sources of Heterogeneity from Large-Scale Replications." *Journal of Educational Psychology* 109 (3): 405–24.

Harden, Kathryn Paige, Benjamin W. Domingue, Daniel W. Belsky et al. 2019. "Genetic Associations with Mathematics Tracking and Persistence in Secondary School." *bioRxiv*: 598532.

Harden, Kathryn Paige, Eric Turkheimer, and John C. Loehlin. 2007. "Genotype by Environment Interaction in Adolescents' Cognitive Aptitude." *Behavior Genetics* 37: 273–83.

Hardyck, Curtis, and Lewis F. Petrinovich. 1977. "Left-Handedness." *Psychological Bulletin* 84 (3): 385–404.

Harris, Judith R. 1998. *The Nurture Assumption: Why Children Turn Out the Way They Do*. New York: Free Press.

Hassett, Janice M., Erin R. Siebert, and Kim Wallen. 2008. "Sex Differences in Rhesus Monkey Toy Preferences Parallel Those of Children." *Hormones and Behavior* 54 (3): 359–64.

Hawks, John, Eric T. Wang, Gregory M. Cochran et al. 2007. "Recent Acceleration of Human Adaptive Evolution." *Proceedings of the National Academy of Sciences* 104 (52): 20753.

He, Y., Z. J. Chen, and A. C. Evans. 2007. "Small-World Anatomical Networks in the Human Brain Revealed by Cortical Thickness from MRI." *Cerebral Cortex* 17: 2407–19.

Hedges, L. V., and A. Nowell. 1995. "Sex Differences in Mental Test Scores, Variability, and Numbers of High-Scoring Individuals." *Science* 269: 41–45.

Hedges, S. Blair. 2000. "Human Evolution: A Start for Population Genomics." *Nature* 408: 652–53.

Heidensohn, F., and M. Silvestri. 2012. "Gender and Crime." In *The Oxford Handbook of Criminology*, edited by M. Maguire, R. Morgan, and R. Reiner. Oxford: Oxford University Press.

Henn, B. M., L. R. Botigue, S. Peischl et al. 2016. "Distance from Sub-Saharan Africa Predicts Mutational Load in Diverse Human Genomes." *Proceedings of the National Academy of Science* 113 (4): E440–49.

Herculano-Houzel, Suzana. 2017. "Numbers of Neurons as Biological Correlates of Cognitive Capability." *Current Opinion in Behavioral Sciences* 16: 1–7.

Herlitz, Agneta, and Julie E. Yonker. 2010. "Sex Differences in Episodic Memory: The Influence of Intelligence." *Journal of Clinical and Experimental Neuropsychology* 24 (1): 107–14.

Hermisson, Joachim, and Pleuni S. Pennings. 2005. "Soft Sweeps: Molecular Population Genetics of Adaptation from Standing Genetic Variation." *Genetics* 169 (April): 2335–52.

Herráez, David L., Marc Bauchet, Kun Tang et al. 2009. "Genetic Variation and Recent Positive Selection in Worldwide Human Populations: Evidence from Nearly 1 Million SNPs." *PLoS ONE* 4 (11): e7888.

Herrera, Alexandra Ycaza, Jiaxi Wang, and Mara Mather. 2018. "The Gist and Details of Sex Differences in Cognition and the Brain: How Parallels in Sex Differences Across Domains Are Shaped by the Locus Coeruleus and Catecholamine Systems." *Progress in Neurobiology.* Advance online publication.

Herrnstein, Richard J. 1973. *I.Q. in the Meritocracy.* Boston: Little, Brown.

Herrnstein, Richard J., and Charles Murray. 1994. *The Bell Curve: Intelligence and Class Structure in American Life.* 1996 ed. New York: Free Press.

Hershkovitz, Israel, Gerhard W. Weber, Rolf Quam et al. 2018. "The Earliest Modern Humans Outside Africa." *Science* 359 (6374): 456–59.

Hettema, J. M., Michael C. Neale, and Kenneth S. Kendler. 1995. "Physical Similarity and the Equal-Environment Assumption in Twin Studies of Psychiatric Disorders." *Behavior Genetics* 25 (4): 327–35.

Heuer, Friderike, and Daniel Reisberg. 1990. "Vivid Memories of Emotional Events: The Accuracy of Remembered Minutiae." *Memory and Cognition* 18 (5): 496–506.

Hill, Carolyn J., Howard S. Bloom, Alison R. Black et al. 2008. "Empirical Benchmarks for Interpreting Effect Sizes in Research." *Child Development Perspectives* 2 (3): 172–77.

Hill, William G. 1995. "Sewall Wright's 'Systems of Mating.'" *Genetics* 143: 1499–506.

Hines, Melissa. 2010. "Sex-Related Variation in Human Behavior and the Brain." *Trends in Cognitive Sciences* 14: 448–56.

Hines, Melissa, Mihaela Constantinescu, and Debra Spencer. 2015. "Early Androgen Exposure and Human Gender Development." *Biology of Sex Differences* 6 (3): 1–10.

Hines, Melissa, and Francine R. Kaufman. 1994. "Androgen and the Development of Human Sex-Typical Behavior: Rough-and-Tumble Play and Sex of Preferred Playmates in Children with Congenital Adrenal Hyperplasia (Cah)." *Child Development* 65 (4): 1042–53.

Hines, Melissa, V. Pasterski, D. Spencer et al. 2016. "Prenatal Androgen Exposure Alters Girls' Responses to Information Indicating Gender-Appropriate Behaviour." *Philosophical Transactions of the Royal Society B: Biological Sciences* 371 (1688): 20150125.

Hittelman, J. H., and R. Dickes. 1979. "Sex Differences in Neonatal Eye Contact Time." *Merill-Palmer Quarterly* 25: 171–84.

Hoffman, M. L. 1973. "Developmental Synthesis of Affect and Cognition and Its Implications for Altruistic Motivation." *Developmental Psychology* 11: 607–22.

Hoffmann, T. J., N. J. Marini, and J. S. Witte. 2010. "Comprehensive Approach to Analyzing Rare Genetic Variants." *PLoS ONE* 5 (11): e13584.

Hogan, Michael J., Roger T. Staff, Brendan P. Bunting et al. 2011. "Cerebellar Brain Volume Accounts for Variance in Cognitive Performance in Older Adults." *Cortex* 47 (4): 441–50.

Holland, John L. 1959. "A Theory of Vocational Choice." *Journal of Counseling Psychology* 6 (1): 35–44.

———. 1977. *Manual for the Vocational Preference Inventory (7th Rev.)*. Palo Alto, CA: Consulting Psychological Press.

Holloway, Ralph L. 1979. "Brain Size, Allometry, and Reorganization: Toward a Synthesis." In *Development and Evolution of Brain Size*, edited by Craig Jensen and Bruce C. Dudek, 59–88. New York: Academic Press.

———. 2017. "In the Trenches with the Corpus Callosum: Some Redux of Redux." *Journal of Neuroscience Research* 95 (1–2): 21–23.

Horn, Joseph M., John C. Loehlin, and Lee Willerman. 1979. "Intellectual Resemblance Among Adoptive and Biological Relatives: The Texas Adoption Project." *Behavior Genetics* 9 (3): 177–207.

Horowitz, Mark, Anthony Haynor, and Kenneth Kickham. 2018. "Sociology's Sacred Victims and the Politics of Knowledge: Moral Foundations Theory and Disciplinary Controversies." *American Sociologist* 49 (4): 459–95.

Horsthemke, Bernhard. 2018. "A Critical View on Transgenerational Epigenetic Inheritance in Humans." *Nature Communications* 9 (1): 2973.

Huerta-Sanchez, Emilia, Xin Jin, Asan et al. 2014. "Altitude Adaptation in Tibetans Caused by Introgression of Denisovan-Like DNA." *Nature* 512: 194–97.

Huguet, Pascal, and Isabelle Régner. 2007. "Stereotype Threat Among Schoolgirls in Quasi-Ordinary Classroom Circumstances." *Journal of Educational Psychology* 99 (3): 545–60.

Humphreys, Lloyd G. 1978. "To Understand Regression from Parent to Offspring, Think Statistically." *Psychological Bulletin* 85 (6): 1317–22.

———. 1983. "Review of *The Mismeasure of Man* by Stephen Jay Gould." *American Journal of Psychology* 96: 407–15.

Humphreys, Lloyd G., David Lubinski, and Grace Yao. 1993. "Utility of Predicting Group Membership and the Role of Spatial Visualization in Becoming an Engineer, Physical Scientist, or Artist." *Journal of Applied Psychology* 78 (2): 250–61.

Hyde, Janet Shibley. 2005. "The Gender Similarities Hypothesis." *American Psychologist* 60 (6): 581–92.

Hyde, Janet Shibley, Daphna Joel, Rebecca S. Bigler et al. 2018. "The Future of Sex and Gender in Psychology: Five Challenges to the Gender Binary." *American Psychologist* 74 (2): 171–93.

Iliescu, D., A. Ilie, D. Ispas et al. 2016. "Sex Differences in Intelligence: A Multi-measure Approach Using Nationally Representative Samples from Romania." *Intelligence* 58: 54–61.

Imperato-McGinley, J., M. Pichardo, T. Gautier et al. 1991. "Cognitive Abilities in Androgen-Insensitive Subjects: Comparison with Control Males and Females from the Same Kindred." *Clinical Endocrinology (Oxford)* 34: 341–47.

Ingalhalikar, Madhura, Alex Smith, Drew Parker et al. 2014. "Sex Differences in the Structural Connectome of the Human Brain." *Proceedings of the National Academy of Sciences* 111 (2): 823–28.

Irwing, Paul. 2012. "Sex Differences in *g*: An Analysis of the US Standardization Sample of the WAIS-III." *Personality and Individual Differences* 53 (2): 126–31.

Irwing, Paul, and Richard Lynn. 2005. "Sex Differences in Means and Variability on the Progressive Matrices in University Students: A Meta-analysis." *British Journal of Psychology* 96: 505–24.

Jablonsky, N. G., and G. Chaplin. 2010. "Human Skin Pigmentation as an Adaptation to UV Radiation." *Proceedings of the National Academy of Sciences* 107 (suppl. 2): 8962–68.

Jackson, Douglas N., and J. Philippe Rushton. 2006. "Males Have Greater *g*: Sex Differences in General Mental Ability from 100,000 17- to 18-Year-Olds on the Scholastic Assessment Test." *Intelligence* 34 (5): 479–86.

Jacobson, Kristen C., and Terrie Vasilopoulos. 2012. "Developmental Changes in Moderating Effects of Parental Education on Individual Differences in Vocabulary IQ from Adolescence to Young Adulthood." *Behavior Genetics* 42: 941.

Jahan, Selim et al. 2016. *Human Development Report 2016*. New York: United Nations Development Programme.

Jahanshad, Neda, and Paul M. Thompson. 2017. "Multimodal Neuroimaging of Male and Female Brain Structure in Health and Disease Across the Life Span." *Journal of Neuroscience Research* 95 (1–2): 371–79.

Jannot, Anne-Sophie, Georg Ehret, and Thomas Perneger. 2015. "P < 5 × 10⁻⁸ Has Emerged as a Standard of Statistical Significance for Genome-Wide Association Studies." *Journal of Clinical Epidemiology* 68 (4): 460–65.

Janssen, Ian, Steven B. Heymsfield, Zimian Wang et al. 2000. "Skeletal Muscle Mass and Distribution in 468 Men and Women Aged 18–88 Yr." *Journal of Applied Physiology* 89 (1): 81–88.

Jencks, Christopher. 1979. *Who Gets Ahead? The Determinants of Economic Success in America*. New York: Basic Books.

Jencks, Christopher, Marshall Smith, Henry Acland et al. 1972. *Inequality: A Reassessment of the Effect of Family and Schooling in America*. New York: Basic Books.

Jensen, Arthur R. 1998. *The g Factor: The Science of Mental Ability*. Westport, CT: Praeger.

Jensen, Jeffrey D., Bret A. Payseur, Wolfgang Stephan et al. 2018. "The Importance of the Neutral Theory in 1968 and 50 Years On: A Response to Kern and Hahn 2018." *Evolution* 73 (1): 111–14.

Joel, Daphna, Zohar Berman, Ido Tavor et al. 2015. "Sex Beyond the Genitalia: The Human Brain Mosaic." *Proceedings of the National Academy of Sciences* 112 (50): 15468–73.

Joel, Daphna, Ariel Persico, Jürgen Hänggi et al. 2016. "Reply to Del Giudice et al., Chekroud et al., and Rosenblatt: Do Brains of Females and Males Belong to Two Distinct Populations?" *Proceedings of the National Academy of Sciences* 113 (14): E1969–70.

Johnson, Wendy, and Thomas J. Bouchard Jr. 2005. "The Structure of Human Intelligence: It Is Verbal, Perceptual, and Image Rotation (Vpr), Not Fluid and Crystallized." *Intelligence* 33: 393–416.

———. 2007. "Sex Differences in Mental Abilities: *g* Masks the Dimensions on Which They Lie." *Intelligence* 35: 23–39.

Johnson, Wendy, Andrew Carothers, and Ian J. Deary. 2008. "Sex Differences in Variability in General Intelligence: A New Look at an Old Question." *Perspectives in Psychological Science* 3 (6): 518–31.

Johnson, Wendy, Matt McGue, Robert F. Krueger et al. 2004. "Marriage and Personality: A Genetic Analysis." *Journal of Personality and Social Psychology* 86 (2): 285–94.

Jordan, Daniel M., Marie Verbanck, and Ron Do. 2018. "The Landscape of Pervasive Horizontal Pleiotropy in Human Genetic Variation Is Driven by Extreme Polygenicity of Human Traits and Diseases." *bioRxiv*.

Joseph, Dana L., and Daniel A. Newman. 2010. "Emotional Intelligence: An Integrative Meta-analysis and Cascading Model." *Journal of Applied Psychology* 95 (1): 54–78.

Kaczkurkin, Antonia N., Armin Raznahan, and Theodore D. Satterthwaite. 2019. "Sex Differences in the Developing Brain: Insights from Multimodal Neuroimaging." *Neuropsychopharmacology* 44 (1): 71–85.

Kahneman, D., P. Slovic, and A. Tversky, eds. (1982). *Judgment Under Uncertainty: Heuristics and Biases*. Cambridge: Cambridge University Press.

Kajonius, Petri, and Erik Mac Giolla. 2017. "Personality Traits Across Countries: Support for Similarities Rather Than Differences." *PLoS ONE* 12 (6): e0179646.

Kansaku, K., A. Yamaura, and S. Kitazawa. 2000. "Sex Differences in Lateralization Revealed in the Posterior Language Areas." *Cerebral Cortex* 10 (9): 866–72.

Kaprio, Jaakko, M. Koskenvuo, and R. J. Rose. 1990. "Change in Cohabitation and Intrapair Similarity of Monozygotic (MZ) Cotwins for Alcohol Use, Extraversion, and Neuroticism." *Behavior Genetics* 20 (2): 265–76.

Karama, S. M., A. R. Lecours, J. M. Leroux et al. 2002. "Areas of Brain Activation in Males and Females During Viewing of Erotic Film Excerpts." *Human Brain Mapping* 16: 1–13.

Karreman, Annemiek, Cathy van Tuijl, Marcel A. G. van Aken et al. 2006. "Parenting and Self-Regulation in Preschoolers: A Meta-analysis." *Infant and Child Development* 15 (6): 561–79.

Katzman, Steven, and George M. Alliger. 1992. "Averaging Untransformed Variance Ratios Can Be Misleading: A Comment on Feingold." *Review of Educational Research* 62 (4): 427–28.

Kawabata, Y., L. R. A. Alink, W.-L. Tseng et al. 2011. "Maternal and Paternal Parenting Styles Associated with Relational Aggression in Children and Adolescents: A Conceptual Analysis and Meta-analytic Review." *Developmental Review* 31 (4): 240–78.

Kazachenka, Anastasiya, Tessa M. Bertozzi, Marcela K. Sjoberg-Herrera et al. 2018. "Identification, Characterization, and Heritability of Murine Metastable Epialleles: Implications for Non-genetic Inheritance." *Cell* 175 (5): 1259–71.e13.

Kerminen, Sini, Alicia R. Martin, Jukka Koskela et al. 2018. "Geographic Variation and Bias in Polygenic Scores of Complex Diseases and Traits in Finland." *bioRxiv*.

Kern, Andrew D., and Matthew W. Hahn. 2018. "The Neutral Theory in Light of Natural Selection." *Molecular Biology and Evolution* 35 (6): 1366–71.

Kettlewell, H. B. D. 1955. "Selection Experiments on Industrial Melanism in the *Lepidoptera*." *Heredity* 9: 323–42.

———. 1956. "Further Selection Experiments on Industrial Melanism in the *Lepidoptera*." *Heredity* 10 (3): 287–301.

Key, Felix M., Qiaomei Fu, Frédéric Romagné et al. 2016. "Human Adaptation and Population Differentiation in the Light of Ancient Genomes." *Nature Communications* 7 (10775).

Khalid, Javaria Mona, Juliet M. Oerton, Carol Dezateux et al. 2012. "Incidence and Clinical Features of Congenital Adrenal Hyperplasia in Great Britain." *Archives of Disease in Childhood* 97 (2): 101.

Kimura, Motoo. 1968. "Evolutionary Rate at the Molecular Level." *Nature* 217: 624–26.

———. 1983. *The Neutral Theory of Molecular Evolution*. Cambridge: Cambridge University Press.

Kimura, Motoo, and George H. Weiss. 1964. "The Stepping Stone Model of Population Structure and the Decrease of Genetic Correlation with Distance." *Genetics* 49: 561–76.

King, Jack L., and Thomas H. Jukes. 1969. "Non-Darwinian Evolution." *Science* 164: 788–97.

Kirkpatrick, Robert M., Matt McGue, and William G. Iacono. 2015. "Replication of a Gene-Environment Interaction Via Multimodel Inference: Additive-Genetic Variance in Adolescents' General Cognitive Ability Increases with Family-of-Origin Socioeconomic Status." *Behavior Genetics* 45 (2): 200–214.

Kliman, Richard. 2008. "The EvolGenius Population Genetics Computer Simulation: How It Works." *Nature Education* 1 (3): 7.

Knickmeyer, R., S. Baron-Cohen, P. Raggatt et al. 2005. "Foetal Testosterone, Social Relationships, and Restricted Interests in Children." *Journal of Child Psychology and Psychiatry* 45 (1): 1–13.

———. 2006. "Fetal Testosterone and Empathy." *Hormones and Behavior* 49: 282–92.

Kodric-Brown, Astrid, and James H. Brown. 1987. "Anisogamy, Sexual Selection, and the Evolution and Maintenance of Sex." *Evolutionary Ecology* 1 (2): 95–105.

Kong, Augustine, Gudmar Thorleifsson, Michael L. Frigge et al. 2018. "The Nature of Nurture: Effects of Parental Genotypes." *Science* 359 (6374): 424.

Korenman, Sanders, and David Neumark. 1991. "Does Marriage Really Make Men More Productive?" *Journal of Human Resources* 26 (2): 282–307.

Korenman, Sanders, and Christopher Winship. 2000. "A Reanalysis of the Bell Curve: Intelligence, Family Background, and Schooling." In *Meritocracy and Economic Inequality*, edited by Kenneth Arrow, Samuel Bowles, and Steven Durlauf. Princeton, NJ: Princeton University Press.

Koscik, Tim, Dan O'Leary, David J. Moser et al. 2009. "Sex Differences in Parietal Lobe Morphology: Relationship to Mental Rotation Performance." *Brain and Cognition* 69 (3): 451–59.

Krapohl, Eva, Kaili Rimfeld, Nicholas G. Shakeshaft et al. 2014. "The High Heritability of Educational Achievement Reflects Many Genetically Influenced Traits, Not Just Intelligence." *Proceedings of the National Academy of Sciences* 111 (42): 15273–78.

Kuhn, Thomas S. 2012. *The Structure of Scientific Revolutions*. 4th ed. Chicago: University of Chicago Press. Original edition 1962.

Kuncel, Nathan R., and Sarah A. Hezlett. 2010. "Fact and Fiction in Cognitive Ability Testing for Admissions and Hiring Decisions." *Current Directions in Psychological Science* 19 (6): 339–45.

Kuncel, Nathan R., Deniz S. Ones, and Paul R. Sackett. 2010. "Individual Differences as Predictors of Work, Educational, and Broad Life Outcomes." *Personality and Individual Differences* 49 (4): 331–36.

Kurdi, Benedek, Shayn Lozano, and Mahzarin R. Banaji. 2016. "Introducing the Open Affective Standardized Image Set (OASIS)." *Behavior Research Methods* 49 (2): 457–70.

LaBar, K. S., and R. Cabeza. 2006. "Cognitive Neuroscience of Emotional Memory." *Nature Reviews Neuroscience* 7 (1): 54–64.

Lachance, Joseph, Ali J. Berens, Matthew E. B. Hansen et al. 2018. "Genetic Hitchhiking and Population Bottlenecks Contribute to Prostate Cancer Disparities in Men of African Descent." *Cancer Research* 78 (9): 2432–43.

Lakin, Joni M. 2013. "Sex Differences in Reasoning Abilities: Surprising Evidence That Male–Female Ratios in the Tails of the Quantitative Reasoning Distribution Have Increased." *Intelligence* 41 (4): 263–74.

Lander, E. S., and N. J. Schork. 1994. "Genetic Dissection of Complex Traits." *Science* 265 (5181): 2037.

Landy, Frank J. 2005. "Some Historical and Scientific Issues Related to Research on Emotional Intelligence." *Journal of Organizational Behavior* 26 (4): 411–24.

Law, David J., James W. Pellegrino, and Earl B. Hunt. 1993. "Comparing the Tortoise and the Hare: Gender Differences and Experience in Dynamic Spatial Reasoning Tasks." *Psychological Science* 4 (1): 35–40.

Lawson, Daniel John, Neil Martin Davies, Simon Haworth et al. 2019. "Is Population Structure in the Genetic Biobank Era Irrelevant, a Challenge, or an Opportunity?" *Human Genetics*. Published online April 27, 2019.

Lawson, Daniel John, Lucy van Dorp, and Daniel Falush. 2018. "A Tutorial on How Not to Overinterpret Structure and Admixture Bar Plots." *Nature Communications* 9 (1): 3258.

Leaper, Campbell, Kristin J. Anderson, and Paul Sanders. 1998. "Moderators of Gender Effects on Parents' Talk to Their Children: A Meta-analysis." *Developmental Psychology* 34 (1): 3–27.

Lechner, Clemens, Daniel Danner, and Beatrice Rammstedt. 2017. "How Is Personality Related to Intelligence and Achievement? A Replication and Extension of Borghans et al. and Salkever." *Personality and Individual Differences* 111: 86–91.

Leeb, R. T., and F. G. Rejskind. 2004. "Here's Looking at You, Kid! A Longitudinal Study of Perceived Gender Differences in Mutual Gaze Behavior in Young Infants." *Sex Roles* 50 (1–2): 1–14.

Lehre, Anne-Catherine, Knut P. Lehre, Petter Laake et al. 2009. "Greater Intrasex Phenotype Variability in Males Than in Females Is a Fundamental Aspect of the Gender Differences in Humans." *Developmental Psychobiology* 51 (2): 198–206.

Lemann, Nicholas. 1999. *The Big Test: The Secret History of the American Meritocracy.* New York: Farrar, Straus, and Giroux.

Lever, J. 1978. "Sex Differences in the Complexity of Children's Play and Games." *American Sociological Review* 43: 471–83.

Lewis, Neil A., and Nicholas M. Michalak. 2019. "Has Stereotype Threat Dissipated over Time? A Cross-Temporal Meta-analysis." *PsyArXiv Preprints.*

Lewontin, Richard C. 1970. "Race and Intelligence." *Bulletin of the Atomic Scientists* 26 (3): 2–8.

———. 1972. "The Apportionment of Human Diversity." *Evolutionary Biology* 6: 381–98.

———. 1974. "The Analysis of Variance and the Analysis of Causes." *American Journal of Human Genetics* 26: 400–411.

Li, Jun Z., Devin M. Absher, Hua Tang et al. 2008. "Worldwide Human Relationships Inferred from Genome-Wide Patterns of Variation." *Science* 319 (5866): 1100–1104.

———. 2008. Supporting Online Material for "Worldwide Human Relationships Inferred from Genome-Wide Patterns of Variation."

Li, Rui, Alexandre Montpetit, Marylène Rousseau et al. 2013. "Somatic Point Mutations Occurring Early in Development: A Monozygotic Twin Study." *Journal of Medical Genetics* 51 (1): 28.

Lim, Vivien K. G., Thompson S. H. Teo, and Geok Leng Loo. 2003. "Sex, Financial Hardship and Locus of Control: An Empirical Study of Attitudes Towards Money Among Singaporean Chinese." *Personality and Individual Differences* 34 (3): 411–29.

Linn, M. C., and A. C. Peterson. 1985. "Emergence and Characterization of Sex Differences in Spatial Ability: A Meta-analysis." *Child Development* 56: 1479–98.

Lippa, Richard A. 2010. "Sex Differences in Personality Traits and Gender-Related Occupational Preferences Across 53 Nations: Testing Evolutionary and Social-Environmental Theories." *Archives of Sexual Behavior* 39 (3): 619–36.

Lippa, Richard A., Marcia L. Collaer, and Michael Peters. 2010. "Sex Differences in Mental Rotation and Line Angle Judgments Are Positively Associated with Gender Equality and Economic Development Across 53 Nations." *Archives of Sexual Behavior* 39 (4): 990–97.

Lippa, Richard A., Kathleen Preston, and John Penner. 2014. "Women's Representation in 60 Occupations from 1972 to 2010: More Women in High-Status Jobs, Few Women in Things-Oriented Jobs." *PLoS ONE* 9 (5): e95960.

Littman, Lisa. 2018. "Rapid-Onset Gender Dysphoria in Adolescents and Young Adults: A Study of Parental Reports." *PLoS ONE* 13 (8): e202330.

———. 2019. "Correction: Parent Reports of Adolescents and Young Adults Perceived to Show Signs of a Rapid Onset of Gender Dysphoria." *PLoS ONE* 14 (3): e0214157.

Liu, X., R. T. Ong, E. N. Pillai et al. 2013. "Detecting and Characterizing Genomic Signatures of Positive Selection in Global Populations." *American Journal of Human Genetics* 92 (6): 866–81.

Lock, Andrew, and Thomas Strong. 2010. *Social Constructionism: Sources and Stirrings in Theory and Practice*. Cambridge: Cambridge University Press.

Locke, John. 1960. *Two Treatises of Government*. Cambridge: Cambridge University Press. Original edition 1689.

Loehlin, John C. 1978. "Identical Twins Reared Apart and Other Routes to the Same Direction." In *Twin Research, Part A: Psychology and Methodology*, edited by W. Nance, G. Allen, and P. Parisi, 69–77. New York: Allan R. Liss.

Loehlin, John C., and Robert C. Nichols. 1976. *Heredity, Environment, and Personality: A Study of 850 Sets of Twins*. Austin: University of Texas Press.

Lombardo, Michael V., Emma Ashwin, Bonnie Auyeung et al. 2012. "Fetal Testosterone Influences Sexually Dimorphic Gray Matter in the Human Brain." *Journal of Neuroscience* 32 (2): 674.

Lombardo, Michael V., B. Chakrabarti, Edward T. Bullmore et al. 2011. "Specialization of Right Temporo-Parietal Junction for Mentalizing and Its Association with Social Impairments in Autism." *NeuroImage* 56: 1832–38.

Long, Jeffrey C., Jie Li, and Meghan E. Healy. 2009. "Human DNA Sequences: More Variation and Less Race." *American Journal of Physical Anthropology* 139 (1): 23–34.

LoParo, Devon, and Irwin Waldman. 2014. "Twins' Rearing Environment Similarity and Childhood Externalizing Disorders: A Test of the Equal Environments Assumption." *Behavior Genetics* 44 (6): 606–13.

Lopez, Saioa, Lucy van Dorp, and Garrett Hallenthal. 2016. "Human Dispersal out of Africa: A Lasting Debate." *Evolutionary Bioinformatics* 11 (S2): 57–68.

Low, Bobbi S. 2015. *Why Sex Matters: A Darwinian Look at Human Behavior*. Princeton, NJ: Princeton University Press.

Lubinski, David, and Camilla P. Benbow. 2006. "Study of Mathematically Precocious Youth After 35 Years: Uncovering Antecedents for the Development of Math-Science Expertise." *Psychological Science* 1 (4): 316–45.

Lubinski, David, Camilla P. Benbow, and Harrison J. Kell. 2014. "Life Paths and Accomplishments of Mathematically Precocious Males and Females Four Decades Later." *Psychological Science* 25 (12): 2217–32.

Lubinski, David, Camilla P. Benbow, Daniel L. Shea et al. 2001. "Men and Women at Promise for Scientific Excellence: Similarity Not Dissimilarity." *Psychological Science* 12 (4): 309–17.

Lubinski, David, Rose Mary Webb, Martha J. Morelock et al. 2001. "Top 1 in 10,000: A 10-Year Follow-up of the Profoundly Gifted." *Journal of Applied Psychology* 86 (4): 718–29.

Luders, Eileen, Arthur W. Toga, and Paul M. Thompson. 2014. "Why Size Matters: Differences in Brain Volume Account for Apparent Sex Differences in Callosal Anatomy." *NeuroImage* 84: 820–24.

Ludwig, Volker, and Josef Brüderl. 2018. "Is There a Male Marital Wage Premium? New Evidence from the United States." *American Sociological Review* 83 (4): 744–70.

Lukianoff, Greg, and Jonathan Haidt. 2018. *The Coddling of the American Mind: How Good Intentions and Bad Ideas Are Setting Up a Generation for Failure*. New York: Penguin.

Luo, Yang, Xinyi Li, Xin Wang et al. 2018. "Estimating Heritability of Complex Traits in Admixed Populations with Summary Statistics." *bioRxiv*: 503144.

Lutchmaya, Svetlana, S. Baron-Cohen, and Peter Raggatt. 2001. "Foetal Testosterone and Vocabulary Size in 18- and 24-Month-Old Infants." *Infant Behavior and Development* 24: 418–24.

———. 2002. "Foetal Testosterone and Eye Contact in 12-Month-Old Human Infants." *Infant Behavior and Development* 25: 327–35.

Lynn, Richard. 1999. "Sex Differences in Intelligence and Brain Size: A Developmental Theory." *Intelligence* 27 (1): 1–12.

———. 2017. "Sex Differences in Intelligence: The Developmental Theory." *Mankind Quarterly* 58 (1): 9–43.

Lynn, Richard, and Paul Irwing. 2004. "Sex Differences on the Progressive Matrices: A Meta-analysis." *Intelligence* 32: 481–98.

Lytton, Hugh, and David M. Romney. 1991. "Parents' Differential Socialization of Boys and Girls: A Meta-analysis." *Psychological Bulletin* 109 (2): 267–96.

Maccoby, Eleanor E., and Carol N. Jacklin. 1974. *The Psychology of Sex Differences*. Stanford, CA: Stanford University Press.

Mac Giolla, Erik, and Petri J. Kajonius. 2018. "Sex Differences in Personality Are Larger in Gender Equal Countries: Replicating and Extending a Surprising Finding." *International Journal of Psychology*. www.ncbi.nlm.nih.gov/pubmed/30206941.

Machin, Stephen, and Tuomas Pekkarinen. 2008. "Global Sex Differences in Test Score Variability." *Science* 322 (5906): 1331.

Madsen, B. E., and S. R. Browning. 2009. "A Groupwise Association Test for Rare Mutations Using a Weighted Sum Statistic." *PLoS Genetics* 5: e1000384.

Makel, Matthew C., Jonathan Wai, Kristen Peairs et al. 2016. "Sex Differences in the Right Tail of Cognitive Abilities: An Update and Cross Cultural Extension." *Intelligence* 59: 8–15.

Malaspinas, Anna-Sapfo, Michael C. Westaway, Craig Muller et al. 2016. "A Genomic History of Aboriginal Australia." *Nature* 538: 207–14.

Malécot, Gustave. 1948. *Les Mathématiques de l'Hérédité*. Paris: Masson.

Mallick, Swapan, Heng Li, Mark Lipson et al. 2016. "The Simons Genome Diversity Project: 300 Genomes from 142 Diverse Populations." *Nature* 538: 201–6.

Mancuso, N., N. Rohland, K. A. Rand et al. 2015. "The Contribution of Rare Variation to Prostate Cancer Heritability." *Nature Genetics* 48: 30.

Marchini, Jonathan, Lon R. Cardon, Michael S. Phillips et al. 2004. "The Effects of Human Population Structure on Large Genetic Association Studies." *Nature Genetics* 36: 512.

Mardis, E. R. 2008. "Next-Generation DNA Sequencing Methods." *Annual Review of Genomics and Human Genetics* 9: 387–402.

Marigorta, U. M., and A. Navarro. 2013. "High Trans-Ethnic Replicability of GWAS Results Implies Common Causal Variants." *PLoS Genet* 9 (6): e1003566.

Marks, G. N. 2008. "Accounting for the Gender Gaps in Student Performance in Reading and Mathematics: Evidence from 31 Countries." *Oxford Review of Education* 34: 89–109.

Marth, Gabor T., Fuli Yu, Amit R. Indap et al. 2011. "The Functional Spectrum of Low-Frequency Coding Variation." *Genome Biology* 12 (9): R84.

Martin, C. L., D. N. Ruble, and J. Szkrybalo. 2002. "Cognitive Theories of Early Gender Development." *Psychological Bulletin* 128: 903–33.

Martin, L. A., H. W. Neighbors, and D. M. Griffith. 2013. "The Experience of Symptoms of Depression in Men vs Women: Analysis of the National Comorbidity Survey Replication." *JAMA Psychiatry* 70 (10): 1100–1106.

Marwha, D., M. Halari, and L. Eliot. 2017. "Meta-analysis Reveals a Lack of Sexual Dimorphism in Human Amygdala Volume." *NeuroImage* 147: 282–94.

Matarazzo, Joseph D. 1972. *Wechsler's Measurement and Appraisal of Adult Intelligence*. New York: Oxford University Press.

Mattern, Krista D., and Brian F. Patterson. 2013. "Test of Slope and Intercept Bias in College Admissions: A Response to Aguinis, Culpepper, and Pierce (2010)." *Journal of Applied Psychology* 98 (1): 134–47.

Matthews, Gerald, Moshe Zeidner, and Richard D. Roberts, eds. 2007. *The Science of Emotional Intelligence: Knowns and Unknowns*. Oxford: Oxford University Press.

Mayer, John D., David R. Caruso, and Peter Salovey. 1999. "Emotional Intelligence Meets Traditional Standards for an Intelligence." *Intelligence* 27 (4): 267–98.

Mayes, L. C., and A. S. Carter. 1990. "Emerging Social Regulatory Capacities as Seen in the Still-Face Situation." *Child Development* 61: 754–63.

McCarthy, Margaret M. 2015. "Sex Differences in the Brain." *The Scientist* (October 1).

McCarthy, Margaret M., and Arthur P. Arnold. 2011. "Reframing Sexual Differentiation of the Brain." *Nature Neuroscience* 14 (6): 677–83.

McCarthy, Margaret M., and Gregory F. Ball. 2011. "Tempests and Tales: Challenges to the Study of Sex Differences in the Brain." *Biology of Sex Differences* 2 (1): 4.

McCarthy, Margaret M., Bridget M. Nugent, and Kathryn M. Lenz. 2017. "Neuroimmunology and Neuroepigenetics in the Establishment of Sex Differences in the Brain." *Nature Reviews Neuroscience* 18 (8): 471–84.

McClure, Erin B. 2000. "A Meta-analytic Review of Sex Differences in Facial Expression Processing and Their Development in Infants, Children, and Adolescents." *Psychological Bulletin* 126 (3): 424–53.

McCoy, Rajiv C., and Joshua M. Akey. 2017. "Selection Plays the Hand It Was Dealt: Evidence That Human Adaptation Commonly Targets Standing Genetic Variation." *Genome Biology* 18 (1): 139.

McCrae, Robert R., and A. Terracciano. 2005. "Universal Features of Personality Traits from the Observer's Perspective: Data from 50 Cultures." *Journal of Personality and Social Psychology* 88 (3): 547–61.

McDaniel, Michael A. 2005. "Big-Brained People Are Smarter: A Meta-analysis of the Relationship Between *in vivo* Brain Volume and Intelligence." *Intelligence* 33: 337–46.

———. 2018. *How to Build a Cognitive Ability Test with Reduced Group Mean Differences*. Presentation to Personnel Testing Council of Metropolitan Washington (February 21).

McDaniel, Michael A., and Sven Kepes. 2014. "An Evaluation of Spearman's Hypothesis by Manipulating G Saturation." *International Journal of Selection and Assessment* 22 (4): 333–42.

McGlone, Jeannette. 1980. "Sex Differences in Human Brain Asymmetry: A Critical Survey." *Behavioral and Brain Sciences* 3 (2): 215–27.

McGue, Matt, and David T. Lykken. 1992. "Genetic Influence on Risk of Divorce." *Psychological Science* 3: 368–73.

McHenry, H. M. 2012. "Origin and Diversity of Early Hominin Bipedalism." In *African Genesis: Perspectives on Hominin Evolution*, edited by S. C. Reynolds, 205–22. Cambridge: Cambridge University Press.

Mecca, Andrew, Neil J. Smelser, and John Vasconcellos, eds. 1989. *The Social Importance of Self-Esteem*. Berkeley: University of California Press.

Merton, Robert K. 1968. "The Matthew Effect in Science." *Science* 159: 56–63.

Migeon, Barbara R. 2017. "Choosing the Active X: The Human Version of X Inactivation." *Trends in Genetics* 33 (12): 899–909.

Mill, John Stuart. 1869. *The Subjection of Women*. London: Longmans, Green, Reader & Dyer.

Miller, Gregory A., and Jean P. Chapman. 2001. "Misunderstanding Analysis of Covariance." *Journal of Abnormal Psychology* 110 (1): 40–48.

Moffitt, Terrie E., Louise Arseneault, Daniel Belsky et al. 2011. "A Gradient of Childhood Self-Control Predicts Health, Wealth, and Public Safety." *Proceedings of the National Academy of Sciences* 108 (7): 2693–98.

Moffitt, Terrie E., Avshalom Caspi, and Michael Rutter. 2005. "Strategy for Investigating Interactions Between Measured Genes and Measured Environments." *Archives of General Psychiatry* 62 (5): 473–81.

Moffitt, Terrie E., Richie Poulton, and Avshalom Caspi. 2013. "The Lifelong Impact of Early Self-Control." *American Scientist* 101 (5): 352–59.

Money, John Williams. 1952. "Hermaphroditism: An Inquiry into the Nature of a Human Paradox." PhD dissertation, Harvard University.

Montagu, Ashley. 1997. *Man's Most Dangerous Myth: The Fallacy of Race*. 6th ed. Walnut Creek, CA: Altamira Press. Original edition 1942.

Moore, Carrie B., John R. Wallace, Daniel J. Wolfe et al. 2013. "Low Frequency Variants, Collapsed Based on Biological Knowledge, Uncover Complexity of Population Stratification in 1000 Genomes Project Data." *PLoS Genetics* 9 (12): e1003959.

Moore, D. S., and D. Shenk. 2017. "The Heritability Fallacy." *Wiley Interdisciplinary Reviews: Cognitive Science* 8 (1–2).

Moran, Carlos, Ricardo Azziz, Enrico Carmina et al. 2000. "21-Hydroxylase-Deficient Nonclassic Adrenal Hyperplasia Is a Progressive Disorder: A Multicenter Study." *American Journal of Obstetrics and Gynecology* 183 (6): 1468–74.

Moreno-Briseño, P., R. Diaz, A. Campos-Romo et al. 2010. "Sex-Related Differences in Motor Learning and Performance." *Behavioral and Brain Functions* 6: 74.

Morrongiello, Barbara A., and Tess Dawber. 2004. "Identifying Factors That Relate to Children's Risk-Taking Decisions." *Canadian Journal of Behavioural Science* 36 (4): 255–66.

Mueller, Claudia M., and Carol S. Dweck. 1998. "Praise for Intelligence Can Undermine Children's Motivation and Performance." *Journal of Personality and Social Psychology* 75 (1): 33–52.

Mundy, P., J. A. Block, C. Delgado et al. 2007. "Individual Differences in the Development of Joint Attention in Infancy." *Child Development* 78: 938–54.

Murray, Charles. 1984. *Losing Ground: American Social Policy, 1950–1980.* New York: Basic Books.

———. 1988. *In Pursuit: Of Happiness and Good Government.* New York: Simon and Schuster.

———. 1997. *What It Means to Be a Libertarian: A Personal Interpretation.* New York: Broadway Books.

———. 2003. *Human Accomplishment: The Pursuit of Excellence in the Arts and Sciences, 800 B.C. to 1950.* New York: HarperCollins.

———. 2006. *In Our Hands: A Plan to Replace the Welfare State.* Washington: AEI Press.

———. 2012. *Coming Apart: The State of White America, 1960–2010.* New York: Crown Forum.

———. 2015. *By the People: Rebuilding Liberty Without Permission.* New York: Crown Forum.

Myrianthopoulos, N. C., and K. S. French. 1968. "An Application of the U.S. Bureau of Census Socioeconomic Index to a Large Diversified Population." *Social Science and Medicine* 2: 283–99.

Nagel, Mats, Philip R. Jansen, Sven Stringer et al. 2018. "Gwas Meta-Analysis of Neuroticism (N=449,484) Identifies Novel Genetic Loci and Pathways." *Nature* 50 (7): 920–27.

Nagy, Emese, Hajnalka Kompagne, Hajnalka Orvos et al. 2007. "Gender-Related Differences in Neonatal Imitation." *Infant and Child Development* 16 (3): 267–76.

Nanney, D. L. 1958. "Epigenetic Control Systems." *Proceedings of the National Academy of Sciences* 44 (7): 712.

Narasimhan, Vagheesh M., Raheleh Rahbari, Aylwyn Scally et al. 2017. "Estimating the Human Mutation Rate from Autozygous Segments Reveals Population Differences in Human Mutational Processes." *Nature Communications* 8 (1): 303.

Nauta, Margaret M. 2010. "The Development, Evolution, and Status of Holland's Theory of Vocational Personalities: Reflections and Future Directions for Counseling Psychology." *Journal of Counseling Psychology* 57 (1): 11–22.

Nave, Gideon, Amos Nadler, David Zava et al. 2017. "Single-Dose Testosterone Administration Impairs Cognitive Reflection in Men." *Psychological Science* 28 (10): 1398–407.

Nazareth, Alina, Xing Huang, Daniel Voyer, et al. 2019. "A Meta-Analysis of Sex Differences in Human Navigation Skills." *Psychonomic Bulletin & Review.* Published online July 3, 2019.

Nédélec, Yohann, Joaquín Sanz, Golshid Baharian et al. 2016. "Genetic Ancestry and Natural Selection Drive Population Differences in Immune Responses to Pathogens." *Cell* 167 (3): 657–69.e21.

Neisser, Ulric, Gwyneth Boodoo, T. J. Bouchard Jr. et al. 1996. "Intelligence: Knowns and Unknowns." *American Psychologist* 51 (2): 77–101.

Neves, Kleber, Gerson D. Guercio, Yuri Anjos-Travassos et al. 2018. "Lack of Correlation Between Number of Neurons and Behavioral Performance in Swiss Mice." *bioRxiv.*

Newman, H. H., F. N. Freeman, and K. J. Holzinger. 1937. *Twins: A Study of Heredity and Environment.* Chicago: University of Chicago Press.

Nguyen, Hannah-Hanh D., and Ann Marie Ryan. 2008. "Does Stereotype Threat Affect Test Performance of Minorities and Women? A Meta-analysis of Experimental Evidence." *Journal of Applied Psychology* 93 (6): 1314–34.

Nielsen, Rasmus, Joshua M. Akey, Mattias Jakobsson et al. 2017. "Tracing the Peopling of the World Through Genomics." *Nature* 541 (7637): 302–10.

Noftle, Erik E., and Phillip R. Shaver. 2006. "Attachment Dimensions and the Big Five Personality Traits: Associations and Comparative Ability to Predict Relationship Quality." *Journal of Research in Personality* 40 (2): 179–208.

Nolen-Hoeksema, S., J. Morrow, and B. L. Fredrickson. 1993. "Response Styles and the Duration of Episodes of Depressed Mood." *Journal of Abnormal Psychology* 102: 20–28.

Nolen-Hoeksema, S., L. E. Parker, and J. Larson. 1994. "Ruminative Coping with Depressed Mood Following Loss." *Journal of Personality and Social Psychology* 67: 92–104.

Novembre, John, and Nicholas H. Barton. 2018. "Tread Lightly Interpreting Polygenic Tests of Selection." *Genetics* 208 (4): 1351–55.

Novembre, John, and Anna DiRienzo. 2009. "Spatial Patterns of Variation Due to Natural Selection in Humans." *Nature Reviews Genetics* 10: 745–55.

Novembre, John, and Benjamin M. Peter. 2016. "Recent Advances in the Study of Fine-Scale Population Structure in Humans." *Current Opinion in Genetics and Development* (41): 98–105.

Okbay, Aysu, Jonathan P. Beauchamp, Mark Alan Fontana et al. 2016. "Supplementary Information: Genome-Wide Association Study Identifies 74 Loci Associated with Educational Attainment." *Nature* 533 (7604).

Olafsen, K. S., J. A. Ronning, P. I. Kaaresen et al. 2006. "Joint Attention in Term and Preterm Infants at 12 Months of Age: The Significant of Gender and Intervention Based on Randomized Controlled Trial." *Infant Behavior and Development* 29: 554–63.

Olalde, Iñigo, and Carles Lalueza-Fox. 2015. "Modern Humans' Paleogenomics and the New Evidences on the European Prehistory." *Science and Technology of Archaeological Research* 1 (1): 1–9.

Oleksyk, Taras K., Vladimir Brukhin, and Stephen J. O'Brien. 2015. "The Genome Russia Project: Closing the Largest Remaining Omission on the World Genome Map." *GigaScience* 4 (1): 53.

Olsson, Andreas, Eleni Kopsida, Sorjonen Kimmo et al. 2016. "Testosterone and Estrogen Impact Social Evaluations and Vicarious Emotions: A Double-Blind Placebo-Controlled Study." *Emotion* 16 (4): 515–23.

Omi, Michael, and Howard Winant. 1986. *Racial Formation in the United States: From the 1960s to the 1980s*. New York: Routledge.

Ones, Deniz, S. Dilchert, and Chockalingam Viswesvaran. 2014. "Cognitive Abilities." In *The Oxford Handbook of Personnel Assessment and Selection*, edited by Neil Schmitt, 179–224. Oxford: Oxford University Press.

1000 Genomes Project Consortium. 2012. "An Integrated Map of Genetic Variation from 1,092 Human Genomes." *Nature* 491 (7422): 56–65.

Otter, Maarten, Constance T. R. M. Schrander-Stumpel, and Leopold M. G. Curfs. 2010. "Triple X Syndrome: A Review of the Literature." *European Journal of Human Genetics* 18 (3): 265–71.

Pagani, Luca, Daniel John Lawson, Evelyn Jagoda et al. 2016. "Genomic Analyses Inform on Migration Events During the Peopling of Eurasia." *Nature* 538: 238–42.

Palmer, Benjamin R., Gilles Gignac, Ramesh Manocha et al. 2005. "A Psychometric Evaluation of the Mayer–Salovey–Caruso Emotional Intelligence Test Version 2.0." *Intelligence* 33 (3): 285–305.

Papagianni, Dimitra, and Michael A. Morse. 2015. *The Neanderthals Rediscovered: How Modern Science Is Rewriting Their Story*. New York: Thames & Hudson.

Parra, Esteban J. 2007. "Human Pigmentation Variation: Evolution, Genetic Basis, and Implications for Public Health." *Yearbook of Physical Anthropology* 50: 85–105.

Paunesku, David, Gregory M. Walton, Carissa Romero et al. 2015. "Mind-Set Interventions Are a Scalable Treatment for Academic Underachievement." *Psychological Science* 26 (6): 784–93.

Pellegrini, Anthony D. 2007. "The Development and Function of Rough-and-Tumble Play in Childhood and Adolescence: A Sexual Selection Theory Perspective." In *Play and Development: Evolutionary, Sociocultural, and Functional Perspectives*, edited by Artin Göncü and Suzanne Gaskins, 77–98. New York: Erlbaum.

Pelphry, K. A., J. P. Morris, and G. McCarthy. 2005. "Neural Basis of Eye Gaze Processing Deficits in Autism." *Brain* 128 (Pt. 5): 1038–48.

Penner, Andrew M. 2003. "International Gender X Item Difficulty Interactions in Mathematics and Science Achievement Tests." *Journal of Educational Psychology* 95 (3): 650–55.

Pennington, Charlotte R., Damien Litchfield, Neil McLatchie et al. 2018. "Stereotype Threat May Not Impact Women's Inhibitory Control or Mathematical Performance: Providing Support for the Null Hypothesis." *European Journal of Social Psychology* 49 (4): 717–34.

Perez, Marcos Francisco, and Ben Lehner. 2019. "Intergenerational and Transgenerational Epigenetic Inheritance in Animals." *Nature Cell Biology* 21: 143–51.

Peterson, Jennifer. 2018. "Gender Differences in Verbal Performance: A Meta-analysis of United States State Performance Assessments." *Educational Psychology Review*. Published online September 3, 2018.

Pettersson, Erik, Jane Mendle, Eric Turkheimer et al. 2014. "Do Maladaptive Behaviors Exist at One or Both Ends of Personality Traits?" *Psychological Assessment* 26 (2): 433–66.

Phillips, Deborah A., Mark W. Lipsey, Kenneth A. Dodge et al. 2017. *Puzzling It Out: The Current State of Scientific Knowledge on Pre-kindergarten Effects: A Consensus Statement.* Washington, DC: Brookings Institution.

Phoenix, Charles H., Robert W. Goy, Arnold A. Gerall et al. 1959. "Organizing Action of Prenatally Administered Testosterone Propionate on the Tissues Mediating Mating Behavior in the Female Guinea Pig." *Endocrinology* 65 (3): 369–82.

Picho, Katherine, Ariel Rodriguez, and Lauren Finnie. 2013. "Exploring the Moderating Role of Context on the Mathematics Performance of Females Under Stereotype Threat: A Meta-Analysis." *The Journal of Social Psychology* 153 (3): 299–333.

Pickrell, Joseph K., Tomaz Berisa, Jimmy Z. Liu et al. 2016. "Detection and Interpretation of Shared Genetic Influences on 42 Human Traits." *Nature Genetics* 48: 709.

Pickrell, Joseph K., Graham Coop, John Novembre et al. 2009. "Signals of Recent Positive Selection in a Worldwide Sample of Human Populations." *Genome Research* 19 (5): 826–37.

Pietschnig, Jakob, Lars Penke, Jelte M. Wicherts et al. 2015. "Meta-analysis of Associations Between Human Brain Volume and Intelligence Differences: How Strong Are They and What Do They Mean?" *Neuroscience and Biobehavioral Reviews* 57: 411–32.

Pike, Alison, Shirley McGuire, E. Mavis Hetherington et al. 1996. "Family Environment and Adolescent Depressive Symptoms and Antisocial Behavior: A Multivariate Genetic Analysis." *Developmental Psychology* 32 (4): 590–604.

Pinker, Steven. 2002. *The Blank Slate: The Modern Denial of Human Nature.* New York: Viking Penguin.

Plomin, Robert. 2011. "Commentary: Why Are Children in the Same Family So Different? Non-shared Environment Three Decades Later." *International Journal of Epidemiology* 40 (3): 582–92.

———. 2018. *Blueprint: How DNA Makes Us Who We Are.* Cambridge, MA: MIT Press.

Plomin, Robert, and Denise Daniels. 1987. "Why Are Children in the Same Family So Different from One Another?" *Behavioral and Brain Sciences* 10: 1–60.

Plomin, Robert, and J. C. DeFries. 1983. "The Colorado Adoption Project." *Child Development* 54 (2): 276–89.

Plomin, Robert, G. E. McClearn, D. L. Smith et al. 1994. "DNA Markers Associated with High Versus Low IQ: The IQ Quantitative Trait Loci (QTL) Project." *Behavior Genetics* 24 (2): 107–18.

Plomin, Robert, and Frank M. Spinath. 2004. "Intelligence: Genetics, Genes, and Genomics." *Journal of Personality and Social Psychology* 86 (1): 112–29.

Polderman, Tinca J. C., Beben Benyamin, Christiaan A. de Leeuw et al. 2015. "Meta-analysis of the Heritability of Human Traits Based on Fifty Years of Twin Studies." *Nature Genetics* 47: 702–9.

Poldrack, Russell A., J. A. Mumford, and Thomas E. Nichols. 2011. *Handbook of fMRI Data Analysis*. Cambridge: Cambridge University Press.

Pomiankowski, Andrew, and A. P. Møller. 1995. "A Resolution of the Lek Paradox." *Proceedings of the Royal Society B* 260: 21–29.

Poropat, Arthur E. 2014. "A Meta-analysis of Adult-Rated Child Personality and Academic Performance in Primary Education." *British Journal of Educational Psychology* 84 (2): 239–52.

Posth, Cosimo, Christoph Wißing, Keiko Kitagawa et al. 2017. "Deeply Divergent Archaic Mitochondrial Genome Provides Lower Time Boundary for African Gene Flow into Neanderthals." *Nature Communications* 8: 16046.

Poznik, G. David, Brenna M. Henn, Muh-Ching Yee et al. 2013. "Sequencing Y Chromosomes Resolves Discrepancy in Time to Common Ancestor of Males Versus Females." *Science* 341 (6145): 562.

Prediger, Dale J. 1982. "Dimensions Underlying Holland's Hexagon: Missing Link Between Interests and Occupations?" *Journal of Vocational Behavior* 21 (3): 259–87.

Premack, David, and Guy Woodruff. 1978. "Does the Chimpanzee Have a Theory of Mind?" *Behavioral and Brain Sciences* 1 (4): 515–26.

Pritchard, Jonathan K., Matthew Stephens, and Peter Donnelly. 2000. "Inference of Population Structure Using Multilocus Genotype Data." *Genetics* 155 (2): 945.

Protzko, John, and Joshua Aronson. 2016. "Context Moderates Affirmation Effects on the Ethnic Achievement Gap." *Social Psychological and Personality Science* 7 (6): 500–507.

Ramachandran, Sohini, Omkar Deshpande, Charles C. Roseman et al. 2005. "Support from the Relationship of Genetic and Geographic Distance in Human Populations for a Serial Founder Effect Originating in Africa." *Proceedings of the National Academy of Sciences* 102 (44): 15942–47.

Ramel, W., P. R. Goldin, L. T. Eyler et al. 2007. "Amygdala Reactivity and Mood-Congruent Memory in Individuals at Risk for Depressive Relapse." *Biological Psychiatry* 61 (2): 231–39.

Ranke, M. B., and P. Saenger. 2001. "Turner's Syndrome." *Lancet* 358: 309–14.

Raymond, Cindy L., and Camilla P. Benbow. 1986. "Gender Differences in Mathematics: A Function of Parental Support and Student Sex Typing?" *Developmental Psychology* 22 (6): 808–19.

Reardon, P. K., Jakob Seidlitz, Simon Vandekar et al. 2018. "Normative Brain Size Variation and Brain Shape Diversity in Humans." *Science* 360 (6394): 1222.

Reich, David. 2018. *Who We Are and How We Got Here: Ancient DNA and the New Science of the Human Past*. New York: Pantheon.

Reilly, David, David L. Neumann, and Glenda Andrews. 2015. "Sex Differences in Mathematics and Science Achievement: A Meta-analysis of National Assessment of Educational Progress Assessments." *Journal of Educational Psychology* 107 (3): 645–62.

———. 2018. "Gender Differences in Reading and Writing Achievement: Evidence from the National Assessment of Educational Progress (NAEP)." *American Psychologist* 74 (4): 445–58.

Reinhold, Klaus, and Leif Engqvist. 2013. "The Variability Is in the Sex Chromosomes." *Evolution* 67 (12): 3662–68.

Reisberg, Sulev, Tatjana Iljasenko, Kristi Läll et al. 2017. "Comparing Distributions of Polygenic Risk Scores of Type 2 Diabetes and Coronary Heart Disease Within Different Populations." *PLoS ONE* 12 (7): e0179238.

Reynolds, Cecil R., Robert L. Chastain, Alan S. Kaufman et al. 1987. "Demographic Characteristics and IQ Among Adults: Analysis of the WAIS-R Standardization Sample as a Function of the Stratification Variables." *Journal of School Psychology* 25: 323–42.

Reynolds, Matthew R., Caroline Scheiber, Daniel B. Hajovsky et al. 2015. "Gender Differences in Academic Achievement: Is Writing an Exception to the Gender Similarities Hypothesis?" *Journal of Genetic Psychology* 176 (4): 211–34.

Rhemtulla, Mijke, and Elliot M. Tucker-Drob. 2012. "Gene-by-Socioeconomic Status Interaction on School Readiness." *Behavior Genetics* 42: 549–58.

Rhodes, Gillian, Linda Jeffery, Tamara L. Watson et al. 2004. "Orientation-Contingent Face Aftereffects and Implications for Face-Coding Mechanisms." *Current Biology* 14 (23): 2119–23.

Richards, M., and A. Sacker. 2003. "Lifetime Antecedents of Cognitive Reserve." *Journal of Clinical and Experimental Psychology* 25: 614–24.

Richardson, Ken, and Sarah H. Norgate. 2015. "Does IQ Really Predict Job Performance?" *Applied Developmental Science* 19 (3): 153–69.

Richter, Daniel, Rainer Grün, Renaud Joannes-Boyau et al. 2017. "The Age of the Hominin Fossils from Jebel Irhoud, Morocco, and the Origins of the Middle Stone Age." *Nature* 546: 293.

Richters, Juliet, Dennis Altman, Paul B. Badcock et al. 2014. "Sexual Identity, Sexual Attraction and Sexual Experience: The Second Australian Study of Health and Relationships." *Sexual Health* 11 (5): 451–60.

Riès, Stéphanie K., Nina F. Dronkers, and Robert T. Knight. 2016. "Choosing Words: Left Hemisphere, Right Hemisphere, or Both? Perspective on the Lateralization of Word Retrieval." *Annals of the New York Academy of Sciences* 1369 (1): 111–31.

Risch, Neil, and Kathleen Merikangas. 1996. "The Future of Genetic Studies of Complex Human Diseases." *Science* 273 (September 13): 1516–17.

Risch, Neil, Donna Spiker, Linda Lotspeich et al. 1999. "A Genomic Screen of Autism: Evidence for a Multilocus Etiology." *American Journal of Human Genetics* 65 (2): 493–507.

Ritchie, Stuart J. 2015. *Intelligence: All That Matters*. London: Hodder & Stoughton.

Ritchie, Stuart J., Simon R. Cox, Xueyi Shen et al. 2018. "Sex Differences in the Adult Human Brain: Evidence from 5216 UK Biobank Participants." *Cerebral Cortex* 28 (8): 2959–75.

Ritchie, Stuart J., and Elliot M. Tucker-Drob. 2018. "How Much Does Education Improve Intelligence? A Meta-analysis." *Psychological Science* 29 (8): 1358–69.

Rivas, Manuel A., Brandon E. Avila, Jukka Koskela et al. 2018. "Insights into the Genetic Epidemiology of Crohn's and Rare Diseases in the Ashkenazi Jewish Population." *PLoS Genetics* 14 (5): e1007329.

Roalf, David R., Raquel E. Gur, Kosha Ruparel et al. 2014. "Within-Individual Variability in Neurocognitive Performance: Age- and Sex-Related Differences in Children and Youths from Ages 8 to 21." *Neuropsychology* 28 (4): 506–18.

Rojas, D. C., S. D. Bawn, T. L. Benkers et al. 2002. "Smaller Left Hemisphere Planum Temporale in Adults with Autistic Disorder." *Neuroscience Letters* 328: 237–40.

Ronald, James, and Joshua M. Akey. 2005. "Genome-Wide Scans for Loci Under Selection in Humans." *Human Genomics* 2 (2): 113–25.

Rosen, Sarah, Boram Ham, and Jeffrey S. Mogil. 2017. "Sex Differences in Neuroimmunity and Pain." *Journal of Neuroscience Research* 95 (1–2): 500–508.

Rosenberg, Alex. 2017. "Why Social Science Is Biological Science." *Journal for General Philosophy of Science* 48 (3): 341–69.

Rosenberg, Noah A. 2018. "Variance-Partitioning and Classification in Human Population Genetics." In *Phylogenetic Inference, Selection Theory, and History of Science: Selected Papers of A. W. F. Edwards with Commentaries,* edited by Rasmus Grønfeldt Winther, 399–402. Cambridge: Cambridge University Press.

Rosenberg, Noah A., Saurabh Mahajan, Sohini Ramachandran et al. 2005. "Clines, Clusters, and the Effect of Study Design on the Inference of Human Population Structure." *PLoS Genetics* 1 (6): e70.

Rosenberg, Noah A., J. K. Pritchard, J. L. Weber et al. 2002. "Genetic Structure of Human Populations." *Science* 298 (5602): 2381–85.

Rosenblatt, Jonathan D. 2016. "Multivariate Revisit to 'Sex Beyond the Genitalia.'" *Proceedings of the National Academy of Sciences* 113 (14): E1966–67.

Rosenthal, Robert, and Donald B. Rubin. 1982. "Further Meta-analytic Procedures for Assessing Cognitive Gender Differences." *Journal of Educational Psychology* 74: 708–12.

Rosip, J. C., and Judith A. Hall. 2004. "Knowledge of Nonverbal Cues, Gender, and Nonverbal Decoding Accuracy." *Journal of Nonverbal Behavior* 28 (4): 276–86.

Rosnow, Ralph L., and Robert Rosenthal. 2003. "Effect Sizes for Experimenting Psychologists." *Canadian Journal of Experimental Psychology* 57 (3): 221–37.

Rothbaum, Fred, and John R. Weisz. 1994. "Parental Caregiving and Child Externalizing Behavior in Nonclinical Samples: A Meta-analysis." *Psychological Bulletin* 116 (1): 55–74.

Rowe, David C., Kristen C. Jacobson, and Edwin J. C. G. Van den Oord. 1999. "Genetic and Environmental Influences on Vocabulary IQ: Parental Education Level as Moderator." *Child Development* 70 (5): 1151–62.

Rowe, David C., and Robert Plomin. 1981. "The Importance of Nonshared (E_1) Environmental Influences on Behavioral Development." *Developmental Psychology* 17: 517–31.

Rubin, Leah H., Li Yao, Sarah K. Keedy et al. 2017. "Sex Differences in Associations of Arginine Vasopressin and Oxytocin with Resting-State Functional Brain Connectivity." *Journal of Neuroscience Research* 95 (1–2): 576–86.

Ruigrok, Amber N. V., Gholamreza Salimi-Khorshidi, Meng-Chuan Lai et al. 2014. "A Meta-analysis of Sex Differences in Human Brain Structure." *Neuroscience and Biobehavioral Reviews* 39: 34–50.

Sabeti, Pardis C., Stephen F. Schaffner, Ben Fry et al. 2006. "Positive Natural Selection in the Human Lineage." *Science* 312 (June 16).

Sackett, Paul R., Chaitra M. Hardison, and Michael J. Cullen. 2004. "On Interpreting Stereotype Threat as Accounting for African American–White Differences on Cognitive Tests." *American Psychologist* 59 (1): 7–13.

Sackett, Paul R., Nathan R. Kuncel, Justin J. Arneson et al. 2009. "Does Socioeconomic Status Explain the Relationship Between Admissions Tests and Post-secondary Academic Performance?" *Psychological Bulletin* 135 (1): 1–22.

Sagi, A., and M. L. Hoffman. 1976. "Empathic Distress in the Newborn." *Developmental Psychology* 12: 175–76.

Sahakian, Barbara J., and Julia Gottwald. 2017. *Sex, Lies, and Brain Scans: How fMRI Reveals What Really Goes On in Our Minds.* Oxford: Oxford University Press.

Sandberg, D. E., and H. F. L. Meyer-Bahlburg. 1994. "Variability in Middle Childhood Play Behavior: Effects of Gender, Age, and Family Background." *Archives of Sexual Behavior* 23: 645–63.

Sandler, L., and E. Novitski. 1957. "Meiotic Drive as an Evolutionary Force." *American Naturalist* 91 (857): 105–10.

Sankararaman, Sriram, Swapan Mallick, Michael Dannemann et al. 2014. "The Genomic Landscape of Neanderthal Ancestry in Present-Day Humans." *Nature* 507: 354–57.

Sapienza, Paola, Luigi Zingales, and Dario Maestripieri. 2009. "Gender Differences in Financial Risk Aversion and Career Choices Are Affected by Testosterone." *Proceedings of the National Academy of Sciences* 106 (36): 15268–73.

Satel, Sally, and Scott O. Lilienfeld. 2015. *Brainwashed: The Seductive Appeal of Mindless Neuroscience*. New York: Basic Books.

Satterthwaite, Theodore D., Daniel H. Wolf, David R. Roalf et al. 2015. "Linked Sex Differences in Cognition and Functional Connectivity in Youth." *Cerebral Cortex* 25: 2383–94.

Sauce, Bruno, and Louis Matzel. 2018. "The Paradox of Intelligence: Heritability and Malleability Coexist in Hidden Gene-Environment Interplay." *Psychological Bulletin* 144.

Savic, Ivanka, Louise Frisen, Amirhossein Manzouri et al. 2017. "Role of Testosterone and Y Chromosome Genes for the Masculinization of the Human Brain." *Human Brain Mapping* 38 (4): 1801–14.

Savic, Ivanka, Alicia Garcia-Falgueras, and Dick F. Swaab. 2010. "Sexual Differentiation of the Human Brain in Relation to Gender Identity and Sexual Orientation." *Progress in Brain Research* 186: 41–62.

Savin-Williams, Ritch C., and Kenneth M. Cohen. 2018. "Prevalence, Mental Health, and Heterogeneity of Bisexual Men." *Current Sexual Health Reports* 10 (3): 196–202.

Savin-Williams, Ritch C., and Zhana Vrangalova. 2013. "Mostly Heterosexual as a Distinct Sexual Orientation Group: A Systematic Review of the Empirical Evidence." *Developmental Review* 33 (1): 58–88.

Sawilowsky, Shlomo S. 2009. "New Effect Size Rules of Thumb." *Journal of Modern Applied Statistical Methods* 8 (2): 597–99.

Sax, Leonard. 2002. "How Common Is Intersex? A Response to Anne Fausto-Sterling." *Journal of Sex Research* 39 (3): 174–78.

Sayre, Anne. 2000. *Rosalind Franklin and DNA*. New York: W. W. Norton.

Scarr, Sandra, and Susan Grajek. 1982. "Similarities and Differences Among Siblings." In *Sibling Relationships: Their Nature and Significance Across the Lifespan*, edited by M. E. Lamb and B. Sutton-Smith. Hillsdale, NJ: Erlbaum.

Scarr-Salapatek, Sandra. 1971. "Race, Social Class, and IQ." *Science* 4: 1285–95.

Scerri, Eleanor M. L., Mark G. Thomas, Andrea Manica et al. 2018. "Did Our Species Evolve in Subdivided Populations Across Africa, and Why Does It Matter?" *Trends in Ecology and Evolution* 33 (8): 582–94.

Scheiber, Caroline, Matthew R. Reynolds, Daniel B. Hajovsky et al. 2015. "Gender Differences in Achievement in a Large, Nationally Representative Sample of Children and Adolescents." *Psychology in the Schools* 52 (4): 335–48.

Scheper-Hughes, Nancy. 1995. "The Primacy of the Ethical: Propositions for a Militant Anthropology." *Current Anthropology* 36 (3): 409–40.

Scherbaum, C. A., P. J. Hanges, K. Yusko et al. 2012. "The Spearman Hypothesis Cannot Explain All Racial Score Differences." Annual Meeting of the Society for Industrial and Organizational Psychology.

Schiffels, Stephan, and Richard Durbin. 2014. "Inferring Human Population Size and Separation History from Multiple Genome Sequences." *Nature Genetics* 46 (8): 919–25.

Schmid, P. C., M. Schmid Mast, D. Bombari et al. 2011. "Gender Effects in Information Processing on a Nonverbal Decoding Task." *Sex Roles* 65: 102–7.

Schmitt, David P., A. E. Long, A. McPhearson et al. 2016. "Personality and Gender Differences in Global Perspective." *International Journal of Psychology* 52 (51): 45–56.

Schmitt, David P., A. Realo, M. Voracek et al. 2008. "Why Can't a Man Be More Like a Woman? Sex Differences in Big Five Personality Traits Across 55 Cultures." *Journal of Personality and Social Psychology* 94 (1): 168–82.

Schraiber, Joshua G., and Joshua M. Akey. 2015. "Methods and Models for Unravelling Human Evolutionary History." *Nature Reviews Genetics* 16 (12): 727–40.

Schrider, Daniel R., and Andrew D. Kern. 2017. "Soft Sweeps Are the Dominant Mode of Adaptation in the Human Genome." *Molecular Biology and Evolution* 34 (8): 1863–77.

Schwartz, C. E., C. I. Wright, L. M. Shin et al. 2003. "Inhibited and Uninhibited Infants 'Grown Up': Adult Amygdalar Response to Novelty." *Science* 300 (5627): 1952–53.

Scutari, Marco, Ian Mackay, and David Balding. 2016. "Using Genetic Distance to Infer the Accuracy of Genomic Prediction." *PLoS Genetics* 12 (9): e1006288.

Segerstråle, Ullica. 2000. *Defenders of the Truth: The Sociobiology Debate.* Oxford: Oxford University Press.

Seguin-Orlando, Andaine, Thorfinn S. Korneliussen, Martin Sikora et al. 2014. "Genomic Structure in Europeans Dating Back at Least 36,200 Years." *Science* 346 (6213): 1113.

Sehlmeyer, C., U. Dannlowski, S. Schöning et al. 2011. "Neural Correlates of Trait Anxiety in Fear Extinction." *Psychological Medicine* 41 (4): 789–98.

Seidlitz, Larry, and Ed Diener. 1998. "Sex Differences in the Recall of Affective Experiences." *Journal of Personality and Social Psychology* 74 (1): 262–71.

Sela, Yael, and Nicole Barbaro. 2018. "Evolutionary Perspectives on Personality and Individual Differences." In *The Sage Handbook of Personality and Individual Differences*, edited by Virgil Zeigler-Hill and Todd K. Shackelford, 203–28. London: Sage Publications.

Selzam, Saskia, Stuart J. Ritchie, Jean-Baptiste Pingault et al. 2019. "Comparing Within- and Between-Family Polygenic Score Prediction." *bioRxiv*: 605006.

Serre, David, and Svante Pääbo. 2004. "Evidence for Gradients of Human Genetic Diversity Within and Among Continents." *Genome Research* 14 (9): 1679–85.

Shanahan, Michael J., Shawn Bauldry, Brent W. Roberts et al. 2014. "Personality and the Reproduction of Social Class." *Social Forces* 93 (1): 209–40.

Shaw, George Bernard. 1891. *The Quintessence of Ibsenism.* London: Walter Scott.

Shaywitz, S. E., B. A. Shaywitz, K. R. Pugh et al. 1998. "Functional Disruption in the Organization of the Brain for Reading in Dyslexia." *Proceedings of the National Academy of Sciences* 95: 2636–41.

Shea, Daniel L., David Lubinski, and Camilla P. Benbow. 2001. "Importance of Assessing Spatial Ability in Intellectually Talented Young Adolescents: A 20-Year Longitudinal Study." *Journal of Educational Psychology* 93: 604–14.

Shewach, Oren R., Paul R. Sackett, and Sander Quint. 2019. "Stereotype Threat Effects in Settings with Features Likely Versus Unlikely in Operational Test Settings: A Meta-Analysis." *Journal of Applied Psychology.* In press.

Shiao, Jiannbin Lee, Thomas Bode, Amber Beyer et al. 2012. "The Genomic Challenge to the Social Construction of Race." *Sociological Theory* 30 (2): 67–88.

Shin, L. M., C. I. Wright, P. A. Cannistraro et al. 2005. "A Functional Magnetic Resonance Imaging Study of Amygdala and Medial Prefrontal Cortex Responses to Overtly Presented Fearful Faces in Posttraumatic Stress Disorder." *Archives of General Psychiatry* 62 (3): 273–81.

Simmons, Joseph P., Leif D. Nelson, and Uri Simonsohn. 2011. "False-Positive Psychology: Undisclosed Flexibility in Data Collection and Analysis Allows Presenting Anything as Significant." *Psychological Science* 22 (11): 1359–66.

Simner, Marvin. 1971. "Newborn's Response to the Cry of Another Infant." *Developmental Psychology* 5 (1): 136–50.

Sirugo, Giorgio, Scott M. Williams, and Sarah A. Tishkoff. 2019. "The Missing Diversity in Human Genetic Studies." *Cell* 177 (March 21): 26–31.

Sisk, Victoria F., Alexander P. Burgoyne, Jingze Sun et al. 2018. "To What Extent and Under Which Circumstances Are Growth Mind-Sets Important to Academic Achievement? Two Meta-analyses." *Psychological Science* 29 (4): 549–71.

Skinner, B. F. 1938. *The Behavior of Organisms: An Experimental Analysis.* New York: Appleton-Century-Crofts.

Smith, Adam. 1776. *An Inquiry in the Nature and Causes of the Wealth of Nations.* London: W. Strahan.

———. 1979. *The Theory of Moral Sentiments.* Oxford: Oxford University Press. Original edition 1759.

Smith, Kerri. 2017. "The Brain Circuit Challenge." *Nature* 548: 150–52.

Smouse, Peter E., Richard S. Spielman, and Myoung H. Park. 1982. "Multiple-Locus Allocation of Individuals to Groups as a Function of the Genetic Variation Within and Differences Among Human Populations." *American Naturalist* 119 (4): 445–63.

Soden-Hensler, Brooke. 2012. "An Examination of Gene × Socioeconomic Status Interactions for Reading Achievement." PhD dissertation, Florida State University.

Sodini, Sebastian M., Kathryn E. Kemper, Naomi R. Wray et al. 2018. "Comparison of Genotypic and Phenotypic Correlations: Cheverud's Conjecture in Humans." *Genetics* 209 (3): 941–48.

Sohail, Mashaal, Robert M. Maier, Andrea Ganna et al. 2018. "Signals of Polygenic Adaptation on Height Have Been Overestimated Due to Uncorrected Population Structure in Genome-Wide Association Studies." *bioRxiv.*

Sosnowski, David W., Carolyn Booth, Timothy P. York et al. 2018. "Maternal Prenatal Stress and Infant DNA Methylation: A Systematic Review." *Developmental Psychobiology* 60 (2): 127–39.

Soutschek, Alexander, Christopher J. Burke, Anjali Raja Beharelle et al. 2017. "The Dopaminergic Reward System Underpins Gender Differences in Social Preferences." *Nature Human Behaviour* 1 (11): 819–27.

Sowell, Elizabeth R., Bradley S. Peterson, Eric Kan et al. 2007. "Sex Differences in Cortical Thickness Mapped in 176 Healthy Individuals Between 7 and 87 Years of Age." *Cerebral Cortex* 17 (7): 1550–60.

Speiser, Phyllis W., Eric S. Knochenhauer, Didier Dewailly et al. 2000. "A Multicenter Study of Women with Nonclassical Congenital Adrenal Hyperplasia: Relationship Between Genotype and Phenotype." *Molecular Genetics and Metabolism* 71: 527–34.

Spengler, Marion, Juliana Gottschling, Elisabeth Hahn et al. 2018. "Does the Heritability of Cognitive Abilities Vary as a Function of Parental Education? Evidence from a German Twin Sample." *PLoS ONE* 13 (5): e0196597.

Spinath, Birgit, Frank M. Spinath, Nicole Harlaar et al. 2006. "Predicting School Achievement from General Cognitive Ability, Self-Perceived Ability, and Intrinsic Value." *Intelligence* 34 (4): 363–74.

Spiro, Melford E. 1954. "Is the Family Universal?" *American Anthropologist* 56: 839–46.

Sporns, Olaf. 2006. "Small-World Connectivity, Motif Composition, and Complexity of Fractal Neuronal Connections." *Biosystems* 85: 55–64.

———. 2011. "The Human Connectome: A Complex Network." *Annals of the New York Academy of Sciences* 1224 (1): 109–25.

Staff, R. T., M. J. Hogan, and L. J. Whalley. 2017. "Childhood Intelligence and Personality Traits Neuroticism and Openness Contributes to Social Mobility: A Study in the Aberdeen 1936 Birth Cohort." *Personality and Individual Differences* 114: 206–12.

Stankov, Lazar. 2013. "Noncognitive Predictors of Intelligence and Academic Achievement: An Important Role of Confidence." *Personality and Individual Differences* 55 (7): 727–32.

Stanovich, Keith E. 1986. "Matthew Effects in Reading: Some Consequences of Individual Differences in the Acquisition of Literacy." *Reading Research Quarterly* 16: 32–71.

St. Clair, D., M. Xu, P. Wang et al. 2005. "Rates of Adult Schizophrenia Following Prenatal Exposure to the Chinese Famine of 1959–1961." *JAMA* 294 (5): 557–62.

Steele, Claude M., and Joshua Aronson. 1995. "Stereotype Threat and the Intellectual Test Performance of African Americans." *Journal of Personality and Social Psychology* 69: 797–811.

Stevens, Jennifer S., and Stephan Hamann. 2012. "Sex Differences in Brain Activation to Emotional Stimuli: A Meta-analysis of Neuroimaging Studies." *Neuropsychologia* 50 (7): 1578–93.

Stewart, J. R., and C. B. Stringer. 2012. "Human Evolution out of Africa: The Role of Refugia and Climate Change." *Science* 335 (March 16).

Stewart-Williams, Steve. 2018. *The Ape That Understood the Universe: How the Mind and Culture Evolve.* Cambridge: Cambridge University Press.

Stewart-Williams, Steve, and Andrew G. Thomas. 2013. "The Ape That Thought It Was a Peacock: Does Evolutionary Psychology Exaggerate Human Sex Differences?" *Psychological Inquiry* 24 (3): 137–68.

Stiles, Joan, and Terry L. Jernigan. 2010. "The Basics of Brain Development." *Neuropsychological Review* 20: 327–48.

Stoet, Gijsbert, and David C. Geary. 2012. "Can Stereotype Threat Explain the Gender Gap in Mathematics Performance and Achievement?" *Review of General Psychology* 16 (1): 93–102.

———. 2013. "Sex Differences in Mathematics and Reading Achievement Are Inversely Related: Within- and Across-Nation Assessment of 10 Years of Pisa Data." *PLoS ONE* 8 (3): e57988.

———. 2015. "Sex Differences in Academic Achievement Are Not Related to Political, Economic, or Social Equality." *Intelligence* 48: 137–51.

———. 2018. "The Gender-Equality Paradox in Science, Technology, Engineering, and Mathematics Education." *Psychological Science* 29 (4): 0956797617741719.

Stormshak, Elizabeth A., Karen L. Bierman, Robert J. McMahon et al. 2000. "Parenting Practices and Child Disruptive Behavior Problems in Early Elementary School." *Journal of Clinical Child Psychology* 29 (1): 17–29.

Strand, Steve, Ian J. Deary, and Pauline Smith. 2006. "Sex Differences in Cognitive Abilities Test Scores: A UK National Picture." *British Journal of Educational Psychology* 76: 463–80.

Strenze, Tarmo. 2007. "Intelligence and Socioeconomic Success: A Meta-analytic Review of Longitudinal Research." *Intelligence* 35 (5): 401–26.

Stringer, C. B., and P. Andrews. 1988. "The Origin of Modern Humans." *Science* 239: 1263–68.

Su, Rong. 2018. "The Three Faces of Interests: An Integrative Review of Interest Research in Vocational, Organizational, and Educational Psychology." *Journal of Vocational Behavior.*

Su, Rong, and James Rounds. 2015. "All STEM Fields Are Not Created Equal: People and Things Interests Explain Gender Disparities Across STEM Fields." *Frontiers in Psychology* 6: 189.

Su, Rong, James Rounds, and P. I. Armstrong. 2009. "Men and Things, Women and People: A Meta-analysis of Sex Differences in Interests." *Psychological Bulletin* 135 (6): 859–84.

Summers, Lawrence H. 2005. "Remarks at NBER Conference on Diversifying the Science & Engineering Workforce." NBER Conference on Diversifying the Science & Engineering Workforce, Cambridge, MA.

Susser, E., and S. P. Lin. 1992. "Schizophrenia After Prenatal Exposure to the Dutch Hunger Winter of 1944–1945." *Archives of General Psychiatry* 49: 983–88.

Swanwick, Helena Maria. 1913. *The Future of the Women's Movement.* London: G. Bell & Sons.

Tang, Hua, Jie Peng, Pei Wang et al. 2005. "Estimation of Individual Admixture: Analytical and Study Design Considerations." *Genetic Epidemiology* 28: 289–301.

Takeuchi, Fumihiko, Masato Akiyama, Nana Matoba et al. 2018. "Interethnic Analyses of Blood Pressure Loci in Populations of East Asian and European Descent." *Nature Communications* 9 (1): 5052.

Tang, Hua, T. Quertermous, Beatriz Rodriguez et al. 2005. "Genetic Structure, Self-Identified Race/Ethnicity, and Confounding in Case-Control Association Studies." *American Journal of Human Genetics* 76: 268–75.

Tay, Louis, Rong Su, and James Rounds. 2011. "People-Things and Data-Ideas: Bipolar Dimensions?" *Journal of Counseling Psychology* 58 (3): 424–40.

Taylor, Howard Francis. 1980. *The IQ Game: A Methodological Inquiry into the Heredity-Environment Controversy.* New Brunswick, NJ: Rutgers University Press.

Telenti, Amalio, Levi C. T. Pierce, William H. Biggs et al. 2016. "Deep Sequencing of 10,000 Human Genomes." *Proceedings of the National Academy of Sciences* 113 (42): 11901.

Tennessen, Jacob A., Abigail W. Bigham, Timothy D. O'Connor et al. 2012. "Evolution and Functional Impact of Rare Coding Variation from Deep Sequencing of Human Exomes." *Science* 337 (6090): 64.

Thaler, R. H., and C. Sunstein (2008). *Nudge: Improving Decisions About Health, Wealth, and Happiness.* New York: Penguin.

Thomas, Duncan C., and John S. Witte. 2002. "Point: Population Stratification: A Problem for Case-Control Studies of Candidate-Gene Associations?" *Cancer Epidemiology Biomarkers and Prevention* 11 (6): 505–12.

Thomas, J. R., and K. E. French. 1985. "Gender Differences Across Age in Motor Performance: A Meta-analysis." *Psychological Bulletin* 98: 260–82.

Thomas, K. M., W. C. Drevets, P. J. Whalen et al. 2001. "Amygdala Response to Facial Expressions in Children and Adults." *Biological Psychiatry* 49 (4): 309–16.

Thompson, Ashley, and Daniel Voyer. 2014. "Sex Differences in the Ability to Recognise Nonverbal Displays of Emotion: A Meta-analysis." *Cognition and Emotion* 28 (7): 1164–95.

Thorndike, Edward L. 1911. *Individuality.* Boston: Houghton Mifflin.

Timmermann, Axel, and Tobias Friedrich. 2016. "Late Pleistocene Climate Drivers of Early Human Migration." *Nature* 538 (7623): 92–95.

Tobi, Elmar W., Roderick C. Slieker, René Luijk et al. 2018. "DNA Methylation as a Mediator of the Association Between Prenatal Adversity and Risk Factors for Metabolic Disease in Adulthood." *Science Advances* 4 (1).

Tooby, John, and Leda Cosmides. 1992. "The Psychological Foundations of Culture." In *The Adapted Mind: Evolutionary Psychology and the Generation of Culture*, edited by Jerome H. Barkow, John Tooby, and Leda Cosmides, 19–136. New York: Oxford University Press.

Trivers, Robert. 1972. "Parental Investment and Sexual Selection." In *Sexual Selection and the Descent of Man*, edited by B. B. Campbell, 136–79. Chicago: Aldine.

———. 2011. *The Folly of Fools: The Logic of Deceit and Self-Deception in Human Life.* New York: Basic Books.

Trut, Lyudmila. 1999. "Early Canid Domestication: The Farm-Fox Experiment." *American Scientist* 87 (March–April): 160–69.

Trzaskowski, M., N. Harlaar, R. Arden et al. 2014. "Genetic Influence on Family Socioeconomic Status and Children's Intelligence." *Intelligence* 42 (100): 83–88.

Tucci, Serena, and Joshua M. Akey. 2016. "A Map of Human Wanderlust." *Nature* 538: 179–80.

Tucker-Drob, Elliot M., and Timothy C. Bates. 2015. "Large Cross-National Differences in Gene × Socioeconomic Status Interaction on Intelligence." *Psychological Science* 27 (2): 138–49.

Tucker-Drob, Elliot M., Daniel A. Briley, Laura Engelhardt et al. 2016. "Genetically-Mediated Associations Between Measures of Childhood Character and Academic Achievement." *Journal of Personality and Social Psychology* 111 (5): 790–815.

Tucker-Drob, Elliot M., Daniel A. Briley, and K. Paige Harden. 2013. "Genetic and Environmental Influences on Cognition Across Development and Context." *Current Directions in Psychological Science* 22 (5): 349–55.

Tucker-Drob, Elliot M., and K. Paige Harden. 2017. "A Behavioral Genetic Perspective on Noncognitive Factors and Academic Achievement." In *Genetics, Ethics, and Education*, edited by Susan Bouregy, Elena L. Grigorenko, Stephen R. Latham et al., 134–58. Cambridge: Cambridge University Press.

Tucker-Drob, Elliot M., Mijke Rhemtulla, K. Paige Harden et al. 2011. "Emergence of a Gene × Socioeconomic Status Interaction on Infant Mental Ability Between 10 Months and 2 Years." *Psychological Science* 22 (1): 125–33.

Tunç, Birkan, Berkan Solmaz, Drew Parker et al. 2016. "Establishing a Link Between Sex-Related Differences in the Structural Connectome and Behaviour." *Philosophical Transactions of the Royal Society B: Biological Sciences* 371 (1688): 20150111.

Turecki, Gustavo, and Michael J. Meaney. 2016. "Effects of the Social Environment and Stress on Glucocorticoid Receptor Gene Methylation: A Systematic Review." *Biological Psychiatry* 79 (2): 87–96.

Turkheimer, Eric. 2000. "Three Laws of Behavior Genetics and What They Mean." *Current Directions in Psychological Science* 5: 160–64.

———. 2011. "Commentary: Variation and Causation in the Environment and Genome." *International Journal of Epidemiology* 40 (3): 598–601.

———. 2019. "Genetics and Human Agency: The Philosophy of Behavior Genetics Introduction to the Special Issue." *Behavior Genetics* 49 (2): 123–27.

Turkheimer, Eric, Brian M. D'Onofrio, Hermine H. Maes et al. 2005. "Analysis and Interpretation of Twin Studies Including Measures of the Shared Environment." *Child Development* 76 (6): 1217–33.

Turkheimer, Eric, Andreana Haley, Mary Waldron et al. 2003. "Socioeconomic Status Modifies Heritability of IQ in Young Children." *Psychological Science* 14 (6): 623–28.

Turkheimer, Eric, Erik Pettersson, and Erin E. Horn. 2014. "A Phenotypic Null Hypothesis for the Genetics of Personality." *Annual Review of Psychology* 65 (1): 515–40.

Turkheimer, Eric, and Mary Waldron. 2000. "Nonshared Environment: A Theoretical, Methodological, and Quantitative Review." *Psychological Bulletin* 126 (1): 78–108.

Twenge, Jean M. 2006. *Generation Me: Why Today's Young Americans Are More Confident, Assertive, Entitled—and More Miserable Than Ever Before.* New York: Free Press.

Udry, J. Richard. 2000. "Biological Limits of Gender Construction." *American Sociological Review* 65: 443–57.

Udry, J. Richard, Naomi M. Morris, and Judith Kovenock. 1995. "Androgen Effects on Women's Gendered Behaviour." *Journal of Biosocial Science* 27 (3): 359–68.

UKK Consortium. 2015. "The UK10K Project Identifies Rare Variants in Health and Disease." *Nature* 526: 82–90.

Unterman, Rebecca. 2017. *An Early Look at the Effects of Success Academy Charter Schools.* New York: MDRC.

U.S. Department of Health and Human Services, Administration for Children and Families. 2010. *Head Start Impact Study: Final Report.* Washington, DC.

Valla, Jeffrey M., and Stephen J. Ceci. 2014. "Breadth-Based Models of Women's Underrepresentation in STEM Fields: An Integrative Commentary on Schmidt (2011) and Nye et al. (2012)." *Perspectives on Psychological Science* 9 (2): 219–24.

Valla, Jeffrey M., Barbara L. Ganzel, Keith J. Yoder et al. 2010. "More Than Maths and Mindreading: Sex Differences in Empathizing/Systemizing Covariance." *Autism Research* 3 (4): 174–84.

van der Linden, Dimitri, Curtis S. Dunkel, and Guy Madison. 2017. "Sex Differences in Brain Size and General Intelligence (g)." *Intelligence* 63: 78–88.

van der Sluis, Sophie, Danielle Posthuma, Conor V. Dolan et al. 2006. "Sex Differences on the Dutch WAIS-III." *Intelligence* 34 (3): 273–89.

van der Sluis, Sophie, Gonneke Willemsen, Eco J. C. de Geus et al. 2008. "Gene-Environment Interaction in Adults' IQ Scores: Measures of Past and Present Environment." *Behavior Genetics* 38 (4): 348–60.

Van Essen, David C. 2018. "Scaling of Human Brain Size." *Science* 360 (6394): 1184.

van Honk, Jack, Dennis J. L. G. Schutter, Erno J. Hermans et al. 2004. "Testosterone Shifts the Balance Between Sensitivity for Punishment and Reward in Healthy Young Women." *Psychoneuroendocrinology* 29 (7): 937–43.

Van Rooy, D. L., and Chockalingam Viswesvaran. 2004. "Emotional Intelligence: A Meta-analytic Investigation of Predictive Validity and Nomological Net." *Journal of Vocational Behavior* (65): 71–95.

Vasta, Ross, and Lynn S. Liben. 1996. "The Water-Level Task: An Intriguing Puzzle." *Current Directions in Psychological Science* 5 (6): 171–77.

Verweij, Karin J. H., Miriam A. Mosing, Brendan P. Zietsch et al. 2012. "Estimating Heritability from Twin Studies." In *Statistical Human Genetics: Methods and Protocols*, edited by R. Elston, J. Satagopan, and S. Sun. Totowa, NJ: Humana Press.

Vinkhuyzen, A. A., S. van der Sluis, H. H. Maes et al. 2012. "Reconsidering the Heritability of Intelligence in Adulthood: Taking Assortative Mating and Cultural Transmission into Account." *Behavior Genetics* 42 (2): 187–98.

Visser, Beth A., Michael C. Ashton, and Philip A. Vernon. 2006a. "Beyond *g*: Putting Multiple Intelligences Theory to the Test." *Intelligence* 34 (5): 487–502.

———. 2006b. "*g* and the Measurement of Multiple Intelligences: A Response to Gardner." *Intelligence* 34 (5): 507–10.

Voight, Benjamin F., Sridhar Kudaravalli, Xiaoquan Wen et al. 2006. "A Map of Recent Positive Selection in the Human Genome." *PLOS Biology* 4 (3): e72.

von Hippel, William, and David M. Buss. 2017. "Do Ideologically Driven Scientific Agendas Impede the Understanding and Acceptance of Evolutionary Principles in Social Psychology?" In *The Politics of Social Psychology*, edited by J. T. Crawford and Lee Jussim, 7–25. New York: Psychology Press.

von Stumm, Sophie, Catharine R. Gale, G. David Batty et al. 2009. "Childhood Intelligence, Locus of Control and Behaviour Disturbance as Determinants of Intergenerational Social Mobility: British Cohort Study 1970." *Intelligence* 37 (4): 329–40.

von Stumm, Sophie, Benedikt Hell, and Tomas Chamorro-Premuzic. 2011. "The Hungry Mind: Intellectual Curiosity Is the Third Pillar of Academic Performance." *Perspectives on Psychological Science* 6 (6): 574–88.

von Stumm, Sophie, Emily Smith-Woolley, Ziada Ayorech et al. 2019. "Predicting Educational Achievement from Genomic Measures and Socioeconomic Status." *bioRxiv*: 538108.

Voyer, Daniel. 1996. "On the Magnitude of Laterality Effects and Sex Differences in Functional Lateralities." *Laterality* 1 (1): 51–83.

Voyer, Daniel, and Susan D. Voyer. 2014. "Gender Differences in Scholastic Achievement: A Meta-analysis." *Psychological Bulletin* 140 (4): 1174–204.

Voyer, Daniel, Susan D. Voyer, and M. P. Bryden. 1995. "Magnitude of Sex Differences in Spatial Abilities: A Meta-analysis and Consideration of Critical Variables." *Psychological Bulletin* 117: 250–70.

Waddington, John. 1942. "The Epigenotype." *Endeavor* 1: 18–20.

Wade, Nicholas. 2014. *A Troublesome Inheritance: Genes, Race and Human History*. New York: Penguin.

Wai, Jonathan, Megan Cacchio, Martha Putallaz et al. 2010. "Sex Differences in the Right Tail of Cognitive Abilities: A 30-Year Examination." *Intelligence* 38 (4): 412–23.

Wainschtein, Pierrick, Deepti P. Jain, Loic Yengo et al. 2019. "Recovery of Trait Heritability from Whole Genome Sequence Data." *bioRxiv*: 588020.

Wallen, Kim. 2009. "The Organizational Hypothesis: Reflections on the 50th Anniversary of the Publication of Phoenix, Goy, Gerall, and Young (1959)." *Hormones and Behavior* 55 (5): 561–65.

Walton, Gregory M., and Steven J. Spencer. 2009. "Latent Ability: Grades and Test Scores Systematically Underestimate the Intellectual Ability of Negatively Stereotyped Students." *Psychological Science* 20 (9): 1132–39.

Wang, B., and J. Degol. 2013. "Motivational Pathways to STEM Career Choices: Using Expectancy-Value Perspective to Understand Individual and Gender Differences in STEM Fields." *Developmental Review* 33: 304–40.

Wang, M. T., J. S. Eccles, and S. Kenny. 2013. "Not Lack of Ability but More Choice: Individual and Gender Differences in Choice of Careers in Science, Technology, Engineering, and Mathematics." *Psychological Science* 24 (5): 770–75.

Warne, Russell T. 2019. "The Mismeasurements of Stephen Jay Gould." *Quillette* (March 19).

Warne, Russell T., Lindsey R. Godwin, and Kyle V. Smith. 2013. "Are There More Gifted People Than Would Be Expected in a Normal Distribution? An Investigation of the Overabundance Hypothesis." *Journal of Advanced Academics* 24 (4): 224–41.

Waterhouse, Lynn. 2006. "Multiple Intelligences, the Mozart Effect, and Emotional Intelligence: A Critical Review." *Educational Psychologist* 41 (4): 207–25.

Waterland, Robert A., and Randy L. Jirtle. 2003. "Transposable Elements: Targets for Early Nutritional Effects on Epigenetic Gene Regulation." *Molecular and Cellular Biology* 23 (15): 5293.

Watson, John Broadus. 1914. *Behavior: An Introduction to Comparative Psychology.* New York: H. Holt.

———. 1924. *Behaviorism.* New Brunswick, NJ: Transaction.

Watson, Neil, and Doreen Kimura. 1991. "Nontrivial Sex Differences in Throwing and Intercepting: Relation to Psychometrically-Defined Spatial Functions." *Personality and Individual Differences* 12 (5): 375–85.

Watts, D. J., and S. H. Strogatz. 1998. "Collective Dynamics of 'Small-World' Networks." *Nature* 393: 440–42.

Weaver, Ian C. G., Nadia Cervoni, Frances A. Champagne et al. 2004. "Epigenetic Programming by Maternal Behavior." *Nature Neuroscience* 7: 847.

Weidenreich, F. 1946. *Apes, Giants, and Man.* Chicago: University of Chicago Press.

Weiner, Jonathan. 1994. *The Beak of the Finch: A Story of Evolution in Our Time.* New York: Random House.

Wellman, Henry M., and David Liu. 2004. "Scaling of Theory-of-Mind Tasks." *Child Development* 75 (2): 523–41.

Whitehurst, Grover J. 2013. "New Evidence Raises Doubts on Obama's Preschool for All." In *Brown Center Chalkboard Series Archive.* Washington, DC: Brookings Institution.

Wicherts, Jelte M., Conor V. Dolan, and Han L. J. van der Maas. 2010. "A Systematic Literature Review of the Average IQ of Sub-Saharan Africans." *Intelligence* 38 (1): 1–20.

Wilde, Sandra, Adrian Timpson, Karola Kirsanow et al. 2013. "Direct Evidence for Positive Selection of Skin, Hair, and Eye Pigmentation in Europeans During the Last 5,000 Years." *Proceedings of the National Academy of Sciences* 111 (13): 4832–37.

Willerman, Lee, Robert Schultz, J. Neal Rutledge et al. 1991. "*In vivo* Brain Size and Intelligence." *Intelligence* 15 (2): 223–28.

Williams, G. C. 1966. *Adaptation and Natural Selection: A Critique of Some Current Evolutionary Thought.* Princeton, NJ: Princeton University Press.

Williams, L. M., M. J. Barton, and A. H. Kemp. 2005. "Distinct Amygdala-Autonomic Arousal Profiles in Response to Fear Signals in Healthy Males and Females." *NeuroImage* 28 (3): 618–26.

Williams, L. M., D. Mathersul, D. M. Palmer et al. 2008. "Explicit Identification and Implicit Recognition of Facial Emotions: I. Age Effects in Males and Females Across 10 Decades." *Journal of Clinical and Experimental Neuropsychology* 19: 1–21.

Willoughby, Emily, Alan Love, Matt McGue et al. 2018. "Free Will, Determinism, and Intuitive Judgments About the Heritability of Behavior." *Behavior Genetics* 49 (2): 136–53.

Wilson, Edward O. 1975. *Sociobiology.* Cambridge, MA: Harvard University Press.

———. 1998. *Consilience: The Unity of Knowledge.* New York: Alfred A. Knopf.

Winegard, Bo, Benjamin Winegard, and Brian Boutwell. 2017. "Human Biological and Psychological Diversity." *Evolutionary Psychological Science* 3 (2): 159–80.

Winkler, Anderson M., Peter Kochunov, John Blangero et al. 2010. "Cortical Thickness or Grey Matter Volume? The Importance of Selecting the Phenotype for Imaging Genetics Studies." *NeuroImage* 53 (3): 1135–46.

Witchel, Selma Feldman, and Ricardo Azziz. 2010. "Nonclassic Congenital Adrenal Hyperplasia." *International Journal of Pediatric Endocrinology* 2010: 625105.

Wolf, Aaron B., and Joshua M. Akey. 2018. "Outstanding Questions in the Study of Archaic Hominin Admixture." *PLoS Genetics* 14 (5): e1007349.

Wood, Wendy, and Alice H. Eagly. 2012. "Biosocial Construction of Sex Differences and Similarities in Behavior." *Advances in Experimental Social Psychology* 46: 56–123.

Wright, Daniel B., and Elin M. Skagerberg. 2012. "Measuring Empathizing and Systemizing with a Large US Sample." *PLoS ONE* 7 (2): e31661.

Wright, John Paul, J. C. Barnes, Brian B. Boutwell et al. 2015. "Mathematical Proof Is Not Minutiae and Irreducible Complexity Is Not a Theory: A Final Response to Burt and Simons and a Call to Criminologists." *Criminology* 53 (1): 113–20.

Wright, Sewall. 1943. "Isolation by Distance." *Genetics* 28: 114–38.

———. 1978. *Evolution and the Genetics of Populations: Variability Within and Among Natural Populations*. Chicago: University of Chicago Press.

Xing, Jinchuan, W. Scott Watkins, Adam Shlien et al. 2010. "Toward a More Uniform Sampling of Human Genetic Diversity: A Survey of Worldwide Populations by High-Density Genotyping." *Genomics* 96 (4): 199–210.

Yan, C., G. Gong, J. Wang et al. 2011. "Sex- and Brain Size-Related Small-World Structural Cortical Networks in Young Adults: A DTI Tractography Study." *Cerebral Cortex* 21 (2): 449–58.

Yeager, Ashley. 2019. "Classic Mechanism of Epigenetic Inheritance Is Rare, Not the Rule." *The Scientist* (March 1).

Yeager, David S., P. Hanselman, G. M. Walton et al. 2019. "Where Does a Scalable Growth-Mindset Intervention Improve Adolescents' Educational Trajectories." In press.

Yeager, David S., Rebecca Johnson, Brian James Spitzer et al. 2014. "The Far-Reaching Effects of Believing People Can Change: Implicit Theories of Personality Shape Stress, Health, and Achievement During Adolescence." *Journal of Personality and Social Psychology* 106 (6): 867–84.

Yeager, David S., Hae Yeon Lee, and Jeremy P. Jamieson. 2016. "How to Improve Adolescent Stress Responses: Insights from Integrating Implicit Theories of Personality and Biopsychosocial Models." *Psychological Science* 27 (8): 1078–91.

Yehuda, Rachel, Nikolaos P. Daskalakis, Linda M. Bierer et al. 2016. "Holocaust Exposure Induced Intergenerational Effects on FKBP5 Methylation." *Biological Psychiatry* 80 (5): 372–80.

Yeo, B. T. Thomas, Fenna M. Krienen, Jorge Sepulcre et al. 2011. "The Organization of the Human Cerebral Cortex Estimated by Intrinsic Functional Connectivity." *Journal of Neurophysiology* 106: 1125–65.

Zhu, Zhaoyu, Robin Dennell, Weiwen Huang et al. 2018. "Hominin Occupation of the Chinese Loess Plateau Since About 2.1 Million Years Ago." *Nature* 559 (7715): 608–12.

Zigerell, L. J. 2017. "Potential Publication Bias in the Stereotype Threat Literature: Comment on Nguyen and Ryan (2008)." *Journal of Applied Psychology* 102 (8): 1159–68.

Zucker, Kenneth J. 2017. "Epidemiology of Gender Dysphoria and Transgender Identity." *Sexual Health* 14: 404–11.

Zuckerman, Marvin, and D. Michael Kuhlman. 2000. "Personality and Risk-Taking: Common Biosocial Factors." *Journal of Personality* 68 (6): 999–1029.

Index

About the Author

Charles Murray is the F. A. Hayek Emeritus Scholar in Cultural Studies at the American Enterprise Institute, where he has worked for thirty years. He was raised in Iowa, educated at Harvard and MIT, and came of age in Thailand. The father of four children, he is married to Catherine Cox and lives in Burkittsville, Maryland.